Money and Growth

Allyn Young is one of the central figures in the development of American economic thought, and is one of the originators of modern endogenous growth theory. However, it has been difficult to appreciate the full extent of Young's work because many of his most significant contributions are buried in obscure journals and unsigned articles.

This volume addresses this by reprinting much of Young's lost work, as well as other selected pieces that reveal the scope of his vision which encompasses two of the grand themes of economics, growth and money. The biggest "finds" are 36 encyclopedia articles, originally published anonymously more than 75 years ago. They are important because they shed light on the unity of Young's thought which is based on the single abstract idea that trade is the source of wealth.

The volume includes sections on:

* the socialist movement
* the First World War and its aftermath
* money
* theories of growth

The volume concludes with some writings that are pointers to the nature of the two treatises Young was planning before his untimely death in 1929. A comprehensive bibliography is also provided.

Perry G. Mehrling is associate Professor of Economics at Barnard College, Columbia University. His research mainly involves the intellectual and theoretical foundations of monetary theory. His most recent book is *The Money Interest and the Public Interest: American Monetary Thought 1920–1970*.

Roger J. Sandilands is Senior Lecturer at the University of Strathclyde, Glasgow, Scotland. For many years he worked closely with Allyn Young's student Lauchlin Currie, and is the author of *The Life and Political Economy of Lauchlin Currie: New Dealer, Presidential Adviser, and Development Economist*. He also edited Nicholas Kaldor's "Notes on Allyn Young's LSE Lectures, 1927–29" which appeared in the *Journal of Economic Studies* in 1990.

Routledge Studies in the History of Economics

Money and Growth
Selected papers of Allyn Abbott Young

Edited by Perry G. Mehrling
and Roger J. Sandilands

London and New York

First published 1999
by Routledge
11 New Fetter Lane, London EC4P 4EE

Simultaneously published in the USA and Canada
by Routledge
29 West 35th Street, New York, NY 10001

Routledge is an imprint of the Taylor & Francis Group

© 1999 Edited by Perry G. Mehrling and Roger J. Sandilands

Typeset in Garamond by
Hodgson Williams Associates, Tunbridge Wells and Cambridge
Printed and bound in Great Britain by TJ International Ltd, Padstow,
Cornwall

British Library Cataloguing in Publication Data
A catalogue record for this book is available from the British Library

Library of Congress Cataloging in Publication Data
Young, Allyn Abbott, 1876–1929.
    Money and growth : selected papers of Allyn Abbott Young / edited
by Perry G. Mehrling and Roger J. Sandilands.
        p.   cm.
    Includes bibliographical references and index.
    ISBN 0-415-19155-6 (alk. paper)
        1. Young, Allyn Abbott, 1876–1929.   2. Economics.   3.
Economists–United States.   4. Economic history–20th century.
5. Endogenous growth (Economics)   6. Economic development.
7. Socialism.   8. Money.   9. World War, 1914–1918–Economic
aspects.   I. Mehrling, Perry.   II. Sandilands, Roger J. (Roger   James),
1945–   .   III. Title.   IV. Title: Selected papers of Allyn
    Abbott Young
    HB119.Y68A25   1999   98-41828
    330–dc21   CIP

ISBN 0-415-19155-6

Contents

Editors' preface

In recent years, in the specialist literature on the history of economic thought, a picture has been emerging of Allyn Young as a central figure in the development of American economics (Blitch 1995). His fingerprints are everywhere: co-author of the best-selling textbook *Outlines of Economics* (Ely et al. 1908, 1916, 1923, 1930) and of two others besides (Riley 1924, Reed 1925); patient builder of professional infrastructure as head of the Stanford economics department (1906–1910) and Secretary of the fledgling American Economics Association (1914–1920); devoted public servant, most notably as chief economist and statistician for the American Commission to Negotiate the Peace at Paris; inspiring teacher of a generation of economists, most notably Frank Knight and Edward Chamberlin but including also Holbrook Working, Lauchlin Currie, James Angell, Arthur Marget, and Nicholas Kaldor.

Modern interest in Young stems less, however, from his contribution to the economics profession, than from his contribution to economic thought. Young's 1928 presidential address to Section F of the British Association, titled "Increasing Returns and Economic Progress" has never lacked fans (Kaldor 1972, 1985; Currie 1981; Sandilands 1990), and the recent flurry of interest in theories of endogenous growth (Romer 1989; Currie 1997; Aghion and Howitt 1998) has brought Young's thinking on growth to the attention of a much broader audience. By contrast, Young's work on money and banking, the area of his special expertise, was largely forgotten. For example, Friedman and Schwartz in their comprehensive *Monetary History of the United States* (1963) make no mention of Young, not even of his book *An Analysis of Bank Statistics for the United States* (1928b). Only recently, with the work of Laidler (1993, 1998) and Mehrling (1996, 1997), has Young begun to come into focus as a figure of fundamental importance in the field of monetary economics, and this side of Young, it is fair to say, is still much less well known than the side concerned with economic growth.

Growth and Money, then, are the two themes of Young's work and of this volume, the main aim of which is to make more widely available a number of key texts that, until now, were accessible only to specialists, and often not even to them. Even in the specialist literature, appreciation of Young has suffered because an unusual fraction of his output has been either unknown, or inaccessible. The bibliography at the end of the volume addresses the first problem, and the major bulk of the volume addresses the second. In this regard, the biggest "finds" are the

36 chapters originally published anonymously in the Grolier Society's *Book of Popular Science* (Young 1924a), and especially the final six chapters on money and banking which constitute a small book by themselves, the longest sustained effort by Young on the subject of his special expertise, and a book previously unknown. (Two new chapters, Chapters 37 and 38, were added later for a revised 1929 edition.) In addition, the 1912 Lectures on Socialism and the 1922 exam questions on money are published here for the first time. A number of the other papers practically qualify as "finds" on account of the obscurity of their publication – the *Cornell Civil Engineer, The [New York] Independent*, and *The New York Times Annalist* are all defunct and difficult to locate.

Mere obscurity was however neither sufficient – we have not reprinted Young's early work for the Bureau of the Census, or his 1923 commencement address at Hiram College – nor necessary for inclusion. Papers can be known and accessible but not adequately appreciated until they are viewed in the context of the author's work as a whole. Scholarly appreciation of Young has, in our view, suffered not only from lack of access but also from lack of context, and we were concerned to present a rounded view of his work. Mindful of space considerations and the budgetary constraints of interested scholars, we have sought to produce a volume for the most part complementary to the collection *Economic Problems New and Old* (1927b) – only the important paper "Economics and War" appears in both. For similar reasons, we have reproduced only a limited selection of Young's LSE lectures and his *Encyclopaedia Britannica* entries, the full text of which is published in a special issue of the *Journal of Economic Studies* (1990; Young 1929c). Nevertheless, subject to those constraints, we have tried to produce a volume that stands on its own as a kind of Young reader that, we hope, will inspire scholars to consult the other collections, as well as the various worthy papers that remain uncollected but fairly readily accessible in back issues of major economics journals.

Growth and Money are the two grand themes of Young's work, but a rounded view of him, a view made possible by the material published in this volume, reveals them to be two sides of a single theme: Trade is the source of wealth. At the highest level of abstraction, growth is nothing more than a cumulative process of trade expansion, a process driven by the progressive cheapening of goods as the ever-widening market opens the way for increasingly productive methods of business organization. From this point of view, the institutions of money and credit are no mere veil hiding from view a world of purportedly "real" transactions, but are instead the key infrastructures that make markets work and enable them to expand. Young never went so far as to say that superior monetary institutions cause growth, but he was quite sure that inferior monetary institutions stymied growth, and for that reason he was intensely interested in monetary reform. Much like Joseph Schumpeter, whose *Theory of Economic Development* (1912) painted a picture of economic development made possible by the allocation of bank credit to business entrepreneurs, Allyn Young saw growth and money as inextricably intertwined.

Life

Allyn Abbott Young was born into a middle-class family in Kenton, Ohio on September 19, 1876 and died aged 52 in London on March 7, 1929, his life cut short by pneumonia during an influenza epidemic. He was then at the height of his intellectual powers and current president of Section F of the British Association. Uniquely, Young had also been president of the American Statistical Association (1917) and the American Economic Association (1925).

As documented in a recent biography (Blitch 1995), Young was a brilliant student, graduating from Hiram College in 1894 at the age of seventeen, the youngest graduate on record. After a few years in the printing trade he enrolled in 1898 in the graduate school of the University of Wisconsin where he studied economics under Richard T. Ely and William A. Scott, history under Charles H. Haskins and Frederick Jackson Turner, and statistics under Edward D. Jones. In 1900 he was engaged for a year as an assistant in the United States Bureau of the Census in Washington DC where he established lifelong friendships with Walter F. Willcox, Wesley C. Mitchell and Thomas S. Adams.

He returned to Wisconsin as Instructor in Economics for the 1901–02 academic session. After graduating in 1902 with a doctoral dissertation on age statistics, he embarked on what Blitch has called a peripatetic academic career, beginning with posts at Western Reserve University, 1902–04; Dartmouth, 1904–05; and Wisconsin, 1905–06. He then assumed the position of head of the economics department at Stanford, 1906–10, followed by a year at Harvard as visitor, 1910–11, and two years at Washington University, St Louis, 1911–13 (with the 1912 summer term at the University of Chicago). From 1913–20 he was professor at Cornell, but war took him to Washington DC in 1917 to direct the Bureau of Statistical Research for the War Trade Board, and to New York in 1918 to head the economics division of a group known as "The Enquiry" under Colonel Edward M. House, which group was charged with laying the groundwork for the Paris peace conference.

After the war, Young moved to Harvard in 1920 where he stayed until 1927 when he accepted William Beveridge's offer of the chair vacated by Edwin Cannan at the London School of Economics. He intended remaining at the LSE for three years before returning to Harvard. In December 1928 he traveled to the University of Chicago to explain in person why he felt unable to accept their invitation to be chairman of their economics department. It was shortly after his return to London that he succumbed to the fateful influenza epidemic.

At the time of his death Young was reputed to have been preparing a treatise on money (Morgenstern 1929; Taussig *et al* 1929); and T. E. Gregory (1929), a colleague at the LSE, wrote that he had in the last few months "begun work on a systematic treatise on economic theory and had resumed the writing of the work upon monetary theory which he had begun at Harvard." He continued:

> A passion for thoroughness would drive him on to explore every inch of the field in which he was for the time interested: he was always convinced that economic truth was not the monopoly of a single school or way of thinking, and that the

first duty of a teacher and thinker was to see the strong points in every presentation of a point of view. Such an attitude of mind, combined with great personal modesty, made for unsystematic writing: for scattered papers and articles and not for a comprehensive treatise. In many respects he resembled Edgeworth, for whose work he felt a growing admiration; and if Young's work is ever collected, it will be seen that, like Edgeworth's, it amounts in sum to a very considerable and impressive achievement.

The nature and scope of economics

The papers reprinted in section I provide a general introduction to Young's thinking, and a framework for understanding the more focused papers that follow. "Economics as a field of research" (1927f) and "English political economy" (1928c) represent Young's mature reflections on the nature of the field and on his own place in it (compare 1925d). Among very many points of interest, it is worth emphasizing two. First, although as a student of Ely's "look and see" method Young was definitely an empiricist at heart, he had a much greater appreciation for the role of theory than did Ely. As he put it: "In any really creative research, however modest in scale, there is this process of continuous give and take between the search for general relations and the scrutiny of particular details, between thinking and concrete observation" (1927f: 13). Second, although as a professional economist Young worked constantly to improve his narrowly economic expertise, he never lost sight of the fact that economic relations are only part of the larger social picture, and that economics is only one of the social sciences. As he put it: "The final terms of every chain of economic inferences reach out into other systems of relations, often non-economic in character, and it is from these other relations that the final terms get their meaning and significance" (1928c: 11).

"National statistics in war and peace" and "Economics and war" both argue, from very different standpoints and for very different audiences, that war and its aftermath were the determining events for the development of economics at the time. Significantly, Young places less emphasis on the purely economic problems (mobilization of resources, control of monetary disorder) and more on the general changes in society which alter the meaning and significance of economic problems (compare 1920a, 1921a, 1921b, 1923b, 1924c, 1924d). "If the war continues it is certain that the field of activity over which the public interest will be deemed to extend must be much further widened" (1918: 2). "Political organization has not kept pace with economic organization" (1926: 11).

This context provides for a rather different reading of the justly famous "Increasing returns and economic progress" (1928h). Posing as a gloss on Smith's dictum that the division of labor depends on the extent of the market, the paper can be read also as a reflection on the likely economic consequences of the gradual restoration of free international commerce in the aftermath of World War I. For Young, the history of American economic development showed what lay ahead for world economic development. Widening the extent of the market would inevitably stimulate economic progress, and economic progress would then stimulate further widening of the market in a cumulative process of endogenous growth. What was needed was an institutional basis, both economic and political, that would do for the world what the hard-won institutional basis at the level of the nation had done for the development of America.

Theory and practice

The papers in Section II backtrack a bit to trace the prewar development of Young's thought. The early extract on "the social dividend" (1908) shows Young's conception of the economy in its "togetherness," a conception remarkable for its synthesis of the individual with the social point of view (his "attribution" theory of distribution), the static with the dynamic (his "waiting" theory of capital), and the real with the monetary (his "money capital" theory of interest). The economy is not only a process in time – Young emphasizes that past sales, not current ones, pay for currently produced output – but also a process of growth (increasing roundaboutness), and a process in which the flow of funds through the financial system from surplus to deficit agents plays a critical role. The extract appeared as an appendix to the chapter on profits in the 1908 edition of the *Outlines*. Later editions (1916, 1923) gave increasing attention to the role of money and credit institutions, but already in 1908 Young's vision was clear of the way strains and maladjustments arise and contribute to business fluctuation, a vision that lies behind his later work on the way the banking system may exacerbate or moderate these strains.

The lectures on socialism (1912) show Young's conception of the nature of the communal problems that, in his view, were directing the development of economics as a science before war intervened. For him, the significance of the socialist movement came mainly from an increased appreciation that "private property is not a simple thing, but a complex thing; not a single right, but a bundle of rights." More specifically, the socialist movement was responsible for the conception that there is a general interest in increasing the social dividend and in distributing it more equitably. The challenge for economics was to figure out how such new goals might best be achieved in the context of a private property market economy.

This context provides for a rather different reading of another of Young's famous articles, his review essay on Pigou (1913b). Posing as a critique of some technical aspects of Pigou's theorizing, the paper can be read more deeply as a byproduct of Young's ongoing reflection about the practical consequences of a commitment to maximize the social dividend. His suggestion that Pigou might have benefited from "more intimate acquaintance with the recent work of American public utility commissions" reveals Young's conception of where the best work on the question was being done, not by theorists but by practitioners. In this regard, his paper on "Public borrowing for road building" (1915c) can be seen as more than just an occasional contribution, and instead part of a more general inquiry into the fundamental principles of public finance (compare 1913d, 1914b, 1914c and 1915a, 1915b, 1915d). The consideration (and rejection) of agriculture as a kind of public utility in the paper on "The economics of farm relief" (1926e) shows that Young carried his prewar viewpoint into the postwar period. The mature essays on "Economics," "Capital," and "Supply and demand" (1929b) show Young returning to the mode of his early "Social dividend" essay, attempting to draw a picture of economics once again in its togetherness after the distorting pressures of war had passed, so he thought.[1]

Commerce: the marketplace of the world

Section III contains selections from the first thirty chapters written by Young for the *Book of Popular Science*. These chapters were the result of an invitation from W.F.Kellogg of the Grolier Society of New York to participate in the production of an American edition of a well-known British encyclopaedia, the *Harmsworth Book of Popular Science* (1913). Young was asked to write thirty-six chapters on "Commerce" that paralleled, for the US and Canadian market, a similar number of chapters that had been written for Harmsworth by Sir Leo George Chiozza Money.[2]

The first versions of Young's original thirty-six chapters for the Grolier Society's *Book of Popular Science* were completed by Young between January and August 1922, but with revisions and updating (and two new chapters) over the next few years as new editions appeared. Young apparently used Chiozza Money's text as a starting point, though his revisions and additions were extensive. By comparing the Grolier edition with the Harmsworth, it was possible to separate Young's contribution. The selections included here represent about three quarters of Young's total contribution. Space considerations regrettably indicated deletion of much purely statistical or descriptive material, as well as the single chapter that surveyed Canada's prospects.[3]

At first glance the chapters appear as a mere compilation of facts about the American economy, but closer reading reveals a fascinating experiment in pedagogy (compare Riley 1925), and more. Rather than beginning, in the manner of most textbooks, with abstract concepts which are then used to illuminate some aspect of lived experience, Young begins in Chapter 1 with a big idea – trade is the source of wealth – and then proceeds to spend the next twenty-three chapters building a statistical portrait of trade in all its dimensions. The level of abstraction rises a notch in Chapters 20 and 21 where the concepts of wealth and income are examined critically for the first time, but the discussion remains largely at the level of statistical measurement. Chapters 25–7 are the first essentially non-statistical chapters since the opening, and only in Chapter 30 on "The meaning of value" do we find the kind of abstract discussion of economic concepts with which most textbooks begin. What is Young doing? In effect, he has arranged his materials in such a way that the reader learns economics inductively, passing from the concrete to the abstract and from the particular to the general, rather than the other way around.

So seductive is the lesson, and so sure is Young's guiding hand, that it is easy to lose sight of how radical and far-reaching the underlying big idea is. Trade is the source of wealth, not the innate fertility of land (Ch. 5), not the diligence of labor (Ch. 25), and not the ingenuity of invention (Ch. 11), but trade. It is trade that determines whether the capacity of soil to produce a particular crop is also the capacity to produce value, and whether labor however diligent or invention however ingenious is labor or invention that produces value. The natural resources of the world, including population, are only potential supplies and potential demands. It is trade that makes those potentialities manifest, and so creates wealth. The extent of the market limits the division of labor, and so also the productivity with which wealth is created. It is a theorem of Adam Smith, but physiocratic blinders limited Smith's vision of its implications. Not so Young, who, in direct contradiction to Smith, viewed Great Britain's specialization in the carrying trade (shipping) as a wise move (Ch. 3). Let the reader beware! There is a powerful theoretical argument lurking within these apparently benign statistical chapters.

Indeed, the theme of the *Grolier* to a large extent anticipates Young's later, and much more well-known, work on increasing returns, which in turn anticipates modern work on endogenous growth theory. Note, for example, his emphasis on what we would call human capital: "industrial and technical knowledge which the members of the community possess, handed down from generation to generation, diffused by education and increased by the advances of science" (Ch. 26). Even more significant, because so unexpected, although Young admits that agriculture faces diminishing returns in the short run and when viewed as a separate sector (Ch. 27), nevertheless he insists on the high elasticity of agricultural supply as population and the size of the entire market economy extends in the long run (Chs 2, 8; see also 1926e). The point is that cost reductions in manu-facturing, services, agriculture, and especially transport interact symbiotically. They depend on each other and they depend on overall growth in the national and international economy, and overall growth is in turn sustained by these sectoral improvements that together extend the size of the reachable markets and thus the size of potential demand. In this regard the discussion of cotton (Ch. 11) is especially revealing – Young is careful to emphasize that technological improvements are not the cause of growth, but rather large markets that make the use of new technologies economically feasible. This is endogenous growth, albeit not via the mechanisms usually emphasized in the modern literature (*see* discussion of Section V below).

Money and credit

Section IV is best approached, at least on first reading, as Young's attempt to work out his own answer to the exam questions he posed for his students, both undergraduate and graduate, in 1922. One sees in the questions that Young was working with the entire gamut of monetary thought, both the quantity theory of money and the real bills doctrine, both the gold theory of money's value and the legal tender theory, both the viewpoint of the monetary theorist and the viewpoint of the practical banker. And he was working with the entire gamut of monetary phenomena, both domestic and international, both long run and short run. One sees in the answers that Young took to heart his own dictum that theories are never completely right nor completely wrong, and that it is better to inquire about the significance of a theory for some particular phenomena. The farthest thing from an eclectic, Young played the entire scale of monetary theory because he was interested in understanding the range of monetary experience "in its togetherness."

The undergraduate questions get answered first in *Grolier* Chapter 31 ("The Value of Money") where Young draws the distinction between money and credit. Defining money by its function as the means of payment, Young includes in the money stock such forms of circulating credit as national bank notes (Ch. 32), but he nevertheless maintains the distinction between banks notes (money) and deposit accounts (credit) on the grounds that the latter depend on the personal credit of the depositor. Although, for historical reasons, the U.S. money stock is comprised of many different types of money (Young counts ten!), all the various types have one thing in common, and that one thing is what fits them all to serve as money, according to Young. They are all elastically "interchangeable" with the standard money, gold.

Elasticity is, for Young, the essential quality of money, the quality that enables money to serve as a means of payment. "An elastic demand in itself creates a safe outlet" (Ch. 31). In primitive monetary systems, the most elastically demanded commodity typically is chosen to serve as money (Ch. 31). The evolution of modern monetary systems (Chs 32–4) is the story of our attempt to perfect institutional mechanisms that ensure the elasticity of modern monies. More specifically, the evolution of modern monetary systems is a story of progress from the currency principle – such as lay behind both the 1844 Peel Act in Britain and the 1863 National Banking Act in the U.S. – to the banking school principle that lay behind the actual practice of the Bank of England (an elastic deposit currency, if not note issue) and both the design and functioning of the Federal Reserve System after 1913 (elastic deposits and note issue both). Young summarizes the difference between the two ways of thinking: "The currency principle stresses the analogy of bank-notes to government paper money, while the banking principle emphasizes the similarity of the bank-note and the deposit" (Ch. 33).

As between the two, there can be little question that Young's sympathies lie with the banking principle as he defines it. Against the currency principle, he finds a world of difference between irredeemable government paper money (a paper standard) and a bank note currency redeemable in gold. In the former case, exemplified for Young by the Greenback Era, Gresham's law operates to drive gold out of circulation and to depreciate the value of paper money against gold. In the latter case, the note issue is not a competing standard but only a subsidiary currency that gains its value from its exchangeability with the single standard. The better analogy is between bank notes and bank deposits – "A bank-note, like a bank deposit, is a bank's promise to pay on demand" (Ch. 31) – which is not to say the analogy is exact in all respects. For example, notes remain longer outstanding and so are more liable to excessive issue (Ch. 32). That said, however, there is no mistaking Young's enthusiasm for the new Federal Reserve System, nor the reasons for that enthusiasm. "Taking the system as a whole, it will be seen that it gives a thoroughly elastic supply of credit. It has all of the necessary elements: elastic note issue, elastic deposits and elastic reserves" (Ch. 33).

The evolution toward greater elasticity represents perfection of the monetary apparatus, which is a good thing in itself insofar as disruptive monetary crises can be avoided, but the really significant gains come from the indirect and longer term effects. Starting from the idea that trade is the source of wealth, it is not too far a stretch to the conclusion that the institutions of money and credit are also a source of wealth, insofar as they support the expansion of trade (Ch. 33). Young takes the lesson of history that the institutions of money and credit tend to follow rather than lead economic development, and often with a considerable lag because politics, not economics, most often drives financial development, at least in the short-run. (The 1926 introduction to Steels contains Young's most forthright account of the political forces involved – the debtor interest vs. the creditor interest, the frontier west vs. the New York "money power.") The elasticity of the monetary system is therefore a good thing insofar as elasticity supports economic development.

Elasticity having been achieved, certain perennial economic problems were solved, but Young saw new problems emerging in their place, namely the problem of the business cycle. Young thought that business cycles were a matter of strains and maladjustments in the dynamic adaptation of the pattern of production to the pattern of demand, and he thought further that the credit system was integrally involved in these strains because credit allowed the pattern of current income to diverge from the pattern of current spending. Starting from this point of view, Young came naturally to ponder the question how the new Federal Reserve System apparatus might be employed in order to smooth, or at the very least not to exacerbate, business fluctuation. This is the subject of Chapters 35 and 36.

As Young approached the problem, the point was to find ways to improve on the kind of automatic regulation of cycles that had occurred in the previous regime. Man's invention of a banking apparatus to ensure elasticity meant that the credit system was no longer automatically regulated by the scarcity of reserves. The point is not that the automatic system worked all that well – it didn't – but rather that regulation now requires conscious and deliberate effort by the monetary authorities. What should they do, if anything? Here it is important to be very clear that Young rejected the laissez-faire policy of passive accommodation. Though he favored an elastic credit system, he also believed (with Hawtrey) that the credit system was inherently unstable, and so required regulation.

More specifically, Young rejected the real bills doctrine as a guide for monetary policy despite his sympathy for the banking principle with which the doctrine is usually associated. Unlike real bills advocates, Young recognized not only the impossibility of drawing a strict line between real and finance bills, but also the undesirability of doing so for the purposes of monetary policy. No real bills advocate would ever have written, as Young did: "the speculator, so far as he operates wisely and shrewdly, is in reality a producer of wealth" (Ch. 35). Young understood business enterprise as a process in time, inherently involving speculation, and so found himself unable to condemn those who made a business speciality out of one dimension of speculation. What then were the principles on which the newly formed monetary authority could rely?

In this regard, Chapter 36 can be understood as an extended contrast between the work of Irving Fisher and Ralph Hawtrey, to the definite advantage of the latter (compare 1920b, 1923a, 1924e; *see also* Mehrling 1997, Ch. 4). Young's sympathies were with those who wanted to manage money, but he realized, as others did not, that managing money was a difficult thing, not a simple thing. Following Hawtrey, Young hoped that judicious discount rate policy, enforced by open market operations, will enable the monetary authority to stabilize the business cycle, raising the rate to slow an unsustainable boom and lowering it to speed recovery from recession. Young's discussion makes clear that the point is not so much to control the outstanding stock of money (notes) issued by the monetary authorities as it is to control the flow of expenditure by controlling the flow of new credit. Modern readers may be misled by Young's use of the framework of the quantity theory of money, a framework nowadays most often associated with the currency principle, so it is worth repeating. To the extent that credit control is successful, expenditure will remain in line with output so prices do not rise. At the same time, slower growth of bank lending means slower growth of bank liabilities, be they bank notes (money) or deposits (credit). Thus money and prices move together, but they do so because they are both effects of a third cause.

Hawtrey of course made much of the "art" of central banking, but in Chapter 35 Young seems to have been looking for more scientific principles by developing a theory of how the price of money, which is the interest rate, affects borrowers' demand for it. ("The price of money means the rate of interest asked for the loan of it." Ch. 34.) The importance of such an exercise follows from the fact that, in a world of elastic currency supply, not the quantity of money but only the price of money can be an instrument of monetary policy. The challenge of developing a theory of money demand comes from the fact that, as Young says, money is not demanded for itself, but only as a means of payment, which means that the usual demand and supply analytical apparatus may be unreliable. Young begins to make analytical progress on the problem by considering the demand for money to be a speculative demand, i.e. a demand based on expectations of price changes, not a demand for the underlying commodity.

The importance of this analytical direction is not fully apparent in the chapter itself, which merely mentions in passing the relation between stock market speculation and the money market, a relation Young deplores. It is only in subsequent work, most notably *Bank Statistics*, that Young spins out the implications for monetary control. Unlike in Hawtrey's Britain, the crux of instability is not in the money (bills) market, but in the long-term capital markets, aided and abetted by bank lending. Furthermore, the instability is not so much a trade cycle as it is an industrial investment cycle, and it is less connected with international swings and more connected with domestic rhythms. Unlike Hawtrey (and unlike his own gloss on Hawtrey in *Grolier* Ch. 36), Young came to think there was "no basis for the belief that these cyclical swings, once under way, were never halted until the resources of the banks had been exhausted." Because the channels of instability were different from those emphasized by Hawtrey, the nature of the instrument for control would also have to be different, not discount rate manipulation to control the pace of bank lending, but rather open market operations to influence the timing of capital refunding operations (see also 1923c).

Young's attempt to bring the theory of speculative asset pricing to bear on the field of money was not confined to the rather specific institutional setting of the United States. Note how, for example, in "Downward Price Trend Probable" Young traces the demand for gold reserves not so much to the quantity of gold relative to transactions but rather to the demand for gold as determined by banking institutions and the degree of confidence in their continued smooth operation. Even more interesting is his account of money demand in the inconvertible paper money system of postwar France (1929g), where foreign exchange speculation played the major role. Here the important difference from the gold standard case is that, as Young says, "There is no 'limiting' or 'ultimate' supply of inconvertible money apart from such restrictions as the government may choose to impose upon itself or upon the banks." For Young, the significant question is not whether a change in the money supply causes a change in prices, but rather whether or not the government is able and willing to impose restrictions and, even more significant, whether or not the (speculative) holders of money believe in the government's ability and willingness to do what needs to be done.

In this regard, Young found it hard to overestimate the importance of the establishment of the Federal Reserve System, a move for which he gives decisive credit to Woodrow Wilson's political skill (1926d). For Young, the establishment of the Fed was about much more than mere technical improvements in the operation of the monetary system. Note the emphasis he places on the fact (as he thought) that the System was designed not so much to mimic European central banks, but rather to mimic the clearinghouse mechanisms that banks had innovated during banking crises (such as that of 1907) in order to overcome the defects of the National Banking System. The Federal Reserve System took over the instruments designed in the very heart of the money power, and ensured that hereafter they would be utilized for the public interest (compare 1927d). A triumph of economics over politics, and of the general interest over merely sectional interest, the Fed would be a force for stability not so much on account of its wise intervention, since it would inevitably err, and not so much on account of its strong control over the system, since its control was anything but strong. Rather, the real importance of the Fed, according to Young, was that no longer would monetary issues be treated as a "football of politics." Stability would come first and foremost from the fact that, given the institution of the Fed, speculators had less reason than ever before to doubt the government's willingness and ability to do what needed to be done. It was to be expected, therefore, that what speculation remained would overwhelmingly be of the "prudent" sort that operates to stabilize markets, not to destabilize them.

Having been for so long a source of monetary instability for the world economy, the United States became after the establishment of the Fed the great bastion of stability, at least as compared with other central banks (compare 1924c, 1924d, 1924f). The next logical step forward, so Young argued in "Downward price trend probable" (1929a), would involve overcoming the merely apparent sectional interests of individual nations in favor of the true international general interest, in effect applying the lessons of U.S. history at the world level. Unfortunately, for lack of any overarching institution capable of taking the general view, atomistic competition of individual central banks for a limited gold reserve was beginning to place completely unnecessary strain on the world's monetary system (much as the defective National Banking system had done previously). Young thought the strain would cause long-term deflation, but he was too optimistic. As it happened, the strain instead led to collapse and worldwide depression, though Young did not live to see it.

Growth and fluctuations

In Section V all these monetary issues are in the background, while Young turns his attention more directly to the questions of economic growth and fluctuation. For both questions, Young seems to have felt that the standard economist's tools had little to offer, designed as they were to handle the rather different questions of value and distribution. Nicholas Kaldor's notes on Young's LSE lectures are best read as an initial attempt to work out an alternative analytical apparatus, with mixed success.

In his discussion of the determinants of long-run growth, Young seems to be struggling, with some misgivings, to adapt the static and microeconomic Marshallian long-run demand and supply apparatus to the dynamic and macro-economic problem of growth.[4] The problem Young faces is that he views growth as fundamentally a phenomenon of increasing returns, and "seeking for equili-brium conditions under increasing returns is as good as looking for a mare's nest." Analytical progress can be made by abandoning the idea of increasing returns, as we know from the neoclassical, constant-returns growth model of Solow (1957), but this direction was not open to Young, given his theoretical priors.

The problem was not just that Young viewed increasing returns as the essence of growth, but also that he would have been uncomfortable building a theory of growth on the neoclassical theory of distribution. Wages and profits measure compensation, which is not the same thing as contribution because of the pervasive externalities involved in the growth process.[5] In this regard, it is instructive to compare Young's growth accounting (*Grolier* Ch. 37) with the more familiar neoclassical growth accounting. Young notes that production per worker increased because workers were better equipped, and he notes that compensation per worker increased as well, but he never uses compensation as a measure of productivity. Further, he carefully avoids the vexed question of measuring capital, using instead a physical measure of horsepower to suggest the degree to which workers were better equipped. In the end, Young was too much the empiricist ever to be comfortable with the kind of analytical abstrac-tions on which modern developments in growth theory have been based.

Young's discussion of fluctuations is more successful, since here analytical progress can be made by viewing fluctuations as deviations from equilibrium (*see* LSE lecture, 1 May), much in the same way that asset price fluctuations can be viewed as temporary speculative deviations from true valuation (compare *Grolier*

Ch. 35). Notably, he presents this analysis only after a critical review of alternative explanations which he suggests don't quite get to the core of the question, despite their useful emphasis on the interplay of expenditure and income, of investment and savings, of purchasing power and output. The alternative view that business cycles are about speculation not only offers a simpler analysis, but also leads directly to the policy conclusion that credit control may be an effective lever of stabilization. Also possibly effective, improvements in business forecasting may help to ensure that prudent stabilizing speculation would come to dominate the imprudent destabilizing sort.

The discussion of deviations from equilibrium may leave the misleading impression that Young thought equilibrium was an achievable policy goal. Not so: in his mind, the essence of a modern capitalist economy was not stability but growth and structural change. For him, not only aggregates but more importantly the pattern of output and the pattern of demand were in constant flux, flux that showed up not so much in the overall price level as in the constantly shifting structure of relative prices. It is the stresses and strains caused by misalignment that give long-run growth its cyclical character, but those stresses and strains are the very stuff of economic growth, and cannot be abolished without abolishing growth. What Young wanted was to use the credit apparatus to buffer the economic system at times of stress, without allowing undue credit expansion or contraction to become an additional source of stress. For Young, fluctuation came with growth, but excessive fluctuation could be a barrier to growth. He hoped to use the new Federal Reserve System apparatus to walk a line between too much fluctuation and too little, both of which stand in the way of achieving potential economic growth.

If the LSE lectures may be viewed as the early stages of an academic treatise, the two *Grolier* chapters 37 and 38 (apparently written at about the same time as the lectures) show the broader vision of growth and fluctuation that lay behind Young's analytical efforts. "Economic changes since the war" poses as an account of the causes and consequences of the shift in the center of the world economy toward America, only to downplay the shift by placing it in the longer context of economic development at the world level. What is most significant, in Young's view, is not the relative rise of America, but rather the continuing expansion of the market at the world level. War, currency instability, and continuing bouts of economic nationalism all pose threats to further expansion, but Young views them as temporary setbacks only. At the world level, just as at the level of the United States, he was confident that economics and the general interest would win out in the long run, even though politics and sectional interests seem so often to win out in the short run.

It is a grand and hopeful vision, but what, one may ask, does it mean for me? "Big business" (Ch. 38) can be read as Young's attempt to answer the question posed by the impatient encyclopaedia reader. Doesn't the expansion of the market mean large-scale business, monopoly that threatens democracy, and standardization that threatens treasured variety of life? No, says Young. The expansion of the scale of production does not necessarily mean expansion of the size of the representative firm. It all depends on the particular product in question. Expansion of production means reorganization of production, which may or may not mean integration and standardization. On a number of specifics, Young's forecast of the future was apparently wide of the mark. The rise of agribusiness certainly contradicts his forecast of the survival of the family farm, and the integration of the printing industry contradicts his forecast of the survival of craft on account of the variety of products. Nevertheless, the larger lesson remains as much worth attending today as it was in his time. Small business does survive, much as Young expected it would, and even in industries apparently dominated by a few very large firms.

In this regard, Young's extended account of the forces changing the face of the retail trade in his time makes fascinating reading even today. Where he writes about the telephone and the automobile, the modern reader will substitute the internet and inexpensive package delivery services. Where he writes about the rise of the department store and the chain store, the modern reader will substitute the rise of large discount retailers (Walmart) and specialty catalogues (L. L. Bean). Young reminds us, as he reminded his own intended audience, that there are diseconomies of scale as well as economies of scale, that expansion of the size of the market does not necessarily mean expansion of the size of the representative firm, that standardization does not only crowd out craft but also provides additional scope for the expression of craft, that increasing returns are realized not just at the level of the firm, but also at the level of the industry, the nation, and, most significantly, the world economy as a whole.[6]

In his togetherness, the lesson of Young may be summarized. Trade is the source of wealth, and expansion of the market is the source of increasing wealth. The point, however, is not wealth *per se*, but rather the civilization that wealth makes possible, and the democratic civilization that a competitive market economy supports. In this respect, expansion of the market is also about expansion of liberty, and about the general interest winning over mere sectional interest. Young's enthusiasm for the market was the farthest thing from the apologetics of a laissez-faire advocate.

Where monopoly threatened competition (railroads and utilities), he sought principles of regulation. Where atomistic private property threatened the general interest (water resources and banking), he sought principles of public management. For Young, the market was always a means to an end, not an end in itself. The role of the state was to ensure that the potential general benefits of the market – in terms of liberty as well as wealth – were actually realized, and not dissipated in merely sectional or individual appropriation.

Notes

1 Taken together, "Social dividend" (1908) and "Economics" (1929) shed some additional light on the origins of Frank Knight's famous circular flow diagram (Patinkin, 1981). Part of Patinkin's search for the "wheel of wealth" led him to Knight's 1951 *Encyclopaedia Britannica* entry entitled "Economics," but this was actually a lightly edited version of Young's 1929 entry. Patinkin's search also missed Young's 1908 "social dividend" discussion

because he consulted only the first (1893) and last (1937) editions of the *Outlines* (Patinkin 1981: 54), and Young's discussion disappeared after the 1923 edition, perhaps because it was found to be too difficult for students (Blitch 1995: 56). Knight studied economics with Young at Cornell and would have known Young's 1908 revised version of Ely's text.

2 Chiozza Money (1870–1944) was, among other things, an economic journalist noted for his writings on the distribution of income in the UK, set forth in *Riches and Poverty*, London 1905. He was elected Liberal Member of Parliament from 1906–18, during which time he served on various official select committees dealing with economic matters. From 1915–16 he was private secretary to the then Minister of Munitions, Mr Lloyd George, and in 1917 he drafted the new Pensions Scheme while serving as private secretary to the Minister of Pensions. He resigned from the Liberal Party in 1918 to stand (unsuccessfully) as the Labour parliamentary candidate for South Tottenham. He was later the editor of the economic, financial, industrial, engineering and sociological sections of the 14th edition of the *Encyclopaedia Britannica*, 1929. Young was familiar with Chiozza Money's work from an early date (see Young 1911a). In addition to his work on Money's text for the Grolier project, Young also contributed eleven entries to the *Encyclopaedia Britannica* under Money's editorship, three of which are reproduced in this volume.

3 We have excluded those *Grolier* chapters where Young made only minor alterations to what was written by Chiozza Money for Harmsworth. These included chapters on coal, cotton goods, wool, and the shipping of the world. The chapters that were written mainly or exclusively by Young but not reproduced in this volume are: Chapter 10 on wheat in international trade; Chapter 12 on the trade in cotton goods; Chapter 15 on America's merchant marine; Chapter 18 on America's water routes; and Chapter 24 on Canada.

4 The diagrams in the lectures on "Particular expenses and supply curves" help explain the famously puzzling diagram and mathematical note at the end of his 1928 presidential address (see Reid 1989, Ch. 8).

5 Compare *Grolier* Chapter 26: "Appraised by his real contributions to wealth and welfare, not in dollars and cents, the scientist may easily outrank the millionaire or the captain of industry. His contributions to society's capital are, in general, free. For that reason they do not fall under the ordinary laws of supply and demand." Similar points were made at the end of his discussion of the "social dividend" (1908).

6 Young's agnosticism over the appropriate size of the individual firm or plant, his stress on the desirability and intensity of competition as the size of the market expands, and his skepticism over the desirability or effectiveness of patent protection, all contrast rather sharply with modern endogenous growth models (*see* Aghion and Howitt's recent survey, 1998) and "new trade theory" (pioneered by Krugman 1990). These models focus mainly on *internal* economies of scale; present a case for investment subsidies, patents and tariff protection; and view monopolistic competition as a necessary and integral part of the growth process.

References

Aghion, Philippe and Howitt, Peter. (1998) *Endogenous Growth Theory*. Cambridge, Mass. and London: MIT Press.

Blitch, Charles P. (1995) *Allyn Young: The Peripatetic Economist*. London: Macmillan Press.

Currie, Lauchlin. (1981) "Allyn Young and the Development of Growth Theory," *Journal of Economic Studies* 8, 1: 52–60.

—— (1997) "Implications of an Endogenous Theory of Growth in Allyn Young's Macro-economic Concept of Increasing Returns," *History of Political Economy* 29, 3 (Fall): 413–43.

Deutscher, Patrick. (1990) *R. G. Hawtrey and the Development of Macroeconomics*. London: Macmillan Press.

Ely, Richard T. (1893, 1908, 1916, 1923, 1930, 1937 editions) *Outlines of Economics*. New York: Macmillan.

Friedman, Milton and Schwartz, Anna J. (1963) *A Monetary History of the United States, 1867–1960*. Princeton, NJ: Princeton University Press (for NBER).

Gregory, T.E. (1929) "Allyn Abbott Young," *Economic Journal* 39: 297–301.

Kaldor, Nicholas. (1972) "The Irrelevance of Equilibrium Economics," *Economic Journal* 82: 1237–55.

—— (1985) *Economics Without Equilibrium.* Cardiff: University College of Cardiff Press.

Krugman, Paul R. (1990) *Rethinking International Trade.* Cambridge, MA and London: MIT Press.

Laidler, David. (1993) "Hawtrey, Harvard, and the Origins of the Chicago Tradition," *Journal of Political Economy* 101, 6 (December): 1068–103.

—— (1998) "More on Hawtrey, Harvard and Chicago," *Journal of Economic Studies* 25, 1: 4–24.

Mehrling, Perry G. (1996) "The Monetary Thought of Allyn Abbott Young," *History of Political Economy* 28, 4 (Winter): 607–32.

—— (1997) *The Money Interest and the Public Interest: American Monetary Thought, 1920–70.* Harvard Economic Studies, 162. Cambridge, Mass., and London: Harvard University Press.

Morgenstern, Oskar. (1929) "Allyn Abbott Young" (as tr. and repr. in A. Schotter (ed.) *Selected Economic Writings of Oskar Morgenstern.* New York: New York University Press, 1976).

Patinkin, Don. (1981) "In Search of the 'Wheel of Wealth', " in *Essays On and In the Chicago Tradition,* Durham, NC: Duke University Press, Ch. 2: 53–72.

Reed, Harold Lyle, (with Allyn Young). (1925) *Principles of Corporation Finance.* Boston: Houghton Mifflin.

Reid, Gavin C. (1989) *Classical Economic Growth.* Cambridge: Cambridge University Press.

Riley, Eugene B. (with Allyn Young). (1925) *Economics for Secondary Schools.* Boston: Houghton Mifflin.

Romer, Paul M. (1989) "Capital Accumulation in the Theory of Long-run Growth," in Barro, Robert J. (ed.), *Modern Business Cycle Theory.* Cambridge: Harvard University Press.

Sandilands, Roger J. (1990) *The Life and Political Economy of Lauchlin Currie: New Dealer, Presidential Adviser and Development Economist.* Durham, NC: Duke University Press.

Schumpeter, Joseph A. (1912: first German edition; English edition, 1934) *The Theory of Economic Development.* Cambridge, MA: Harvard University Press.

Taussig, Frank W., Bullock, Charles J. and Burbank, Harold H. (1929) "Allyn Abbott Young," *Quarterly Journal of Economics.* August.

Young, Allyn A. For these references, see Chapter 47, Bibliography of Allyn Young's writings at the end of this volume.

Acknowledgements

Chapter 1 first appeared in *The Quarterly Journal of Economics* 42:1, (November 1927), pp. 1–25 and is reprinted with the kind permission of MIT Press Journals © 1927 by the President and Fellows of Harvard University.

Chapter 2 first appeared in *Economica* (March 1928), pp. 1–15, and is reprinted with the kind permission of Blackwell Publishers.

Chapter 4 first appeared in the *American Economic Review* 16:1, (March), pp. 1–13 and is reprinted with the kind permission of the American Economic Association.

Chapter 5 first appeared in the *Economic Journal* (December 1928) and is produced with the kind permission of Blackwells Publishers on behalf of the Royal Economic Society.

Chapter 8 first appeared in *The Quarterly Journal of Economics* 27:4 (August 1913) pp. 672–86.

Chapters 11, 12 and 13 are reprinted with permission from *Encyclopaedia Britannica*, 14th edition © 1929 by Encyclopaedia Britannica, Inc.

Chapters 14–31, 33–38 and 45–46 first appeared in *The Book of Popular Science*, 1924 edition. Copyright by The Grolier Society. Reprinted with permission.

Chapter 32 is part of the Allyn Young Papers and is reprinted courtesy of the Harvard University Archives.

Chapter 39 first appeared as two journal articles in *The Review of Economics and Statistics* 6:4, (October 1924), pp. 284–96 © 1924 by the President and Fellows of Harvard College and *The Review of Economics and Statistics* 7: 1 (January 1925), pp.19–37 © 1925 by the Presidents and Fellows of Harvard College. This material is reprinted with the kind permission of MIT Press Journals.

Chapter 40 first appeared in Steels, J. *La Banque à Succursales dans le système bancaire des Etats-Unis* (1926), and is reprinted with the kind permission of the Faculteit Rechtsgeleerdheid, Universiteit Gent.

The publishers have made every effort to contact authors/copyright holders of works reprinted in *Money and Growth*. We would welcome correspondence from any individuals/companies we have not been able to trace.

Part I

The nature and scope of economics

1 Economics as a field of research

Quarterly Journal of Economics (1927) 42, 1 (November): 1–25. Read before the Institute for Research in the Social Sciences, of the University of Virginia, on May 20, 1927, as the second of a series of lectures dealing with the fundamental objectives and methods of research in the social sciences.

I. The social sciences differ from the physical in that the observer's interest lies within them. – The contractual and the institutional views of society. – Corresponding types of investigation. – The genetic point of view. – II. Group research and its promise. – Induction and deduction. – Fruitful hypotheses essential. – Individual research; the constructive imagination. – Promising types of research. – The limitations and promise of research.

I

The social sciences, like the natural sciences, proceed upon the one great premise that the intricate flux of events can in some way be explained. What appear to be arbitrary or capricious happenings can be fitted into a scheme which has no room for anything but dependable uniformity and regularity. Such is the first article of the scientist's creed. The second article of that creed is that the one way to come to a knowledge of these hidden uniformities is by means of those patient and methodical inquiries which we call research.

The social sciences, however have to be distinguished from the physical sciences, not only because the phenomena with which they deal are more complex, because their data are less exact, and because the experimental method which the more rigorous physical sciences employ is generally not available to them, but also because they encounter problems of *orientation* which are peculiar to them and from which the physical sciences are free. The physical scientist sets himself, as an impartial observer, outside of nature, inquires into nature's processes, and tries to reduce them to simple general relations. He does not hope to be able to change nature, or even in any literal sense to gain "increased power over nature." But he knows that as we come to understand nature's processes better we are able to make better use of them – which means merely that in our ways of doing things we take account of our new knowledge. The data of the physical sciences are physical phenomena, but the problems which these sciences seek to solve are born of human interests, and so far as the knowledge which they yield has instrumental value, it serves human ends and leads to modifications of human arrangements.

The social scientist cannot, in any comparable way, put himself, as an impartial observer, outside of society, so as to get a view of social processes as a connected whole. His interests, his values, his ends, lie *within* that connected whole. Every occurrence in the contemporary life of a society enters into two separate sets of relations. In the first place, every such occurrence is a phenomenon, a scientific datum, which has to be fitted into the ordered scheme of social processes. In the second place, every such occurrence has its own immediate and concrete significance, and has to be accorded its due weight in any system of social values. We seek to understand the impersonal processes of nature and to take account of them, but we neither approve nor disapprove of them. We also seek to understand and to take account of social processes, but we reserve the right to approve or disapprove of them. We do not hope to change nature's uniformities; but the processes of organized society, we believe, are in some degree plastic. So far as the knowledge which the social sciences yield has instrumental value, it serves social ends and leads to modifications of social arrangements. In any complete view the realm of the phenomena of organized society and the realm of ends are coterminous. The great first premise of the scientific method compels us to view these phenomena as rigidly determined and predictable, while the interests that prompt our scientific inquiries imply that they are in some measure amenable to control.

Upon the general philosophical aspects of the predicament in which the social scientist finds himself I do not propose to dwell. My present concern is with the practical devices by means of which men interested in social problems have been able to get something of value out of the scientific study of social processes. These devices all involve some particular orientation and some particular ordered scheme of abstraction. The traditional type of economic theory, for example, rests upon the common interest in increasing the production of wealth and securing its juster distribution. The data which it submits to scientific scrutiny (the pertinent aspects of the physical environment, along with other commonplace facts, being taken as given) are the reciprocal relations between certain types of human conduct that appear to be fairly stable and dependable in the mass, and the variations of such economic magnitudes as product, prices, wages, costs, profits, and interest rates. The economic processes of society are thus viewed as constituting an intricate but reliable mechanism, operating in an orderly and predictable way.

But this economic mechanism is something more than an object for scientific analysis and contemplation. It may be controlled, directed, or interfered with. It is a social instrument, to be *used* as our communal interests may dictate. Above the economic man stands the political man, free to limit and define the field of the economic man's activity, to impose conditions upon him, to prevent him from doing certain things, to encourage him to do others. It is incorrect, therefore, to say that the traditional political economy implies a wholly mechanistic view of human society. All that it implies is a particular orientation, with one particular set of social processes viewed as a mechanism by free agents who want to understand the workings of the mechanism because they want to know how best to control it and use it. They want to know how far to control it and how far to leave it alone, and it is desirable that they should be able to predict the more remote as well as the immediate effects of particular measures of control. Agents, mechanism, instruments, and ends are thus all in the picture. Doubtless they are seen in a one-sided and partial way, and yet this view of things has proved itself to be practically serviceable, and the traditional political economy which embodied it was one of the great intellectual achievements of the nineteenth century.

Every social science has to be defined in terms of its problems, and accordingly includes agents, instruments, and ends, as well as a mechanism, among its postulates. But every social science has its own particular orientation. Thus for political science the behaviour of the political man may well be an object of scientific scrutiny, just as educational science may focus its attention upon the learner and criminology upon the law breaker. The same human activities which one science regards as sufficiently uniform and dependable in the mass to make scientific analysis of them profitable, appear in other social sciences as free or plastic. To the economist the citizen, the voter, may be a free agent; to the political scientist his conduct may be in some measure determinate; to the student of education he may be a bit of malleable human material.

There is no necessary conflict between these different views, for each is a partial view. Held to consistently, they would separate the different social sciences rather more narrowly and rigidly than is practically desirable. A worker in any part of the field of the social sciences needs to be aware of the importance for his own problems of more orientations than one. But I venture to hold that no complete *scientific* synthesis of all the different social sciences is possible, if only for the reason that, as I have said, the inquirer, with his interests, must stand somewhere *within* society and its processes.

There is another problem of orientation, which cuts across all the social sciences, for there are two different possible views of the general structure of society. Both views can be traced back as far as the Greeks, but sometimes one view and sometimes the other has been dominant. These two views, or ways of conceiving the structure of society, are the contractual and the institutional. In the contractual view social arrangements are deliberate contrivances resting upon voluntary agreements – instruments which men use in attaining their purposes. In the institutional view these same arrangements appear as social habits, the products of history, not really shaped by the rational prevision of men, but dominant factors, themselves, in determining what men's purposes and values shall be, and establishing the patterns which human behavior follows. In the one view, the institutions which make up the structure of society are human expedients; in the other view, man himself, except for his endowment of native powers and propensities, is the product of life in society. These views are variously distinguished, as individualistic and social, rational and genetic, atomistic and universalistic, mechanistic and organic. Each pair of names conveys a particular emphasis, or invokes a particular analogy, but each expresses the same fundamental contrast or opposition.

I see no satisfactory ground for any other position than that both of these opposed views take account of necessary aspects of the structure and the processes of organized society, and that neither view, taken by itself, is adequate. Yet the opposition between these two views has at one time and another divided social scientists into two warring camps. We have had, and still have, too much of what Mill, in his essay on Coleridge called "the noisy conflict of half-truths, angrily denying one another." Mill added these wise words: "All students of man and society who possess that first requisite for so difficult a study, a due sense of its difficulties, are aware that the besetting danger is not so much of embracing falsehood for truth, as of mistaking part of the truth for the whole." These are words for all inquirers in the field of the social sciences to remember. Our work is retarded and our intellectual energies are dissipated in useless quarrels because of our intolerance of methods and points of view other than our own. There are only two things of which we have a right to be intolerant: first, positive errors of fact or of inference; second, intolerance itself.

Since the two views of which I have spoken are really supplementary, one to the other, it follows that in the social sciences we must make room for two different general classes or types of investigation. In the first type we concern ourselves with certain aspects of the nature and the operations of a complicated social mechanism. We search for uniform and dependable relations that will help to explain the degree of order that is apparent in our social environment. In the second type of inquiries we seek to get an understanding, not of those general and dependable relations among things which we call "laws," but of specific events, particular institutions, and unique situations. We look for explanations of *differences*, of the *new* forms which our institutions and our activities assume from time to time.

What am I trying to emphasize is the distinction between the field of "science," in a narrow and strict sense, and the field of "history" – a distinction which many philosophers have recognized, but which has been curiously neglected in current American discussions of the problems and methods of the social sciences. Because both the natural and the social sciences, as commonly defined, extend over both fields, I prefer to follow Cournot in distinguishing, not between science and history, but between the abstract sciences and the historical sciences, between the sciences which have to do with those dependable abstract general relations which we call laws, and the sciences which deal with given situations or particular events in terms of their specific relations to situations and events which have preceded them.

Now it is a capital error to hold (with Thorstein Veblen and some of his followers) that the explanation of things in terms of their historical antecedents is in some special sense a scientific mode of explanation; that, as Veblen puts it, modern sciences are characteristically "evolutionary sciences," and concern themselves primarily with "unfolding sequences" and "cumulative causation." The truth is, of course, that the goal towards which the natural sciences are always pressing – even though it may be an unattainable goal – is the explanation of this world of changing and evolving forms and types of organization in terms of some simple and stable mechanism. Mathematical physics has not abdicated to descriptive genetics its place as the perfect type of science, and in a manner the ultimate type.

It is far from my purpose to belittle the importance of historical and genetic inquiries for the social sciences. I am merely trying to correct what seem to me to be prevalent misconceptions respecting the part they play in increasing our knowledge. I shall not even attempt to support the thesis that the unique and special character of historical events make "historical laws" impossible – for that thesis seems to depend partly on the way in which we define "history," and partly on what we mean by "law." There can be no doubt, however, that the sort of knowledge that we get from those historical inquiries which assume the institutional view of the structure of society, is not the sort of knowledge that we get from those inquiries into abstract general relations which assume a mechanistic or contractual view of the structure of society.

The mechanistic or contractual view of society is of necessity an instrumental view. The knowledge we get from researches into the nature of the general form of the economic relations that obtain in such a society is practical working knowledge, and can be formulated in working rules. It tells us what the general character of effects of a particular measure of control will be, what will happen if we pull a particular lever. Historical and genetic inquiries do not lead to working rules. They extend the range of our experience, they give us a better understanding of ourselves and of our possibilities and our limitations, they lead to new appraisals of our social arrangements, but they tell us little or nothing about means. At their best they add to our wisdom, to our judgment respecting what things are worth accomplishing, but they add little to the technical equipment required for successful accomplishment.

Researches into the "unfolding sequence" of institutional forms encounter the difficulty that the results they give are never scientifically verifiable. Wholly different interpretations of the course of history may have equally good credentials. A countless number of threads of continuity ramify backward into the past, and are woven together into what Maitland called the seamless web of history. Selection among them has to be made on the ground of present interests, and there is always the danger that it will be made on the ground of present predilections or present prejudices. Every account of the origins and the development of any of our contemporary institutions involves a revaluation of the past as well as of the present. (Consider, for example, the contrast between Alfred Marshall's summary account of what he calls "the growth of free industry and enterprise," and any one of the various socialistic accounts of the origins of what the socialists prefer to call "modern capitalism.")

Of course, the worker in this field cannot give free rein to his imagination, for he is controlled and limited by the facts. But his task is not merely to ascertain the facts: he has to select them, evaluate them, and relate them so that they will tell their story. His task is not merely one of research, but of esthetic construction as well. What he sees and reproduces will depend not only upon what there is to be seen, but upon what he looks for, and that will depend upon himself, his training, and his interests.

I do not mean to suggest that within the limits set by the facts the historical or genetic interpretation of our existing economic order depends solely upon the personal equation of the investigator. If he is an honest workman he will be controlled by the circumstance that all of the knowledge he gets, by whatever methods of inquiry, must fit together so as to be a consistent whole. In practice the lines between different views of the structure of economic society and different methods of inquiry cannot be drawn so sharply as I may have seemed to suggest. The economic theorist does not "deduce" his results from a few simple premises. Even when he controls his findings by using statistics, he works in the midst of a context of experience, and the system of general relations which constitutes his theory is empty of meaning unless it is consistent with that body of experience, and explains and organizes some part of it. Similarly, whatever new views of the structure of economic society we get by looking backward to its development must supplement and be consistent with that abstract and general view of economic relations which we call economic theory. Every economic theorist ought to be something of an historian, and every student of the development of economic institutions ought to be something of a theorist.

It may be that I have dwelt overlong on these preliminaries, but this has seemed to me to be an appropriate occasion for entering a protest against the fruitless quarrels of the methodological sects, against their intolerance, and against their pretensions to exclusive possession of the only right points of view and the only effective methods of research. We ought to welcome sound work in the field of economics – work that really contributes to our understanding of economic problems, – whatever its orientation and whatever method or technique it employs. The prerequisite to this degree of tolerance is the recognition of the fact that no one orientation can possibly lay bare the whole field of the economist's interests.

II

I hesitate to try to say towards what particular economic problems research could most profitably be directed just now. The difficulty is partly in the necessity of fitting research problems to the interests and equipment of the individual investigator and to the resources available to him, and partly in the rich diversity of important problems. Much depends, moreover, upon whether group research or individual research is contemplated.

Group research is an important and promising new development. It involves a common attack upon a particular problem or set of problems, by an organized body of investigators who apportion their work so as to get some of the advantages of the division of labor, and who may be able to turn over routine parts of their tasks to a corps of clerical assistants. This sort of organized research undoubtedly has advantages when what is wanted is a definite answer to a definite question, and when the question is one of fact. The task then is one of assembling materials and of putting them through appropriate technical processes so as to get a finished product. The form, though not the precise content, of the product is known in advance. The product must always be got by assembling facts in a particular way, or by relating them in a particular way. Doubtless research of this kind, directed toward a definite objective, will often yield important by-products; and doubtless, also, individual investigators who are engaged in this kind of research, will often hit upon new methods of dealing with their materials, or will find that new explanations and possible new inquiries come into their minds. But the specific goal of such research, as I have said, is a definite answer to a definite question of fact.

We have made hardly more than a beginning in organized group research in economics, and I look for a considerable increase in the number and importance of such undertakings. There are many important tasks which are beyond the powers and the resources of the individual investigator and which call for the coöperation of a number of investigators, with different capacities and different training. The advantages of this kind of organized coöperation are so obvious that I need not enlarge upon them. Its limitations are, or ought to be, equally obvious. These limitations are bound up with the fact that effective research is more than mere routine, more than a manufacturing process. The multiplication of research activities and the increase of endowments for research will not of themselves afford any assurance that there will be a corresponding increase of our understanding of the economic life of society. The assembling and systematic ordering of historical documents and statistical data is not enough. Willingness and industry are not enough. A perfected scientific technique is not enough. The really important thing is that research be directed towards the answering of significant questions, and it is hard to frame significant questions except in the light of definite hypotheses. Formulating questions and hypotheses is the first and most important task of the investigator.

Just because we can make a formal logical distinction between deduction and induction, we are prone to exaggerate the difference between deductive and inductive methods of inquiry. In the practical work of getting knowledge, we pass from a generalization to the facts and from the facts back to new generalizations in a way that blends deduction and induction. We begin, let us say, with a hypothesis – a tentative generalization. We then look into the facts, knowing that if the hypothesis is sound the facts we find within a certain range will not be inconsistent with it, and we determine our field of inquiry accordingly. This much is deduction. If the facts prove to be consistent with the hypothesis, our tentative deduction is transformed into an induction (or, as we say when we are testing some existing theorem, into a "verification"). If the facts are inconsistent with the hypothesis we cast about for a new hypothesis, for a generalization that brings the facts into some sort of orderly relation. In any really creative research, however modest in scale, there is this process of continuous give and take between the search for general relations and the scrutiny of particular details, between thinking and concrete observation.

But the process is generally not nearly so orderly and schematic as I have made it appear. Whatever the degree of perfection to which we have brought our methods of investigation, however conscientiously we try to conduct our inquiries so that our findings shall be impartial and objective, we have to proceed in the directions in which our interests and our questioning minds lead us, and we have to rely upon the subtle and obscure processes by which new hypotheses, new perceptions of possible relations among things, build themselves upon our minds as we bring new materials under survey.

Moreover, the materials which we consciously scrutinize, and which lie, perhaps, on the table before us, are only a part of the materials on which we levy. We work, as I have said, in a context of experience. Some of it may be formulated in general principles or in a consistent system of theory, some of it be organized in the form of orderly views of historical sequences. But a considerable part of it must be made up of that unsystematized knowledge of the relations of things which we get out of the immediate experience of life, as well as out of what we hear and what we read. The new knowledge which our researches yield has to be fitted into, not merely added onto, a comprehensive view of economic life, into which all our knowledge enters. This remains true regardless of whether, as in what we call deduction, we scrutinize such experience as is already at hand, and try to discern more clearly the systematic relations which run through it, or whether, as in what we call induction, we reach out for new experience and use it in testing and extending our knowledge.

In any case, the prerequisites to really successful research are significant questions and fruitful hypotheses. Successful research, of course, calls for industry and a command of the appropriate technical methods. But if it is to be anything more than mere fact-finding, it calls also for imagination, for the ability to see a problem and to devise hypotheses that are worth testing. Industry fortunately is not an uncommon virtue. Technique may be acquired. But imagination, and especially the kind of imagination that keeps its moorings, is rare. That is one reason why we ought to put our emphasis upon the individual investigator rather than upon a fixed program of research; why we should try to make it possible for the man with ideas to do the particular things he wants to do rather than the things we want to see done.

On the other hand, because men with really fruitful ideas are rare, and because there are a few men who combine a clear vision of some of the major economic problems with the ability to direct research effectively, it may sometimes be wise economy to make it possible for these exceptional men to control and direct the work of other investigators. In this way apprentice investigators may learn their trade while devoting themselves to more important tasks than they might have hit upon if left to find their problems for themselves. There are wastes in such arrangements, however. The energies which men of first-rate capacity give to directing the work of others might sometimes be employed more profitably in their own work. The largest contributions to economics have been, and, as I believe, always will be products of individual scholarship and research. There is no substitute for first-hand and intimate knowledge of one's own materials. Everyone who has undertaken a piece of original research knows how, even in the course of the routine handling of materials, the active mind notes at one point an apparent discrepancy, which calls for some recasting of hypotheses, while at another point it finds a suggestion of some hitherto unsuspected relation. The technical processes of research play a rôle auxiliary to that of the constructive and co-ordinating powers of the mind. Withdraw the investigator from immediate personal touch with his materials and, while you may increase his output, you are sure to impair the quality of his work.

In what I have just said I have had statistical research particularly in mind. In historical studies the case for individual research is, of course, even stronger. Constructive imagination counts for more, for the reason that in historical research it has a freer range. However objectively the investigator controls his findings by his materials, the task of appraising their significance, of relating them, and of fitting them together so that the finished product shall be history and not merely an enumeration of events, calls in a peculiar way for insight, imagination, and judgment. History is true in the way in which a picture is true; not in the way in which a physical law is true.

It will be apparent now, I trust, just why I hesitate to point to certain particular economic problems and say that those are the problems to which investigators could best devote their energies. The man who has hit upon a significant problem and who sees its significance has already taken a long step forward in research. Now there are of course a number of research problems in which I have an especial interest and which seem to me important. But I could not make their importance, as I see it, clear to anybody else, without a long preliminary account of the general setting of each problem and particularly of its relation to the other problems and the tentative hypotheses which are in my mind. I prefer, therefore, not to attempt to suggest specific problems, but to speak instead of certain inviting general types or fields of research.

I shall put my emphasis on what might be called neglected types of research, for there is no danger that the fields which just now are being more actively cultivated will escape anyone's attention. At any one time economists as a group have certain central interests in common. These central interests change as economic science advances, as the passing years bring new economic problems into the foreground, or when brilliant and challenging work by one economist attracts the attention of others. The war and the problems it bequeathed to the world have done more than anything else to determine the present central interests of economists. Problems in the fields of money and banking, of public finance, and of international trade have come into fresh prominence, as has commonly happened after long wars. Our war-time experience with government control of production and trade has helped to turn the attention of economists toward such questions as the future adequacy of the world's food supply, the distribution and control of supplies of raw materials, and the possibility of reducing wastes by introducing a larger element of conscious planning into the economic life of organized society. There is a new interest, also, in the nature of the national economic rivalries that make for war, and in ways of getting rid of them or controlling them.

Even before the war an increasing amount of attention was being given to the nature of the commoner types of industrial fluctuations, and, as everyone knows, a large number of investigators are now at work upon problems in that field. It is a field that lends itself particularly well to exploration with the aid of statistical methods. New materials are being put under survey, statistical technique is being perfected, and some of the intricate relations between the fluctuations of different series of economic phenomena are beginning to be perceived more clearly. This new interest in establishing empirical correlations between different economic variables with some approach to quantitative precision has been carried over into other fields. A promising beginning has been made, for example, in extracting from statistics a more precise knowledge of the relations between supply and demand and price. In general, there has been a notable growth of interest in determining empirical uniformities of relation that are sufficiently stable to afford some basis for prediction. We can safely count upon a steady increase of research activities in such fields. For this reason I shall say nothing about the alluring possibilities in these fields, or the unsolved problems with which they teem.

The neglected fields to which I want to call attention lie close about us on every hand. One only has to look to see great stores of unexplored materials, rich with the crude ore of knowledge, awaiting only patient delving and artful refining. More than once a promising young economist has complained to me that, where he lived and taught, the materials for research were inadequate. To one such I said recently that a set of census reports contained enough material to occupy his energies for the rest of his life. In our preoccupation with time series and correlation coefficients we are forgetting other aspects of what Sir Robert Giffen called "the utility of common statistics." A glance at the apportioning of space in some of the recent textbooks on statistics will suggest that we are unduly narrowing our notions of the field of profitable statistical inquiry.

The reports of our federal Census constitute, as a whole, the best general record that any country has of its economic life. Few economists use them, however, for other than reference purposes. I cannot think of any other research task that would promise surer or more valuable results than a systematic use of census materials in an inquiry into any one of an indefinitely large number of problems. Some years ago the Advisory Committee of the Bureau of the Census (a committee made up of representatives of the American Economic Association and the American Statistical Association) recommended that the Bureau undertake to publish a series of monographs, each to be the work of a competent scholar, in which census figures were to be analyzed and interpreted. The Bureau has now published seven of these monographs, and a few more are to follow. Anyone who looks through them will appreciate their importance and value. There is room for almost any number of studies of this kind, for the materials are well-nigh inexhaustible, and endowments for economic research would be wisely used in promoting them.

With the recent general growth of interest in population problems it is to be hoped that a larger number of investigators will occupy themselves with problems in the general field of demography – a field which American scholars, with a few conspicuous exceptions, have unaccountably neglected. It is to be hoped also that inquirers endowed with patience and insight and adequately trained in economic theory will make a first attempt to get from our successive censuses of manufacturers and agriculture a new comprehension of some of the forces that have been transforming the economic life of the United States. And there are large economic and social questions upon which careful studies of the changing importance of different ways of earning a living, as reported in the Census, would be certain to throw light. I shall not particularize further, but I think that it would be fairly easy to name as many as a hundred different important studies for which the reports of the federal Census would supply the more important part of the materials.

Of course there are other accumulating statistical records, imperfectly explored as yet by economists, which also provide inviting fields for research. I cannot dwell upon them or even specify them in detail. Many of them are by-products of the administrative work of governments. In the aggregate they cover a great variety of economic activities, and we should know more about a wide range of economic problems if investigators who have ideas and whose minds are open to new ones would address themselves to the study of these easily available materials.

Outside of the statistical field there is special need just now, I think, of careful and scholarly historical studies. There is always the temptation to paint on a large canvas, although painstaking work in miniature may have a larger permanent value. The man of genius may be able to see new sequences in the old materials that have been combed over by others, but the average investigator is surer of making his contribution if he gets hold of new materials, and uses them with the utmost care. This means, in practice, monographic work on a rigidly defined and limited subject. In my reference to the "average investigator" I did not mean to imply that the miniature may not be on every account as important an achievement as work on a larger scale. I think that I have learned more about some important aspects of the economic development of the Middle West from Professor B. H. Hibbard's history of agriculture in a single Wisconsin county than from any of the larger and more ambitious accounts. I do not see why the economic history of some American town or village should not be written in a way that would make it a contribution of the first importance to our under- standing of the development of the economic life of the United States.

Many of our monographs on economic history have dealt with states. This is inevitable, of course, when the inquiry is concerned with the legislative or administrative aspects of some matter within the control of the state, such as taxation or banking or poor relief. Furthermore, some of the materials that are most easily available for the investigator are records of the law-making and administrative activities of states. But a state, after all, is an economic unit only in respect of matters of public economy. There is need for a series of concrete studies of various aspects of the economic development of carefully defined homogeneous regions and communities. There is also need for careful historical studies, not only of industries, but of individual business undertakings, of the careers of successful captains of industry and finance, of particular products or commodities, and of changing modes of consumption as well as of changing forms of production.

Perhaps I can make clear what is in my mind by saying that we need to supplement our statistical inquiries, which have to do with aggregate and averages, by historical studies in which the individual and concrete aspects of economic activities shall be emphasized. Or if I have not yet made my meaning clear, look again into the *Wealth of Nations*, and ask yourself how much of the power of that book comes from Adam Smith's ability to take a broad and general view, how much of it comes from the rich concreteness of his interests and his knowledge, and how far it is born of his rare capacity to see things in *both* their general and abstract and their immediate and concrete relations.

It may be objected that to discover and bring to light *new* knowledge by means of these researches, so that the past shall not only "live again" but shall disclose new aspects of itself, requires not only the methodical study of sources but a degree of creative genius. Now I have to grant, of course, that most historical writing is imitative, just as most literature is imitative, for the power to see things at once truly and as no one has seen them before is given to few men. But in historical research, as I have already suggested, the investigator of average ability has it in his power to make substantive contributions. It is necessary only that he should be insistent in his search for new and fresh materials, and that he should weigh and ponder those materials until they fall into place in some consistent account of the particular episode or series of episodes with which he is concerned.

In the history of banking for example, it is not so important to us as economists that we should know more about banking laws or about the administrative control of banking by public authorities, as it is that we should know more about the actual operations of banks and the actual uses of credit in representative communities in different parts of the country. The careful study of the records of some particular bank – and it need not be a large bank – over a period of years would establish a basis for an important and useful contribution to economics. There is opportunity for research of this kind, involving the gathering and careful scrutiny of new materials, in a large number of other fields.

I put special stress upon the requirement that some, at least, of the materials used shall be *new*. I mean that they should be not merely first-hand materials, "original sources," but new kinds of materials. If an investigator uses only materials of a kind that have often been exploited, he is likely to write, let us say, just another history of banking, of a familiar standardized sort, adding little or nothing to our understanding of the complicated structure of the economic world in which we live. Best of all, of course, is the capacity to ask really new and significant questions, and to attack one's materials with new and pregnant hypotheses in one's mind. But that capacity is rare, and any conscientious and thoughtful investigator is sure to find that new materials have a way of asking their own questions and of falling into new sets of relations. The goal of such research, of course, is not the mere accumulation of records, such as might delight the heart of the antiquarian, or even the disclosing of the "lessons of history," but rather a new and fresh perception of some of the different factors that have entered into the total economic situation and have helped to make that situation what it is.

I shall not attempt to particularize further, for I do not want to try to list a series of specific problems. The difficulty, as I have said, is not that problems are scarce, but that they press in upon us in such abundance and variety that selection is difficult. If I were to point to some of them and say that in my judgment those particular problems are the ones to which investigators could most profitably devote their energies, I might be diverting attention from other problems which equally deserve investigation. The important things are that the investigator concern himself with a real problem; that some goal be seen, however dimly, towards which his inquiries should converge; that he be openminded enough to permit new evidence to lead him in new direction; that he remember that successful economic research calls for thinking as well as for routine processes.

In an economist's opinion there could be, of course, few wiser uses of money than in endowing economic research. Yet we must remember that our first and most difficult task is that of developing trained economists, so that the interests and energies of an increasing number of really competent investigators may be turned towards the study of economic problems. And it is not sufficient that the investigator be a "trained" economist, for he must have, of course, a native endowment of judgment and insight. In fact, as I look back over what I have written up to this point, I find that much of what I have been trying to say has probably been prompted by my fear that we are in danger of expecting from systematic research more than systematic research can possibly give us. There appear to be some who think that through research, and research alone, the social sciences might be as completely revolutionized in the course of the twentieth century as the physical sciences were during the nineteenth. As a result, we are asked to believe, society would be in command of its own destinies, in the same way that, in a sense, man is getting a better command of the forces of physical nature. Now all this seems to rest upon a failure to see certain fundamental differences between the physical and social sciences, and especially upon a misapprehending of what we really mean when we speak of "controlling" the processes of nature. But I shall not enlarge upon that topic here. My concern is merely with the rôle allotted to research.

Now research of itself – as a mere formal process, I mean – never accomplished anything. Routine research will give a routine product. The only kind of research that really advances our working knowledge of the economic mechanism or that really adds to our understanding of the complex structure of our economic society, is research that serves as the tool of the active, questioning, and relating mind of the investigator. Let the individual investigator, therefore, if he has passed his apprenticeship and proved his quality, have all the encouragement, all the freedom, and all the assistance we can give. In short, in the actual administration of funds for economic research, let us put our emphasis upon the quality and promise of the investigator, and let us be careful not to hamper him by prescribing too narrowly just what he shall do and how he shall do it.

I recognize, of course, that the young investigator's interests are likely to be narrow, and that if he is put to work upon new problems, he will acquire new interests. For this and other reasons it appears to be desirable that a group of research workers should try to agree upon the general range of problems to which they are to devote their effort. As their studies proceed, a common field of interests will be created; new methods and new ideas will become common property; one good piece of work will set a standard for others. As a result of building up a group interest in a common range of problems in this natural way, the work of the group will have a natural unity, and will itself grow in a natural way. I should expect that the results would be better than if a fixed and detailed program of research were drawn up at the beginning, into which the work of each individual investigator would have to be fitted.

Some eighteenth-century philosophers professed to believe that all the imperfections of human society might be got rid of, if only men would put their trust in reason. The same faith is held today, but the word "reason" has been replaced by the word "research." One does not have to subscribe to this creed – and I cannot subscribe to it – in order to believe that the increase in the number of able men who are bringing the spirit of scientific inquiry into the study of economic problems gives us ground for hoping that we shall learn how to deal with those problems more effectively and more wisely. I say "more wisely" as well as more effectively, because I believe that social wisdom as well as a better knowledge of ways and means ought to be one of the goals of research in the social sciences.

2 English political economy

Economica (1928) 8, No. 22 (March): 1–15. Inaugural lecture delivered at the London School of Economics and Political Science on October 11th, 1927.

Two thoughts contend for the uppermost place in the mind of an economist who turns aside from whatever special problems have been engaging his energies and steps away a little so as to get a general view of the present state of economic science.

In the first place there is an oppressive sense of the utter inadequacy of his own knowledge, and even of the knowledge which he could anywhere lay hold of. Economic science is still in its infancy, and despite the increasing numbers of its students, its growth is slow and uncertain. The world is asking more questions of the economist than it ever asked of him before, and it is asking its questions more insistently. There are old questions among them, and for these the economist has some sort of an answer, although not always an answer upon which economists would be agreed, and hardly ever a really complete and adequate answer. The new questions may not even reach his ears. So far as he does attend to these new questions the economist often finds that except in one respect – and I shall want to return later to that saving exception – he is little better equipped than a layman to deal with them effectively.

Then comes the more comfortable thought that, after all, the old problems about which economic science has something fairly definite and positive to say are exceedingly important problems. They are persistent problems, too, though they often recur in new forms and in new relations. There is much in the experience of the past twelve years from which the economist may draw confidence and courage. The economic problems of the war and of the period of readjustment were new in their magnitude and sometimes in their form. But in their essentials they were mostly old problems, such as economists had encountered before. Economists in general have held pretty definite opinions with respect to most of these problems. When – as happened frequently – their opinions were at variance with the policies of governments, in practically every instance the event has proved that the economists were right. Again and again, under the pressure of circumstances, governments have veered around until they have come close to the positions marked out for them in the beginning by the economists.

Despite his comparative helplessness in the face of some of the new problems that press in upon him, the economist has some things to say that he can say with confidence. Ahead of him are unexplored territories of limitless extent. Back of him are some lands, however narrowly circumscribed, which his predecessors have surveyed and charted and in which they have established some kind of order. What more could be said of a worker in any field of science?

It may be objected that the economist of whom I have spoken is a mythical person, a fictitious average of a heterogeneous group rather than a true type. Economics has it warring schools, and economists appear to devote no small part of their energies to differing among themselves. Now, although I suspect that we are prone to exaggerate the significance of these differences, I am frank to admit that the economists whom particularly I have had in mind are those who, whatever the different fields they cultivate or the different special tools they use, look at that extraordinary intellectual structure, nineteenth-century English political economy, as the one most important element in their common scientific heritage. An economist from another country who has been honoured by an appointment to a chair of political economy in this country and in this University is bound to feel that he has been admitted to the freedom of a great intellectual tradition, in which he, in common with economists of all lands, has found strength and leading. It is of that tradition, therefore, or of certain of its aspects, that I shall speak to-day.

English political economy, through all its own changes, held a central place in the midst of the various currents of nineteenth century economic thought. The other "schools," for the most part, took over its doctrines and built upon them, modifying here and rejecting there, or seized upon some of its obscurer elements or upon elements to which it seemed to give too little weight and elaborated them into what appeared at first to be competing systems, or frankly defined their own position largely in terms of opposition to its methods and disagreement with its findings. The central position which English political economy held was in fact a position at a storm centre. The romanticists urged that English political economy was too hard, too little mindful of other values than those of the market place. The positivists challenged its scientific credentials. It was too soft, they said, too much coloured by ethical and metaphysical prepossessions, not confined as it should be to the search for observable uniformities in the behaviour of economic phenomena. Some of the mathematical economists held that it was insufficiently abstract and general, or at any rate that its abstract and general elements needed to be disentangled from what was particular, local, or merely immediately practical. The historical economists insisted that it was too abstract and general in its form and too absolute in its pretensions, that it gave too little attention to the particular differentiating circumstances of time and place, and that it missed its mark because it tried to explain the phenomena of economic life in terms of simple and stable systems of general relations instead of by assigning them to their appointed places in some long historical series of changing institutional forms.

Despite the virtually continuous cross-fire of criticism directed against it by these and other hostile schools, English political economy has continued to show extraordinary vitality. More than once it has been pronounced dead or moribund, and it has sometimes been the fashion to allude to it only in the past tense. But its influence has continued to grow and to become more widely diffused. Even where its findings are mostly rejected, its general method, its categories, its modes of thought, its way of resolving complex economic problems into manageable elements, are commonly part of the working apparatus of competent economists. It has been a fortunate circumstance, I suspect, that British economists (never a large group) have rarely given more than passing attention to the controversies of the opposed schools, but have continued to work at their own problems in their own way. There were gains as well as losses from the scientific insularity which was characteristic of British political economy during a considerable part of its history. It would be particularly ungracious for me to-day to say anything which might seem to suggest that internationalism in economic science is something to be avoided. I mean merely that the worker who hopes to accomplish anything in so difficult and disputatious a field as economics must close his ears to some of the clamour round about him. The comparative insularity of British economics would have been its undoing if it had not within itself lasting sources of strength. It is worth our while, therefore, to try to discern some of the characteristic qualities which help to distinguish English political economy from such systems as appear already to have had their short day.

I shall not speak of particular doctrines or tenets. It is an error to identify the history of political economy with the history of doctrines. A system of political economy is not so much a set of doctrines as it is an intellectual or scientific apparatus, a way of arranging the complex facts of economic life so that some sort of discernible order appears in them and so that we can foresee some of the probable effects of dealing with them in one way or another. Furthermore, a doctrine severed from its context, like a branch torn from a tree, is dead wood, brittle in the hands of anyone who tests its strength. By the context of an economic doctrine I mean not only the whole visible structure of thought of which the doctrine is a part, but also the specific issues to which it had at first some sort of living functional relation, the opposing theses to which it was a reply or a challenge, the whole dim background of things consciously or unconsciously assumed or premised, and even the particular cluster of relations or pattern of ideas for which each word or phrase was a symbol. A summary review of doctrines, therefore, would not advance us in our quest.

Turning then to its more general aspects, we may observe first that English political economy has always been an eminently practical subject. It did not come into being because men decided that here was a gap which the existing sciences left uncovered. It was not created *in vacuo*, but grew out of men's attempts to deal intelligently with large questions of national concern. The distinguished economist who was my predecessor in this chair has made clear how the economic problems which confronted Britain in consequence of the Napoleonic wars did much to determine the form which economic theories took in the early part of the nineteenth century. The renewed interest lately observable almost everywhere in the study of the economic writings of that period has been prompted, of course, by an interest in modern problems, again the heritage of war, which are curiously like the problems with which those earlier writings dealt.

The periods when political economy has ceased its frontal attacks upon the communal problems of economic life and has turned inward upon itself to contemplate its own perfections or imperfections, or has occupied itself with questions of its proper "method" or of its standing as a "science" have been sterile periods. Economic theory, divorced from its functional relations to economic problems, or with those relations obscured, is no better than an interesting intellectual game. It gives endless opportunities for dialectical ingenuity. But it cannot advance knowledge, for it leads up a blind alley.

The distinction which some economists like to make between "pure economics" and "applied economics" is largely artificial. There is and can be no such thing as an economics embodying only pure analysis and description, uncoloured by any of the human interests which mark off the field and point to the relations which are to be described and analysed. I do not want to be understood as questioning the usefulness of general and abstract modes of economic analysis. Without the broad and general view, the short-range view, which takes in only a small part of the field and sees it in only a limited set of relations, is almost sure to be misleading. I suspect, however, that in the future the largest contributions to economic theory will be made, as they have been made in the past, not by professional "theorists," but by men who have set themselves the task of forging instruments that will help towards a better knowledge of how to deal with the communal problems of organised economic life. English political economy has been built up for the most part in precisely that way, and its instrumental or pragmatic character has always been one of its dominant qualities.

Another of its qualities is closely linked to what for lack of a better name we must call its method. Most of its critics and some of its defenders appear to be agreed that it was and has remained essentially deductive, proceeding from a few questionable assumptions about human nature, and that it has assigned an especially important rôle to a lay figure, the economic man. Now the truth is that English political economy has never been, in any real sense, deductive or *a priori*, and that it has never put a very heavy burden upon the economic man.

Its method was determined by the circumstance that it proceeded upon the basis of a mechanistic or contractual as contrasted with an historical or institutional view of the structure of economic society. The mechanistic view of the ordering of the relations that obtain among men was no new thing. Some hints or traces of it, at least, can generally be found wherever trade has been a conspicuous factor in the life of a community. But only after the new worlds had been found across the seas and the Commercial Revolution had created a new world in Europe was this view of things extended so as to include a field broad enough to invite systematic exploring. As the forms of economic activity changed, as larger fields were opened for business enterprise, as men came more and more to govern their activities by agreements made among themselves, the general aspect of the social structure became profoundly altered. The new forms of activity and the new nexus of contractual relations became dominating elements in the general scheme of affairs. It was a characteristic flash of insight which led Bagehot to observe that English political economy was "an analysis of that world so familiar to many Englishmen – the "great commerce" by which England has become rich."

Some sort of order or balance was discernible in this new economic system, though not an order imposed upon it from above, and not necessarily an order conforming to some rational (or, in the old sense, "natural") pattern. It was the task of economists to inquire into the secrets of that order and to acquaint themselves with the operations of the mechanism by which it seemed to be controlled. Only so could they deal intelligently with the issues which were their main concern.

They did not proceed by drawing inferences from assumptions about the nature of man or of the universe. Instead they inquired into the commonplace facts of the world about them and into such others as they could conveniently lay hold of. They drew upon their own observations of the behaviour of themselves and of their neighbours. Some of them made occasional use of history and records, or pressed into their service such statistics as were at hand. Many of their facts, of course, came to them already tied together in some way: in shrewd observations which other writers had made, or in commonsense generalizations such as serve us well enough in the daily routine of life. Like other writers they were misled sometimes by these stereotyped commonplaces, taking them to be first-hand elements in experience. But facts were not gathered blindly. Facts generally are significant to the economist only in so far as he finds that they are consistent or inconsistent with some thesis with respect to the inter-relations of economic phenomena. The economist, like any other inquirer, goes from hypothesis to facts and from facts back to hypothesis – although even that simple statement makes the subtle processes of constructive thought appear to be more formal and schematic than they really are.

I have rehearsed these commonplaces in order that we may remind ourselves that the method, as distinguished from the technique, of the English political economy of the nineteenth century was in no sense peculiar to it, but was and is the method – the inevitable method – not only of the sciences generally, but of all intelligent inquiries into the general aspects and relations of events.

When economists point to "strict reasoning" and "rigid logic" as one of the prime requirements of their subject, they put the emphasis in the wrong place. Political economy, like other systems of scientific thought, is held together by inferences. But except in some of the higher reaches of mathematical economics, most of these inferences, in their purely formal aspects, are of an elementary and obvious sort, such as generally give us no concern, outside of treatises on formal logic. The grounds on which an economist's conclusions are more commonly open to attack are that he has erred in his facts, or has seen only one aspect of their many-faceted surfaces, or that he has failed to take account of other facts that would have altered his findings, that he has asked and therefore answered the wrong questions, or that, tricked by the duplicity of words or his own limited vision, he has misread the meaning of his results or has overestimated their significance. At any rate, such are the issues upon which the major controversies of economics have generally turned. Doubtless a place might be found for most of these lapses among the fallacies of logical inference. But we put the emphasis better and get closer to the heart of the matter when we say that the economist, in even greater measure than the worker in more narrowly circumscribed fields of scientific inquiry, has need of insight, imagination, breadth of view, and complete intellectual honesty. It is worth remembering that one great English economist, especially distinguished for his achievements in mathematical economics, quoted approvingly the observation of another great English economist that much economic work "has less need of elaborate analytical methods than of a shrewd mother-wit, of a sound sense of proportion, and of a large experience of life."[1]

An attempt to appraise the extent to which a whole school of thought is open to or immune from attack on account of such lapses as those to which I have just referred is apt to be no more than a confession of prejudice. I hazard the opinion, however, that despite the solid foundations they laid in many departments of economic inquiry, the nineteenth-century English economists of the orthodox line, taken as a group, concerned themselves with a more narrowly limited range of problems than they realised. Some of their results, therefore, did not have the particular significance, or the full significance, which they attached to them, and, as everyone knows, they did not leave political economy in as well-rounded or complete a form as some of them appear to have thought.

The most promising recent development in economics is the increasing use of statistics. W. S. Jevons hoped to revolutionise economic theory. But he could not have foreseen that some of his path-making statistical inquiries might count for more towards that end than his *Theory of Political Economy*. This new development, however, is not really a revolution. It is wholly consistent with the spirit and method of the older political economy. But it calls for a broadening of the empirical outlook of economists, and this broadening is sure to have important consequences.

Sometimes the advantages of using statistics are supposed to be conveyed by such phrases as the "quantitative method" or the "exact method," but these phrases themselves are curiously inexact. Economic theory has always had to deal with quantitative rather than qualitative problems, and statistical inferences, though generally reducible to precise (i.e. numerical) terms, are rarely exact. What we loosely call the statistical method might seem at closer view to have two different tasks.

In the first place, the statistician brings new facts into view, some of which may be highly organised combinations of more elementary or more nearly unitary facts. Sometimes these new facts have a direct concrete significance of their own. More often, however, they get their significance from the way they enter into our systematic knowledge and supplement it or modify it. They enable us sometimes to say how much or how little instead of merely more or less. They help us to test not the truth but the significance of our theorems. They often make us aware of the appalling extent to which we have pushed our abstractions, of how deep some of the "tendencies" which we discover lie submerged below the surface of life. They challenge the accuracy of our observations and the adequacy of our systems; they put new problems before us, and as we use them they lead us on into the exploring of new territories.

In the second place, the statistician concerns himself with the behaviour of averages and aggregates, and especially with their inter-relations. The increase of interest in this field of work has been astonishingly rapid and enough has already been done to give promise of very large achievements. There is danger, I fear, not so much that we shall overestimate the importance of this new tool of economic research, as that we shall misinterpret its significance. There are some enthusiasts who seem to believe that we are just at the dawning of a completely new day in economic science, and that all of its yesterdays might well be forgotten. The new science is to rest upon the analysis of the behaviour of the objective phenomena of economic life, as reported by the arithmetically precise and verifiable aggregates and averages of the statistician. The orbits of these aggregates and averages are to be calculated, gravitational forces are to be measured by correlation coefficients, and a new empirical economic mechanics is to emerge, less exact and less reliable than the celestial mechanics of Newton and La Place, but sufficiently trustworthy to serve as a basis for prediction and for estimating the effect of planned interferences.

Such expectations are bound to be disappointed. They rest upon a misapprehending of the character of the empirical foundations of scientific knowledge. Such knowledge is not made up of separate bits, each bit supported merely by an isolated series of experiments or by the observation of a series of detached facts. Each new finding has to be fitted into the existing system of knowledge. If it does not fit, its own special credentials become suspect. If these credentials withstand the most rigid scrutiny, consistency may have to be secured at the cost of an overhauling of the whole systematic structure. When certain careful measurements of the velocity of light gave unexpected and at first inexplicable results, men were driven to attempt to alter the fundamental assumptions of Newtonian mechanics. The old distinction between a "merely empirical law" and a "law of nature" remains significant, for it points to the difference between a generalisation which has only its own legs to stand on and a generalisation which finds a place in a systematic view of nature (or of society), and is supported, therefore, by all of the experience which that systematic view interprets and harmonises.

We are prone to forget how weak a basis for inductive inference averages, aggregates, and the observed relationships among them generally provide, if taken only by themselves, without the support of other knowledge. In fact, outside of the pages of Mr Keynes's *Treatise on Probability*, I know of no really adequate analysis of the matter.

The movements and relationships of averages and aggregates are, in the first instance, merely historical facts. Like other historical facts they may be unique. Or a series of such facts may show enough stability to suggest inferences with respect to their tendencies. That is, they may have some prediction value. But the circumstances under which we can be assured that their prediction value is high are rarely met with in economic statistics. They need to be treated, therefore, merely as a special class of facts, which suggest tendencies but hardly ever define them. They need to be "explained," which means that they need to be woven into the general texture of knowledge. What appear to be the two different tasks of the statistical method are really one task – the task of collecting and preparing fresh materials for economic theory, not the task of weaving its fabric.

With the growth of statistical inquiries economic theory will have to concern itself more and more with explaining the behaviour of averages and aggregates. For that very reason it will not be able to turn aside altogether from that careful scrutiny of the common experience of life with which it has largely occupied itself in the past. But the bridging of the gap between economic statistics and the type of economic theory which we have found useful in the past will be no easy task. Economic theory has dealt mostly with what appear to be the inevitable results of the interplay of a limited number of important factors. The "laws" or "tendencies" which it discovers are merely statements of what would happen if the particular factors of which it takes account were the only factors really at work. Statistical facts, on the other hand, are the net resultants of the play of all of the factors and of the special combinations of factors that are operative at particular times and in particular places. Economic theory has never professed to deal with the temporal succession or the spatial distribution of unique combinations of circumstances, while statistics has to deal, in the first instance, with nothing else.

The statistician has his own way of laying bare the structural elements of his general facts, while the economic theorist has his own way of building up his generalisations. The abstractions of economic theory have always been in some degree arbitrary, although imposed in part by the nature of the particular problem in hand, and in part by the materials which the economist has had to work with. Economics will have to make room for new conceptions and new sorts of abstractions if it is to make effective use of the new facts which the statisticians are uncovering. If theorist and statistician continue to work apart, the gap between them will not be bridged, The structures built out from one side and the other will not meet, and neither structure alone will reach across to the opposite bank.

Economic theory, then, is bound to take account of this new range of facts and problems, even though in consequence its own lineaments must be profoundly altered. Such a development, as I have already suggested, would be wholly consistent with the empirical outlook and general temper of English political economy.

A third general characteristic of English political economy will suggest itself to anyone who reflects upon the curious oppositions among the principal criticisms which have been directed against it. Too abstract to please some, it is not abstract enough to please others. Some critics deplore its neglect of moral values. Others are vexed because it has never pruned itself of just such intrusive non-scientific elements. Not as abstract as the pure sciences, not as concrete as history, it has occupied a position logically vulnerable, perhaps, but practically advantageous.

A perfectly abstract economics is impracticable. A system concerned merely with the relations of variables which are defined only by their mathematical attributes is not economics, any more than pure mathematics is mechanics. The variables have to be taken, of course, as representing economic phenomena, or events, and they cannot always be taken altogether abstractly, with regard only to a selected set of their quantitative variations. The final terms of every chain of economic inferences reach out into other systems of relations, often non-economic in character, and it is from these other relations that the final terms get their meaning and significance. Except within a very narrow field, no economics can be practically useful in which these final terms are handled loosely, or in which difficulties are evaded by treating them as though they were mere algebraic symbols, or as though a single set of relationships could exhaust their meaning.

There have always been large non-scientific elements in English political economy, as there must be in any system of economic thought which concerns itself with questions of economic policy, and is not content to limit itself to a certain type of specific questions having to do with ways and means. This circumstance, in itself, does not open the door to criticism, any more than the circumstance that English political economy, like any science, has concerned itself with abstract quantitative relations.

The importance of what I have designated as non-scientific elements in economics will doubtless diminish as economists extend the range of experience which they take into account, and as the borderlands between economics and other sciences come to be more thoroughly explored. But the economist will always have need of wisdom, as well as of scientific acumen. And wisdom, as wise men have told us, is not to be had by contemplating only those measurable or numerable aspects of things with which the abstract or mechanistic sciences deal. Wisdom requires also a balanced view of the concrete diversities of life. So far as this important element in wisdom can be gained or imparted, it must largely be through historical studies.

History, in the broadest sense, is concerned with precisely those concrete differences, those special appurtenances of place or time, which the general and abstract view mostly has to ignore. History has its own way of explaining why particular events have occurred or why particular institutions have emerged or survived, and its way is not the way of the abstract sciences. History explains the present in terms of its specific relations to the past, and in so doing it reinterprets the past in terms of the interests and problems of the present. Its quality (except in certain special fields where it deals with numbers, and thus becomes statistics) is aesthetic, rather than (in any rigorous sense) scientific. But that does not mean that historical interpretation is merely a matter of taste, that there is no discoverable difference between the history which illuminates and the history which misleads, any more than it means that there is no difference between the literature which reveals life and the literature which falsifies it or conceals it under a conventional gloss.

History leads to new appraisals of our economic order, and to a realisation of the variety and mutability of the institutional patterns which direct our energies into one path rather than another, and which thus establish the general framework within which, at any given time, the economic life of society proceeds. The old question of the relative importance of the work of the economic theorist and the work of the economic historian is one of those questions which ought not to be asked. Each makes his contribution to our understanding of economic life, but the two contributions are altogether unlike, so that one supplements the other. The adherents of the older historical schools, in the criticisms which they directed against English political economy, were right in whatever stress they put upon the importance of historical studies. But they failed to see the practical value, the compelling necessity even, of inquiries into the mechanism of economic life, and some of them, at least, missed the real value of historical studies while attributing to such studies certain formal scientific virtues which generally they do not have.

English political economy of the orthodox line has never concerned itself much with history in any formal way. Individual writers differ, but taking something like an average of the six or eight great nineteenth-century treatises, I should say that English political economy has not been altogether unhistorical in its outlook or its general temper – at any rate not unhistorical in the degree that either the more abstract mathematical systems of political economy or the doctrinaire philosophies of history that have been proffered as substitutes for such economic theory are unhistorical. Such use as English political economy has made of history has been unsystematic and casual. But historical elements are woven, almost indistinguishably, into its general contexture. It is the presence of these concrete elements, along with the special character of some of its problems and the peculiarly British lineage of some of its general conceptions, which makes one of Cournot's penetrating observations especially applicable to English political economy. "The science of the economists," he said, "more than other sciences, without being, as has been wrongly said, a literature, is permeated by that flavour of the soil, marked by that stamp of time and place which distinguishes one literature from another... Other sciences also have their history, their growth, which is linked to the progress of society, but not in such degree that their physiognomy reflects, like a literature, the physiognomy of society."[2] Just as a country's literature is its own national heritage, imperfectly communicable across the barriers set up by differences in history and language, so, I suspect, some of the controversies of the various schools of economic theory are not much more than a confusion of tongues.

It is scarcely to be supposed that one looking back a hundred years from to-day at the development of economic science in the twentieth century would be able to say that it had kept closely to the general pattern set by the English political economy of the nineteenth century. Some of the findings that once were thought important have already been rejected on the ground that they were mistaken or misleading. Others have been forgotten, because they had lost whatever significance they once had. There remains a substantial body of other findings, however, which appear to us to-day to be both true and important, and which, so far as our limited vision goes, will be permanent elements in economic science.

But what the economist of to-day inherits from that older economic science is not so much a set of keys which open each its particular door as a set of clews which help the inquirer to find his way about in the intricate mazes which he has to explore. These clews will lead him to the end of no single passage, but generally they will turn his face in the right direction and will save him from making false starts. The most important thing a student of political economy gets from his training is not the possession of a body of "economic truth" but command of an intellectual technique. Confronted by a new problem he knows how to find his bearings and how to work his way through to some sort of reasoned conclusion. He knows how to pick up new facts and find a place for them in some consistent view of the mechanism of economic life. That is why economics is on the one hand a discipline to be taught, and on the other hand an almost limitless field of research.

Economics has its iconoclasts who would destroy in order that they may build anew. It also has its guardians of the established faith. But unless they be men of exceptional genius, ardent destroyers are never builders. And English political economy will not be preserved by its guardians but by men whose interest is not so much in political economy as in the problems with which political economy has to do. Carried beyond a certain point – a point impossible, of course, to know with any precision – the study of economic theories ceases to be an important element in acquiring the technical equipment of an economist, and becomes, according to the method pursued, an exercise in dialectics or an inquiry into an interesting chapter in the history of human thought. I am not questioning the value of the latter type of inquiry, which appears to me to be capable of throwing light upon a number of persisting problems. But neither the dialectical nor the historical pursuit is in the tradition of English political economy, which in the hands of its masters has characteristically turned away from itself and focused its attention on the world about it.

The economic science which has its strongest roots in English political economy will keep itself alive only by growth. Its growth will be at the hands of scholars who use the territory it has already conquered only as a point of vantage, not as a resting place, and who try to take account of new classes of facts and to bring a wider range of experience into an orderly view of economic processes. Because they will be building an organon they will continue to seek for dependable general relations, but they will be mindful of how the abstract method lays bare only certain formal aspects of the swirl and flow of economic life, and they will not carry scientific purism so far as to refuse to make room for concreter views of some of the manifold relations of economic phenomena. Nor will they dwell overmuch on such questions of interpretation and method as I have discussed today. The working apparatus which we call economic science will be made into a more perfect instrument only by continually renewing and extending its contacts with life.

Notes

1 Edgeworth, F.Y. (1925) *Papers Relating to Political Economy*, London: Macmillan.
2 Cournot, Antoine Augustin (1877) *Revue sommaire des doctrines économiques*, Paris: Hachette et cie, pp. 336–7.

3 National statistics in war and peace

American Statistical Association (1918) 16, No. 121 (March): 873–85. Presidential Address at the seventy-ninth Annual Meeting of the American Statistical Association, Philadelphia, December 27, 1917.

Our national participation in the war has brought with it an enormous demand for prompt and exact statistical information. Such a demand is, of course, an inevitable accompaniment of a war waged under modern conditions. War has come to be a conflict of directed masses, – of aggregates. Men, money, munitions, food, railways, shipping, raw materials, and manufactured products in great variety are impressed into the service of the nation. The problems of the effective control and use for war purposes of these varied national resources is intimately dependent upon a knowledge of their quantities, that is, upon statistics. Like chemistry, physics, and the applied sciences, statistical knowledge and the statistical method have come to be important tools of modern warfare. Just as this war is our largest national undertaking, so its statistical demands constitute, in the aggregate, the largest statistical problem with which we have had to deal.

The statistical activities of the federal government in times of peace cover in the main only those phases of national life which are deemed to be of public and especially of political moment. Our census of population is taken primarily to afford a basis for congressional apportionment; our census of manufactures and our foreign trade statistics still bear the marks of tariff controversies, and our federal statistics of wages and prices may be traced back to the same origin. In other fields, as diverse as immigration and railway transportation, our federal statistics are at once a by-product of federal control and a guide in the exercise of that control. In the fields of federal finance, money, and banking, our statistics are largely administrative by-products. The statistical work of the Department of Agriculture is a recognition, inadequate as yet, of a public interest which is probably only in small part political, and so with the statistical work of the Geological Survey and the Bureau of Mines. The work of the Bureau of the Census in the field of vital statistics is the most noteworthy example of the recognition of a large social interest which is not primarily either economic or political.

Thus the federal government, in its statistical work, has touched the current of our national life at only relatively few points, and at some of these only intermittently. For the most this current flows on in its own channels, free from disturbance or questioning or measurement by the government. Except to the tax-gatherer, a large part of the productive and business activities of the country have not been deemed to be matters of public concern, even as group aggregates.

The changes brought by our entrance into the war have been profound. Other activities have had to be subordinated to the necessities of the efficient and successful conduct of the war. This subordination, we may well believe, is only imperfectly realized as yet. If the war continues it is certain that the field of activity over which the public interest will be deemed to extend must be much further widened.

Our national problem, in its essence, is that of directing our efforts and output into new channels, of focusing all of our national energies on the one supreme task before us. Individual desires and whims are no longer masters of our economic life. Instead of doing what it is most profitable to do, men are beginning to do, and to do willingly, what they are bidden to do.

This new ordering of life works through such diverse forms as the drafting of men, the commandeering of ships and workshops and supplies, the control of prices and output, the restriction of exports and imports, the supervision of the processes of market distribution, the regulation of consumption, the coördination and administration of transportation agencies, the solution of labor difficulties, the raising of vast sums of money through taxes and loans, and the creation of priority rights.

The successful execution of such a program calls for a degree of national self-knowledge far beyond anything that we might have imagined necessary or possible in the past. We have been suddenly thrust into a situation in which we find ourselves in urgent need of a complete inventory of our national assets and a complete record of our productive activities. In this need we find the explanation of that enormous demand for prompt and exact statistical information to which I have referred.

In this emergency we turned first to our existing stocks of statistical information and to the current statistical output of our government bureaus, and have realized, perhaps for the first time, how woefully incomplete and inadequate our federal statistics are. With our latest population figures seven years old, our latest statistics of manufacturing output three years old – and it is surprising to find how antiquated and how useless for present purposes this latest manufacturing census is – and with no information whatever respecting important fields of trade, we were in a state of statistical unpreparedness.

Under these conditions a war statistical service had to be improvised. With no centralizing and coördinating agency at work, the boards and commissions created to take charge of the various fields of war work have had to procure for themselves, as best they could, the statistical information needed for their purposes. In part, it is true, these inquiries have taken the form of assembling information furnished by other organizations, and more especially by the permanent statistical offices of the government. But there is scarcely a war board or commission in Washington that has not had to make independent statistical investigations of its own, involving the collection, tabulation, and analysis of necessary facts. In many instances this work has been of sufficient magnitude to lead to the organization of separate statistical bureaus or divisions within these war organizations. A few of these rival in the size of their staffs and of their statistical output the larger of the permanent statistical offices.

I shall not attempt to describe in any detail the work of these new statistical agencies. Hurriedly organized, confronted by really formidable tasks and by the necessity of getting quick results, it was inevitable there should have been much misdirected energy. In particular there has been, admittedly, much duplication of inquiries. Each war organization, needing information of a kind not immediately available, has very naturally proceeded to obtain it at first-hand by direct investigation and inquiry. Because there is a large measure of overlapping in the statistical needs of the different war organizations there has been some overlapping of inquiries. Business men and trade organizations have found themselves required to furnish information, essentially similar, but with just enough differences to require the work to be done over again, for two or more Washington offices. These wastes are now becoming smaller, as a result of increasing knowledge on the part of each war organization of the activities of others. A less excusable form of duplication has come from the neglect on the part of some of the new organizations to inform themselves fully respecting the work of the established statistical bureaus, or, at any rate, from their failure to make use of the material that these permanent bureaus might easily have furnished them.

As for the work of these permanent bureaus, out of my own experience in the work of one of the war organizations, I can vouch for their unfailing attitude of helpful and generous coöperation. Certain of them, in fact, have taken on heavy additional burdens in this way. Thus one may cite the more adequate and more promptly published statistics that are now available for the production of minerals and metals, and the prompter tabulation of foreign trade statistics. These are merely examples, for there is hardly a statistical bureau in Washington that has not been called upon for some new or increased service. It must nevertheless be said that some of these bureaus have not risen to the full recognition of their opportunities. With so much that needs to be done, and so much that is being badly done by others by reason of insufficient experience or inadequate equipment, some of our permanent bureaus are giving virtually all of their energies to routine work, much of which is of relatively little present importance, or are merely marking time.

What I have just said should not be taken as imputing any blame to the men who are immediately responsible for the policies of these bureaus. Most of them are handicapped by inadequate appropriations and find it difficult for that reason to arrange for any considerable increase in their functions. And in many instances the available appropriations are for specific purposes and cannot be transferred to new undertakings. Not only has it been easier to obtain funds for the new war offices than for the established organizations, but the new offices have been encumbered by fewer restrictions respecting the precise way in which they should use their funds. In this way they have virtually been compelled to do for themselves what might, in many cases, have been more economically and efficiently done by one or another of the permanent statistical bureaus. In statistical work, as in other fields of government activity, the new war organizations have been superadded to the preëxisting administrative machinery rather than merged with it, – a policy which has its disadvantages as well as its advantages.

Returning now to the topic of the work which has been done and which remains to be done by the different war statistical bureaus, it is to be observed that despite the differences in their tasks, a common thread of interest runs through their work. They are all concerned, fundamentally, with the general tasks which I have mentioned earlier in this discussion: the measurement of our national resources, whether in men, money, or goods; the determination of our actual and potential output of the immense variety of things that are important, directly and indirectly, in the conduct of the war; the gauging, so far as may be, of our own needs and those of our allies and of the other countries that have to be recognized as in some measure dependent upon us. The problems of raising and equipping a fighting force, of providing ships and munitions, of food and fuel control, of the regulation of exports and imports, of the organization of transportation, of industrial priority, of the adjustment of labor difficulties, of national economizing, and of war finance, are all inextricably interwoven. Back of all these special problems is the general problem of the relative urgency of different national needs, – the problem of priority in the widest sense. Here not only successful administration but even the right choice of policies depends upon full and accurate knowledge, and in particular upon statistical knowledge.

It is partly, perhaps, because this statistical problem is usually discussed in terms of its parts, rather than as a whole, that its enormous importance has not been fully realized. When compared with our aggregate annual expenditures for war purposes, our expenditures for statistical purposes are seen to be almost pitifully inadequate. It is easy to see the wastes and the duplications in such statistical work as has been done. It is harder, perhaps, to realize the indispensable character of most of this work. It is even harder to visualize the real advantages and economies that would result from the organization of statistical inquiries on a vastly greater scale than now obtains.

Many of the mistakes that have been made – and some of them have undoubtedly been very costly – have been due to the lack of full and exact statistical information. Our expenditures for statistical purposes are not a thousandth part of our aggregate war expenditures. It might easily be wise economy to increase them ten or twenty fold. This much at least is certain: in range, in completeness within the fields which they cover, and in accuracy, the statistics now available furnish a wholly inadequate basis for the most efficient conduct of the task in hand. Our statistical apparatus has not expanded in any such degree as the field of public interest has grown. Confronted as we are by the necessity of making the most effective disposition of our national energies, we have not attempted to secure anything like a complete and accurate statement of the forces at our disposal.

In some special fields our knowledge may be fairly complete, but in other fields it is either incomplete or non-existent. Most of all we lack the materials for a picture of the whole economic situation, invaluable as it would be as an aid in the shaping of national policies.

To make the point clear, imagine, if you will, what might have been accomplished if, when we entered the war, or even when our participation in the war came to be a serious possibility, there had been created a central statistical commission, instructed to develop a scheme for a comprehensive war statistical service. In the light of the experience of the other belligerents – for there are few elements of novelty in our own war problems – the greater part of our statistical needs might have been foreseen. Plans for the utilization and extension of the work of existing statistical bureaus, as well as for the creation of new ones for special purposes, would very likely have been made. To begin with, there would have been a complete census of population, with inquiries respecting sex, age, marital condition, citizenship, nationality, occupation, and income. The schedule would have been simple and the tabulations would have been merely those which threw direct light upon the problems in hand. Among other things this would have afforded a definite basis for a genuinely selective draft and for the right construction of a war income tax. Then there should have been a general census of production, covering extractive as well as manufacturing industries, especially for the whole field of staple products, neglecting some of the customary inquiries, but putting special stress on such points as stocks and consumption of raw materials, stocks and output of finished products, capacity, existing contracts – foreign and domestic – and number of employees. Similar inquiries might advisably have been made in the field of market distribution, at least so far as the wholesale, jobbing, brokerage, commission, and storage trades are concerned.

In the second place, provision should have been made for keeping much of this information up to date, through some system of weekly or monthly reporting, thus doing for important fields of industry and trade what is already done for agriculture and mining. The population census, even, might well have been used as a starting point for continuous local population registers, under the charge of the police or of local registration officials. In all of this work it would be sufficient if the general tabulations showed classes only, but information respecting individuals and firms ought to be available, by means of proper formalities, to the appropriate branches of the war administration.

This may seem to be an ambitious statistical program, but, in view of the unprecedented magnitude of the interests involved, it is perhaps unduly modest. Certainly it would have to be supplemented, in any adequate scheme, by provisions for a more elaborate centralization of statistics of railway operations and of the general movement of goods, for very much more detailed statistics of foreign trade than we now have, for more comprehensive official records of wages and prices, and for the compilation of all available statistics bearing upon economic conditions in other countries. I have left out of account the enormous mass of information that has to be gathered with reference to individual persons and firms and transactions, rather than to groups or aggregates, as primarily non-statistical in character. I have also omitted reference to the use of statistics in purely military operations, as a subject apart. It may be worth noting, however, that Napoleon put as much emphasis upon the value of complete statistics as a basis for military strategy as he did upon their use in the administration of civil affairs.[1]

Under such a scheme of organization as I have in mind the central statistical commission would have other functions than that of planning and apportioning the work to be done. It would remain as a centralizing and coördinating body, a clearing house for the national war statistical service. As new statistical demands arose they would be referred by it to the bureaus best qualified to secure the desired information. It would confer with the organizations asking for statistical service and with the bureaus furnishing this service respecting such practical matters as the best construction of schedules and the best tabulation of returns. Upon it would devolve the duty of making synthetic statistical studies of the whole national situation, the importance of which I shall try to indicate later.

I hope that I shall not be interpreted as meaning that no separate war statistical organizations should have been created, that all of the work should be done by established bureaus under the general direction of the suggested central commission. This would be manifestly undesirable and impossible. Some war organizations need statistical divisions for compiling and tabulating the records of their own activities. Some of them need special statistical inquiries or special statistical information that is of importance and interest only to themselves. In many instances, too, statistical material, wherever obtained, has to be combined and organized so as to meet the special needs of a particular organization.

The purpose of the suggested central commission would be, not to displace, but to coördinate and especially to supplement such statistical work as would naturally and necessarily be done if no such commission existed. Nor is the matter of economy through avoidance of duplication the most important factor. The inevitable duplication of work on the part of bureaus that are concerned primarily with their own particular problems is a matter of relatively small moment compared to the fact that no number, no matter how large, of isolated bureaus will adequately cover the whole field of necessary statistical information, so far as that field is one in which their interests are common. Each separate organization may cover the field in which its own interests are special, but this is no guarantee that it will be able to find anywhere or to provide for itself such fundamental statistics as are of common interest to itself and to other organizations.

The difficulties under which war statistical work has been carried on in Washington have come very largely from the absence of any organization with power to formulate the statistical problem as a whole. But apart from the particular advantages which the existence of this fundamental general statistical information would give to the separate branches of the war administration, there is the yet larger gain that would come from a comprehensive view of our national assets, and more especially of our annual national product. This kind of view is essential to the wisest national strategy, to the most effective use of our available powers. Only in this way can we find the materials for an estimate of our possible national savings, – not in terms of money, but of labor and resources and goods. Only in this can we gauge the maximum amount that the government may wisely spend for war purposes as indicated by the part of the national product and of the national productive forces that it can divert to its own uses. Such a statistical survey would indicate not only the foods, but also the raw materials, finished products, and classes of productive agents of which the supply is short as well as those of which there is a surplus. It would suggest, at least, where national waste exists. In short it would point the way, as I have already suggested, to the most effective marshalling and redistributing of all of our national energies.

To summarize: our governmental statistical work has been largely concerned with such affairs as have happened to be matters of public or political concern. War not only enlarges the field of public interest, but it also creates a new set of values. These new values are not the outcome of the "normal forces of supply and demand," but are, or should be, the expression of conscious decision respecting the relative worth of different things and different activities for the dominant national purposes. These values can be effectively recognized and expressed in action only on the basis of a far more comprehensive mass of statistical information than has been available or is likely soon to be available. A practicable if not the only method of planning for and obtaining these statistics on an adequate scale is through the agency of a central statistical commission. The cost, however great, would be small as compared merely with the magnitude of the economic problems dependent for a right solution upon the knowledge such statistics would give, and wholly negligible in view of the larger interests involved.

What light does this review of the problem of statistical organization in war time throw upon the problem of statistical organization in time of peace?

It is not to be presumed that after peace is to be concluded we shall continue to want precisely the sorts of statistics that are now needed, that the field of public interest will be wholly unchanged. Nor is it to be presumed that we will be interested, as a nation, in just the things that were deemed most important before the war. The boundaries of the field of public interest will be narrower, undoubtedly, than they now are, but they will not be just what have been in the past. The lapse back from thoroughly awakened national consciousness will not be complete. However large the measure of freedom restored to individual enterprise and to the individual conduct of life, we shall realize, as we have not in the past, the possibilities of doing things on a national scale, of rationally adapting the mechanism of national life to fit national ends. And there will be new national interests springing from our new participation in world affairs. There will be, in short, new fields of statistical inquiry.

It is possible that there will not be a ready and general acceptance of a premise implicit in what I have said: namely, that the organization of national statistics should, in fact, correspond in scope to the field of public interest. Is no weight to be given, it may be asked, to purely dispassionate and scientific interests? I confess to being somewhat skeptical with respect to the reality of a what is sometimes appropriately called "idle scientific curiosity." There is an interest in technique and there is an interest in problems, and may it not be that our "idle scientific curiosity" is merely a name for an interest in technique strong enough to make the choice of problem a matter of indifference. But without venturing further on disputed and dangerous ground one may safely observe that the function of a national statistical service is primarily that of securing and purveying statistical information; that is, in a large sense, of answering questions and of providing the material for the solution of problems. As statisticians I fear that we have sometimes permitted our interest in technique to blind us to the social importance of the right choice of the problems to be covered in our federal statistical service. There is much satisfaction to be derived from doing our best with bad statistical material, from replacing the missing facts by careful inference and shrewd conjecture. One can even sympathize with the scholar who complained that the modern wealth of printed bibliographies had destroyed scholarship. But as a guide to the choice and administration of national policy, verifiable facts are infinitely better than estimate and conjecture. If statistics is not to be merely an occult science, statisticians must interest themselves in enlarging the scope of their sources of information and particularly in what we may describe as the national choice of statistical problems.

Although before the war our national statistical activities could be explained in terms of past and present phases of public interest, it can not be said that all important phases of public interest were adequately represented. Even then, I think we shall all admit, our national statistical service had not kept pace with the fast-flowing current of economic and social change and with the accompanying development of new national interests. And with yet more profound changes impending in the near future, some form of method of statistical reorganization and adjustment will be urgently needed. This is because, in general terms, the formulation and administration of wise national policies must depend upon the national self-knowledge that only statistical information, gathered on a much larger scale than we have been accustomed to think possible, can give. Nor must the importance of an elastic and comprehensive scheme of statistical organization as an element in preparedness for war be forgotten.

A committee of this Association, coöperating with committees of other associations, has been studying the problem of the organization of statistical work in Washington. I am informed that it has given favorable consideration to proposals looking toward the creation of a central statistical commission. It is to be hoped that its efforts will help to secure tangible progress toward that end. But the functions of such a commission ought to include more than merely introducing some measure of coördination into the work of the existing Washington offices. It should be empowered to make recommendations to Congress for the inauguration of new statistical activities, utilizing either established offices or new ones, according to the circumstances of the particular case. It should control some discretionary funds, to be used in special inquiries made by its own staff or, more frequently, by one or more of the established statistical bureaus. Its fundamental interest should be less in the statistical work that is being done than in the work that is not being done. It should try to eliminate some of the statistical dead wood that now cumbers the reports of many of the Washington bureaus. It should not refrain, even, from attempting to introduce an element of national prophecy as well as of national history into our statistics.

If the statistical problems brought sharply into the foreground by the war hold any lesson that has a significance for times of peace, it is that we have not yet begun to realize the possibilities of federal statistics as a general scheme of national accountancy, or the responsibilities which the future holds for the statistician.

Note

1 Cf. de Foville, A. "Napoléon Statisticien," in *Journal de la Société de Statistique de Paris*, December, 1911.

4 Economics and war

American Economic Review (1926) 16, 1 (March): 1–13. Presidential address at the thirty-eighth annual meeting of the American Economic Association, New York, December 29, 1925.

"Peace is the natural effect of trade," said Montesquieu.[1] Not is, but should be, said Adam Smith. "Commerce, which ought naturally to be among nations as among individuals, a bond of union and friendship, has become the most fertile source of discord and animosity."[2] More than a century later one of the wisest of historians reaffirmed the Scotch economist's verdict. "It is not true that the development of material interests promotes peace. Commerce, as the messenger of peace, is a mythological character. In its origin it was brigandage; in ancient, mediæval, and modern times it occasioned wars. Men fought on the Baltic for herring, and on all the seas for spices. In our day the growth of industry creates the question of foreign markets, which, in turn, brings the interests of the states into conflict. Commercial rivalry and rancor thus strengthen national hatred."[3]

In what measure is this a true finding? In what measure must it remain true? These are the questions I propose to discuss. They are difficult questions, and the literature of economics throws surprisingly little light upon them. There appear to be two general classes or types of opinions, and little else beside.

One view – which might be called the popular or naïve view – sees in war one of the normal, or even one of the rational, economic activities of men. Nations are pictured as behaving like the economic man of our methodological mythologies, each consistently and relentlessly seeking its own interests. The interests of different nations clash, conflicts arise, and conflicts grow into war.

In one way or another this view is persistently thrust before us. We encounter it in our newspapers, where it serves as one of the useful stock scenarios into which the ordinary humdrum incidents of economic and political intercourse among nations are fitted, and which give to such incidents a meaning, an element of dramatic interest, an easily recognizable place in the general course of events. We meet it in some of our books on international politics and in some of our histories – particularly in those that have been written during the last thirty or forty years. We find it in the reports by which a country's representatives in other lands keep their own government informed of matters which may be presumed to affect its interests. It even has a special literature of its own – a literature which had a mushroom growth during the war.

Such interpretations of the economic relations of nations utilize a set of familiar phrases: commercial warfare, the struggle for markets, the control of raw materials, surplus products, surplus population, economic imperialism, economic penetration, and the like. Phrases such as the struggle for (national) existence and the survival of the fittest are also pressed into service, carrying with them the suggestion that international economic rivalries have an appointed place in the processes of nature.

There are two different ways of handling this apparatus of ideas. The characteristic of one of these methods is that nations are depicted as alert and intelligent personalities, conscious of their purposes and deliberately choosing the means of achieving those purposes. Their foreign policies are conceived in terms of strategy, of calculated economic advantage. They are, in short, rational, or Machiavellian, states.

The other way of dealing with this common stock of notions uses the apparatus of historical determinism. Causes, not purposes, rule. National policies and national destinies are shaped by the cumulative pressure of antecedent forces. The fruits of this method are a variety of pseudo-scientific dogmas respecting the "ultimate" causes of war. I call them pseudo-scientific because, although they borrow the mask of science, they are and must be arbitrary and unverifiable.

Of these various dogmas the one which has had the most pervasive influence is the Marxian. This doctrine is to the effect that changes in industrial technique, coupled with the private ownership of those instruments of production through which alone the fruits of technical progress can be realized, bring about a disparity between a country's power to produce and its power to consume. The surplus product accumulates in the market, where it leads periodically to crises. Endeavours to find an outlet for it lead to economic rivalries among nations, to the exploiting of undeveloped or backward countries, to colonial expansion, to economic imperialism, and to wars.

The rational state does not appear in this picture. Instead there is the capitalistic or class state, itself only an historical incident, marking a certain stage in the development of economic and political institutions. The abiding thing is the conflict of the interests of different economic classes. Modern wars are undertaken to secure the advantage, not of a nation, but of a class. The real lines of cleavage are to be found, not at national frontiers, but in the horizontal stratification of society.

One element in this Marxian doctrine, namely the notion of surplus products pressing outward across national boundaries under military convoy, has an especially wide vogue. Writers who do not count themselves followers of Marx, as well as those who do, employ it as a routine formula.

The second general class or type of opinions to which I have referred is distinguished, not by a special emphasis upon some particular view of the nature and purposes of the aggressive activities of states, but by a very definite thesis with respect to the wisdom and the consequences of such activities. If wars are waged for economic advantage, it is held, they defeat their own purposes. So, too, in general, with all national policies designed to advance the economic interests of one state at the expense of other states. The truth is, it is alleged, that a nation gains by the prosperity of other nations, not by their poverty.

This general thesis, if stated with some necessary qualifications, would be subscribed to by most economists. It was brilliantly expounded in Mr. Norman Angell's book, *The Great Illusion*. If in the days of its first vogue that book seemed to be given little attention by the economists, it was not because they disagreed with its conclusions, but rather because most of those conclusions seemed to them to be fairly commonplace economic doctrines. Doubtless Mr. Angell weakened a good case by pushing it a little too far. He gave too little weight to the special interests (not necessarily or even generally class interests) that may be served by a belligerent or imperialistic policy, even when other interests, larger but more diffused, are injured. He did not adequately distinguish between immediate and ultimate gains and losses. But taking his argument in the large, it would command, I believe, the general assent of economists. Some of the policies he finds unwise are, in fact, policies economists are accustomed to disparage by lumping them together and calling them neo-mercantilism.

Assuming that Mr. Angell and the economists are right, is there ground for hope that, as the result of a slow process of education, the world would become convinced that aggressive economic nationalism is profitless? Is there reason to believe that in this event the so-called economic causes of war would be done away with? Such hopes, we may be fairly sure, would be vain. For one thing, we have learned in other fields that progress which has to wait upon men's becoming more reasonable is likely to be delayed indefinitely. For another thing – and here I pass to one of the central themes of this paper – there is ground for challenging the common views of the nature of international economic competition and of its relation to war. The facts are too complex and too tangled to be fitted into the concepts and formulas which we ordinarily use.

We get those concepts and formulas, for the most part, from the market place. We use them in describing and analyzing the mechanism of money-making, of business competition. Here we find uniformities, rational rules of conduct, out of which we build the framework of economic science. That reliable mechanism, the "economic man," is merely the average man, taken in his business relations – taken, that is, as buyer and seller. Now, save under very exceptional conditions the economic relations of national groups are not like those of buyer and seller. Not since the days of the crudest types of mercantilism have they been so regarded by economists.

We concern ourselves with what nations *should* do in order to secure their maximum economic advantage, we take account of some of the things they actually do, and we even venture to explain or find reasons for certain of these activities. But unless we are the bigoted devotees of some dogmatic philosophy of history, we do not expect that the behaviour of national groups will conform to some rational rule, that it will be stable and predictable.

The values of the world of international rivalry are more like the irrational values of the world of consumers' choices than they are like the money profits and the other money incomes for which men contend in the world of commerce. Consider such phrases as economic dominance, empire, economic independence, a place in the sun, territorial expansion, control of markets, freedom of the seas. These phrases denote some of the things for which men are supposed to fight. Each has an economic significance. And yet, what discernible relation is there between their potency for war and their economic significance? Their real meaning appears only when they are projected against an historical background; but there they lose any peculiarly economic quality, and become merged in the general picture of national prejudices and passions.

What I am trying to say has been put more skillfully by Walter Lippman: "How does it happen that the people not concerned in a special interest are so ready to defend it against the world?... The most obvious reason is that the private citizens are in the main abysmally ignorant of what the real stakes of diplomacy are. They do not think in terms of railroad concessions, mines, banking, and trade.... Each contest for economic privileges appears to the public as a kind of sporting event with loaded weapons. The people wish their team, that is, their country, to win. ... Business is the chief form which competition between nations can assume. To be worsted in that competition means more than to lose money; it means a loss of social importance as well.... The way to increase national prestige is to win economic victories by diplomatic methods.... Armament is added as an "insurance' for diplomacy, and of course military preparation always calls forth military preparation. Every international incident is seen then, not on its "merits," but in its relation to the whole vast complicated game, forever teetering on the edge of war." [4]

It may be that some of the interests which arouse these belligerent emotions and around which they cluster are the rational economic interests of different national groups. It is plain that some of them are the real interests of particular men or particular classes. But, as I have said, there is no correlation between the economic importance of these interests and their power to rally a people to their defense. They may be wholly factitious, and yet be potent.

There is instruction to be had from recent developments in the field of sports. I mean, of course, inter-collegiate and other inter-group sports, in which small teams of selected competitors carry with them into their contests the rivalries of the groups they represent. Members of these rival groups like to absorb themselves in these conflicts by reading about them. The purveyors of sporting news have found that this is an appetite which can be stimulated, that the interests of persons outside the rival groups may be engaged, and even that the number of partisans may be increased.

They have found also that the number of *competitions* may be fruitfully multiplied by bringing existing contests into new relations. An intricate system of mythical regional and class "championships" has been invented. Teams are ranked by the percentage of victories, by the total scores they have made, and in various other ways. Ingenious methods of rating the achievements of individual players have been devised.

These artifices succeed in entrapping the interests of readers. And they accomplish more than that. Some of these make-believe competitions become real. The spirit of rivalry reaches out and takes hold of them. They supply new criteria of superiority, new symbols of prestige. Some of them come to be regarded as expressions of inevitable "natural rivalries." The facts, however, suggest that though there may be a vaguely circumscribed field of potential rivalries, within that field competitive alignments are free to arrange themselves in various patterns, while one thing or another may come to be adopted as an emblem of success.

In the larger field of international economic rivalries group psychology retains its characteristics. The world in which national groups strive to realize their opposed interests is in large part a world of man-made patterns and symbols. It is a new world, for nations as we know them are only a few hundred years old – no older than the new world-commerce which helped to bring them into being and which remains one of the fields in which their oppositions and rivalries feed and grow.

Among the architects of this world have been the historians. They have played a rôle not unlike that of the contemporary newspaper annalist of competitive sports. Most histories have been histories of nations. By abstracting the nation from the other forms which human relations take, by emphasizing the peculiar and differentiating elements in a nation's institutional heritage, they deepen the cleavages between national groups. Many histories have put disproportionate emphasis upon wars. And in explaining wars they have often put more reliance upon "economic motives" then either economics or psychology would warrant.

"It is possible to study a multitude of histories," says John Dewey, "and yet permit history, the record of the transitions and transformations of human activities, to escape us. Taking history in separate doses of this country and that,... we miss the fact of history and also its lesson; the diversity of institutional forms and customs which the same human nature may produce and employ. An infantile logic, now happily expelled from physical science, taught that opium put men to sleep because of its dormitive potency. We follow the same logic in social matters when we believe that a war exists because of bellicose instincts; or that a particular economic regime is necessary because of acquisitive and competitive impulses which must find expression.... We have constructed an elaborate political zoology as mythological and not nearly as poetic as that other zoology of phœnixes, griffins, and unicorns. Native racial spirit, the spirit of the people, or of the time, national destiny are familiar figures in this social zoo. As names for effects, for existing customs, they are sometimes useful. As names for explanatory forces they work havoc with intelligence."[5] And so, we may add, do such names as economic motives and the economic causes of war.

William James wrote a famous essay on the "The Moral Equivalents of War." Conceivably we might speak of equivalents or substitutes for economic antagonisms. But what we need most are substitutes for the habitual patterns which elicit and direct those antagonisms.

Something may be accomplished, undoubtedly, by continued emphasis upon the wasteful stupidity of most of the efforts national governments make to secure economic advantages outside of their own territories, although this something is not very much. There is reason to hope, moreover, that with the increase in the number and variety of contacts between the peoples of different countries, national antagonisms will diminish. Not, however, that the growth of concreter forms of knowledge, born of such contacts, can be counted upon to dissipate our abstract notions of alien types of men and of rational but malevolent states. The real ground for hope is rather that with the growth of communication and of economic interpenetration, new forms of organization will have to be devised.

Organization generally provides a mechanism by means of which some measure of external control can be exercised over men's activities. But that is only a small part of its significance. Organization *directs* activities as well as controls them.

Political organization has not kept pace with economic organization. Increasing interdependence asserts itself in economic life. Raw materials, markets, borrowing and lending, trade routes, price, monetary and banking policies are things in which the different peoples of the world have a joint as well as a separate interest.

National states, each acting only for itself, are inefficient guardians of these joint interests. Within a nation's own boundaries it manages to bring the conflicting interests of different sections and groups into some sort of balance and to enforce general standards and rules governing the conduct of business enterprise. Just because there are these rules of the game, because political organization is nation-wide, the game takes on a different character, the nature and the meaning of sectional conflict is changed. An American scholar who has thrown a new and transforming light on our national history has said: "We must frankly face the fact that in this vast and heterogeneous nation, this sister of all Europe, regional geography is a fundamental fact; that the American peace has been achieved by restraining sectional selfishness and assertiveness and by coming to agreements rather than to reciprocal denunciations or to blows.... Statesmanship in this nation consists not only in representing the special interests of the leader's own section, but in finding a formula that will bring the different regions together in a common policy." [6]

But the nation, in its larger relations, is itself a section. Outside of its own borders its interests, real or supposed, conflict with the interests of other nations. Here statesmanship becomes sectional leadership. The rôle which the statesman finds easiest to play is often one which is assigned to him in the popular dramatization of the facts of international economic intercourse. His task would be harder, however, if his countrymen insisted or expected that the foreign policy of their own government should have the same degree of design and purpose, the same elements of plot and strategy, that they see in the foreign policies of other states.[7]

There is a modern animism which imputes malign intent, not to the forces of nature, but to personified "nations." The preposterous myth that Pan-Germanism was a definite national policy could not have found lodgment except in minds patterned to receive it. In a newspaper which lies before me as I write, there is a short dispatch telling that a new German company has been organized which proposes to operate in Russia. The headline reads: "Germany Getting Grip on Russia." Not long ago another dispatch told of a rather notable increase of some relatively unimportant German exports to Sweden. The headline and an introductory paragraph interpreted this ordinary incident of trade as meaning that Germany was getting "control" of Swedish markets. And when it is not Germany it is England or Japan or some other country. A clipping bureau, I suppose, could supply hundreds of such items each year. No one country has a monopoly of these childish absurdities. Running through the pre-war files of an important German commercial journal I found an astonishing number of references to the "conquest" (*Eroberung*) of Latin America by the United States; and that interpretation of our plans (not of our achievements) is common in Latin American countries.

A good deal of what passes for information respecting the purposes and activities of other nations is no better than malicious gossip. Such is the character of some of the information which governments receive through diplomatic channels. Bismarck said, "I have often not shown dispatches from our representatives in German Courts in the highest quarters, because they had a tendency to be piquant, or to relate and give importance to annoying expressions or occurrences, rather than to foster and improve the relations between the two courts, so long as the latter, as in Germany is always the case, was the task of our policy."[8] But even when a government's policy is "to foster and improve relations," no such censorship is possible over the open channels of communi-cation through which the people of a democracy gain their impressions of the purposes of other states.

However slight their foundation, these impressions, like our general views of the nature of international economic competition, help to determine our attitudes and to shape our conduct. Fear of the power and the purposes of American trusts was one of the reasons Germans gave for the organization of cartels in some of their export industries. The German cartels, in turn, figured largely in the discussions which led to the Webb-Pomerene Act of 1918 – a particularly invidious piece of legislation, which permits in American export trade combinations of a type that is illegal in domestic trade, with the proviso that such combinations shall not "restrain" the trade of or compete unfairly with *American* competitors.

In a hundred other incidents where retaliation leads to retaliation, any one who cares to look may see part of the actual process by which a world of gossip and of myths becomes the world of national policies. Nothing else is possible so long as each separate state is not only the guardian of its own interests but is also the interpreter of the interests and purposes of other states. There is no more ground for hoping that these types of economic friction will be done away with by changes in the policies of separate states than there is for expecting that armaments can be reduced effectively in any other way than by common agreement among nations.

In certain limited fields of economic activity, common agreements have already been reached and organs of international administration have been established. This is notably true in respect of communications and transport, where elementary considerations of convenience and economy, as well as the common interest in uniform and nondiscriminatory rules, make agreements imperative. The advantages of conformity are plainly visible, while there is little in nonconformity to which even a fictitious "national interest" can be attached. There is more significance in what has been accomplished in freeing transit trade from duties and from unreasonable transport charges and in creating international easements in important rivers and canals. Here the interest of a particular state may sometimes be opposed to the interests of other states. Taking advantage of a favorable geographical position, it might take tribute from the commerce which crosses its territory (as states often have in the past). There has been an element of compulsion – sometimes the compulsion of stronger states and sometimes the compulsion of circumstances – in the progress that has been made in these matters. To take only one example, the provisions relating to freedom of transit in the treaties concluded at the end of the World War, one-sided though those provisions were, helped to prepare the way for the general European agreement embodied in the Barcelona Convention of March, 1921.

Agreements for the suppression of the use of unfair methods of competition in international trade have been limited, for the most part, to the protection of patents, copyrights, trade-marks, trade-names, and the like. In these matters the interests of different states are not so much joint as they are reciprocal, and they are unevenly reciprocal. Substantial inequalities remain, particularly in the effectiveness with which the provisions agreed to are enforced.

International agreements with respect to labor legislation may possibly be regarded as tending toward fairer standards of international industrial competition. But that is not their chief significance; and I can do no more than mention them here. Nor can I discuss the important preparatory work done under the auspices of the Economic Committee of the League of Nations on commercial arbitration, export and import prohibitions, double taxation, and other matters.

It will be observed that few of the operative agreements which I have discussed thus far cut deeply into what are generally deemed to be important national interests or have come to be symbols of national prestige. None of them has much news value. The history of the international agreements that have sought really to limit the scope of international commercial "strategy" has been a record of halting achievement. Like price agreements and pooling arrangements among business concerns, such covenants appear to remain effective only so long as that situation serves the interests of the more important signatories. Such was the history of the Berlin Act of 1885, of the Brussels Sugar Convention of 1902, and of the Act of Algeciras of 1906.

In the absence of general agreements, the international economic relations of a large part of the world have been governed by a complex network of bilateral commercial treaties, held together and made at all consistent and tolerable only by most-favored-nation clauses. The system thus set up, especially in continental Europe was unstable; for a single important new treaty would upset things until, by the revision of other treaties, a condition of temporary equilibrium could again be reached. The system was uneven; for the strong states were able to bargain more effectively than the weaker ones. In particular, industrial states had a more advantageous position than agricultural states. Questions of commercial policy were recurrently projected into the field of international politics, so that they were quite commonly discussed in terms of *Machtpolitik*. Commercial treaties were regarded as instruments by which a state's power could be projected across its own boundaries.

Such a system often has undesirable economic effects. The present tariffs of some of the new states of eastern Europe afford an illustration. These tariffs are much higher than the real economic interests of those states demand. Artificial barriers set up at new boundary lines, these new tariffs block long-established channels of trade and hinder the economic recovery of that part of the world. Not all the blame can be put upon the newly stimulated spirit of nationalism. For these are bargaining tariffs. Some of the highest duties are imposed, not upon goods which the tariff-making country particularly desires to keep out, but upon goods which another country desires to get in. Aimed at one another, these new tariffs are an example of wasteful futility. Commercial treaties, coupled with most-favored-nation provisions, will gradually reduce them. In the meanwhile the costs are heavy. And experience has shown, I think, that tariffs made in this way generally have an upward trend. New vantage points are sought from time to time; special industrial interests look upon the reductions made in treaties as ground regrettably lost; national sentiment, also, learns to look upon concessions as retreat, so that there is a cumulative pressure upward.

The United States has stood aloof from this system. We have held, though not with complete consistency, to the policy of the equal treatment of the commerce of all other nations. But the Tariff Act of 1922 empowers the President to impose retaliatory duties upon imports from any country which discriminates against our commerce; and the same general principle was embodied in the Tariff Act of 1909. We determine the other country's guilt; and we impose what we consider an appropriate penalty.

Students of these problems have become pretty well convinced, I think, that the most important single step toward their solution lies in the adoption of multilateral conventions defining the conditions of economic intercourse among the nations of the world. The first principle, the irreducible minimum, in such agreements is the doing away with a nation's power to discriminate against the trade of any other nation. This was the meaning of the third of President Wilson's

Fourteen Points: "The removal, so far as possible, of all economic barriers and the establishment of an equality of trade conditions." This, beyond doubt, is part of the meaning of the clause in the Covenant of the League of Nations which binds the signers of that covenant to "make provision to secure and maintain freedom of communications and of transit and equitable treatment for the commerce of all Members of the League." [9]

The League's word "equitable" is better in some ways than President Wilson's word "equality." It does not carry with it so clear and definite a commitment; but for that very reason it does not suggest precise limits to the scope of international economic agreements.

In fact, the phrase "equitable treatment for commerce," suggests different things to men in different countries. To some it means equal, that is, general most-favored-nation treatment. Some would add national treatment in respect of certain matters, such, for example, as the rights of foreign vessels in national ports, the taxes imposed upon foreigners, or the protection given them against unfair competition. To others it includes anti-dumping arrangements, the removal of restrictions on exports, unrestricted access to raw materials, or the open door in undeveloped parts of the world. But just now the content of international economic agreements is not so important as it is that agreements should be reached.

I have already said that the more important agreements of this general sort made before the war were unsuccessful. The difficulty with them was that they were *exceptional* arrangements. Belgium in the Congo and France in Morocco were hampered by restrictions that had the character of special disabilities, such as had not been attached to the colonial expansion of other countries. The Brussels Sugar Convention was an anomaly in a world in which nations were generally left free to determine their commercial policies as they pleased. To be really effective, such agreements must establish a general rule, not an exception to a rule. They must in some way create a new standard pattern of thought and conduct.

The resolution by which a few months ago the Assembly of the League of Nations invited the Council of the League to institute preparations for an international economic conference referred to the "economic difficulties which stand in the way of the restoration of general prosperity," and expressed the conviction that "economic peace will contribute largely to ensuring the security of peoples." As matters now stand in Europe, these two objects, economic restoration and economic peace, are closely connected. But of the two, economic peace is the more important, for it is the condition of the other.

Consider what has already been accomplished toward financial reconstruction. The real significance of the plans for the financial rehabilitation of Austria, Hungary, and Germany is that they embody international agreements. The securing of these international agreements was both a more difficult and a more important achievement than the formulating of the particular economic remedies that were to be administered. It is easier to determine what economic procedure is wise than it is to change national attitudes.

In these instances the changing of national attitudes was achieved by organizing and giving expression to the common interests of nations. The hopelessness of other methods had to be shown before this could be accomplished, but once done, it is not easily undone. The new attitude creates a new interest. Even if some of its economic provisions should break down, as is altogether likely, the Dawes plan probably will have solved the reparation problem.

The significance of these achievements for the general problem which I have undertaken to discuss is obvious. The attitudes and activities which we have in mind when we speak of "the economic causes of war" are not inevitable and unyielding expressions of permanent traits of human nature. They are forms or patterns of conduct and are correlated with particular modes of organization. Other forms and patterns, associated with other modes of organization, are within the bounds of practicable achievement. This does not mean that the task is simple, or that it can be accomplished merely by finding a magic formula. No sensible person expects that sectional interests or international economic antagonisms will disappear. But it is not unreasonable to hope that some day they may be subordinated to new and larger interests which will grow out of new forms of organization. At any rate, the only way to secure economic peace is to turn our eyes towards it.

Notes

1 Montesquieu, Charles de Secondat, Baron de (1750) *Esprit des Lois*, Edinburgh: G. Hamilton & J. Balfour, Book xx, chap. 2
2 Smith, A. (1776) *Wealth of Nations*, Book iv, chap. 3.
3 Lavisse, E. (1891) *General View of the Political History of Europe* (transl. C. Gross), New York: Longmans, Green & Co., p. 163.
4 Lippman, Walter (1915) *The Stakes of Diplomacy*, New York: H. Holt and Co., pp. 76–83.
5 Dewey, John (1922) *Human Nature and Conduct*, New York: Henry Holt and Co., pp. 110–12.
6 Turner, F. J. (1925) "The Significance of the Section in American History," *Wisconsin Magazine of History*, March, vol. xiii, pp. 275, 279.
7 "Whoever has been inside British foreign policy is familiar with the emotion of indignation, amusement, or contempt with which he reads of the deep motives and the clever schemes that are invented for present-day British diplomatists and attributed to them by ingenious writers in foreign, and sometimes even in the British, press. One who is conscious of this may well be cautious in attributing deep and sinister designs to the action of foreign Governments." – Grey, Edward, Viscount Grey of Fallodon (1925) *Twenty-Five Years, 1892–1916*, New York: Frederick A. Stokes, vol. i, p. 230.
8 von Bismarck, Otto Furst (1899) *Reflections and Reminiscences* (Eng. transl.), New York: Harper and Bros. vol. ii, p. 248.
9 I have given an account of the history of this clause in Temperley, Harold William Vazeille (Ed.) (1924) *A History of the Peace Conference of Paris*, London: Frowde, Hodder and Stoughton, vol. v, chap. 1, part 3.

5   Increasing returns and economic progress

Economic Journal (1928) 38, No. 152 (December): 527–42. Presidential Address before Section F (Economic Science and Statistics) of the British Association for the Advancement of Science, Glasgow, September 10, 1928.

My subject may appear alarmingly formidable, but I did not intend it to be so. The words economic progress, taken by themselves, would suggest the pursuit of some philosophy of history, of some way of appraising the results of past and possible future changes in forms of economic organisation and modes of economic activities. But as I have used them, joined to the other half of my title, they are meant merely to dispel apprehensions, by suggesting that I do not propose to discuss any of those alluring but highly technical questions relating to the precise way in which some sort of equilibrium of supply and demand is achieved in the market for the products of industries which can increase their output without increasing their costs proportionately, or to the possible advantages of fostering the development of such industries while putting a handicap upon industries whose output can be increased only at the expense of a more than proportionate increase of costs. I suspect, indeed, that the apparatus which economists have built up for dealing effectively with the range of questions to which I have just referred may stand in the way of a clear view of the more general or elementary aspects of the phenomena of increasing returns such as I wish to comment upon in this paper.

Consider, for example, Alfred Marshall's fruitful distinction between the internal productive economies which a particular firm is able to secure as the growth of the market permits it to enlarge the scale of its operations and the economies external to the individual firm which show themselves only in changes of the organisation of the industry as a whole. This distinction has been useful in at least two different ways. In the first place it is, or ought to be, a safeguard against the common error of assuming that wherever increasing returns operate there is necessarily an effective tendency towards monopoly. In the second place it simplifies the analysis of the manner in which the prices of commodities produced under conditions of increasing returns are determined. A representative firm within the industry, maintaining its own identity and devoting itself to a given range of activities, is made to be the vehicle or medium through which the economies achieved by the industry as a whole are transmitted to the market and have their effect upon the price of the product.

The view of the nature of the processes of industrial progress which is implied in the distinction between internal and external economies is necessarily a partial view. Certain aspects of those processes are illuminated, while, for that very reason, certain other aspects, important in relation to other problems, are obscured. This will be clear, I think, if we observe that, although the internal economies of some firms producing, let us say, materials or appliances may figure as the external economies of other firms, not all of the economies which are properly to be called external can be accounted for by adding up the internal economies of all the separate firms. When we look at the internal economies of a particular firm we envisage a condition of comparative stability. Year after year the firm, like its competitors, is manufacturing a particular product or group of products, or is confining itself to certain definite stages in the work of forwarding the products towards their final form. Its operations change in the sense that they are progressively adapted to an increasing output, but they are kept within definitely circumscribed bounds. Out beyond, in that obscurer field from which it derives its external economies, changes of another order are occurring. New products are appearing, firms are assuming new tasks, and new industries are coming into being. In short, change in this external field is qualitative as well as quantitative. No analysis of the forces making for economic equilibrium, forces which we might say are tangential at any moment of time, will serve to illumine this field, for movements away from equilibrium, departures from previous trends, are characteristic of it. Not much is to be gained by probing into it to see how increasing returns show themselves in the costs of individual firms and in the prices at which they offer their products.

Instead we have to go back to a simpler and more inclusive view, such as some of the older economists took when they contrasted the increasing returns which they thought were characteristic of manufacturing industry taken as a whole with the diminishing returns which they thought were dominant in agriculture because of an increasingly unfavourable proportioning of labour and land. Most of them were disappointingly vague with respect to the origins and the precise nature of the "improvements" which they counted upon to retard somewhat the operation of the tendency towards diminishing returns in agriculture and to secure a progressively more effective use of labour in manufactures. Their opinions appear to have rested partly upon an empirical generalisation. Improvements had been made, they were still being made, and it might be assumed that they would continue to be made. If they had looked back they would have seen that there were centuries during which there were few significant changes in either agricultural or industrial methods. But they were living in an age when men had turned their faces in a new direction and when economic progress was not only consciously sought but seemed in some way to grow out of the nature of things. Improvements, then, were not something to be explained. They were natural phenomena, like the precession of the equinoxes.

There were certain important exceptions, however, to this incurious attitude towards what might seem to be one of the most important of all economic problems. Senior's positive doctrine is well known, and there were others who made note of the circumstance that with the growth of population and of markets new opportunities for the division of labour appear and new advantages attach to it. In this way, and in this way only, were the generally commonplace things which they said about "improvements" related to anything which could properly be called a doctrine of increasing returns. They added nothing to Adam Smith's famous theorem that the division of labour depends upon the extent of the market. That theorem, I have always thought, is one of the most illuminating and fruitful generalisations which can be found anywhere in the whole literature of economics. In fact, as I am bound to confess, I am taking it as the text of this paper, in much the way that some minor composer borrows a theme from one of the masters and adds certain developments or variations of his own. To-day, of course, we mean by the division of labour something much broader in scope than that splitting up of occupations and development of specialised crafts which Adam Smith mostly had in mind. No one, so far as I know, has tried to enumerate all of the different aspects of the division of labour, and I do not propose to undertake that task. I shall deal with two related aspects only: the growth of indirect or roundabout methods of production and the division of labour among industries.

It is generally agreed that Adam Smith, when he suggested that the division of labour leads to inventions because workmen engaged in specialised routine operations come to see better ways of accomplishing the same results, missed the main point. The important thing, of course, is that with the division of labour a group of complex processes is transformed into a succession of simpler processes, some of which, at least, lend themselves to the use of machinery. In the use of machinery and the adoption of indirect processes there is a further division of labour, the economies of which are again limited by the extent of the market. It would be wasteful to make a hammer to drive a single nail; it would be better to use whatever awkward implement lies conveniently at hand. It would be wasteful to furnish a factory with an elaborate equipment of specially constructed jigs, gauges, lathes, drills, presses and conveyors to build a hundred automobiles; it would be better to rely mostly upon tools and machines of standard types, so as to make a relatively larger use of directly-applied and relatively smaller use of indirectly-applied labour. Mr. Ford's methods would be absurdly uneconomical if his output were very small, and would be unprofitable even if his output were what many other manufacturers of automobiles would call large.

Then, of course, there are economies of what might be called a secondary order. How far it pays to go in equipping factories with special appliances for making hammers or for constructing specialised machinery for use in making different parts of automobiles depends again upon how many nails are to be driven and how many automobiles can be sold. In some instances, I suppose, these secondary economies, though real, have only a secondary importance. The derived demands for many types of specialised production appliances are inelastic over a fairly large range. If the benefits and the costs of using such appliances are spread over a relatively large volume of final products, their technical effectiveness is a larger factor in determining whether it is profitable to use them than any difference which producing them on a large or a small scale would commonly make in their costs. In other instances the demand for productive appliances is more elastic, and beyond a certain level of costs demand may fail completely. In such circumstances secondary economies may become highly important.

Doubtless, much of what I have said has been familiar and even elementary. I shall venture, nevertheless, to put further stress upon two points, which may be among those which have a familiar ring, but which appear sometimes to be in danger of being forgotten. (Otherwise, economists of standing could not have suggested that increasing returns may be altogether illusory, or have maintained that where they are present they must lead to monopoly.) The first point is that the principal economies which manifest themselves in increasing returns are the economies of capitalistic or roundabout methods of production. These economies, again, are largely identical with the economies of the division of labour in its most important modern forms. In fact, these economies lie under our eyes, but we may miss them if we try to make of *large-scale* production (in the sense of production by large firms or large industries), as contrasted with *large* production, any more than an incident in the general process by which increasing returns are secured and if accordingly we look too much at the individual firm or even, as I shall suggest presently, at the individual industry.

The second point is that the economies of roundabout methods, even more than the economies of other forms of the division of labour, depend upon the extent of the market – and that, of course, is why we discuss them under the head of increasing returns. It would hardly be necessary to stress this point, if it were not that the economies of large-scale operations and of "mass-production" are often referred to as though they could be had for the taking, by means of a "rational" reorganisation of industry. Now I grant that at any given time routine and inertia play a very large part in the organisation and conduct of industrial operations. Real leadership is no more common in industrial than in other pursuits. New catch-words or slogans like mass-production and rationalisation may operate as stimuli; they may rouse men from routine and lead them to scrutinise again the organisation and processes of industry and to try to discover particular ways in which they can be bettered. For example, no one can doubt that there are genuine economies to be achieved in the way of "simplification and standardisation". Or that the securing of these economies requires that certain deeply rooted competitive wastes be extirpated. This last requires a definite concerted effort – precisely the kind of thing which ordinary competitive motives are often powerless to effect, but which might come more easily as the response to the dissemination of a new idea.

There is a danger, however, that we shall expect too much from these "rational" industrial reforms. Pressed beyond a certain point they become the reverse of rational. I have naturally been interested in British opinions respecting the reasons for the relatively high productivity (per labourer or per hour of labour) of representative American industries. The error of those who suggest that the explanation is to be found in the relatively high wages which prevail in America is not that they confuse cause and effect, but that they hold that what are really only two aspects of a single situation are, the one cause, and the other effect. Those who hold that American industry is managed better, that its leaders study its problems more intelligently and plan more courageously and more wisely can cite no facts in support of their opinion save the differences in the results achieved. Allowing for the circumstance that British industry, as a whole, has proved to be rather badly adjusted to the new post-war economic situation, I know of no facts which prove or even indicate that British industry, seen against the background of its own problems and its own possibilities, is less efficiently organised or less ably directed than American industry or the industry of any other country.

Sometimes the fact that the average American labourer works with the help of a larger supply of power-driven labour-saving machinery than the labourer of other countries is cited as evidence of the superior intelligence of the average American employer. But this will not do, for, as every economist knows, the greater the degree in which labour is productive or scarce – the words have the same meaning – the greater is the relative economy of using it in such indirect or roundabout ways as are technically advantageous, even though such procedure calls for larger advances of capital than simpler methods do.

It is encouraging to find that a fairly large number of commentators upon the volume of the American industrial product and the scale of American industrial organisation have come to surmise that the extent of the American domestic market, unimpeded by tariff barriers, may have something to do with the matter. This opinion seems even to be forced upon thoughtful observers by the general character of the facts, whether or no the observers think in terms of the economists' conception of increasing returns. In certain industries, although by no means in all, productive methods are economical and profitable in America which would not be profitable elsewhere. The importance of coal and iron and other natural resources needs no comment. Taking a country's economic endowment as given, however, the most important single factor in determining the effectiveness of its industry appears to be the size of the market. But just what constitutes a large market? Not area or population alone, but buying power, the capacity to absorb a large annual output of goods. This trite observation, however, at once suggests another equally trite, namely, that capacity to buy depends upon capacity to produce. In an inclusive view, considering the market not as an outlet for the products of a particular industry, and therefore external to that industry, but as the outlet for goods in general, the size of the market is determined and defined by the volume of production. If this statement needs any qualification, it is that the conception of a market in this inclusive sense – an aggregate of productive activities, tied together by trade – carries with it the notion that there must be some sort of balance, that different productive activities must be proportioned one to another.

Modified, then, in the light of this broader conception of the market, Adam Smith's dictum amounts to the theorem that the division of labour depends in large part upon the division of labour. This is more than mere tautology. It means, if I read its significance rightly, that the counter forces which are continually defeating the forces which make for economic equilibrium are more pervasive and more deeply rooted in the constitution of the modern economic system than we commonly realise. Not only new or adventitious elements, coming in from the outside, but elements which are permanent characteristics of the ways in which goods are produced make continuously for change. Every important advance in the organisation of production, regardless of whether it is based upon anything which, in a narrow or technical sense, would be called a new "invention", or involves a fresh application of the fruits of scientific progress to industry, alters the conditions of industrial activity and initiates responses elsewhere in the industrial structure which in turn have a further unsettling effect. Thus change becomes progressive and propagates itself in a cumulative way.

The apparatus which economists have built up for the analysis of supply and demand in their relations to prices does not seem to be particularly helpful for the purposes of an inquiry into these broader aspects of increasing returns. In fact, as I have already suggested, reliance upon it may divert attention to incidental or partial aspects of a process which ought to be seen as a whole. If, nevertheless, one insists upon seeing just how far one can get into the problem by using the formulas of supply and demand, the simplest way, I suppose, is to begin by inquiring into the operations of reciprocal demand when the commodities exchanged are produced competitively under conditions of increasing returns and when the demand for each commodity is elastic, in the special sense that a small increase in its supply will be attended by an increase in the amounts of other commodities which can be had in exchange for it.[1] Under such conditions an increase in the supply of one commodity *is* an increase in the demand for other commodities, and it must be supposed that every increase in demand will evoke an increase in supply. The rate at which any one industry grows is conditioned by the rate at which other industries grow, but since the elasticities of demand and of supply will differ for different products, some industries will grow faster than others. Even with a stationary population and in the absence of new discoveries[2] in pure or applied science there are no limits to the process of expansion except the limits beyond which demand is not elastic and returns do not increase.

If, under these hypothetical conditions, progress were unimpeded and frictionless, if it were not dependent in part upon a process of trial and error, if the organisation of industry were always such as, in relation to the immediate situation, is most economical, the realising of increasing returns might be progressive and continuous, although, for technical reasons, it could not always proceed at an even rate. But it would remain a process requiring time. An industrial dictator, with foresight and knowledge, could hasten the pace somewhat, but he could not achieve an Aladdin-like transformation of a country's industry, so as to reap the fruits of a half-century's ordinary progress in a few years. The obstacles are of two sorts. First, the human material which has to be used is resistant to change. New trades have to be learnt and new habits have to be acquired. There has to be a new geographical distribution of the population and established communal groups have to be broken up. Second, the accumulation of the necessary capital takes time, even though the process of accumulation is largely one of turning part of an increasing product into forms which will serve in securing a further increase of product. An acceleration of the rate of accumulation encounters increasing costs, into which both technical and psychological elements enter. One who likes to conceive of all economic processes in terms of tendencies towards an equilibrium might even maintain that increasing returns, so far as they depend upon the economies of indirect methods of production and the size of the market, are offset and negated by their costs, and that under such simplified conditions as I have dealt with the realising of increasing returns would be spread through time in such a way as to secure an equilibrium of costs and advantages. This would amount to saying that no real economic progress could come through the operation of forces engendered *within* the economic system – a conclusion repugnant to common sense. To deal with this point thoroughly would take us too far afield. I shall merely observe, first, that the appropriate conception is that of a *moving* equilibrium, and second, that the costs which (under increasing returns) grow less rapidly than the product are not the "costs" which figure in an "equilibrium of costs and advantages".

Moving away from these abstract considerations, so as to get closer to the complications of the real situation, account has to be taken, first, of various kinds of obstacles. The demand for some products is inelastic, or, with an increasing supply, soon becomes so. The producers of such commodities, however, often share in the advantages of the increase of the general scale of production in related industries, and so far as they do productive resources are released for other uses. Then there are natural scarcities, limitations or inelasticities of supply, such as effectively block the way to the securing of any important economies in the production of some commodities and which impair the effectiveness of the economies secured in the production of other commodities. In most fields, moreover, progress is not and cannot be continuous. The next important step forward is often initially costly, and cannot be taken until a certain quantum of prospective advantages has accumulated.

On the other side of the account are various factors which reinforce the influences which make for increasing returns. The discovery of new natural resources and of new uses for them and the growth of scientific knowledge are probably the most potent of such factors. The causal connections between the growth of industry and the progress of science run in both directions, but on which side the preponderant influence lies no one can say. At any rate, out of better knowledge of the materials and forces upon which men can lay their hands there come both new ways of producing familiar commodities and new products, and these last have a presumptive claim to be regarded as embodying more economical uses of productive resources than the uses which they displace. Some weight has to be given also to the way in which, with the advance of the scientific spirit, a new kind of interest – which might be described as a scientific interest conditioned by an economic interest – is beginning to infiltrate into industry. It is a point of controversy, but I venture to maintain that under most circumstances, though not in all, the growth of population still has to be counted a factor making for a larger *per capita* product – although even that cautious statement needs to be interpreted and qualified. But just as there may be population growth with no increase of the average *per capita* product, so also, as I have tried to suggest, markets may grow and increasing returns may be secured while the population remains stationary.

It is dangerous to assign to any single factor the leading rôle in that continuing economic revolution which has taken the modern world so far away from the world of a few hundred years ago. But is there any other factor which has a better claim to that rôle than the persisting search for markets? No other hypothesis so well unites economic history and economic theory. The Industrial Revolution of the eighteenth century has come to be generally regarded, not as a cataclysm brought about by certain inspired improvements in industrial technique, but as a series of changes related in an orderly way to prior changes in industrial organisation and to the enlargement of markets. It is sometimes said, however, that while in the Middle Ages and in the early modern period industry was the servant of commerce, since the rise of "industrial capitalism" the relation has been reversed, commerce being now merely an agent of industry. If this means that the finding of markets is one of the tasks of modern industry it is true. If it means that industry imposes its will upon the market, that whereas formerly the things which were produced were the things which could be sold, now the things which have to be sold are the things that are produced, it is not true.

The great change, I imagine, is in the new importance which the *potential market* has in the planning and management of large industries. The difference between the cost per unit of output in an industry or in an individual plant properly adapted to a given volume of output and in an industry or plant equally well adapted to an output five times as large is often much greater than one would infer from looking merely at the economies which may accrue as an existing establishment gradually extends the scale of its operations. Potential demand, then, in the planning of industrial undertakings, has to be balanced against potential economies, elasticity of demand against decreasing costs. The search for markets is not a matter of disposing of a "surplus product," in the Marxian sense, but of finding an outlet for a potential product. Nor is it wholly a matter of multiplying profits by multiplying sales; it is partly a matter of augmenting profits by reducing costs.

Although the initial displacement may be considerable and the repercussions upon particular industries unfavourable, the enlarging of the market for any one commodity, produced under conditions of increasing returns, generally has the net effect, as I have tried to show, of enlarging the market for other commodities. The businessman's mercantilistic emphasis upon markets may have a sounder basis than the economist who thinks mostly in terms of economic statics is prone to admit. How far "selling expenses", for example, are to be counted sheer economic waste depends upon their effects upon the aggregate product of industry, as distinguished from their effects upon the fortunes of particular undertakings.

Increasing returns are often spoken of as though they were attached always to the growth of "industries", and I have not tried to avoid that way of speaking of them, although I think that it may be a misleading way. The point which I have in mind is something more than a quibble about the proper definition of an industry, for it involves a particular thesis with respect to the way in which increasing returns are reflected in changes in the organisation of industrial activities. Much has been said about industrial integration as a concomitant or a natural result of an increasing industrial output. It obviously is, under particular conditions, though I know of no satisfactory statement of just what those particular conditions are. But the opposed process, industrial differentiation, has been and remains the type of change characteristically associated with the growth of production. Notable as has been the increase in the complexity of the apparatus of living, as shown by the increase in the variety of goods offered in consumers" markets, the increase in the diversification of intermediate products and of industries manufacturing special products or groups of products has gone even further.

The successors of the early printers, it has often been observed, are not only the printers of to-day, with their own specialised establishments, but also the producers of wood pulp, of various kinds of paper, of inks and their different ingredients, of type-metal and of type, the group of industries concerned with the technical parts of the producing of illustrations, and the manufacturers of specialised tools and machines for use in printing and in these various auxiliary industries. The list could be extended, both by enumerating other industries which are directly ancillary to the present printing trades and by going back to industries which, while supplying the industries which supply the printing trades, also supply other industries, concerned with preliminary stages in the making of final products other than printed books and newspapers. I do not think that the printing trades are an exceptional instance, but I shall not give other examples, for I do not want this paper to be too much like a primer of descriptive economics or an index to the reports of a census of production. It is sufficiently obvious, anyhow, that over a large part of the field of industry an increasingly intricate nexus of specialised undertakings has inserted itself between the producer of raw materials and the consumer of the final product.

With the extension of the division of labour among industries the representative firm, like the industry of which it is a part, loses its identity. Its internal economies dissolve into the internal and external economies of the more highly specialised undertakings which are its successors, and are supplemented by new economies. In so far as it is an adjustment to a new situation created by the growth of the market for the final products of industry the division of labour among industries is a vehicle of increasing returns. It is more than a change of form incidental to the full securing of the advantages of capitalistic methods of production – although it is largely that – for it has some advantages of its own which are independent of changes in productive technique. For example, it permits of a higher degree of specialisation in management, and the advantages of such specialisation are doubtless often real, though they may easily be given too much weight. Again, it lends itself to a better geographical distribution of industrial operations, and this advantage is unquestionably both real and important. Nearness to the source of supply of a particular raw material or to cheap power counts for most in one part of a series of industrial processes, nearness to other industries or to cheap transport in another part, and nearness to a larger centre of population in yet another. A better *combination* of advantages of location, with a smaller element of compromise, can be had by the more specialised industries. But the largest advantage secured by the division of labour among industries is the fuller realising of the economies of capitalistic or roundabout methods of production. This should be sufficiently obvious if we assume, as we must, that in most industries there are effective, though elastic, limits to the economical size of the individual firm. The output of the individual firm is generally a relatively small proportion of the aggregate output of an industry. The degree in which it can secure economies by making its own operations more roundabout is limited. But certain roundabout methods are fairly sure to become feasible and economical when their advantages can be spread over the output of the whole industry. These potential economies, then, are segregated and achieved by the operations of specialised undertakings which, taken together, constitute a new industry. It might conceivably be maintained that the *scale* upon which the firms in the new industry are able to operate is the secret of their ability to realise economies for industry as a whole, while presumably making profits for themselves. This is true in a way, but misleading. The scale of their operations (which is only incidentally or under special conditions a matter of the size of the individual firm) merely reflects the size of the market for the final products of the industry or industries to whose operations their own are ancillary. And the principal advantage of large-scale operation at this stage is that it again makes methods economical which would be uneconomical if their benefits could not be diffused over a large final product.

In recapitulation of these variations on a theme from Adam Smith there are three points to be stressed. First, the mechanism of increasing returns is not to be discerned adequately by observing the effects of variations in the size of an individual firm or of a particular industry, for the progressive division and specialisation of industries is an essential part of the process by which increasing returns are realised. What is required is that industrial operations be seen as an interrelated whole. Second, the securing of increasing returns depends upon the progressive division of labour, and the principal economies of the division of labour, in its modern forms, are the economies which are to be had by using labour in roundabout or indirect ways. Third, the division of labour depends upon the extent of the market, but the extent of the market also depends upon the division of labour. In this circumstance lies the possibility of economic progress, apart from the progress which comes as a result of the new knowledge which men are able to gain, whether in the pursuit of their economic or of their non-economic interests.

Note

In the accompanying construction (which owes much to Pareto), a collective indifference curve, *I*, is defined by the condition that, at equal cost, there would be no sufficient inducement for the community to alter an annual production of *x* units of one commodity and *y* units of another in order to secure the alternative combination of the two commodities indicated by any other point on the curve.[3] Each commodity might be taken as representative of a special class of commodities, produced under generally similar conditions. Or one commodity might be made to represent "other goods in general", the annual outlay of productive exertions being regarded as constant. Alternatively, one commodity might represent "leisure" (as a collective name for all non-productive uses of time). The other would then represent the aggregate economic product.

There will be equilibrium (subject to instability of a kind which will be described presently) at a point *P*, if at that point a curve of equal costs, such as *d*, is tangent to the indifference curve. The curve of equal costs defines the terms upon which the community can exchange one commodity for the other by merely producing less of the one and more of the other (abstraction being made of any incidental costs of change). Negative curvature, as in *d*, reflects a condition of decreasing returns, in the sense that more of either commodity can be had only by sacrificing progressively larger amounts of the other. Although a sufficient condition, the presence of decreasing returns is not a necessary condition of equilibrium. There would be a loss in moving away from *P* if equal costs were defined by the straight line *c*, which represents constant returns. Increasing returns, even, are consistent with equilibrium, provided that the degree of curvature of their graph is less than that of the indifference curve. It might happen, of course, that returns would decrease in one direction and increase in the other. Curve *d*, for example, might have a point of inflexion at or near *P*.

Consider now the conditions of departure from equilibrium. The curve *i* is drawn so as to represent *potential* increasing returns between *P* and *P₁*, which lies on a preferred indifference curve. If these increasing returns were to be had merely for

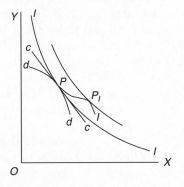

Figure 5.1

the taking, if i were, for example, merely a continuation of the upper segment of d or c, P would not be a point even of unstable equilibrium. The advance from P to P_1 would be made by merely altering the proportions of the two commodities produced annually. To isolate the *problem* of increasing returns it is necessary to assume that P is a true point of equilibrium in the sense that it is determined by a curve of equal costs, such as d or c. The problem, then, has to do with the way in which the lower segment of d or c can be transformed into or replaced by such a curve as i. This requires, of course, that *additional* costs be incurred, of a kind which have not yet been taken into account. To diminish the amount of the one commodity which must be sacrificed for a given increment of the other, some of the labour hitherto devoted to its production must be used indirectly, so that the increase of the annual output of the one lags behind the curtailing of the output of the other.

This new element of cost might be taken into account by utilising a third dimension, but it is simpler to regard it as operating upon Δx, the increment in x accompanying the movement from P to P_1, so as to move the indifference curve upon which P_1 lies towards the left. It would be an error, however, to think that the combinations of x with y and $x + (\Delta x)$ with $y - \Delta y$ (where (Δx) is the contracted form of Δx) are themselves indifferent, so that P_1 is, in effect, brought over on to the original indifference curve, I, and no advantage is reaped. The path from P to P_1 is a *preferred* route, not merely a segment of an indifference curve. The cost of moving along that route is a function of the *rate* (in time) of the movement. An equilibrium rate (which need not be constant), such as would keep the movement from P to P_1 continuous and undeviating, would be determined by the condition, not that (Δx) and $- \Delta y$ should negate one another, but that either an acceleration or a retarding of the rate would be costly or disadvantageous. Because a mountain climber adjusts his pace to his physical powers and to the conditions of the ascent, it does not follow that he might as well have stayed at the foot. Or, alternatively but not inconsistently, the movement from P to P_1 may be conceived as made up of a series of small steps, each apparently yielding no more than a barely perceptible advantage, but only because the scale of reference for both costs and advantages depends at each step upon the position which has then been reached.

Several sets of circumstances will affect the amount and direction of the movement. (1) Even if i has no point of inflexion, such as has been indicated at P_1 (merely to simplify the first stages of this analysis), it will sooner or later (taking into account the "contraction" of Δx) become tangent to an indifference curve. In the absence of any other factor making for change, progress would then come to an end. (2) There may be another possible alternative path of increasing returns extending upwards from P and curving away from I. The most advantageous route will then be a compromise between (or a resultant of) the two limiting alternatives. In such circumstances the only effective limitation imposed upon the extent of the movement may come from the failure of elasticity of demand on one side or the other. (3) Successive indifference curves cannot be supposed to be symmetrical, in the sense that dy/dx remains the same function of

y/x. If, for example, the slope of successive indifference curves at points corresponding to given values of y/x decreases (indicating that the demand for the commodity measured in units of y is relatively inelastic), freedom of movement in the direction of P_1 is reduced, while it becomes advantageous to move a little way in the opposite direction along even such a path as c or d. Under inverse conditions (with $-dy/dx$ increasing relatively to y/x for successive indifference curves) the extent of the possible movement in the direction of P_1 is increased. This conclusion amounts to no more than the obvious theorem that the degree in which the decreasing returns encountered in certain fields of economic activity operate as a drag upon the securing of increasing returns in other fields depends upon the relative elasticities of demand for the two types of products. But this consideration, like the others of which note has been made, serves to make clear the general nature of the reciprocal relation between increasing returns and the "extent of the market". (4) Discoveries of new supplies of natural resources or of *new* productive methods may have either or both of two kinds of effects. They may tilt the curves of equal cost and they may modify their curvature favourably. In either event a point such as P is moved to a higher indifference curve, and the paths along which further progress can be made are altered advantageously.

Notes

1 If the circumstance that commodity a is produced under conditions of increasing returns is taken into account as a factor in the elasticity of demand for b in terms of a, elasticity of demand and elasticity of supply may be looked upon as different ways of expressing a single functional relation.

2 As contrasted with such new ways of organising production and such new "inventions" as are merely adaptations of known ways of doing things, made practicable and economical by an enlarged scale of production.

3 The collective indifference is to be taken as an expository device, not as a rigorous conception. The relative weights to be assigned to the individual indifference curves of which it is compounded will depend upon how the aggregate product is distributed, and this will not be the same for all positions of P.

Part II
Theory and practice

6 The social dividend

Richard T. Ely, Thomas S. Adams, Max O. Lorenz and Allyn A. Young, *Outlines of Economics* 2nd edn. (1908), New York: Macmillan. Appendix to chapter XXV, "Profits": 448–56

The significance of the statement made in an earlier chapter, that the distribution of wealth is a matter of valuation, should now be clear to the reader. But since the detailed character of the analysis may make a broad and inclusive view of this valuation process somewhat difficult, it will be worth our while to bring together the more important conclusions we have reached, and to try to see them from a somewhat different point of view.

The *social dividend* is made up of the scarce and valuable things (commodities and services) that are of direct use in the satisfaction of human wants. The process by which the claims of different individuals against the social dividend are adjudicated is the process of the distribution of wealth. We have seen that these claims rest upon various grounds. Some men give of their own time and energy to the production of goods. Others permit the use of the scarce and valuable natural agents (especially land) which they own. Still others exchange part of their present claims against the social dividend for future claims, thereby permitting part of the productive work of society to be turned toward the creation of indirect goods, the use of which operates, in the long run, to greatly increase the social dividend.

A unifying characteristic of these three different kinds of claims is the fact that the wages of labor, the rent of land, and the interest on capital are simply different forms of money income, paid for the services of land, labor, and capital in the production of valuable things. The valuations which society puts on the productive services of its members or of their productive goods are determined through the activities of entrepreneurs.

The relation of the activities of entrepreneurs to the money incomes of the members of society is twofold. On the one hand, the purchasing power of consumers is derived from their money incomes, which in this way constitute the means by which the demand for the entrepreneur's products expresses itself. On the other hand, the money incomes received by laborers and by those who supply capital and land are paid by entrepreneurs in return for productive services. The wages, rent, and interest expended by any one entrepreneur for these productive services are in turn paid over by the individuals who receive them to other entrepreneurs in return for their products. There is thus a continuous flow of money income through the hands of entrepreneurs, appearing first in the form of the prices that are paid for an entrepreneur's goods, then emerging in the form of the rent, wages, and interest that the entrepreneur pays for the service of the factors in production, then reappearing in the prices paid for other goods, and so on in a continually recurring cycle of income and outgo.[1]

This process is made more complicated, however, by the fact that not all of the entrepreneur's expenses appear directly as rent, wages, or interest. A considerable part, and in many cases (as in mercantile establishments), the largest part of such expenditures are for various concrete forms of capital, – raw materials, dealers' stocks of goods, machines, and the like. Here a part of the money income received by the entrepreneur in the form of the prices paid for his own goods emerges in the prices which he pays for the goods sold by other entrepreneurs, and which, in turn, make up a part of their money incomes. But this other class of entrepreneurs – who supply capital goods rather than consumption goods – are subject to the same necessity of expending their money incomes in the payment of wages, rent, and interest, and in the purchase of different kinds of capital goods. To push the analysis still further would obviously lead us only into needless repetition. One important fact, however, appears clearly: If we could trace the expense of producing any consumption goods back through all the long series of services and of production goods that have contributed to its making we would find that this expense reduces itself, ultimately, to rent, wages, and interest, not counting what remains in the entrepreneur's hands as profits. Part of the "flow of money income" passes through the hands of a chain of entrepreneurs, but it nevertheless originates in the prices that consumers pay for the things that satisfy their wants and emerges in the form of the payments made for the productive services of land, labor, and capital.

Yet another correction must be made, however, to fit this picture of part of the economic process more closely to the facts. The money which consumers pay for particular commodities does not usually constitute the actual fund with which the entrepreneur pays for the labor, the land, and the capital goods used in the production of those commodities. Still less does it constitute the actual fund from which the entrepreneurs who supply the necessary capital goods pay their expenses, or from which the expenses of still more remote stages in the process of production are paid. The roundabout, indirect methods which characterize modern production, and which involve the division of the productive process among countless different undertakings, take time. The goods which consumers buy to-day are the result of a long series of productive efforts extending back indefinitely into the past. Similarly the productive efforts of to-day avail but relatively little toward the satisfaction of present wants, for they are in large part directed to forwarding, often in the most indirect ways, the production of things that will come to a final fruition in the satisfaction of human wants only in the more or less remote future.

Viewed in this way the *annual product* of society is something very different from the social dividend. The year's work is begun with an equipment of economic goods of all kinds, – finished goods in the hands of dealers and manufacturers, goods in all stages of completion, growing crops, factory and mercantile buildings, machines, and all the auxiliary apparatus of production in a finished or unfinished state. The annual product includes all the additions made to this stock of goods, and all that is accomplished in forwarding such goods as are destined for human consumption towards the form, place, and time in which and at which they are wanted. It includes all that is done in a similar way to forward, replenish, and increase the stock of production goods. It includes also all the personal services that command a money payment which are not embodied in concrete goods, but which confer their benefits in the very instance of their performance.

But while the productive efforts of society are thus constantly building up and modifying the stock of economic goods, this stock is continually being depleted in various ways. The instruments of production are constantly wearing out, or are being cast aside on account of the introduction of either more efficient appliances, or more efficient methods which utilize other kinds of appliances. Then, too, as the final outcome of this productive process there is a constant stream of finished consumption goods passing into the hands of consumers. The social dividend consists of this flow of consumption goods, together with those direct personal services which do not have to do directly or indirectly with the fitting of *goods* for human consumption, but which nevertheless satisfy wants and command a money payment. While the social dividend is to a large extent the outcome of past work and effort, the annual product is very largely a provision for future wants.

What is the effect of all these considerations upon our analysis of the flow of money income? It still remains true that the money which consumers pay to entrepreneurs is in turn used by them in the payment of their expenses of production, and that the money which they in turn pay to other entrepreneurs for various forms of capital goods are used in the payment of expenses of production. But the prices consumers are paying are for goods, the expenses of producing which have (at least in greater part) already been paid, and some of them (such as the prices paid for some kinds of capital instruments) may have been paid some considerable period of time back in the past. If in turn we should trace back the expenses of producing the capital goods used in producing these consumption goods our search would lead us into the more remote past, while still further analysis of the expenses of production would discover an increasing number of ramifications running back into the still more distant past. The present flow of money income, originating in the prices paid by consumers, passes, as we have seen, through the hands of a chain of entrepreneurs and in this process gets ultimately into the lands of laborers, capitalists, and landlords. But most of the productive services which are thus remunerated are services which will avail toward the satisfaction of future rather than of present wants. In other words, the prices paid for consumers' shares in the *social dividend* constitute (save for an important exception to be noted presently) the fund which pays for the *annual product*. The productive efforts of the past, which satisfy the wants of to-day, were paid for out of past income, while the present work of producing goods that will be ripe for consumption only in the future is paid for out of present income. In this fact lies the explanation of the nature and necessity of one of the various kinds of claims against the social dividend – interest.

The outlays which entrepreneurs make in producing goods, so far as they are paid before they receive an income from the sale of the goods, are commonly called investments of capital. Not only, as we have seen, does the entrepreneur invest capital in production goods such as machines and buildings, but his purchases of raw materials, his advances of wages to laborers, the interest which he pays on borrowed capital, and the rent or the purchase price which he pays for land, are usually investments of capital. No such investments can be regarded as remunerative unless the entrepreneur gets in the selling prices of his products enough to provide interest upon such outlays as well as to cover the outlays themselves. These facts were noted in connection with the discussion of interest in an earlier chapter, but there, for simplicity's sake, the analysis was confined to the capital expenditures of the individual entrepreneur. The full significance of the rôle which capital plays in production does not appear until we view the activities of the individual entrepreneur as only a link in the continuous chain of activities that make up the productive process.

The point of special significance in this connection is the fact that the finished products sold by some entrepreneurs constitute the capital goods (raw materials, productive appliances, etc.) bought by other entrepreneurs. When one entrepreneur sells his products to another entrepreneur his period of "waiting" is completed, so far as his advances of capital funds in the production of these particular units of goods are concerned. But the "waiting" is only transferred to the other entrepreneur, who adds further expenditures of capital and, in turn, gets his remuneration from the sale of his product. The important conclusion to which this analysis leads is that (so far as the entrepreneurs have been accurate in their estimates) the prices which consumers are paying to-day for finished goods cover not only all the actual money expenditures which have been made in the past in the production of these goods, but also the interest on all such expenditures from the time they were made up to the time of the sale of the finished goods to the ultimate consumer.

Similarly the expenditures made by entrepreneurs to-day in the production of goods that will directly or indirectly satisfy future wants will (so far as these entrepreneurs and those who will control the remaining steps in the productive process are accurate in their estimates) be covered, together with accrued interest, by the prices which consumers will pay in the future. Present wants are satisfied by means of the productive efforts of the past. These productive efforts were paid for out of past income, but the outlays were made in the expectation that present prices would suffice to repay them, with interest. A particular entrepreneur may be interested only in disposing of his products at remunerative prices to the entrepreneurs who stand next to him in the productive series, but this does not alter the essential nature of capital investment, which, from the social point of view, is a cumulative process.

The flow of money income which originates in the prices consumers pay to the entrepreneurs with whom they deal emerges in the form of capital expenditures, and so far as these take the form of the purchase of capital goods they constitute the fund from which other capital expenditures are made by other entrepreneurs. The gross money income of entrepreneurs, then, furnishes by far the most important part of the current supply of capital funds, and the most important form of capital investment is the entrepreneur's customary practice of "putting money back into the business." That this way of investing capital is customary, even habitual, does not mean that the amount as well as the particular forms of such investments is not a matter subject to the discretion of the entrepreneur. So far as the entrepreneur is not hampered by contracts (with customers, other entrepreneurs, money lenders, landlords, or laborers) he is free to do as he pleases with his income. As a matter of fact he is apt to devote a fairly constant proportion of it to the replacement of the capital goods that are being used up or worn out and to the other necessary expenses of continued production.

It rarely happens, however, in any undertaking, that income and expenditure are so nicely adjusted and so evenly distributed through the year that the one always suffices to provide for the other. A temporary surplus may be followed by a temporary deficit. Transfer of goods on credit smooth over some of these irregularities, while the institution of banking provides a mechanism whereby the temporary surpluses of some entrepreneurs are made use of in meeting the temporary deficits of others. Moreover, while the entrepreneur need not continue to renew his capital investments unless he chooses, he is at liberty to do even more than this if he deems it advisable. That is, his profits – the excess of his gross income over and above his current and normal capital expenditures – may be used for additional capital expenditures.

Still another source of capital funds is found in the rent, wages, and interest into which, as we have seen, the expenses of production ultimately resolve themselves. For so far as these forms of income are saved, rather than expended immediately for consumption goods, they may be loaned directly or through savings institutions to entrepreneurs for productive employment. This is the important exception, previously mentioned, to the statement that "the prices paid for consumers' shares in the social dividend constitute the fund which pays for the annual product." The truth is that as the flow of money income passes from entrepreneur to entrepreneur, a part only, although the larger part, is put into productive expenditures. The residuum is used by entrepreneurs in paying for their own shares in the social dividend. In much the same way the money incomes received by those who furnish labor, land, or capital is only in part paid back to entrepreneurs in return for consumption goods, the residuum being put (through loans to entrepreneurs) into productive expenditures.

It will be seen, then, that as the flow of money income passes through the hands of entrepreneurs, laborers, capitalists, and landowners, it is divided into two streams, one of which goes to pay for the present goods that have been produced in the past, while the other goes to pay for the present expenses of forwarding the production of goods for future consumption. This division represents a kind of social balancing of possible present satisfactions over against the larger future satisfactions which the productive use of capital makes possible. On the one hand we have the entrepreneurs' estimates of how much specific amounts of capital funds are worth to them, – estimates which involve judgments as to the amount of product dependent upon the use of these specific amounts of capital funds, the prices that can be got for such products, and the period of time that will elapse before they will be remunerated for such investments. On the other hand we have the estimates of those who supply capital funds as to the relative importance of future and present wants. The interest rate will normally be fixed, of course, at a point where the supply and demand of money capital will be in equilibrium.

In dividing his capital expenses between labor, land, and capital goods the entrepreneur will again be influenced by his estimates of how much the use of specific quantities of each of these factors in production will add to his money income. Here he has to reckon with the fact of diminishing productivity. He can get the same amount of product from different combinations of land, capital goods, and labor, but the larger the proportion of his expenditures he devotes to any one of these things (labor, for example), the smaller will be the increment of product dependent upon any one unit of it (any one laborer, for example). The most economical combination of labor, capital goods, and land is reached, of course, when the marginal expenditures for each add equal quantities to his product. All this, however, was discussed in detail when the activities of the individual entrepreneur were taken as the point of departure for the analysis of distribution in an earlier chapter. When we take the social point of view, so that production is made to appear as a cumulative process of capital investment, the expenses for capital goods become reduced to the more fundamental expenditures of rent, wages, and interest, involved in the production of such goods. In this view capital goods might, by a legitimate figure of speech, be said to be embodied rent, wages, and interest.

The social process of production involves the expenditure of rent, wages, and interest for returns of all possible degrees of futurity, and a consequent comparison and balancing of the productivity of investments for shorter and longer periods of time. That is, social estimates of productivity are estimates of the value of the amounts of the ultimate products, realizable at different periods of time in the future, that are dependent upon specific present expenditures in the form of rent, wages, or interest. Or, in other words, there is a continuous effort to make the most profitable of all the various possible combinations of land, labor, and waiting. For just as rent, wages, and interest are the ultimate expenses of production, so the ultimate factors in production may be said to be land, labor, and waiting.

The money incomes which individual laborers, landlords, and capitalists receive, and which constitute the claims (or, more accurately, the potential claims) against the social dividend, are determined by this social estimate of the specific amounts which they add to the value of the annual product, or, ultimately, to the value of finished products. Here again, on account of the law of diminishing productivity, the marginal product of land, labor, or waiting is the measure of the specific product attributed to a unit of land, labor, or waiting.

It must be remembered, however, that marginal productivity does not depend alone on the technical efficiency of labor, the fertility and accessibility of land, and the greater technical or physical productivity of the roundabout, indirect methods which waiting makes possible.[2] It also depends, just as fundamentally, upon the amount and elasticity of the supply of land, labor, and waiting. It has been shown in earlier chapters that the conditions of supply are very different in the case of each of the three factors in production. No account of the distributive process can be complete that does not lay special stress on these differences, for these are the things that become of most importance when economic theory is utilized in the untangling of the practical social problems growing out of the distribution of wealth.

Moreover, we cannot insist too strongly that the statement of the tendency toward an equality of the specific product attributable to a unit of land, labor, or capital funds and the price paid for its use is, after all, only an illuminating way of stating the real problem of distribution. Just as marginal utility is at the same time the cause and effect of price, so marginal productivity is at the same time the cause and effect of wages, rent, and interest. From one point of view it is seen that the competition of producers makes it necessary that specific units of land, labor, and capital should get a reward proportionate to the value of the amounts which they contribute to the social dividend; from another point of view it is equally clear that the necessary expenditures for land, labor, and capital are, in the long run, potent factors in determining the value of the things that make up the social dividend.

Furthermore, we are apt to forget that the word "productivity" as used in economics (and generally in current discussions of economic topics) has a distinctly limited meaning. To digress for a moment in order to make the point clearer: In the theory of consumption we emphasize the fact that many of the most important human wants are satisfied by "free goods," which, simply because they are free, lie outside the proper field of economic investigation. But the enjoyment of these free goods is usually dependent upon the possession of economic goods. Air is a free good, – to any one who can demand the economic goods necessary to life. The glorious scenery of the Alps is a free good, – to any one who can afford traveling expenses and hotel bills. In general, the enjoyment of many of the finer pleasure of life, involved in the common human relations of an individual to his physical and social environment, are "free," but free only to the individual who can afford the leisure and the economic goods without which many of these "free" pleasures are impossible.

For present purposes, however, the important point is that there are free production goods as well as free consumption goods. Nature furnishes some of these. The oceans and lakes furnish free pathways for commerce; natural forces of all kinds are freely utilized by men in the work of production. As was pointed out in an earlier chapter, we do not call these things productive, because no part of the annual product is dependent on the utilization of any particular unit of them. In this technical sense the wind is not productive, but windmills are. In order to utilize the ocean we have to invest capital in vessels and docks. We have to impute productivity to these things because they will not be furnished unless it is estimated that they will yield a remunerative income, and because the annual product will obviously be reduced if they are not furnished. But we would have to impute productivity to the Strait of Gibraltar if England were able to charge a toll for its use!

Somewhat analogous to these "free productive goods" is society's fund of accumulated knowledge of productive methods, – the heritage of centuries of economic evolution. This accumulated industrial experience is an infinitely more precious possession than the existing store of productive goods. Compare the productive possibilities of a community of men possessing this knowledge, but forced to begin work absolutely without a ready-made stock of capital goods, with those of a tribe of savages suddenly and miraculously equipped with all the productive appliances of modern civilization. Yet this vast fund of productive knowledge, so far as is common property, is not thought of as "productive." The social dividend is continually being increased as a result of the discovery of new natural forces, or new ways of harnessing and utilizing natural forces. Secrecy or government patents make it possible for those who first introduce these new methods of production to reap an income from the temporary advantage it gives to them as producers. For the time being these new methods themselves have to be regarded as "productive," although they contribute much more to the increase of the social dividend after they have become matters of common knowledge and use, and hence have ceased to be called "productive."[3] Disinterested scientists, especially those in the employment of the government or of universities, have often given the results of their improvements in industrial methods freely to the world, thereby swelling the social dividend, but not reaping for themselves the pecuniary reward which goes to those who patent their improvements and thereby render them "productive." Moreover, many of the world's greatest advances in the technique of production have been made possible only by the patient researches of investigators in the "unproductive" field of pure science, working solely for love of the work, and without hope of pecuniary reward.[4]

We impute productivity, in the technical economic sense, only to goods or services which are the objects of property rights or of analogous rights of control, – such as a man's power to dispose of his own labor. The fact is that just as the benefits of free consumption goods are bound up with the possession of larger or smaller quantities of economic goods, so the utilization of free productive agencies is possible only in combination with labor, waiting, and scarce and appropriable natural objects, – and these have to be paid for. We harness natural forces for the work of production, but we impute productivity only to the harness. We continually learn better and better methods of doing our productive work, but we impute productivity only to the expenses involved in utilizing these methods, – not to the methods themselves.

It is important that the reader should see the truth in the statement that the laborer, the landlord, and the capitalist get paid in proportion to their respective products. It is equally important that he should see clearly that there are definite limitations to the meaning and significance of the statement.

Notes

1 To a very large extent, this "flow of money income" does not take the form of the actual circulation of concrete forms of money. For the most part it takes place through the creation and cancellation of credit obligations.

2 Whether roundabout, indirect methods of production are inherently more efficient (that is, whether they necessarily yield a larger product with the use of a given amount of labor and land) has been recently a matter of debate among economic writers. The fact that a process is roundabout does not in itself make it more economical. But that many roundabout processes are economical is proved by the simple fact that entrepreneurs find it profitable to use them. This fact is all that is needed to establish the importance of the greater technical productivity of indirect, time using methods of production for the theory of interest.

3 The discussion of the social dividend in the preceding page relates only to "normal" or purely competitive production and distribution, and no account has been taken of the "productivity" of monopoly rights.

4 See a note on this point in Merz, John Theodore (1896) *History of European Thought in the Nineteenth Century*, Edinburgh: W. Blackwood, vol. I, p. 92. The list there given could be greatly extended.

7   Socialism

Lecture notes, Washington University, St Louis, April 1912

Best general account: Oscar Douglas Skelton: *Socialism; A Critical Analysis.* [Boston: Houghton Mifflin, 1911] (anti-socialist)

Most brilliant exposition: Werner Sombart: *Socialism [and the Social Movement in the 19th Century.* [Chicago: Charles H. Kerr, 1902] (strong socialistic leanings)

Best *Socialistic* account: Morris Hillquit: *Socialism in Theory and Practice.* [New York: Macmillan, 1909]

John Spargo: Various books.

Utopian socialism

1   Difficulty in saying definitely and precisely just what socialism is. Lack of agreement among scholars and among socialists themselves. [American Economic Association meeting in St. Louis.] [a]

2   Illustration of (two widely differing definitions)

(a) Professor Adolph Wagner of the University of Berlin: "It [Socialism] is a principle which regulates social and economic life according to the needs of society as a whole, or which makes provision for the satisfaction of those needs, whereas, individualism is a principle which, in social and economic life, places the individual in the foreground, takes the individual as a starting-point, and makes his interests and wishes the rule for society."

(b) *Most common definition*: "Socialism means the public [common] ownership of all the means of production." This defended by Professor Carver: "Any one who will take the trouble to read the propagandist literature of socialism will find that nine out of ten, or possibly 99 out of every hundred, books, articles, or speeches, propose nothing short of complete common, or public, or government ownership of all means of production." [b]

3 To compare these two definitions,

(a) "Socialism is a *philosophy*," – a point of view
(b) "Socialism is a *program*."

Is socialism *both* a philosophy and a *program*? *No*, for the philosophy and the program are two different things. Socialism (as a *social philosophy*) is vs. *individualism*. Socialism (as a program) is to be set over against the competitive system.

Those who believe in the *program* of socialism may be, and often are individualists. [Ex. of German Social Democracy]

4 [Taking up here socialism as a philosophy.] – At the present time socialism (as a social philosophy) seems to occupy the dominant position. We hear much of "social welfare," of the "interests of society."

Modern thinking on social and economic problems seems like Nature in Tennyson's phrase:

> "So careful of the type she seems
> So careless of the single life." c

Individualism is identified with selfishness; the social view point with altruism. The very existence of the individual is even denied, except as a unit in Society. Importance of the "social heritage" – language, literature, art, economic technique – civilization in short. Further, the mind of the individual grows by a process of give and take, of imitation, of absorption.

Urged that the individual realizes himself only so far as he *absorbs* this common social heritage; sinks himself in the sea of communal relations and interests.

"Humanity" is now "society," – that and nothing more; and society is an organism, of which the life of the individual is a temporary function. Society, in other words, is the concrete reality, of which the individual is a mere abstraction.

We are therefore prepared to hear from contemporary ethics that "all morality is social"; that goodness is synonymous with altruism; and that reason and duty can now dictate nothing but self-sacrifice for the good of society and of the race. And logic tells the same story. For truth is also social; it turns out now to be nothing but the opinion of the race as against that of the individual. Along the same line history, economics, and sociology treat the individual as an episode in a social and economic movement, a merely passing detail of an essentially social process. Likewise for psychology mental development is social. The individual is the product of society. Through heredity society provides him with a set of "social" instincts to begin with, and then carefully guides the development of these instincts into a "socially-formed" personal character. Child-psychology, so-called, fairly wallows in the social, and condemns the poor child to an exclusively social life. I have somewhere seen a pedagogical treatise in which the child rose in the morning, donned his social vestments, ate a social breakfast, and went about his social occupations, indulging later in the day in some social recreation and some further social reflection, – after which, I should say, it remained only to put on his social night-gown and tuck him into his social bed.

The term "social" has thus become only a piece of academic slang. Yet beneath this indiscriminateness of usage there is implied still an antithesis and contradiction between the social and the individual, to the disadvantage of the individual. As the social has come to stand for positive values the individual has been relegated to the negative.

… And thus it has come about that in ethics "individualism" is, with "egoism," a popular synonym for selfish meanness, – in fact a generic term for moral evil. "Individualism" is the term used to describe the tendencies of the trusts, the stock-jobbers and the corrupt politicians, while the honest citizen, and particularly the unfortunate citizen, is supposed to be "performing a social function."

[Quotation from Warner Fite's *Individualism*, pp. 3–5] [d]

5   This new social philosophy had its excuse. After that blazing up of the passion for individual liberty and individual rights in the latter half of the 18th century – that movement which showed itself most spectacularly in the French Revolution – individualism came to be identified with the assertion of so-called natural rights; and natural rights were identified with "laissez faire"; – "let-alone-policy" of government.

A formal kind of *political* freedom was taken to be all sufficient, forgetting that social control is economic rather than political.

"Negative freedom" (absence of restraint imposed by political superiors) vs. "Positive freedom" – the right and the power of a man to make the most of himself.

It was forgotten that men, however free, may not in fact be equal; that inherited wealth, privilege, unequal opportunities, may impose handicaps. A game played without rules is not apt to [be] a fair game! In order that the rules of the game be *fair* we need positive action; political action, positive law, – and a good deal of it! [for the game is complex, and the rules must be complex.]

In other words: individualism, narrowly and wrongly interpreted, became the bulwark of privilege, the cloak of class selfishness, the rallying cry of reaction, of the opposition to most of the humanitarian movements of the nineteenth century.

6   Conceding all this: Danger in other extreme. Today we talk about "social welfare," not "individual rights." But "social welfare" is a vague term, that might be used by the advocates of almost any policy! In the absence of a clearly defined social ideal, "social welfare" often meaningless. Too often used to apply to any projected reform, wisely and carefully thought out. Too often

a symbol for a mushy sentimentalism in one's attitude toward social problems. Too often "social welfare" means the interest or the supposed interests of the "masses," without reckoning the cost to the so-called "classes" or to the forgotten middle layer of society – most numerous of all.

Confused thinking upon economic problems not a mere matter of phraseology, of course. Immature, half thought out schemes, – plans in which an obvious small good obscures a less obvious great evil, plans in which temporary are set above long-time interests: – These always will be.

7 But, danger in vague abstractions. Just as there have been crimes in the name of "liberty," crimes in the name of "society"! Granting all that is said about the individual's debt to others, granting that an isolated man is not a man but a rather helpless and inferior animal, granting even Hobbes' statement that apart from society the life of man is "solitary, poor, nasty and brutish," it still remains that "society" is in the last analysis only an abstraction, a name for all [of] us, taken together. Admit that "all of us taken together" are not just what "all of us taken separately" would be; admit that the individual is a socialized unit, a communally living and thinking unit, he yet remains a unit. He counts for one.

It is the individual who feels pleasure and suffers pain, who finds life worth living or not worth living. There are no values, no things worth while, except as they affect the individual and his life, or some other individual and his life.

It is probably well that we are ceasing to talk of "natural rights" in the sense of definite, unchangeable rights, fixed by the very nature of things. But it is hard to imagine a state of society which shall have outgrown any interest or concern in the matter of individual rights, interpreted as the old and abiding problem of justice as between man and man.

Hundreds of proposed reforms are discussed today with special reference to their supposed effect upon "social welfare." I know few such problems which could not be discussed with reference to the effect of the proposed reforms upon individual men and women and upon the problem of justice as between individuals. The discussion would not be so easy, so glib, in many cases, as the discussion of "social welfare," but it would be correspondingly more thorough-going, – reaching more directly at the roots of the matter, and there is another side to it:

The current stress on the responsibility of society for individual ills marks a wholesome reaction from the atomistic attitude which threw on the pauper or the criminal the whole responsibility for his shortcoming. Yet, as is the way with reactions, it has already gone to an extreme, and at present we are in danger of losing sight of the *responsibility of the individual* ᵉ by shouldering all the blame on that intangible and ungrieving entity Society, absolving *A* by holding *B* and *C* at fault and *B* by *A*'s and *C*'s neglect.

[Skelton, p. 61]

[Read Wagner again, p. 1 of ms. (above)] So far as Professor Wagner's definition goes I, for one, am willing to call myself an individualist.

8 Rather dangerous for one today to proclaim himself an individualist.[f] "Reactionary." i.e. opposed to progress, or to change of any kind. This springs from the confusion previously mentioned between "individualism" and the belief in "natural rights," – in the "let things alone" policy.
[Explain again the fact that believers in the socialist program may be, and often are, individualists.]

9 Really three things to be kept distinct, which may be illustrated by three "ultimate grounds" of social obligation, which have held currency at different [times].

   1 Crude Individualism. The right of a man to do as he pleases. Logically – anarchism. Formerly held by many; – a minimum amount of governmental restraint being necessary.
   2 "Socialism". The greatest "happiness" of the greatest number. Utilitarian. Connected with "social welfare" – *Indefinite*.
   3 The new individualism. The right of an individual to make the most of himself. [Thomas Hill Green.[g]] Equality of opportunity, – equitable "rules of the game."

10 *Socialism as a Program*. Even here no one thing on which one can put one's finger and call it socialism. *Socialism not one thing but many things*.

Definition again. "Socialism means the public [common] ownership of all means of production." Altho this a common definition, especially common among socialists themselves, yet, as socialism has grown and faced its concrete practical problems more squarely, the proposition has usually been modified.

I should state it in this way (not a "definition" of Socialism except as it describes a common element in most "socialisms"): "Socialism means the communal ownership of the great national instruments of production, – including those forms of property the ownership of which carries with [it] a substantial amount of social power."

Included. Roads, public utilities, factories.

Not included. Things bought for one's personal use. Houses, Books, Pictures, Furniture.

Land(?)

Besides the general program, most kinds of socialism contain two other common elements:

(1) Socialism proposes the *communal control* of the *distribution of income*. Contrast with present condition of free contract [controlled at some points] and free competition. Socialists would not agree as to standard – equality, needs, service – but some standard there must be.
(2) Socialism places less reliance than do the defenders of the existing economic system upon egoism – selfishness – as the main-spring of human action. The

theory of the modern competitive struggle is that the desire to get an income, to amass wealth, to achieve the power that wealth gives will spur men on to their best endeavors as laborers, as business and professional men. Money profits are today the main prize in the race; under socialism more reliance would have to be put upon the love of work for the work's sake, upon the sense of duty, interest in the public service, and altruism in its various forms. That these forces operate today cannot be denied. But would they be sufficient?

[Eds: Mss. pages 12 and 13 are missing here. Page 14 has two headings, "Utopian Socialism" and "Fabian Society." The text continues as follows.]

... acquired advantages of the country be equitably shared by the whole people.

Therefore (1) National ownership of land. And (2) Transfer to the community of the administration of such industrial capital as [can] conveniently be managed socially.

Exceptionally brilliant group including Sidney Webb, Sydney Olivier, Bernard Shaw, William Clarke, Graham Wallas, Hubert Bland, Edward R. Pease [These in the original group – Add such men as H.G. Wells and G. Lowes Dickinson.]

Really scientific principles. Careful methods. "For the attaintment of these ends, the Fabian Society looks to the spread of socialist opinions, and the social and political changes consequent thereon. It seeks to promote these by the general dissemination of knowledge as to the relation between the individual and society in its economic, ethical and political aspects."

The *name* "Fabian" in some ways a misnomer. Not to "wait" idly with folded hands [as a Marxist might] but to achieve socialism gradually.

> "Prophets, now-a-days, do not found a partial community which adopts the whole faith; they cause rather the partial adoption of their faith by the whole community. Incomplete reform is effected in the world of ordinary citizens, instead of complete reform outside of it... In England to-day the comparatively small avowed Socialist army obtains most of its influence by the unconscious permeation of all schools of thought. In all three countries the development of Socialistic institutions is gradual, persistent, and carried out by legislative enactments."
>
> Quote Webb: *Soc. in Eng.* p. 7–8: [h]

> "They [the Fabians] do not believe, like their Hegelian cousins, that a day will ever come when it can be said, there was unsocialism, here will be socialism. It has been their political tactics to endeavor to lead the progressive parties to socialism, to convince the Liberal and the Radical and the Tory Democrat that socialism is the logical successor of their now outworn creeds. They have labored ingeniously to show that an unconscious socialism is already in full swing in Britain, in post-office and public school, in hawkers'

licenses and factory inspection and income taxation, drawing the deduction that the nation may as well be hanged for a sheep as for a lamb, and go consciously to the end of the socialist road. Instead of founding a party, they have preferred to remain a coterie, permeating the existing parties and forcing the pace by insistent pressure from within of a resolute and purposeful minority."

Skelton, p. 289

Extraordinary success. National and municipal activity. Present achievement and *"liberal"* proposals in England equal to most of the *immediate* proposals of the English S.D.F.[a] in '89. [cf Webb, p. 15.]

Movement educational, bureaucratic, middle classed. Based on a thoroly *socialistic "philosophy"*.

Effect on other Socialistic Parties [Many members of which are also members of the Fabian Society.]

[Eds: Here follows a twenty-page survey of utopian socialists, such as St. Simon, Fourier, Owen, Plato, which concludes the section on "Utopian Socialism." The second section on "Scientific Socialism" begins with the biography of Karl Marx (17 pages), drawn largely from John Spargo, and continues with "Economic Interpretation of History" (6 pages), a list of Marx's economic theories (1 page). The second section concludes with the following.]

General Estimation of Marx

The most notable single thing about the mass of dogma that makes up Scientific Socialism is its pretentiousness. The "bourgeois" political economy. It is an attempt, and on the whole an unsuccessful one, to prove by dialectic the inevitableness of socialism. Yet its significance does not stop there. Marx was by nature a revolutionist, and passionately so. Of the honesty and sincerity of his purpose there can be no question.

To the one who reads *Das Capital* with attention to more than the intricacies of the dialectical argument, the work makes an impression of tremendous power. Despite its avowedly scientific purpose, the reader finds that the book is a passionate outcry against injustices (real and imagined) in the present social order. It is an attempt to make them stand forth so clearly that once impressed upon the consciousness of the workers they will... The appeal of the theory of surplus value, of the exploitation of one class by another is emotional rather than intellectual. It is as though Marx were applying the goad relentlessly to the unawakened proletariat, as tho he were attempting to fill it with an overpowering sense of injustice done them, and then preaching, in the words of the Communist Manifesto, "Workingmen of the World, Unite."

I am inclined to agree with John Spargo (the latest biographer of Marx) that Marx, despite his obvious pride of authorship, would have been ready to throw overboard his own theories if he were convinced that they stood in the way of the socialist movement.

[Example of his attitude toward Russian revolution without passing through the throes of capitalism. Based on Russian commune.]

Nor did he agree with those who opposed "social reform".

Marx a Fabian, with a set of dogmas and an ultimate program.

Marx's influence has made many socialists, but have they been of the [...] socialist type – [...] intellectuals, content to wait with folded hands for the social revolution. The true Marxians are [...] the militant socialists.

[Eds: The third section on "Militant Socialism" concerns the history of the socialist movement in Germany (18 pages), France (7), England (1) and the US (1). Also Syndicalism (1) and International Congresses (2). The third section concludes with the following, which also concludes the course.]

Conclusions

However important socialism as a dogma, as a prophecy of an ideal of a future state, or as an assertion of an inevitable social revolution may be, it will be easily concluded, I think, that socialism as a movement is for us today a thing of much greater present weight. We may close our ears, if we wish, to socialistic preaching; we cannot close our eyes to what is going on all around us. There are those undoubtedly who see in this rising tide of socialism a danger which they think will eventually engulf the state and destroy social order unless prompt and energetic measures be taken against it. There are others, undoubtedly, who seek to explain away the facts of the growth of socialism; – who will see it only [as] the expression [of] a more or less temporary dissatisfaction with the promises, and, still more, with the achievements of the older political parties; or who see in it not much more than a protest against certain admitted wrongs of our present system, against the grosser forms of economic injustice and political corruption. Still others see in socialism only the greedy efforts of the members of one social class, conscious of their numerical power, to get all they can for themselves, regardless of any considerations of social justice and of the ultimate, permanent, welfare of society.

Such men, I think, see only *parts* of the socialist movement, and close their eyes to its *larger unity*. That many men have voted the socialist ticket who are not themselves socialists cannot be denied; in many American cities, as in Germany, a vote for the socialist ticket has often been the only way of lodging an effective protest against things as they are. Certain elements of the socialist movement, *syndicalism* more especially, seem to [be] based on little more than class greed; – on the envious spleen of those who have not against those who have.

These things, however, are but parts. A movement so vast and so spontaneous as what I have called militant socialism must be traced back to some more general and fundamental cause than those I have yet mentioned. The socialist movement, in its most general aspects, seems to me to be nothing more or less than the natural and inevitable continuation of that great movement of the eighteenth and nineteenth centuries toward *democracy*. Individual rights are now, as they were a hundred years ago, the fundamental things in the situation. Talk as much as we will of "social progress," of "social welfare," of the superiority of the claims of society over those of the individual; it yet remains that the driving power of the social movement today comes from individuals who imagine, or who know, or who are being taught that they, in common, perhaps, with millions of others have *rights* that are implicit in the very notion of democracy, but rights which, for one reason or another cannot be realized under existing social arrangements.

Just as is the case of the individual, every step forward in the attainment of desires, in the satisfaction of wants, opens up vast fields of new and previously unfelt wants, so every step in the realization of that great abstraction, democracy, has brought into the field of vision a continually enlarging view of its yet unrealized possibilities.

Political democracy, the right of each to count for *one* in the determination of government policies has as yet been only imperfectly achieved. But even if machine politics, and the undue power of certain kinds of special interests, and other remaining obstacles to the complete expression of the will of democracy were swept away; even, further, if we had learned, as we have not yet fully learned, that a real democracy must be an efficient democracy, that the mere expression of popular will means nothing unless there be the means of converting that will into action; – that the democracy, having decided broadly on the things it wants done, must entrust the doing of these things to a *centralized, expert*, even *bureaucratic* **administration**; even having achieved all these things, it would yet be felt, that we had only the form and not the substance of democracy, only the frame and not the concrete content.

In short the emphasis is already shifting from political democracy to industrial democracy. We have come to see that one man's control over another is more often *industrial* than *political*. Private property means more than the individual well-being of its possessor, it gives to him a certain amount of *social power*, varying not only with the amount of the property, but also with its nature. There is this much truth to the socialist contention: a bargain between a propertied man and the propertyless, even tho in legal theory a free contract on both sides, is not, in fact, a bargain between equals. The advantage is all on one side. Now, economic relations today are very largely the result of contract and there can be no such thing as equality of opportunity unless the conditions of contract, – the rules of the game, are so adjusted that every handicap is removed. Said Anton Menger, a distinguished Austrian jurist, "there is no greater inequality than the equal treatment of unequals."

Now the socialistic diagnosis, seizing the simple and obvious surface fact, comes to the conclusion that private property itself is the root of the evil, and so the socialist proposes to *abolish* private property in the great material instruments of production. But aside from such personal forms of property as might be left to private ownership, as at present, the installation of the common ownership of property would bring with it the problem of the proper adjustment of individual rights in the income of this communally owned property. In reality, the problem would be that of the recognition and the measurement of individual equities, – individual property rights, virtually, in the communal possessions. What, after all, is the profound socialist guarantee of the right of every man to "the full product of his labor" but an assertion, a guarantee of one kind of property right?

And if socialism should ever go so far as to have to face the concrete question of measuring and allotting to each man the full product of his labor, it would find I think, that a workable and permanent system of distribution would not differ so very widely from that which the present system of private property, pruned of its grosser forms of injustice, would tend to bring about.

As for the proposed abolition of the "rent of land" and of the "interest on capital," that, I am confident, is *inherently impossible*. There will always be land rent so long as the use of better lands gives an economic advantage over the use of poorer land; – there will always be interest on capital so long as the present use of money is worth more than its future use, so long as a dollar today is valued more highly than a dollar ten years from today. Yes, the advanced (revisionist) Socialist will say, but when land and capital are owned by the community, the *private receipt* of rent and interest will have been abolished! But communal receipt of rent and interest involves the ultimate distribution of these forms of income among individuals. Aside from the amount needed to pay the expenses of government and for communal expenditures (even tho these be greatly increased under the Socialist regime) what will be done with the tremendous fund arising from the real earnings of land and capital? It may be *added* to the real wages of labor, but it can never be a part of the real wages of labor. How shall the ultimate *private* property rights (for such they would be) in rent and interest be adjusted?

I shall not attempt to answer this question, but leave it to the socialists.

Moreover, I believe it is a question they will never have to face. Socialism, after all, is an abstraction, as democracy is. The socialist movement everywhere, as we have seen, when facing concrete questions of policy and tactics has tended to become opportunist. At one time it said that such things as factory laws, 8 hour laws, compulsory education laws, minimum wage laws, universal franchise laws, taxation reforms, the public control of monopolies, were bourgeois, middle class reforms, which at best were palliatives, making the rough road of social progress a bit smoother, and which, at worst, might act as sedatives, – might delay the finally inevitable coming of socialism. Now socialism is coming to say: "this is a part of socialism; that is a part of socialism, let us get what we can." The victory seems to be with Lassalle, with Jaurès, with the Fabians, rather than with Karl Marx. Unless all the signs fail, socialism will not come in the form of the abolition of private property. This, as we have seen would involve (1) a taking away, and (2) a regranting, of private property rights. Socialism will realize itself in the recognition of the fact that private property is not a simple thing, but a complex thing; not a single right, but a bundle of rights. For some forms of property we may expect a larger measure of social control (which the most avowed believer in laissez faire, in economic individualism, might logically wish. Example of the […] – "Rules of the game."

For some kinds of property there may be an extension of national or municipal ownership; but for all kinds of property there will be a larger limitation of a man's supposed right to "do what he will with his own." Doctrinaire socialism proposes the communal ownership of property and the re-establishment of individua.lrights or equities in this communally owned property. The actual socialism which seems to be already at work among us looks rather to the retention of private property as the fundamental economic institution, and to the creation of *communal* rights or equities in this individually owned property, – and this is an ideal which the *true* individualist, intent upon the equalization of opportunity, might well claim as his own. Upon all the details of the practical program there can be as yet no general agreement. In the Erfurt Program, for example, there are many things about the desirability of which there is probably little question. Mingled with them are undoubtedly a number of quack nostrums, remedies which might alleviate present distress at the price of future disaster. My task is not the discussion of particular measures of social reform. But it is fairly certain that socialism will realize itself, not in a revolution, but along the lines of specific social reforms. So far as these reforms represent the unfolding of democracy; so far as they strike only at discriminating privileges, and strive merely to remove the handicaps which make the present economic struggle an unfair one, – to that extent they will undoubtedly be given a growing measure of support.

The real supporters of the violent revolutionary socialism, as embodied in that dangerous movement called Syndicalism, are the reactionaries, the stand-patters, who consistently refuse to get out of the way of the movement toward democracy. Our fundamental institutions are too deeply rooted; too carefully selected in the long process of social evolution, to give way under the pressure of the moment, unless the forces making for change have been dammed up and held back by an obstinate and unreasoning reaction. Socialism at work, socialism as the unfolding of democracy is socialism with its teeth drawn. Or, better, perhaps, socialism as a doctrine, as a creed, is an abstraction. Give to this abstraction a concrete content, and it ceases to be Socialism!

Editors' notes

a Refers to a session organized to discuss the paper of Martin, John (1911) "An Attempt to Define Socialism." *American Economic Review* 1 No. 2 (June): 347–354.

b Carver, Thomas Nixon (1911) "Discussion of Martin," *American Economic Review* 1 No. 2 (June): 362.

c Tennyson, Alfred, Lord, *In Memoriam*. Part LV Stanza 2.

d Fite, Warner (1911) *Individualism; Four Lectures on the Significance of Consciousness for Social Relations.* New York: Longmans, Green.

e Young's emphasis.

f This sentence replaced one scored out by Young: "But one may be an individualist without being, in general, a reactionary."

g Cf. Green, Thomas Hill (1895) *Lectures on the Principles of Political Obligation.* New York: Longmans, Green.

h Webb, Sidney (1893) *Socialism in England,* 2nd edn. Reprinted by Gower Publishing Co., Brookfield, Vermont, 1987.

i Social Democratic Federation, a Marxian group led by H.M. Hyndman.

8 Pigou's wealth and welfare

Quarterly Journal of Economics (1913) 27, 4 (August): 672–86

Six years ago, in a review of the fifth edition of Marshall's *Principles of Economics*,[1] Professor Pigou said: "The conception of the National Dividend is not an academic toy, but a practical instrument of great power designed for service in the concrete solution of social problems." This statement accurately defines the purpose, scope, and method of Professor Pigou's new book.[2] Its spirit, like that of Marshall's great treatise, is one of sane conservatism, tempered by an attitude of open-minded receptivity toward such new proposals as seem to stand the test of careful analysis. Yet the boldness of Professor Pigou's theoretical analysis and the fact that the practical problems he discusses are suggested, for the most part, by very recent proposals for social reform give to his book a distinctly fresh and unconventional flavor.

The book will find an audience more limited, I fear, than it deserves on its merits. No one not thoroly familiar with the concepts and technical apparatus of Marshall's *Principles* will be able to read it intelligently. Moreover, altho Professor Pigou writes in a simple and straightforward fashion, he possesses neither an especially attractive style nor any marked skill in exposition. The argument is well ordered, but the whole discussion is closely knit and the subject matter full of inherent difficulties.[3] Mathematical formulae are used sparingly (tho skilfully) and are relegated to the footnotes.

In the formal discussion of his premises the author posits a sophisticated sort of utilitarianism, in which welfare is held "to include states of consciousness only," and *economic* welfare appears as the "psychic return of satisfaction." Grounds of dissent from both the psychological and the ethical implications of these theses suggest themselves, but are not worth stating: first, because Professor Pigou hedges his doctrines about with so many safeguards that the really vulnerable points are, at most, few; and, secondly, because these debatable points play but a small rôle in the general argument and conclusions of the book. In fact, save for a carefully guarded statement of the familiar doctrine that a transference of shares in the dividend from the rich to the poor will, *ceteris paribus*, increase the sum total of satisfactions, he deals only incidentally with the subjective aspects of wealth. The difficult questions connected with the meaning, variations, and practical significance of consumers' and producers' surpluses are for the most part disregarded, altho these are questions which Professor Pigou has shown himself peculiarly competent to discuss.

The chief task which Professor Pigou sets himself is the discussion of the effects of different forces upon the magnitude and stability of the *national dividend*, – which is conceived (after Marshall) as identical with the net annual product of such commodities and services as are measurable in terms of money value.[4] Even with so concrete a concept Professor Pigou cannot entirely escape the old familiar dilemma that confronts the utilitarian when "greatest good" and "greatest number" seem to point in opposite directions. For example, after showing clearly that an increase in the supply of the factors of production, other than labor, is likely to increase both the national dividend and the aggregate real earnings of labor, he examines the effect of an increase in the supply of labor itself and concludes[5] that, since the elasticity of the demand for labor is high, and since an increase in the population (of England) would affect the price of imported food supplies but slightly, "the diminution of real wages per head would be very small;" and that, consequently, "it seems reasonable to conclude that an increase in the absolute share of labor, even when it results from an increase in the number of the population, carries with it an increase in the economic welfare of working people." Surely this is enough to show the need of a more clear cut conception of what "economic welfare" really is.

In general Professor Pigou's treatment of the population problem is the most unsatisfactory feature of his work. It seems less thoro and candid than the other parts of his analysis. There is, it is true, an admirable chapter on "The National Dividend and the Quality of the People," dealing with the claim of some of the apostles of Eugenics that economic inquiries, concerned as they are in the main with environment rather than heredity, are relatively unimportant. I know of nothing on this topic more incisive than this chapter, with its summary statement: "Environments, as well as people, have children." But the fundamental questions relating to the *quantity* of the laboring population Professor Pigou, it may fairly be said, neglects or evades. The economic tendencies with which he deals are "long-time" tendencies, but nevertheless distinctly limited either in duration or scope. He postulates (implicitly) mobility of capital, of employing power, and of "uncertainty bearing" (save where monopoly prevents), and takes account of such movement of labor as its degree of mobility permits from industry to industry, from locality to locality, and even, in some slight degree (fitting English condition), from one country to another. But the effect of large population movements either in place or in time, such as are shown in American and Australian immigration or were postulated as the basis of the Ricardian theories relative to "long-time" tendencies are comparatively neglected. It is doubtless true that, as Professor Pigou argues,[6] an increase in the dividend not itself caused by an increase in the supply of labor, will not be *entirely* absorbed by an increase of population.[7] But, in relation to some of the economic proposals discussed in the book, such as the establishment of a national minimum (conceived as a minimum standard of living conditions) the population question remains of fundamental importance.

The general run of the introductory part of Professor Pigou's carefully articulated argument is to the effect (1) that whatever increases "economic welfare" will in general increase "total welfare," (2) that whatever increases the magnitude of the national dividend, or decreases its variability, or increases the absolute share of the relatively poor, is likely to augment economic welfare. Despite his attempt to confine his own analysis to "economic welfare," which, it will be remembered, is defined in terms of subjective "satisfactions," Professor Pigou, like every other sensible person who has dealt with the subject, is forced to take some account of the obvious fact that some of the "satisfactions" people want are injurious to themselves or to others.[8] His device for maintaining logical consistency is that adopted by Dr. Marshall and others: some expenditures diminish the sum total of satisfactions by adversely affecting the physical health and vigor of the people and thereby diminishing the future national dividend. Similarly, public expenditures for education, sanitation, and the like, are justified as tending to increase the national dividend and (indirectly) the sum total of satisfactions. All this is along familiar lines, and I would not mention it here, if it were not that, in my opinion, complete logical consistency demands either a thoro and consistent recognition of the varied relations of present "satisfaction" of *all kinds* to efficiency in future production, or, better, an abandonment of the "satisfactions" conception of economic welfare. But Professor Pigou, as I have already said, deals mainly with a national dividend of concrete goods and services, and no one, whatever his philosophy of economic welfare, can question the fundamental importance of such a study.

Professor Pigou discusses two general classes of concrete problems: first, the conditions of business organization and control under which the dividend is a maximum; second, the way in which the dividend and, consequently, real incomes are affected by attempts to improve its distribution.

In the first of these two general studies Professor Pigou introduces a new and powerful instrument of economic analysis, the *curve of marginal supply prices*,[9] which might with equal accuracy and greater simplicity be called the curve of aggregate expenses. His own account of this curve is, I think, so abstract and general as to suggest imaginary difficulties to the reader. I shall venture, therefore, to describe what I take to be the principles involved in somewhat simpler terms.

The facts to be observed are those connected with the increase of the *aggregate expenses* of an industry as a whole. These must be distinguished from the general fact of the diminishing productivity of the particular factors of production and also from the tendency to diminishing (or constant, or increasing) returns per unit of expense as the size of the individual business unit increases. Furthermore, we do not have in mind precisely the same thing as when we speak of diminishing (or constant, or increasing) returns in a given industry as a whole during a period of time; altho the basic facts involved in both conceptions are in part identical.

Take, for example, an industry of diminishing returns, say wheat growing. By "diminishing returns" we mean of course, to imply that if an aggregate annual product of x units of wheat is increased to an annual product of $x + \Delta x$ units, more capital and labor per unit of product must be "applied to the land" to produce the Δx units than be were required to produce the final increments of the original x units.

Now the fact of present importance is that, through the rise of land rent (and possibly, also, through an increased expense per unit of labor and capital, caused by the increased demand) the *aggregate expenses*, including land rent, of producing $x + \Delta x$ units will exceed the expenses of producing x units by much more than the expenses specifically attributable to the production of the Δx units. The curve of aggregate expenses, or of "marginal supply prices," as Professor Pigou prefers to call it, is so constructed that as successive increments of product are measured, on the horizontal axis, the successive ordinates represent the amounts by which aggregate expenses are increased. Thus, in the accompanying diagram (Figure 8.1), the area inclosed by the curve (SS_2), the two axes, and the ordinate at any point M represents the aggregate expense of producing OM units of product. For industries of diminishing returns the curve has a positive slope, which is greater than the slope of Dr. Marshall's "particular expenses" curve or that of the ordinary long period competitive supply curve as used to represent conditions of diminishing returns.

In similar fashion the curve of aggregate expenses may be used to describe conditions of increasing returns. In this case the aggregate annual expense of producing $x + \Delta x$ units exceeds the aggregate annual expense of producing x units by *less* than the amount of expense that can be specifically attributed to the production of the additional Δx units. I imagine, however, that cases of increasing returns in this sense (*i.e.*, diminishing aggregate expenses per unit of product as production increases) must be rare, if not altogether lacking, in competitive industry, unless an increase in the size of the representative establishment be taken into account as a natural concomitant of increased production in the industry

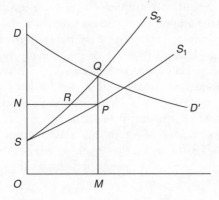

Figure 8.1

in question.[10] For monopoly, where one undertaking is identical with the "industry at large," the curve of diminishing aggregate expenses has real significance.

Contrasted with the curve of aggregate expenses is the ordinary long period supply curve, *i.e.*, the curve for which the ordinate at any point M represents the price which, in the long run, tends to maintain an annual output OM. Since, under competition, the receipts in a given industry tend to equal the total expenses (including the rent of land and payment for any other differential advantages), and since, furthermore, each unit of a given product must be supposed to be sold at the same price as any other unit, it follows that the total receipts for OM units (represented by the rectangle OMPN where SS_1 is the supply curve) must equal the amount of expenses represented by the area OMQS.[11] That is, the area PRQ is equal to the area SRN. "It follows that, when SS_1 is a horizontal line, SS_1 and SS_2 coincide: when SS_1 is inclined positively, SS_1 lies below SS_2: when SS_1 is inclined negatively, SS_1 lies above SS_2. Furthermore, the rapidity with which SS_1 and SS_2 diverge from one another, as they move towards the right, is greater, the sharper is the inclination of SS_1 in either a positive or a negative direction."[12]

We are now equipped to examine the use to which Professor Pigou puts this new construction. Here we may advisably follow his own exposition:[13]

> Under simple competition – where the output of each supplier is so small that he accepts, and does not attempt to modify, the price of the market – the exchange index necessarily stands at the point of intersection of the demand curve with the supply curve, and the output is such as to correspond with this position of the index. Hence, the actual output tends to be equal to the ideal output when the supply curve and the curve of marginal supply prices coincide, and it tends to diverge from the ideal output when these curves diverge from one another. This implies that the measure in which the actual and the ideal output of any industry approximate to one another is determined by the measure in which the supply curve and the curve of marginal supply prices approximate towards one another.
>
> ... The general result is that, in industries of constant returns, the supply price and the marginal supply price of all quantities of output are equal; in industries of increasing returns the supply price is greater than the marginal supply price; in industries of diminishing returns the supply price is less than the marginal supply price. This result is, of course, equally valid, whether the supply price and marginal supply price in question refer to an operation yielding a single product or to one yielding several products jointly. It follows that, other things being equal, in industries of increasing returns the marginal net product of investment tends to exceed, and in industries of diminishing returns to fall short of, the marginal net product yielded in industries in general. Furthermore, the "error" in either case is greater, the more sharply diminishing or increasing returns, as the case may be, are acting.

This means, of course, that in competitive industries of diminishing returns investment tends to be pushed too far, and in competitive industries of increasing returns, not far enough, to secure that equality of marginal net products which makes the national dividend a maximum. These conclusions lead naturally to the suggestion that the equality of marginal net products might be increased by appropriate taxes upon industries of diminishing returns, coupled with appropriate bounties upon industries of increasing returns.

When Professor Pigou passes to the consideration of monopoly he reaches results which are quite as interesting and important. The simplest case is that of a monopoly which has complete power in the matter of price discrimination, *i.e.*, power to charge a different price for each successive unit of output, so as to leave no consumers' surplus. Referring again to the diagram, it is clear that the increase of total receipts accompanying increasing output will be represented[14] by the increasing total area included between the curve DD' and the axis as the ordinate at M is moved toward the right, while the increasing total expenses of production will be represented by the area between the curve SS$_2$ and the axis. It is evident that the point of maximum profits will be fixed by the intersection of DD' and SS$_2$; so that the marginal net product is equal to "the marginal net product of resources invested in industries in general." "In cases of constant returns the result is exactly the same as that attained under simple competition, but in cases of diminishing and of increasing returns, that is to say, in the generality of cases, it is both different and socially more advantageous."[15]

In fact, of course, no monopoly possesses this complete power of discrimination. Very frequently a monopoly must sell its product at a uniform price; in other cases it may be able roughly to classify its customers or its products or services into a number of grades, charging a separate price to each group of buyers. It might naturally be inferred that such monopolies, altho falling short of the standard of perfection set by the hypothetical monopoly with ideal powers of discrimination, would, nevertheless, be apt to set their marginal investments somewhat nearer the socially desirable point of equal net products than would competitive concerns in industries of diminishing or increasing returns. But Professor Pigou shows, in a careful analysis,[16] too lengthy to be summarized here, that such will not, in general, be the case.[17] Thus competition is again awarded the primacy, altho it emerges with a less perfect score than in former reckonings.

I now pass to the discussion of the validity of some of the conclusions just outlined, but I do so with some hesitancy, especially in view of the fact that in regard to certain results which I find difficulty in accepting, Professor Pigou's own weighty authority is reinforced by the no less weighty approval of Professor Edgeworth.[18] I do not, of course, deny the significance of the "curve of marginal supply prices." Professor Pigou's own work shows it to be a powerful aid in the analysis of the tendencies of monopoly. It might also be used advantageously, I imagine, in the discussion of certain problems relating to the *distribution* of the national dividend, but I fail to see that its use is appropriate in the analysis of the extent to which competition tends to secure the maximum national dividend.

A possible difficulty (altho a minor one) is attached to the meaning of the "marginal net product in industries in general," which Professor Pigou postulates as the standard to which the marginal product of particular industries should conform. If it is true that only the relatively unimportant industries of constant returns tend to meet this standard, while industries of increasing returns tend to exceed, and of diminishing returns to fall short of it, what *is* the marginal net product of industry in general? It might possibly be conceived as a general average of actual net products, were it not that industries of diminishing returns (in the sense of increasing aggregate expenses per unit of product in the industry at large) are probably much more important than those of increasing returns, and the extent of deviation from constant returns larger in the case of diminishing returns than of increasing returns. I do not stress this objection, however, for the existence of an ideal standard is easily possible, even if the marginal products of actual industries do not in general tend to approach it.

A more serious difficulty appears when we inquire as to the precise content of the "resources" which are devoted to the work of production. Is equality of marginal aggregate expenses the equality which we have in mind when we say that the maximum product will be achieved when marginal net products are equal? Does Professor Pigou mean by the term "resources" the services of labor and capital which are used up in production or does he refer to the money expenses of entrepreneurs? Examination shows that his use of the term is not altogether consistent. In his general discussion of production and distribution[19] he states that the factors of production consist of the services actually used in production.[20] Nor is there any indication that in the following chapter, in which is developed the proposition that "the more nearly equal marginal products in all uses are, the larger the dividend is likely to be,"[21] there is any change in the meaning attached to "resources." But in the description of the curve of marginal supply prices,[22] altho Professor Pigou continues to speak of the "investment of resources," and the "net product of resources" it is clear that he has in mind merely the aggregate money expenses of entrepreneurs.

For illustration, take again the example of industries of diminishing returns. The significance of the curve of marginal supply prices consists, it will be remembered, in the fact that the expense of producing $x + \Delta x$ units exceeds the expense of producing x units by more than the amount of expenses specifically incurred in producing the additional Δx units. This excess cost is due to the fact that increased production is only possible at an increased price per unit for the product, which makes possible and necessary an increased annual price for the land (and, under some conditions, for other resources) used in production. This is not a case, it is important to note, in which the money measure of a given quantum of resources can, in order to simplify the analysis, be supposed a constant. Changes in the prices of product and of resources are the very essence of the situation. Increased prices for the use of land and the other factors in production do not represent an increased *using up* of resources in the work of production. They merely represent *transferences* of purchasing power. The resulting changes in distribution may, of course, indirectly affect production, but Professor Pigou's discussion of the curve of marginal supply prices is not concerned with these indirect effects.

To have achieved consistency Professor Pigou should have adhered consistently either (1) to the viewpoint of entrepreneurs' costs, and have measured *product* as well as resources in terms of price, or (2) to a more distinctly social point of view and have measured *costs* as well as product, in terms of physical units.[23] In either case, I think, he would have reached a result more in harmony with the traditional theory relative to competition and the maximum product. The second of these two points of view may seem to be the more significant, but it is impossible to adhere to it without encountering great difficulties in the analysis.

When, for example, one takes account, as Professor Pigou does, of the general fact of diminishing returns in an industry at large, one explicitly or implicitly postulates changes in the price of the product, and as soon as one does this it becomes impossible any longer to view the national dividend in a purely (physically) quantitative aspect. For (neglecting consumers' surplus) we have to admit that (on Professor Pigou's premises) a dollar's worth of one commodity is as important to society as a dollar's worth of another. Concretely: *when measuring the effect of diminishing returns* in agriculture upon the national dividend, we cannot assume that a bushel of wheat at 60 cents is as large a part of the dividend as a bushel of wheat at one dollar.

On somewhat different grounds, it can be shown that it is difficult entirely to avoid the use of a money measure for the "resources" devoted to the work of production. The maximum product will be attained, it is true, when the values of the net marginal products of equal *quantities* of *comparable sorts* of labor, waiting and other forms of productive energy are equal. But there is no way in which the proper apportioning of the different *kinds* of resources which contribute to production can be discussed, except in terms of a money measure.[24] The problem as a whole, it seems to me, is one to which the general theory of the diminishing productivity of individual factors in production is appropriate, rather than the curve of marginal supply prices.

Wholly admirable, however, is Professor Pigou's discussion of the various sorts of economic friction that tend to prevent the perfect equality of marginal net products.[25] But it is when he passes to such practical problems as those connected with purchasers' associations, state intervention, public control of monopoly, and public operation of industries[26] that his rare judicial faculty of taking fairly into account the varied considerations that weigh for and against a given proposal is seen at its best. I have no space here even to summarize these admirable chapters, with their discriminating conclusions. Professor Pigou here, as elsewhere, has primarily in mind British national problems. I am inclined to think that a more intimate acquaintance with the recent work of American public utility commissions would have made Professor Pigou's conclusions as to the range and variety of the considerations that can be taken into account in the public regulation of monopoly prices and services somewhat more favorable.

In his discussion of the distribution of the national dividend[27] Professor Pigou deals almost exclusively with labor problems, and especially with "attempts to improve the distribution of the dividend by the deliberate transference of resources from the relatively rich to the relatively poor, first through interference with the natural course of wages and secondly through taxation, and so forth." In this field Professor Pigou is thoroly at home, and shows familiarity with an unusual range of modern economic literature. The problems he discusses are those suggested by recent labor union policies and by recent achievements and proposals in the field of social legislation, particularly in England. These chapters constitute what is beyond question the best discussion to be found anywhere of the economic principles involved in this new social program. The lack of an adequate treatment of the population problem is the only serious blemish on this admirable discussion.

Professor Pigou has in a rare degree the power of forcing his way through to some positive conclusion in cases where at first no conclusion seems possible. That many of his results are stated merely as probabilities is a testimonial as much to the courage with which the analysis is pushed through to the end as it is to the caution with which inferences are made. Nowhere do the advantages of the particular type of economic theory in which Professor Pigou is an adept appear more clearly. Theory of this sort (if I may characterize it briefly) is not concerned with the vain attempt to formulate concepts so general and abstract that the whole economic process may be viewed as a relatively simple mechanical system. The purpose is, rather, that the fabric of theory shall be a yielding garment, fitting the varied and complex reality of economic life as closely as is demanded by the criterion that the conclusions to which the theory leads shall be both useful and general.

The book is not without indications that it was put through in some haste. Typographical errors and small slips of one sort and another are more common than one expects in a book of dignity and importance. The most serious lapse of this kind which I have noticed is the loosely demonstrated statement[28] that Pareto's measure of inequality in the distribution of incomes gives results that are in general agreement with those indicated by the standard deviation. Applied to actual income statistics these measures are rather more apt than not to give precisely opposite results.[29]

Notes

1 Economic Journal, Dec., 1907, vol. xvii, p. 532.
2 Wealth and Welfare, by A. C. Pigou, M.A. London: Macmillan and Company, 1912 pp. xxxi, 493.
3 Professor Pigou rightly observes (p. 487): "It is a popular delusion, that, while economic science itself is a difficult subject, the discussion of practical problems, in which economic forces play an important part, can safely be undertaken without special preparation. There is no warrant for this view. The study of economic theory is, indeed, difficult; but the application of the knowledge, which that study wins, to the guidance of practical affairs, is an even heavier task; for it needs, not only a full understanding of the theory, but also the

trained judgment that can balance against one another a large number of qualifying considerations. This would be the case, even if human life were such that economic welfare and welfare in general were coincident terms."

4 Professor Fisher's concept of a dividend consisting only of such services of goods (and persons) as enter directly into consumption within the year is appreciatively discussed, but dismissed as unmanageable for the purpose in hand. In the opinion of the reviewer, when questions relating to the magnitude and effects of *savings* are involved, much is to be gained by distinguishing the "annual dividend" (conceived as the valuable goods and services coming into the possession of ultimate consumers within the year) from the "annual product," which includes (in addition to direct personal services) the results of all that is done within the year in forwarding goods, directly and indirectly, toward completion.

5 P. 94.

6 Pp. 28–32.

7 Professor Pigou possibly gives too much weight to Brentano's conclusions relative to the effect of the increased prosperity of any social class in diminishing the birth-rate. This matter has been carefully surveyed by K. Oldenberg in the Archiv für Sozialwissenschaft und Sozialpolitik, vol. xxxii, pp. 319–77; xxxiii, 401–99. See also the controversy between Oldenberg and Mombert in the same journal, vol. xxxiv, pp. 794–7. After all, however, the problem centers around the net increase of the population rather than the birth-rate. On this point the general experience of the last century (in England, as well as elsewhere) has been so explicit that Professor Pigou's failure to deal seriously with the problem is hard to defend. Cf. Ely, Outlines of Economics, rev. ed., pp. 373–6.

8 See, for example, pp. 163, 165.

9 Also described in Professor Pigou's article on "Producers' and Consumers' Surplus," Economic Journal, vol. xx, pp. 358–70.

10 The economies of large scale production affect industry at large (if competitive) only by reducing the expense per unit in individual establishments. It is scarcely logical to treat these economies in the same general manner as the increasing expense of agricultural production, which arises from causes external to the individual undertaking. Professor Pigou says (p. 177): "Provided that certain external economies are common to all the suppliers jointly, the presence of increasing returns in respect of all together is compatible with the presence of diminishing returns in respect of the special work of each severally." I cannot imagine "external economies" adequate to bring about this result.

11 In general, $\int_0^x f_2(x)dx = x.f_1(x)$.

12 P. 175

13 Pp. 174, 176, 177.

14 Subject to some qualifications which do not affect the result.

15 P. 206.

16 Pt. II, chs. xi, xii.

17 Professor Pigou makes an important application of this conclusion in his discussion of railway rates (in Pt. II, ch. xiii). The important aspects of his treatment of this question have been ably reviewed by Professor Taussig in the Quarterly Journal of Economics, May, 1913, and by Professor Edgeworth in the Economic Journal, June, 1913, and will not be discussed here. With reference to the controversy between Professor Pigou and Professor Taussig, I may say, however, that I see no inconsistency in granting both Professor Taussig's contention that railway costs are largely joint costs and Professor Pigou's contention that railway rates form a special case of discriminating monopoly price. [See also Professor Pigou's note in the present issue of this Journal. – *Editor.*]

18 Loc. Cit.

19 Pt. II, ch. ii.

20 "For our purpose it is convenient to divide the factors of production, from whose joint operation the national dividend results, into two broad groups, labor and the factors other than labor, or, as we may say for brevity, non-labor.... Labor embraces the work both of

unskilled casual workpeople and of numerous sorts of skilled artisans. Non-labor embraces, along with the work of Nature, the work of many kinds of mental ability, the service of waiting and the service of uncertainty-bearing" (p.79).

21 P. 108.

22 Pt. II, ch. viii.

23 Thus Professor Pigou might well have adhered, in the case of "waiting," to his own formal statement (p.79, note): "The unit of waiting is the use of a given quantity of resources for a given time."

24 Unless we assume that the marginal units of the various sorts of productive energy represent equivalent amounts of ultimate cost or sacrifice, – an assumption which does not seem to me to be of significance for the analysis of actually existing conditions.

25 Pt. II, chs. iv–vii.

26 Pt. II, chs. xiv–xvii.

27 Pt. III.

28 P. 125.

29 The more evenly income receivers are distributed throughout the income scale the lower will be Pareto's index, and the more closely they are concentrated about the average income the lower will be the standard deviation. Whether these two measures will agree in indicating that the distribution of wealth has moved in a particular direction will depend largely upon the difference between the modal income and the average income, together with the extent of the change. Tests applied to a number of typical cases indicate that disagreement is more probable than agreement.

9 Public borrowing for road building

Cornell Civil Engineer (1915) 23, Nos 6–7 (March/April): 301–15

This topic has nothing to do with the practical problems of construction and administration, nor does it have more than an indirect bearing upon the general merits of the movement for good roads. We all know how inefficient and unprogressive this country has been in the development of a decent system of highways and country roads; we all know how slow we have been to so arrange things that the expert task of planning the construction of these roads and the no less important task of supervising their maintenance after they are constructed could really be entrusted to experts. And we all rejoice in the splendid progress that has been made in the last twenty years, and in the nation-wide interest that has been aroused in this great public problem.

We all want good roads, but good roads are expensive. And they are particularly expensive in America, where distances are long, and labor costs high. That we are so far behind most regions of western Europe in the matter of road building seems to me largely attributable to two obstacles we have had to contend with: (1) our absurd, though long-continuing reliance upon local initiative and local supervision, and (2) the extraordinarily high *per capita* cost of modern road construction in this country, arising, as I have suggested, from the high wages that have to be paid, from the distances that separate our cities and towns and from our thinly-scattered farming population. The first obstacle – local inertia – we have squarely attacked – and with a large measure of success – by putting large powers of supervision into the hands of state boards. The second obstacle – expense – still remains, and in the nature of the case it is bound to remain. What I have to say will have to do with this aspect of road-building – with financial ways and means.

Public borrowing for road-building is not a new thing in this country. In the first half of the nineteenth century it played a part in one of the most discreditable episodes in the history of the finances of American states. The story is a familiar one, but I shall venture to recall some of its general outlines, because it has its lessons for us today.

Soon after the Revolution we began to build roads, and from the accounts of travelers of the time we must have needed good roads as badly then as a country ever did. Most of these roads were built by small private corporations, – "turnpike companies," – which expected to operate them for a profit. Some of these roads were good, others were indescribably bad; some of the companies succeeded, others failed; some were organized to sell their own stock rather than to build roads. But as our rapidly growing population began to spread toward the west men began to plan means of internal communication on a larger scale, and to call on the state and federal governments for assistance. Especially was this true after the war of 1812. The federal government built the old National Pike running west from Cumberland, Maryland, and for some years a running fight was kept up in Congress over the constitutionality of federal activities of this sort. A few things were accomplished, but the whole movement for federal construction was brought to a sudden stop when Andrew Jackson became president in 1829.

Then the pressure upon the states for aid to these projects was increased. New and larger demands began to be heard. The newly settled regions of the West wanted a market; they wanted to exchange their surplus agricultural products for some of the comforts and luxuries of the East and of Europe. The tremendous success of the Erie Canal, completed in 1825, and especially the rise of New York City to the position of the first market-place of the continent led Philadelphia and Baltimore to cast jealous eyes upon the western trade and to develop schemes for transportation routes that would rival the Erie Canal. And back of all there was the impelling force of American optimism and the pernicious influence of land speculation. American capital was inadequate for investments so large as those proposed. Funds had to be obtained from Europe. American business corporations did not have an established European credit. Moreover, many of the improvements proposed offered so little hope of profits that they would never have been undertaken by private corporations. But American states were able to borrow in Europe, for up to this time their debts had been paid promptly. And so the thing was done. Within fifteen years Pennsylvania created a state debt of over $40,000,000 in constructing state roads, a state canal system, and two short railroads. Badly planned, wastefully constructed, and improperly maintained, Pennsylvania's system of internal improvements was unprofitable from the start. In 1857 the state was glad to sell the main line of its canal system to the Pennsylvania Railroad (which parallels it) for $7,500,000.

Maryland's experience was similar. (One curious feature is that both Maryland and Pennsylvania, as well as other states, required the banks which they chartered to subscribe to the stock of turnpike companies.) In fact there were few states in the Union which were not drawn into extravagant and largely unprofitable expenditures for roads and canals. But the wildest excesses were found in the states of the old Northwest, – Ohio, Michigan, Indiana, and Illinois. Here each frontier village saw itself a future metropolis, and land speculation, aided by easy loans from irresponsible banks, was the dominant fact of the situation. Michigan's first state legislature, in 1837, authorized the construction of an enormous system of roads, canals, and railroads. Similar laws were enacted at about the same time in Indiana and Illinois. In this legislation, as in many of our federal tariff laws and our "pork-barrel" appropriations for rivers and harbors the old American system of vote-trading was seen at its worst. Thus in Illinois the scheme of canals, railroads, and state roads was so worked out that every county in the State, except one, was reached by some part of the state system. And the one county left out was consoled by being given the state capital.

The outcome of all these ambitious undertakings was disastrous. Construction was slower and more expensive than had been estimated. Revenue from tolls had been counted on to pay the larger part of the interest on the bonds and to provide for their retirement, but the actual revenues received were utterly inadequate for the purpose. Aid from the federal government in the form of the distribution to the states of the surplus revenues arising from the sales of public lands and a percentage of the money received from such sales was suddenly stopped. And the whole country found itself in the grip of the prolonged business depression which followed the great panic of 1837. By 1842 the work of constructing these state improvements was almost everywhere brought to a stop. The states found themselves loaded down with debts amounting to over $200,000,000, – and with very little to show for it. Some of this was ultimately paid; for some of it a compromise was effected with the bondholders, and, worst of all, some of it was shamelessly repudiated.

Now I have not cited these familiar facts because I think there is any danger of our repeating this experience. The conditions which made such excesses possible can never exist again. They were the offspring of a period of rapid growth and of buoyant optimism; of inflated currency and unsound credit conditions; of strong local and sectional rivalries; of ignorance of the real costs and the real possibilities of improvements in the means of transportation. The routes to be improved were in many cases chosen without reference to the natural channels of commerce and communication. And although the commercial practicability of these projects was thus ignored, it was vaguely expected that their profits would be sufficient to pay interest on the borrowed capital and ultimately to repay the capital itself. That such improvements should be paid for immediately or ultimately out of taxes was a thing never contemplated. In other words, these extravagant public works were masquerading as commercial enterprises. This in itself is enough to mark the fundamental difference between these old projects and the present-day plans for highway improvement. I have ventured to recall this experience to you, merely *because* it is an extreme case; because on this account it puts in clear relief the dangers – not so great now as then – that inhere in the use of the borrowing power for the construction of works of internal improvement.

These dangers are much greater when the borrowing power used is that of the state than when it is that of a private corporation. Private corporations may easily go too far in this matter, still there are rigid limitations to the borrowing power of such enterprises. These limitations come from the fact that when a railroad or other large corporation wishes to borrow money for new construction by selling bonds it has to convince bankers and underwriters and, through them, the investing public that the new construction will add enough to the earnings of the corporation to enable it to pay the interest on the bonds. In general, it must be shown that the money borrowed will be put to a profitable use. And, despite some exceptions, the broad statement will hold that if the investment of private capital in new construction is profitable it is because the new construction meets a real public need. Otherwise, still speaking broadly, the public would not make sufficient use of the new improvement to afford a return on the investment.

The conditions under which public borrowings are made are quite different. Here the lender – the bond buyer – looks only to the legality of the bond issue and to the good faith of the state, backed by its taxing power. The profitableness of the undertaking is not in question. Neither is its utility. Through public borrowing, funds can be secured quite as easily for extravagant and foolish expenditures as for real needs or real emergencies. Please do not misunderstand me at this point. I am not saying that large public expenditures for road building are extravagant and foolish, I am merely emphasizing the fact that the borrowing power of the state is a powerful instrument, easily liable to abuse; that the only effective limitations upon it are the good sense and caution with which it may be used. It is easy for a state to borrow money, and it is correspondingly difficult always to make sure that a proposed borrowing can be justified.

Authorities on public finance are agreed that there are three purposes for which a government is justified in borrowing money on long-term bonds: (1) For refunding some existing debt which is either necessarily permanent in character or which it is uneconomical or unwise to pay off, now or in the near future. (2) For meeting extraordinary expenses in connection with some great public emergency, such as an important war. (But even in such cases it is recognized that bond issues must be supplemented and supported by a vigorous use of the taxing power). (3) Public borrowing is justified for the purpose of paying for expensive permanent improvements of a sort that are not made regularly, but only at infrequent intervals. Note that the conditions are that the improvements paid for from the proceeds of borrowing should be both permanent and unusual. With respect to permanency, its probable life should be no less than that of the bonds issued to pay for it, and even under such conditions full provision should be made for the accumulation of a sinking fund with which to retire the bonds when due. In saying that the improvement should be unusual I mean merely that there should not be a regularly recurring need for further improvements of the same type; otherwise it would be better to provide for these regular needs out of annual taxes. It is entirely proper to issue bonds for a school building, but not for teachers' salaries; for a court-house, but not for the normal costs of county government; for an electric-light plant, but not for its fuel; for the construction of a barge canal – if that be deemed a wise expenditure of money – but not for its maintenance. The essential point is that it is legitimate to borrow money for the purpose of spreading the burden of a large expenditure over a period of years, whenever the benefits derived from that expenditure will likewise endure for a period of years. But under any but the most extraordinary conditions it can never be sound public policy to issue long-time bonds for the sake of putting off into the future the burden of paying for some present service or improvement which will yield most of its benefits now or in the near future.

These general principles are clear enough, and I imagine that nearly everyone would admit their soundness. But when we come to certain classes of concrete problems it is not always easy to determine just what effect the application of these principles would have. Highway construction, in my opinion, is one of these difficult problems. The original construction of improved highways is not, perhaps, one of those normal and regular expenses of government which should always and without question be paid for by current taxes. But neither is it in all ways like those permanent and unusual expenditures which may, beyond question, properly be provided for by public borrowings.

Let me cite an extreme case. The other day I happened upon a pamphlet in the University Library entitled "Good Roads and How to Obtain Them." The pamphlet itself is of no particular importance. It was published in 1898, and the scheme which it proposes is only one of the dozens of projects for currency reform born of the great contest over the free coinage of silver, which had reached its climax in 1896. The author of this pamphlet believed in a bank-note currency; he wanted this sort of currency largely increased; and he wanted to retain the principle of our national-banking system which required each bank desiring to issue notes to invest in government bonds as a security to guarantee the final redemption of the notes. But the supply of government bonds was running short; and the author of the pamphlet did not foresee the refunding operations authorized in 1900 by which we postponed the payment of a large part of our outstanding government debt; nor did he foresee the large bond issues made for the purpose of constructing the Panama Canal. So he proposed the issue and sale of new bonds for the purpose of building a system of "national country roads" connecting Washington and the capitols of all the states in the Union. The cost of this modest plan was to be $500,000,000. Of the bonds to be issued $100,000,000 were to mature at the end of fifty years, another hundred million at the end of one hundred years; one hundred million, in short, at the end of each fifty-year period, so that the last hundred million would mature at the end of two hundred and fifty years. We should all call his proposals absurd, but mainly, I think, because of the arbitrary routes which his national highways were to take and because of the financial improvidence of incurring a two-hundred-and-fifty-year debt for the purpose of constructing an improvement so little certain to have permanent value as even the best of modern roads. This is, of course, an extreme case; but are we altogether sure that it is so extreme as to constitute a difference in kind rather than merely a difference in degree from the present situation in the State of New York? Is it not possible that in our state bond issues for good roads we have set a dangerous precedent?

The answer to this question depends in part, though not wholly, upon the permanency of the roads we are building. This is primarily an engineering question, and most of my hearers are much better qualified to discuss it than I. But some facts that seem to me to bear upon the question are obvious even to the layman. In the first place, it is inaccurate to speak of the probable life of a modern highway. Some parts of it are relatively permanent; other parts are short-lived. Suppose, for example, that the chief task of highway improvement in this state were that of resurfacing all existing improved roads. No matter how expensive this might be, none of us, I suppose, would think that the cost should be covered by an issue of fifty-year bonds. The improvement itself would be too short-lived to justify us in such a postponement of the final payment. At the other extreme, I suppose, would be the heavier work of grading, and especially of cutting and filling, much of which might be said to be permanent in character. In difficult and expensive mountain construction (such as the road around Storm King Mountain) there may be heavy expenditures for cutting through rock, for building retaining walls, and the like. Wherever roadmaking with such high initial costs is justified at all, there is no reason why bond issues should not furnish all or a large part of the funds needed for construction. In such a case it is *relatively* unimportant whether or not annual repairs are expensive, and whether resurfacing or even partial rebuilding are frequently recurring costs. The important thing is that by far the largest part of the initial expenditure on such a road is permanent; it is made *once for all*. Under such conditions, and especially where the aggregate cost of construction is heavy, the use of bond-issues is entirely in accord with sound financial principles.

I do not know that we can get a better general rule than this: the more permanent the construction, – that is, the larger the proportion of the total expenditures for construction which are made "once for all," – the greater will be the propriety of using the proceeds of long-time loans for such construction. The best way of measuring this in practice might be to take the proportion which average annual maintenance bears to the total original construction costs. By average annual maintenance I mean to include the cost of ordinary repairs, of resurfacing, and of such rebuilding as may be necessary, averaged over a sufficiently long period of time to give a fairly representative result for a given type of road under given traffic conditions. The higher the ratio of probable average annual maintenance to the expense of the original construction the more difficult it is to justify the use of the borrowing power in obtaining the money for construction purposes. And, conversely, the lower the ratio of average annual maintenance to original construction costs, the sounder are the reasons for resorting to bond issues. Moreover, the lower the ratio, the longer is the length of time which may properly be allowed to elapse before the bonds mature. It may be unwise to lay down a more definite rule, but I venture the tentative suggestion that the bonds should not run for more years than it takes for the aggregate maintenance expenditures to equal the original cost of the road. If, for example, annual maintenance expenditures average about five per cent of the original cost of construction, at the end of twenty years an amount equal to the original cost will have been expended for maintenance. In a physical sense the road as a whole will not have been replaced, for although some *parts* will have been replaced several times over, other parts will not have been replaced at all. But it is not altogether incorrect to say that the road has been replaced, in the sense that as much additional money has been put into it as would have sufficed to build another road like it. Twenty years, then, may be called the "replacement period" for such a road. I suggest that if bonds are issued to build a road of this type it would be better to issue twenty-year bonds, or bonds maturing in not more than twenty years. And for other types of roads, the replacement period, whatever it may be, furnishes a reasonable maximum term within which bonds issued for construction should be paid off. Not enough experience has been accumulated as yet to enable one to estimate the replacement period of the various types of roads that have been built in this state out of the proceeds of our fifty-year bond issues. But I infer from the State Highway Commissioner's reports that it is apt to be as low as ten years on some types of roads with a heavy traffic, and I am inclined to think that in general it is rather more apt to be under twenty years than over it. If bonds had to be issued, twenty- or twenty-five-year bonds would have been better. They would have sold, I think, as well as the fifty-year bonds. The principle difference would have been that the annual sinking-fund accumulations for the purpose of retiring the bonds would have been much larger.

Thus far I have dealt with the relation of what may be called the physical depreciation of highways to the question of the use of bond issues. But there are other kinds of depreciation to be reckoned with; depreciation in value, in utility, and more particularly depreciation from obsolescence. He would indeed be a rash prophet who would venture to infer from our present conditions and present knowledge just what kind of highways will be desirable fifty or even twenty-five years from now. Recent changes in the standards of highway construction should be enough to enforce that point. Twenty years ago, if I am correctly informed, waterbound macadam was standard construction, even for through routes, subjected to heavy traffic. The rise of the motor vehicle has made that old standard inadequate. Would it have been an altogether fortunate thing if twenty-five years ago we had sold a hundred million dollars' worth of fifty-year state bonds for the purpose of constructing a system of state and county highways, – all of waterbound macadam? If this had been done we would now be contributing and for the next twenty-five years would still be contributing toward the payment of the interest and principal of a debt incurred to construct a system of public works, already partly obsolete. And who shall say what changes in the *use* of our roads may occur in the next twenty-five or fifty years? There may be, for example, a considerable development in the use of steam or gasoline tractors, such as are already used in England. More than that, if again I am correctly informed, a considerable portion of the highway construction paid for from the proceeds of our state bond issues has been frankly experimental in character. I am told that the standards first adopted for the important avenues of heavy travel have been found to be inadequate and that heavier and more expensive construction has been found necessary in order to bring maintenance costs down to a reasonable point. I am also told that for some types of county highways it has been found desirable to change to cheaper types of construction in order to make the available funds cover a greater mileage. But even for given standards I am informed that many different types of construction have been used, partly because of differences in local conditions and in the materials locally available and partly because of a desire to secure a wide variety of experiments.

Much progress has undoubtedly been made. Certain types of construction have been discarded and I suppose that there has been a tendency to center more and more upon the use of a few apparently successful types. And yet would it be going too far to say that the construction of the type or types of road best adapted to modern traffic conditions, taking into account both construction and maintenance expense, remains an unsolved engineering problem? Of course on this point I speak out of ignorance. It may be that some engineers would agree with me and that some would not.

At any rate, I do not mean that we should not experiment. Nor do I mean that we should wait for good highways until we are through experimenting. Road-building and experimentation on a large scale must in the nature of the case go hand in hand. Part of the expense must be charged off to social profit and loss as the cost of progress. But I venture to suggest that experimentation had better be paid for in other ways than by the sale of fifty-year bonds. We want experimentation, and we want good roads, but do we want more of either than we can pay for as we go along? Is it not possible that the general cause of road improvement would have been about as far advanced if we had paid for our state and county road-building out of taxes, and had gone a little slower and a little more carefully?

There is one thing, however, which should be said on the other side. By far the most important economic problem relating to the roads of the state is that of the improvement of a reasonable portion of the seventy-five thousand miles of town roads not included in state or county systems. This has a larger bearing upon the prosperity of our farming regions than has any other part of our good roads program. The adoption of the principle of state aid in the enaction of the Fuller-Plank law of 1898 did much; the extension of the supervision of central authorities over the work of local construction and maintenance, beginning in 1904, has also done much; but it is possible that the rapid construction of state and county highways has done even more, by furnishing an object-lesson; by spreading abroad the general spirit of community progress in road-building. This much is to the distinct credit of the bond-issue system. Anything slower in its operation, more tentative in its methods would not have accomplished so much. Yet here, of course, is the largest and most fruitful field for still further accomplishment.

I am inclined to think that the resort to bond issues for road building in this state was due in part to a peculiar combination of circumstances, although of course full recognition should be given to the successful efforts of the leaders of the organized movement for good roads. The legislative resolution which led to the adoption of the constitutional amendment authorizing the first fifty-million dollar bond issue was passed in 1903, and followed closely upon similar action taken with reference to the $101,000,000 bond issue for the construction of the barge canal. That bond issue had set the example. It was felt that highways had at least an equal claim to generous treatment, especially since the canal, at best, would primarily benefit the large cities, while improved highways would be of special service to the smaller cities and country districts. Moreover the state had abandoned the use (for state purposes) of the direct tax upon general property and was getting its revenues from a variety of indirect special taxes. These indirect taxes furnish a large and increasing revenue, but they are inelastic, in the sense that the amount of revenue derived from them cannot easily be increased at will so as to cover a substantial increase in public expenditures. It was not thought desirable, even if it were possible, to reintroduce the direct tax in order to secure funds for road-building.

In this respect the situation remains substantially unchanged, and the question arises as to what other sources of state revenue are available for road-building in case no further resort should be made to bond issues. Our principal indirect taxes now are the liquor traffic tax, the special tax on corporations, the inheritance tax, the mortgage recording tax, the secured debts tax, the stock transfer tax and the motor vehicles tax. The revenues from this last tax are now devoted to road maintenance. This tax yields almost $2,000,000 annually, and this amount is steadily increasing. But it could be still further increased without injustice by increasing the tax on all classes of motor vehicles, but especially on heavy commercial vehicles. Under the present law these are assessed at the same rate as the lightest class of pleasure cars although they are notoriously destructive to roads. Instead of five dollars a year the tax on some of these vehicles might with entire propriety be made twenty-five or even fifty dollars a year. It should be remembered that motor vehicles are exempted from the property tax; so that despite their destructive effect on highways they are not taxed so heavily as other forms of property. The revenues from the tax on motor vehicles could easily be doubled without the slightest injustice to the owners of such vehicles.

Let me pause to say that I think we are apt to *underestimate* the full responsibility of the automobile for the increased expense of road building and road maintenance. It is not only that some of our through roads and many of our branch roads are primarily for automobile traffic; or that this traffic is a chief cause of need of frequent resurfacing. For, in addition to these things, we must remember the needs of automobiles have largely *set the standards of construction* on a large part of our state and county highways. Without this traffic cheaper types of construction could have been used in many places with a resulting saving to the taxpayers of the state. Despite the rapidly growing amount of motor traffic the owners of motor cars constitute a very small class, for whom the state has expended and is expending many millions of dollars. There could be no reasonable objection, I think, to a marked increase in the annual taxes imposed upon motor vehicles. And I see no sound objection to Commissioner Carlisle's plan for taxing the motor cars of other states.

In general, however, I do not think that our reliance on indirect taxes for our current state revenues is altogether commendable. Easily assessed, for the most part, not directly *felt* by individual tax-payers, these taxes furnish an easy method of paying the ordinary expenses of the state. They furnish a large and increasing revenue and tempt to legislative extravagance. And yet, as I have said, they are inelastic in that their yield cannot be increased by a definite amount so as to provide for large special expenditures, such as those necessary to carry out a comprehensive scheme of road improvement.

I believe it is a real misfortune that we have abandoned the use of the direct personal tax on the ownership of real property as a regular part of our state revenue system. If we had retained it the needed element of elasticity in the state revenues could have been secured by raising or lowering the direct tax rate. But now that it has been abandoned it is difficult to reinstate it. Some part of the state revenues, I think, ought to come from the direct contributions of the citizens of the state. Under an autocratic form of government it may be desirable to make use of a multitude of indirect taxes, and so to "pluck the goose with the minimum amount of squawk." But in democracy the personal taxation of every property-owning citizen – of every citizen, even, whether property-owning or not, if that were possible – is a much more wholesome ideal. And at most the tax rate for state purposes would be exceeding low. A tax rate of half a mill on the dollar, that is of fifty cents on every thousand dollars of assessed valuation, would yield a revenue of about $6,000,000. I do not think that so good a cause as that of good roads should depend for success upon our ability to achieve a painless extraction of money from the taxpayer's pocket by the use of bond issues supported by indirect taxes. Not that I think that our two $50,000,000 bond issues have been productive of much harm. They have at least launched the work of state road improvement with a momentum which might not have been achieved in any other way. But now that the initial inertia has been overcome and that the advantages of good roads are generally known and appreciated as never before, would it not be best for the active supporters of the movement to say: "Yes, we want the work of road-building on a state-wide scale continued; want more state-built roads, and after that we will probably want yet more state-built roads. But we want to pay for them as we go along. We want the taxpayers of the state to vote for them, not because they think they can shift the burden of paying for them upon somebody else or upon the next generation, but because they honestly want good roads, and want them badly enough to be willing to help pay for them."

Discussion

Q. How much would the 50 cents on a thousand valuation amount to in New York?

A. About $6,000,000; this amount at present would pay for the annual cost of maintenance on the state roads and leave a considerable margin for new construction. The 50 cents on a thousand valuation seemed to me a fair amount.

Q. What part should the national government play in the support of highway construction?

A. I am not sure that the national government should do anything more than, if possible, take upon itself the building of certain national highways through thinly populated parts of the country where they can not be otherwise built, such as across the great plains of the west. I think the national government should keep up the educational work in the matter of experimental construction primarily through the Department of Agriculture.

Q. Don't you think they would have a large field in experimental work?

A. Yes, of course. But in experimental work in applied science of all kinds the National government ought to be a center of activities.

Q. What do you think about the government helping to maintain that portion of the road used by rural delivery carriers?

A. I believe that is not a fair basis for federal help. There is little relation between the use of the road by rural delivery carriers and the wear and tear on the roads. That argument is very incidental and quite secondary.

Q. Would it be fair to tax the farmers for vehicles that they use on the state highways?

A. I think it would be fair but it would be unnecessary in a way. Of course, in this state we have a peculiar situation in that the personal property tax is not very well imposed. Still, the farmers pay rather more of it than any other classes. If the law was strictly enforced they would pay a tax upon their vehicles which would be larger proportionally than the owners of motor cars pay. The question is difficult because we have a conflict between law and practice. As a matter of fact many farmers do not pay tax at all. I see no injustice in exempting that class of personal property from the operation of the personal property tax and levying a small direct tax. It seems to me to be not a bad plan.

Q. Referring to your suggestion to tax motor bus lines more than the pleasure vehicles, would it be legal to grant a franchise to those lines, renting them the highway the same as a railroad line?

A. And refuse them the use of the road unless they had a franchise? I think it would be perfectly practicable. A franchise is not necessarily an exclusive right, but most franchises of the kind with which we have been familiar have been exclusive. The franchise of the kind we have in mind is primarily the right to use the public property. I believe it would be right to require a license and to require from bus lines a payment either based upon the weight or character of their busses or possibly upon the mileage.

Q. Would it be fair to ask the national government for assistance in building highways as a help to the national defense?

A. Yes. Curiously enough, in 1816–29, when the constitutionality of federal appropriation was so much discussed, there were three federal powers that were emphasized in the debates. Several of the bills were vetoed by presidents because they did not believe in the constitutionality of such bills. The men who did believe such bills constitutional, among them John C. Calhoun, the strictest of all strict constitutionists of the constitution, based their belief that it was proper for the federal government to aid such undertaking upon three powers: first, the general welfare of the federal government; second, the power to establish post roads; and third, the power to establish military roads. Now of course, the power to establish military roads is largely, I should say, a power to build and construct railroads, and the large grants to the Union Pacific railroad were justified in the view of many constitutional lawyers on the ground that that was a military necessity. It may be that there are certain regions of the country – mountainous or near the coast – where highways would be of military use. It is a question for the military experts as to whether such are needed.

Q. Sometime ago there was a bill proposed in the House of Representatives to bond the government to the amount of a billion dollars, this in turn to be loaned to the states for use in building good roads. What was the object of that, to centralize the bonding?

A. It may have been done to get better terms and lower rates of interest because of the better credit of the Federal Government. That may have had some effect upon the situation in some states though it would not materially affect the situation here. The state of New York can not borrow on quite as good terms as the federal government, but now that our national banks no longer have to invest part of their capital in United States government bonds, I doubt if there would be more than half of one per cent difference in the net rate.

Q. Some of the advocates of long term bond issues for roads back up their arguments by saying that the original construction of the road involves about 52% of permanent construction.

A. I think that is not an entirely fair way of getting at it. Suppose we say that 52% of the original cost is permanent; nevertheless the remaining cost may be divided into parts which are of different degrees of permanency. Some parts of the road, to borrow a commercial term, have a much more rapid rate of turn over. It seems to me that this should be taken into account. It is not only the permanency of the permanent part, but it is the degree to which the less permanent parts are short lived. That affects what I call the replacing period.

Q. If you carried that argument a little farther, could you not say that a road with no pavement – only graded, culverts improved, and afterwards taken care of, would justify a long term bond issue while a brick pavement would not?

A. I should say, take a concrete case, if a fairly well-to-do town wanted to borrow money for the purpose of bringing its roads into good shape – all dirt roads where it is only a matter of grading and building culverts – with the expense large enough to make it worth while it is an entirely proper case for the use of borrowing power provided this power is properly carried out. On the other hand, the ordinary maintenance and care of town roads seem to me to be the farthest of all removed from the class of cases in which the use of borrowing power is possible.

Q. Which do you think is the wiser, greater mileage and cheap roads with greater cost of maintenance, or permanent roads with lower cost of maintenance?

A. This is an engineering problem. I think it depends largely on individual cases.

Q. Well, you believe the bonds should be used for the permanent type and direct tax for the other?

A. Yes, but even the more permanent type of construction – that which we are apt to call so – is used because it is subject to unusual traffic conditions, and the so called permanent type of construction is, as a matter of fact, likely not to be any longer lived than the more fragile types. I do not believe that any general principle can be laid down. The answer would vary depending on individual cases.

10 The economics of farm relief

The Independent (1926) New York: 117, No. 3972 (July 17): 64–6

Sir Josiah Stamp has a distinguished place among the world's economists. He deserves that place, for his work reflects a remarkable combination of qualities – knowledge, judgment, and analytical power. Much weight, therefore, has properly been given to his finding that an essential part of the scheme for agricultural relief embodied in the recently defeated Haugen bill is "economically feasible and not fallacious."

This finding was announced in a letter to Vice President Dawes, with whom Sir Josiah had been associated as a member of the commission which formulated the Dawes Plan. Few economists, I am sure, would quarrel with Sir Josiah's conclusion, provided proper emphasis is put on the reservations with which he safeguards it; and few economists, I am equally sure, would see in it sufficient ground for supporting the Haugen bill or any similar project.

Price discrimination, where conditions make it feasible, is generally a profitable business policy. It is feasible, however, only when different groups of buyers can in some way be segregated in different markets, so as to separate those who are willing to buy at high prices from those who are unwilling to buy except at lower prices. In a competitive market, segregation of different classes of buyers is impossible. But it is a familiar practice in monopolistic fields where price discrimination goes under such names as "class price," "dumping," and "charging what the traffic will bear."

The Haugen bill proposed to erect machinery which would so modify existing competitive conditions as to give farmers the advantage of discriminatory prices for their staple products. With foreign competition shut out of the domestic market by the tariff, that market was to be further segregated by establishing agencies which would bid up prices in the domestic market and dump the surplus on foreign markets for whatever it would bring. Now, within reasonable limits domestic consumers will pay higher prices for wheat without greatly decreasing the amounts they will buy. Within reasonable limits, again, the foreign market will absorb additional quantities of wheat without any large reduction of price. The amount of wheat exported – for which prices would be somewhat reduced –

is small as compared with the amount consumed within the country – for which considerably higher prices would have to be paid. It is clear, therefore, that, with price discrimination of the kind proposed, American farmers would get more money for a wheat crop of given size than if they had to sell in a completely open market not fenced off from the rest of the world. This is what Sir Josiah Stamp meant when he said that the scheme was "economically feasible and not fallacious," and this, I infer, was about all that he meant.

But this is by no means all that there is to the problem. For one thing, although a necessary condition, it is not a sufficient condition for the success of such a plan that the demand for wheat be relatively inelastic – little affected by changes of price. It is also necessary that the supply of wheat should be relatively inelastic – relatively insensitive to the stimulus of higher prices. If higher prices lead to larger crops, there will be a larger export surplus and larger losses on that surplus. In the measure that such increased losses appear, the plan would fail of its objective. Sir Josiah Stamp says that he was given "as a statement of fact" that the agricultural industry "is for the most part in an economic condition of decreasing returns: that is, stimulus does not bring in new supply at lower average cost," and he is careful to say that he expresses no opinion as to "the efficiency of the maintenance of price," if this assumption – or any of several other assumptions given him – is incorrect.

This particular assumption may be incorrect. Agriculture is now burdened with an excessive overhead in the form of taxes, interest on indebtedness, and the cost of maintaining a surplus farm population. There is room for a very considerable increase in agricultural production without any comparable increase in these fixed charges. A definite prospect of higher prices would promptly evoke a larger output, and under the price-fixing scheme all of the increase would have to be marketed abroad at a loss. Probably, in the case of wheat, the increase would not be large enough to absorb all the profits which might be derived from the operation of the plan. But it would lessen the profits; it would put a heavy strain upon the administration of the plan; and it would, at best, create a thoroughly unsound situation. The situation would be unsound because, with production thus overexpanded, there would be a serious collapse if the Government's prop were at any time removed.

The fundamental obstacle to successful price regulation or price maintenance in any purely competitive field of industry is that it is impracticable to regulate output or to close the doors to the entry of new labor and new capital. Successful price maintenance calls for something like a unified monopolistic control of production, and that is out of the question in an industry like agriculture.

Weak at its best, the case for the economic possibilities of the control of agricultural prices is strongest in the case of wheat. But even if it were feasible to give these advantages to wheat growers alone, the amount of land devoted to wheat growing would promptly be increased at the expense of other products. Attempts to control the prices of other agricultural products would encounter special difficulties. The demand for meat – and hence for livestock – is much more elastic – that is, more affected by price advances – than the demand for wheat. The export market for some products – corn, for example – is so small as compared with the domestic market that unsalable surpluses would be piled up as a result of buying quantities large enough to raise domestic prices to the desired point. Other farm products, notably cotton, are raw materials for American industries. The net effect of controlling the prices of these particular products would be that while the American manufacturer would have to pay more for his raw materials, his foreign competitors would get the same materials on the bargain counter. This situation would call, first, for some definite system of refunding to the American manufacturer the excess, or price differential, paid by him on raw materials used in making goods for export, and, second, for higher tariff protection against goods of foreign manufacture. And this is not the only point at which price control would tend toward the piling up of complications.

There are other circumstances, too, which make cotton a peculiarly refractory subject for price control. The United States produces so large a part of the world's total supply that any notable increase in our own exports would amount to a rather large percentage increase in the aggregate amount of cotton – from all sources – offered on foreign markets. These markets would not absorb this additional supply except at markedly reduced prices. So much of our cotton crop is exported that the losses incurred in this way might easily eat up all the profits derived from the higher prices domestic consumers would have to pay. It is so obvious that price control would work badly in the case of cotton that some of the advocates of price control have suggested that the cotton might be left out, and that cotton growers might be compensated by a direct bonus.

An obstacle to the success of any method of controlling the prices of agricultural products is the absence of any criterion of a "fair and reasonable" price. Such criteria are always loose and uncertain. In the case of agriculture, they are virtually non-existent. A few years ago, when the prices of agricultural products were lower than they are now, proposals for price fixing usually embodied the notion that agricultural prices were to be brought back into supposed harmony with other prices. That is, some past period, when agriculture was prosperous, was to be taken as affording a norm, or standard. The task of the price fixer, then, would be to keep agricultural prices in about the same average relation to other prices as obtained in the supposedly "normal" period. I am not sure just what the advocates of price fixing would propose to do in a situation in which the ordinary forces of supply and demand, if unimpeded, would raise agricultural prices measurably *above* the point indicated by the so-called "norm."

Dubious at best, the notion that the movement of agricultural prices should be kept within a groove, always maintaining a fixed relation to the movement of prices in general, fails completely in the case of the prices of separate agricultural products. Who would care to maintain that the size of the crop, the extent of foreign demand, the activities of the boll weevil, and the new competition of rayon should have no effect whatever upon the price of cotton? We do not have to take these questions seriously, however, for the proponents of price control no longer rest their case upon the "maladjustment" that now exists between agricultural prices and other sorts of prices. Agricultural prices now, as a group, are not very far below the supposed normal points, and some agricultural prices are distinctly above normal. It is clear that a normal adjustment would be unsatisfactory. What appears really to be wanted is a guarantee of a satisfactory return upon the "capital" invested in agriculture. That is, it is held that prices should be high enough to provide the farmer reasonable profits over and above his costs of production. It is upon some such basis that we regulate the rates and the earnings of railways and of public utilities. Is not the American farmer entitled to a fair return upon his capital, quite as much as the public service corporation?

Apart from the fact that the public service undertaking is a monopoly while the farmers are engaged in the most competitive of all businesses, the task of determining what should justly be counted as invested capital, difficult enough in the case of public utilities, becomes simply impossible in the case of agriculture. The farmer's largest investment is in his land, and the price of land depends upon how profitable agriculture is; that is, upon the crops the farmer can grow and the prices he can get for them. The farmer's land is like the public utility's franchise. Its ownership carries with it an opportunity to engage in an undertaking for profit. Whether the land or the franchise is worth much or little depends upon the prospective profitableness of the possible undertaking. And that in turn depends upon a number of different things.

If one could effectively control agricultural prices, one would, in fact, control land values. This is the vital fact behind the price-control movement. The real significance high or low prices have for the American farmer is that a new level of prices and profits, continued over a short period of years, is quickly reflected in changed land values. The unduly heavy overhead costs which the farmer now has to carry, are, in considerable part, a sequel of the postwar agricultural boom and the accompanying rise of land values. It was then that agriculture became heavily overcapitalized and an enormous structure of fixed charges was created. The current proposals for price control, such as the Haugen bill, are, in effect, proposals for the artificial valorization of a part, at least, of what is already an inflated system of land values.

These proposals, though recently defeated in the Senate, are likely to be revived again. I believe them to be in large part unworkable, and so far as they are workable, I believe that they would, if put into practice, do more harm than good. But the discussion of them has had a profoundly useful educational influence. Agricultural depression is real, and one cannot disprove it merely by pointing to the fact that agricultural prices are higher than they were a few years ago. Professors Warren and Pearson of Cornell University have made abundantly clear in a recent work that agricultural depressions are necessarily longer lived than depressions in other fields of industry and trade. In agriculture, liquidation is a slower and more painful process, not to be accomplished in a moment.

The farmers of the country were not primarily responsible for the overcapitalization of agriculture. That was an inevitable fruit of our postwar inflation. Nor can one blame the farmers for asking that something be done for them. They have seen the protective tariff readjusted so as to take some account of changes in world prices and in the conditions of international competition. They have learned that the tariff on agricultural products is, for the most part, a formal and empty thing. They hold that agriculture should be given favors commensurate with those which the protected manufacturing industries enjoy.

A quarter of a century ago David Lubin, remembered as the founder of the International Institute of Agriculture, preached a doctrine which came to be known as Lubinism. The doctrine was, in effect, that the Government should pay a bounty upon agricultural exports so as to compensate the farmer for the loss of foreign markets and for the higher cost of living which come as the results of the restrictions the protective tariff puts upon imports of manufactured goods. The adoption of Lubinism would put a direct burden upon taxpayers, and Lubin suggested that a considerable part of that burden might be properly borne by the protected industries. Price-fixing proposals, like those of the Haugen bill, would put the burden directly upon American consumers of agricultural products. But, although Lubinism and price control employ different techniques, they have a common purpose and a common logic.

The farmer is right when he holds that some of the things proffered as substitutes for price control, such as coöperative marketing and further improvements in the machinery of agricultural credit, are at best mere palliatives. And yet it is difficult to see just what, aside from reducing the tariff, the Federal Government can do that will really afford the farmer the relief he asks for and needs. The present situation is one of the results of the war. The burdens of war are never equitably distributed, and an undue proportion of them have fallen upon the American landowning farmer. If I knew of any really effective way of redressing the balance, I would support it. As things are, I think, the farmer has a genuine interest in two things: first, sizable tariff reduction; second, the maintenance of generally stable conditions and, in particular, the avoidance of another period of inflated prices necessitating further readjustment and distressing unrest.

11 Economics

Encyclopaedia Britannica (1928) London: The Encyclopaedia Britannica Company. 925–32

Because economics has to do with the wealth-getting and wealth-using activities of men, it is often defined as "the science of wealth". This is not a wholly satisfactory definition, for the special characteristics of economics are determined not so much by its subject matter as by the particular interests which have prompted the enquiries of economists and the particular questions which they have tried to answer. We define economics better, therefore, when we say that it is a science which is concerned with the communal problems of economic life. The ordering of the economic affairs of the household and the planning and management of business undertakings come alike under its purview, but its interests and problems are not the interests and problems of either household economy or business enterprise. How men acquire wealth and how they use it are matters of fundamental importance for economics, but its principal concern is with the intricate interrelations of various wealth-getting and wealth-using activities and with the ways in which these activities affect the welfare of the community. The attention which economics gives to the general or social aspects of the interplay of economic activities is born of its central interest in the wisdom or unwisdom of measures which governments take or which conceivably they might take with a view to regulating, controlling or participating in them or to directing them into one channel rather than another. The older name, "political economy", still gives a right impression of the kinds of problems with which economics is mostly concerned.

Like every science, economics proceeds upon the assumption that there is some sort of order in the phenomena with which it deals. Just as and because the economic activities of men are not altogether aimless or directed wholly by chance, so the economic life of the community, viewed as a whole, is not sheer confusion, but has a discernible ordered pattern, showing itself in dependable "laws" or "tendencies" which are discoverable by means of careful observation and analysis. That there is some measure of regularity and predictability in economic phenomena is a commonsense assumption, one upon which men act in the daily conduct of their affairs. But there was only a very small field for economic science so long as the economic order, in its larger features, merely reflected the social or political order – so long, that is, as men's different economic activities and their economic relations were determined largely by their political status, by the position in the general institutional structure of society into which they were severally born or which they might be able to attain. Under such circumstances economic problems appeared in the guise of juristic and ethical problems. Economic activities were rated good or bad, not so much by their ultimate effects upon the economic welfare of the community as by their consistency with some supposedly rational or "natural" view of the general structure of society. Thus Aristotle's conclusion that trading for gain, as contrasted with trading to exchange goods, is "unnatural" was merely a corollary in his views of the nature and the functions of the family and the state. In the Middle Ages economic matters were discussed by some of the patristic writers and later by the schoolmen, but both groups were concerned almost wholly with the ethics of trade and of money-lending, and their criteria were drawn either from authority or from their own systematic philosophies.

The new economic order and its problems

What made the development of a science of economics possible was that transformation of the economic structure of society which, better than anything else, marks off the modern period from the mediaeval. This transformation is referred to, with emphasis upon one or another of its aspects, as the rise of modern capitalism, or of the competitive system, or of the system of free business enterprise. The dominating factor in it was the growth of trade, especially the growth of inter-town and inter-regional trade. With the growth of trade and the widening of markets the advantages of the division of labour and of local and regional industrial specialization became more and more pronounced. With the increasing ramifications of the market men were brought into a new nexus of relations, more intricate and more impersonal than the mediaeval system of prescriptive rights and duties, and giving the individual man more freedom of choice and action than that system had given him. Men became more dependent upon one another, not in any direct personal way, but in the sense that with the expansion of markets and the progress of the division of labour the welfare of each became intricately related to the activities of an increasing number of others. They came to realise that they had common economic interests and oppositions of economic interest as well. What were these interests and how best could the interests of the community or of a particular group or class within the community, be furthered? Such questions created problems of public policy for the new national states which the transformation of economic life had helped to bring into being, and out of the discussion of such problems the new science of political economy was born. There was need of such a science, because the mechanism of economic life had become so intricate that the deeper-reaching as contrasted with the surface effects of particular economic policies were difficult to discern. The task of economics was that of finding whatever dependable ordered relations might lie beneath the baffling complexity of the surface of economic life, so that public policies might be based upon knowledge and understanding.

Long before there was anything deserving the name of economic science, however, there was much writing, mostly controversial, as there has been ever since, about such matters as the monetary, fiscal and commercial policies of governments. Among the participants in these early controversies were some of the ablest men of their time – philosophers, public administrators and successful men of affairs. At one point or another the best of them probed deeply into the mysteries of the world's economic mechanism and reached conclusions which the economists of a later day have reaffirmed. For the most part, however, the early writers were too heavily handicapped by the lack of a scientific organon. They had no consistent general view of economic processes taken as a whole, so that their views of particular issues were likely to be partial and short-sighted. Take for example the writings which had the purpose of expounding or defining the principles of that general system of governmental economic statecraft known as "mercantilism", which flourished from the sixteenth century down to the nineteenth and which was exemplified in the restrictive policies of such statesmen and rulers as Colbert, Burleigh, Cromwell and Frederick the Great. Whether mercantilistic measures met the immediate needs of the times, whether they helped or hindered the task of nation-building, are disputed questions; but there can be no doubt respecting the weakness of the grounds upon which the case for such measures was commonly supposed to rest. It is not quite true that, as their critics have often said, the mercantilists held that money alone is wealth; but as a group they concerned themselves largely with the ways in which a country might secure and maintain a favourable balance of trade so as to conserve and increase its stock of money. They identified the economic interests of the nation with the interests of its merchants and they looked mostly at the immediate rather than the enduring interests of the mercantile classes themselves. The things which they thought conducive to national welfare were those they thought would stimulate trade and increase profits: plentiful supplies of money, low interest rates and low wages. Some of them appear to have thought of the nation as though it were itself a great trading firm, profiting from the excess of its foreign sales over its foreign purchases. Mercantilism, as the reader may have observed, is even now not wholly dead, but its errors were exposed long ago.

The beginnings of economic science

Sharply contrasted with the mercantilists' naive confusion of economic welfare and money profits were the conceptions employed by a small but influential group or philosophical sect, which flourished in France in the second half of the eighteenth century. They called themselves *les Économistes*, but the world now calls them the Physiocrats. Compared with the tracts of the mercantilists, who used the language of the world of trade, their writings seem abstract and doctrinaire. Their principal tenets were erroneous, and the modern economist finds less that has permanent value in their work as a whole than in that of some of their predecessors (e.g. Richard Cantillon, whose *Essai sur le commerce* was written between 1730 and 1734). But though they saw the processes of economic life imperfectly, they saw them as a whole. Not the buying and selling of the marketplace, but the continuing flow of goods through various channels from producer to consumer, was what they fixed their attention upon. The welfare of the community, in their view, was measured, not by the profits of trade, but by the excess of the community's annual product over its cost. In commerce and manufactures, they thought, there is no net product or surplus, for those activities add no more to the aggregate product than is required to support the people who are engaged in them. But in agriculture more is produced than is required to support the cultivators, and the surplus, which goes to the landowners as rent, is the only true net product which the community reaps from its efforts. Upon this disposable surplus the burden of all public expenditures, through the shifting of taxes from one producer to another, must inevitably fall. The Physiocrats were mistaken, for there were inconsistencies in their ways of measuring product and costs; they are important in the history of thought, not because they gave the right answers, but because they asked important questions – questions which in themselves were a challenge to the naive assumptions of mercantilism; and they had a considerable influence upon thoughtful men of their own day and of the period immediately following. Turgot, renowned for his courageous but abortive economic and fiscal reforms, fell just short of discipleship. His work, *Reflexions sur la formation et la distribution des richesses* (1766), is an exceedingly able treatise.

In 1776 Adam Smith published *An Inquiry into the Nature and the Causes of the Wealth of Nations*, a work in which wisdom, learning and power of analysis were joined as they are in few books. Sharing the physiocratic prejudices ("in agriculture nature works with man" – as though she did not work with him in his every pursuit!) and holding that the interests of business men, as a class, are more often opposed to the interests of the community than the interests of landowners are, Adam Smith nevertheless gave the world a new interpretation of the advantages of trade, a new "philosophy of commerce". But he saw in commerce a means to welfare, not an end, and his book was, in effect, a formidable tract directed against mercantilism. Money, from the communal point of view, he held to be merely an instrument, a "wheel of trade". The real source of a country's wealth, he said, is its "annual labour", and its wealth could be increased only by making its labour more effective and by husbanding and accumulating the products of labour. The division of labour, i.e. the specialization of tasks, is the principal factor in its effectiveness, and the degree in which the division of labour is practicable depends upon the extent of the market. These were Adam Smith's fundamental principles. He elaborated them with extraordinary skill, always discussing concrete problems, showing unusual powers of fresh observation in his selection and use of illustrative material, and passing large sections of economic history and the whole range of the contemporary commercial and fiscal problems of Great Britain under survey. Although the book is the most powerful brief ever formulated for unimpeded trade, neither hampered nor coddled by governments, its greatest importance is not to be found in that circumstance, but in the general picture, at once simple and comprehensive, which it gives of the economic life of a nation. The apparent chaos of competition, the welter of buying and selling, are resolved or transmuted into an orderly system of economic co-operation by means of which the community's wants are supplied and its wealth increased. This general picture has been in the minds of economists ever since, whatever their opinions with respect to the efficiency of the competitive system. Despite some sweeping phrases which invite a different interpretation, Smith's real concern was for the establishing and maintaining of competitive conditions rather than for a vigorous observance by governments of a hands-off policy in respect of economic matters. He was discussing a special set of problems. He was opposed to monopoly, to exclusive combinations, and special privileges of all kinds, quite as much as to the type of legislation which aims at fostering a country's prosperity by restricting its trade. Often styled the "apostle of self-interest", he took no pains to conceal his dislike for some of the forms in which self-interest manifests itself in trade and industry. What his attitude would have been under the later conditions of the nineteenth and twentieth centuries towards the factory acts, social insurance, and measures intended to help onward equality of competitive opportunities, we cannot tell. Bu there is very little in these newer types of legislation which runs counter to his principal contentions or is inconsistent with his general economic philosophy.

The older political economy

Adam Smith's work had a profound influence, not in Britain alone, but in almost every part of the Western world. It was probably partly responsible for some radical changes in the commercial policies of governments, although one cannot be certain about this, for the current of the times was moving in a direction favourable to Smith's contentions. Its effect upon scientific thought and upon the character and quality of public discussions of economic questions was unmistakable. Men like J.B. Say in France and K.H. Rau in Germany based their own work very largely on Smith's and helped to diffuse his influence. Say, however, was more than a mere popularizer. He had some clear-cut views of his own, and developed Smith's work in directions other than it took in the hands of Smith's British successors. In the United States, Say's work came to be about as widely read as Smith's.

The particular trend which the development of economics took in Great Britain was determined very largely by the character of the economic problems which confronted the nation, partly by reason of swiftly progressive changes in its own industrial structure and partly in consequence of the Napoleonic wars. The rapid growth of population, the extension of agricultural cultivation and the rise of land rents, the expansion of industrial activities, the depreciation of the currency, the variations of prices, of interest rates and of profits, and, after the wars, the depression in both agriculture and industry, were phenomena at once conspicuous and important. Some of these developments commanded the attention of Parliamentary committees; all of them attracted the interest of thoughtful men. With Adam Smith's impressive picture of the mechanism of organized economic life in their minds, it was natural that men should think of such phenomena as interrelated and as susceptible of being explained in some consistent and comparatively simple way. At any rate, out of the discussions of the period, out of the pamphlets and the controversial tracts, there emerged a coherent system of political economy, owing much, of course, to Adam Smith, but putting stress on matters to which he had given little or no attention, and emending his views at a number of important points. This newer political economy was more formal and systematic than Adam Smith's, and was concerned more largely with abstract general relations, but it dealt with real problems and dealt with them in what was intended to be a practical way. There is an appearance of paradox, but only an appearance, in the circumstance that the particular type of economics which grew out of attempts to deal intelligently with the problems of a period of economic storm and stress should be one which gave particular attention to "normal tendencies" and to the conditions of economic equilibrium rather than to the causes of economic maladjustments. A parallel may be found in the way in which the study of pathology has contributed to men's knowledge of normal physiology.

For convenience the period of which we are now speaking may be taken as having definitely begun when David Ricardo's *Principles of Political Economy and Taxation* was published (1817) and as having culminated with the publication of John Stuart Mill's *Principles of Political Economy* (1848). One who compares the economic tracts and the systematic treatises of that period with the *Wealth of Nations*, will be impressed with the increased importance given to a group of problems which have remained ever since among the principal concerns of economics, problems now commonly grouped under the head of "the theory of value and distribution". The theory of value, of course, has to do with the explanation of why goods exchange at particular ratios, why some goods are expensive and other goods are cheap. The theory of distribution is really an extension of the theory of value so as to explain the magnitude of the shares of the total national product which are secured by those who contribute either their own services or the use of their property to the communal task of production. With the problem of personal distribution, the problem, that is, of why some men are rich and some are poor, economic theory, of the type which we are now discussing, has not directly concerned itself. Its problem has been that of the distribution of the product among the so-called factors of production. These factors and their respective shares were classified as labour and its wages, capital and its profits, and land and its rent. Later on the conception of a fourth share, the profits of enterprise, or of the successful direction of production, was taken over from the French economists, the earnings properly imputable to capital, as distinct from enterprise and direction, being put down as interest. But British economists, more than those of other countries, still continue to speak, in realistic fashion, of "the profits of capital", and there is no general agreement among economists anywhere that enterprise should be treated as a separate factor in production, even though the profits of enterprise be conceded to be a separate distributive share. The three-fold, or four-fold, classification of factors is in some respects arbitrary. Some economists use a two-fold classification, treating land as a particular form of capital, while others hold that a really adequate classification would take account of many different kinds of capital and of various grades or qualities of labour. The truth is that the three-fold classification is adequate in the analysis of some problems (the simple contrast between labour and capital, taken as including land, is all that is needed to bring certain important problems into clear relief), and inadequate in the analysis of others. It has been suggested that the three-fold classification was in its origins merely a reflection of the actual political and social structure of the society of the day. Be that as it may, the classification still corresponds very closely to the way in which some of the most important of communal economic problems present themselves.

An element in the theory of value which, for a long time, was stressed to the comparative neglect of almost everything else was the tendency for the exchange values or relative prices of goods produced and sold under competitive conditions to be equal or at any rate proportionate to the respective costs of producing them, as a result of the continuous shifting of productive resources from less profitable to more profitable channels. By costs were meant not the money outlays of employers but "real" or communal sacrifices. At first these real costs were conceived to be measured by or proportionate to the amounts of labour required to produce different goods, but later the "abstinence" or waiting involved in accumulating capital by using resources so as to get a larger future product instead of using them in providing for immediate wants was held to be a distinct and separate cost. This innovation was first suggested by N.W. Senior in 1836. At this point, it may be observed, the economic theory of the "scientific" socialists, including the predecessors a well as the followers of Karl Marx, branches off from that of the more orthodox economists, for the socialists refused to adopt the innovation.

The distribution of the product was held also to be determined in considerable part by costs. Thus the doctrine that in the long run the standard of living of the labouring people determined their wages was in effect a cost-of-production theory of the value or price of labour. This doctrine rested upon the theory of population generally associated with the name of T.R. Malthus, and particularly with the revised form which Malthus gave his theory in the second edition (1803) of his famous *Essay on Population*. In its revised form the theory was to the effect, not that population would normally increase faster than the means of subsistence could be increased, but that it would normally increase at least as fast as the means of subsistence would permit. For "means of subsistence" read "standard of living", understanding by that term the general scale or standard which labourers think must be maintained if a family is to be supported, and the essential basis of the standard-of-living theory of wages is obvious. If wages fall below that level, it was thought, the rate of growth of the population will fall off, the supply of labour will be relatively smaller, and wages will rise. If wages rise above that same fixed point, the increase of the population will be quickened (except so far as a better standard of living may become effective) and wages will fall.

The rent of land, however, was held not to be governed or determined by the principles of cost. This was because (1) the supply of land is fixed, so that a rise of rents does not tend to counteract itself by stimulating supply, and because (2) the prices of agricultural products cover the costs of cultivation on lands which, prices and wages being what they are, are barely worth using, and hence yield no rent. Rent, from the communal point of view, was held to be neither determined by cost nor itself a determining element in the prices of commodities, but to be a surplus arising from the circumstance that the value of the produce of the better lands is more than enough to pay the cost of cultivating them. Closely connected with the doctrine of rent – although in point of historical fact preceding it instead of deriving from it – was the law of diminishing returns. With the growth of population and the extension of cultivation, the theory ran, resort must be had to poorer lands, or lands already in use must be cultivated more intensively, or more probably both things must occur. In any case the increase of product would not be proportionate to the increase of the amount of labour required. In manufactures, it was thought, increasing returns were normally operative, because a larger population, with a larger demand for goods, affords larger opportunities for the economies of the division of labour, and for the inventions and the applications of the fruits of scientific progress to industry which the division of labour facilitates. Agriculture, too, benefits by technical progress, but here the possibility of improvements in methods were thought to be somewhat smaller and to be more than counterbalanced by the increasingly disadvantageous proportioning of labour and land which comes as an inevitable result of the growth of population. Some of the older economists, including both Ricardo and Mill, went so far as to hold, in what is perhaps the most vulnerable part of their analysis, that with the increase of the amounts of labour required to produce the labourer's own subsistence, coupled with advance of land rents, the profits of capital must decline. This would dampen men's desire to accumulate capital, and finally the growth of population and of wealth would come to an end. In the law of diminishing returns, taken as a statement of a tendency, there was nothing fallacious. Taken as a prophecy, however, it was, or has been thus far, mistaken. The possibilities of improvements in agricultural techniques were underestimated, and the rapid extension of the cultivation of new lands of good quality, brought nearer to the world's industrial centres by cheap transport, was unforeseen.

It was recognized, of course, that at any given time the prices of goods and of productive services might be considerably out of line with the norms established by long-run tendencies. But these deviations were held to be self-correcting and for the most part the older economists were content to attribute them to "variations of supply and demand". In some instances, however, they pushed their analysis of the factors which control the temporary state of the market a little further. Thus, for the time being, the supply of labour is determined by the present numbers of the working population. The demand for labour was held to be determined, not by the demand of final consumers for the products of labour, but (since most labour has to be paid for and the labourers supported before their products are ready for the market) by the amount of capital that can be devoted to the making of "advances" to labour. This was the famous wages-fund doctrine. It was found to be so misleading, however, that it has been pretty generally abandoned, the elements of truth which it contained being taken account of in other ways. Again, the equally famous doctrine (which has withstood criticism better) that the value or purchasing power of money at any given time depends, other things being equal, upon its quantity as compared with the volume of production and trade, may be regarded as a supply-and-demand theory of money. It was supplemented by the doctrine that the "normal" value of money, i.e. its value in the long run, is determined, when gold or silver is the monetary standard, by the marginal costs of mining; that is, by the costs of producing that portion of the supply which would not be produced if the metal were a little less valuable. Similarly, and quite naturally, short-lived fluctuations of the rate of interest were ascribed to temporary changes in the supply of and demand for loanable funds.

It would be an error, however, to think of these earlier economists as altogether preoccupied with theories of value and distribution, and it would also be an error to fail to recognise that their interest in those theories was born of their interest in practical problems. In general, moreover, they were not such uncompromising opponents of any sort of interference by the government in industry as some of their critics and some of the lesser writers who pretended to expound their views might lead one to think. Their attitude towards legislation intended to improve the condition of the working classes was sometimes sceptical but rarely hostile.

The critics

Before reviewing the later progress of economics it will be helpful to look at the principal types of criticism which have been directed against the older political economy and which are still maintained as against some of the newer developments of economics. In the first place, romanticists like Adam Müller and John Ruskin and their followers disliked the new modern economic mechanism, into the working of which the economists were trying to probe, and they also disliked the economists" conception of communal welfare, which, one might say, involves no challenge of the particular conception of individual economic welfare which prevails in a competitive society, but merely substitutes the point of view of the community for that of the individual. They preferred an ordered society with economic subordinated to religious, moral or aesthetic values – such as some of them thought was implied, even if not fully realized, in the social structure of the later Middle Ages. Work, some of them insist, is not merely a means to an end, particularly when the end is what is commonly called wealth, for good work is worth doing for its own sake and for its effect upon the character of the worker. What the romanticists offer is a moral or aesthetic creed, not a science. They do not impugn the fitness of economics to serve as an instrument of attack upon its own problems, but they belittle its problems.

Another group of writers, for whom there is no better general descriptive name than "the critical school", come much closer to meeting the economists of the orthodox line upon their own grounds. One of the earliest and easily the most influential of them was Sismonde de Sismondi (*Nouveaux principes d'économie politique,* published in 1817, and other works). Other able writers, often without any conscious discipleship, have taken a position much like Sismondi's. These critics urge that insufficient attention is given to the defects of the existing economic mechanism, even if it be viewed merely as a means of providing for the material needs of the community. They suggest that the economists, in their contemplation of such things as "long-run" or "normal" tendencies, the advantages of the division of labour, and the seeming perfections of the automatic processes by means of which the things men do in the pursuit of their own economic interests become knit together into a vast scheme of communal economic co-operation, forget how often the mechanism breaks down and the "normal" progress of the community's economic life is interrupted by a crisis; how unemployment, partly chronic and partly epidemic, is a persisting disease of the present economic order; how unequally the aggregate product is distributed among the members of the community; and how many of the things which men do in pursuit of their own economic advantage are, in point of fact, inimical to the economic interests of the community. As some contemporary critics put the matter, men today are interested first of all in making money, and only incidentally in making goods. To look at the activities of a competitive, acquisitive, society as though such activities constituted, in their entirety, a communal process of wealth production, requires, it is urged, rather more rationalizing and sophisticating of the facts than the orthodox economists and their followers realized. Such criticisms undoubtedly go too far. They give an incorrect impression of the place of the more abstract parts of the older economics in the general view of the community's economic activities which one finds in the works of the economists. No economist of the first rank has ever been a devotee of the "economic harmonies". The critical school, nevertheless, has had a wholesome influence upon the progress of the science. This school, it may be observed, occupies a position midway between that of the economists of the more orthodox line and that of the socialists who denounce the parts of economics that are inconsistent with their tenets as being merely an apologetic for and a product of the existing economic order.

Another angle of attack was adopted by the "historical school" – using that term broadly so as to include critics who might easily be put into several different groups. This school has had and still has adherents in all countries, but it has been especially influential in Germany. The most important of the early exponents of its views were Friedrich List (*Nationales System der politischen Oekonomie,* 1841) and Wilhelm Roscher (*Grundlagen der Nationaloekonomie,* 1854, and other works). The structure of a nation's economic life, said these critics, is a "historical category", something peculiar to a given nation at a given time, a product of its past, and to be understood, therefore, only by the study of that past. The wisdom of particular economic policies is relative to place and time, and the general or supposedly universal "laws" of abstract economics need to be supplemented by or even subordinated to an analysis of the concrete facts of each nation's economic growth. If they had gone no further these critics would have found many to agree with them. But the founders of the school (Karl Knies, whose work, *Die politische Oekonomie vom Standpunkte der geschichtlichen Methode*, appeared in 1853, is a notable exception) made of what they called the historical method something peculiarly arbitrary and doctrinaire. Instead of looking to history for the particular antecedents of those concrete differences of economic structure in which they professed to be interested, they proposed to derive from history universal and binding laws, akin to the laws of the physical sciences. In naming certain stages of economic development through which they thought every nation must pass they were really elaborating suggestions which they got, not from historical research, but from the Greeks. Like some of their followers, they regarded the forms which economic life has taken in the past as inevitable products of historical forces, while at the same time they contended for a rather heavy-handed control of economic activities by the state. The French and British economists had looked upon the way in which the economic life of the community is organized as being shaped and determined by the interplay of the activities and interests of individual men, and they had treated the state as though it were an instrument of men's purposes, a utilitarian device. The spokesman of the historical school, on the other hand, strongly influenced by Hegel, ascribed a prior and independent value to the state, and looked upon the economic activities of individuals as though moving in grooves determined by the general structure of society and expressing at the same time the controlling purposes of the state. Despite the extremes to which they pushed their contentions, the historical economists gave a needed emphasis to what may be called the institutional as contrasted with the free or contractual aspects of economic activities. Their work, and that of their successors, has made economists more mindful of the way in which institutions are the masters as well as the servants of men, and less ready to assume that the particular economic order with which their analysis is mostly concerned is inevitably permanent or final. The historical economists also gave a needed impetus to the study of economic history – a most valuable complement to the study of economic theory. With the growth of careful and painstaking historical research the old dogmatism of the historical economists has pretty generally given way to a realization of the variety and complexity of the fabric of economic history, and the new schools of historical economics under the leadership of such scholars as Gustav Schmoller in Germany and George Unwin in Great Britain (to name only men who are no longer living) are, as they should be, schools of historical research.

The methods of economics

Not only its critics but also some of its expounders have held that economics (i.e. analytical economics, allied in its methods and its aim, even if not in all of its findings, to the older political economy) is essentially abstract and deductive, proceeding from the premise that men's activities are prompted mostly by self-interest, and that it posits an "economic man", whose behaviour under given circumstances is completely rational or predictable. Economics is indeed abstract, as any science must be, but it has never been in any real sense deductive or a priori, and the "economic man" will be found upon scrutiny to be a fairly complex sort of person, whose behaviour is taken to be strictly self-regarding only in respect of certain aspects of the relationships into which he enters as buyer or seller, borrower or lender. In fact it might be urged plausibly that the older political economy, of which the Malthusian theory of population was an integral part, erred by underestimating the part which the rational prevision and weighing of economic consequences plays in human conduct. When we say that economics is abstract, we mean merely that economists do not pretend to take account of all of the factors which, in their entirety, might be supposed to account completely for every happening and every outcome in economic life. Their principal interest is in uncovering factors and relationships which are so general and important that the community cannot afford to remain in ignorance of them.

Economics makes use of two general classes of data: (1) observed facts respecting the behaviour of men in their various economic activities and relationships, including all classes of activities that have economic consequences; (2) such economic phenomena or events as movements of population, production, trade, incomes, prices, wages, profits, interest rates, etc. The most trustworthy evidence respecting the characteristics of human behaviour is often supplied by its results, and so the second class of data has often been drawn upon for knowledge respecting the first class. In the actual processes of constructive thought men doubtless pass forward and backward from one sort of knowledge to the other. The earlier economists, however, presented their findings in such a manner as to show that the known phenomena of the second class could be explained by (i.e. were consistent with) the known facts of the first class – the known characteristics of human behaviour. This circumstance undoubtedly accounts for the mistaken impression that they "deduced" their findings, including the second class of facts, from the first. What they really did, of course, was to examine such experience as was at hand and seemed relevant to their problems, with a view to discerning the systematic relationships which ran through it and to explaining the more puzzling or apparently more complicated happenings in terms of their relationships to what was familiar or more easily understood.

The growing accumulations of precise numerical information covering a wide variety of economic facts, coupled with the advance of statistical technique, bids fair to accomplish a notable change in the character and content of economics. More and more it is found that records of measurable economic phenomena, carefully interpreted, may be used to provide a basis for more reliable and in some respects more sensitive accounts of the economic activities of the community than can possibly be derived from even the most careful observation of how individual men conduct their affairs. The economic science of the immediate future, it is safe to say, will give a relatively larger place to the study of the movements of averages and aggregates. It should not be supposed, however, that this means that economics will be or can be altogether statistical – a new kind of "political arithmetic". Every average or aggregate is in some measure unique, the resultant of the play of a particular combination of circumstances, such as may never be encountered again. In order that we may know just how dependable and how significant the variations of these statistical magnitudes are, we need to analyse them so that we can explain them. That is, we need to weave them into the general texture of our knowledge, so as to relate them to other things which we know. In short, although economics is beginning to utilize new materials effectively, and although some of these new materials call for the use of a new technique, it cannot change its general logical method, for outside the field of the experimental sciences there is no other method of getting useful and reliable knowledge.

The progress of economic theory

"Economic theory" is the rather misleading name now commonly given to the more general and abstract parts of economics. These more general parts are no less practical than what is sometimes called "applied economics", but the problems with which they have to do are less immediate and particular. The general problems of value and distribution, referred to above, have continued to hold a place among the central concerns of economic theory, but there has been a notable change in the general character of the analyses. The older economists, as we have seen, had a special interest in the long-run relations between value and costs and, save in a few notable instances, were content to dispose of the other factors governing the variations of prices and values by invoking the formula of supply and demand. One of the tasks which a newer generation of economists set for themselves was the careful examination of the mechanism of supply and demand, with special emphasis on what had been the relatively neglected factor of demand. One of the most important steps in the new analysis was taken independently but almost simultaneously (towards the end of the third quarter of the nineteenth century) by W.S. Jevons (England), Carl Menger (Austria) and Léon Walras (France and Switzerland), although it came to be known later that they had been anticipated by some earlier but forgotten writers. Adam Smith, in a famous passage, had contrasted "value in use" (high for water and relatively low for diamonds) with "value in exchange" (high for diamonds and low for water). The new analysis found a definite relation between value in use (or "utility") and exchange value. The point was that neither use value nor exchange value is an attribute of things conceived generally or abstractly, but only of specific units or increments. Water, for example, has a variety of different uses, and its exchange value at a particular time and place is directly related to the importance of its marginal uses, i.e. the uses which would have to be foregone if the supply of water were just a little smaller. Under conditions of scarcity the value of water might be exceedingly high, but only because its marginal uses were exceedingly important. In this way many an ingenious theory of value was built up by the economists whom we have named and their followers in Europe and America. Some of these writers also took another and more doubtful step. Having explained values by relating them to the choices and preferences of consumers, they pictured the economic behaviour of men, including the choices which they make as consumers, as governed by the aim of maximizing pleasure and avoiding pain, so that the fullest possible satisfaction of consumers' wants was held to yield "maximum happiness". This, it is now pretty generally agreed, is dubious psychology.

Starting with this new way of explaining the values of the goods and services which consumers buy and use, a new type of explanation of the distribution of the aggregate product among the various productive factors was developed. The central point in this new analysis was the thesis that the value of productive agents, including labour, capital and land, is derived from or, we might say, reflects the value which consumers attach to the final products of such agents. The problem of distribution, viewed from this particular angle, is the problem of discovering the general relations between the values of the final products of trade and industry and the values of the productive agents. If the demand of consumers for finished products could be construed to be a demand for definite quantities of land, labour and instruments, combined in fixed proportions, the problem would be relatively simple. But because, in fact, goods can be produced in different ways, and because, within limits, one factor can be substituted for another (as a given amount of agricultural produce can be grown by using more labour and less land or more land and less labour, or as simple and direct or highly roundabout methods, requiring small or large amounts of capital, may be used in industry) the problem is really exceedingly complex.

One general principle which has been found to help towards clarifying the problem is nothing more than an extension or generalization of a principle which the older economists had taken account of in their doctrine, previously noted, that the expansion of agricultural production is attended by diminishing returns. It came to be seen that if it is true that the amount of product dependent upon the efforts of any one labourer or any one day's labour becomes smaller when the amount of labour "applied" to or combined with a given amount of land is increased, it must also be true that the amount of product dependent upon the use of any one particular acre of land becomes smaller when the available supply of land of equal quality and accessibility is increased more rapidly than the supply of labour. Similarly, the larger the supply of capital as compared with the supply of labour and land, the smaller is the amount by which the product would be decreased if any one unit of capital were not available. How much of the aggregate product will have to be assigned to any one labourer or to the owner of a certain productive instrument or a certain piece of land will be determined, if competition is free and frictionless, by the extent to which the product really depends upon the work of that particular labourer or the use of that particular productive agent. The individual labourer, for example, counts for more, and indeed produces more, when there is a plentiful supply of productive agents other than labour. He produces less – for less depends upon his own efforts – when labour is relatively plentiful and other productive agents relatively scarce. What he earns will depend, of course, upon the value of what he produces, and his real wages – what he is able to buy – will depend as well upon the values of other products. But – assuming again that competition is unimpeded and frictionless – labour, like capital and land, will move or be moved away from employments where the value of its product is relatively small, and will move or be moved into employments where the value of its product is relatively large. There is thus a tendency – effective in a measure, though never working itself out completely – towards an equality of the values of the products attributable in different employments to labourers of comparable efficiency and to other productive agents of comparable kinds. The significant outcome of this newer analysis is not the doctrine that everyone who contributes to the communal product tends to get as his allotted share an amount equal to "what he produces". It must be remembered that differences in respect of training and of opportunity still affect men's productive capacities; that institutions, such as inheritance, help to determine how the products imputed to capital and land shall be distributed; that the swift process of industrial change often robs men of the advantages of acquired skill; that impediments of one kind or another often prevent men from transferring their labour to employments in which its product would have a higher value; that capital once fixed or invested in permanent forms is generally irretrievably committed to the fortunes of a particular type of enterprise, whatever those fortunes may prove to be. No, the doctrine that "rewards tend to be proportionate to products", taken by itself has no particular significance, except as a corrective to the even more misleading notion that rewards are in no manner related to or dependent upon productivity. The real significance of this new way of sketching the outlines of the problem of distribution is that it brings clearly into view the general form, at least, of some very important relations between production and distribution and between one distributive share and another. Relations such as these have to be kept in mind when analysing the probable repercussions of almost any projected scheme for economic betterment.

Any short summary is bound to make economic theories appear thinner and more remote from the concrete facts of economic life than they are. The structure of abstract general relations which constitutes the framework of modern economic theory has been built up, not like pure geometry, by a wholly intellectual process, but by a patient and persistent scrutiny of the complicated facts of economic life. In what is generally called "mathematical economics", however, one finds a comparatively high degree of abstraction. The one great advantage of the use of mathematics in economics is that in that way alone is it possible to depict the variety, the complexity and most of all the interdependence of the factors which determine prices, costs, supply, demand and distributive shares. Elaborate mathematical formulations of the conditions of "general economic equilibrium" have been devised, notably by Léon Walras (*Éléments d'économie politique pure*, 1874, and later editions) and Vilfredo Pareto (*Manual d'économie politique*, 1909, and other works). The principal value of these elaborate and highly abstract systems is that they put the enquirer on his guard against over-simplifying his problems, as for example, by forgetting that a change of almost any economic variable has its indirect as well as its direct effects. Other writers, notably Alfred Marshall (*Principles of Economics*, 1890, and later editions) have shown that it is possible to put a proper emphasis upon the interdependence of economic phenomena while yet examining more closely and realistically the operations of the different parts of the economic mechanism, and while taking account of factors which make for change as well as of factors which make for stability.

Among the economic phenomena to which a largely increased amount of attention has been given are interest and profits. In connection with interest, two different though related types of questions present themselves. First, is interest a necessary or in any sense an "earned" income? For what sort of productive service or sacrifice is it a payment? Is there any perceptible relation between the amount of the payment and the amount of service or sacrifice? Second, what factors govern the fluctuations of interest rates, and what determines their general level or their movements, upward or downward through longer periods of time? The first of these two types of problems was brought into prominence by the attacks of the socialists upon the private receipt of income from capital. Profits, as the term is used in the world of affairs, are generally a mixed form of income, containing elements of interest and sometimes of wages (as for superintendence or managerial direction) along with a special element (which may be positive or negative) of what the economist calls "pure profits". The distinguishing characteristic of profits is that they are not paid in accordance with any contract or agreement, but are contingent upon the success of particular undertakings. Pure profits are what is left after allowance is made for the interest and wages which would have to be paid for capital and management upon a contractual instead of a contingent basis. Pure profits, therefore, are determined by all of the factors which make for the success of an undertaking, such as foresight, fortune, quickness to see opportunities for gain and to take advantage of them. In a completely stationary and unchanging economic order, it is pretty generally agreed, the advantages of different employments of capital and of managerial ability would be so completely equalized by competition that there could be no pure profits.

The problems of modern economics

The more general and abstract parts of economics cannot be taken to be completely true and adequate accounts of the mechanism of modern economic life. They are at best serviceable approximations to partial, though important aspects of truth. There are other true generalizations which might be made. Some of these are obvious but unimportant; others, doubtless, are important, but require further scrutiny of the facts or a more penetrating insight to bring them to light. But even in their present imperfect and incomplete state the generalizations which the economist has at his hand constitute an organon of proved effectiveness, an instrument by means of which some of the results of economic changes, whether planned or not planned, may often be predicted with a fair degree of certainty. The practical problems of communal economic life are many and various. At any given time they appear to fall into a number of fairly well defined groups or classes, but as new problems challenge attention and new interests emerge, new groups appear and some of the old problems fall into new relations. Each group or class of problems has its special literature, and each engages the attention of a corps of specialists.

Among the classical problems of economics are such subjects as the mechanism of money and credit and its proper management, the incidence and the effects of various kinds of taxation, the nature of international trade and the economic consequences of protective tariffs and other devices for controlling it. In none of these fields is the ground completely explored or all of the issues definitely settled. But in each field important findings have been reached which appear to have permanent value. The outcome of the various fiscal and monetary measures to which governments resorted during the World War, and the results of the various restrictions imposed at that time upon trade and industry were in general just about what competent economists predicted they would be. Post-war experience, too, in respect of such problems as reparations and monetary stabilization, were such as to give new confirmation of some long-established economic principles.

The general form which economics took at first was determined very largely by its preoccupation with certain special types of problems, notably problems of national commercial policy. But as new types of economic problems have forced themselves upon the attention of the community, economics has had to deal with them, and in the process not only its scope, but its general pattern has inevitably been altered. The way in which a new group of "labour problems" has emerged from the labour movement of the nineteenth century is a case in point. Up to the last quarter of that century there was very little careful analysis of those problems, apart from discussions of the general theory of wages. Now, however, there is hardly a field of economic enquiry which is more thoroughly cultivated. The trades union movement and its significance, the possible gains of collective bargaining, the length of the working day, factory legislation, profit-sharing, the organization of control within the factory and its administration, labour turnover, the minimum wage, the prevention and settlement of industrial disputes, compulsory arbitration, the causes and possible cures of unemployment and social insurance in its various forms are subjects which suggest the increasing range of this new field of economic interest. It is important to observe that the attention now given to these subjects marks a change of interest rather than a change of attitude. The earlier economists, interested as they were in the exploding of popular fallacies with respect to the ways in which the prosperity of the community can best be secured and (with that end largely in view) in showing how the economic activities of individuals are so interrelated that they constitute, in their entirety, a great communal economic mechanism, often give the impression – an impression which careful study of the writings of the ablest of them will dispel – that they regarded that mechanism as self-sufficient, needing neither interference nor any sort of direction on the part of the community. They concerned themselves more with what governments could not do than with what they could wisely attempt. Modern economics strikes a different note. Its tone is less negative; it is more insistent in its search for and scrutiny of possible ways of altering the organization of the community's economic life for the better. Almost every gain has its cost, and accordingly almost every such problem resolves itself into a question of a balance of advantage. The advantages and disadvantages are hardly ever purely economic, and no purely "scientific" analysis, therefore, can completely dispose of such questions. The economist, however, may be able to gauge the general character of the probable effects of a specific change upon the production of wealth or its distribution, so that the wisdom of proposed changes can be discussed upon the basis of some knowledge of their probable consequences.

Questions associated with monopoly – its roots, its various types, its effects, its possible advantages in some circumstances, the ways in which it may be controlled – are matters with which economics have long been concerned. Economists have learned, for one thing, to distinguish between the types of monopolies which are inevitable, and have to be recognized and treated as such, and the types of monopolies which might be prevented or suppressed, in so far as the maintenance of competitive conditions in fields where competition is feasible is held to be a sound public policy. Changing methods of business organization and particularly the rise of the limited liability company have created new problems for economics. On the one hand there is a new opportunity for large numbers of people, not merely to put their savings out at interest, but to participate in the profits (and losses) of large undertakings. On the other hand, along with this larger diffusion of industrial ownership, there are new opportunities for the concentration of industrial control. This situation gives rise to new communal problems, and these, in turn, create new fields for economic enquiries. The general theory of economic equilibrium, which includes an analysis of how exchange values and distributive shares "tend" to be determined under the operation of the forces which make for a general balancing of supply and demand, retains its importance in economics. But in recent years economists have come to give increased attention to the factors which make for economic change and to the persistence of maladjustments in the mechanism of production and trade. The recurring phenomena known as industrial fluctuations or business cycles, with their attendant costs and wastes, are receiving a very much larger amount of study than was formerly given to them.

The most striking and possibly the most important characteristic of the newer work in economics, as contrasted with the older, is its greater realism. Not that it manages to do without abstract conceptions, but that it takes its conceptions, so far as it can, from the world of affairs. The older economists, for example, in their efforts to dig beneath that surface view of economic life which had deceived the mercantilists, held that money was merely a convenient instrument or tool.

From their point of view, which remains a significant point of view, they were right. They also held that money prices were "exchange values" expressed in terms of money, making value the basic and price the derived conception, and thus inverting their real relation. This procedure, again, was not without reason, and in some special types of economic analysis it remains convenient to assume that trade is conducted by barter, without the use of money. In general, however, modern economists find it better to deal with money prices rather than "exchange values". They have observed that modern processes of price-making and distribution depend upon the use of money and credit, not only in the sense that processes so complex would be unthinkable otherwise, but also in the further sense that the use of money and credit has certain special and discernible effects upon the outcome. Reliable records of economic activities – or at any rate of their results – are now brought together and published by governments or made public by business organizations on a scale, in respect of both volume and variety, which would have excited the envy of the older economists. A much wider range of economic experience is now available for study and analysis. In dealing with this new material – virtually a by-product of the activities which it records – economics again has to accommodate itself to a more realistic view. It has to deal with economic events in the forms in which they really occur, and it has to search for the systematic relations which run through these masses of real events. But although the interests of economics have become more varied and concrete, and although its conceptions have become better adapted to the handling of the facts of economic life in the form in which those facts present themselves, economics remain a communal or political science. Particular findings or tenets have been discarded, and new ones have been set up in their stead. But the general picture of a scheme of communal economic life, sufficiently ordered to make an analysis of it possible, and imperfect enough to give point and purpose to such an analysis in spite of changes of view-point and method, remains.

Bibliography

Monroe, Arthur Eli, (Ed.) (1924) *Early Economic Thought*, New York: Gordon Press, a compilation of well chosen selections from economic literature prior to Adam Smith; Gemähling, Paul (Ed.) (1925), *Les grands économistes*, Paris: L. Tenin, with excellent bibliographies, covers the subsequent period also. For the history of the earlier period the best single reference is Oncken, August (1922) (3rd edn.) *Geschichte der Nationalökonomie*, Leipzig: C.L. Hirschfeld; for the later period the *Histoire des doctrines économiques* by Gide, Charles and Rist, Charles (1926) (5th edn.), Paris: Societé anonyme du Recueil Sirey, is similarly useful. An English translation (1915) *History of Economic Doctrines*, Boston: Heath, of an earlier edition of the last-named work is available. Recent developments are treated in detail in Surányi-Unger, Theo (1927) *Die Entwicklung der theoretischen Volkswirtschaftslehre im ersten Viertel des 20 Jahrhundert*, Jena: G. Fischer; a more accurate though less complete survey will be found in Mayer, Hans, and others (Eds.) (1927–29) *Die Wirtschaftstheorie der Gegenwart*, Wien: J. Springer. See also for special branches, Cannan, Edwin, (1917) *A History of the Theories of Production and Distribution in English Political Economy from 1776 to 1848* (3rd edn.), London: P.S. King and Son; Lewinski, Jan Stanislaw (1922) *The Founders of Political Economy*, London: P.S. King; Bonar, James (1922) *Philosophy and Political Economy* (3rd edn.), London: G. Allen and Unwin; Bagehot, Walter (1879) *Economic Studies*, London and NY: Longmans, Green and Co; Altmann, S.P. and others (1908) *Die Entwicklung der deutschen Volkswirtslehre im neunzehnten Jahrhundert* (2 vols.); Bousquet, G.H. (1927) *Essai sur l'évolution de la pensée économique*, Paris: M. Girard; and the following standard treatises: Ingram, J.K. (new edn. 1919) *A History of Political Economy*, London: A & C Black; Haney, L.H. (1911) *History of Economic Thought*, NY: Macmillan; Dubois, A. (1903) *Précis de l'histoire des doctrines économiques,* Paris: A. Rousseau; Denis, Hector (2 vols., 1904, 1907) *Histoire des systèmes économiques et socialistes*, Paris: V. Giard and E. Briere; Gonnard, René (3 vols., 1921–27) *Histoire des doctrines économiques*, Paris: Nouvelle librairie nationale; Rambaud, J. (2 vols., 1907–8) *Histoire des doctrines économiques*, Paris: L. Larose; Bücher, K., Schumpeter, J.A. and von Wieser, F. (1913) *Epochen der Dogmengeschichte* (in *Grundriss der Sozialökonomik*, Tübingen: J.C.B. Mohr. Articles on various special topics, with bibliographies, will be found in the *Handwörterbuch der Staatswissenschaften* (4th edn., 3 vols., 1923–8), Jena: Fischer; and in the *Dictionary of Political Economy*, edited by Sir R.H.I. Palgrave (revised edn., edited by Henry Higgs, 3 vols., 1926) London: Macmillan.

12 Capital

Encyclopaedia Britannica (1928) London: The Encyclopaedia Britannica Company.
793–7

In economics, capital may be defined as produced wealth used productively for gain. It is thus distinguished from land and other natural resources, which are not "produced", and from consumers' goods, which are not used productively for gain. The economist's conception of capital is unlike the conceptions which govern the practice of accountants. The reason is that many things which are properly counted as part of the capital of a person or a firm make no part of the aggregate capital of society. A house occupied by a tenant is part of its owner's capital, but it is not for that reason any more a part of the productive apparatus of the community than it would be if it were owned by its occupant. A may include what B owes him in an inventory of his capital, but in the aggregate view A's claim and B's liability cancel. Patents, copyrights, the franchises of public service companies, and other exclusive privileges, or the goodwill of a business undertaking, its established claim upon the preferences of buyers, have similar status. Such things are sometimes called "acquisitive capital", to distinguish them from the things which constitute the true capital of the community.

There is a sense in which a community's whole stock of accumulated wealth, including durable goods in the possession of consumers, may be said to be its capital. A consumer who buys durable goods – a house, a piano, a piece of furniture – from which he expects to get a long series of uses, is thereby providing for the future, and so far as a community is supplied with such goods its future wants are in that measure provided for. Whether such accumulations should be called capital is a question of convenience, not of principle. The distinction between goods which provide for future wants and the goods and services which merely provide for the present is doubtless important, but the distinction between using goods in production for the market, i.e. in production for gain, and using them as part of one's own equipment for living is also important, and most economists have preferred to emphasise this last distinction by drawing a line between capital and consumers' goods. The line cannot be drawn with perfect precision, however. It is impracticable to make a sharp distinction either between the capital which a farmer uses in producing food for the market and the equipment which he uses in producing food for his own household, or between the latter and the equipment which a housewife uses in preparing food for the table. But these are small matters and do not affect the practical utility of the conception of a special category of produced wealth which is used productively for gain.

There is also a sense in which personal qualities, as well as goods, may be said to be capital. Expenditure for education or for any training which makes a man a more efficient producer may properly be regarded as an "investment of capital". The personal earnings which are attributable to acquired qualities of skill and efficiency might easily be treated as interest or profits upon "personal capital". Economists have found it more convenient, however, to adhere in this particular to the practice of the business world, and to treat such earnings as elements in wages. Similarly, while it is important to take account of the motives which lead men to employ capital in improving land (e.g. in fertilizing or draining it), no useful purpose is served by attempting always to distinguish between the return attributable to the capital which has been incorporated in land and the rent of the land itself.

The varieties of capital

Historically, the distinction between commercial capital and industrial capital is of prime importance, for capital was employed on a large scale in trade and transport long before any considerable use was found for it in industry. What date should be assigned to the beginnings of "modern capitalism" or of "capitalistic institutions" depends upon what is meant. Most of the history of industrial capitalism falls within the last 200 years, while many of the characteristic institutions of commercial capitalism can be traced back to the towns of the later middle ages, or even to the ancient civilizations of the eastern Mediterranean. The distinction between commercial and industrial capital remains important for an understanding of the part which capital plays in modern economic life, but it is better to draw the line, not between the capital used by traders and the capital used by manufacturers, but between stocks (raw materials, auxiliary materials, goods in process, finished goods) and instruments (machines, tools, railways, factory buildings, etc.). Much the same distinction is conveyed by the terms circulating capital and fixed capital. The characteristic which gives circulating capital the quality of capital, however, is not that it "circulates" (whether in the way in which raw materials reappear in the finished product or in the way in which goods pass from manufacturer to merchant and from merchant to consumer) but that the processes of production and distribution require that large stocks of it shall be maintained.

Next in importance to the distinction between instruments and stocks is the distinction between specialized capital and unspecialized capital. A railway track or a complicated machine is serviceable only within the narrow range of uses for which is was constructed. Its value depends upon the demand for the special services which it is capable of rendering. Raw materials that enter into different sorts of finished products, tools and machines of standard types, are examples of less highly specialized capital. The difference is one of degree. Most capital is partly specialized, in the sense that it has only a certain range of uses and that it is better adapted to some uses than to others. Money, because it can be used in acquiring goods and services of whatever sort, is sometimes held to be a wholly free and unspecialized form of capital. But is money capital? It is true that stocks of ready money as well as stocks of goods are required for the operations of industry and trade, and that these stocks are not maintained without expense. But it is also true of some of the most important forms of money (including the notes of banks and governments and bank deposits subject to cheque) that the holder's capital is offset by the issuer's debt or liability. Furthermore, the supply of money may be increased without there being any attendant increase of the real wealth of the community or even of the aggregate serviceability of its stocks of money. In short, money may properly be counted as capital if it is recognised clearly that it constitutes a separate category, with special characteristics of its own.

The earnings of capital

That capital contributes nothing to the production of wealth beyond the labour which it embodies, that it merely enables its owners to appropriate an unearned share of the total product, is a tenet held by disciples of Karl Marx and by other critics of the existing economic order. This tenet appears to rest upon a misconception of the services which both labour and capital render. Neither labour nor capital is inherently productive. Just as land will grow thistles as well as figs, so labour and capital alike may be wasted in making things which no one wants and which therefore have no value. Labour and capital are without value except as their products are valuable. In one sense, therefore, labour and capital may be said to derive their value from the value of their products. Taken by itself, however, this is a misleading statement. No product will have value if it can be reproduced without diverting any part of the supply of scarce and valuable productive agents (labour, capital, and natural resources) from other possible uses. When we say that capital is productive we imply not only that capital can be used so as to increase the supply of valuable goods but also that the supply of capital itself is in some degree limited or inelastic.

Nature furnishes free productive agents which, merely because no economy need be practised in our use of them, are not productive in an economic as distinguished from a purely physical sense. Thus in the economic sense the wind is not productive but windmills are. We harness natural forces so as to use them in production, but we attribute the product wholly to the harness. This is inevitable, for the harness is the only factor in the situation which we can add or take away or which we can vary as we please, so that the product depends upon it. Capital would not be deemed productive if its supply were not limited, nor would it be deemed scarce if it were not productive. Whether the earnings of capital are attributable to its productivity or to its scarcity is therefore a meaningless question. That a larger (physical) product can be got by using capital does not explain why a specific part of the product has to be attributed to capital and assigned to it as its earnings. The economic productivity of capital, its scarcity, and its earning power are merely different aspects of the way in which the amount of the product depends upon the supply of capital. For an understanding of this relation of dependency between product and capital it is necessary to take account both of the productive uses of capital and of the circumstances which limit its supply.

The uses of capital

Consider first the uses of instruments – tools, machines, prime movers, and auxiliary apparatus. Inert and passive in themselves, from the point of view of economics, instruments are goods which are produced and used in the producing of other goods for the reason that such procedure is economical. A conspicuous characteristic of the procedure is that it is indirect or roundabout. There is nothing inherently economical in roundabout methods, but the most economical methods often happen to be roundabout. The degree of roundaboutness which is most economical generally depends upon the amount of a particular kind of work which is to be done. And also the making and use of instruments involves an extension of the principle of the division of labour, and the division of labour, as Adam Smith observed, depends upon the extent of the market. The use of capital on a large scale in industry came later than its use in commerce, for the reason that not until there were markets which were able to absorb large outputs of standard types of goods was it profitable to make any extensive use of roundabout methods of production. Once established, however, industrial capitalism showed that it had within itself the seeds of its own growth. Cheaper goods, improved means of transport, and the increased advantages of specialization led to larger markets, so that the economies of industrial capitalism grew in a cumulative way. The increasing division of labour, by breaking up complex industrial processes into simpler parts, not only invited a larger use of instruments, but also prompted the invention of new types of instruments. Along with these changes and holding with respect to them the dual relation of cause and effect, the exploitation of the world's stores of mechanical energy extended enormously the effective range of the use of instruments. Improvements in industry and in transport made the world capable of sustaining a larger population, while the growth of population, in turn, by creating larger markets, made it profitable for industry to use methods of a higher degree of roundaboutness.

The uses of stocks are various. (1) Stocks are held in order to give time for spontaneous or induced changes of a desirable kind to occur. The maturing of wine or tobacco, the fructifying of the seed in the soil, the drying and seasoning of the wood used in cabinet work, are examples of a very large number of processes which either cannot be hastened or cannot advantageously be hastened beyond a certain point. (2) Stocks have to be held in order that the products of agriculture and of other seasonal industries may be spread throughout the year in accordance with the requirements of consumers. (3) The technical requirements of production make it necessary that stocks of "goods in process" be held. (4) At various points in the linked chains of agencies through which goods pass on their way from the producer of raw materials to the ultimate buyer of the finished product stocks are accumulated. This helps to safeguard buyers, at whatever point in the chain, against the inconvenience and losses of delays, and it makes for economy in transport and handling. Furthermore, even if production and trade were always managed with complete efficiency and if producers and traders always had complete knowledge of the market, it would be impracticable and uneconomical to keep all of the various processes of production and distribution moving together so as to maintain a smooth and even flow of goods from the first producers to the final buyers. Stocks are like the reservoirs in which the waters from variable and intermittent streams are impounded so as to guard against both floods and drought.

The supply of capital

The use of capital saves time, in the sense that a larger product can be had with a given amount of labour. But it increases the average interval of time which elapses before the products of a given day's labour reach their final form and pass into the hands of consumers. Present work, however far away its final fruition in a finished product may be, has to be paid for in the present, and so do the present uses of land and capital – unless, indeed, the owners of land and capital can be induced to defer their claims. These present payments are advanced in anticipation of the payments which consumers will make later for finished products. This is the central fact of the capitalistic system of production.

Interest is the premium which is paid for advances. The money incomes which employers, labourers, capitalists, and landowners receive are used in part to pay for immediate personal services and for the finished goods that have been produced in the past, and in part to pay (as advances) for the present expenses of forwarding the production of goods for future markets. In those future markets, it is expected, the goods will sell for enough to cover the advances, with interest added. If the returns finally secured prove on the whole to be inadequate, or even promise to be inadequate, the demand for advances will fall off and the rate of interest will decline. But if industry is prosperous, if the prospect is that in general some net profit will be left after the cost of advances has been met, the demand for advances will increase and the rate of interest will rise, so that a smaller part of the current stream of money incomes will be expended for finished goods and personal services and a larger part will be used in producing instruments and in increasing stocks. There is thus an effective tendency towards an unstable sort of equilibrium, in which the most important variable factors (human nature being taken as constant) are, first, the economies of capitalistic methods of production, and second, the rate of interest. In the long run, however, what part of the product is imputed or attributed to capital rather than to labour or to natural resources will be determined by the rate of interest. How much larger the total product is than it would be if no capital were used is mostly a matter of technology. How much of the product is, in the economic sense, attributed to capital as its product, is largely a matter of the price which has to be paid for advances.

The operations of banks have an important effect upon the way in which advances are made. Banks are more than mere intermediaries between lenders (depositors) and borrowers. So far as their own obligations (notes and deposits) will serve as money, and within the limits set by the necessity of maintaining their own solvency, they can make advances to industry and trade without there being any prior saving. In fact, because consumers' incomes will be increased as the funds advanced by the banks are paid out to cover the expenses of producing goods, the demand (in terms of money offered) for goods and services will be larger than before. If stocks cannot be increased as rapidly as the demand for finished goods increases, prices will rise, and a disguised form of involuntary saving will thus be imposed upon all consumers whose incomes have not increased proportionately. Furthermore, if manufacturers and traders gain by reason of the rise of prices (their expenses not having increased proportionately), they are fairly sure to reinvest some of their profits. The real burden of the saving which makes these new advances possible falls more heavily upon the persons who lose (in purchasing power) because of the rise of prices than upon the manufacturers and traders who gain. But profits, of course, do not depend upon price fluctuations alone. A high general level of profits, brought about as the result of whatever causes, will increase both the demand for and the supply of advances. In consequence there may be an unduly rapid increase of instruments and stocks – a circumstance which probably plays a part in the recurring industrial fluctuations which have come to be known as trade cycles. Business profits are probably the largest single source of investment funds. Estimates made by A.L. Bowley, Sir Josiah Stamp and W.I. King indicate that in Great Britain and the United States fully half of the current supply of advances comes from that source.

Non-productive uses and forms of capital

No simple and consistent view of the nature and uses of capital can be altogether true to the complicated facts of economic life. The conception of capital as a productive agent is justified because it emphasises what are, in fact, the most important uses of capital. Advances are made mostly so that capital may be used in furthering the production of goods. In some important fields of business enterprise, however, large amounts of money are invested, not in producing goods which consumers already want, but in inducing them to buy certain particular things. The purpose of a considerable part of what are commonly called selling expenses is not to supply goods to satisfy an existing demand, but to shift demand from other channels. Such expenditures are not always wholly productive. Scrupulously truthful advertising may be of real service to the consumer, perplexed by the wide range of alternative choices and without firsthand knowledge of the qualities of competing goods. Advertising, furthermore, by helping to create larger markets for particular types of goods which can be produced much more economically if produced on a large scale, may itself be a factor in the economising of the productive resources of the community. But these are incidental and by no means necessary results of what are primarily competitive or acquisitive uses of capital. Advertising may lead sometimes to the education of the consumer, but it may also lead to the exploitation of weakness and ignorance. While it may sometimes open the way to real economies in production, it may at other times involve a pure waste of resources which might otherwise have been used productively. Its importance has been fully recognised in all forms of productive business.

One other qualification of what has been said about the nature of capital remains to be noted. A nation's capital may be taken to be either (1) the capital within the nation's boundaries, irrespective of its ownership, or (2) the capital owned within the nation, irrespective of its situation. In the second sense a nation's capital includes the net excess of its external or foreign assets (property and credits) over its external liabilities (domestic property owned abroad plus foreign debts). In two respects this view is inconsistent with the definition of capital "as produced wealth used productively for gain". In the first place, credits are included, which, in an international stock-taking, would cancel against debts. In the second place, foreign holdings of land, of mineral rights, of concessions, and of other valuable privileges, as well as of instruments and stocks, are included. There is nothing unreasonable in this. Investments in landed property or in mineral rights outside of a nation's own boundaries make part of its national savings and affect the amount of its annual national income. In short, in determining the amount of a nation's capital, it is necessary, for some purposes, to abandon at the national frontiers the communal conception of capital, and to adopt a private or acquisitive conception, such as is employed in accountancy. Similarly, while the phrase, "the export of capital", might conceivably be taken to refer to the movement of instruments and stocks from one country to another, it is more generally taken to denote the increase of the net foreign investments of the people of a given country.

Bibliography

von Böhm Bawerk, E. (1921) in *Kapital and Kapitalzins,* 4th edn., Jena: G. Fischer, provides an acute critical analysis of the principal theories of capital and interest. An English translation of an earlier edition of this important work is available in two separate volumes, *Capital and Interest* (1890) and *Positive Theory of Capital* (1891), London and NY: Macmillan. Standard modern treatments will be found in Marshall, A. (1920) *Principles of Economics,* 8th edn., London: Macmillan; Cassel, G. (1903) *The Nature and Necessity of Interest,* London and NY: Macmillan, and (1923) *Theory of Social Economy* (trans. J. McCabe), London: T. F. Unwin; Ely, R.T. and others (1920) *Outlines of Economics,* 4th edn., NY: Macmillan; Taussig, F.W. (1921) *Principles of Economics,* 3rd edn., NY: Macmillan; Landry, A. (1904) *L'intérêt du Capital,* Paris: V. Giard and E. Briere; Clark, J.B.

(1899) *The Distribution of Wealth*, NY and London: Macmillan, distinguishes between capital, viewed as a "fund", and the specific capital goods, including land, in which at any given time the fund is embodied. Fisher, Irving (1906) *Nature of Capital and Income* and *The Rate of Interest*, NY: Macmillan, identifies capital with wealth, measured in terms of its money value. Schumpeter, J. (1912) *Theorie der wirtschaftlichen Entwicklung*, Leipzig: Dunker and Humblot, emphasizes the parts which progress and enterprise play in making capital productive. Davenport, H.J. (1913) *The Economics of Enterprise*, NY: Macmillan, holds that in a competitive society capital must be defined as an instrument of acquisition rather than of production. The most influential statement of the view that income from capital is unearned and is based on exploitation is Karl Marx's *Capital*. For older views of the nature and services of capital see especially Adam Smith, *The Wealth of Nations* (1776), Book II, and J.S. Mill, *Principles of Political Economy* (1848), Book I. Some of the differences in the views of modern economists, it may be observed, are more apparent than real, and come from differences in definitions, in emphasis, or in the particular problems which the different writers have attacked.

13 Supply and demand

Encyclopaedia Britannica (1928) London: The Encyclopaedia Britannica Company. 579–80

Economics or political economy, is sometimes defined as the science of supply and demand. Although this is an inadequate definition it cannot be said to be altogether misleading. A very important part of Economics, and the part which probably has the best title to the name of science, has to do with the operations of supply and demand and with the way in which variations of supply and demand are related to the movements of prices and to changes in the production and distribution of wealth. The "law of supply and demand" was not invented or discovered by the economists, however, nor do they lean very heavily upon it as a general explanatory formula. Long before there was any systematic analysis of economic processes men had observed that prices vary with supply and demand, and from the earliest days, traders have had to take account of that circumstance. The economist's task has been to scrutinise those characteristics of human behaviour and of the physical environment which determine the various forms or patterns in which supply and demand appear and to enquire into the complicated interactions of the demand for and the supply of different commodities and services.

Elementary principles

Consider the familiar theorem that the price of a commodity must be such as to make supply and demand equal. If supply is taken to mean the amount sold and demand the amount bought the theorem is mere tautology, for supply and demand become different names for the amount transferred from sellers to buyers at any price whatever. But if it be understood that demand means the amount which buyers would be willing to take at a specified price, that supply means similarly the amount which sellers would be willing to part with at a specified price, and that demand and supply vary in some systematic and continuous way and in opposite directions as the price is raised or lowered, the theorem has meaning and significance, for there will be one price, and only one price, at which supply and demand will be equal.

In another elementary theorem, namely that an increase of demand for a commodity will raise its price, that an increase of supply will lower it, and that a decrease of supply or of demand will have an opposite effect, other meanings are attached to changes of supply and demand. Here an increase of demand or supply means an increase of the amounts which will be taken at given prices, not an increase which is dependent upon a reduction of price. The general state of supply and demand, in the sense specified in the preceding paragraph, can be represented by lists or "schedules" of "supply prices" and "demand prices". In this other sense, however, supply and demand are regarded as independent variables, and a change of supply or demand means an alteration of the schedule of supply prices or demand prices, such as might come on the one hand from a change of consumer's preferences or an enlarging of the market or, on the other hand, from a change of costs of production.

It is proper to assume that at any given time the immediate general condition of supply might be represented by a schedule in which the progressively higher prices which are required to evoke a progressively larger supply are set forth. But if the commodity is one which can be produced more economically if produced in large quantities, the ultimate effect of an increase of demand, in the sense of an increase of the amounts which will be taken at specified prices, will ordinarily be to reduce the price per unit at which these larger amounts will be supplied. In a schedule of supply prices constructed on the assumption that sufficient time is allowed to permit the necessary economies to be effected, larger supply will be associated with lower prices. When the long-period schedule of supply prices is of this type, the commodity is said to be produced under conditions of decreasing costs or of increasing returns. When, on the other hand, because of the scarcity of some necessary productive factor, increased supply cannot be had, even in the long run, except at a higher price, the condition is described as one of increasing costs or of diminishing returns. The factors which give rise to increasing returns should not be confused with the circumstance that in many industries certain outlays (e.g. for plant and equipment) have to be incurred in advance or with the further circumstance that in a growing industry such outlays are ordinarily considerably larger than the volume of output immediately in prospect would require. Under such circumstances the additional or "prime" costs incurred by reason of an increase of output may be relatively small. Furthermore, with a progressive increase of output there will be a progressive diminution of costs per unit of output, because the general, supplementary, or "overhead" costs will be spread over a large number of units. But although when the market is sluggish or when competition is especially keen, prices may be cut to a point where they barely suffice to cover the additional or "prime" costs, this condition, which cannot be lasting, should not be confused with a true condition of increasing returns, for this last condition is to be found only when a gradual increase of output is attended, in the long run, with genuine economies.

Interactions of supply and demand

The results obtained by taking account only of the supply of and demand for a particular commodity in relation to its price are no more than a first approximation to the truth. In isolating, for reasons of practical convenience, the factors which determine the price of any one commodity, taken by itself, economists are accustomed to assume that the value of money, to both buyers and sellers, is constant. This means that no account is taken of the way in which changes in the amount of money which consumers expend for the one commodity will affect their ability to buy other commodities, or the way in which an increase of the production of the one commodity will affect the ability of producers to supply other commodities. There are many instances of joint or complementary demand, as for fruit and sugar or for automobiles and petrol, and of joint supply, as of mutton and wool, of coal-gas and coke, of cotton and cottonseed. The general rule is, however, that consumers' outlays for any one commodity can be increased only by reducing the amounts which they expend for other commodities, and that more of any one commodity can be produced only by displacing other possible uses of productive resources. This general rule is not inconsistent with the fact that, making abstraction of the use of money as a medium of exchange, the supply of any one commodity is an expression of the demand of its producers for other commodities and services.

There is a sense in which supply and demand, seen in the aggregate, are merely different aspects of a single situation. It is for this reason that some of the older economists held that general overproduction is impossible – a theorem which, though not really erroneous, has proved to be misleading. The *effective* demand of the producers of one commodity for other products depends not only upon how much they produce, but also upon the relative demand of other producers for that particular commodity as compared with other products. Only so far as the demand for a particular commodity is elastic is it true in any significant sense that an increase of its supply is an effective increase of demand for other commodities. There may be and often are maladjustments of supply and demand. Furthermore, production in general may at one time outrun and at another time fail to keep pace with the expansion of money incomes. In either event there will be general fluctuations of prices, attended, as experience shows, by changes in the relative levels of the prices of different classes of goods and services.

The general form of the relations of supply, demand and price which obtain when all products are taken into account can be depicted mathematically in systems of equations, and thus the general character of the whole interdependent structure of prices can be laid bare. But empirical (statistical) studies of the relations between the fluctuations of the production of various staple commodities and fluctuations of their prices have shown that the first approximation previously referred to is generally a useful and often a surprisingly accurate approximation. It is necessary, of course, to allow for the effects of contemporaneous changes of the general purchasing power of money, and it is sometimes necessary to allow also for the effects of other important disturbing circumstances. But it is not necessary to take account of complications of a secondary order of importance in order to obtain "empirical laws of demand" for such commodities as wheat, cotton, sugar, beef and potatoes which appear to be fairly reliable, at least over periods of some years.

Inelastic supply

The rule that supply and demand may be regarded as functions of or dependent upon price must be so interpreted, of course, as to allow for the circumstance that the supply of something is fixed and is in no way responsive to an increase of price. As the production of other goods increases the prices of these non-reproducible forms of wealth must inevitably increase, unless the demand for them falls off. If these non-reproducible things are necessary instruments in the production of other goods, as land is, then other goods will be produced under conditions of diminishing returns, unless this disadvantage can be offset by improvements in productive processes or by cheaper supplies of other necessary productive instruments. For some purposes it is convenient to assume that the aggregate supply of reproducible goods, or of reproducible productive goods, is fixed for the time being. The problems of supply and demand then have to do merely with the apportioning, by exchange, of an existing stock of goods, or with the assigning of productive instruments to the most important of their various possible uses. Thus the increase of the supply of labour in a given industry or a given locality may be taken to depend largely upon a possible transfer of workers from other industries or other localities. Whether labour in the aggregate may be said to have a supply price (i.e. to be responsive in the long run to an increase of wages) is a question to which the Malthusian theory of population gave a more nearly unqualified affirmative answer than would be supported by the present opinion of scholars.

Part III

Commerce: The marketplace of the world

14 The creator of wealth

The vast traffic between nations upon which the prosperity of the world depends

How the world goes to market

The Book of Popular Science (1924; revised 1929) New York: The Grolier Society. Group IX Ch. 1: 110–16

We are accustomed to think of the farmer, the miner, and the manufacturer as the real producers of wealth. The trader and the transporting agent seem to us to be concerned merely with the distribution of wealth already produced. We may be forced to admit that their services are necessary, but we think of them as in some way taking toll from the wealth others have produced. A little reflection. however, will show us that such a view of things is wholly false. Neither the farmer nor the manufacturer creates anything really "new." Utilizing the forces of nature, they merely give new forms to things, forms which fit things better for use in the satisfaction of human needs. But it is not alone sufficient that things should be in the form in which they are needed. If a thing is really to constitute an article of wealth, it must be brought to the place at which it is needed and be available at the time at which it is needed. The creation of wealth, then, involves not only changes in form, but also changes in place and in time.

Within the boundaries of the United States there is the widest variation of natural products and advantages. No other nation has been so richly endowed by nature. But our coal and our iron, our copper, our precious metals, our oil fields, our cotton, wheat, and corn are rarely found in close juxtaposition. They are distributed over wide areas. If our people, like those of the Middle Ages, lived in village communities, with little or no exchange of commodities between different communities, the amount of wealth we could produce would be small indeed. For in order that there may be wealth there must be markets. Commerce creates markets. It makes the products of any one region available for the rest of the country.

The United States is in itself an economic empire. It is more nearly self-sufficient, economically, less dependent on outside sources of supply, than any other country of advanced economic civilization. And yet it is wholly lacking in certain metals, in many valuable woods, in a variety of fibers, in some indispensable miscellaneous articles, such as rubber or coffee or tea, in a number of important vegetable oils, and in various fruits and spices. Without these things the United States might have developed a relatively high economic civilization, but at vastly more toil and cost.

But we shall still fall short of seeing the full significance of commerce in modern civilization if we see in it merely an important factor in the world's growth in wealth and in population. The quality of modern living, the structure of our political institutions, the liberties we cherish, are in no small measure the outcome of the growth of commercial enterprise. The typical medieval village was economically self-contained and self-sufficient. It was economically isolated. Now no isolated community can be wholly free. Robinson Crusoe was not free; or better, perhaps, such a statement means nothing. Liberty is a social fact. It has no meaning except as an aspect of human relations. Isolation, moreover, makes for stability and conservatism, for the hardening of habit and custom into a fixed and rigid scheme of life.

In isolation, as Professor C.H. Cooley has suggested, ideas descend vertically, that is, they come down from the past, transmitted from generation to generation. Thus they are old ideas. With free communication between communities ideas tend more and more to come in sidewise, that is, they come from the outside. They are new ideas. Communities without commerce stagnate.

In the isolated village, with its fixed system of tradition and custom, a man could live his life only by conforming to what custom and tradition required. But when trade developed it brought new contacts, new problems, calling for initiative and energy, giving opportunity and meaning to human freedom. Rightly enough were the early traders called "adventurers."

In the advance of civilization the trader leads the way

Political freedom, as we understand it, appeared first in the towns of the later Middle Ages. These towns were communities of traders. There men found a freedom from the restrictions which obtained in the isolated country villages. There they found new and varied opportunities. Trade between the towns became world trade in the modern sense after the discovery of America and of the sea route to India at the end of the fifteenth century. In the advance of civilization into the new worlds thus opened up, the trader, along with the missionary, led the way.

Doubtless economic civilization today remains far short of its goal of equality of opportunity for all. But it is important for us to remember that such a goal could not be conceived of, even as a remote ideal, by the men of antiquity or of the Middle Ages. Freedom of commercial enterprise has brought with it enlarged and enriched notions of the meaning and significance of life. That the world now ranks men according to their own achievements and only in small measure by the status into which they were born is to be attributed in no small measure to the fact that commerce and the system of free enterprise that has grown up along with and as a part of commerce gives little weight to anything but achievement and success.

How the Law Merchant differed in spirit from other systems prevalent

An illustration of the significance of the relation of the growth of commerce to the growth of freedom is found in the history of the Law Merchant. This was in the beginning merely a body of rules laid down by medieval merchants for regulating their relations one with another. The old rules of medieval law hampered them. Moreover, their trade created new situations and problems to which the old rules did not apply. The Law Merchant was different in spirit from the then prevailing systems of law. It made little of distinctions of outward form, of the status of the parties to a litigation, of title or sex, in order that it might deal with rights and duties on a broadly human basis. It had to do very largely with contract, that is, with free agreement. It has long been absorbed into the general body of our law, where it has had a most wholesome influence and effect.

Quite in keeping with what we have seen to be the general character of free commercial activity is the fact that in the growth of our economic civilization it has been commerce, rather than agriculture or industry, that has led the way. Production is limited by the market. It can advance only as markets are increased. Commerce creates markets. The industrial revolution at the end of the eighteenth century, when the factory system came into being and when the use of power was first successfully applied to manufactures, cannot be ascribed merely to the great inventions of Watt, Kay, Hargreave, Arkwright, and Crompton. These mechanical improvements were, from one point of view, really called into being by the fact that the growth of English commerce, and especially the development of the Indian market, had, for the first time, made the factory system and large-scale production possible.

Men do not produce or manufacture goods in the blind hope that in some way buyers will be found. In manufacturing and agriculture alike production increases only when larger markets are available. The history of commerce has been the history of the growth of markets. Markets can grow either extensively or intensively. One sort of growth is a broadening of the territory which affords the market to the commerce of the nation; the other sort of growth is bound up with the creation of new wants and new standards of living. It is commerce more than anything else that has given men new wants. The status of economic civilization is determined by the number, character, and quality of the wants which constitute a people's standard of living. Just so far as commerce has taught men to know and to want more things and better things, just so far it has been the moving force in the progress of economic civilization.

In medieval times the merchant "suffered even more," as Professor Clive Day has put it, "from bad men than from bad roads." Government was weak; traders were often strangers, and strangers were suspect. There was an old English law, "If a man come from afar, or a stranger, go out of the highway, and he then neither shout nor blow a horn, he is to be accounted a thief, either to be slain or to be redeemed."

Now, save in time of war, every civilized country undertakes to give full and adequate protection to the trade and the traders of other countries. For the most part these undertakings are embodied in commercial treaties between different nations. A feature very commonly found in commercial treaties is the "most-favored nation clause," by which each party to the treaty undertakes not to discriminate against the trade or the traders of the other party. A nation often binds itself to give the traders of other nations as favorable treatment in some respects and as adequate protection as it gives its own citizens.

A very important and interesting development of the principle of the commercial treaty is found in a number of multilateral treaties or conventions which are designed to prevent different forms of unfair international commercial competition. It is in this way that international protection is given to such valuable commercial rights as patents, trade-marks, firm names, and brands.

The modern trader thus has back of him the countenance and support of his own government and the protection of the governments of the other nations with which he trades.

15 The rise of population in great countries

The Book of Popular Science (1924; revised 1929) New York: The Grolier Society. Extract from Group IX Ch. 2: 254–5

In the last century and a quarter the population of the United States has grown by over one hundred million. We are too likely to think of this phenomenal increase as something unique and unparalleled. It is, in fact, merely an unusually striking example of the way in which the development of commerce and communication, the opening up of new resources and the resulting industrial cooperation of the whole world have brought about an enormous increase in the number of human beings.

In the last two hundred years or so the population of the world has just about doubled. This is possibly the most significant single fact of modern history.

In 1760 there were probably not more than 130,000,000 people in all of Europe. In 1914 there were 450,000,000. Half of this increase was subsequent to 1872. The population of England in 1761 was only 6,700,000, and it was probably as much as 6,000,000 two hundred years before that date. By 1831, when England had come to rely more largely upon commerce as a source of wealth, although she was still trying to raise most of her own food supply, the population had more than doubled. Since that time England has developed her manufacturing and commercial interests and has imported a larger and larger proportion of her food supply and raw materials from newer countries. As a result, England now supports a population of nearly 40,000,000 people on a higher average level of comfort and well-being than was possible for her 7,000,000 inhabitants a hundred and fifty years ago.

It must not be thought that this growth of the populations of the western world has been at the expense of the more backward peoples. Whenever commerce has carried western civilization and industrial methods the numbers of the native population have more often increased than decreased. Such, for example, is true of the Indians of Mexico and of South America, who are more numerous than they were at the time of the discovery of America. Such also is true of the native population of the Philippines, of India and of Egypt. Japan offers a striking illustration. For at least a hundred and fifty years before it opened its doors to the commerce of other nations its population had remained nearly stationary. Since 1871 it has increased from 33,000,000 to approximately 60,000,000.

Japan is not an isolated instance. The island of Java has grown from about 4,000,000 in 1800 to nearly 35,000,000. That island, only one-third as large as the state of California, now contains about one-third as many people as the whole United States. Viewing the whole experience of human history, we are entitled to say that millions now live where nature grudged existence to thousands.

For hundreds of years it had been thought that the white man could not live or at least could not work effectively in a tropical climate. Climatic considerations, therefore, seemed to indicate that the tropics must forever remain in a relatively undeveloped condition; that the temperate zones alone could be the home of an advanced economic civilization.

But we have now come to realize that the barriers to the economic development of the tropics have not been so much excessive heat or excessive rainfall as the presence of insects that have conveyed such dread diseases as yellow fever, malaria, and sleeping sickness. A new chapter, therefore, seems to be opened in the history of the advance of man's control over nature. If the white man can successfully wage war on the mosquitoes and other flies which introduce these diseases into his blood, he can live and work in tropical countries. The history of these researches is a magnificent story of heroic devotion to the cause of science and of human progress. It was through the heroism and martyrdom of Reid, Carroll, and Lazear that it was proved that yellow fever could be spread only by the bite of a mosquito and only by a single species of mosquito. Havana, formerly a plague center, was cleaned up and rid of the disease during the period of American occupation. By far the largest and most significant test, however, is to be found in the elimination of yellow fever and malaria from the Panama Canal Zone by United States government enterprise.

16 The three great powers

The tremendous share of the world's commerce controlled by the United States, Great Britain and Germany

The foundations of industrial supremacy

The Book of Popular Science (1924: revised 1929) New York: The Grolier Society. Group IX Ch. 3: 397–403

Before the recent Great War three nations stood out preëminently in the world of trade, the United States, Great Britain, and Germany. Germany's position was, of course, adversely affected as a result of the war. Through the Treaty of Versailles she has lost the rich iron deposits of Lorraine and important coal reserves in Upper Silesia. Nevertheless, she is left in a position stronger than that of any other nation, aside from the United States and Great Britain. From the point of view of commercial leadership, she must still be reckoned one of the three great powers.

[*Chiozza Money: In reviewing the wealth of the world as a whole, we saw how all-important is the possession of natural stores of energy. Despite the present importance of petroleum and the future possibilities of electric energy developed from water power, the largest source of energy utilized by the industries of the world is supplied by coal. Coal is so heavy and bulky that its transport is costly. For this reason machine industry is chiefly carried on in the countries which have large coal deposits.*]

Estimates of the coal reserves of the different countries are subject to an uncertain margin of error. The following estimate, however, is as recent and as authoritative as any:

United States	3,500,000,000,000 tons
Great Britain	190,000,000,000 tons
Germany	400,000,000,000 tons

Since the known coal reserves of the whole world are estimated as only slightly over 7,000,000 million tons, it appears that the United States has about half of the world's coal. Add to this the fact that the coal reserves of Canada are estimated at 1,250,000 million tons, and that there is coal in Alaska and Mexico, and it will be seen that two-thirds of the world's coal is contained within the continent of North America. This is the first and most fundamental fact which any one undertaking to prophesy respecting the future industrial leadership of the world and the future distribution of the world's population must take into account. Half of the coal reserves of the United States, like three-fourths of the Canadian reserves, are lignite. But this fact does not materially modify the significance of the figures as given.

Outside the North American continent, the largest coal reserves of the world are probably those of China, estimated to be between 1,000,000 million and 1,500,000 million tons. Some of the Chinese coalfields are near the coast, and there is no reason why Chinese coal should not at some time become an important article of export. The larger utilization of coal within China itself must wait upon the development of better means of internal transportation.

[CM: When we come to coal production, as distinguished from coal possession, the element of uncertainty disappears. The latent power supplies of the United States and of Germany have been developed so rapidly that the coal production of Great Britain has been altogether out-distanced by that of the United States and approached by that of Germany.]

Table 16.1 gives the figures for 1913, which, as the last year before the war, is more significant than a later year would be as indicating the position that had been attained through the operation of economic and commercial forces alone.

So far as its importance for industry and commerce is concerned, the quality of coal is very nearly as significant as its quantity. Coal varies greatly in its burning qualities and in its steam-producing powers. Especially important in its relation to the development of the iron and steel industries is the coking quality of coal. There are only a few deposits of coal in the world from which coke of high quality can be made efficiently and cheaply. Here again, it is significant to observe, the United States, Great Britain, and Germany have an advantage over other countries.

Great Britain's especial advantage is found in its possession of high-grade coal immediately adjacent, on the one hand, to important deposits of iron ore, and exceptionally close, on the other hand, to her coast ports. In no other country can coal be brought from the mine to the seaboard and put on board ship so cheaply as in Great Britain. This gave her a great advantage over other countries in the coal export trade. The coal export trade, in turn, has been the most important single factor in the prosperity of the British mercantile marine, and it

Table 16.1 The world's coal output: 1913

United States	570,000,000 tons
Great Britain	322,000,000 tons
Germany	306,000,000 tons
Total for the three nations	1,198,000,000 tons
Rest of the world	280,000,000 tons
Total for all the world	1,478,000,000 tons

had a good deal to do with Great Britain's ability to carry and handle other sorts of international commerce effectively. During the Great War, when English ships were needed for other purposes, her coal export trade, especially to Latin America, had to be almost entirely cut off. Since the war Great Britain has been regaining her former position in the coal trade, in part at least, but the recovery of her coal exports has been relatively slow by reason of increased costs of operating her mines.

[... *Turning from coal to agriculture*], the United States has been growing so rapidly in population that the world will not long be able to expect from her the large export of grain which America now puts on the market. But for a wide range of other food crops, notably corn, as well as for live stock, the United States produces much more than she consumes. Despite the fact that the standard of living of her people, the quality and variety of the food consumed per capita, are higher in the United States than in any European country, the United States, unlike the nations of western Europe, produces a *food surplus*.

[CM: *The magnificent area and range of climate of the United States give her in other respects great economic advantages over her competitors. Great Britain and Germany alike have to look to the United States for their main supplies of cotton. In her forests and fisheries the United States is equally fortunate, and if her forest areas have been too rapidly denuded, she has at last awakened to the necessity of conservation, and drastic steps have been taken to assure the future of her timber supply.*]

In all of these ways Great Britain and Germany seem alike to be at a disadvantage. In the first quarter of the nineteenth century Great Britain raised more grain than she consumed and exported her surplus. But with the growth of her industry and her commerce, and the consequent increase of her population, she has found it more profitable to devote her energies to other things than agriculture. Not only relatively but absolutely she raises less food than she did a hundred years ago.

Great Britain's unfortunate position in regard to raw materials

In the domain of raw materials Great Britain is even worse furnished than in respect to foods. Very little indeed of British work and industry is done upon purely native materials. But the commercial miracle has become an everyday, unregarded commonplace. Products foreign to her soil and climate or which, if found there, are present in exceedingly limited measure, are everywhere built into her environment. Palace and cottage alike are largely supplied with imported materials.

A very great part of the industrial work of Great Britain is done upon iron and steel. She possesses great supplies of native iron ores. Nevertheless, of her total consumption of iron ore in a normal year, about one-third is imported. More than that, the iron ores which Great Britain imports are much richer in metallic content than the ores mined at home, so that, broadly speaking, about one-half of her production of iron and steel is based upon ores obtained by overseas commerce.

Great Britain has frankly accepted this situation. More than that, she has made of her very limitations the foundations of her commercial policy and power. Producing little of her own raw materials and of her own food, she has become the great commercial *specialist* among nations. By opening her ports freely to the trade of the world, putting her energies into the carrying trade and into the manufacturing and merchandising of the goods of foreign origin, she has become the world's great commercial entrepôt. There are dangers, of course, in such a policy. To Great Britain more than to any other nation a blockade, involving a complete shutting off of commerce, would mean starvation. Hence her dependence and reliance upon her fine navy. Even before the Great War and the realization of the possibilities of the submarine if used ruthlessly in destroying merchant shipping, Great Britain had come to feel more and more concerned with respect to the dangers involved in her dependence upon the maintenance of untrammeled national commerce, and upon the absence of commercial discriminations against her by other nations. This disquietude showed itself in various proposals and tentative steps toward organizing the British Empire as a relatively self-sufficient and intradependent economic unit. No single nation, not even the United States, begins to have the magnificent resources of the British Empire taken as a whole. So far, however, the proposals and tentative steps to which we have referred have had little or no visible effect in altering the nature and the direction of the main currents of British trade. Nor is there any likelihood that in the near future Great Britain will find it worth her while to turn her energies more and more into imperial trade at the expense of her enviable position in the general trade of the world. She remains the best single example of a nation whose wealth is built on commerce. Her very life-blood flows through the arteries of commerce.

Germany, unlike England, aimed for economic self-sufficiency

While England has thus deliberately discarded the goal of economic self-sufficiency and has built her prosperity upon commerce and industrial specialization, Germany, like most of the countries of continental Europe, has aimed at as large a degree of economic self-sufficiency as circumstances would permit. Nevertheless, she has been able to develop her industries and to increase her population some measure only by accepting some measure of dependence upon other countries. The word "dependence" is, in a way, misleading. The dependence of each country upon others means the intradependency of all. Intradependence is merely another name for international economic coöperation. It is through such coöperation, making the wealth of each section available for every other section, that the enormous progress of the last hundred years has been possible.

With Germany, however, economic independence or self-sufficiency was part and parcel of adequate preparedness for war. Not England's equal on the sea, she tried to lessen her dependence upon the outside world, encouraging her agriculture, for example, by imposing high protective tariff duties upon imported foodstuffs. In the eighties of the last century she was spending from two million to two hundred and fifty million dollars a year on imported food; in the nineties three hundred and fifty to four hundred million. Just before the war this figure had reached the sum of eight hundred million. This, however, was much less than the similar outlay upon the part of Great Britain, whose annual expenditures for foreign food were often as much as a billion and a quarter of dollars.

Germany is not, aside from her coal, richly endowed by nature. Of other minerals, except iron, zinc, and potash, her native supply is small, in most cases insignificant. Her economic progress is for this reason all the more phenomenal. It reflects not merely the energy, industry, and organizing ability of her people, but also the fundamental significance of coal. In Germany's case her supplies of coal have done much toward offsetting other natural disadvantages. Particularly was this true because a large part of her trade is with other west European countries, and many of these are less advantageously placed with respect to supplies of coal than is Germany. Commerce is delicately and sensitively responsive to slight differences in natural advantages.

It was through the skillful use of such advantages as she had, rather than through the presence of such overwhelming advantages as nature has given to the United States, that Germany reached her position as one of the three great commercial nations. Her factories, like those of England, are dependent in very large measure upon imported raw materials. Her population, though in less measure, is dependent upon imports for food. These facts were a source of fundamental weakness in her position in the Great War. Despite the accumulation of vast stores, her supplies of food, of copper, of rubber, and of other things which a country must have if it is to wage war, were inadequate, and it was only by the exercise of marvelous energy and ingenuity that these supplies were eked out, or substitutes found, so that the war could be continued as long as it was. There are no two greater enemies than commerce and war. Not only does war destroy commerce, but commerce, by increasing the intradependence and coöperation of the peoples of the world, makes war more difficult, more expensive, and more hopeless.

War differs from commerce in that both sides lose

Commerce itself involves international competition, and the rivalries thus created are sometimes discussed as though they constituted a sort of "warfare." This is only a superficial aspect of international commerce. We are fond of "dramatizing" the facts of economic life. By emphasizing the competitive side of commerce, the element of international rivalry involved, we dramatize it, or rather, we make it into an exciting game with prizes and victors and losers. The real difference between commerce and war is that both the victors and the defeated lose incalculably by war. They lose in human life and they lose in wealth. In commerce, although some of the rival nations, it must be admitted, gain more than others, *all* are winners. Where war takes toll of life and wealth, commerce multiplies both.

No better illustration of these fundamental truths can be found than the economic relations of the three great commercial nations themselves. America's advance toward national prosperity was not at the expense of Great Britain. Rather the growth of American wealth brought larger markets and new and better sources of supply to Great Britain. In a similar way the rise of Germany has increased the wealth both of Great Britain and the United States. True, these different countries have been rivals for the trade of Latin America and the Far East. But their largest and most lucrative trade has been among themselves. To cite one example, in itself convincing, Germany before the war sold more goods to England than she did to any other country; she bought more goods from the United States than she did from any other country. Great Britain, also, bought more goods from the United States than from any other country, and the United States was also her largest and most profitable market, aside from British India and Australia. And both as a market for British goods and as a source of supply for British imports, Germany stood next to the United States.

Turning to the statistics of American trade, we find a similar situation. The United States bought more goods from Great Britain than from any other country, but, on the other hand, the United States sold more goods to Great Britain than to any other country. As a market for the products of the United States, Canada stood second to Great Britain, but Germany was the third largest of our markets and she was the second largest of our sources of supply. The trade rivalries of these three great countries were in fact of relatively little significance as compared with the benefit each one of them derived from the trade of the other two.

These facts appear clearly in the following table which shows, in millions of dollars, the annual trade of these three great commercial nations just before the war. The pre-war figures are more instructive for our present purposes than more recent statistics would be. In interpreting their significance it is important to note that the aggregate trade of these three great countries constituted one-third of the total trade of the world and that a very large proportion of their trade was with each other.

Table 16.2 Position of three leading commercial nations in the world's trade (figures are in millions of dollars)

Source of Exports	Destination of Exports				
	United States	*Great Britain*	*Germany*	*Other Countries*	*Total*
United States		650	425	1,375	2,450
Great Britain	290		260	2,000	2,550
Germany	180	380		1,865	2,425
Other Countries	1,330	2,270	1,915	8,410	13,925
Total	1,800	3,300	2,600	13,650	21,350

17 America's natural endowment

The material environment in which the American people live and work

Wealth: collaboration of nature and man

The Book of Popular Science (1924; revised 1929) New York: The Grolier Society. Group IX Ch. 5: 677–89

It is but a commonplace to remark that the two essential factors in any country's material progress are, first, the character of its people and, second, the extent of its natural resources. Both human and natural qualities must be estimated in any appraisal of a nation's wealth. For only when the gifts of nature are bountiful and are intelligently utilized by man can industry function at its maximum.

Not infrequently does it happen, however, in countries upon which nature has frowned, that man, by the exercise of his own industry and talents, achieves more than in countries where nature has more beneficently bestowed its products. The presence of rich natural resources alone was not sufficient to render industrially efficient the sport-occupied American Indian nor the ease-loving tribes of warmer regions. For nature reacts upon man. Where the gifts of nature are superabundant, and may be called forth with little difficulty, man may not be impelled to exercise to the full his own innate resources; a bountiful nature may, as but too commonly in the tropics, only render man slothful.

Nevertheless, it is still true that where nature has been niggardly no people can achieve other than a mediocre industrial development. For man can mine only where there are minerals, build houses of wood only where there is timber, fish only where there is water. A bold, vigorous race like the Scandinavian has not been able to achieve great industrial success in a barren, inhospitable country such as Iceland; the semi-arid districts of western United States can never become the seat of a dense population. "No man by taking thought can add a cubit to his stature;" nor can he make good any great deficiency in the natural resources of his country.

Continental United States, not including Alaska, contains 3,026,789 square miles of territory, an area only slightly less than that of Europe, with its land surface of 3,700,000 square miles. Geographically it is most advantageously situated. Practically all of its area lies in the warmer half of the temperate zone. Its southern extremities, Texas and Florida, do not quite touch the tropics, but are much nearer the equator than is any point of Europe. The latitude of New Orleans is the same as that of Cairo, Egypt. In the north, the forty-ninth parallel, the northernmost boundary line, is the latitude of Paris. But, removed from the warming Gulf Stream, only a narrow belt of the American territory north of the United States and southern Canada is suited for an intense cultivation or a dense population. Only a small portion of the United States, however, lies north of the corn belt; and other cereals, such as wheat, oats, rye, may be grown throughout four-fifths of its area. For the grazing of cattle and sheep, districts in all parts of the country are suitable. It is remarkably well supplied with minerals, particularly in those essentials of industry, coal and iron. Lying in the temperate portion of the continent, the United States is much more richly endowed than the slightly larger territory of Canada, full of magnificent promise as that region is.

The eastern and western boundaries, the Pacific and the Atlantic, provide the country with an enormous coast line, altogether 18,000 miles in length. Europe, the most favored of the continents in this respect, has 19,500 miles of seacoast, but 3000 of these are within the Arctic Circle and not, therefore, available for commerce. Deducting the arctic frontier, Europe has only one mile of coast for each 224 miles of land area, whereas the United States possesses one mile of coast for each 165 miles of area. And not only is the United States thus favored with many magnificent harbors, but it is also well provided with a system of long and navigable rivers. The Mississippi River system alone drains over 1,000,000 square miles of territory.

A resident of western Europe, asked to describe our climate, would likely utter the single compound word, "tropicalarctic." In summer there is intense heat, in winter extreme cold. Particularly in the states of the Mississippi Valley is the temperature scorching in summer, but it is not at all uncommon in winter to find the thermometer at twenty degrees below zero in such cities as Minneapolis, Omaha, and Chicago. Practically all the Southern States are liable to cold waves in winter, the only states with uniformly mild winters being those of the Gulf and Pacific coasts.

The wide range of our climate a great aid to the diversification of crops

But varied as is the climate, the months of summer heat are sufficiently long and intense to render the country the world's greatest corn-producing area. And the wide range of climate has aided greatly in the diversification of the crops. The danger of a general crop failure is lessened by the probability that deficiencies in one part of the country will be offset by bountiful yields in another. Only countries possessing both a broad expanse of territory as well as a great variety of climate may hope to become self-sustaining.

Regions with an average yearly rainfall of less than eighteen inches are not suited for the normal processes of agriculture. In the more arid districts crop-growing is usually subordinated to grazing. The average annual rainfall of the United States is about thirty inches; east of the hundredth meridian, which passes through the Dakotas, Nebraska, Kansas, Oklahoma, and Texas, the average is much higher than this. West of the hundredth meridian, as far as the tablelands of the Rockies, the rainfall decreases; this intervening area is the "dry lands" region, where cultivation must be suspended because of the prevalence of droughts and the irregularity of the rainfall. In the sub-arid zone lies about one-third of the territory of the country. By the processes of irrigation or dry farming, however, much of this semi-desert territory is being reclaimed for cultivation, and much more of it will unquestionably be reclaimed in the future.

Scarcely less important than the amount of rainfall is the length of the growing season. This is determined by the dates of the last killing frost in spring and of the first killing frost in the fall. The United States Department of Agriculture has made an elaborate investigation of this important subject. In this one respect the agricultural possibilities of the United States are in some measure limited as compared with those of the larger part of Europe, where the extremes of heat and cold are less, and where the growing season in general is longer. The dates at which killing frosts occur do not depend alone upon latitude. Altitude is nearly as important, and even in the case of comparatively small differences of elevation, the severity of the frost may be less on the hillsides, or even the hilltops, than on the valley bottoms by reason of the tendency of the coldest air to collect at the lowest levels.

The average growing season varies from three hundred and sixty-five days at Key West, Florida, to considerably less than ninety days in the extreme northern portions of the country and in some of the high plateau regions of the West. Where the growing season is less than ninety days, general agriculture is usually not profitable. Such regions may be more profitably devoted to forests. The longest safe growing season is found in the states bordering on the Gulf of Mexico, in southern Arizona, and in parts of California. The safe growing season in the eastern part of the United States varies from about two hundred and forty days along the Gulf of Mexico to one hundred days or less in Minnesota or the Dakotas, and ninety days or less in parts of the Appalachian Mountains and in the higher altitudes of northern New York and New England. In many of the more elevated regions of the West the safe growing season is less than ninety days.

The localization of our industries due to sectional physical characteristics

With its broad expanse of territory, broken up by two great mountain chains, its varied climate and rainfall, industrial United States must inevitably have developed a great diversification. To gain even a rough picture of the localization of industries in the United States necessitates a consideration of the peculiar physical characteristics of the different sections. For our purposes we may divide the country into the following sections, the North Atlantic, the Southern, the North Central, and the Western.

The North Atlantic section includes the New England States and New York, New Jersey, and Pennsylvania. In gross area it is only 5.6 per cent of that of the entire country. In this section, however, nearly 30 per cent of the American people obtain their livelihood. Such density of the population as this is made possible only by the great development of the manufacturing industries. If we glance at the recent census figures, we shall find that the value of its manufactured products amounts to nearly half of the total for the entire country. And in its shops and factories are employed half the workers engaged in the manufacture of goods.

Why 30% of the people earn their living in an area only 5.6% of the whole country

But what qualities make for the manufacturing supremacy of this section? Assuredly it is not its nearness to the sources of raw materials. For neither in minerals nor in soil fertility is this section comparatively rich. New England is an ancient mountain region worn down by long exposure to the elements; its lowlands are small and its climate harsh. In the Middle States the glaciers of the ice age stripped the uplands of their original soil and scattered a deep layer of glacial drift or rock waste over the entire country. Only a small part of New England where the glaciers passed is fit for the plow. The Middle States, possessing a milder climate and a more level surface, are better situated in this respect, but are still not to be compared in soil advantages to the Middle West and South.

The explanation of the manufacturing supremacy of this comparatively small region we find then to consist in, first, the abundance of its mechanical power; second, its excellent shipping facilities; and, lastly, the impetus of an early start.

In a previous chapter it has been pointed out that where mechanical power resides, there manufactures must go. Coal cannot be economically transported any great distance, and science has not yet discovered any means of conveying electrical power far from the site where it was generated, without undue loss. In both coal and water-power the North Atlantic region is well endowed. Many of the rivers are narrow and swift and descend rapidly from considerable elevations. The lakes, formed by glacial action, furnish natural reservoirs and thus insure a constant flow. Indeed New England makes a larger use of water-power than any other section and in the Niagara section of western New York the water-power advantages are unexcelled.

In shipping facilities, also, nature richly endowed this section. In the possession of numerous natural harbors the North Atlantic States possess great advantages over the South Atlantic.

South of the Hudson the coastal plain is broad, extending in some places more than 200 miles. For the most part approach to the shore is permitted only where buried river channels lie. South of New York City good harbors are therefore few. But north of the Hudson the coast is "drowned," and is exceedingly indented. These drowned valleys make the best of harbors. And so it is that this section possesses the country's greatest ports, as New York, Boston and Portland. Through New York alone half the foreign trade of the country is conducted, and of the others, Boston is surpassed by very few of our ports.

But even the best harbors in the world would be of little avail without ready access to the interior. In mountainous sections railroads seldom penetrate great distances, except along river valleys. But in this respect the North Atlantic is well cared for. The chief route to the West was from earliest days the Mohawk Gap. For more than a century this has been a dominant factor in the commerce of the continent. Used by the Indians, when it was known as the "Iroquois Trail," it later furnished the route of the Erie Canal. Along its course there developed a row of prosperous cities – Albany, Troy, Cohoes, Schenectady, Utica, Syracuse, Rochester and Buffalo. Through it there run six lines of rails, constituting a great highway to the West which crosses the Divide where the grades are least.

Ever since the building of the Erie Canal through the Mohawk Gap, New York's supremacy as the great market-place of the continent has been unchallenged. These railway lines, together with the New York State Barge Canal, constitute, in reality, an extension of the Great Lakes route to the East. Chicago and Duluth, therefore, may be said to stand at the western end of the Mohawk route. Turning farther south, other gaps through the mountains, utilized in turn by Indian trails, canals, turnpikes and railways, connect the great ports of Philadelphia and Baltimore with the Ohio River at such important gateways as Pittsburgh and Wheeling.

With all the natural advantages, the North Atlantic States must sooner or later have turned from agriculture and shaped their industries largely for manufacturing. But in the early days there was still commerce, shipbuilding, and fishing to engage the productive activities of the people. With numbers of fine harbors and a wealth of timber, shipbuilding was bound to thrive. Fish were always in demand in Europe, and with the lumber and agricultural supplies of this region, its ships were guaranteed adequate outward cargoes. To render the inward cargoes sufficient, European manufactured goods had to be carried. Thus New England began to compete with England for the carrying trade of the world.

But the War of 1812 and the Embargo Act very nearly destroyed our fleets. Protected, however, during the war from European competition, manufacturing began to thrive. Capital and labor were withdrawn for a while from commerce; and as the country grew and its peculiarly great natural advantages began to tell, the North Atlantic States soon gained prominence in the manufacturing industries.

When we turn from the North Atlantic to the Southern States we find some economic facts reversed. The North Atlantic States are densely peopled; on a relative basis the population of the South is sparse. In the North the manufactured products outweigh the agricultural in importance: in the South the reverse is true. The large cities in the North, as New York, Boston, Philadelphia, are seacoast ports; few of the large cities of the South front the ocean. In the North no single crop holds the preëminence that cotton does in the South, where there is less diversification in agriculture as well as in industries.

The Southern section includes the states south of Mason and Dixon's line and the Ohio, and, in addition, Texas, Oklahoma, Arkansas and Louisiana. In these states there live 50 persons for each square mile of territory, whereas in New England the density of population is 120, and in the Middle Atlantic 223.

The area of the Southern section is over four times as great as the North Atlantic, but the value of the manufactured products in the latter accounts for about half that for the entire country. The South, on the other hand, can boast of only a little over one-eighth of the total. But in the value of its agricultural products the South, with over a third of the total crop values of the entire country, holds a notably high position, easily surpassing all other sections with the single exception of the North Central.

It must be remembered, however, that before the Civil War the South was organized on a wholly different economic system, with slavery as the foundation. This made the plantation system profitable and in itself tended to retard the development of manufactures. The Civil War impoverished the South, not only because it drained it of its resources, but because by eliminating slavery it destroyed at one blow a large part of the wealth of the South and undermined its system of economic organization. Aside from that, the Civil War gave a severe setback to the development of manufactures in the South, and little progress was made during the period of political restoration which occupied the two decades immediately following the war – a period of marked industrial expansion in the North.

Since 1880, however, the commerce and industry of the South has progressed by leaps and bounds. The new commercial and industrial South presents in many respects as wonderful a picture of the achievements of human enterprise and progress as can be found anywhere. Since 1900 the manufacturing industries of the South have increased between three and four-fold; whether that increase be measured in capital invested, in horse-power used, in wage-earners employed, or in value of products.

Nevertheless this industrial progress of the South has been made in the face of what might seem to be insurmountable obstacles. As has been said, good harbors are not common on the southern Atlantic. In general the only good approaches to land arise where river channels are drowned by the general sinking of land. But because of the prevalence of sand-bars, these channels require frequent dredging in order to permit the approach of large vessels.

Indeed, in the Southern Atlantic States, south of the Chesapeake, the most important cities, such as Richmond, Raleigh, Columbia, Augusta and Macon, do not lie on the coast but are situated on the "fall line," on the margin of the coastal plains, where the rivers running to the Atlantic descend from the uplands over a ledge of rock in falls or rapids. This fall line stretches from the Delaware as far as northern Georgia, retreating farther westward from the coast.

In earlier years the fall line got its importance because it marked the head of navigation for large boats and necessitated portage for smaller boats. Now its importance comes more largely from its cheap water-power, which has encouraged the development of manufactures. Nearer the coast, however, we find that such cities as Charleston and Savannah have been and are important ports, and the volume of their commerce is likely to continue to increase as rapidly as it has in the recent past.

The Gulf States are much more favorably situated from the standpoint of ready access to the sea. New Orleans, indeed, stands next to New York in the handling of the country's foreign trade, and its importance is bound to increase. It stands at the foot of the Mississippi River, which, being ice free and of sufficient depth, is likely again to be a great artery of commerce, as it has been in the past. In Texas, Galveston is the natural outlet for the commercial products of a large part of the Southwest. Mobile and Pensacola owe their importance primarily to the large coal and iron deposits around Birmingham; Mobile is growing through the increase of commerce with Cuba and Central America, and Tampa and Key West also owe their commercial importance to this southerly routed trade. Tampa also is situated close to the most valuable phosphate deposits in the world. As the Panama Canal trade develops and commerce is more largely diverted in a southerly direction, these gulf ports are bound to assume prominence as trade outlets of the South and Central West.

In minerals the South is well provided, even though its coal districts probably cannot hope to provide power quite so cheaply as the Pennsylvania and West Virginia deposits do for the manufactures of the North.

But coal can be mined so cheaply there that a great increase in the manufacture of bulky raw materials which cannot be cheaply transported considerable distances is inevitable. At Macon, where water-power is abundant, the manufacture of iron ore has already assumed large proportions. The lumber industry of the South is wresting the leadership from the Great Lakes states. The Louisiana sugar industry has made necessary the development of sugar refineries in New Orleans. The beef from Texas ranches should in time go in larger part to packing houses in such cities as Fort Worth and Dallas. At Charleston the production of phosphate fertilizers has a splendid future.

The South more dependent than other sections upon a few great staple crops

In agriculture, as we have seen, the South is more dependent upon a few great staple crops than are other sections of the country. The principal crop is, of course, cotton. The northern limit of cotton growing follows closely the mean summer temperature line of seventy-seven degrees. Very little cotton is grown where the average frostless season is less than two hundred days. On the west the spread of cotton culture has been stopped approximately at the line where the average annual rainfall is twenty-three inches. Cotton growing demands fertile soil. So we find cotton in the Piedmont and the coast plains of the South Atlantic States, on the black prairie soils of Alabama and Mississippi, in the Yazoo-Mississippi delta, in the Red River Valley of Arkansas, and in the Black Prairie of Texas. Recently the cultivation of fine grades of cotton has been successfully introduced into the Southwest, especially California and Arizona. In many of the states of the South cotton exceeds in value any other crop, or the product of any industry.

Practically the only limitation in the South upon the production of cotton is the difficulty and expense of securing sufficient pickers; man can cultivate more cotton than can be economically picked. Cotton growing has been so intimately bound up with the history of the South and has been in so peculiar a way the economic basis of its civilization that it is hard to find elsewhere any single crop or product which has the same economic, social, and political significance.

Corn ranks next to cotton, and indeed rivals it, in acreage. Cotton, however, is the principal export. In fact, the United States produces normally two-thirds of the world's cotton. But corn is the chief crop for local consumption. Corn bread and pork form the staple diet of many a southern farm laborer. Winter wheat is also grown extensively in the Appalachian uplands, as well as in parts of Texas and Oklahoma. Although the general climate is not exceptionally favorable to the winter grains, they possess the advantage of not requiring attention during the seasons when cotton is being cultivated.

Just as cotton growing has been the dominating industry of what might be called "the southern South," so tobacco growing has had a similar significance in the northern South, especially in Kentucky, North Carolina, Virginia, and Tennessee. Kentucky produces burley tobacco, used in the manufacture of chewing and smoking brands, while Virginia and the Carolinas grow flue-cured or bright tobacco, used for cigarettes as well as for chewing and smoking. Virginia and Maryland tobaccos, in particular, have an important export market. Such tobacco as is grown in the North, especially in Ohio, Wisconsin, and the Connecticut Valley, is used largely in the making of cigars, as is the high-grade tobacco which is being grown in increasing measure in Florida. Tobacco, like cotton, requires intensive cultivation and hand labor.

The North Central section

The North Central section includes two census divisions, the East North Central and the West North Central. The former is made up of states in the basin of the Great Lakes: Ohio, Indiana, Illinois, Wisconsin and Michigan. The Western North Central States lie west of the Mississippi and include the Dakotas, Nebraska, Kansas, Minnesota, Iowa and Missouri.

Altogether the twelve states occupy one-fourth of the total area of continental United States and furnish homes for about one-third of its people. The density of the population is accordingly somewhat greater than the average for the entire country.

In geographical structure the most important feature is its unrivaled system of natural waterways. The Mississippi provides a natural outlet to the Gulf, the Great Lakes to the East. No country in the world has more splendid arteries of commerce, and the Great Lakes Basin is already one of the world's greatest trade highways. Measured due east and west, the Great Lakes afford a navigable waterway six hundred miles long. The St. Lawrence in Canada connects Lake Erie with tide-water; in the United States the New York State Barge Canal affords water transportation to New York Bay.

North of the Ohio and the Missouri the soil is mostly of glacial origin. Glacial soil contains rock waste of many lands. As this slowly decays the quality of the soil is improved. This section is therefore extraordinarily fertile, and its soil is not easily exhausted by tillage. Glacial action has made the surface generally level, and particularly in the treeless prairies of the Dakotas and Iowa grain farming on a large scale is invited. The climate in summer is hot, rapidly maturing the crops, and the cold winters pulverize the soil. No equal area in the world possesses greater natural farming advantages than this. The Middle West is the world's greatest granary.

A few census figures will serve to indicate in striking fashion the agricultural predominance of this section. The two North Central sections contained at the time of the Thirteenth Census two-fifths of the farm land of the country, and the proportion improved is greater than in any other section. The estimated value of its farm property was more than one-half the country's total. Table 17.1 brings this out clearly.

In the production of cereal crops this section has no rival. In corn, Illinois, Iowa, Indiana, and Missouri produce more than two-fifths the total for the entire country. In wheat production the first five states, North Dakota, Kansas, Minnesota, Nebraska, and South Dakota, are all in this division. Washington comes next, but is followed by four other states of the North Central division. In oats the leading ten states are in this section, in barley six of the first ten, in rye eight of the first ten. Since cereals represent more than half the total value of the country's crops, the agricultural supremacy of the North Central division stands unrivaled. Altogether the United States produces about three-fourths of the world's corn supply, and it grows more wheat and oats than any other country. Cereals are to these states what cotton is to the South.

Great cities of the Middle West

The Eastern North Central States occupy a prominent position in the country's manufacturing. Their shops and factories produce more than a fourth of the

Table 17.1 The way in which the total value of farm property is distributed among the grand divisions of the United States. (in per cents of totals for the whole country)

Division	All farm property	Land	Building	Implements and machinery	Live stock
North Atlantic	9.3	6.4	20.8	17.2	9.4
Southern	21.9	20.8	22.5	23.3	26.9
Western	11.1	12.0	6.0	9.1	12.7
North Central	57.7	60.8	50.7	50.4	51.3
Total	100.0	100.0	100.0	100.0	100.0

goods manufactured in the country, and employ nearly a fourth of the wage earners engaged in manufacturing industries. The position of the West North Central States in this division is naturally less important.

The large cities of the Middle West are prevailingly lake ports, together with those possessing unusually important positions on the Mississippi, Ohio and Missouri rivers. Of these, Chicago is the greatest, being both the largest food market and the greatest railway center in the world. About thirty great trunk lines enter the city, and daily several thousand trains enter and depart from its stations. The location of Chicago at the southern end of Lake Michigan is such as to make it necessary for railways to converge at this point.

Next to Chicago as a lake city stands Detroit. The strait upon which it is situated carries the heaviest traffic in the world. From the West it is one of the gateways to Canada. The magic of Detroit's growth from a commercial center of ordinary importance to a magnificent city with over a million population is, of course, bound up with the history of the automobile industry. In this respect men of energy, ability and vision, as well as Detroit's natural advantages of location, must be taken into consideration. In this account of the industrial geography of our country we are of necessity emphasizing physical factors. The significance and influence of these must be taken into account first of all in any scientific discussion of our economic situation and progress. But it is well to remember that economic progress comes only from the coöperation of man with nature. Human energy and ability may often compensate for some measure of natural disadvantage. It is wrong to say that man dominates nature, just as it is wrong to say that nature dominates and defines all human efforts. It is nearer the truth to say that human effort is conditioned by nature. The world of human effort is a world of purpose, of striving, and of accomplishment. Human progress cannot be explained unless both factors are taken into account.

Cleveland is another lake city whose industrial rise has been no less marvelous than that of Detroit. Situated with respect to Lake Erie much as Chicago is situated with respect to Lake Michigan, the northern outlet for the densely populated agricultural and industrial regions of Ohio, at the point where the coal of Pennsylvania naturally meets the iron ore of Lake Superior, the rapid rise of Cleveland to the fifth city in point of size in the United States is a striking illustration of the combined influence of natural factors and human energies.

On the Ohio River is Cincinatti, historically as well as in the present, one of the great commercial centers of the Middle West. In its earlier history it was a center of dispersion for the population and the goods that flowed from the East into the new West through the passes of the Alleghenies and down the Ohio River. Now it is the great gateway from the Middle West to the South and Southeast.

St. Louis, situated near the point where the Missouri and the Mississippi meet and where the convergence of river valleys has made the entrance of railways easy, close to the coal deposits of Missouri and southern Illinois, is of necessity a great commercial and industrial center. Kansas City and Omaha likewise owe their importance to such a convergence of river valleys. These cities, together with St.

Paul and Minneapolis in the Northwest, are distributing points for a large part of the Mississippi Valley, and are the gateways for transcontinental traffic.

West North Central States bound to increase enormously in manufacturing

Despite the natural emphasis on agriculture, the West North Central States are bound to increase enormously in manufacturing. Industries continually tend to migrate toward the seat of the bulky raw materials. As water-power comes to be more extensively used in manufacturing, the coal advantages of cities further east will become much less pronounced. In the meat packing industry there has already been a marked westward trend, especially toward such cities as St. Paul, Omaha, St. Joseph, and Kansas City. Since the use of compressed air has become common in the chilling of fresh meat, it has been found economical to dress the meat near the cattle feeding areas. Live cattle require more space and more attention and are subject to greater dangers in transportation.

The Western section extends from the Pacific Coast to Texas and the western limit of the North Central division. It occupies about two-fifths of the area of continental United States, but is the home of only a twelfth of its people. It is increasing in population, however, more rapidly than any other section. During the thirty years from 1900 to 1930 it just about tripled in population – the rate of increase, in fact, was more than 290 per cent, while that for the whole United States was a little more than 66.

Topographically this section may be divided into two districts, the Plateau region and the Pacific Slope. The Plateau region is the "land of little rain," and extends as far west as the white crest of the Sierra Nevada Mountains. In all this vast expanse, land is generally arid; it is only in the higher regions that enough moisture is condensed to support the forests. Farming is therefore confined very largely to old lake beds, river-flooded plains, and irrigated districts.

As in the days of Mexican and Spanish domination, agriculture in the Plateau region is subordinated to grazing. The lofty plateaus furnish many of the cattle shipped later to the corn belt for fattening. In wool the Western section produces about three-fifths of the total for the country. Sheep raising may have tended to restrict the growth of the cattle industry; the young sheep crop the grass so closely that cattle cannot graze after them.

Many fertile tracts of soil are to be found in this section and, accordingly, the limitations upon agriculture are largely fixed by the rainfall. To remedy this, the government is continually utilizing the proceeds of land sales in the arid states for the construction of irrigation reservoirs for the impounding of stream waters now running to waste. Dry farming is being extensively developed in certain fertile sections. The science of winter irrigation is also being invoked. The rain of two winters is stored in the soil – if the rain fell in the summer it would evaporate – and held there over one summer by a dust-mulch. In this way a good crop can often be obtained every two years.

The Pacific Slope

On the Pacific Slope the climate is oceanic, comparatively cool in summer and mild in winter. This is the only section of the country having really but two seasons, the rainy and the dry. In the great valleys of California there abound many level and fertile expanses sufficiently watered by rainfall. Such tracts are unsurpassed for the growing of wheat. In the past a large part of this wheat went to Great Britain by the long route around Cape Horn. In California wheat growing, however, is yielding in relative importance to fruit growing. This is not because wheat growing has in itself become unprofitable, but merely because fruit growing has become even more profitable. So fertile, so favored in respect to climatic conditions are the lands of California, that it involves an economic waste to use them for other than the most intensive forms of agriculture, such as gardening and fruit growing. Fruit is the most important single product of California; its oranges, lemons, peaches, olives, figs, and grapes give it the fruit leadership of the country. The invention of the refrigerator car has given an enormous stimulus to this industry. The crop is transported in special cars attached to fast trains and distributed through such centers as Minneapolis, Chicago, St. Louis, and New York.

Another important crop of the West is its minerals. Since the discovery of gold and silver in this region, it has produced about four billions of dollars in gold and silver bullion. California, Colorado, Nevada, Arizona, Montana, and Utah, in the order named, have been the largest producers of gold in recent years. South Dakota is the only state outside of this district with an important gold production. In silver production the leading states are, in order, Montana, Utah, Nevada, Idaho, Arizona, Colorado, and California. The importance of some of these western states as producers of coal has been discussed in another connection. In the Southwest too, especially in Southern California, there is much petroleum. The presence of this petroleum has been an economic factor of the first importance. It has done much to offset the high cost of coal on the Pacific Coast. Not only is it used as fuel for locomotives, but in an increasing measure it is the fuel for industries, for the heating of homes, and for the production of gas. Its increasing utilization in the bunkers of ocean-going steamers is a commercial fact of the first significance.

It would take too much space to describe in detail the wonderful mineral wealth of this western region. The rarer as well as the commoner minerals are found in extraordinary abundance and variety.

The navigable waterways of the West are few, as the country is in the main a lofty tableland. The Columbia and Sacramento river systems are most fortunate exceptions to this statement. The Columbia is navigated by sea-going vessels as far as Portland on the Willamette, and by river steamers to Lewiston on the Snake. In the absence, however, of a general system of inland waterways, western industrial development depends largely on the railroads.

High freight costs are at once the salvation and the handicap of local manufactures. They prevent to a certain extent the competition of eastern finished goods. Likewise they prevent western manufactured products from seeking eastern markets, except in cases where the power of the West, either coal or water, can be cheaply obtained. Manufactures in the Far West are accordingly, for the most part, dependent upon the western market for the disposal of their output.

The Pacific Coast is characterized by mountains rising straight from the sea. It is at most points rugged and forbidding and might therefore seem to be unfavorable to commerce. Only in three places – Puget Sound, the mouth of the Columbia, and San Francisco Bay – is it pierced by navigable rivers. Here lie ports of enormous future possibilities. Spokane and Walla Walla are commercial centers on the Columbia River. At Spokane railways converge which gather the wheat and the grain of the "inland empire." San Francisco Bay and Puget Sound afford naturally better harbors, larger and more accessible, than New York. Steamship lines connect them to Panama, the Hawaiian Islands, Japan, and Australia. They are the centers likewise of a large coastwise ocean traffic. Other ports of importance are Los Angeles, where human energies have made a splendid harbor where nature had been none too generous, and San Diego, whose natural harbor is one of the safest as well as one of the most beautiful in the world.

As the fertile areas of the Far West are more extensively developed by irrigation and dry farming, as its mineral wealth is more and more drawn upon, as our Pacific traffic increases, the West is bound to increase enormously in population. Local manufactures must also grow with the increasing density of the population. Discovery of new coal fields, more scientific utilization of the old, and the more extensive development of its water-power facilities may in time do much to overcome its relative disabilities in respect of power manufacturing.

Of all the natural divisions of the world few even approach North America in physical endowment. And the United States occupies the heart and the richest portion of the continent. With its untold mineral wealth, its preëminence in coal and iron, its vast fertile plains, its strength in cereals and cotton, its magnificent ports and internal waterways, the United States has been so richly endowed by nature that its peoples must feel that before them lie not only magnificent opportunities but also responsibilities of wise use and trusteeship, which, rightly viewed, are equally splendid.

18 Our wealth in minerals

Supremacy of the United States and the rapid development of its sources of supply

Need of public regulation of consumption

The Book of Popular Science (1924; revised 1929) New York: The Grolier Society. Group IX Ch. 6: 817–27

Pierre Leroy-Beaulieu, a noted French economist, has remarked that the United States owes its industrial greatness more largely to its minerals than to any other single factor. And well justified appears this belief when we consider the striking supremacy of this country in this particular field of natural resources. Not only is the United States the leader in coal and iron, but it also surpasses in the production of petroleum, natural gas, silver, sulphur, molybdenum, arsenic, salt, and lime phosphates; it manufactures the largest share of the world's aluminum, and in gold it is rivaled only by Australia and South Africa. The United States produces more than one-half the world's copper, holds primacy in lead, and in zinc has wrested the lead from Germany. No other country can hope to rival the United States in its mineral wealth.

Minerals comprise an exceedingly large part of the nation's annual production. At the present time the value of our annual product of the mines is over five billions of dollars. In only one industry, agriculture, is this mark exceeded.

Mineral resources are not to any appreciable extent the result of existing natural forces; they were manufactured by the work of agents operating millions of years ago. Before the earth's crust had hardened, rocks were hurled by volcanic action from the interior and spread over the surface. Thrusting aside the solid rocks, the igneous rocks became a part of the earth's crust, the deposits ready for man's exploitation millions of years later. Volcanic action also caused vapors, bearing minerals in solution, to issue forth. In the Carboniferous Age vegetation was abundant. Trees grew and fell. This tree fiber is the source of our present coal.

But all this is the result of the past work of natural forces. Mineral wealth is a mere accident of creation; what nature has granted or denied cannot be appreciably changed by man. All man can do is to utilize intelligently and thoughtfully these gifts of nature.

[Eds.: There follows a detailed survey of the stocks of these minerals and their depletions. The section on precious metals alone is reproduced here.]

The precious metals now demand our consideration. Here we find the United States surpassed only by the Transvaal. Until recently, however, the United States has occupied first place. The supreme position of this country in the past has been due to the fact that it is one of the few countries which has been a great producer both of gold and silver. Indeed, in no other continent but America are there to be found rich deposits of gold and silver so interlocked with each other that the cost of extraction for each is considerably reduced.

From the beginning of the science of political economy the question has continually been propounded, What is the real value to a country of its precious metals? Is a nation richer because its gold yield is abundant? The mercantilists of the seventeenth and eighteenth centuries indeed argued that gold and silver were the most important of all commodities, that the commercial policy of nations should have for its principal purpose the maintenance of a large stock of gold or of silver. And so we witnessed an era of high protective tariffs, of liberal bounties and subsidies to home industry, of laws seeking to restrict colonies from purchasing finished goods from merchants in rival manufacturing countries.

But in the liberalistic period, following the publication in 1776 of Adam Smith's epoch-making work, "The Wealth of Nations," mercantilism declined. Statesmen were convinced that it was not masses of gold or silver that contributed to the wellbeing of the people, but rather the sum total of the goods capable of satisfying their people's wants and needs. The principal use of gold is not found in the arts; its primary service is to furnish the counters of exchange. What real difference did it make whether the number of these counters was large or small? Assuredly gold does not to any large extent increase man's goods, the things necessary to satisfy his wants. And so, how is it that the great gold production of the United States can be said to contribute to its wealth, to minister unto its industrial welfare?

The answer is that no nation lives by itself; it cannot be isolated in trade from its neighbors. Were the United States virtually self-sufficing and without foreign trade connections, its vast silver and gold would indeed contribute little to its wealth. But gold mined in the United States permits the purchase of goods from abroad without the sacrifice of other materials. The gold-mines of California and Colorado yield a mortgage upon the labor of the coolie in China, of the white man in Europe, of the black man in the tropics. A country without the precious metals must continually exchange the other products of its labor and its capital for the so-called "sterile wealth" of other countries. And that is why we cannot omit mention of America's gold when taking stock of its natural resources.

[Eds.: Young concludes this chapter with comments on the need for conservation.]

... From the standpoint of nature's beneficence, the people of the United States have only cause for self-congratulation. But it cannot be too strongly emphasized that these gifts are the mere accidents of creation; in the present régime of man they cannot to any considerable extent be repeated. A nation which draws upon these resources without foresight is like the spendthrift who barters future capital for the sake of present income.

As the original chemical elements cannot be created by man, neither can they be destroyed. Doing all in his power, man cannot add or subtract a single atom from the physical mass of the universe. But he can destroy utilities; he may so change combinations and forms that their capacity to gratify wants will be lessened.

It is not then from the principle of the inviolability of matter, but rather from that of the destructibility of utilities that the true policy of conservation should proceed. The use of metals for some purposes does not mean their withdrawal from future use. It is not always a question of wresting these materials from nature; it is often primarily a question of the use to which they shall be put. The utilization of lead for paints means that after one act of consumption its utility to man is destroyed. When devoted, on the other hand, to the making of water pipes, the material is available for future use. Copper devoted to chemical purposes is rarely available more than once; for other uses it can be drawn upon again and again. And so likewise with zinc.

Most of the minerals may be utilized for several purposes. True conservation policy again demands their use for the most indispensable services. Petroleum for fuel or power is not absolutely indispensable; for both purposes alcohol may very well be substituted. So far as economically possible, petroleum should be saved for lubricating purposes and for the other uses for which it has no adequate substitute. Likewise either copper or aluminum may serve for conducting electricity; but if future chemical discoveries should render aluminum the more common metal, the use of copper for this purpose should be abandoned. And likewise with the nitrates; conservation of sewage and manure should relieve as far as possible the pressure upon our mineral deposits.

In these and other ways the principle of utilizing first that which is at present the cheapest or the most available is being modified. The thoughtful nation must consider not merely what is for the present the most economical, but what is also likely to be dearest in the future.

19 Our water and forest wealth

The Book Of Popular Science (1924; revised 1929) New York: The Grolier Society. Group IX Ch. 7: 951–60

In discussing the nation's mineral wealth we found that, to prevent the impairment of our heritage, public policy must look with clear-sighted vision into the future. Private enterprise sometimes thinks too largely of immediate profits, and the competitive system is apt to operate with an insufficient regard for future resources. When we come to our riches in forest and water, we find similar need of looking ahead...

The problem of conserving our material resources is vastly different in regard to water from what it is in regard to the minerals. In the case of minerals it is primarily a question of abstention, of substituting wherever economically feasible some non-mineral material. But the water supply renews itself constantly; the rain which falls upon land, the snow which gathers in banks and glaciers, must sooner or later, whether in a day or in the course of hundreds of years, return to the ocean and be again available for evaporation and precipitation. The water supply, being perpetually renewed, should then be utilized fully; wherever possible it should be substituted for other materials...

To our savage predecessors obliged to descend a canyon and gather the trickling water in a jar, or make a long trip to a spring, how marvelous would it appear to see the present city dweller gather water anywhere by merely turning a faucet.

Prior to the age of the industrial revolution, water was the principal motive force used by man. Indeed, until toward the end of the eighteenth century, only water and, to a lesser degree, wind were utilized in industrial establishments. Mechanical power was then, however, confined largely to milling and to very small factories. It was not until the age of coal that there was any noticeable lessening in the use of man power. But today the productivity of factories depends less than at any former period upon human power. Man has become a director and a distributor rather than a mere producer of power. And in recent years there has been a decided turning to the earlier source – to the use of water as a mechanical power.

A special investigation made by the Bureau of the Census in 1912, covering 5,221 central electric light and power stations, discovered that of the 7,530,000 total horse-power employed, 2,470,000, or practically a third, was developed by water-wheels. Over nine-tenths of the water-power was used by 225 large hydro-electric stations, each of which reported water-power of over 1000 horse-power. Since 1912 the creation of hydro-electric power has proceeded even more rapidly than before. It is true that the use of steam and gas has also grown remarkably, but we must remember that the knowledge of how to render water-power available at any considerable distance from the place at which it is generated is largely a recent discovery. The possibilities of water-power have only recently been unfolded, but its increasing use in the future is certain.

In an earlier chapter [a] it was shown how conclusively industrial leadership depends upon cheap mechanical energy, and how this country's recent tremendous strides have been largely due to its remarkably large supplies of cheap coal. We cannot be at all certain, however, how long the United States can hold its relative advantage in fuel-power, great as that advantage is. Many authorities have stated that at the present rate of increase in consumption all our coal will he gone before the middle of the next century.

And who can tell to what extent the coal resources of the United States will be drawn upon by the rest of the world as the European reserves approach depletion and as South America and Africa – lands of little coal – support denser populations? If it be true, as Leighton asserts, that one-third of the coal now used could be saved by the wise utilization of water-power, too much emphasis cannot be placed upon the necessity of developing these "white coal" resources.

It is often predicted that the future will witness the development of other sources of power which will render less important our coal and our water. For instance, the wind may be still further utilized, and it may become economically feasible to harness by motors the direct energy of the sun. Be this as it may, the direct utilization of the wind and sun possesses difficulties insuperable under our present knowledge. We cannot wisely risk our national future upon improbable or at least uncertain discoveries...

The secret of industrial leadership will in the future, even more than in the past, depend upon mechanical energy. Since water bids fair to become the most important source of energy, the question of its control assumes daily added importance. Some have even regretted that governments ever surrendered to private hands the title to coal lands. After these resources are once developed as legitimate fields of private ownership, the problem of recovering them for public use, even if that were desirable, becomes exceedingly difficult. Vested interests, the rights of property originally acquired without restriction, may not altogether be ignored. The proper time for the assertion of public rights is *before* rights of private ownership are created.

Already there has been a considerable concentration of the private ownership of water-powers. In 1909, Herbert Knox Smith, Commissioner of Corporations, reported that 35 per cent of the horsepower then utilized was controlled by a relatively small group of proprietors. And the water-power sites so utilized were the strategic sites, holding the advantage over others by reason of their nearness to markets and the adequacy of their stream flow. Further delay in the assertion of public control can only mean the building up of legitimate private property rights which may, perhaps, stand in the way of the larger interests of power conservation.

Advantages of public control of natural water-power sites

What now are the advantages of public control? First of all, such control is necessary in order to secure for the public reasonable charges. He who controls mechanical energy controls its price. The monopolizing of natural water-power sites means that the public cannot always rely upon the competition of private firms to secure reasonable prices. Public regulation, of some sort, is the only alternative. State control is also necessary to secure the full development of water-power sites.

In many parts of the country water-power sites have been held for purely speculative purposes and are not being devoted to immediate use. Moreover, private parties may establish dams here and there in such a way as to interfere with the plans of others. Public interest demands that before franchises be given for dam construction the assent of competent government engineers be obtained.

Old English law of riparian rights

The old law of riparian rights, which we inherited from England, gives to the adjoining owners full rights to the flow that occurs past their holdings. When waterpower was used almost exclusively for milling purposes, this law was not grossly out of harmony with public interest. But today the use of water-power has completely transcended former bounds and the old law is a fetter binding enterprises conducted for the public interest. When cities wish to acquire power for lighting or other municipal purposes, they are forced to pay the private owner millions of dollars in damages for water-powers unused and undeveloped. Thus a free gift of nature must sometimes be paid for before the public has a right to utilize its advantages. This method of obtaining water-power rights is unduly expensive. The country from which we inherited our law of riparian rights is today not hampered in this way. An English city may build a water reservoir and, without purchase of water rights, may turn from the stream enough water to maintain unimpaired the "low water" power. In this way both public and private interests are subserved...

Our forest wealth and the indirect utilities subserved by forests

Let us now consider our forest wealth. The general public has only recently begun even to comprehend the enormous value of our wooded tracts. The annual value of the forest products of the United States is over $2,000,000,000, and the industries which subsist wholly or mainly upon wood yield employment to more than a million and a half of workers. But the services of our forests can by no means be measured solely by the value of the wood products; and it is the recognition of this fact which has brought the question of forest care to the forefront in the conservation problem.

The indirect utilities subserved by forests are many and great. It has already been shown how greatly forests tend to prevent the dissipation of water into the run-off. The forest floor has often been likened to a blanket, and a blanket will hold more moisture than the porous soil of treeless tracts. Because of its roots and undergrowth, the forest encourages the absorption into the underground reservoir which furnishes the water for wells, and from which springs and streams are fed. Mention has also been made of how forests check the frequency of floods and regulate the flow of streams. Indeed, in the absence of forests, reservoirs, either natural or artificial, often become useless through the washing in of great quantities of silt. It has been found, too, that a forest moderates the extremes of temperature. Its presence retards the melting of snow in the spring. Snowbanks in the forest remain until late in the summer. From them little rivulets trickle, carefully and gradually feeding the streams...

Except in the Rocky Mountain and the Pacific areas forests are now mere remnants of their original splendor. The stand of board feet has, by clearing for agriculture, by fires and logging, been reduced over one-half; the forest acreage has been lessened by 350,000,000 acres. Our yearly consumption is three and one-half times as great as the yearly growth, and we export more lumber than we import. Particularly large has been the destruction of the rarer and better grades, woods which in some cases require centuries to mature. In 1928 yellow pine lumber cost 130 per cent more than in 1904, white pine 100 per cent more, walnut 200 per cent more. The extinction of many of the hardwood grades is already threatened.

It is not difficult to explain this unprecedented destruction of our timber resources. In colonial days the forest was the enemy of the settler. It retarded his agriculture, and therein lurked wild animals and hostile savages. Wood was the superfluous commodity; cleared land rare.

The woodsman could not fail to sink his ax into the tree with a feeling of malicious satisfaction. But industrial progress has meant an increasing consumption of wood, so that today the problem is not to clear the forests away, but rather to lessen the timber waste...

Editors' note

a Chapter 4 of the Grolier *Book of Popular Science*, entitled "Our Industrial Future" (not included in this selection).

20 Our wealth in cereals

*Why the food cost of living is ever
increasing; the outlook for the future*

How the laboratory may save

The Book of Popular Science (1924; revised 1929) New York: The Grolier Society.
Group XI Ch. 8: 1101–12

Except for a few richly endowed tropical islands, the most thickly settled regions
of the world are those whose economic activity is predominantly manufacturing.
Agriculture alone will not support a dense population. The greatest centers of
industry may therefore be located in regions where the soil is comparatively
unfertile and the climate not well adapted to large crop yields. This is merely a
corollary of the principle that food and raw materials can be more cheaply
transported than the coal which yields the power for manufacturing.

When we take a long-time view of the situation, however, we can readily
understand the tremendous advantage of a country able to produce more food
than it itself consumes. Unless crop growing is pushed too rapidly, and insufficient
attention is paid to fertilizing, the soil does not become impoverished. It is capable
of producing its harvests perpetually. With proper care soil may be cultivated
without destroying its properties. Some of the best agricultural lands of northern
France – and there are none richer in the world – have been intensively cultivated
for more than a thousand years.

Coal seams and iron mines, however, wear out. A nation which holds its
industrial supremacy by exporting coal and manufactures is slowly but surely
mortgaging its future. Thus Jevons, several decades ago, was led to write: "We
[the people of England] have to make the momentous choice between brief but
true greatness and longer continued mediocrity."

The United States is not merely rich in the basic minerals of manufacturing,
coal and iron, but it possesses vast tracts of fertile agricultural land. Its farms are
able to produce more food than its people require to consume. It need not,
therefore, diminish its mineral resources to maintain its trading strength. If we
analyze the country's agricultural wealth, the first fact to impress us is the
tremendous importance of the cereals. According to the Census, the farm area
devoted to cereals is more than 43 per cent that of all improved farm land and 55
per cent of all the land devoted to crops.

Not merely in domestic trade, but in international commerce as well, is grain a leading commodity. As far back as 1897 the international trade in cereals amounted to 1615 millions of bushels. In value it amounted to $1,275,600,000, about one-tenth of the total world's trade.

All this is largely a result of the development of steam power. Before the days of the steam locomotive, bulky articles could only be transported at great expense across the face of the globe. Then populous communities could only arise in regions capable of producing at least the larger part of the food required by their people. Now man is much less dependent upon nature in the choice of a home. Food, refused occasionally by a temporarily adverse climate, or constantly by an unfertile soil, can be supplied by imports from other parts of the world. Development of transportation has brought the food granaries of the world – India, Argentina, Egypt, North America, Russia – to the doors of the densely populated portions of Europe.

Civilized countries no longer in danger of bread famine

International trade in grain has now practically freed civilized countries from the danger either of famine or of prohibitive prices of bread. This fact is of tremendous significance. Except where war cuts the arteries of international commercial communication, modern trade among nations performs its work of distributing the world's products so smoothly and so efficiently that our attention is rarely drawn to the wonder of its intricate mechanism. The more perfectly a machine operates, the less it calls for attention. The more we become accustomed to its operations, the smaller the trouble it gives us, the more we are likely to overlook its very perfections. But to savage man, directly dependent upon the bounty of nature, life was an alternating recurrence of periods of plenty and periods of famine. The savage took whatever nature had to give him, be it much or little. The progress of economic civilization has been in essence the growth of man's purpose and power to control nature and bend its forces to meet human needs.

We are likely to forget, too, how new a thing in human history the world market for food products is. It is really a development of the last century and a half. It had to wait upon the discovery and utilization of means of transporting bulky goods cheaply and quickly between distant parts of the world. One thing that must impress every student of medieval times is the small size, the distinctly limited or local nature, of the market for food products. Thus Professor U.S.B. Gras, who has studied the evolution of the English grain market, found that in medieval England there were at least fifteen "local price areas."

The price of grain in one of these areas, East Suffolk, for example, might be distinctly lower on the average than the price of grain in another area, East Essex, for example. And within these local price areas the variations in the supply and the price of food products were such as we should regard with amazement today.

Professor A.P. Usher, who has made a detailed study of the grain trade in France from the fifteenth to the eighteenth century finds that there was an elaborate market mechanism, with local and royal regulations, designed primarily to solve the difficult problem of assuring a regular and adequate supply of food to the cities of France. Under the least strain, however, the system broke down. Not only might the cities be inadequately supplied, but in the non-commercial regions, not regularly supplying the city market, there were likely to be periods not only of shortage but of famine.

As things are now, nothing short of a general world shortage – an exceedingly improbable event – can, under ordinary conditions, mean famine for any large part of the civilized world. War, as we have seen it, may cut the lines of communication so that particular countries may be forced to rely upon their own inadequate food resources.

Or a complete breakdown of the mechanism of modern commerce, coupled with economic isolation, such as has characterized Russia under the Soviet government, may lead to a similar result. But examples like these serve only to make it absolutely clear and certain that the modern mechanism of international commerce has now conquered the specter of famine – a specter which had haunted man since the earliest days of the race. That mechanism does not break down except when it is wantonly injured or destroyed...

Not only has international trade in grain practically freed the world from the danger of famine, but it has also reduced the seasonal fluctuations in prices. When each country depended upon its own production alone, its supply of grain was limited to a few harvest weeks. During the rest of the year demand alone was prominent. Now the world's wheat is marketed in many months of the year. In January it comes from Argentina, New Zealand and Australasia; in February and March from the East Indies; in April from Mexico, Egypt, Persia and Asia Minor; in May from Texas, China, Japan and northern Africa; in June from California, Spain, Italy and southern France; in July from most of the United States, upper Canada, Hungary, southern Germany and northern France; in August from western Canada, western Russia and northern Germany; in September from Scotland, Scandinavia and northern Russia; in November from Peru and South Africa; and in December from India. In similar manner the other cereals are harvested throughout the world at different seasons. International trade in grain, therefore, does much to stabilize prices...

The advantages of the United States in cereal production, even though they are elastic, are proportionately decreasing. New acres may be devoted to the growing of grain, but the cultivation of less fertile districts can only be at an increasing cost. The superiority of the United States has also been due in part to the use of labor-saving implements and machinery. In time these can be more largely utilized in European culture, even if its farming is more intensive and accordingly not so easily adapted to large-scale planting and harvesting...

Europe of recent years, however, has become alarmed not because of a plethora but rather because of a threatened scarcity of our grain yield. In 1898 this view was most forcibly presented by Sir William Crookes in his presidential address before the British Association at Bristol. Sir William's view was exceedingly pessimistic from the standpoint of a wheat-importing country, such as England. He showed that the United Kingdom grew but 25 and imported 75 per cent of its annual wheat supply. Because of the natural increase in the population, its annual requirements were increasing by some 2,000,000 bushels; and the possibilities of an increasing yield per acre were also limited because cultivation in England was already comparatively intensive. The limited acreage of the British Isles could not be expected to increase sufficiently to compensate for the growing deficit.

Great Britain must then depend more and more largely upon wheat importations. But what will be the conditions in a few years in the countries to which England habitually looks for its imports? The United States and Russia have in the past been the dominant factors in the foreign supply of wheat. At the time of Sir William Crookes's address, the United States was growing about one-fifth of all the world's wheat, and contributing about one-third of all wheat exportations. But even then the indications were that far from increasing its exportations the time must soon come when no surplus wheat would be available from the United States to make up the shortage elsewhere.

"Almost yearly since 1885 additions to the wheat-growing area have diminished, while the requirements of the increasing population of the States have advanced, so that the needed American supplies have been drawn from the acreage hitherto used for exportation. Practically there remains no uncultivated prairie land in the United States suitable for wheat growing. The virgin land has been rapidly absorbed, until at present there is no land left for wheat without reducing the area for maize, hay, and other necessary crops."

And then Crookes estimated that if the present increase of population in the United States continued it would, within a generation, be obliged to suspend its exportations and, in fact, begin to compete for the surplus supply of the world.

In his book "Highways of Progress," James J. Hill, late president of the Great Northern Railway, arrived at a similar conclusion. Owing to the later date at which Hill wrote, his detailed argument should be more applicable to the particular conditions of the United States. Mr. Hill begins by predicting that by the middle of the twentieth century this country will be obliged to support two hundred millions of people. This figure he estimates by assuming that the natural increase of population by births over deaths is 15.2 per thousand per year, and that an annual increase of 750,000 can quite conservatively be attributed to probable foreign immigration.

What will be the wheat requirements of this vast population? The average annual per capita consumption of wheat has been about seven bushels. Assuming it to be six and one-half bushels, these two hundred millions of people would require by 1950 an annual wheat supply of thirteen hundred million bushels. For a country producing less than seven hundred million bushels, and whose wheat lands were almost entirely exploited, a scarcity of food seemed to be one of the certainties of the future...

In view of Mr. Hill's broad experience and ripened judgment, these apprehensions demand the most careful consideration. Most thinkers on the subject will not, however, accept all of his assertions without challenge. First of all, we may reasonably doubt whether by 1950 the population of this country will be anything like 200,000,000.[a] The excess of births over deaths is not likely to be 15.2 per thousand per year, for the birthrate is decreasing much more rapidly than the death-rate.

The per cent of increase in the population of the United States has been: 1880–1890, 25.5; 1890–1900, 20.7; 1900–1910, 21; 1910–1920, 14.9; 1920–1930, 16.1. If Mr. Hill's conclusions were correct, the rate of increase from 1900 to 1930 would have been much higher than it actually was. There is really no scientific basis for the assertion that the population of the country will even approach 200,000,000 in 1950. Changes now in progress will make it fall short of this estimate by many millions.

Neither is American agriculture the land butchery which Mr. Hill represents it to be. It is true that in some of the Eastern States many acres have been taken from wheat growing. As the price of wheat rises, it may become profitable to return these to wheat culture. It is also true that the yield per acre in the United States is much less than, perhaps not even one-half of, that of foreign countries, such as Germany, Austria and France. But conditions in the United States have not been such as to render intensive cultivation profitable. In this country land has been cheap, but labor dear. When the pressure of the population upon the land becomes as intense as in Europe, then it will pay the American farmer to employ more labor per acre. He has merely recognized that under past conditions an intensive cultivation was not profitable.

In one respect, however, it is difficult to refute Hill. Undoubtedly Europe will be required eventually to depend less and less upon American wheat exports. And so we are led to inquire with Sir William Crookes, from what districts can England and the other European countries obtain their wheat. Sir William examines successively country after country – European Russia, Siberia, Australasia, Roumania, northern Africa and Egypt. In all of these he reaches the same conclusion: under present methods of cultivation, the wheat exports of these countries, far from expanding, must actually fall, as the requirements of their own peoples become more intense.

What then is to be the future food of the present wheat-eating nations? "If bread fails – not only us, but all the bread eaters of the world – what are we to do? We are born wheat eaters. Other races, vastly superior to us in numbers but differing widely in material and intellectual progress, are eaters of Indian corn, rice, millet and other grains; but none of these grains have the food value, the concentrated health-sustaining power of wheat, and it is on this account that the accumulated experience of civilized mankind has set wheat apart as the fit and proper food for the development of muscle and brains."

The way out, then, lies only in increasing the yield of wheat per acre, not in changing the kind of food. It is here that the chemist must be called upon – only in the laboratory can the wheat problem be solved...

Only a relatively slight increase in the pressure of population upon subsistence, resulting in a slightly higher average price of grain, will be sufficient to make the production of artificial nitrogen compounds on a large scale not only possible but profitable. Society's demand for food will be transmuted, as it were, into a demand for nitrogenous fertilizers. This is, in itself, an excellent example of the wonderfully balanced mechanism of supply and demand through which human energies, utilizing the materials of the forces of nature, are drawn into those channels of effort where they will be most efficient – that is, where they will go furthest in providing for the satisfaction of human needs.

Possibility of producing artificial nitrogen compounds on a large scale profitably

Such a success is by no means beyond the range of possibilities. If it is realized, solicitude over the wheat supply for the immediate future should be largely quieted, for the atmosphere possesses unlimited quantities of nitrogen, whereas in any other form its supply is limited. More intensive wheat culture is largely a problem of nitrogen. The mere application of more labor without more rich and abundant fertilizer will merely result in cheapening the product of labor. The problem of the future is to increase rather than to decrease the productivity of labor. This can only be accomplished by rendering more available for man's use the free gifts of nature. In the wheat problem the free gifts of nature are soil, climate, and nitrogen. The first two are fixed in supply – only the latter holds out hope to the growing populations of the future.

The fundamental error in the forecasts of Sir William Crookes and James Hill

The fundamental error in the forecasts made by both Crookes and Hill should now be obvious. They assume, without adequate evidence, that the future growth of population will be quite independent of and uncontrolled by the advance of science. In an earlier chapter[b] we have seen how the increase of the population in the last century and a half has been a thing absolutely without precedent in the world's history. Population has advanced because commerce and communication have brought new sources of food supply into being, because the power stored in the coal deposits of the world has been unloosed, because with the advance of scientific knowledge the forces of nature have been made more and more subservient to man. Without this growth in scientific knowledge the population of the country would be very much smaller than it is. Mr. Hill assumes that population is going to increase, while the advance of scientific knowledge has come to a standstill. As a matter of fact, the two things are intimately bound up with one another. In view of what has already been accomplished, it is less reasonable now to doubt that the economic progress of the next century will be vastly greater than that of the last hundred years than it was for the economists of a hundred years ago to hold the pessimistic views respecting the possibilities of human progress that some of them did hold.

Most of all, it is important to remember that there are no absolutely fixed and definite limits or barriers to human progress. Such obstacles as exist are elastic rather than rigid. The prospect before us is not that of a high precipice, impossible to surmount, but rather that of a long road which may have a gradually increasing upward gradient, although this increase in steepness may be only apparent, an optical illusion born of our inability to see clearly into the future.

This general view of the situation will be illuminated if the reader will take pains to study with some care the figures in the accompanying table, giving a survey of the world's wheat acreage and production in 1929ᶜ... Speaking generally, it is not the largest producers of wheat that have the largest production per acre. In comparison with the fifty-five bushels per acre achieved in Denmark and the per acre production of twenty-five to forty-five bushels in Germany, Great Britain, Belgium, Egypt, and Japan, our own record of bushels seems extremely small.

What is the explanation? Does it mean that American soils are less fertile? Or that American farming is less efficient? It is not the opinion of soil experts that the wheat-growing areas of America are, in respect to their natural fertility, less productive than the wheat-growing areas of other countries. Nor can it be assumed that the average American farmer, usually well educated and enterprising, is less efficient than the peasant farmer of some of the European countries which show a higher yield of wheat per acre.

A moment's thought will suffice to show that this test of productivity, the number of bushels raised per acre, is a very poor one. If the showing were on the basis of the number of bushels raised per man, that is, per unit of human labor utilized in wheat growing, the ranking of the different countries in respect of the productivity of their agriculture would be very nearly the inverse of what is shown in the table. Product per acre and product per man are generally opposed or reciprocal ratios. In this country, as compared with the much more densely populated countries of Europe, labor is relatively scarce and land is relatively plentiful. In Europe labor is relatively plentiful and land is relatively scarce. The American farmer has to economize in respect of labor, that is, he has to spread labor rather thinly over a large area of land. The European farmer has to economize in respect of land, that is, he has to employ a large amount of labor upon a relatively small area of land. It is an inevitable result, of course, that the product per acre in densely populated countries, where land is expensive, is bound to be greater than the product per acre in more thinly populated countries, where land is relatively plentiful.

The American farmer has been subjected to a good many unfair criticisms in the past. Persons without economic training have had their attention called to figures such as we give and have inferred that the American farmer is careless, wasteful, inefficient. It is frequently urged that "more intensive" farming is needed in this country.

But after all this is hardly a matter with respect to which the outside observer is qualified to advise the American farmer. The degree of intensivity of cultivation which is most profitable is determined very largely by the relative costs of labor and of land. If land becomes dearer as the country's population increases, the American farmer will turn to more intensive farming, not because his farming is not sufficiently intensive at the present, but merely because under changed conditions the more intensive cultivation of the soil will become more profitable.

There may even be some reason to suspect that changes in the immediate future may be in the direction of a decreased rather than an increased intensivity of cultivation. The invention and development of farm labor-saving machinery is now changing the situation rapidly. In many cases larger farms than those now in use may become profitable.

The general conclusion is that the future of the world's food supply is safe

In general we must conclude that the American farmer is a fairly good judge of his own interests. In serving his own interests, that is, by utilizing the best proportions of land, labor and capital, he also serves the interests of the nation. Farming is rather better standardized and is probably more efficiently conducted on the whole than are most of the other types of industry.

What is the bearing of these considerations upon the future of the world's cereal production? Merely this: there is an elastic and indefinitely large source of future increase in increased intensity of agricultural cultivation. This does not mean that efforts should be made to secure increased intensivity of cultivation now, without regard to its immediate profitableness. The point to be emphasized is that as the population of the world grows, as the demand for cereals and other food crops increases, increased intensivity of cultivation is going to become profitable in just the same way and for just the same reasons that it will be profitable to extend cultivation to certain lands, not of the first class, on which it is not now profitable to grow cereals. Even if we assume that science stands still, that there are no advances in our knowledge of how to utilize the powers of nature to best advantage, there nevertheless remains an elastic reserve of indefinitely large extent which may be drawn upon for the food of the future. This means, to use the figure that we have used before, that, while the road ahead of us may be uphill, it does not lead toward a precipitous wall, but up a gentle and almost imperceptible gradient. If the possible or even probable advances in science are taken into account, we may not even be altogether sure that the road, when we come to it, will be uphill! All in all, there is no reason for present pessimism respecting the future of the world's food supply, or respecting any limits which that food supply may set upon human progress and achievement.

Editors' notes

a Actually the US population reached 152 million in 1951 and 205 million in 1971.
b Chapter 2 of the Grolier *Book of Popular Science*, entitled "The Rise of Population in Great Countries" (included in this Selection as Chapter 15).
c Not reproduced. The data in the table are for 1929 which suggests that this chapter was updated after Young's death.

21 The economic interdependence of nations

The ideal of national economic self-sufficiency and its limitations

Minerals and military preparedness

The Book of Popular Science (1923; revised 1929) New York: The Grolier Society. Group IX Ch. 9: 1243–52

The history of human society in its economic aspect is a history of an increasingly complex system of economic interdependence. From savagery to civilization man has progressed – has found an opportunity to make the most of his own personal powers – only by restricting and narrowing the field of his own personal endeavors, by learning to depend more and more upon the increased coöperation of his fellows. His steps forward have been in the path of increased division of labor, increased specialization, increased dependence upon exchange and commerce.

The first division of labor, very likely, was a division of labor between the sexes. Among savage tribes everywhere it is found that even though one man may occupy himself with the same activities that occupy other men of the tribe, and one woman's work may be precisely like that of the other women of the tribe, there is nevertheless a sharp distinction between the activities of the men and of the women. Speaking generally, what were deemed to be the more honorable activities, including hunting and fishing as well as war, were monopolized by the men, while activities of a more humble order, such as the preparing of food and the cultivating of the fields – if the tribe had advanced to the stage where it practised some crude form of agriculture – were left to the women. The next step upward in respect of the division of labor is not quite so certain.

Some have thought that among nearly all savage peoples trade began in the shape of intertribal exchange, – a development, perhaps, of ceremonial reciprocal gift-making as among different tribes. In this way a tribe which had cultivated the art of wickerwork or of pottery might exchange its products for those of a tribe which, in some way, had stumbled upon the art of making crude implements out of iron. There is evidence that intertribal trade of this sort sometimes occurs in exceedingly primitive conditions, even before trade of any recognizable sort takes place within the tribe. But it is easy to be too dogmatic with reference to problems like these. It is not safe to try to describe any stage in human history by any one single sweeping formula. As a matter of fact we know that, in some cases at least, a considerable division of labor within the tribe accompanied or even preceded the stage of intertribal trade.

When division of labor proceeds beyond the stage of differentiation in the work assigned to the sexes, or beyond the stage of tribal specialization, it takes, in many cases at least, the form of a division of labor as among families. For a long time, and despite the gradual growth of specialized crafts, men seem to have held firmly to the notion that the family should be a self-sufficient economic unit. In economic organization, as well as in political life and in legal relations, the ancient family was a social unit of prime importance.

The family, aided by slavery, the self-sufficient economic unit

It must be remembered, of course, that the ancient family, the patriarchal for example, might comprise a very large number of individuals bound together by blood relationship. And in the classical period slavery could be utilized to increase the economic strength of a single family so that it would be more nearly self-sufficient and independent than would otherwise have been possible.

The American reader will find it easy to imagine the possibilities of an economic organization of this sort if he will think of the plantation system of the Southern States before the Civil War. In this respect, as in many others, the economic history of the United States has been in some measure a recapitulation of the economic history of western civilization. Professor F. J. Turner has said: "The United States lies like a huge page in the history of society. Line by line, as we read this continental page from west to east, we find the record of social evolution. It begins with the Indian and the hunter; it goes on to tell of the disintegration of savagery by the entrance of the trader, the pathfinder of civilization; we read the annals of the pastoral stage in ranch life; the exploitation of the soil by the raising of unrotated crops of corn and wheat in sparsely settled farming communities; the intensive culture of the denser farm settlement; and finally, the manufacturing organization with city and factory system."

The medieval town becomes the economic substitute for the family

Passing to the Middle Ages, the thread of development becomes stronger and more easily traced. The medieval village, with a little outside trade, became subordinate finally to the trading town, itself a product of the human quest for adventure and for expanding opportunities for life. The burghers of the town safeguarded their freedom jealously not only against feudal overlords but against outsiders of whatever sort. Thus freedom within the town was a monopoly as against outsiders.

Economic self-sufficiency was the frankly avowed goal of the medieval town. Its "freedoms" were identical with its "privileges." Its artisans and traders insisted, so far as they could, that strangers should not come into the town to compete with them, and they also tried to see that the different crafts were all represented, so far as practicable, within the town.

Commerce made the towns; it now was to make the nations

The growth of the towns had itself been one of the factors tending to undermine feudalism. By the irony of fate, the towns lost their authority and prestige through precisely the same general forces through which they had gained them. Commerce had made the towns, commerce now was to make the nations. First, the Mediterranean trade with the East, and second the new opportunities for world trade which followed upon the discovery of America and of the sea route to India at the end of the fifteenth century, created problems that were altogether too large for the towns to handle. Foreign trade became of necessity a national enterprise. With the strengthening of the powers of national governments there came, in the sixteenth and seventeenth centuries, a new insistence that the nation rather than the town was the natural economic unit, that it should be so far as possible economically self-sufficient. The new colonial domains beyond the seas were viewed as part of or more literally as appendages to, the national economic system.

The pursuit of this ideal of national economic independence resembled in many respects the quest of the corresponding goal on the part of the towns in earlier centuries. There was the same growing emphasis upon freedom within the economic unit – freedom, that is, within the nation, and the same attitude of jealous aggression as against outsiders or "foreigners."

Now during the past few centuries international commerce has vastly increased. The division of labor is no longer wholly a division of labor within the family, or within the town, or even within the nation. The world's economy is founded in very large part upon a division of labor among different nations. Nevertheless, the ideal of national economic self-sufficiency has by no means perished. On the contrary, it has in recent years shown renewed vitality. How shall we explain this? Is this merely a survival of older ideals and of older modes of thought? Is there nothing in it beyond a stupid refusal to accept the advantages and economies of the international division of labor and to use those advantages to the very fullest extent possible?

The question we are discussing, it should be observed, is not the question of protection versus free trade, although, of course, a protective tariff is one of the obvious methods of securing a measure of economic isolation. But many of the more cogent arguments in favor of protective tariffs would retain such significance as they have even though national economic independence as an ideal should be definitely repudiated. The problems, then, are related, but they are not identical.

The advantages of international economic coöperation are obvious. They are, in a strict sense, economic advantages. Reliance upon international commerce leads the way to national specialization, and national specialization is, from the point of view of the economic interests of the world as a whole, just as advantageous as personal specialization, or regional specialization, or the division of labor in any other of its manifold forms. Only through international economic coöperation are the world's fuel deposits, its sources of energy, brought into the most efficient relation with its raw materials, its food products, its varying degrees of national abilities and aptitudes. Its disadvantages must be sought from the point of view not of the world as a whole but of the interests of particular nations. These interests may be worthy or unworthy, real or imaginary; generally they are of both orders. In particular they are associated with the idea of the preservation of the integrity of the nation's existing political, economic and cultural institutions.

In the first place, commerce makes for progress. That means that it makes for change. Progress and change may not always be desired by a nation conscious of its past as well as of its present, desiring to hold fast to the institutions which it has proved to be good and which at any rate are its own. But commerce makes not only for progress. It makes for standardization, for a leveling of life within different nations. Standards of living tend to approach a common level; tastes, literature, art, music, all of the institutions of a nation's civilization, tend with unrestricted commerce and communication more and more to become internationalized, as it were, that is, to approach a common international level. "Local color" fades. For those who value just those local and national differences that unrestricted commerce and communication tend to eliminate, the world seems to be tending toward a monotonous uniformity.

Fichte's views on the ideal conditions in the closed industrial state

It was thus that Fichte, the great German philosopher, writing in the last year of the eighteenth century of "The Closed Industrial State," held that under ideal conditions foreign intercourse would be dispensed with, so far as possible, and that such as remained should be in the hands of the government. The German people, he thought, could make their largest and best contribution to the civilization of the world by developing their own civilization and, through self-imposed isolation, preserving that civilization free from contact with or, one might say, from dilution by, the civilization of other peoples.

In the second place, it is perfectly clear that just so far as a nation participates in the world's commercial system, by just so much it makes itself economically dependent upon other nations, just as these other nations become economically dependent upon it. Now a nation whose normal economic life is bound up with that of other nations is not so well prepared for suddenly enforced isolation as is a nation which has cultivated self-sufficiency to the best of its ability.

Economic self-sufficiency an essential to adequate preparedness for war

Putting it plainly, economic self-sufficiency is of enormous military value. It is properly to be regarded as an essential part of adequate national preparedness for war.

Take, for example, the position of the South at the time of the Civil War. The Southern States at that time were more largely dependent than any other part of the country upon external trade. They had a specialized agriculture; they raised cotton and other staples and shipped them to Europe as well as to the Northern States in exchange for manufactured goods and even for a good many ordinary and necessary food products. Cut off by the war and the attendant blockade of southern ports from their outside markets, the whole basis of the economic life of the Southern States was shattered. Cotton that cannot be marketed is not wealth; it is merely waste. Purchasing power which has no access to markets in which goods may be bought is valueless. The miracle was that under these conditions the Southern States were able to prolong the struggle so gallantly and for so many years as they did.

Or, to take a more recent example, turn to the position of Germany. The idea of maximum preparedness for war touched and colored German imperial policies of many different sorts. For example, the problem of the "industrial nation" as compared with the "agricultural nation" was discussed and debated through long years in Germany as an essential problem of maximum preparedness for war. Should the German government encourage industry? Or should it encourage agriculture, with a view of making Germany less dependent upon imports from other nations? It cannot be said that the partisans of either policy won a clean-cut victory. But it is true that the agrarian party won a partial victory in the German tariffs which imposed rather high duties upon imports of foreign foodstuffs, especially wheat and rye. This policy was intended and frankly admitted to be "war insurance."

The partial success of Germany's encouragement of agriculture

In part, at least, it most certainly accomplished its purpose, for from the beginning of the twentieth century up to the fateful year of 1914, Germany, along with the magnificent strides her industries were making, was increasing the production of the fundamental cereals.

The war, although it resulted in such a way as everlastingly to discredit the soundness of the military argument for national self-sufficiency, gave, for the time being at least, a new power to that ideal. New states have been set up in eastern Europe within national boundaries that inevitably had to be drawn right across what in the past had been free and unimpeded channels of commerce. These new states asserted their national independence by taking measures looking toward larger economic independence. And a country like France, rich in historical traditions, rightly jealous of the interests of its own splendid civilization, continues to withdraw itself, just so far as it can, within the boundaries of an economic system which includes not only France but its great colonial possessions. For a while at least it seemed as though the war had given a new impetus toward the movement to make of the British Empire a self-sufficing economic unity, set off from the rest of the world by high differential or discriminatory tariffs, producing in large measure its own raw materials and its own manufactured products. But there does not seem to be any evidence that the movement has really gained in lasting strength.

How the war for a time affected Great Britain's economic policy

As a matter of fact, England has gone farther than any other country in fitting herself into the international commercial system. A hundred years ago she abandoned the ideal of economic self-sufficiency. Her coal mines, her textile mills, her ships and her banks, rather than her tilled fields, were to be the sources of her wealth and strength. Everyone knows the enormous success of England's economic policy. Quickly assuming industrial and commercial leadership, and manufacturing, banking, supplying fuel, and carrying goods for the rest of the world, she has been able to bring to her shores vastly larger supplies of food products and of raw materials than she could possibly have produced within her own narrow boundaries. But in a world not yet freed from war a national economic system built up upon international commerce has its penalties. The life of England, more than that of any other country, depends upon keeping the inlets and outlets of her trade open. England's navy, expensive and burdensome as it has been, was part of the price she had to pay for her commercial supremacy.

The development of international commerce has given a new significance to sea power, the place of which in human history has been portrayed in so masterly a manner by the great American expert, Admiral Mahan. The enormous growth of international commerce during the nineteenth century, and the accompanying increase of the dependence of one nation upon another, have greatly increased the significance of the control of the seas. Blockades and embargoes are more than ever the most potent weapons of warfare.

Should we draw the conclusion, therefore, that so long as the peoples of the world live under the shadow of possible war only those countries whose naval or military position is impregnable can afford to refuse to limit and confine their commerce with a view to securing the largest possible measure of economic independence and self-sufficiency? A little investigation of the facts will show that this conclusion does not follow – that under modern conditions economic self-sufficiency is something absolutely impossible for a nation to attain or even to approximate. The difficulty is that we are too likely to think of economic self-sufficiency in terms merely of food supplies. Now for only a very few highly industrialized countries, of which England is the best example, is the domestic food supply so small that, in an emergency, it would not be sufficient to carry the nation through a fairly prolonged war.

Under old conditions of warfare a siege might force a city to surrender, for the city would have only its accumulated stores of food to draw upon. But it is difficult or well-nigh impossible to starve a whole nation into submission. The experience of European countries during the Great War showed how far it is possible to get along with reduced food consumption by substituting cheaper foods for dearer ones, and by using possible sources of food that had formerly been allowed to waste. In other words, for most countries the domestic food supply is, within limits, elastic.

Not shortage in food supply the real difficulty in time of war

The fundamental difficulty, then, is not likely to be with the food supply, but with the supply of some of the highly specialized products that enter into the mechanism of modern industrial life. With the development of the application of the sciences, especially chemistry, to warfare, some of these specialized products are military essentials. Food, after all, is produced in larger or smaller quantities almost everywhere. These other products to which we have referred have been distributed by nature in a more miserly fashion. No one country has all of them; most countries must get their share of them through international trade.

Take, for example, the position of Germany in the Great War. Germany, as we have seen, had consciously pursued a policy supposed to lead to economic self-sufficiency. She never became wholly self-sufficing even in respect of food. In particular, certain important kinds of food – for example, animal and vegetable oils and fats – were obtained by import. Nevertheless, her difficulties during the war, when she was shut off from ocean-borne trade, were less serious in respect of food than in respect of other necessary commodities...

The fact is that under modern conditions there is no such thing as complete economic self-sufficiency. It is an absurdly impossible goal. The complexity of modern life, utilizing hundreds of different sorts of commodities and materials drawn from all parts of the earth, has forever removed the possibility that any nation can live of its own. The world is now a world of interdependent nations. To cut the lines of international commercial communication is to cut the arteries of national life. There are superficial thinkers who hold that commerce, the competition of the great nations for markets, is the fundamental cause of modern wars. But rightly viewed, any one nation gains more than it loses by the growth of the wealth and the trade of other nations. With respect only to a minor factor of the world's trade are the great nations in a strict sense competitors. The bulk of the world's trade is among the great trading nations themselves. Each of these nations is a market for the others. Commerce and war are opposites.

22 The reign of king cotton

America's great staple crop and its place in international trade

The methods of the cotton market

The Book of Popular Science (1924; revised 1929) New York: The Grolier Society. Group IX Ch. 11: 1529–36

Next to iron and steel, cotton has been the largest single factor in the industrial and commercial changes of the last century and a half. Only within recent times, comparatively speaking, has cotton become an important article or product of commerce in the western world. Grown and used long ago in the Orient, cotton and cotton goods were little known in Europe until the seventeenth century. Before that cotton had been grown in Spain by the Moors, and Italian traders had brought small quantities of Oriental cotton into Europe. But at no time was this early trade important.

It was the development of England's trade with India that first acquainted Europe with the fine cotton fabrics of the Orient. A demand quickly arose for them, even though they were then more expensive than the ordinary domestic fabrics made of wool or linen. In England the woolen interests asked Parliament to protect them against the competition of these imported East Indian goods, and so there was passed in 1721 the so-called "Calico Act": "An act to preserve and encourage the woolen and silk manufactures for the more satisfactory employment of the poor, by prohibiting the use and wear of all printed, painted, flowered, or dyed calicoes in apparel, household stuffs, furniture, or otherwise." Even though it remained possible to import white goods, the net effect of the Calico Act was not so much to protect the woolen industry as to bring into being within England a new cotton industry that became a more serious competitor than the foreign cotton would have been.

The subsequent rise of cotton to a predominant position in world trade was accomplished through one of the most dramatic series of events of modern economic history. It affords a striking illustration of the elasticity of the world's productive and commercial mechanism, of the way in which new human needs are met by advances in science and technology. The "great inventions" – so called not because they were in themselves surpassing technical achievements, but because of their influence upon later history – were identified in a peculiar way with the new cotton industry of eighteenth century England. Not complete in themselves, not suddenly perfected, they were as much a result as a cause of the expansion of the cotton trade; they were a reaction to the stimulus of demand.

But even the roller spinning machine of Wyatt and Paul (1758), Hargreave's jenny (1767), the water-frame of Arkwright (1769), Crompton's mule (1780), and Horrocks's improved power loom (1803), very important steps forward though they were, would not have sufficed in themselves to make cotton the cheap and universal fabric that it is today. The great difficulty that remained was the preparation of the raw cotton; not the growing of the cotton, but the separating of it from the seed. So long as the laborer could not prepare more than a pound of cotton fiber in a day, cotton was bound to remain a relatively expensive luxury. Again, however, need brought forth a solution of the problem. Eli Whitney's cotton gin (1793) was a very simple invention indeed.

But it is fairly certain that if Whitney had not hit upon its fundamental principle someone else very soon would have done so. Nevertheless, as history stands, there is truth in Macaulay's judgment that, "What Peter the Great did to make Russia dominant, Eli Whitney's invention of the cotton gin has more than equaled in its relation to the power and progress of the United States."

With cotton, then, it happened, but not wholly by chance, that a cheapening of the cost of producing the raw material came along with the reductions in manufacturing costs. Furthermore, the fertile soils of the southern part of the United States were waiting, one might say, for the growth of cotton culture, while, on the other hand, the populations of the world were waiting, it may with equal truth be said, for this new and wonderful and cheapest of all textiles. An enormously elastic demand on the one hand, and enormously elastic possibilities of supply on the other hand! The result was the rise of what was destined in a few years to become one of the world's most important industries.

In Georgia and the Carolinas the early settlers grew cotton as an ornamental plant. Not until after the Revolution did the United States raise cotton on a commercial scale. As a matter of fact, eight bags of cotton shipped from Charleston to London in 1774 were seized at the custom house on the charge of false entry, the ground being that it was impossible to raise so much cotton in the United States!

The rapid spread of American cotton culture westward under the stimulus of a growing world demand has been an important factor in the political as well as the economic history of the United States. In the North, people of New England origin went westward, following the route of the Erie Canal and the Great Lakes. Their migration westward was marked by a wonderful expansion of our wheat-growing areas.

Similarly the people of the southern Atlantic States, moving westward into the great cotton-growing regions of the Gulf States, took with them cotton and the plantation system. Cotton led the westward movement in the South, as did wheat in the North. Is it to be wondered at that the conflict out of which grew the Civil War came first in the regions just west of the Missouri River, – that section where wheat growing and cotton culture met? ...

One very important economic peculiarity of cotton growing has been much discussed. Wherever cotton is an important crop it becomes the one important crop. It is satisfied with nothing less than dominance, and will tolerate no rivals in its field.

Thus cotton-growing regions are regions of highly specialized agriculture. Now specialized agriculture has its advantages and its disadvantages. In prosperous years the profits from specialized agriculture, that is, from some one dominant "money crop," are usually larger than could be got from the expenditure of a similar amount of labor and capital in diversified farming. But diversified farming is safer and surer. If the chance of large profit is less, so too is the chance of large loss. Specialized agriculture, then, necessarily involves a large speculative element. The farmer or the planter stakes everything upon the success or failure of one particular crop and upon the chance that the crop will sell at a profitable price.

The farmers of the South have long been criticized for their adherence to this unstable and uncertain "one-crop" system. Throughout most of the cotton belt from one-half to three-fourths of the cultivated land is devoted to cotton. The land not planted to cotton is devoted to corn, which is the foundation of the food supply of cotton-field labor. It is often asked why the southern farmer has not grown a larger diversity of crops and thus released himself from his dependence upon the uncertainties of the cotton crop and of the cotton market. The answer is that under favorable conditions, or even under average conditions, wherever cotton can be grown at all, cotton is the most profitable single crop. Moreover, if the farmer is to grow cotton at all, he will be able to grow but little else. Always and everywhere in American agriculture the limiting factor in determining how much land shall be devoted to one crop and how much to another is found in the relative demands these different crops make upon the available time of the farmer. The farmer in the northern states plans his crops, so far as possible, on a non-competing basis. Wheat, oats and corn, for example, can be fitted into the calendar in such a way that there will be very little overlapping of the demands which the different crops make for attention. Not so with cotton. It requires labor throughout almost the entire year. Its picking in particular, demands a large amount of hand labor. Therefore, wherever it is profitable to produce cotton at all, it becomes difficult or relatively unprofitable to devote much land or labor to the growing of other crops.

It is quite possible, of course, that conditions may change so that cotton growing will become relatively less profitable or that the growing of other crops will become more profitable. Changes of this sort may lead to more diversified farming in the cotton-growing region. In general, the uninformed outsider, lacking special knowledge of local conditions, has no right whatever to tell the farmers of the South or of any other region that they would find a more diversified agriculture or a less diversified agriculture more profitable than the sort of agriculture they are now practising. ...

The methods by which the cotton crop is marketed may seem at first sight simple and even primitive. But more careful study will show that in between the cotton grower of the South and the cotton mills of the world there is a complex and intricate marketing organization which, although doubtless not perfect, and operating with some wastes, nevertheless fulfils its purpose admirably and never breaks down under stress.

Cotton growing is largely done upon credit. Planters, especially the small planters, must usually borrow money in order to pay for tools and machinery and labor before the crop is sold. Sometimes the credit is furnished in the form of "charge accounts" by local merchants. This is likely to be true of tenant farmers especially. There is, however, a growing use of bank credit, especially on the part of the larger growers. The inauguration of the Federal Reserve System, by liberalizing the terms upon which agricultural credit can be granted by the banks, has been of very great advantage to the cotton grower. When the cotton is picked and baled it is sold to local buyers or sometimes shipped directly to a mill or warehouse. The buyers pay cash, enabling the planter to pay off his accumulated debts and often to begin his preparations for the next crop with a surplus of profit.

The small local cotton buyers sell to larger buyers, who are purchasing cotton for mills or for exporters. Many of these large buyers advance a good deal of money during the growing season to help finance the crop, but when they finally purchase it themselves they need help from the banks. ...

Organized speculation in staple crops tends to stabilize prices

The great central cotton markets of the world are New York, New Orleans, Liverpool (England), Bremen (Germany), Havre (France), Alexandria (Egypt) and Bombay (India). Some of these great cotton markets, however, are concerned with the buying and selling of cotton primarily for the manufacturers of a particular country or region (Bremen or Havre, for example), or they deal almost exclusively in the cotton grown in a particular country (Alexandria and Bombay, for example). The three great world markets, properly so called, then, are New York, New Orleans and Liverpool. Each of these cities is not only an important market for actual cotton, but is also a center of speculation in cotton "futures." The nature and effects of organized speculation in cotton and other staples will be discussed in a later chapter. It is sufficient here to say that, despite very real evils and abuses, organized speculation in staple crops is unquestionably of very real advantage both to producers and consumers.[a] Its effects, on the whole, are to stabilize prices rather than to unsettle them. Moreover, the speculative market makes it possible for sellers and buyers of actual cotton who do not desire to be burdened with the risks of changing prices to "hedge," that is, to shift such risks on to the shoulders of professional speculators in staples.

Editors' note

a Young's treatment of this subject is very different from that of Chiozza Money, who emphasizes the evils of speculation. Young's detailed discussion of speculation was in Chapter 35 of *The Book of Popular Science*, reprinted in Chapter 37 below.

23 Trade and the railroad

The Book of Popular Science (1923; revised 1929) New York: The Grolier Society. Group IX Ch. 19: 2529–37

[Eds: This chapter, mostly by Chiozza Money, emphasizes the importance of transport to commerce and civilization, records the inventions that made the railway possible, and gives details of the growth of railways around the world. Allyn Young gives a history of the railroad in the United States. Here we reproduce the section in which he explains why countries have subjected their railway systems to public ownership and control.]

It is important to observe that in those countries where railroads are not owned by the government, they are subjected to rigorous public control of a kind unheard of in the case of ordinary industrial undertakings. In fact, no one any longer claims that railroads are in all respects like other business undertakings, or that they should be free to do as they please, or as their business interests dictate, with respect to such important matters as the rates they charge and the services they offer.

It is commonly said that the excuse for the rigorous public control exercised both by the federal govermnent and the individual states is that railway companies are "quasi-public corporations," and as such properly subject to an unusual measure of supervision. But on examination this supposed explanation turns out to be no explanation at all. There remains the fundamental question, just why our railways are singled out as quasi-public undertakings, or as businesses "affected with a public interest." Surely railway transportation is no more vital to the nation than is the growing of grain, the milling of flour, or the baking of bread or a host of other necessary occupations.

As a matter of fact all ordinary business undertakings are subject to the control exercised by *competition*. The prices the farmer, the miller and the baker can charge are fixed within fairly close limits by the forces of supply and demand. The individual producer has little control over them. He has to sell at the market price, be that price profitable or unprofitable.

Railways, by contrast, have a large measure of monopoly power. Most of the towns in any country have only one line of railway; many industries have convenient access to only one line; many sections of the country, and many cities, are dependent for their trade outlets on a very few railway systems.

More than that, where railroad competition would seem to be possible, as where two or more lines connect two important cities, experience has shown that it works very badly. Slight differences in rates will send nearly all of the through freight traffic over one line or another, provided that the services and facilities afforded are at all comparable. From the point of view of any one railroad, rate cutting, under such conditions, is profitable, in the sense that it is better to earn even a small income than to earn none!

A large part of the expenditures of a railroad has to be paid whether it carries much or little freight. This is true of interest on its bonds, of much of its taxes, of a considerable proportion of its office expenses, of much of its outlays for maintaining its way and structures and even its equipment. Of course over a long period of years, such fixed charges, or "overhead costs" increase as the railway's traffic increases; that is, as it improves its track, or builds additional tracks and better stations, and buys more and heavier cars and locomotives. But from the point of view of the railway traffic manager it is profitable at any one time to secure additional freight if rates can be secured that are high enough to pay the "prime costs" of moving it, that is, the *actual additional* costs created by the added freight. If this much, and just a little more, can be obtained, it will be more profitable to carry the freight than not to carry it.

The result is that even where competition between railway lines would seem to be possible, such competition sets no efficacious or practicable limit to rate cutting. It is clear that what we have called fixed charges and overhead must be paid in some manner. Some part if not all of the traffic must contribute more than the actual prime or "additional" costs of conducting transportation. But in the case of two parallel and so-called "competing" lines there is relatively little traffic which cannot be drawn from one road to the other by rate cutting. Railway history supports this analysis. Railway competition degenerates into rate wars, and leads to the inevitable bankruptcy of the competing roads. The only alternative on the part of the roads is combination. This takes on different forms: the pooling or division of competitive traffic in agreed proportions; the pooling of gross or net earnings; the leasing of one line to another; the ownership of the majority of the stock of various lines by a "holding company" organized for that purpose, etc. Whatever the form, the purpose is the same – monopoly and the unity of policy which monopoly gives.

Thus we see that in the railroad field monopoly is inevitable. In some industries, the public may think it better to tolerate a measure of monopoly than to burden itself with the trouble and expense of control. But not so with respect to railways; the economic power they wield is too enormous to be left unregulated and unchecked. Railways, by using the simple device of discriminations in rates, have the power to make or unmake the prosperity of industries, cities and of whole sections of the country. A guarantee of equal and fair treatment in respect to railway rates and service, of unimpeded access to the transportation facilities of the country, are fundamental conditions of the maintenance of wholesome competition in the nation's industry and trade. Likening the competitive struggle to a game, railways *have the power to lay down the rules of the game.* This power is too vast and too important to be permitted to be lodged anywhere except in the hands of the government. The point is not that the government always does these things well. It is rather that the power of control, whether for good or ill, cannot be lodged in any other hands than those of a government which represents all of the people and all of the interest of a state or nation. It would be as logical to permit private corporations to determine what our taxes and our tariff duties shall be as to give them the absolute power to determine what our railroad rates shall be.

24 Wealth and well-being

The true nature of wealth, and the
end and aim of human effort in trade
and industry

The value of American accumulations

The Book of Popular Science (1924; revised 1929) New York: The Grolier Society. Group IX Ch. 20: 2665–74

[Eds: The Harmsworth and Grolier editions have a common introduction about the meaning of wealth, and attack the mercantilist view that wealth is money (as opposed to commodities that give us health and pleasure). Young has a section explaining the paradox of value. Chiozza Money fulminates against the evils of the machine age and the need to promote greater leisure for workers. At this point Young offers a more optimistic view of the effects of mechanization:]

...[T]houghtful observers and students of the problem have questioned whether the advent of machinery has really had in general a degrading effect upon the industrial employments. Thus, for example, Professor T. N. Carver, dealing with this very case of the making of shoes, has suggested that other considerations should be taken into account:

> Looked at broadly, is the average work of a laborer in a machine industry less dignified, less agreeable, less humanizing than it was before the industry reached the machine stage? From the nature of the question, it is dangerous to dogmatize because neither the affirmative nor the negative is capable of being demonstrated. The negative view seems to rest mainly upon the assumption that it is more dignified to be occupied with a great many purely mechanical operations than with a very few. The old-fashioned shoemaker, for example, was largely occupied with purely mechanical operations, most of them of a very elementary nature, such as a machine can do quite as well as a man. Each of these operations required great concentration of attention, leaving him very little opportunity for other forms of mental activity. He was the slave of each particular task as truly as a modern machine worker can be said to be the slave of his single task. But the old-fashioned shoemaker had to turn from one kind of work to another. This increased the difficulty, and, on the whole, required of him a greater amount of concentration than is now required of the operator of a machine. The latter, who has but one routine task to learn, learns it easily, and can carry it out without

very intense concentration of mind. His mind, therefore, would seem to be freer than that of the old hand worker, though there was more variety to the work of the latter. Whether this greater variety is to his advantage or disadvantage would be difficult to determine off-hand. It looks as though the operator of a machine in a shoe factory, being relieved of the necessity of acquiring several forms of specialized manual dexterity, would be in a better position for free mental activity than the old-fashioned shoemaker.

... It is [also] possible ... that in present day discussions of economic problems we attach too much importance to an increase in leisure. The working hours of the day absorb, and will continue to absorb, a large part of humanity's energies. The peoples and the nations which have succeeded in the struggle for existence are not those which have put a high value on leisure, but those which have combined the qualities of industry and thrift. Rightly seen, the economic problem is not so much that of lessening the amount of work to be done as that of making it more agreeable and attractive to the worker, and of directing it into channels which will be of maximum usefulness to society. From time immemorial the world's wise men have observed that there is no happier man than he who delights in the work he has to do, and who is therefore able to put his energies and his enthusiasm into it with all his heart.

The radical social reformers who count upon the ultimate reduction of the working day not only to four or five but even to two or three hours are not only over-optimistic but also are failing to see the real goal of human progress. Not less work, but better work and happier work are more serviceable ambitions for any people. It may be too much to hope that what we may call the artistic instinct, the irresistible impulse toward the expression of one's personality in one's work, may come to be the common possession of the world's workers. But progress toward such a happy condition is probable.

One of the greatest present disadvantages of the machine system may ultimately become one of its greatest advantages. By subdividing, simplifying and standardizing manufacturing processes, it reduces them to routine. It introduces monotony of occupation. It calls for a large number of routine tasks. But it happens that it is just these monotonous and routine tasks which invite the further use of machine processes. When a task becomes simple and standardized it is fairly certain to be taken over sooner or later by machinery. Mechanical stokers, mechanical press feeders, mechanical filling and bottling devices and other machines have already taken over certain monotonous employments. Further applications of machinery to simple and standardized processes are inevitable. It may well be that the cure of some of the evils of the machine system may come through its own further perfection.

Adam Smith and John Stuart Mill on productive and unproductive work

[Chiozza Money: The desirable commodities which constitute wealth may be material goods or immaterial goods (services), and we may find immaterial goods in a concrete form. The services of a carpenter, bricklayer, machinist, or longshoreman satisfy wants,

and are properly termed wealth. We may see any or all of these embodied in material form. Ten thousand bricks in a brickyard are worth less than ten thousand bricks built up as a wall, because not only has other material been incorporated in the wall, but the bricklayer's labor has taken a concrete shape. So it is also with the services rendered by postmen, policemen, doctors, or lawyers, whether or not they take concrete form.]

Such has not always been the opinion of political economists. Both Adam Smith and John Stuart Mill – the two greatest names in the history of English economic thought – held that those services only are truly productive which are embodied in "durable and vendible commodities." Adam Smith said:

> The labor of some of the most respectable orders in society is, like that of menial servants, unproductive of any value, and does not fix or realize itself in any permanent subject, or vendible commodity, which endures after that labor is past, and for which an equal quantity of labor could afterwards be procured. The sovereign, for example, with all the officers both of justice and war who serve under him, the whole army and navy, are unproductive laborers. They are the servants of the public, and are maintained by a part of the annual produce of the industry of other people. Their service, how notable, how useful, or how necessary soever, produces nothing for which an equal quantity of service can afterwards be procured. The protection, security, and defense of the commonwealth, the effect of their labor this year, will not purchase its protection, security, and defense for the year to come. In the same class must be ranked some both of the gravest and most important, and some of the most frivolous professions: players, buffoons, musicians, opera-singers, opera-dancers, etc. The labor of the meanest of these has a certain value, regulated by the very same principles which regulate that of every sort of labor; and that of the noblest and most useful produces nothing which could afterwards purchase an equal quantity of labor. Like the declamation of the actor, the harangue of the orator, or the tune of the musician, the work of all of them perishes in the very instant of its production.

Various writers since Smith and Mill have called attention to the inconsistency and absurdities that are inherent in such contentions. For example, by Smith's criterion, a violin maker is productive, and a violinist unproductive, although, the only purpose of making the violin is that it may be played upon! In a similar way, the engineer who designs a bridge is productive, but the professor in a technical school who taught him how to design bridges is unproductive! Caruso was unproductive when he sang in the Metropolitan Opera House, but he was productive when he sang for a phonograph record! It is clearly impossible to qualify services as productive and unproductive simply because some are directly rendered to the consumer, while others take the intermediate form of marketable commodities. After all, everything that satisfies a human want must be held to possess utility, and from one point of view it is unimportant whether the want be satisfied by a service directly rendered, as by a musician, a teacher or a physician, or result in the increase of more or less durable commodities, as do the services of artist, author, and the manufacturer of medical supplies.

Nevertheless, there is a fundamental truth in the doctrine advanced by Smith and Mill, although their use of the words "productive" and "unproductive" is misleading. The distinction they sought to make is really one between work which provides for present wants, and work which adds to a country's stock of capital. From the point of view of the consumer, the difference appears as the distinction between spending and saving. The accumulation and increase of national wealth depends not only upon production; it also necessitates thrift. No nation, any more than an individual, can "eat its cake and have it, too." There would, of course, be no purpose in producing solely with an eye to the increase of future wealth; thrift should not become parsimony. But, as human nature is constituted, there is little likelihood that the people of a nation, taken as a group, will need to be exhorted to save less and spend more. No one has ever assigned too large a measure of thrift as the cause of the decline of any people. For practical purposes, the lesson which needs to be taken to heart is that which Smith and Mill taught.

[Eds. There follows a section on the need to include public as well as private wealth in computing total national wealth. Young then presents and discusses statistical estimates of the growth of the stock of wealth in the United States, 1850–1922, making allowance for the general movement of prices, and also noting "the paradoxical fact that an increase in wealth may come from increasing scarcity as well as from increasing abundance. Such, for example is the case of the enormous increase in the figures for land values between 1900 and 1912." After presenting Josiah Stamp's estimates of the total and per capita wealth of the most important countries in 1914, Young concludes as follows:]

The high position occupied by the English-speaking peoples is notable. [United States per capita wealth, $2,060; United Kingdom, $1,550; Australia, $1,550; Canada, $1,460.] This is not only because, with characteristic enterprise, they have sought out and settled those portions of the earth where nature has been most generous. It is also because, in their political and economic organization, they have left a reasonably free scope for individual enterprise and initiative, and because they have been quick to develop and make use of the methods which science furnishes. Germany [$1,200], whose natural resources, aside from coal, are in no way notable, nevertheless makes an extraordinarily good showing. Her relatively high position is to be attributed in large measure to the scientific organization of her industry and of her economic life. France, with respect to per capita wealth [$1,500], occupies even a higher position than Germany, – a position comparable to that of Australia and Canada. In France thrift, industry and fertile soil have done much to offset a paucity of coal and a resulting handicap in the development of large-scale industries.

The net result of our study is to put new emphasis on the dominating importance of the human element in the wealth of nations. Bountiful supplies of the sources of mechanical power, fertile soils, favorable climate, harbors and waterways – these and other gifts of nature remain merely dormant and potential elements of a nation's wealth until they are quickened into life by the touch of human energies, guided by the knowledge science alone can give.

25 The annual wealth product

The income of the people and its distribution among them

An achievement of statistical science

The Book of Popular Science (1924; revised 1929) New York: The Grolier Society. Group XI Ch. 21: 2793–2800

In the last chapter we examined such facts as were available respecting the accumulated wealth of the United States, of Canada, and of other important countries. In the present chapter, we have to deal with a different, though related, subject: namely, the annual production of wealth, and the distribution of the annual wealth product among the people of the country. The two subjects are related because, of course, accumulated national wealth, or national capital, is created by annual increments of produced and saved wealth. As with an individual, so with a nation, capital is the resultant of a net difference between production and consumption; that is, it is built up by income and depleted by expenditures.

For a long time the United States had no reliable statistics of the distribution of incomes among persons or families, although, on the basis of the results of the decennial census of manufactures, agriculture and mining, it was possible for statisticians to make up fairly adequate estimates of the annual production of wealth. It was not until the United States adopted a federal income tax that trustworthy estimates of the distribution of incomes became possible. For our present knowledge of the size and distribution of the national income we are indebted to the National Bureau of Economic Research which published in 1921 its findings respecting the amount and distribution of income in the United States. The work of this research institution is itself a noteworthy example of the way in which science may be enlisted in the solution of economic as well as technical problems.

The bureau is a non-partisan institution. Its aim is merely to ascertain fundamental facts in its field, and to make its findings known. By so doing, the officials of the bureau state they hope "to aid all thoughtful men to base their discussions on objective knowledge as distinguished from subjective opinion." To insure impartiality, the directors of the bureau are chosen by such diverse organizations as the American Economic Association, the American Statistics Association, the American Bankers' Association, the Engineering Council, the National Industrial Conference Board, the American Federation of Labor, the

Periodical Publishers' Association and the American Federation of Farm Bureaus. Professional economists and statisticians, bankers, accountants, businessmen, labor leaders and socialists are numbered among its directors.

In attacking the difficult statistical problem to which we have referred, the bureau made use of a simple, fundamental principle: the total amount of *wealth produced* during a year must be equal to the total amount of *incomes received* during the year. This will be clear to the reader if he will note, first, that for all of the wealth produced, so far as it is sold on the market, its producers receive money incomes, and second, that the money incomes of any year are expended (counting investments as a form of expenditure) for the wealth produced within that year. Certain adjustments are necessary to take account of marketable goods not actually marketed, as, for example, wealth produced and consumed on the farm. Account must also be taken of the fact that sales of land or securities at increased values may create "income" which has no exact offset or counterpart in the "wealth product."

The bureau's statisticians made independent estimates of the national income or national wealth product by two different methods: (1) by sources of production, utilizing largely census results and similar material, and (2) by incomes received, utilizing income tax statistics and similar facts.

It is high testimony to the scientific quality of the bureau's work that these two independent estimates, made for each of the years from 1909 to 1919 inclusive, agreed very closely, the maximum difference between the two in any one year being 7 per cent. For the year 1916, the difference between the two estimates was one-tenth of 1 per cent! This is surely enough to show that the results reached by the bureau are entitled to an unusual measure of confidence. For this reason, we shall make them the basis of our own discussion.

Before discussing the details of income distribution in the United States it will be well for us to take a glance at the size of the annual wealth product of the United States as compared with that of certain other leading nations. Here again we shall avail ourselves of figures carefully brought together by Sir Josiah Stamp, which we have summarized in the accompanying table. It must be remembered that these are pre-war figures. An increase in physical production accompanied by a much larger increase in the general level of prices has led to a corresponding increase in the money value of the wealth product of all countries. Thus for 1918, the aggregate wealth product of the United States was not less than sixty billions of dollars, – not far short of twice what it was before the war. It is probable that not more than from 10 to 20 per cent of this extraordinary growth can be accounted for by an increase in the actual volume of the output of the products of the farms and industries of the country. The bulk of the increase – from 80 to 90 per cent of it – is merely apparent, being a result of the diminished purchasing power of the dollar.

Similar changes have likewise occurred, generally on a more violent scale, in other countries, for everywhere the war led to inflation of currencies and to depreciation of the value of money.

Table 25.1 The income of the leading nations: 1914

Country	Estimate based upon the work of	Approximate accuracy grade*	National income, millions of dollars	Per capita income, dollars
United States	NBER	I	$33,200	$335
United Kingdom	Bowley, Stamp	I	10,950	243
Germany	Helfferich	I	10,460	146
France	Pupin	II	7,300	185
Italy		IV	3,890	112
Austria-Hungary		IV	5,350	102
Spain	Barthe	IV	1,120	54
Australia	Official, Knibbs	I	1,260	263
Canada	Giffen	IV	1,460	195
Japan	Stamp	III	1,580	29

* Grade I. Estimate is not likely to be inaccurate to a greater extent than 10 per cent.
Grade II. Estimate is not likely to be inaccurate to a greater extent than 20 per cent.
Grade III. Estimate is not likely to be inaccurate to a greater extent than 30 per cent.
Grade IV. Estimate may be inaccurate to a greater extent than 40 per cent.

On the basis of the pre-war figures, which are more instructive than any yet available for the period after the war, the aggregate national income of the United States was three times that of either the United Kingdom or Germany, and four times that of France. This astonishing difference can be ascribed only in part to the larger population of the United States, for its per capita income was 38 per cent more than that of the United Kingdom, 80 per cent higher than that of France, 130 per cent higher than that of Germany, and three times as great as that of Austria-Hungary. Australia, whose per capita income was 80 per cent that of the United States, makes a better showing. The estimate quoted for Canada is, in the opinion of the present writer, much too low; he believes that the per capita annual product of Canada is probably as large as that of Australia. The very low figure assigned to Japan is a matter of interest. Even before the war, the per capita income of less than $30 per year would have hardly sufficed for the meanest necessaries of life in either the United States or Canada. This astonishing figure is explained by the vastly lower standard of living that prevails among the peasants and laboring classes of that country.

Turning now to the consideration of the structure of the national income of the United States, we may note first of all the fact that the United States is by this test predominantly a manufacturing, rather than an agricultural country. In fact, agriculture and mining taken together account for only between a fourth and a fifth of the national product, while manufacturing, including the hand trades, accounts for nearly a third. It will be understood, of course, that these figures are so compiled as to avoid duplication, so that the value of the agricultural and mining product is not again counted in the value of the product of the industries to which agriculture and mining furnish

Table 25.2 The sources of wealth product of the United States

Source	Amount in millions of dollars			Per cent distribution		
	1900	1912	1922	1900	1912	1921
Agricultural Products	1,455	5,240	5,466	1.64	2.81	1.70
Mining Products	327	816	730	.36	.43	.22
Manufactured Products	6,087	14,694	28,423	6.87	7.88	8.87
Real Estate	52,538	109,237	176,415	59.35	58.63	54.99
Livestock	3,306	6,238	5,807	3.73	3.34	1.81
Transportation and Transmission						
Railroads and Their Equipment	9,036	16,149	19,951	10.20	8.66	6.25
Street Railways	1,576	4,597	4,878	1.78	2.46	1.52
Telegraph and Telephone	612	2,304	1,950	.69	1.23	.60
Motor Vehicles	–	–	4,567	–	–	1.42
Water Transportation	538	1,491	2,951	.60	.80	.91
Pipe Lines and Water Works	268	290	861	.30	.15	.26
Electric Light and Power	402	2,099	4,229	.45	1.12	.13
Unclassified Industries and Miscellaneous Income	12,372	23,145	64,576	13.97	12.43	20.12
Total	88,517	186,300	320,804	100.00	100.00	100.00

Charts and material in this chapter are from "Income in the United States" by W. C. Mitchell and other members of the staff of the National Bureau of Economic Research Inc. (Harcourt, Brace & Co., N. Y.).

raw materials. The product assigned to manufacturing is merely the value *added* by the manufacturing process.

An estimate made some years ago by Dr. W. I. King indicates that in 1850 agriculture furnished about a third of the national income, while manufacturing was responsible for less than a fifth. The most notable change since 1850, if Dr. King's estimates may be trusted, is the decreasing share assigned to transportation, which formerly seems to have created something like 20 per cent of the wealth product, but which now can claim less than 10 per cent. This change is in the face of the enormous development of our transportation systems. The truth would seem to be that, despite the fact that we are using vastly more transportation, measured in ton-miles, than we did in the middle of the last century, our transportation is now so much more efficient and so much cheaper that it costs us, as a nation, relatively less than formerly. Seventy-five years ago something like a fifth of the income of the average citizen was absorbed by transportation costs; at the present time, the corresponding proportion is not more than a tenth. This is an excellent example of true economic progress: a product increased in quantity and bettered in quality, furnished at vastly decreased cost per unit.

One necessary limitation of these figures, as of all statistics of income, must be borne in mind. They take account only of such contributions to the national product as are sold for money, that is, for which a price is commonly paid. So far as goods and services are given freely, like the services of friendship or of parental care, they do not enter into the statement. Nor is the work which one does "for himself" taken into account, except where its money value can properly be estimated, as in the case of produce both raised and consumed on the farm. It is clear that in this way we omit some of the most important factors in real wealth-production, including, for example, the work of housewives. Sir Josiah Stamp has said:

> If we suppose that in one country one million wives stay at home, and one million women work in industry, and there are no domestic servants, the total "income" will differ from that of a country where half the "wives" work in industry, and half the other women are domestic servants in the homes of the absent wives, despite the fact that the total "work" being done is the same in both cases.

On account of the interest attached to this particular item, the statisticians of the National Bureau of Economic Research attempted to make a rough estimate of its possible importance. It seems likely that there were some twenty million women in the United States engaged in housework in their own homes in 1918. If the average pay of domestic servants, including their subsistence, was, say, $500 per year, the total annual value of the housewives' services would on that basis amount to some $10,000,000,000. If the market price of work like that done by the average housewife was as much as $750 per annum, the value of the wealth product of the housewives of the country would have been approximately $15,000,000,000 – a contribution larger than the aggregate value of the agricultural product of the country and nearly as large as that of the factories of the country in the same year.

Turning now to the statistics respecting the distribution of the national income among individuals, we enter a field of discussion in which advocates of one side and the other are accustomed to make assertions without troubling themselves about the actual facts. Socialists and other radicals have been inclined to paint a picture in wholly dark colors; advocates of the existing economic order have too often erred by using none but roseate tints.

What is Labor's share? No direct answer to this question can be given. But the investigations of the National Bureau of Economic Research show that payments to employees are equal to about one-eighth of the total value of the product in agriculture, to about two-thirds of the total in railway transportation, and to about three-fourths of the total in water transportation, manufacturing and

Table 25.3 Changes in the wealth product attributed to different sources (wealth product in 1900 = 100)

	1900	*1912*	*1922*
Agriculture	100	363	378
Mining	100	249	223
Manufacturing	100	241	466
Transportation and Transmission	100	215	308
Real Estate	100	207	331
Livestock	100	188	175
Other Sources	100	186	521

mining. In large-scale industries, the pay of employees (including salaries of officials) amounts to about seven-tenths of the value of the product, the remaining three-tenths going to interest, rent and profits. Of the share going to employees, about 8 per cent goes to officials.

The accompanying table[a] shows the way in which personal incomes in the United States were distributed in 1924. The table accounts for about $25,000,000 distributed among 7,298,481 persons. The figures include only those incomes reported to the Collector of Internal Revenue for the year 1924. The commonest size of income reported was between $1000 and $2000. This may seem surprisingly small, but it should be remembered that we are dealing with statistics of *personal* rather than family incomes, and that in many cases family incomes combine the incomes of two or more persons. It will be noted, furthermore, that the income group in which the largest amount of income falls is the group whose limiting figures are $2000 and $3000. Over one-fourth of all personal incomes fall into this class. As we advance toward the higher income groups, the number of persons in the group and the total amount of their incomes decrease rapidly. These facts have a bearing upon public policy with respect to income taxation.

It is quite clear that no system which relies largely upon heavy "super-taxes" imposed upon the exceedingly wealthy can tap the largest sources of public revenue. Moderate rates imposed upon the great mass of income receivers would be more productive than extremely high rates imposed upon the relatively few persons who have very large incomes. This does not mean that large incomes should not be taxed at a higher rate than moderate incomes; it merely means that if an income tax is to yield a maximum amount of public revenue it must rely largely upon fair and equitable rates reaching the millions of persons who cannot be counted among the wealthy.

Only 74 persons had incomes of over a million. But the table reveals 21,328 persons who might be counted "millionaires" in the sense that they had incomes of $50,000 or over, equivalent to a 5 per cent return on an investment of a million.

The same facts are tabulated in another form in the table showing the cumulative distribution of incomes in 1924. It appears that less than $1000 constituted less than 1 per cent of the aggregate amount of income. Incomes of over $2000 were 85 per cent of the aggregate income, while incomes of more than $5000 were 38 per cent, incomes of over $100,000 were 2 per cent, and incomes of over a million were only about half of 1 per cent of the sum of all incomes. When we turn to the distribution of income *receivers,* however, we find different results. Persons receiving incomes of over $2000 constituted only 63 per cent of all income receivers. Those whose incomes were over $5000 belong to a favored 9 per cent of the population. Persons whose incomes were more than $100,000 constituted but seven hundredths of 1 per cent, while persons whose incomes were over $1,000,000 were only one one-thousandth of 1 per cent of all receivers.

Putting the same facts in another way, it would appear, according to the statistician, that the most prosperous 1 per cent among the income receivers got nearly 16 per cent of the total income; the most prosperous 10 per cent received about a third of the total; the group including the most prosperous fourth of all income receivers got about 50 per cent of the total income. Put in this way, the statistics may seem to indicate that income is concentrated to an alarming degree in relatively few hands. But a closer inspection of the facts gives them a different color. That prosperous 1 per cent of all income receivers includes all persons who get more than $25,000 per year. To get the most prosperous 9 per cent of the income receivers, we have to include everyone who has an income more than $5000. The most prosperous 30 per cent includes persons who are getting incomes of $3000 or a little less, and the most prosperous 60 per cent includes persons who are getting incomes slightly under $2000. All of these figures are summarized in what is called the "Lorenz curve," so named because it was first used by Dr M. O. Lorenz, statistician of the Interstate Commerce Commission. Both the vertical and horizontal scales represent per cents ranging from zero to 100. The horizontal scale corresponds to income receivers, the vertical scale measures per cents of the sum of all incomes. Thus, for example, a point which we may take arbitrarily, such as the point located by measuring three squares toward the right on the horizontal scale, and two squares upward on the vertical scale, would indicate both 30 per cent of all income receivers and 20 per cent of all incomes. Now it is clear that if all incomes were of exactly equal size, 10 per cent of the population would have 10 per cent of the income, 40 per cent of the income receivers would have 40 per cent of the total income, etc. So the "line of equal distribution" on the diagram would represent this hypothetical situation, for the points through which it passes are equal distances from both the vertical and the horizontal scales. The actual distribution of incomes in 1924 is indicated by the curved line on the chart. The extent to which this line departs or curves away from the line of equal distribution may be taken as an index of the degree of inequality of the distribution of incomes in the country.

The defect of this Lorenz curve is that it lends itself to misinterpretation. Like the tables of the cumulative distribution of incomes on which it is based it compares actual distribution of incomes with an impossible and really absurd state of affairs in which every person gets just as much income as every other person. A dead level of equality in the distribution of incomes is an impossible ideal. It is hardly ever urged even by extreme radicals. Some measure of inequality is necessary by reason of differences in ability and in energy. Incomes in an ideal state need not, perhaps, be absolutely proportionate to ability only, but there must at least be differences enough to serve as prizes or incentives for the abler and more energetic.

The chart of the "frequency distribution" of income is much less likely to be misleading. On this chart, the horizontal scale merely represents the different sizes of incomes, beginning with zero at the left, and increasing by uniform intervals to the maximum income at the right. The vertical scale represents the number of income receivers. Thus, a vertical distance measured upward from a given point on the base line or horizontal scale represents the number of income receivers who have incomes of the size indicated by that point. The diagram appears made up of "steps" merely because the statistics are for income *groups*.

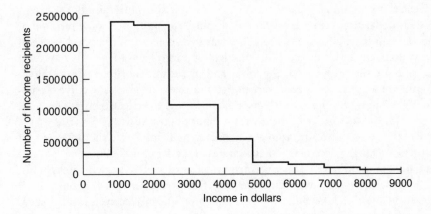

Figure 25.1 Frequency distribution of personal incomes in the United States as shown by the income tax returns for the calendar year 1924

However, if these groups were exceedingly small, that is to say, if, for example, there were a difference of only a dollar or ten dollars between the upper and lower limits of each income group, the diagram would appear as a fairly smooth curve.

Now the most striking aspect of this diagram to one who is a student of statistics is the general similarity of this curve of frequency distribution to many other sorts of frequency distribution curves that are found in nature. If its center were moved toward the right so as to fall at about $4000 rather than at about $1000, and if the curve were symmetrical instead of being much steeper on the left than on the right, it would be an example of what is called a "normal frequency distribution." A normal frequency distribution is like the "curve of errors" or the "probability curve." If the distribution of incomes were purely a matter of chance, we should expect that the statistics would reveal a normal frequency distribution. If, moreover, incomes were exactly proportionate to the difference in ability, and if ability, like many measurable physical traits, were itself distributed "normally," we should again expect that incomes would be distributed with normal frequency.

The fact is, however, that the curve is distinctly "skewed." The real extent of its skewness is not shown in the diagram, which does not extend above $9000, while incomes run up to many millions of dollars. In order to include incomes of a million dollars, the diagram, if drawn on the present scale, would have to extend to the right 100 times as far as it does! Long before reaching that point, however, the curve, if drawn on any practicable scale, would have come so close to the base line as to be indistinguishable from it. It is clear, then, that the incomes most frequently found are very much nearer the minimum than the maximum income. It also appears that the small incomes are huddled together, as it were, that is, that the differences in the incomes of persons in the lower part of the income range are extremely small, and that these differences increase with undue rapidity as the view is shifted to excessively higher income groups.

The alarming thing in these statistics of income distribution is not the extent of their departure from a condition of absolute equality – for some measure of inequality is inevitable in any properly organized society – but rather the general skewness of the income curve. The problem of poverty and the problem of great fortunes are the problems of the lower and upper limits of this income curve. Even more serious, however, is the fact that the extent to which the curve departs from normality throughout its whole extent seems to reflect the presence of a high degree of inequality in the distribution of opportunity.

Another way to put the whole matter may be helpful. We should expect in any properly organized society that incomes of moderate or "average" size would be more common than either extremely small or extremely large incomes. This, we may be fairly sure, would be the case if incomes were proportioned at all closely to the different abilities of the different income receivers, and if these different income receivers enjoyed anything like equal opportunities. Of course, the "spread" of income distribution, that is, the extent to which incomes in general are larger or smaller than the average or most common size of income, is also a matter of importance. The smaller the spread, that is, the greater the degree of closeness with which incomes are grouped around the average income, the less will be the real inequalities in the distribution of wealth.

Now the difference between this distribution of incomes in an ideal state of society and their actual distribution in the United States is not so great as to indicate that things are wholly out of joint, that nothing remotely approaching equality of opportunity exists, that there is "no justice in the world." But on the other hand, the skewness of the curve of income distribution, the concentration of large groups of people just below the average, and the way the curve stretches on so far toward the right by reason of really absurdly large incomes, indicates that we have not fully solved the problem of social justice, that even in our democratic social organization real inequalities exist, and that one's income, while partly a matter of deserts and earnings, is likely to be determined to some extent by the advantages of inherited wealth, or by the disadvantages of being born in poverty or of having before one only a "blind alley." Equality and inequality, justice and caprice, are undoubtedly present together in our existing economic order. The actual facts in the case give little comfort either to revolutionary radicals or to extreme conservatives. They indicate that the structure of our economic life is fundamentally sound, that it would be foolish to wreck it and attempt to erect a new structure based on nothing better than revolutionary theories and class prejudices. But it indicates also that we should not rest satisfied with things as they are, that the structure must be repaired and improved. In this work, we shall do well to keep constantly in mind the fact that the knowledge which science yields affords the only sure basis of permanent progress.

Editors' note

a This table and a Lorenz curve derived from it and discussed below, are not reproduced here.

26 Our foreign trade

Position of goods made in the United States in the different markets of the world

The changing character of our exports

The Book of Popular Science (1924; revised 1929) New York: The Grolier Society. Group IX Ch. 23: 3117– 25

The reader will find that this chapter is largely made up of statistics. Imperfect though they are in some respects, statistics of foreign trade are sufficiently complete and reliable to give us a more accurate picture of this particular phase of our national economic activities than can be found for almost any other field of economic life. We really know much more about the nation's foreign trade than we do about the nature and volume of its purely domestic commerce. The statistics that record the history of the foreign trade of the United States are by no means lacking in interest. In fact, they will reward the careful reader with facts that will impress and stimulate his imagination.

[Eds: There follows a detailed survey of the statistics (not reproduced here) on the growth and changing composition of external trade in the history of the United States through to recent times (1800–1924).]

... [I]n yet more recent years... [o]ur older export staples – agricultural products – have lost in relative importance, even though the actual amounts exported may be as large as ever. The continued growth of population and the unloosing of nature's stores of energy in the form of coal and petroleum have turned us more and more toward manufacturing. A larger and larger proportion of our food products and raw materials find a domestic market. It is now our manufacturing industries which have outgrown the home market, and are seeking the markets of the world.

The change in the character of American exports brings with it new national economic problems. For the first time in our history, we find ourselves face to face with a class of "foreign trade problems" with which older nations have long been familiar. There is a very great difference between selling agricultural products and selling manufactured goods in the world's markets. The market for agricultural goods is highly competitive, but it is ruled by competition of a mechanical or automatic and highly impersonal sort. The mechanism is very perfect, for, under normal conditions, most of the differences in the prices that prevail for agricultural products in different parts of the world are no greater than the expense of transporting the products from one part of the world to another. The world's markets will always take agricultural products. If crops are unduly large, it may be that the price will be unprofitably low, but, nevertheless, there will be no difficulty in selling the crops. Supply and demand distribute agricultural products over the world in much the way that water, flowing into a series of reservoirs, will find a certain level. For agricultural products in general there is no "selling problem." Staple crops need no advertising and no traveling salesmen. They sell themselves.

International competition for markets for manufactured products is of a very different sort. Such goods are products in large measure of great corporations rather than of small farmers. Differences of soil and climate, which lead inevitably to international specialization and international trade in agricultural products, are less important in the case of manufactured goods. Given the possession of coal or other sources of mechanical energy, any nation may well attempt to compete in the international market for manufactured goods. It may be for this reason that the organized activity of promoting foreign trade, whether conducted by private corporations, by associations of business men, or by governmental agencies, has been concerned very largely with securing outlets for exports of manufactures. While agricultural products, as we have seen, may be said in a fashion to sell themselves, it often happens that manufactured goods can be sold in foreign markets only as the result of active and aggressive efforts to secure buyers for the goods of a particular country rather than for similar goods made in other countries. It is highly probable that even in the case of manufactured goods natural advantages and disadvantages count for more, and that the active efforts of traders in the long run count for less than is commonly supposed. But the fact remains that international competition for markets for manufactured goods come to be of surpassing political as well as economic importance. So far as trade breeds international jealousies and rivalries, so far as international economic competition is in any measure to be blamed for war, it is trade in manufactured goods, rather than in raw materials or foodstuffs, which must be be held responsible.

This aspect of international trade in manufactured goods may be perhaps attributed to the fact that, in general, it is the manufactured goods rather than the agricultural products of the western nations that are brought into competition in the markets of the less advanced regions of the world. Of course, even the most cursory survey of the figures will show that, in respect to manufactured goods, trade among the great industrial nations themselves is vastly more important than is the trade of these industrial nations with the regions that are industrially less advanced. Even for manufactured goods it remains true that, properly seen, international trade is a form of international coöperation, rather than of international rivalry. This is one of the great lessons which the peoples of the world must learn before trade and warfare, now joined in an unnatural union, can be divorced. The competition of individual traders of one nation and another in the markets of Latin America, of Asia or of Africa, are as nothing as compared with the great flow of economic goods from one nation to another in channels that are determined by the hundred advantages and disadvantages of different countries with respect to different types of industry.

... So far as the trade balances with particular countries are concerned, the figures for 1913 are a safer guide than those for 1924, distorted as these figures still are by the effects of the war. It will be seen that the countries with which the pre-war trade of the United States was noticeably favorable were Great Britain, Canada, Germany and, in general, most of the countries of continental Europe. On the other hand, the trade of the United States was "unfavorable" with Latin America and the Far East. It should not be inferred that trade with certain regions of the world should be encouraged and that trade with other regions should be discouraged. The words "favorable" and "unfavorable" are misleading. From the point of view of the nation as a whole, the import trade of a nation may be just as profitable as its export trade, and it is certain that a country's import and export trade are in large part determined one by the other. It is a short-sighted view which sees in import trade a source of national losses and in export trade the only source of national profits.

27 The making of wealth

How industry and trade have always been checked by misdirected effort

The possibilities of expansion

The Book of Popular Science (1924; revised 1929) New York: The Grolier Society. Group IX Ch. 25: 3377–85

[Chiozza Money:[a] *The essence of the production of material wealth is to form new combinations of the matter supplied by nature, and industry and commerce alike are concerned with a useful exercise of motion. On analysis we see that all manufacturing is the issue in the form of useful articles of work done by moving into new positions the materials which nature supplies. We cannot either create or destroy matter, but with increasing effectiveness we can create or destroy utilities. We do not create matter when we cut down a tall tree and turn its trunk into timber, but we do create a new utility – timber. We do not destroy matter if we burn the timber; the matter is indestructible, and all that we do is to reduce it to other forms – gases, smoke (unconsumed carbon) and mineral ash. The burning, however, has destroyed utility, although it has not destroyed matter.*

It is not possible for man to waste matter, it is only possible for him to create or waste utilities by changing the form of matter.

But man is ever filled with a desire for new forms and kinds of goods. As his powers increase, and as his command of nature increases, he demands an ever increasing complexity of manufactured articles. His desires are without limit. He calls for houses of the most complicated description, for clothes and personal ornaments of constantly changing type and of great elaboration; he demands for the fuller enjoyment of his powers the constant use of an enormous range of utilities in the shape of prepared foods, furniture, utensils, books and papers, instruments of sport, musical instruments, vehicles, etc. The ever-growing facilities for the conduct of agriculture therefore serve to set free an increasing proportion of working people to devote themselves to manufacturing. The call for agricultural work has decreased, and must, relatively, decrease. The call for the products of industry is ever growing.

Well-ordered movements produce wealth, but labor consists of movements not always well ordered. Labor, then, is a source of wealth; but it would be a mistake to suppose that all labor produces wealth, for much of it is not well ordered.]

When we say that labor is not well ordered, we mean that it is wasted, that is, that it is not exerted in such a way as to contribute directly or indirectly toward increasing the stock of utilities which consumers are demanding. It requires as much labor to sink a deep well in a region in which, for geological reasons, there is no possibility of finding oil as to sink as deep a well into rich oil-bearing strata. But in one case the labor is wasted, and in the other it is productive. Men confined to their homes by illness, or in prison by a court sentence, sometimes while away the tedium of their lives by carving absurdly intricate and fanciful articles of wood. Even though they may have cost years of labor, such articles generally have no value, except perhaps in unusual cases as curiosities. We should see clearly that it is *not labor that gives value to goods.* It is the value of the goods produced which gives value to labor. Labor does not create value; the value of labor is nothing but the reflected value of what labor produces.

[Chiozza Money: We have the further complication that what is a utility to an individual may not be a utility to the society of which the individual forms a part; and, as we have seen, when we have estimated the wealth of a country and expressed it in currency, we have an estimate of wealth which may not be in entire accord with well-being.

In this connection arises the very important considerations connected with productive and unproductive labor. We pointed out in an earlier chapter that a person may be a useful "producer" although he is not directly engaged in constructing material commodities. This necessarily follows from the consideration that it is just as important to move an article into the place where it is wanted as to make the article itself. The pair of shoes at the factory in Massachusetts[b] is useless to the person in Virginia, where they do not make boots. The Virginian could not walk to Brockton or Lynn to obtain the shoes; and the labor exerted, therefore, in conveying them from Lynn to a store in Virginia is obviously just as "productive" as that employed in making the boots themselves. The railway men, the teamsters and eventually the storekeeper, are seen to be truly productive in their movements.

But that by no means exhausts the treatment of this important point. It remains to add that while it is true that a conveyer of goods, or a storer of goods, or a dealer in goods may be a truly productive laborer, it does not necessarily follow that every such conveyer or dealer is a wealth producer. He may be producing something which has utility in relation to the circumstances in which he is employed, but it does not necessarily follow that those circumstances are justifiable or that they could not easily be dispensed with.

Take, for example, the case of two small manufacturing firms engaged in making the same product. If we consider the nature of their operations, we see them renting two separate factories and two separate offices, and each employing a certain number of work-people. Thus established, they compete in the same markets for an amount of trade which is limited by the consuming power of the buyers in the market. They each keep, of course, separate accounts, and find it necessary to print separate stationery, and separate labels. They have also to employ separate clerical staff, separate sets of traveling salesmen, and they issue separate advertisements. It will readily be perceived that each of the persons engaged by the two firms is producing utilities under the given circumstances; each of the clerks and travelers is necessary under the given circumstances.

The point remains, are the given circumstances necessary? And from the point of view of society, is each of the persons employed by the two firms producing social utilities? If we imagine the two firms to combine their operations, we see that they would not require separate offices or separate accounts, or separate traveling salesmen or separate advertisements, and that it would probably be as simple, or even simpler, to manage the two businesses as one than to manage the aggregate business as two. Given fresh circumstances – viz., amalgamation of the two economic units into one economic unit – and a certain considerable amount of the labor before employed by the two separate firms is seen to be economically useless, and productive not of social utilities but of social waste.]

Wastes of this kind, however, – wastes that arise from the unnecessary duplication of manufacturing or distributing units – are probably less important in the aggregate than is sometimes supposed. That such wastes do persist in some fields is not, properly speaking, a fault inherent in the competitive system. The wastes are to be attributed, rather, to the fact that the competitive system is not perfectly and rigorously enforced. Take, for example, the case of the two manufacturing competing firms just discussed. If there were real savings to be effected by their consolidation, it is perfectly clear that it would pay the proprietors of one firm to buy out the other, for, by reason of the savings which consolidation would introduce, the competing plant would be worth more to the buyers than to its original and separate owners. Or if the proprietors of the first plant lacked the capital necessary for such a transaction, some enterprising promoter would be fairly sure to see an opportunity for profit in the operation of buying both establishments, consolidating them, and selling the consolidated business, at a profit, to a new group of investors. Such transactions are, in fact, being carried out every day. If consolidation always meant economy, there would be no effective limit to consolidation. That means that competition would inevitably everywhere end in monopoly. But, as we all know, in most fields of economic life competition maintains its health and vigor. This proves that the supposed benefits of consolidation are often illusory.

The number of people who work hard but add nothing to the country's wealth

Take the case of the corner drug store. It happens that on some kinds of the large variety of proprietary goods carried by drug stores, the margin between the wholesale cost and the retail selling price is fairly large. That is, what the accountant calls the "profit on the turnover" is relatively high as compared with the profit to be had in some other fields of retail trade. Does this mean that the druggist is always a man who makes abnormal profits? By no means. Just so far as the average profit per unit of sales is high, just so far will there tend to be a multiplication of drug stores. A drug store can survive on a relatively small gross volume of sales because the average profit per sale is fairly high. Retail stores in other fields need a larger volume of sales. But is not this apparent duplication of distributing agencies, such as we find in the case of retail drug stores, an economic waste? Would society not be better off if the business of retailing drugs were in the hands of a relatively small number of "cut-rate" drug stores? From some points of view, yes; from other points of view, no. The wastes are obvious, but there is a real social advantage, it is proper to say a real social utility, in having retail distributing units conveniently accessible. Loss in the duplication of clerks, of rentals, etc., is offset, to some extent at least, by the time and effort saved consumers.

The problem, therefore, is complicated. It is clear, however, that

[CM: *the mere fact that a man is at work, and working strenuously in that work, does not necessarily mean that he is a productive worker. Through no fault of his own, but through the imperfect organization of trade, he may be doing work no more valuable to society than if he were digging a hole, and filling it up again. There can be no doubt that in a community of over 100,000,000 people, such as the United States, the number of persons who, although they work arduously, are not really engaged in adding to the wealth of the country, is very large.*

It is never enough to say that people are employed or unemployed; it is all important that we should know how the employed are employed. We sometimes[c] *find economists, in their anxiety to abridge the distinction between productive and unproductive labor, denying that man can "create" anything, and asserting that it is a careless use of the language to speak of a carpenter, for example, as "making" a table. As a matter of fact, a carpenter who asserts that he has made a table is much nearer the truth than the economist who denies the fact. It is perfectly true that a carpenter does not create the matter out of which the table is formed, and that the table is an expression of his skill in utilizing natural materials and his wisdom in so fashioning the materials that they take form as the entity we call a table. A table, however, is not wood, but a created utility embodying the skill, the experience and the judgment of men; and as such it is a real creation. That cannot be said of the products of the unnecessary clerk making a superfluous invoice, or of ten shopkeepers doing a distributive trade which could be conveniently carried on by one-fifth of their number.*

It is false to conclude that all those whose labors satisfy existing wants are to be truly regarded as taking part in production, or that they can be called "productive laborers." It cannot be too strongly insisted upon that honest and arduous work may be, and undoubtedly is, often exerted in forms which are without advantage to the wealth of a nation, and that it may but serve to attenuate the earnings of those who produce usefully.

It is only too true, unhappily, that in the United States, or in any of the great modern civilizations, a limited number of economically employed workers carry on their backs a host of workers whose work is poured out in waste, and who, themselves not really producers, consume the products made by others.]

The fault, however, does not reside in the organization of production so much as in the organization of consumption. In a literal sense, we must admit, commodities for which people are willing to pay, commodities which they demand, are by that very test commodities which satisfy human wants. In other words they are commodities which have utility. The economist can distinguish between higher and lower utilities only by involving some non-economic criterion, – in general, some moral ground of distinguishing between utilities which are useful and utilities which are not useful and which may be even harmful. In most cases there is little doubt in the mind of the man of common sense as to the fact that some things are more useful than other things. There are marginal cases; there may be some disagreement about the utility of certain forms of recreation, of the drama, or even of different kinds of foods and beverages. But these are matters to be decided, not by the economist, but by the moralist, or, in some instances, by the physiologist...

The greater call for labor that comes from the most widely distributed wealth

[CM: It will be realized that a call for commodities is, in effect, a call for labor. As we spend our money, so we direct people to work for us. If we call for clothes, we employ men and women in the textile and clothing trades, and indirectly we call planters to grow cotton and herders to raise sheep. If we elect to be less fine in our persons in order to secure better houses, then we command men to come into the building trades, and we command the various trades of brick and tile making, the making of glass, the making of cement, of lumber, etc., to supply materials to the builders of our homes. If we become a pleasure-loving people, and spend a considerable part of our incomes upon amusements, then we inevitably turn men and women into actors and actresses, professional singers and dancers, builders and furnishers of places of amusement, professional baseball players, jockeys and so forth. Clearly realizing this, we perceive that the total production of the country, the nature of the production of the country, and therefore the character of its trade, must vary with the manner of the distribution of wealth.

The man of small and moderate means – we speak of the average, healthy, decent man – spends by far the greater part of his income upon the necessaries of life. Indeed, he is compelled to do so if he is to keep his home together and his family in modest comfort. The first requisite is a home, and so much has to go in rent; the second is food; the third, fuel and light; the fourth, clothes. As incomes rise in the scale, the proportion of the expenditure of income upon these things varies, and other things are called for in increasing proportion. We may note that, however big a man's income gets, he does not increase the call for certain things very materially. He does not grow additional feet with his additional income; and even though he has ever so ample a supply of footgear, there is not the same proportion of his income spent upon boots as in the case of the man with twenty dollars a week. The existence of a limited number of very large incomes taking a great share of the national dividend, and of a large number of very small incomes, must mean that the industries providing necessaries are not nearly as large as they would be if there were a more equal division. The rich man, by his expenditure, encourages the industries providing luxuries more than those providing necessities.]

Engel's laws; how the average family budget is made up in different countries

In 1857, Dr. Ernst Engel, a distinguished head of the Prussian Statistical Bureau, published statistics showing the way in which the expenditures of working men's families in Saxony were distributed. From these tables and others like them, he deduced certain conclusions to which the name of "Engel's laws" is sometimes given. His first conclusion was that families with larger incomes spend a smaller proportion of their incomes for subsistence than do families with smaller incomes. This conclusion, the reader will say, might be derived from common observation, and scarcely needs to be bolstered up by elaborate statistics. But Engel's second conclusion is not so easily derived from general observation. It is that the per cent of a family's income spent for clothes is approximately the same, whatever the income. His third conclusion is even more striking, namely, that the percent of the income spent for housing, or rent, and for fuel and light is almost invariably the same, whatever the income. The reader will understand that these statements are intended to apply to average families, and that individual cases may deviate considerably from these "laws." Engel's final conclusion is nothing but a simple corollary of the others, namely, that families with larger incomes spend not only absolutely but relatively more for sundries and luxuries of various sorts.

Since Engel made these pioneer investigations many similar studies of family budgets have been undertaken. The findings, in general, agree with those of Engel. Take, for example, some figures relating to the standard of living in New York City.

The per cent of income spent for food decreases as we pass from lower to higher income classes, – except that the very poorest, being confronted by what may be called an irreducible minimum of necessary expenditures for other purposes, find themselves compelled to get along with the cheapest kind of food, and therefore spend relatively less for it than do persons in slightly higher income classes. Engel's conclusion that the per cent of family income spent for housing and rent is constant has been found by most later investigators to be an

Table 27.1 Expenditures of 12,000 families in 92 cities (From U. S. Bureau of Labor Statistics)

Family income	Per cent of income expended for			
	Food	Clothing	Rent	Sundries
$ 900–$1200	42.4	14.5	13.9	29.2
$1200–$1500	39.6	15.9	13.8	30.7
$1500–$1800	37.2	16.7	13.5	32.6
$1800–$2100	35.7	17.5	13.2	33.6

extraordinarily accurate generalization. It holds true not only for working men's families, but also for persons in much higher income classes. But because housing of any sort in an American city has, under practical conditions, a minimum below which it is impossible to go, the poorest classes have to spend a somewhat larger per cent of their incomes for rent than do those who are better off.

On the manner of distribution of wealth depends the ordering of production

It is clear, therefore, that the demand for goods and the consequent ordering of production will depend in very large measure upon the way in which wealth is distributed. We do not propose in this chapter to bring under review again the facts relating to the present distribution of wealth, for these have already been discussed in Chapter 21.[d] We found, it will be remembered, that, while inequalities in the distribution of income are great enough to be matters of serious national concern, they are far from being as irremediably bad as the exaggerations of pessimists would have us believe. In general, the lower the average family income and the more equality there is in the distribution of incomes among families, the greater will be the demand for the necessaries as contrasted with the luxuries of life, and the larger, therefore, will be the proportion of the nation's labor force which is utilized in the production of unquestionably useful goods.

Observe, however, that it is necessary not only that the average family income should be relatively small, but also that there should be no large degree of inequality in the distribution of wealth. The first condition is necessary because, even if the distribution of wealth is fairly uniform, relatively large incomes would give a *surplus* to be spent for things in addition to the obviously necessary utilities of life. The further condition, that incomes must be evenly distributed, is necessary because it is possible to have a relatively low average family income together with a high degree of inequality in the distribution of wealth; if the mass of the people were in poverty and if a relatively small number received very large incomes, the "average" income might easily be low, and yet a large proportion of the nation's labor might be utilized in the production of luxuries of more or less doubtful social utility.

An even distribution of wealth would result in monotonous uniformity of life

One should not too hastily conclude, however, that it is certain that the nation's labor would be best utilized if there was an approach to something like a dead level in the distribution of wealth, and if no family had at its disposal any large surplus income above the amount necessary to provide for its fundamental and immediate wants. Under such circumstances it is hard to see how there could be anything beyond a dull, drab, monotonous uniformity in the conditions of life. The mere multiplication and perpetuation of a large population living in a routine fashion, providing itself only with the necessaries of a humdrum existence, is not an ideal to stir the imagination of one who is honestly interested in the progress of his country and of humanity.

A surplus somewhere in the economic system necessary for the higher interests

Somewhere in the economic system, there must be a surplus which can be used to provide for the higher interests and values of the community, for the advancement of pure science and the increase of human knowledge, for the sustenance of art and music and letters, for the achievement of public works of lasting beauty. Those periods in the world's history which have bequeathed rich cultural legacies to later generations have been periods in which a disposable surplus, over and above the amount necessary to provide for fundamental human wants, existed. Athens built the Parthenon out of funds confiscated from, or, shall we say, embezzled from, other Greek cities. In the Italian Renaissance, literature and the arts developed under the patronage of men who had amassed their fortunes in ways which, judged by modern standards, were often no better than robbery. Even in our own day, no small proportion of the wealth which has been concentrated in the hands of the extremely rich has gone ultimately to libraries, to art museums, to the promoting of education and to the advancement of science.

Just what is a productive laborer in the ultimate analysis?

Facts like these must arouse reflection. Is not the artist or the poet, from the point of view of the long-time interests of the human race, quite as productive as the Purveyor of food or clothing? And when we think of the way in which modern industry is built upon and supported by modem science, must we not conclude that the scientist himself may be a very important producer of wealth? We should remember, too, that the largest advancements in science have often been made by men who were working only for love of the work, who had in mind no important practical application of their results to industrial problems. The man with the practical problem in mind is likely to have his vision somewhat narrowed. The largest view is possible only to the man who works with his eyes upon no near goal, but who has them lifted to the distant horizons which limit human knowledge.

Must we conclude, therefore, that large and permanent inequalities in the distribution of wealth are necessary in order to dispose of the surplus upon which progress of human civilization seems largely to depend?

No, not at all, for there are other and better ways of achieving the same end. One is through education of a sort that will gradually raise the level of popular taste so that things which are beautiful as well as immediately useful will be numbered among the real necessaries of life. To direct production into the best channels it is necessary only to change the tastes, the standards, and desires of the consumers who command the productive army. A second way of achieving the same end is through the increase of public expenditures for higher education, for science, for art, for music and for wholesome recreation.

Public expenditures of this kind have the great advantage that they lead to the production of utilities which are *in-*, rather than exclusive. The picture in the rich man's private gallery is a utility – to him and to his friends. The same picture in a public museum is a larger utility. Public expenditures are becoming more and more wisely adapted to achieve the important ends we have discussed. New and better standards are being maintained for public buildings, for public memorials of various sorts, and new emphasis is given to public expenditures that bring utilities of the finer sort within the reach of all the people.

Economic and social progress require surplus of production over bare necessities

A surplus of production over and above the routine necessaries of life is, as we have seen, prerequisite to economic and social progress. But the surplus need not be procured by robbery or extortion, nor should it make necessary a perpetuation of extreme inequalities in the distribution of wealth. A surplus, in other words, may be democratized. It may be concentrated in part in public revenues and expenditures, or, better yet, it may be made up of the small individual surpluses which separate individual consumers may be able to amass and to expend for things which, even if not immediately and practically "useful," may nevertheless enrich and ennoble human life.

Not all luxurious expenditures are to be condemned as extravagant. Luxury, as has been said, is a vague something which society has always viewed with mingled tolerance and condemnation. Just what things are luxuries and what things are not, depends upon conditions of time and place. With the growth and diffusion of wealth, there has been a continual transfer of articles from the list of luxuries to the list of comforts and necessaries. Careful analysis will reveal to the reader how much of his own consumption is, strictly speaking, unnecessary. Every year increases the list of what are appropriately called "conventional necessities." A very few dollars a year would suffice for satisfying the absolutely necessary minimum of physical wants. Everything above that low minimum must be classed as "comforts" and "luxuries."

Extravagant expenditures of whatever sort, however, have to be condemned. They are sometimes condoned on the grounds that they give employment to labor.[e] This is just one form of the "make-work" fallacy prevalent in much popular economic reasoning. There seems to be a general impression that the welfare and prosperity of the country can be increased merely by increasing the amount of work to be done – as though we were interested in work rather than its fruits. This make-work fallacy is found in some (not all) of the arguments of trade-unionists, in discussions of a protective tariff, in various quack remedies for unemployment and other economic ills. One would gather from some of these arguments that social policies should be so framed as to make the production of wealth just as laborious and just as unproductive as possible.

   Bastiat, a brilliant French economist, satirized these notions in his story of the glass-fitter. The glass-fitter argued that the more window panes were broken, the more employment he and his brethren would have, and the greater would be their demand for the labor and products of others. From this reasoning, it is an easy step to the conclusion that the nation can be made prosperous if only enough windows are broken so as to give employment to the glass-fitters, who, in turn, would give employment to others! The absurdity of the notion that national economic policies should be framed so as to "make work" ought to be obvious.

Society's costly amusements when poor are having "a hard winter" immoral

Some twenty years or more ago, an elaborate fancy dress ball was given in New York City in the midst of a winter in which an unusually large number of people were in poverty. The more sensational newspapers entered into a controversy over the morality or immorality of the extravagant expenditures connected with the ball. They estimated that the total cost, including costumes, ran into the hundreds of thousands, and possibly into the millions, of dollars. And yet many of these newspapers came to the conclusion that these extravagant expenditures were justifiable on the ground that they gave employment to workers in textile mills, to dressmakers, to milliners, to caterers, and the like. Money, it was urged, was in this manner taken out of the hands of the "idle rich" who did not need it, and distributed to persons who could use it to better advantage, and, through the expenditures of this latter class, it gave employment to many others. Now this type of economic reasoning, though frequently encountered, is utterly fallacious. It is perfectly clear that neither the family which gave the ball nor the guests that attended it, were in the habit of keeping their money locked up in strong boxes like misers. Just as far as they expended money on account of the ball, they *diverted* their expenditures from other objects. Dressmakers, milliners and the rest were given employment at the expense of others who would have been given employment if expenditures had been for other objects. But, the reader may say, even though the money was not taken out of hiding, it may have been taken out of savings, or out of investments, and its expenditure, even for a relatively wasteful purpose in the midst of a season of distress, must have done some good. No, for we must not forget that saving and investment, under modern conditions, are merely certain forms of expenditures. Neither the savings bank, nor the insurance company, nor any other custodian of savings holds any large amount of idle money. The funds contributed by different savers are concentrated and set to work in public works, in industry and in agriculture. If, in order to make an extravagant expenditure, a man has to sell securities or other investments, he adds just that much to the supply of investments on the market. Someone must buy them and buy just that much less of something else.

   In the last analysis we cannot help concluding that in modern economic life there is no choice between spending and not spending; the choice is merely between different objects of expenditures. Wasteful and extravagant expenditure is therefore never justifiable. It does not and cannot increase the aggregate amount of employment; it weakens the moral fiber of the spender and of those who foolishly try to emulate him, and this harm is not offset by any positive contribution to the nation's wealth. And in addition, we must take account of the further loss of the objects of real utility which might have been called into existence if the spender had so willed.

The largest problem of the present day are those of consumption rather than of production. What matters it how large a fund of wealth be produced annually, if that wealth is not of the kind that will really benefit the community? Labor and the productive energies of nature can be used for high or for low purposes, just as we, the consumers of wealth, the ultimate directors and governors of the productive process, decide. Large public expenditures on education are to be justified not merely because education, as statistics show, makes for productive efficiency, but also, and chiefly, because education of the right sort ought to make for increasingly higher and better standards in the expending of money and consuming of wealth.

Editors' notes

a The italicised sections of this chapter are by Sir Leo George Chiozza Money.

b Young changed the place names from British to American ones.

c Here Young replaced the word "often" with "sometimes."

d Chapter 21 of the Grolier *Book of Popular Science* entitled "The Annual Wealth Product" (included in this selection as Chapter 25).

e It is interesting to note that here Young discarded Chiozza Money's line of argument (in the Harmsworth encyclopaedia), that the very unequal distribution of income means that the mass of the British workers cannot purchase the necessities of life and that therefore there is a great problem of under-consumption: *"As soon as a limited number of people, by obtaining an undue lien upon the national dividend, call out of the trades of luxury a large proportion of the population, it must necessarily follow that production is checked, and further, that what production there is cannot be of the most desirable kind."* By contrast, Young argues that the distribution of income normally affects only the composition of spending and employment, not their totals. Young's critical attention here focuses on the socially desirable composition of spending rather than on the problem of its total. (This is a similar position to that held by R.G. Hawtrey, though Hawtrey modified his position somewhat in the depths of the depression of the 1930s.)

28 The sources of wealth

The necessary parts played by land, capital, and labor in the production of wealth

The problems of our savings

The Book of Popular Science (1924; revised 1929) New York: The Grolier Society. Group IX Ch. 26: 3505–13

[Chiozza Money:[a] The requisites of wealth-production are broadly, land, capital and labor. More broadly still they might be defined as land and labor. It is convenient to describe by the term "land" every natural agent – that is to say, not only the soil of a given area, but every gift of nature utilized by man, on, in or under the land or sea. It is well to bear clearly in mind that labor is not, as is sometimes loosely said, the only source of wealth. Labor has to be exercised upon the world's natural resources; and those resources are so unevenly distributed as between one country and another, and as between one locality and another, that labor exerted at one place may be very ineffective in wealth-production as compared with labor exerted at another place. It may help clarity of definition if we express our meaning, in other words, by defining "land" as that which owes nothing to labor.

So far as the surface of the earth is concerned, great parts of it have been worked over in minute detail for long periods of time, in some cases for periods stretching back beyond the confines of human history. Year by year, an increasing part of the earth's surface is being brought within the scope of man's civilization. There is perhaps no more wonderful thought connected with an old and developed country like England, or France, or China, than the reflection that almost every acre of it has been in some way scraped, or pared, or cultivated, or mined, or drained, or built upon. Here and there one may find a small spot which has remained undisturbed for a generation or more, but even that has probably been subjected to cultivation or alteration at some not very remote period.

Land is the source of all our materials, and of all our food. To the agriculturalist it is, of course, the prime material. To the industrial captain, it is a fixed base upon which to do certain work, and, in its broader sense, the source of raw materials. To everyone, whatever his calling, it means so much space upon which not only to work but to live. If we inquire what are the distinguishing attributes of land, we find it in the elements of area and location. A certain piece of land is a definite space of the world's surface, the position of which cannot be changed in relation to other pieces of land. We see that these properties are unalterable, and that they inherently attach to land. Whatever else man may do to land, he cannot affect these distinguishing properties. The fertility of land may be increased or decreased. The amount of work to be done upon a certain piece of land may be increased by erecting a building of many floors, multiplying the working space available in respect to it. A definite piece of land, again, may be mined, and minerals brought up for utilization from far below the surface. A swamp or lake may be drained, and what was water-surface converted into more useful land-surface. These and many other things can be done by way of changing the character of land and the use of land. Through them all, however, it will be seen upon consideration that the unalterable qualities of area, or extension, and of situation remain. ...

Land is obviously limited in extent. The land area of the world amounts to only about one-fourth of the entire surface of our not very large globe. Land is thus a commodity of which there is a distinctly limited supply.[b] As the population of a country grows, the land remains the same in area. Every addition to the population, other things remaining the same, raises the degree of use to which the land of a country is put, and therefore increases its value. Consequently, in a growing country, the value of land and the rent of land must grow, and the owners of land must be able to secure an increased income from it. Great political and social problems thus naturally arise in connection with the forms of its ownership or tenure; and in all the countries of the world these problems are being worked out with very great difficulty and in many different ways.

We pass from land – from the gifts of nature – to the labor which, intelligently exerted upon natural gifts, produces material wealth. We picture man in his primitive condition ruling over what were practically unlimited quantities of land, and, by the aid of a few very simple arts, wringing from great natural wealth a bare subsistence.

We are reminded here that, just as it is true that labor alone is not the source of wealth, so it is true that a great and bountiful natural store of wealth may be used but little, and yield a scarcity of material wealth to unintelligent labor. Time was when the extraordinarily wealthy areas of the United States and of Canada were the happy hunting-ground of peoples who knew not how to employ the natural abundance which encompassed them. We must recognize that they obtained freely the means of physical health and development, but they were only able to do this because they were few in number. Land was to them unlimited, and the chase, combined with rude forms of cultivation, yielded them in ordinary times a sufficiency of food. Even in such a primitive form of life, however, we see the beginnings of those storings of the fruit of labor which we call "capital"...

The progress of science and machine production has elevated capital into an entire supremacy over land as a factor of production. Before the industrial era, land and labor and a very little capital sufficed for the operations of mankind. Today, large amounts of capital are necessary for the conduct of every business...

It demands not only intelligence but self-denial to store the fruits of labor. Interest has been sometimes defined as a reward of abstinence. That, of course, it certainly was in the preliminary stages of capital accumulation, and that is how saving presents itself even today to the man of small and moderate means. It requires no little abstinence for the man with $20 or $30 a week to put by any proportion of his earnings, however *small. But the greater amount of saving today is done by persons who already have incomes large enough to command much more than the necessaries of life, and it is not very appropriate to regard their further accumulations as "abstinence."]*

The difficulty, however, is with the word "abstinence," and especially with the self-denial or parsimony which it suggests. A better word is "waiting," and some economists use the term "time preference." The fundamental principle involved is very simple. No one, whether rich or poor, can "have his cake and eat it, too." We are always confronted by the alternative of spending today or saving for tomorrow.

It is likely that much money would be saved, much capital accumulated, even if no interest, or a very low rate of interest, were paid. Some men are so constituted that they really find more pleasure in keeping and in accumulating than in the present consumption of things. The miser is merely an extreme case of the type of man in whom what J. S. Mill called the "effective desire of accumulation" is strongly developed. But fortunately or unfortunately the men who, on any terms, would rather save than spend are rare.

But there are many men who, even if interest did not exist, would save in order to provide for their families, for their own old age, or to insure against the loss of earning power resulting from sickness or accident. The wise man, the man who plans his life rationally, looks into the future, and even if he cannot hope to hand any considerable estate on to his heirs, he will he able, if he plans carefully, to equalize his expenditures and his income through his years of life. After middle life, very likely, his earning capacity may be lessened. In old age, he may become unable to earn an income. Therefore, unless he wishes to be dependent upon the bounty of others, he will save, even if interest on his savings is not held out to him as a further price or inducement for saving.

Other motives necessary to supply the capital needed by a modern community

It is very certain, however, that motives of the kind we have discussed would not suffice to supply the modern community with all the capital it needs. The proof of that simple statement is found in the fact that men are willing to pay a price for saving, and it is fair to assume that the price is no higher than it need be to induce the necessary amount of saving.

Many men have to be induced to save, or to save more than they otherwise would. The fact is that more of us, given the choice between a dollar today and a dollar a year from today, will without much hesitation take the dollar today. To some extent this general preference for present rather than future wealth – a preference which stands in the way of capital accumulation – is irrational. It is highly developed among savage tribes, who are wont to alternate between periods of feasting and surfeiting and periods of famine. Regard for the interests of the future has developed as the rational element in man has developed. It remains unfortunately true, however, that many men are too short-sighted, too much obsessed by the interests and pleasures of the moment, to give the future its reasonable and rightful due. At one social extreme is the miser, at the other is the spendthrift.

No price or premium in the form of interest however high would suffice to induce all men to save, but society has found by experience that a fairly moderate price or interest premium will suffice to induce enough additional saving (over and above the saving that would be made if no interest were paid) to replenish, maintain and slowly to increase society's stock of capital. The man who would refuse to exchange a dollar today for a dollar a year from today might be willing to give a dollar today for a dollar and five cents a year from today.

Although at various points in this chapter and elsewhere we have referred to capital as the product of labor, this is merely to distinguish capital from land, which in its original state is not a "product" at all, but is given by nature. The fact is, as we have seen, that capital requires for its production both labor and waiting. Capital is saved labor, or rather, it is the saved product of labor, and the word "saved" is quite as important as the word "labor." Of course any particular bit of capital, like a machine or factory building, or a ton of coal, may be viewed as the product of labor, land and capital, as well as of waiting, but the capital that is used in the production of new capital is itself the product of factors that lie yet further back in the productive series. If we push our analysis remorselessly back to the origins of economic life, we must find that there are three, and only three, original factors or elements in the production of wealth. Those three original factors are nature (land), labor and waiting.

[Eds: At this point Young retains a few paragraphs by Chiozza Money in which he complains of the inadequacy of capital accumulations relative to the need. Chiozza Money's text then continues:

As things are, the country is supplied with capital for the various purposes of social life, trade and industry, as it were, casually. There is no set purpose in saving; there is no specific national or social aim in accumulation. The thing resolves itself seemingly into a more or less spasmodic and chance investment by various individuals, who spend and invest upon no fixed principle, and whose sole object, of course, is individual gain. No one surveys the country as a whole, and forms an estimate of what capital stock is needed to render the labor of its people more productive. There is absolutely no means of organizing capital-saving. It is often questioned whether this plan, or lack of plan, can forever continue to be regarded as satisfactory by an intelligent and advanced people. The proper use of capital, of stored labor – of, in the words of J. S. Mill, the "accumulated stock of the produce of labor" – is essential. If labor is to be economically exercised, it must be put forth in connection with the use of the best-known appliances that have been devised by the genius of man. Any labor which is not so applied is wasted in some degree.]

The difficulty is, however, that there seems to be no really practical substitute for this apparently planless system of capital accumulation. There are some socialists, of course, who teach that the interest on capital is always unearned; that it represents nothing more than the exploitation of the laborer. We cannot accept this view, for reasons which will be made clear presently. Capital – properly utilized – is productive in just the same way that labor – properly utilized – is productive. Even in a socialistic state, with all industries the property of the government, capital accumulation would nevertheless be necessary and interest would still exist, although it might be hidden or disguised in one way or another. A socialistic state could not repair, maintain, replace and increase its railways, its industrial plants and its distributing establishments without saving, that is, without storing up labor. Labor which might otherwise have been utilized in providing for the satisfaction of immediate wants must, even in the socialistic state, be turned aside or diverted. Some labor must be assigned the task of maintaining and increasing the capital equipment of the nation. This labor produces no immediately consumable good; its benefits will come to fruition only in the future. But in the meanwhile the laborers must be fed, and clothed and housed. In some way or other, *advances* must be made them.

No form of social organization can eliminate the sacrifice of waiting

In the socialistic state, therefore, there must be savings. The community as a whole must wait for the final product of much of its work. The sacrifice of waiting, or the postponement of consumption, cannot be eliminated by any possible form of social organization. In our present competitive society waiting is a matter of free contract. Some men agree to save and wait and are paid a price for waiting. In the socialistic state, waiting might be enforced by means of taxes, the proceeds of the taxes being used in maintaining and increasing the nation's capital. Or some other device might be used. The essential thing is that waiting would be compulsory. It would be a matter of law, of national decision, rather than a matter of free agreement.

Of course just so far as public expenditures are today made for permanent public works there may be said to be a degree of compulsory "waiting." In general, however, most of our capital supplies come through free contract. Now, the method of free contract has its disadvantages. It appears, as has been said, planless. But the planlessness is in part only apparent. We must remember that the direction which the investment of capital takes is really determined by the estimates which business men make of the varieties and kinds of things consumers will demand. The investment of capital today, so far as it is successful, is really governed or controlled by the community as a whole through the community's demand for the products of capital. In a way, the community "votes" that such and such things will be produced and that capital shall be created in such and such forms. But the ballots the community uses in this voting are the dollars which the community spends for consumable goods.

In this kind of voting, the individual voter's power is measured by the number of dollars he has. The wealthy man has a disproportionate influence. There are undoubted evils and obvious waste in the system. Their cure, however, is in the general extension of higher education in the community and in the equalizing of opportunity, rather than in introducing a new system of control which would be based upon political votes in place of dollar votes.

One very important, but frequently neglected element in the accumulation of capital is the retention and reinvestment of business profits. As a matter of fact, the line between principal and interest is more or less arbitrary. When the business man or investor only gets his money back, we say merely that the principal of the money has been returned, and we see nothing in the phenomenon that gives rise to any peculiar economic or social problem. But when he, in addition to his principal, gets 5 or 10 per cent more, we discover the "problem of interest." Now, anyone who can give a satisfactory explanation of just how the organization of economic life makes it possible for the business man to get back 100 per cent, should be able to explain how it is possible for him to get back 105 or 110 per cent on his investment. There is no essential difference between one problem and the other.

We have been careful throughout this discussion to treat the repair, maintenance and replacement of capital goods as ways of investing capital. As a matter of fact, they are. Capital is not created once for all. Saving is a continuous and really perpetual process. There is nothing except business prudence to prevent the storekeeper from gradually selling his stock of goods without replacing it, pocketing not merely the "profits," but also re-pocketing the principal of his investment. There is nothing to prevent the manufacturer from wearing out his machinery or from using up his stock of raw materials without replacing it. The ordinary maintenance of the national stock of capital is, in practice, so largely a routine matter, so largely an accepted business practice, that it goes on, for the most part, silently and efficiently. And yet the largest part of the nation's annual investment of capital consists of just such replacement of older stocks.

In addition to the replacement of existing capital, prudent business men are accustomed from time to time to put part of their earnings "back into the business." Professor David Friday estimates that of the enormous profits made by American corporations during the Great War and the years immediately following, not over one-third have got into the hands of the stockholders, and that third, he says, was subject to the heavy surtaxes imposed by the government on personal incomes.

> A substantial portion of what the stockholder had left went to furnish the great body of the investment funds of the country. It is no exaggeration to say that not more than one-fourth, and probably not more than one-fifth, of the whole volume of corporate profits was actually spent by the stockholders of these concerns. The other 80 per cent went for taxes, for loans to finance the war and to furnish the funds for industrial expansion.

All together, Professor Friday estimates, business corporations in the United States, in the 11 years from 1909–1919, turned back from their profits about $23,000,000,000, this sum constituting a net increase in the invested capital of the country. Similar practices, of course, were not only common but habitual among individual business men and farmers. Everyone at all familiar with American agriculture realizes the extent to which the American farmer puts the year's surplus back into the improvement of his farm. His profit is in the increase of his capital.

The reader should note that a large part, unquestionably the largest part, of modern savings comes, not from investors or capitalists "living on their incomes," but is caught, turned aside as it were, in the active process of modern business. Private property in capital is the condition of and a stimulus to the saving done by the modern community. Private property undoubtedly has its abuses, but thus far no one has been able to show clearly how we are to have the enormous advantages of the productive power of large masses of capital without the stimulus and the safeguards which the rights of private property give.

From one point of view, of course, a nation's real capital does not consist so much of buildings, machines, railways and the like, as of the industrial and technical knowledge which the members of the community possess, handed down from generation to generation, diffused by education and increased by the advances of science. Our knowledge and our science are infinitely more precious possessions than the whole aggregate of our accumulated capital. Destroy our material accumulations and in a generation they will have been replaced. Destroy our knowledge, annihilate our science, and man, reduced to the intellectual status of the savage, would not even know how to use the tools which he has made for himself.

Science teaches how to harness nature, and to use her powers for our own needs. For a short time, the advance of scientific knowledge may be "capitalized" in the form of valuable technical secrets, or in patent rights, but, in the long run, scientific knowledge, of whatever sort, becomes diffused. We pay no rent, interest or royalty to science as such. We merely have to pay for the technical equipment, for the capital, which is required if we are to make effective use of our accumulated fund of scientific knowledge. Appraised by his real contributions to wealth and welfare, not in dollars and cents, the scientist may easily outrank the millionaire or the captain of industry. His contributions to society's capital are, in general, free. For that reason, they do not fall under the ordinary laws of supply and demand. There is no limitation of supply; there is no question of a larger or a smaller number of increments of supply. The scientist's contribution is, or becomes, a free good. Just because it is diffused and free, its *apparent* utility to society may be less. Ordinary capital, in order to have value, must have both utility (productivity) and scarcity. The scientist's contribution has productivity without scarcity.

But that certainly gives us no reason for excluding it from its rightful position as the most important single element in the "social capital" of the day.

Editors' notes

a The first part of this chapter, italicised here, is by Chiozza Money, except that Young made some minor changes, mainly to convert from British to US place-names and values.
b The Harmsworth version here reads: "Land is thus a commodity which can be very easily monopolised."

29 Labor and wealth

How the progressive economy of labor
is the only means of increasing the
supply of commodities

The machine and the man

The Book of Popular Science (1924; revised 1929) New York: The Grolier Society. Group IX Ch. 27: 3627–36

[Eds: This chapter begins with an eloquent critique by Chiozza Money of the "make-work fallacy": "we shall do well to remind ourselves that the primary object of trade and industry is not to make but to save work... The royal road to wealth is by the saving of labor." It is not work so much as income that the working man requires. He goes on to explain that "the division of labour has largely and increasingly helped man to economise effort." The specialization of workmen into particular callings necessitates trade. But the division of labor also finds expression "in the devotion of entire districts to a particular form of industry, the products of which are sent out of the district in exchange for the subsistence of the district." Allyn Young then continues:]

The United States affords many excellent examples of the localization of industries, which is really another name for the geographical division of labor. Thus the boot and shoe industry is predominant in Massachusetts; collars and cuffs are made in Troy, New York; gloves are produced in Gloversville and Johnstown, New York; brassware in Waterbury, Connecticut; carpets in Philadelphia; jewelry in Providence, Rhode Island, and the neighboring towns of Attleboro and North Attleboro, Massachusetts; plated silverware is made in Meriden, Connecticut; silk, in Paterson, New Jersey. Other examples might be given, and, of course, the generally recognized division of the country into industrial and agricultural sections, characterized by different types of industries, and by the dominance of different crops is itself an example of the territorial division of labor.

Different causes explain the localization of different industries. The proximity of raw material or of fuel may be the determining factor. Or it may be the accessibility of markets or the presence of water-power. The availability of a trained labor supply counts for much, and so does what has been called the "momentum of an early start." These last two causes explain the persistence of a particular industry in a certain locality generation after generation. Frequently, however, no one of these factors, and no combination of these factors, is adequate to explain the presence or the development of a certain industry in a certain place. Here we have to fall back upon the human factor, – the variable in so many economic laws. Physical and economic facts will sometimes suffice to explain just why some industries should be distributed as they are, but, in other instances, the only possible explanation is that men of energy have set themselves at work to build up a great industry in a particular locality, and have succeeded.

[Eds: The next section is by Chiozza Money and explains that Adam Smith's principle of the division of labour – or the saving of labor – is carried very much further in the machine age. And today the principle of standardization (for example in the making of automobiles) carries the division of labour further still. Young continues:]

The standardization of products has introduced great economies, not only in the machine industries, but in other fields as well. The whole tendency of the routine, mechanical methods of the modern factory system is to turn out products of definite kinds and of definite grades. Great economies are thus effected at the loss sometimes of the opportunity for personal expression on the part of the workman, and for the full and accurate satisfaction of the personal tastes of the consumer. The machine process is standardizing consumption as well as production. Economy and abundance are purchased at the expense of individuality and variety. To anyone who has viewed the problem without prejudice the conclusion must be that there has been a large net gain. Never before in the world's history have so many people been supported at so high a general level of comfort as in those modern countries which have best mastered and utilized the principles of the division of labor and of the factory system.

[Eds: There follows further examples given by Chiozza Money of the division of labour and use of machinery, followed in turn by a discussion of the international division of labour. Chiozza Money observes that international exchanges rest on three very different bases, two of which are permanent, namely differences in natural resources and differences in "race genius," while the third, acquired skills, may not give a particular country a permanent advantage. In respect of the first of these bases for trade, Young discusses the particular position of the United States:]

It is conceivable that the United States, with its greater area, its larger variety of climates and soils and natural resources, might be able, with relatively less disadvantage, to produce all that it consumed. But in such case it would have to get along without many tropical products (or produce them for itself at extravagant cost) and it would find itself handicapped by the absence of certain important minerals and certain fertilizers. Most of all, it would find that it was producing for itself, with wastefully high expenditure of capital and labor, many commodities which it could have got more easily and more cheaply by exchanging its own best products – the goods it can produce to best advantage for goods made by other nations. It is especially important to emphasize the fact that, even if *absolutely* the United States had an advantage over every other country in the world in the production of every conceivable commodity, it would, nevertheless, be profitable for it to let other countries produce those commodities in which the advantages of the United States were *comparatively* least. By devoting itself to the production of the commodities in which its comparative advantages were greatest, the United States would be able through international exchange to get the maximum total wealth product, the maximum national income with a minimum expenditure of capital and labor, and with the small drain upon its natural resources. *Comparative advantage,* not absolute advantage, governs international trade.

[Eds: Chiozzo Money summarizes his discussion, in this chapter and the last, of the ways in which labor may be "saved and set free by continuous processes" as follows: (i) The storing of the products of labor as capital or stock; (ii) the division of labor; (iii) the invention of new machinery and processes; (iv) the exchange of commodities, which has its roots in the division of labor. He says that "the setting free of labor by the saving of labor need not cause unemployment or distress to any man, but may easily do so through lack of proper social and industrial organization." He goes on to say that if a country's population were to increase five-fold but the proportions in which the population was allocated among the different industries were to remain unchanged, there would be no saving of labor and therefore the community would not be a penny better off. Young at this point interposes thus:]

It must be admitted that the example that we have just given is fanciful and even impossible. With the growth in the size of industries, there come changes in their organization, increased applications of the principle of the division of labor and further economies. We are not referring here to the increase in the size of the individual plant. This may be economical and advantageous up to a certain point. But the reader will have noticed that the largest industrial establishments he knows are, after all, of limited and fairly definite size. Further growth is accomplished by duplication, by building more plants, rather than by extending old ones. The advantageous size of plants varies, of course, with different industries.

Nor are we discussing agriculture, where, as we have seen, a large increase in product can generally not be secured except at a considerable increase in the cost of production per unit. In agriculture, the "law of diminishing returns" is at work. Larger crops cannot be had without resort either to poorer soils than those already in use, or without the more thorough and intensive cultivation of lands already cultivated. Either alternative means more cost per unit of product.

We are discussing, then, neither agriculture nor the single industrial establishment. We are focusing our attention upon manufacturing industries as wholes. Now, within any industry an increase in the demand for its product will almost invariably lead to important economies. For example, even if the only result is to multiply the number of plants, there will be some gain, for it may be assumed that there will result a better distribution of plants so that the costs of transportation for the average unit of product will be decreased. In general, however, a growth in the output of an industry as a whole will result not only in an increase in the number of plants, but also in a further *differentiation and specialization* as among the different establishments. When the shoe industry of the United States reached a certain size, it became possible to build large factories specializing in certain grades of shoes, in men's shoes, or women's shoes, or children's shoes. It became profitable to build separate establishments for the making of lasts, and for the making of shoe machinery. With the development of the American iron and steel industry, we have had not merely the multiplication of blast furnaces and rolling mills, but we have had the further development of tube mills, rod and wire mills and mills turning out other finished products of different types. The growth of the automobile industry has been accompanied by the development of specialized industries making motors, bodies, clutches, axles, and other parts.

In short, with the growth of an industry, division of labor as among the different plants in the industry becomes not only possible but profitable, and, because profitable, inevitable. The division of labor and the roundabout methods involved in the machine process, – "the making of machines to make machines to make machines," – are feasible only when there is a market for a fairly large output. With an increase in the market, the possible and practicable economies of the division of labor increase and multiply. No one factory can afford to equip itself with a large outfit of special machines and tools unless it is assured of large sales for its products. With only a small market, the slower and most wasteful methods of direct production, involving less "roundaboutness," less division of labor, must persist.

But these considerations, important as they are, do not lessen the significance of the fundamental truth that

[*Chiozza Money: a new industry can be started in a country only by freeing labor from an old industry.*

Every inventor, therefore, who displaces labor is a servant of mankind... But while all this is true, it is also true that for a specific individual a new invention may spell disaster and ruin... We see, therefore, that while it is quite necessary for the progress of society, and for the increase of the wealth and comfort of the community, for labor to be continuously and progressively displaced and set free to engage in new occupations, what is on the whole and in the long run a beneficent process is attended for a minority of individuals by quite undeserved loss and, possibly, acute suffering.

If the community as a whole thoroughly understood the importance of the matters of which we have been speaking, it is surely clear (i) that they could not stand in the way of new inventions, and (ii) that they would see to it that there should be no individual loss through the application of new inventions. It is not impossible, it is not even difficult, to make social and industrial arrangements by virtue of which men who are thrown out of their trade by the march of invention may be tided over until they can find a new employment.

When our organization has reached a higher degree of development, the essential truth, that the object of trade and of industry is not to make work but to create a plentifulness of utilities with the least possible amount of work, will be realized, and, when it is realized, few difficulties will stand in the way of its accomplishment.]

To this we must add, however, that the provision of work which shall in itself be pleasurable, which will afford an avenue of self-expression for the workman, which will unleash his energies, enlist his interests, and enrich his life, is, in itself, an object of social policy comparable in importance with the provision of a plentiful supply of utilities. We may increase utility by the simple, even if difficult, device of making work itself less of a disutility.

[Chiozza Money: Nothing can ever make the attendance upon machinery a task fit to be prolonged in all cases for many hours at a time… Civilization must… abolish the machine slave. Attendance upon machines would be a different matter if it were so reduced to a thorough economy, and so shared as a social duty, that no man or woman had to do more than man or woman can bear without losing his or her well-being.]

The most practicable method, however, of lessening the evils of the machine system is to bring about a more thorough utilization of that system. The routine work of machine tending, where it is work of a kind that does not enlist the interests and imagination of the workers, is itself precisely the kind of work which may itself be reduced to a machine process. The engineer, the foreman, the man in responsible charge of a complicated machine, finds in his work a plentiful opportunity to develop his own interests and powers. The kind of machine tending that, from a social point of view, must become unendurable is the kind in which the worker becomes frequently a part of the machine, repeating a simple and monotonous physical movement minute after minute, hour after hour, and day after day. It is just these small routine movements which, with the perfection of the machine process, may be delivered over more and more completely to machinery. One way, perhaps the most important way, out of the admitted evils of the machine system is through the more thorough utilization of the possibilities of that system.

30 Combination and monopoly

The use and abuse of large-scale industry and its relation to national wealth

Sound and unsound control of prices

The Book of Popular Science (1924; revised 1929) New York: The Grolier Society. Group IX Ch. 29: 3971–80

[Eds: The first part of this chapter is mainly by Chiozza Money who notes that Adam Smith had said that the joint-stock company could not rise to prominence because they were compelled to act through hired servants. J.S. Mill had disagreed and had correctly foreseen the growth of large capitalistic corporations and their dominance in manufacturing industry. Chiozza Money, in his original Harmsworth essay, surmised that eventually "the small farm would pass even as the small factory has passed." Young noted that many small factories have in fact survived in the United States, and stressed that in the field of agriculture the small farm possesses many advantages over the large farm. "In fact," writes Young, "the notable absence in agriculture of any movement toward concentration or a large scale industry is a stumbling-block to that type of socialist who sees in the present organization of economic life a general and irresistible tendency toward concentration and monopoly, culminating inevitably, he believes, in socialism. Everywhere socialism has had to make terms with agriculture. The small-landed proprietor, now as always, is a bulwark resisting the forces which tend toward revolutionary social changes. There is little or no possibility that the small farm will pass in the manner in which the small factory has passed in some fields of industry."

Chiozza Money stresses the general advantages of large size. Young inserts a caveat: that the advantages of larger size not only grow more slowly, but eventually disappear, such that further increase becomes a detriment rather than a benefit. Chiozza Money says that combination may lower cost, and this is good. But what is evil is that they may also raise price. The rest of this chapter consists of Young's own analysis of combinations.]

Experience shows tendency of successful combination is to raise not lower prices

The only way to get a trustworthy answer to the question of whether or not a combination tends to increase prices is by turning to the records of past experience.

It has been the almost universal opinion of contemporary observers that monopoly in most cases has meant higher prices. Popular hostility to the numerous monopolies created by the royal favor of Queen Elizabeth was based in part at least upon the extortionate prices some of the monopolies charged. Hume says that the price of salt was multiplied tenfold by monopoly action. In later years, the problem of the effect of monopoly on price has been very carefully investigated by Professor J.W. Jenks for the United States Industrial Commission. Professor Jenks found that the old whisky trust, which had a distinctly checkered career, advanced the price of spirits whenever it felt that its domination of the field was strong enough to make such action feasible. A sugar trust was formed in 1887. A decline in the price of sugar between 1882 and 1887 reflected the strong competition which then dominated the market. But as soon as the trust had been formed, the price of sugar rose 65 percent. But high prices made high profits, and these attracted new competitors so that the price of sugar fell in 1890 to a new low level. In 1892 the trust absorbed its principal competitors, secured again a temporary monopoly, and once more the price was advanced. Again competition came into being, and prices fell. It would be tedious to examine in detail the history of the prices of other products. But in general there seems to be adequate evidence that the whole tendency of combination, just so far as it is successful, is to raise prices, and the hope of the profits resulting from increased prices has been one of the principal stimuli to the formation of combinations. In theory, as we have seen, it is conceivable that the economies of combination would be such that the most profitable monopoly price, – that is, the price which would yield maximum profits for its product, – would be lower than any price that would be possible if production were parceled out among a large number of competitive concerns. In general, however, this advantage remains just a logical possibility, not a fact of experience.

Further evidence that combination makes for higher prices is found in the fact that most of the great modern trusts are grossly over-capitalized. In other words, the par or nominal value of the outstanding shares of stock in these enterprises is very much greater than the actual amount invested in their plants and other properties. In fact, the capitalization of the leading trust is in the aggregate possibly twice their total actual investment of capital. Nevertheless, even though certain trusts which never achieved any measure of permanent monopoly of power have failed, the successful trusts of which we are now speaking have been able to pay dividends upon their inflated capitalization. This is direct evidence that their profits have been high, and from this conclusion we may pass safely to the further inference that the prices they have charged have been higher than would have been feasible if they had been subjected to the pressure of effective competition.

The fact that the great trusts have generally been over-capitalized suggests that another motive for their organization was at work in addition to the hope of the profits to be obtained through the power to increase prices. This other incentive to the organization of combinations lay in the *immediate* profits of combination. In general, these great combinations have issued both preferred stock, with a first claim upon the earnings of the company after its operating costs are paid, and common stock, having only a residual claim upon earnings but having an equal voice, and sometimes a dominating voice, in the control of the policies of the combination. The preferred stock was issued by the typical combination in quantities large enough to represent the actual purchase price of the different plants brought into the combination. In some instances these actual purchase prices were unreasonably high because certain important producers had to be bribed, one might say, to sell out to the combination. While the preferred stock was thus based upon a liberal estimate of the actual value of the investment, the common stock represented nothing but future expectations. The common stock was often said to be a "capitalization of the advantages of combination." You could take this statement in one way or another. The "advantages of combination" might be the real or alleged economies of combination. To the investor, the buyer of trust shares, however, the "advantages of combination" were just as likely to mean its power to charge monopoly prices.

After a combination was formed its promoters or organizers would usually find that they had left, after paying for the different plants absorbed, and for all of their expenses, a very considerable block of the common stock of the corporation. This was theirs to sell or to do with as they pleased. It represented promoter's profits or what we have called the "immediate" profits of the combination. A quarter of a century ago, when the profits made by a few of the older and successful combinations had led the investing public to believe that there was some sort of financial magic in the process of combination, that combinations in whatever industry held out almost unlimited possibilities of future profits, a number of energetic promoters were able to organize combinations in different fields with no other purpose in mind than that of selling them to the public. Many of these, it is hardly necessary to say, have failed, and after passing through the hands of receivers, have disintegrated into their constituent parts.

Then as now the advantages and economies of combination were popularly exaggerated. Moreover, then as now, there was a child-like confidence that the mere fact of size would in itself be sufficient to give monopoly power. Monopolies, it was hoped by some, and feared by others, could be *made* by combination. A relatively small number of clearer-visioned men saw that, just as on the one hand the advantages of combination are often grossly exaggerated, so on the other hand their power for evil is also commonly over-estimated.

Mere size or mass of capital gives no permanent monopoly

The truth is that mere size, mere mass of capital, can never give permanent monopoly power. Back of any real monopoly there must be some definite source from which it derives its immunity from the pressure of competition. Mere size may give advantages up to a certain point, but beyond that point, as we have said, those advantages diminish and vanish. The great combination with its elaborate organization, its many different departments, its complex arrangements for the placing and sharing of responsibility, its intricate systems of checks, of cost keeping, of accounting, etc., is likely to be unwieldy. It is well adapted to processes of a routine nature, to the turning out of standardized products on a large scale for the general market. But in the production of special types of goods, it is likely to be at the mercy of the alert small competitor. Even if the combination succeeds in suppressing or eliminating its older competitors, it always has before it the *potential competition* of a new competitor coming into the industry with fresh capital, fresh ideas, and fresh enthusiasm. In the long run, the success or failure of business undertakings, large or small, is determined not by size, not by natural or artificial advantages, of one kind or another – for in the long run these advantages have to be *paid for* – but by the caliber of the men in responsible charge of the policies of the undertaking. The large establishment has no monopoly on brains. It may be able to attract first class men by paying larger salaries, but it cannot corner or exhaust the market for ability.

What are the real sources of monopoly power? Some of them are clearly artificial; some are natural in the sense that they are inevitably associated with certain types of business undertakings. The clearest of the artificial sources of monopoly power is the exclusive privilege to engage in a certain specified calling. Such monopolies, like the old Elizabethan monopolies mentioned above, might be given as a mark of favor, or for a special royalty or tax to be paid into the royal treasury. Monopolies of this wholly artificial and arbitrary type are now almost everywhere illegal. But we still have artificial monopolies, not created directly by governmental grant, but *based* on special privileges granted by the government, such as patents and copyrights. The inventor is given a patent for a limited number of years on the principle that it is worth while to reward and stimulate invention even at the price of the possible evils of temporary monopoly. The author and his publisher are similarly protected. Otherwise authorship would be a most unremunerative calling, and men without independent incomes could not afford to write books.

Another type of artificial monopoly is sometimes created by the State primarily for fiscal or revenue purposes. Such monopolies may, on occasion, be leased or sold to private firms, but more commonly, and more properly, they are operated by the government itself. In many different countries and at many different stages in the world's history, the production and sale of salt has been monopolized by governments. The tobacco monopoly which obtains in France and certain other countries is an artificial monopoly maintained for fiscal purposes. Japan maintains a number of fiscal monopolies.

The fact that salt and tobacco have been selected as the objects of fiscal monopolies illustrates an important economic principle. Salt is a necessity of life; tobacco, though not a true necessity, is what has been called a "conventional necessity." Its consumption is very largely based on habit. The demand for both salt and tobacco is of the type which the economist calls *inelastic*. This means that relatively large changes in price will have relatively small effects upon the aggregate amount of salt or tobacco consumed. Goods for which the demand is thus inelastic are the most profitable objects of monopoly, whether the monopoly be public or private. A high price will be exceptionally profitable because it will not curtail the demand to any large extent. In general, goods which are true necessities, goods for which there are no satisfactory substitutes, and goods whose consumption forms a habit or custom, are goods for which the demand usually is inelastic and are therefore goods for which a monopoly price is likely to be very much higher than a competitive price.

Aside from artificial monopolies such as we have considered, there are monopolies which, we may say, exist "in the nature of the case." These we may call natural monopolies. The owner of a mineral spring of exceptional value, of land which produces grapes of unusual flavor, of a mine which furnishes all or substantially all of the world's supply of some rare mineral, has a natural monopoly. Extreme and unusual limitation in the supply of some raw material may thus lead to monopoly.

We should be careful to observe, however, that land in itself does not constitute a monopoly despite many thoughtless assertions to the contrary. The ownership of land is, as a whole, minutely subdivided. There is hardly any other important productive good the ownership of which is so evenly distributed as the ownership of land. This is true despite the glaring differences in land ownership which any observer may easily note for himself. There are differences in land, but differences do not constitute a monopoly. One man may be abler than another, but we do not on that account say that the first man has a monopoly of brains. In a similar way, one piece of land may be better than another, but that does not give its owner a monopoly. As a matter of fact, the owner of the land in most cases will have paid for whatever differential superiority it may have.

Finally, we come to the group of so-called public service industries, including railways, street railways, water works, electric lighting plants, gas plants, etc. It is now generally understood that these public service undertakings are monopolistic rather than competitive in nature.

Are they naturally monopolistic, and if so, how may we explain that fact? Some writers have proffered an explanation based on the fact that the industries in this group sell services which cannot be divorced or separated from the industries' plants. Thus, one can avail himself of railway services only by traveling or shipping goods over the railway line. To secure water or gas, or electric or telephone service, one must have the company's plant virtually extended into one's own home. Where the plant itself becomes a factor of such importance, its unnecessary duplication on account of competition is so obviously wasteful and inconvenient that monopoly seems to be inevitable. In many of these public service industries there are physical difficulties in the way of actually multiplying competing plants.

But the unusual importance of the plant is not the only reason why these industries are almost inevitably monopolistic. We may note that the services they render are of a standardized sort. There are no such things as differences in trademarks or brands. A small difference in price would lead buyers to purchase from one producer rather than from his competitor. These facts mean that if competition operated in these fields, it would operate rigorously and remorselessly; that no particular enterprise could build up a clientele of its own and shelter itself in any measure from the pressure of competition by falling back upon its established prestige and the good-will of its customers.

Finally – and this point is very important – the proportion of *fixed charges* in the expenses of these industries is relatively great. Wherever this condition exists, competition is likely to be of a wasteful and destructive type. Businesses that have large fixed charges – costs like interest and other forms of "overhead" that do not vary perceptibly with the amount of business done – find that a large part of their expenses continue even when their output is exceedingly small. This being the case, it is relatively better to produce and sell at any price which yields a small margin over and above the variable expenses – such costs as labor, raw material, etc., which vary as the volume of output changes – than not to produce at all. It is obviously better to get business away from your competitor than to let him get it away from you.

There will be no effective limit to your price-cutting if you are engaged in such an industry except that set by the actual *additional* costs which new business creates. Under such conditions competition destroys itself and monopoly is the only possible outcome. All of these conditions are present in the operation of railways and of the so-called local public utilities. If there are only a few competing establishments in an industry, if fixed charges are relatively large as compared with variable expenses, if the market is quick to take advantage of price-cutting on the part of one establishment or another, competition will be impossible.

Public policy should be based on careful discrimination between types of monopoly

The public has learned slowly, and perhaps has not yet learned fully, that public policy toward monopoly must be based upon careful discrimination between different types of monopoly. For example, artificial monopolies and natural monopolies must receive different treatment. It is absurd to attempt to get rid of the evils of monopoly by enforcing competition in such fields as railway transportation and the municipal public services. In these fields competition is wasteful and in the long run impossible. What we have to do in these instances is to recognize the fact of monopoly and then to rob monopoly of its power for evil by public regulation of the rates charged and the services given by these industries. There is no alternative save governmental ownership and operation.

On the other hand, where monopoly is artificial, we may sometimes get rid of it by eliminating its roots. Reforms of the patent system are undoubtedly sorely needed. It should not be possible for any one company to secure lasting domination of an industry by getting control of so many patents that future improvements and inventions affecting that industry have no market and no value except to the one company already in control. A situation like this virtually perpetuates the life of patents long beyond the years which the law contemplates. It is likely that some day we shall have to come to a system by which the users of important patent rights shall be licensed by the government, which will administer the patent system in such a way as to eliminate the evils of artificial monopoly.

Many so-called monopolies have proved, on actual test, not to be real monopolies at all. Some of the unsuccessful trusts found that the monopoly power they counted upon vanished as soon as they attempted to wield it. Potential competition exists as a threat against any combination which, without any real basis of monopoly power, nevertheless attempts to use that power. Some large businesses, however, having once by artificial combination achieved a monopolistic position in their respective industries, have attempted to perpetuate it by ruthlessly attacking and eliminating all would-be competitors.

There is no particular harm in ordinary price-cutting. It is an essential part of the methods of competition. Yet when price-cutting is used with the purpose not of increasing one's own profits but of destroying a competitor, it becomes one of the weapons of unfair competition. The small new firm just beginning to get a foothold in a given locality may be thus remorselessly crushed out of existence by price-cutting on the part of a large combination, operating in other parts of the country as well as in that particular locality. Its immediate losses from its price-cutting operations will be offset in the long run by the increased profits which can be gained by maintaining and perpetuating its monopoly power. One way, then, of preventing purely artificial monopoly is to prevent the use of unfair methods of competition. Weapons which can be wielded only by a large combination and not by the business establishment of normal size should be outlawed.

The Sherman Anti-trust Act

The federal government, since 1890, has waged a more or less successful warfare against artificial combinations, using as its principal weapon the Sherman Anti-trust Act, which declares that trusts or combinations in restraint of interstate or foreign trade or commerce are illegal. For many years little progress was made because the chief efforts of the prosecutors were given merely to "trust smashing." It is of little use to destroy a combination only to have it appear again in a new form – and such was the history of many of these earlier efforts. But in later years the government prosecutors have learned through experience that the most important thing is not so much flatly to forbid combination as to eliminate the hidden sources of monopoly power, such as special privileges or favors of one kind or another, or unfair methods of competition. The Federal Trade Commission, established in 1914 to assist in the control of combinations, has been given the power to restrain the use of unfair methods of competition.

We are gradually learning also that it is useless to try to force competition into a field that is inevitably monopolistic. To secure the undeniable benefits which combination, and even monopoly, give in certain types of industry, while guarding ourselves against the equally undoubted dangers of private monopoly power should, at least, be the *goal* of public policy.

Finally we should remember that these questions cannot be decided wholly upon the basis of the relative economic efficiency of one type of organization or the other. Monopoly and competition differ in their effects upon the distribution of wealth and upon the quality of economic life. They affect a host of economic, political, and social relations. In most of these respects, we believe, the advantage rests with competition. At any rate, we may be sure that we are making no mistake if we continue to endeavor to raise the level of competitive standards, to eliminate unfair competition as a basis of monopoly, and to recognize and control monopoly where monopoly is naturally inevitable or advantageous.

31 The meaning of value

The remarkable and all-important
interplay of supply and demand

Paradoxes of value and price

The Book of Popular Science (1924; revised 1929) New York: The Grolier Society. Group IX Ch. 30: 4097–105

[Chiozza Money:] *In its economic sense "value" does not mean usefulness; indeed, things may even be useless for any good purpose and yet have economic value. To the economist, a thing possessing value must have value in exchange. A commodity which cannot command other commodities in exchange has no economic value. Thus the water of the ocean, which is so valuable in the ordinary sense that without it the world could not exist and navigation could not be conducted, has no economic value. Similarly, the atmosphere, without which all organisms would perish, although invaluable in the ordinary sense, has no economic or exchange value.*

Using "value," then, in its economic sense, we see that it is a relative term. One commodity is exchangeable for varying quantities of other commodities at different times. At any one time it will exchange for more of this or less of that. A very large quantity of things easily secured will exchange for a very small quantity of things difficult to obtain. Broadly speaking, some kinds of commodities are in general produced easily, and large quantities of them, therefore, are needed if we desire to exchange them for other things which are difficult to procure or to manufacture. At different times the ratios vary considerably, however; in one year a much larger quantity of wheat may be required to purchase a piece of iron than in another year. ...

When all values become an expression of what we can exchange everything for in terms of money, we get the phenomenon of price, *which is simply the* exchange ratio of the article we select as money to some other commodity at any given moment. *Now we see why people talk loosely of a fall in "values," when what they mean is a fall in "prices" – i.e., an increased plentifulness of things in general in relation to the accepted monetary standards.*

If we have a clear perception of "value" as a relative term, and of "price" simply as an expression of the relation of commodities in general to a particular commodity – money – at any particular moment, we are helped to think clearly upon many common phenomena which otherwise escape our comprehension. For one thing, it helps us to see that a rise in prices does not in itself make people richer, or a fall in prices make them poorer, as is so often loosely thought. Properly understood, this would save us

*from imagining that by artificially holding up the prices of commodities we do good
to industry or commerce...*

*A general rise or a general fall of prices simply means an alteration in the purchasing
power of money, and does not matter except as it affects contracts for receiving and
paying fixed sums of money]...*

As a matter of fact, the phrases "general rise" and "general fall" of prices are loose
and vague. All prices do not move upward together, nor do they move downward
in even order. Some prices rise more rapidly and rise further than others; some
prices lag behind or even decrease during a general advance. Thus it usually
happens in periods of rising prices not only that investors and earners of wages
and salaries lose relatively, but that industrial producers, farmers, for example,
the prices of whose products are increasing less rapidly than are the prices of
other products, are also adversely affected. Rising prices bring prosperity to some,
but only at the expense of hardship inflicted upon others. The appearance of
general prosperity and of business activity which often accompanies a period of
rising prices is often illusive and deceptive. Below the surface, changes may be
going on which will breed a crisis and a subsequent period of prolonged depression.

The wide differences between economic value and utility

*[Chiozza Money: It will also be apparent from the considerations we have advanced
that economic value is not a measure of utility. It is a most important consideration
that primary utilities have small economic value. Beginning with the first necessities
of organic existence – air and sunshine – we have invaluable utilities with no economic
value. Proceeding next to food, we have invaluable utilities which have small economic
value. At the other end of the scale we have utilities which can easily be dispensed
with, which many people dispense with as a matter of choice, and which yet have a
very high economic value. We may instance a ruby, an emerald or a rare old piece of
china. As utilities these commodities satisfy a sense of beauty or a sense of curiosity, but
we can exist both comfortably and conveniently without them; many of the highest
types of mind do not value them at all.]*

The reader should remember, however, that when we say that air and sunshine
are utilities of the highest importance, while precious stones have relatively little
utility, we are speaking of air and sunshine in the abstract and that we are speaking
of precious stones in an equally abstract and general way. In an earlier chapter we
have seen that the conception of utility which is important to the student of
economics is not that of utility in the abstract, but the utility of particular, concrete
units or increments of commodities. Under abnormal conditions, a little sunshine
or even a cubic yard of air might have a very high utility indeed. But in general
their supply is so nearly unlimited that the withdrawal or addition of a single
unit makes no difference whatever in our happiness or welfare. Rubies and
emeralds are scarce. Any one emerald or any one ruby thus comes to have a
relatively high degree of importance, that is, of utility. There is the widest

discrepancy, frequently the most amazing contrast, between the general utility or usefulness of goods viewed in a general and abstract fashion and their prices, but there is necessarily a very close correspondence between the utility or importance to us of particular units or increments of goods and their exchange values. We value goods not in proportion to their general usefulness, but *in proportion to our desire for more or less of them.* The utility that is important for economic analysis is *marginal utility*, – the utility of the final or marginal increment of a supply.

Relation between marginal utility and exchange value, or price, very close

If I am a householder and purchase ten tons of coal for the winter's use, what is the utility of coal to me? Quite obviously, in an abstract, general way, the answer might be that without coal or fuel of some sort I could not use my house. More definitely, however, we may say that the utility of coal to me is the utility of the tenth ton of coal. If I have ten tons in my coal-bin, any one ton, of course, may be regarded as the tenth ton. It is this tenth ton which serves the least important use to which I put coal. If I had only nine tons of coal I might decide not to heat one of the less important rooms in my house. The importance of having that particular room heated is a fairly good measure of the importance of the tenth ton of coal, and when I have ten tons, the utility of the tenth ton is identical with the utility of *any other one ton.* Now it is obvious that the utility of this tenth or marginal ton must be closely related to the price I am willing to pay for coal. If the price had been higher I might have got along with eight or nine tons; if the price had been lower, I might have bought twelve tons. I balance the utility of the marginal ton of coal against the utilities of other things which the same expenditure of money would buy. It is clear that the relation between the marginal utilities of different goods and their exchange values, or prices, must be exceedingly close.

The diminishing satisfaction to be obtained from great wealth

It is because the bulk of the necessaries of life can be obtained at relatively small expense, in other words, because their economic value is relatively low, that a diminishing satisfaction is obtained from the possession of income as income grows. For every uniform addition to an income the satisfaction it gives, its importance, we may say, diminishes. Add $500 to an income of $500 and the recipient is overjoyed and feels immediately enriched. Add $500 to an income of $1000 and the addition, although highly appreciated, is nevertheless not so important as it was in the preceding example. Add $500 to an income of $5000, and the increase in satisfaction will be relatively small. Add $500 to an income of $50,000, and the increase of satisfaction will be absolutely unnoticed. A famous mathematician, J. Bernouilli, once suggested that there might be a mathematical relation between the size of an income and the importance attached to an increment of given size. He ventured the guess that equal proportionate increases in income yielded equal amounts of added satisfaction. That is, under this hypothesis, a man would attach as much importance to an addition of $5000 to an income of $10,000 as he would to an addition of $500 to an income of $1000. Of course, there is no way of determining the truth of Bernouilli's hypothesis. At best it is a plausible guess, but it is likely that most critics would hold that it is not very far from the truth. If true, it would have an interesting bearing upon the problem of justice in the distribution of wealth, and upon problems of taxation. Thus, *proportional* taxation might be justified on the ground that as much pain or discomfort might be caused by taking away, say, 5 per cent of the income of a relatively poor man as by taking away the same *proportion* of the income of a relatively rich man. ...

The annual production of wealth is at once a measure of the present limitations of industry and of the present limitations to humanity's capacity to satisfy its wants. From what we have said respecting the law of diminishing satisfaction, it follows that the sum total of satisfactions resulting from the annual wealth product depends in no small degree upon the way in which that wealth product is distributed. In general, the increase of inequalities in the distribution of wealth diminishes the sum total of satisfactions. Changes, on the other hand that tend in any measure to equalize incomes, tend necessarily to lessen the demand for luxuries and to increase the demand for the necessaries and comforts of life.

But, as we have already seen in an earlier chapter,[a] it does not follow that a dead level of equality in the distribution of income would give us a contented society or one in which the full possibilities of economic welfare would be realized. Some differences of income there must be, if only to serve as incentives, as prizes, for efficiency, industry and thrift. Somewhere in society, moreover, there must be the power of expending a surplus for goods other than the necessaries of life, if life is to be anything more than a standardized, unprogressive and generally drab scheme of existence. Somewhere and in some way society must make provision for the production of those goods that do not minister to the most urgent and immediate of human wants, but upon which the lasting progress of civilization is built. ...

Sometimes the most profound of business errors are made through inaccurate estimates of supply and demand. These mistakes are often responsible not only for the shortage in the supply of some commodities and the oversupply of others, and for the failures of many business undertakings, but also for the recurring visitations of those industrial crises and depressions which, more than almost anything else, make us realize that man has not yet completely mastered the problems of the organization of his economic life.

Nevertheless, when we take the whole world of business into account, the wonder is not that so many mistakes are made, but that supply and demand are as dependable and that prices are as constant as in fact they really are. Two factors, in all probability, account for this relatively satisfactory condition: First, the aggregate amount of goods supplied to market in all competitive industries is the net resultant of the decisions of thousands of individual producers, just as the aggregate demand of the market is the outcome of the preferences and desires of millions of individual consumers. In all human affairs in which chance, luck, miscalculation and the like play any part, particular irregularities and abnormalities, mistakes in the individual decision, are absorbed and offset one against the other in the mass.

The "law of large numbers," as statisticians call it, shows itself in the constancy of such ratios as the annual death rate, and the marriage rate. A particular marriage may be thought to be the outcome of an individual decision – rather, of *two* individual decisions, – but year by year in a given country and under given economic conditions, the marriage rate remains as steadily constant as though it were the outcome of some definite physical law. And so with supply and demand. One producer may overestimate the market; another producer may underestimate it. The net result of their combined estimates is likely to be somewhere near the truth.

In the second place, men fortunately learn by experience in their economic conduct, as in other activities. The number of seats that will be sold at a given price in stands erected for those who want to view a great procession is a problem upon which there is no *continuous* experience. But the number of seats which should be provided in the average theater or in the stands at baseball grounds is determined not so much by guesswork as by a definite knowledge of actual facts, based upon experience of drawing power of similar attractions.

It should not be inferred that costly mistakes are not made by producers in the aggregate as well as by individual producers. In certain periods business optimism is contagious, just as pessimism is contagious at other periods. Following a profitable year, when high prices have been paid them for wheat and cotton, the farmers of the country are likely to produce wheat and cotton crops too large to be sold at profitable prices...

Some paradoxes of supply and demand

What we have just said brings us to the consideration of one of the most interesting of the paradoxes of value. It frequently happens that an increase in the physical quantity of a good is accompanied by a decrease in its aggregate selling value. Its real utility in the sense of its real *usefulness* increases as its quantity is increased, even if, as we have seen, at a diminishing rate. But its market value may *decrease*. As an item in society's real wealth, the good may bulk larger than ever before; as an item of wealth, measured by the monetary yardstick, it is smaller. A classical example of this paradox was the destruction of half of their spice crop by the Dutch East Indian Company because it estimated that the remaining half would sell for more money on the market than the whole crop would have brought. It has frequently happened that the farmers of the United States have received less in the aggregate for a large cotton crop than for a smaller one.

The important factor in this problem is the degree of the *elasticity* of the demand for the article in question. We have already seen that if a relatively large advantage in price is accompanied by a relatively small change in demand the latter is said to be "inelastic." If the change in price and the resulting change in the amount demanded are so related that the *aggregate selling value of the total output* of the commodity remains unchanged whatever the price per unit, we have an example of what is called "unitary elasticity of demand." If the aggregate selling value of a product decreases as the amount of the product increases, the demand may be said to be "inelastic."

A second paradox of value appears in the fact that it often happens that an increase in price creates increased demand, while a decrease in price diminishes demand. A rise in the price of stocks, for example, is likely to stimulate the buying of shares, while a decline in price is likely to lead to a cessation of buying. In the year 1921 (as in other years of business depression) declining prices were followed by a decreasing rather than increasing demand for goods.

This particular type of paradox, involving a seeming inversion of the general law of supply and demand, resolves itself upon examination into a phenomenon of speculation. When the prices of stocks are advancing, many people buy because they infer, rightly or wrongly, that for some time at least prices will continue to advance. When prices begin to decline, speculators unload their holdings precipitately on the market in order to avoid loss from a yet further decline. The net resultant of their combined "buying for a rise" is, of course, to push the price yet further up, and to lead to yet further buying. When prices turn downward, the net resultant of the combined efforts of speculators to realize on their holdings, or to save some part of their profits before they disappear entirely, is, of course, to precipitate a more rapid decline of prices. When prices are falling, consumers refuse to buy, reserving their purchasing power for use at a later period when, they hope, prices will have reached their minimum. But when the movement of prices turns upward, consumers hasten to purchase. "Consumers' speculation," as it may be called, is coming to be recognized as an important factor in the ebb and flow in the demand of the market for commodities, just as producers' speculation on the other hand is an equal factor in determining their supply. Another way of putting the matter is that this apparent paradox of supply and demand relates only to the distribution of supply and demand *in time*. The withholding of present demand is fairly certain to be accompanied by increased demand in the future. It is just the temporary withholding of the power of demand that leads to the paradoxical situation that the lower price is accompanied by a diminution in demand.

There are certain cases, however, in which a diminution in price brings about a real and permanent diminution in demand. This occurs in the market for commodities which are valued not so much because they minister to human needs as because they are the objects of passing fads and fancies or because their possession is a convenient means of displaying to the world the consumers' means of spending money freely.

If diamonds were less expensive, if artificial diamonds of good size could be produced at low cost, the demand for diamonds for personal adornment would be likely to decline rather than increase. If the price of admission to moving picture theaters were, by reason of a supposedly high cost of production, greater than the price of admission to grand opera, doubtless it would follow that moving pictures would become rather more fashionable than grand opera, and would be given in theaters offering every opportunity for the ostentatious display of wealth. But we should not allow the undoubted truth of these facts to lead us to the conclusion that the expenditure of money over and above the amount used in the purchase of necessaries is merely a form of competition in what Thorstein Veblen calls "conspicuous consumption." There are many people who love diamonds and other precious stones, not because they are expensive, but because of their real beauty. And doubtless the great majority of those who listen to grand opera will continue to go there because of the real appeal of that combination of musical and dramatic art and not for any less worthy reason. It is easy to be cynical, but the thorough cynic rarely sees more than the surface of economic life.

A long-time view of supply and demand

It may at first thought seem to be somewhat paradoxical that in the long run an increasing demand for a commodity lowers its price. In all economic analysis, we have to distinguish very carefully between the short-time view of things, in which our attention is focused upon the immediate phenomena of the market, and the long-time view which is concerned with the ultimate effects and repercussions of these different economic phenomena.

The relation of supply to demand often involves both action and reaction, and although an increase of demand may immediately produce a rise in price, it may lead eventually to a fall in price by stimulating a better supply, as in the case of books and newspapers, after the invention of printing brought into existence a large potential reading public.

But, it may be asked, has then the cost of producing an article no relation to its value? Is a producer compelled to take a price which is arrived at quite independently of his costs? The answer to this question is that the *cost of production is an essential part of the conditions of supply,* and that when we speak of demand and supply we use the latter term as conditioned by cost of production...

It should be clear from this brief analysis of the relation between price and the cost of production that, although such a relation exists, and although it has, in the long run, a dominating influence upon the prices of different commodities, it is, nevertheless, wholly untrue that cost of production in any sense "creates" value. Things have value, they command a price in the market, not because they are expensive to produce, but because there is a demand for them. Business men incur costs of production because they estimate that the goods produced will sell for enough to recoup the costs and return a profit. Costs, therefore, do not create values. We should be closer to the facts if we should say that value creates costs. Demand is the cause of value, but cost, or, in some instances, artificial scarcity, is a necessary condition of the existence of value. Productive costs unwisely incurred, production unwisely administered, will give no valuable product. It is only in so far as production correctly anticipates demand that it yields not merely a commodity but a valuable commodity.

Diminishing and increasing returns

We must note a very important difference between different types of industries with respect to the ultimate effects of increased demand and increased production upon price. In many industries, notably manufacturing, an increase of demand, by stimulating invention, by making possible large-scale operations, by leading to a better division of labor within the average plant, most of all by securing a better division of labor *as between* different plants, by securing a more elaborate organization of the industry viewed as a whole, leads to very greatly reduced prices.

The printing and publishing industry will again serve as an example. The early printers made their own type, their own ink, even their own paper. Today, we find great printing establishments utilizing ingenious and highly specialized machinery. We find within each establishment a detailed division of labor as between hand compositors, monotype and linotype operators, proofreaders, electrotypers, engravers, pressmen, press feeders, binders, etc.

Even more important, however, is the fact of *specialization within the industry as a whole* whereby the business of making paper is elaborately organized as a separate industry; type-founding is another industry; the making of the various machines used in the printing industry, and we may even say the making of machines that will be used in the making of printing machines occupies yet further industries. To push the analysis further would lead us into endless ramifications. But we have gone far enough to suggest the general nature of the economics, both within the individual plant and within the industry as a whole, which have accompanied the growth in the size of the printing industry.

What is true of the printing industry is true of manufactures in general. Such industries are properly called "industries of *increasing returns*" because with the general growth in the output of the industry, the return to a given expenditure of capital and labor increases. That is, in the long run the product increases more rapidly than the real and ultimate costs of production increase. On the other hand, there are the industries characterized by *diminishing returns,* of which agriculture affords the most conspicuous example. Under given conditions it is impossible largely to increase the agricultural output without having resort either to poorer and poorer land or to more thorough and more intensive cultivation of the land already in use. Either alternative means rapidly rising costs. But these rapidly rising costs will not be incurred, in other words increased production will not be undertaken, unless justified by the hope of securing higher prices. Of course, in agriculture – as in industry – invention, the use of improved fertilizers, of improved types of farm machinery and the like, has an effect precisely like the effect of improvement in manufactures. But there is the important difference that in manufactures generally the effect of improvements, of the external and the internal economies that accompany increased output, dominates the situation.

In agriculture, on the other hand, technical improvements, while they tend to diminish costs and prices, encounter a more potent force operating in precisely the opposite direction – the relatively small supply of the better lands.

It is true that the general course of agricultural prices during the last hundred years has, as compared with the prices of other commodities, been downward. This fact does not, as some superficial observers allege, disprove the validity of the law of diminishing returns in agriculture. Any economic law is merely the statement of a tendency. The phrase "other things being equal" must always be understood to be implied. Now the last hundred years have been periods of rapid and even marvelous change. The world's population has expanded as never before; the world's land area has been gridded with railways and its waters plowed for the first time by steam vessels. Vast areas of fertile land in all parts of the world, previously "poor lands" merely because they were distant from markets, have been made accessible and brought under cultivation. The world can never repeat this particular episode in its history. Not all of the world's cultivable land is in use, but its location, its extent, and its limitations are known with fair accuracy. The law of diminishing returns has not, through the last hundred years, ceased to operate. Its operation, however, has been frustrated by the dominance of new and unusual factors.

If the world's population is to continue to increase, we must frankly and courageously face the fact that the world's supplies of food and of raw materials will be got only at increasing costs. But this does not, as we have already seen in other connections, justify undue pessimism. The law of diminishing returns is not likely to operate sharply and suddenly. It is not true, for example, that a small increase in the world's food supply can be won only at a greatly increased cost per unit. The truth is rather that enormous additions to the world's annual supply of food and raw materials are possible at a relatively small increase in cost per unit.

Editors' note

a Chapter 21 of the Grolier *Book of Popular Science* entitled "The Annual Wealth Product" (included in this selection as Chapter 25).

Part IV
Money and credit

32 Exams in money and banking

Harvard University, 1922

Economics 3 – November 3, 1922 – Hour Examination

Money, Banking, and Commercial Crises

1. "In view of the evident fact that legal-tender acts do not preserve the value of money, it is clear that the demand created by such legislation must be insignificant. And this must be so in principle as well as in fact." From the report of the Indianapolis Monetary Commission, in Phillips.[1] Explain.
2. Define: – deposits, reserves, clearing-house loan certificates; acceptance; guaranty savings banks.
3. "That governments have so frequently felt it their duty to take measures for the protection of the holders of bank-notes against the insolvency of the bank, but have so seldom legislated for the protection of depositors, is due to several reasons." – Dunbar.[2] What reasons?
4. Dunbar describes the way in which a bank creates deposits by discounting commercial paper.[3] A practical banker is likely to refer to his deposits as measuring his ability to lend or discount. Are these two views mutually inconsistent?

Economics 38 – June 13, 1922 – Final Examination

The Principles of Money and Banking

1. "The level of prices, therefore, depends on two sets of influences: (1) the volume of currency available in any country, and (2) the total volume of transactions which have to be performed."[4] In your opinion, is the form of the quantity theory thus stated by Layton true? Is it significant? Is there any other formulation of the quantity theory which you prefer?
2. Explain and discuss critically Marshall's account of the mechanism by means of which new supplies of gold affect the price level.[5] Would Marshall's

explanation account for a long-time movement such as that from 1897–1914, or is it of more significance in its relation to the business cycle?

3. "We have to balance the stimulating effect of rising prices on industry, against the disadvantage to the great mass of persons whose incomes are more or less fixed. The verdict must, of course, be a matter of judgment, but we may conclude that on the whole the social well-being is best advanced when prices are stationary, or slightly declining."[6] The foregoing is Layton's opinion. Do you agree? Discuss.

4. What is your opinion of the efficacy of the mechanism proposed by Fisher for stabilizing the dollar?[7] Why?

5. Why did Walker insist that money is a "common denominator of value" rather than a "measure of value?"[8] What is your opinion?

6. Discuss the dictum that there can be no over-issue of bank credit if bank loans are made only for the purpose of "financing actual commercial transactions."

7. Give Robertson's classification of the varieties of money, or, as an alternative, give a classification of your own which you prefer to Robertson's.[9]

8. "People sometimes speak as though a country which is getting behindhand with its payments to its neighbours can somehow manage to get square, provided it is willing to see the exchanges turn sufficiently against itself. This is untrue."[10] On what reasoning is the opinion which Robertson holds to be untrue based? On what ground does he hold it to be untrue?

Editors' notes

1 Phillips, Chester Arthur (ed.) (1916) *Readings in Money and Banking*, New York: Macmillan, p. 30.
2 Dunbar, Charles F. (1906) *Chapters on the Theory and History of Banking*, 2nd edn., New York: Putnam's, p. 58.
3 Ibid., Ch. 2, "Discount, Deposit, and Issue", pp. 9–19.
4 Layton, Walter T. (1920) *An Introduction to the Study of Prices*, London: Macmillan, p. 30.
5 Young probably had in mind here Alfred Marshall's "Memoranda and Evidence before the Gold and Silver Commission" (1887). Reprinted as Chap. 2 in *Official Papers by Alfred Marshall*. London: Macmillan, 1926.
6 Layton, Walter T. (1920) *An Introduction to the Study of Prices*, London: Macmillan, p. 106.
7 Cf. Fisher, Irving (1920) *Stabilizing the Dollar; A Plan to Stabilize the General Price Level without Fixing Individual Prices*. New York: Macmillan.
8 Walker, Francis A. (1883) *Money*, New York: Henry Holt, pp. 280–90.
9 Cf. "The Kinds of Money", pp. 39–47 in Robertson, Dennis H., (1920) *Money*, New York: Harcourt, Brace and Co.
10 Ibid., p. 145.

33 The mystery of money

*How modern methods of making
payments economize the use of money.
The role of checks and bank-notes*

The enormous edifice of credit

The Book of Popular Science (1924; revised 1929) New York: The Grolier Society.
Group IX Ch. 31: 4231–40

For a long time, it was the habit of writers on the subject of money to picture an
imaginary stage of barter which continued for a long period before it became
possible to agree to use one particular commodity as the medium of exchange or
measure of value, and thus to adopt money.

This view of things, that men *invented* money in order to rid themselves of
the difficulties and inconveniences of barter, belongs, along with much other
conjectural history, on the scrap-heap of discredited ideas. Men did not invent
money by reasoning about the inconveniences of barter any more than they
invented government by reasoning about the inconveniences of some mythical
primitive state of anarchy. The use of money, like other human institutions, grew
or evolved. Its origins are obscure. It is, nevertheless, fairly certain that at no
period in his history has man ever conducted any considerable volume of trade
by means of barter. There was a very small gap, perhaps no gap at all, between the
beginnings of trade and the origin of money.

Of course, traders dealing with regions where civilization has scarcely appeared
may even now find it possible to exchange beads, cheap bright-colored calicoes,
knives, mirrors, etc., for goods which are in modern markets vastly more valuable.
But the trader, unless he be a trained observer, is likely to disregard the fact that
the savages with whom he barters have some crude, primitive monetary system
of their own. In fact, it is not at all uncommon for the beads, or other (to them)
rarities, which the savage tribe obtains by way of barter from civilized peoples, to
become, by reason of their scarcity and desirability, the money, for the time being
at least, of the tribe.

A host of different commodities have been used at different times, and by
different peoples, as money. If we scrutinize a list of such commodities ever so
carefully, we shall find it difficult to see that they have any common characteristics
beyond the fact that, for various reasons, the commodities have all had, at a given
time and place, an assured market or outlet.

Consider the fact, noted by the great German historian of Rome, Mommsen, as well as by other observers, that the peoples of the early civilizations of the world, like the moderns, almost uniformly selected for use as money commodities that were ornamental rather than useful. This fact calls for explanation, and the explanation may throw some light upon at least one of the mysteries of money. If there is any one clear-cut and fundamental difference between necessary commodities and luxuries, it is that human wants for necessaries are satiable, while the desire for ornaments, as for other goods that minister to the love of distinction and display, is insatiable. Of course, it is not true that normal men place luxuries above necessaries. It is simply true that when one is provided with the necessaries of life, the normal man, in adding to his goods, will increase his stores of luxuries rather than his supplies of necessaries. To use a technical phrase explained in earlier chapters, the demand for ornaments, and consequently the demand for the metals from which ornaments are made, is elastic, while the demand for the necessaries of life is, by comparison, inelastic. There is a surer market and a surer outlet for ornaments and for their materials. Their value is less variable than that of necessaries. Especially is this true in communities with little foreign trade. Wheat might be a drug on the market; but such could never be the case with respect to precious stones or ornaments of gold.

The definition of money and its essential characteristic

Money may be defined as a commodity or group of commodities customarily paid and received in exchange for other commodities and services without reference to the personal credit of the one who offers it. That is, a personal note is not money, but a bank-note is. It is necessary to observe further, however, that not only the credit of the one who offers it, but also the desires and intentions of the persons who receive it, have an important bearing upon the question of what is and what is not money. The person who receives money in exchange for commodities or services takes it with no other thought than that of passing it on again in exchange for other goods and services. No one, except the miser, values or wants money on its own account, even though the materials of which some forms of money are made may have utility and value of their own.

The one really essential characteristic of money is that the holder should be able to get rid of it without undue loss. Other commodities have their ultimate consumers; money never finds an ultimate destination or resting-place: it is tossed about from person to person until finally, worn out, lost, or melted down, it passes out of use.

Illustrations showing money is not primarily valued for itself

If, with these fundamental principles in mind, we survey such facts as are available respecting the monies of the primitive peoples and the diverse types of money used even by modern peoples, we shall find that they have just that one essential characteristic. The precious metals, almost from earliest times, have been used as the materials of ornaments, and so also from almost the earliest times, they have been used as money. The precious metals could always be passed on to the man whose wealth and standing in the community were estimated, as today in some parts of India, by the number and the weight of the silver and gold ornament worn by his wife. An elastic demand in itself creates a safe outlet. Why was tobacco used as money in early colonial Virginia; or furs in some of the northern colonies and in Canada? Or rice in the Carolinas? Why did the New England colonists sometimes use the Indians' ornamental strings of beads – wampum – as a medium of exchange in certain of their own transactions? Utilizing again our unifying principle, the answer to each of these questions is obvious. Tobacco was the most important Virginia product for export. It was the medium by which English goods, of which the colonists were in sore need, could be obtained. It was the one product for which there was, for the time being, a certain and undisputed market. What more natural than that accounts as between the colonists themselves should be transferred by means of this particular commodity, their best embodiment of purchasing power? And so with furs, obtained by trappers or bought from the Indians, and sold in the export market: they also came to have a local currency as a means of getting other things. They could be passed on from hand to hand with the certainty that the holder for the time being could pass them on again when he so desired. The case of wampum is a little different. There was, of course, no European outlet for it; but it had purchasing power in dealings with the Indians, and it is very likely that, for that reason, some of the colonists were not unwilling to accumulate a stock of it. All of these illustrations serve to make it tolerably clear that money is not primarily a thing that is valued for itself. The value of money *is* its purchasing power. Just so far as any commodity serves as money, it is because it is wanted, not for personal or permanent use, but for passing on. The material of which money is made may have its own use. This merely makes it all the more certain that money itself may be passed on, that someone may always be found who is willing to take it in exchange for goods or services.

With respect to another problem – the economic functions of money – there has also been unnecessary confusion of thought. Money is an important part of our commercial mechanism. The "functions" of any piece of mechanism are properly determined, not by what we think that particular bit of mechanism *ought* to do, but by what it actually *does*. In economics, as in the natural sciences, we shall see farther and see more clearly if we consistently try to avoid the use of loose, vague and general terms, and fix our attention upon concrete facts, upon what actually takes place in this complicated world.

The money price of commodities is final criterion of relative values

Money is often said to be a medium of exchange and a measure of value. Taken loosely, these descriptive phrases are not objectionable, but when we use them we should try to see back of them into the actual facts they loosely summarize or describe. Otherwise we are likely to forget that after all the "values" of things *are* their money prices. We do not, in actual fact, determine the relative values of different kinds of commodities and services, and then bring in money as a means of "measuring" the different values or of reducing them, as General Francis A. Walker preferred to say, to a common denominator. The general exchange values of the commodities that are bought and sold in modern markets are, in fact, merely relations that we derive or infer from their money prices. The money price of a commodity is the fundamental original fact with which the economic scientist must deal. Interpreted generously and *understood,* however, there is no real difference between the two functions of serving as a medium of exchange and as a measure of value.

It is only in the actual exchange of goods for money, or in deciding whether or not to make such exchanges, that we really use money as a "measure of value." In the same way, of course, it is proper to say that a yard-stick is both a measure of length and an instrument used in measuring. Anyone would say at once that these two alleged functions of the yard-stick are really but one function. Precisely so with money: measuring values and serving as a medium of exchange are only one function, not two.

It is better to avoid these word-wasting controversies over the meanings of terms by recognizing money for just what it is, namely, a *means of payment.* The prices of goods and services are stated in terms of money and we pay for them with money. Debts are promises to pay money, and we pay our debts with money.

Money is sometimes said to serve also as a standard of deferred payments. Properly understood, again, there is nothing objectionable in this statement. It merely emphasizes the fact that debts which run for many years, like short-time debts, are usually made payable in money. The farmer who borrows money on mortgage security and agrees to pay off the loan at the end of ten years, will gain or lose according as prices in general, especially the prices of agricultural products, move upward or downward during the ten-year period. If prices move downward, he has to pay his creditor in money which costs more, which will buy more, and which therefore is worth more than the money he borrowed. If the debt had been contracted in terms of bushels of wheat, the relative positions of the creditor and debtor at the end of the transaction would have been very different. If prices move upward, rather than downward, it is, of course, creditors who lose and debtors who gain. In saying that money serves as a standard of deferred payments we are really doing little more than calling attention to the importance of this particular problem. As a matter of fact, this function of money, like the others, is really covered by the simple statement that money is the ordinary means of payment.

It would be possible, of course, to divorce the *standard* of deferred payments from the ordinary *means* of payments. Thus, the law might prescribe that debts stated in terms of money should be increased or decreased according as the general purchasing power of money declined or advanced. In such case, although money would remain the means of payment, the standard of deferred payments would really consist of the list of goods whose prices were taken and compounded to measure the general purchasing power of money. Or, as some have proposed, the cost of money, or the amount of labor required at different periods to earn a specified amount of money, might be made the basis of a standard of deferred payments. The problem of the standard of deferred payments has had in the past a very large political as well as economic importance, as we shall see when, in a later chapter, we examine some of the outstanding facts in the monetary history of the United States.

What gives different kinds of money its value

We now pass to the consideration of certain problems associated with the coinage of money. There is a widespread illusion that the essential characteristic of a coin is the government stamp, that it is the power and authority of the government which give the coin its value. This notion has done a vast amount of harm, and more than once it has been used by governments as an excuse for unsound monetary policies. On some peculiar kinds of coins, as we shall see, as well as on most kinds of paper money, it is the government's stamp which, in a sense, gives money its value. But in precisely the same way, it is the solvent debtor's name on his promissory note that gives the note its value. We must distinguish carefully between two wholly different kinds of coins: standard coins and subordinate coins.

Put a ten-dollar gold piece upon an anvil and deface it with a heavy sledgehammer. The shapeless lump of gold you will have left will not be a coin, but it will be worth precisely ten dollars. By defacing the coin, you will have removed merely a useful and convenient label. But treat a silver dollar in the same fashion, and you will have left sixty cents' worth of silver or more, the exact value depending upon the price of silver at the time. In defacing the government stamp you will undoubtedly have destroyed some of the value the coin had.

The fact is that the coinage of standard coins, such as the gold eagle, is nothing but a dependable official certification of their weight and fineness. They are in reality nothing but pieces of precious metal.

Anyone can take gold to the United States mint, and if it is of the required standard of fineness, the government will pay him for it at the rate of one dollar for 23.22 grains of fine gold. Silver coins, however, are made from metal purchased by the government. There is less than a dollar's worth of silver in the silver dollar and in a dollar lot of smaller silver coins, just as there is less then five cents' worth of metal in the nickel and less than one cent's worth of bronze in the cent. The details of the process by which these coins are kept at a parity with gold will be discussed in a later chapter. We may note here, however, that just so far as the government in its own transactions does not discriminate among these different types of coins and, in particular, just so far as it remains able and willing to exchange any one type of coin for any other sort, just so far will the business world accept these coins as of identical value per dollar. But it is important to observe that in foreign trade the subordinate coins are at a disadvantage. Save in exceptional cases, such as in border trade with neighboring countries, the general rule is that they will be taken only at the value of their bullion content. Gold also passes in foreign trade at its bullion value, but in its case, as we have seen, bullion value and coined value are identical. For this reason, gold, whether in coins or in bullion form, is the international monetary standard and the means of paying the final trade balances between different countries.

We have assumed thus far that the government makes no charge for the coinage of gold. Such, in fact, is the case in most modern countries. The United States, like most other countries, makes a necessary charge for assaying and refining the gold if it does not conform to the required standard. France and a few other countries make a very small additional charge called "brassage" to cover all or a part of the actual expense of coinage. The operations of the English mint, in principle, are gratuitous like those of the United States mint. There is the essential difference, however, that in England one who takes gold to the mint would supposedly be asked to wait until his bullion had been converted into coin. In practice, the Bank of England acts as intermediary between the mint and the public. An ounce of gold suffices to make £3 17s. 10½d. in English gold coins. The Bank of England will at all times buy gold at the price of £3 17s. 9d. and it may give somewhat more than this price when it desires to strengthen its own gold reserves.

Seigniorage and its results

Modern nations, it is clear, view the maintenance of the coinage as a public function to be performed in large measure at public expense. Very different has been the attitude of governments in earlier times. The monopolistic power of coining money was often held as a prerogative of the sovereign not because in this way only would the people have the advantages of a uniform and dependable currency, but rather in order that the sovereign might use his prerogative as a means of securing profits. A common practice was that of making a high *seigniorage* charge – a charge much more than covering the expenses of coinage. When seigniorage is charged, more bullion must be deposited at the mint than is contained in the coins received for the bullion. The surplus bullion went as profits to the sovereign to be made into coins for his own use. A more flagrantly unfair practice was that of calling in all coins in circulation for recoinage into smaller coins.

Royal monetary legerdemain

One who had thus been forced to turn his money into the mint was repaid the same number of coins, and the coins were of the same denomination, but they were of lighter weight. The bullion taken out of the coins of the people was made into money for the sovereign. It is probable that in purpose and principle these transactions were not thought to be the barefaced robbery which to us they seem to have been. Kings, like other men, were misled by the notion that it was the royal stamp that gave value to the coin. They believed and were often told by their advisors that the new light-weight coins would be worth as much as the old, and that they could thus reap profits without imposing any real burdens upon their peoples. Of course such doctrines were and are no better than pernicious nonsense. By no sort of monetary legerdemain can wealth be created, as it were, out of thin air. The recoining operations, it will be noted, resulted in an increase in the number of coins in the country, just as when seigniorage was charged, a given volume of metal was made ultimately into a larger number of coins than would otherwise have been minted. The sovereign obtained *purchasing power* that he otherwise would not have had. It is absurd to suppose that he could have expended this purchasing power for goods and services without correspondingly reducing the purchasing power remaining in the hands of his subjects. The king's shillings, or florins, or whatever the coins might be, came into the market, we may say, as new competitors of the coins of the king's subjects. Prices rose to a level which they otherwise would not have reached. Seigniorage, like the debasement of the currency, thus operated as a tax upon the people. Coins subjected to a seigniorage charge always fell in value. Their purchasing power was determined, in the long run, not by what they cost at the mint, but by the amount of bullion they actually contained. Under such conditions, bullion was not brought to the mint except under compulsion.

The fact is that a seigniorage charge of any magnitude is not practicable. The point is important, not so much because seigniorage is today a live issue, but because precisely the same principles are involved in various proposals to substitute for gold another type of standard money consisting of irredeemable paper currency, that is, paper currency which involves no promise to pay on the part of the government, nor any governmental responsibility for maintaining its value. Such paper money, sometimes called "fiat money," is very much like metallic money subjected to a 100 per cent seigniorage charge, if such a thing can be imagined. Precisely the same considerations which counted so heavily against the policy of charging seigniorage on the coinage of standard metal hold with really fatal force against any proposal for a standard money of irredeemable paper.

Credit and its big role in business

We shall find it convenient at this point to set aside for the moment these problems of money, properly so called, and turn to the related subject of credit. Nine-tenths of the business transactions in a country like the United States are performed with the aid of credit rather than of money. From the purely quantitative point of view, credit is vastly more important than money. And yet that should not blind us to the fact that credit without money is impossible. Proposals to do away with money and to use credit only as a means of payment reveal a complete misunderstanding of the nature of credit and of its relation to money. There is, in fact, so much confusion respecting the real nature of credit that we shall do well to observe that credit is in fact a very simple thing. Credit is merely the other side of debt! In a borrowing transaction what appears to the lender as a credit, appears to the borrower as a debt. Much confusion would be avoided if, in discussing monetary problems, we should use the word "debt" in place of "credit." The real facts discussed would be unchanged. But the mode of discussion would necessarily steer us clear of a number of dangerous fallacies.

For example, who would be willing to say that we could dispense with money and get along very well by the use of debts as means of payment? The objection is obvious. A debt can hardly be a means of payment, for it itself is something to be paid.

Institutions which deal in debts

Nevertheless, we shall see that there is a *certain sense* in which we may speak of making payments by means of debts. But this is a misleading way of stating the matter unless it is clearly understood that we are using the words "making payments" in a rather loose way. Debts, very naturally, are means of avoiding, rather than of making, payments. And the greater the extent to which we can avoid immediate payments by utilizing credit, the more we will be able to avoid the necessity of making final payments, not because we fail to honor our debts, but because the accumulated debts of persons in the community are offset or canceled one against another. This cancellation or offsetting process is accomplished easily and inconspicuously by the mechanism of banking.

A bank is an institution which deals in debts. It buys the debts of its customers and sells its own debts. Its customers' debts come to it in the form of promissory notes and bills of exchange. A promissory note is, of course, a promise to pay money either on demand or, more usually, on or before a certain date. A bill of exchange or draft is an order to pay, drawn by a creditor upon a debtor. When acknowledged or accepted by the debtor, as by writing his name upon it, it becomes an "acceptance", and then, for all practical purposes, is like a promissory note.

Growth in use of bank acceptances

A bill of exchange drawn by a jobber or manufacturer on account of a shipment of goods and accepted by the buyer – a retail merchant, perhaps – is called a "trade acceptance." It may happen however, that instead of accepting the bill of exchange on his own account, the buyer will arrange with some bank to accept the bill of exchange on his behalf.

The bank, of course, will be fully protected by the deposit of securities or by some other satisfactory arrangement. The bank gets a small commission for thus lending the use of its name and the buyer may get better interest rates or more favorable terms of sale because he can furnish an acceptance so satisfactory to the creditor.

Such "bank acceptances," as they are called, have a large and growing use in financing international trade.

In exchange for its customers' debts, in the form of notes and bills of exchange, the bank gives its own debts in the shape of bank deposits and bank-notes. It will be worth our while to examine these two forms of banking indebtedness rather carefully, for they play a very large part in modern economic life. We are accustomed to think of a bank deposit as "money in the bank." In fact, however, it is nothing but a claim or credit, – a right to receive money on demand from a bank. A bank deposit is the depositor's credit or asset and the bank's debt or liability. It often happens that when some rumor, true or false, has started a run upon a particular bank, the depositors who have stood in line, perhaps for hours, in order to withdraw their deposits before the bank collapses, are perfectly satisfied when they find the bank is able to pay them. They do not want their money, they merely want the assurance that "their money is still there." Of course this shows a profound ignorance of the nature of banking. No bank could afford to have on hand at any one time cash sufficient to satisfy all of its depositors. A certain amount of cash must be in its vaults or must be easily available elsewhere, – somewhat more than enough to meet the ordinary day-to-day demands of its depositors and creditors. This relatively small amount of cash – 10, 15, or even 25 per cent of the bank's debts to its depositors – is the bank's "cash reserve." The proportion it should bear to the bank's total deposit debts is regulated in the United States by law, but in many countries it has been found wiser to leave it to be decided by the practical experience of the banks themselves.

Three ways of obtaining a bank deposit

One may purchase a bank deposit in any of three different ways. In the first place, one may from time to time turn surplus cash over to the bank as many merchants are accustomed to do daily. This may seem like actually depositing money in the bank. But the real transaction is an exchange: the depositor's cash is paid into the bank, not with any understanding that the cash shall be kept intact and separate, but in exchange for the right to demand the same amount of cash, or any part of it, from the bank at any time. Or, in the second place, a bank deposit may be obtained by turning over to a bank checks signed by depositors in the same bank or in other banks. It is clear that transactions of this type merely result in transfers of deposit credits from one depositor to another and, incidentally, from one bank to another. The total volume of bank deposits within the community is not affected by these transfers.

In the third place, depositors' credits are *created* by banks in favor of their borrowers. The business man brings to his bank, let us say, his own promissory note for $10,000, payable at the end of 90 days. Or it may be a note which the business man has taken from one of his customers and to which he has added his own endorsement, or it may be an accepted bill of exchange representing a shipment to the customer. The bank discounts the note or bill of exchange. In other words, it buys it and pays for it, not its face value, but a somewhat smaller sum. The amount of the difference or discount is substantially like interest, except that it is deducted in advance from the face value of the loan instead of being added to the principal of the loan at its maturity. In the imaginary case under discussion, if the rate of discount were 6 per cent per annum, the note or bill of exchange for $10,000, running for three months, would be subjected to a discount of $150 (one-fourth of 6 per cent of $10,000), so that the business man would receive credit for $9850 and would be obligated to repay $10,000. But it must not be supposed that the bank dips down into its vaults and advances cash to every borrower. The common practice is that the borrower is given the right to draw checks upon the bank up to the agreed amount, – in this case $9,850. In other words, he is given a bank deposit. The bank grants him the right to demand money from it at any time in exchange for the right to demand from him or from some third party a somewhat larger sum of money at a definite future date.

Eighty-five per cent of aggregate United States bank deposits due to borrowing

We may have gone into unnecessary detail in describing these elementary business practices, but it is because it is important that the reader should understand the real nature of the operations of depositing and discounting. These are the fundamental things in banking and are, moreover, the fundamental facts that determine the amount and the nature of the bulk of our present-day media of payment. This third method of securing deposit credit at a bank is vastly more important than the other two. Actual cash is continually flowing out of the bank, just as it flows in, so that except in unusual periods, the first method of making deposits referred to above does not have a large net effect. The second method, as we have seen, involves merely the transfer, rather than the creation, of deposits. Probably as much as 85 per cent of the aggregate volume of bank deposits in the United States (amounting to nearly $13,000,000,000 in national banks alone in 1921) have been created by discounting and by similar methods of making advances to borrowers. If we should examine the books of any one individual bank we should hardly find as much as 85 per cent of its deposits represented by advances to borrowers. But we must take into account the fact that the deposits of any one individual bank are created in no small part by transfers from other banks, and if we should trace these transfer deposits back to their ultimate origin we should find that in the beginning many of them started as borrowings. Thus, although our statement is approximately true of the banks of the country taken as a whole, it is not necessarily true of any one individual bank.

The banks' issuance of promissory notes

The other important form in which the banks utilize or sell their debts is that of bank-notes. A bank-note, like a bank deposit, is a bank's promise to pay on demand. There are important differences, however.

The bank-note passes into general circulation; it passes from hand to hand without indorsement; it is engraved and printed in a way that makes it a convenient and a safe medium of exchange; in short, it really serves in hand-to-hand payments as part of the money of the community. Banks issue notes in very much the same way they make deposit credits, with, however, a few differences of detail. Some borrowers, as for example the manufacturer who has a large payroll to meet, may want cash rather than the right to draw checks. Or it may be that borrowers and other depositors are drawing so many checks upon a bank that its cash reserve is becoming dangerously low; in such a case, the bank may find it desirable to pay out its own notes over the counter in lieu of other money. In this case, what really happens is that a depositor who asks for cash is satisfied by having his deposit claim against the bank exchanged for another form of claim – the bank-note – which will serve his purpose as well as would any other sort of money.

The difference between deposits and bank-notes will concern us in other connections in later chapters. It is well that we should observe at this point, however, that, although they are alike liabilities or debts of a bank, the ways in which deposits and notes respectively are actually used creates problems peculiar to each. Thus, the depositor has an opportunity to acquaint himself with the bank's reputation and with the character of its officials, and to learn what he can about its probable solvency before he intrusts his funds to the bank's care. But if banknotes are to be in common use, if they are to pass from hand to hand, they must come into the possession of persons who have no knowledge of the particular banks which are responsible for them. It is for this reason more than for any other that certain governments, including that of the United States, have thought it wise to impose certain restrictions upon the issue of bank-notes while leaving the creation of bank deposits subject, within reasonable limits, to the discretion of the banks themselves.

Some of these matters we have been treating may be made clearer if the reader will glance for a moment at the statement of the condition of a typical national bank in a city of moderate size.

Most of the stated resources and liabilities are self-explanatory. In the list of assets there will be noted United States government securities. Some of these this bank, as a national bank, is required by law to hold to cover its note issue of

Table 33.1 Statement of the condition of a National Bank: September 12, 1925

Resources	
Loans and discounts	$655,920
United States government securities	165,150
Other bonds, investments and real estate	53,400
Cash and exchange, exclusive of lawful reserves	65,151
Lawful reserve with federal reserve bank	30,816
Other assets	27,565
Total Resources	997,565
Liabilities	
Capital	100,000
Surplus and undivided profits	74,426
Circulation	100,000
Demand deposits	167,062
Time deposits	542,524
Due to banks, and all other liabilities	13,553
Total Liabilities	997,565

$100,000, which appears among the liabilities under the name "circulation." In the cash the bank has on hand there is included its "exchange," consisting of checks payable by other banks and other similar claims against them. Its "lawful reserve" under the present laws does not include all of its actual cash on hand, but consists wholly of deposit credit which this particular bank has in a federal reserve bank. Loans and discounts, it will be noted, constitute the most important item of the bank's assets. This item designates the sum total of the bank's holdings of the notes and bills of exchange of borrowers. Deposits, classified as demand and time, bulk as large in the bank's liabilities as do loans and discounts in its assets.

Capital represents the original investments of the bank's shareholders. The undivided profits are accrued earnings not yet paid out in dividends. For these, of course, the bank is liable to its shareholders. Profits come largely as the result of discounting and other lending and investment operations. Profits which the bank's officials have not decided to pay out in dividends, thus reducing their cash or their other resources, but which instead they have determined to retain in the business as further investments of capital, are called "surplus." Banks are required by our law to accumulate a certain amount of surplus. A large surplus is, generally speaking, a sign of strength. Where surplus is large the depositors' claims are a smaller *proportion* of the bank's liabilities than would otherwise be the case, and thus the depositor is better protected.

But sometimes a large surplus is a sign of weakness rather than strength. Bank officials, knowing that some of their loans are non-collectible, or that some of their other assets are not really worth the amount at which they appear on the statement, may be unwilling to put an increased strain upon the bank by paying dividends. The accumulated profits – really only paper profits because they depend upon an over-valuation of the bank's assets – may be "passed to surplus" without arousing suspicion or without affecting the bank's strength or weakness. A surplus as large as or somewhat larger than a bank's capital is not uncommon and is, in general, an indication of sound banking. But a bank with an abnormally high surplus, four or five or even ten times its capital, is one that should be investigated rather carefully by a depositor before he intrusts his funds to the bank's keeping. In general, however, we can congratulate ourselves that the standards of honesty in the conduct of the banking business are, as they should be, somewhat higher than the standards which prevail in most other types of business.

This is as it should be, we say, because the bank is in a very real sense a public trustee, performing an important and necessary public function.

34 Monetary system of the U.S.

How the various elements of its money circulation first came into being

The evolution of the gold standard

The Book of Popular Science (1924; revised 1929) New York: The Grolier Society. Group IX Ch. 32: 4291–303

To the ordinary layman, the principal obstacle to a correct understanding of our currency system arises from its complexity, from the very multiplicity of its elements. Our circulation is made up of silver dollars, gold dollars, and various forms of paper dollars; all together, ten different forms of currency pass freely from hand to hand in the transaction of business. What has been the course of events by which these various forms of currency have been made component parts of our general media of exchange; and what the mechanism by which they have been rendered of equivalent value as means of payment? To gain an understanding of these first principles of American finance, the reader must open the pages of history, and unfold from the tangle of confusing events the dominant threads of financial tendencies.

The life of our country as a nation nominally began on March 4, 1789. The new government was, however, exceedingly slow to assume many of its most urgent duties. Not until the last day of April was Washington inaugurated President, and five months more passed before legal provision was made for a Treasury Department. But the first Secretary of the Treasury, Alexander Hamilton, set himself at once to the task of devising a comprehensive federal monetary system. On January 1, 1791, he presented to Congress his famous report upon the establishment of a mint and a coinage system for the United States. The recommendations of Hamilton in this report formed the basis of our first Coinage Act.

The need of a uniform currency system was pressing, for under the colonies and the confederation, the mechanism of payments was confused and disorganized. In fact the colonies had known almost as many systems of money as there were different colonies. In some accounts men reckoned according to the English system of pounds, shillings and pence; in others the Spanish decimal system prevailed. The principal media of exchange were coins bearing the stamp of a foreign government, as the French guinea and pistole, the Portuguese moidore and joe, the Spanish doubloon, and the various English pieces. The resulting difficulties in the way of trade and commerce were fully recognized, but attempts made under the confederation to remedy the situation proved inadequate. Not until 1787 could the states be induced even to surrender to the general government the sole right to coin money. Indeed, the disorganized condition of the currency was as compelling a factor as any in inducing the people to accept a form of government equipped with stronger, and more centralized powers.

With some alterations Hamilton's recommendations were accepted by Congress in its Coinage Act of 1792. The features of this act which deserve special emphasis were the following:

1 The decimal system was adopted with the dollar as the unit of value. The choice of the dollar rather than the English pound sterling was but natural inasmuch as the people had become familiar with the Spanish dollar, obtained in trade with the West Indies. Furthermore, the simplicity of the decimal system gave it the advantage in the reckoning of accounts over the more cumbersome English system.

2 The mint, whose establishment was authorized by the terms of the act, was to be open to the unlimited coinage on private account of both gold and silver. The holder of either of these metals possessed the right to bring his bullion to the mints and have it struck into dollars. The coinage ratio of 15 to 1 was adopted in the following words:

That the proportional value of gold to silver in all coins which shall by law be current as money within the United States shall be as fifteen to one, according to quantity in weight, of pure gold or pure silver; that is to say, every fifteen pounds weight of pure silver shall be of equal value in all payments, with one pound weight of pure gold, and so in proportion as to any greater or less quantities of the respective metals.

The silver dollar was to contain 371¼ grains of pure silver, the gold coins 24¾ grains of pure gold per dollar. The reader can easily ascertain by the simple process of division that the relative value of the two metals for coinage purposes was as 15 to 1. Both the gold and silver coins were given full legal tender power for all debts, public and private. The unlimited coinage of both silver and gold into the same currency units is known to finance as "bimetallism."

Why the Coinage Act of 1792 failed to bring much gold to the mint

Congress adopted the bimetallic ratio of 15 to 1 because Hamilton believed that such was the commercial ratio between the two metals, that by establishing the same mint ratio sufficient quantities of both metals would be brought to the mints to give us an adequate circulation of new and standard coins. Before the mint had begun to manufacture the new coins, however, a change took place in the relative values of the two metals in the commercial market. As a commodity needed for the arts, gold became worth more than fifteen times as much as silver per ounce. In fact, the actual bullion ratio stood closer to 15½ to 1 than 15 to 1. Under such circumstances little gold was brought to the mints, and the Coinage Act did not succeed in securing any considerable circulation of gold.

This phenomenon is merely an exemplification of the operation of Gresham's principle, that cheap money drives out the good. More accurately stated for our purposes, the law is that the metal relatively the more valuable as bullion will not be brought to the mints for coinage. The comparatively expensive gold bullion would not be brought to the mints; it was more profitable to sell the gold as bullion and mint the silver. As a means of payment a silver coin would be as valuable as a gold coin of similar denomination. The metal *overvalued* by the mint ratio will thus, in fact, be the actual monetary standard; the *undervalued* metal will not be coined.

As events finally turned out, the Coinage Act also failed to secure any considerable circulation of silver. It is true that a large amount of silver bullion was brought to the mints, but the newly coined silver dollars did not remain long, here, in circulation. At this time merchants of this country were conducting a flourishing trade with the West Indies, where both the Spanish and the American dollar were accepted as of equivalent value. Despite the fact that the Spanish dollar contained slightly more silver, the natives were willing and even desirous of obtaining the bright, new American dollars, only recently come from the mint. American merchants and money dealers accordingly found it profitable to exchange the American dollar for the heavier Spanish coins and send the latter back to the mint of this country for coinage into a greater number of American dollars. So flagrant did this practice become that in 1806 President Jefferson directed the mint to suspend the coinage of silver pieces.

The Act of 1792 had not succeeded in securing a circulation either of gold or silver. Gold coins had either been hoarded or exported, and what metallic currency we had was made up of miscellaneous foreign coins, many of them clipped and debased. A great part of our bank notes were, moreover, irredeemable in specie. For in the latter part of the War of 1812, most state banks, except in New England, had discontinued specie payments. After the war the continued scarcity of "hard cash" rendered difficult the task of redemption.

In order to bring gold back into circulation, Congress passed in 1834 an act reducing the weight of the ten-dollar gold piece from 24.75 to 23.22 grains of gold, thus establishing a mint ratio of 16 to 1. The commercial ratio at this time remained closer, however, to 15¾ to 1. The new mint ratio overvalued gold in precisely the same manner as the earlier had silver. Silver coinage was now unprofitable for silver was worth more as bullion than as coin. In fact it was not until the passage of the Bland-Allison Act of 1878, more than fifty years later, that there was any considerable coinage of silver dollars. The new ratio was, however, favorable to gold, and, particularly after the Californian and Australian discoveries in the middle of the century, large quantities of gold coins came into circulation.

Under the new ratio, the country was even despoiled of its small change. The dimes, quarters and half dollars were all silver coins and silver was now worth more as bullion. As stated by Thomas Corwin, Secretary of the Treasury: "This state of things has banished almost entirely from circulation all silver coins of full weight, and what little remains in the hands of the community consists principally of the worn pieces of Spanish coinage of the fractional parts of a dollar, all of which are of light weight, and many of them ten or twenty per cent below their normal value."

To remedy this situation Congress passed in 1853 a subsidiary currency act, whereby the principle of the free coinage of the fractional currency was abandoned. Hereafter, the small coins were to be struck only at the discretion of the government, from bullion purchased by it at the market price, and in amounts dictated by the convenience of the business community. To render unprofitable the melting down of these coins into bullion, they were reduced in weight by about seven percent. They were not to be a legal tender for amounts exceeding five dollars. Later the law was changed to make them a legal tender for amounts not exceeding ten dollars.

The act of 1853 did not close the mints to the coinage of silver dollars, but for all practical purposes this effect had already been accomplished. For, by the ratio of 1834, the silver in the dollar was worth as bullion from $1.01 to $1.05, and silver could not profitably be coined. The country was only nominally on a double or bimetallic standard. The motive of Congress in passing the acts of 1834 and 1853 is not absolutely clear, but there is a great deal of evidence that it deliberately intended to dethrone silver as standard, and to establish the country on a gold basis. The Chairman of the Ways and Means Committee of 1853, Mr. Dunham had said:

> We propose, so far as these coins are concerned, to make silver subservient to the gold coin of the country. We intend to do what the best writers on political economy have approved, what experience, where the experiment has been tried, has demonstrated to be the best, and what the Committee believe to be necessary and proper, to make but one standard of currency and to make all others subservient to it. We mean to make gold the standard coin, and to make these silver coins applicable and convenient, not for large but for small transactions.

By the time of the Civil War the country had thus, with its circulation of gold, overcome the early difficulty – the famine of a metallic currency – and, moreover, had found a means of securing an adequate supply of subsidiary coins. But in the necessities of the Civil War further difficulties arose, difficulties unfamiliar only because earlier experience was forgotten, and for years the country was to be haunted by the specter of inconvertible paper currency. Enormous issues of greenbacks drove out of circulation the larger part of the gold currency, and left the people with no medium except bank notes and government promises to pay, but promises for which no date of redemption was stated.

Few epochs of history are more instructive from a financial standpoint than this paper standard period. Few periods shed more light upon proper and improper methods of war finance, upon measures governments should seek to avoid.

Until the period of the Civil War our government had made no issues of legal tender notes. Of all countries none were more amply forewarned of their inherent danger. In the pre-revolutionary period some of the colonies had issued legal tender bills of credit, but their experience was so unfortunate that the historian Ramsay was impelled to write: "It is hoped that in consequence of the present increasing means of diffusing and perpetuating knowledge, the like will not occur again."

The "like" did occur again, however, this time during the Revolution. Then, however, the justification for such issues was sufficient if ever it was. Because of its lack of power to levy taxes the Continental Congress was really driven to emit bills of credit. But however real the justification, the results were disastrous. The Continental currency became practically worthless, and the strongest appeals to patriotism were impotent to induce the people to accept them. After the formation of the national government a few of them were redeemed on the basis of one cent on the dollar.

In view of this unfortunate experience it is not surprising that the framers of the Constitution inserted the provision forbidding the individual states to issue bills of credit or to make anything but gold and silver legal tender in payment of debts. There is, furthermore, good evidence that the framers never intended the federal government to exercise this power. For the Constitution nowhere expressly delegates to Congress the right to issue bills of credit, whereas, under the Articles of Confederation, this power was expressly conferred on the general government. Even Alexander Hamilton, who believed in an elastic interpretation of the Constitution, believed that the spirit of this instrument was adverse to such issues. And before 1862 only once had it been proposed to Congress to issue legal tenders. This single occasion was in 1814, in the dark days of the war with England, and then the House refused even to consider the resolution.

The events which preceded the issues of war currency in 1862

It will, therefore, be interesting to consider the events which preceded the issues of the "war currency." The strife between the sections began in 1861. In August of that year, the Secretary of the Treasury, Salmon P. Chase, conferred with a committee of bankers and negotiated with them three loans of fifty million dollars each. At about the same time Congress passed a law virtually authorizing the secretary to handle the proceeds in whatsoever manner he deemed most expedient. The loans might either have been left on deposit with the banks and checks drawn against them for the Treasury's disbursements, or the funds might be withdrawn and placed with the various subtreasuries. Against the remonstrance of the bankers, Secretary Chase chose the latter course, and, in the judgment of many historians, virtually forced the banks to suspend specie payments.

It is not difficult to ascribe this suspension of payments in specie to Chase's action. Every dollar in the reserves of banks serves as the basis for the extension of credit to the business public to an amount several times this amount. By withdrawing specie an enormous contraction of credit was inevitable. The general public could not but become exceedingly alarmed; in some places runs on banks took place, quite generally creditors refused to renew loans. With the government withdrawing millions of specie the banks were unable to alleviate this general feeling of insecurity.

Suspension of specie payments and the depreciation of the greenback

The suspension of specie payments inevitably closed, at least in large measure, one avenue of borrowing – loans from the banks. Further means were necessary to obtain funds to meet the government's disbursements, and in this extremity a bill was introduced in Congress providing for the issue of legal tender notes. Again the bankers remonstrated. This time they proposed that the government should sell to the general public its long-time bonds at whatever price they would command in the open market. Fears that any large sale of bonds would lower their value and, to outward appearances, undermine the public credit served, however, to frighten the purse holders of the nation from this course. Accordingly on the 25th of February, 1862, the bill providing for the issue of $150,000,000 in legal tender notes became law. On the 7th of June provision was made for the issue of another batch of $150,000,000. In the short space of less than six months Congress had opened the floodgates for the issue of $300,000,000 of this currency.

Before the war came to an end further issues were made, so that by the time the army was paid off and disbanded, there were 400 millions of these legal tenders in circulation. Almost from the date of the first issue they depreciated in gold value; in 1864 they were worth in gold less than fifty cents on the dollar. By law the greenbacks were made a tender for domestic transactions. They could not be made acceptable for foreign payments, however. Dealings with merchants abroad must be balanced in gold; in making foreign payments our bankers and exchange houses were forced to go into the market and purchase gold. In order to pay the interest on its loans the government was also forced to bid for gold. The depreciation of the greenback in terms of gold was thus measured by the increase in the number of greenback dollars that had to be paid for a given number of gold dollars. Prices of goods imported from and exported to gold-using countries promptly rose and, through the complex mechanism of the market, other prices, and ultimately wages and other forms of money payments made in greenbacks, had to rise also, following the increase in the price of gold.

During this period the greenbacks were not redeemable in gold, and trade was virtually on a paper basis. Inasmuch as the greenbacks did not command a gold value of a hundred cents on the dollar, gold would not be tendered in payment of domestic debts; for such purposes greenbacks would be used. All this furnishes yet another illustration of Gresham's Law.

The bitter struggle to restore the gold parity of the legal tenders

The struggle to restore the gold parity of the legal tenders was bitter and prolonged. When the war closed, Hugh McCulloch, Secretary of the Treasury, stated his belief that the justification of such issues lay only in the necessities of war; that the war being over they should be retired as rapidly as possible. In response to this recommendation Congress passed an act authorizing their retirement at the rate of four millions per month. As greenbacks were received by Treasury in payment of taxes they were canceled instead of being reissued. Under this policy forty-four millions of notes were retired from circulation.

It is almost needless to recount that such course met the most bitter opposition. Accustomed to the stimulus of high prices, business could not look upon the retirement of any considerable part of the currency without general alarm. Debtors, too, including many farmers whose lands were mortgaged, claimed that it was unjust to ask them to pay off their debts in money of greater value than the money they had borrowed. Congress was informed that the country had absorbed the paper issues, that it was a function of government to supply the country with the needed amount of currency. As in other periods of inflation, the most strenuous of demands for further issues were made at a time when the currency was already inflated.

In response to these demands Congress provided in 1868 that the retirement of the greenbacks should cease. But this was not all. In 1874 a bill passed both the Senate and the House authorizing the reissue of all the greenbacks which had been retired under McCulloch's policy of contraction. Herein was involved the whole question of further issues of this currency in time of peace. That the country was not plunged into the abyss of a permanent fiat currency was due perhaps to President Grant, who vetoed the bill. This veto practically killed greenback inflation and is worthy of all the praise which has been bestowed upon it.

The reversal of policy demanded by the public results in Resumption Act

The public condemnation of the Inflation Measure was strikingly indicated in the elections of 1874, in which the Republicans lost heavily. A reversal of policy was clearly demanded by the people. The net result was the passage of the Resumption Act in 1875. By this law the Secretary of the Treasury was authorized to sell bonds without limit in order to obtain gold sufficient in amount to redeem the notes. By the first of January, 1879, the Secretary had accumulated $133,000,000 of gold to be used for that purpose. By the latter part of December, 1878, the premium on gold had disappeared, and speculation in currency was discontinued.

At last, seventeen years after the first issues, the gold parity of the greenbacks had been restored.

Disastrous results to all concerned of the flood of greenback issues

Space permits us here to consider in only the briefest fashion the disastrous effects of these issues. For one matter, it has been estimated by a leading authority that they increased the cost of the war by $600,000,000. In floating its loans the government received greenbacks, whose purchasing power was in gold fifty, sixty or seventy cents on the dollar. Eventually both the interest payments and the principal of these loans were paid in gold. The government was borrowing a cheap dollar and repaying with a dear one. In the same manner disturbances were wrought in private finance.

Among the particularly heavy sufferers were those whose incomes were derived from fixed investments, investments made prior to the war. Labor also suffered, for the time being, in that wages did not advance proportionately with the general rise in prices, even though, as it is only fair to add, wages did not *fall* as rapidly or as far as did prices after the effects of inflation had passed. But regardless of these costs, the issue of the notes was a fortunate episode, if it taught the country the danger of an irredeemable currency.

The depreciation in silver and the loss in bullion value of the silver dollar (Table 34.1)

The bimetallic controversy must now reengage our attention. We have previously noted that very little silver had been coined since 1806, when the minting of the silver dollar was suspended by action of President Jefferson. Nominally the mints were reopened to the coinage of silver in 1834, but only at a ratio which made silver coinage unprofitable. As a matter of coinage statistics, in the period 1861 to 1867 only a little more than 300,000 silver dollars were minted, against a gold coinage in the same period of 230,000,000 dollars. Silver coinage increased somewhat after 1867, but, of the 3,200,000 dollars struck between 1868 and 1872 practically all were exported.

The results of the Franco-Prussian War, and the "Crime of 1873"

During this period events in other countries proved unfavorable to silver. The Franco-Prussian War of 1870–1871 had resulted in victory for the Hohenzollern banner, and immediately German commercial ambitions rose to the high level of their military aspirations. As Great Britain, the chief commercial nation, possessed the single gold standard, what could be more natural and necessary than the reorganization of the finance of the new empire on the same basis? The coinage of the country, which differed in the separate states, was unified, and it was

Table 34.1 The depreciation of silver 1840–1924

Year	Market Ratio	Bullion Value of the silver dollar	Year	Market Ratio	Bullion Value of the silver dollar
1840	15.62	$1.023	1905	33.87	.472
1845	15.92	1.004	1906	30.54	.524
1850	15.70	1.018	1907	31.24	.512
1855	15.38	1.039	1908	38.64	.414
1860	15.29	1.045	1909	39.74	.402
1865	15.44	1.035	1910	38.22	.418
1870	15.57	1.027	1911	38.33	.417
1875	16.64	.961	1912	33.62	.475
1880	18.05	.886	1913	34.19	.468
1885	19.41	.824	1914	37.37	.428
1890	19.75	.809	1915	39.84	.401
1895	31.60	.506	1916	30.11	.531
1897	34.20	.467	1917	23.09	.692
1898	35.03	.456	1918	21.00	.761
1899	34.36	.465	1919	18.44	.867
1900	33.33	.480	1920	20.27	.788
1901	34.68	.461	1921	32.75	.488
1902	39.15	.408	1922	30.43	.525
1903	38.10	.420	1923	31.69	.505
1904	35.70	.448	1924	30.62	.519

resolved to sell the greater part of the old silver pieces. In order not to be swamped by the influx of the cheapened white metal the mints of France were closed to the coinage of silver, and the other countries of the Latin Union followed her example. An international monetary conference held in Paris in 1867 had previously recommended the adoption of the single gold standard.

Contemporaneously with these events a committee of Congress was undertaking the task of revising our coinage laws. This work resulted in an act whereby the silver dollar was dropped from the list of authorized coins. There is every evidence that the committee deliberately intended to render gold, legally, as in fact, the sole standard. In the words of Representative Kelley, who reported the bill from the committee – it was "impossible to retain the double standard." And, furthermore, "every coin that is not gold is subsidiary." This act, which became known as the "Crime of 1873," merely gave legal recognition to the fact that the silver dollar was not a part of our circulating medium.

The pressure brought to bear on Congress by the advocates of "cheap money"

That this law passed Congress without a great deal of public attention was due to the fact that coining silver had been unprofitable. But after 1873 a great change occurred in the silver market. Many rich lodes of silver were developed in Colorado and other Western states, so that if the mints had been open to silver coinage much silver bullion would have been taken thither.

But if the Act of 1873 was to become law without attracting unusual notice, it was later to receive more than passing attention from the public. The silver miners and the advocates of "cheap money" uttered charges of fraud; they declared the act the outcome of a surreptitious conspiracy to dethrone silver, that by making gold the sole standard of value the creditor classes had been successful in their endeavors to defraud the debtors by compelling payments in a constantly appreciating dollar. Apace with the increasing silver production of the Western states arose the demands for the reopening of the mints to the free and unlimited coinage of the white metal.

The Bland-Allison Act and its effects upon national finance

The silver advocates were not of sufficient influence in Congress to secure this, but they were able to secure a compromise measure. Under the terms of the Bland-Allison Act of 1878 great quantities of silver were added to the country's circulation. By this act the Treasury was directed to purchase monthly not less than two nor more than four million dollars' worth of silver bullion and coin it into silver dollars. Recognition was made of the fact that it might be difficult to "popularize" the bulky coin by the insertion of the provision that the metallic dollars might be deposited with the Treasury and that silver certificates, virtually like warehouse receipts for silver, redeemable on demand into dollars be issued in their place.

It would be interesting to examine in detail the history of the Bland-Allison Act from the standpoint of its effects upon the national finance. In the light of subsequent events we cannot, however, fail to realize how seriously it endangered the nation's gold reserve, how difficult it rendered the task of maintaining the gold parity of our currency. Under the terms of this act, more than three hundred and seventy-eight millions of dollars were coined, – dollars worth intrinsically less than their face value in gold. Their gold parity could only be maintained by redeeming them in gold. The bulk of our trading, it should be remembered, was conducted with gold-standard countries, countries to which payments in silver would be accepted only on the basis of the commercial value of silver.

The Sherman Act and the treasury note of 1890 issued under its authority

Our present task, however, is merely to explain the origin of our various forms of currency. We have now seen how there came into being gold coin, subsidiary silver, the standard silver dollar and the silver certificate. In 1890 the country was to have yet another form of currency, the Treasury note of 1890. This currency was issued under the authority of the Sherman Act, which superseded the Bland-Allison Act. It, like its predecessor, was a concession to the silver party.

The Sherman Act authorized the Secretary of the Treasury to purchase monthly 4,500,000 ounces of silver bullion and to issue in payment treasury notes of full legal tender power. From the bullion so purchased dollars were to be coined for one year, and thereafter in such quantities as might be required to redeem the notes. The money of redemption was to be either gold or silver coin, depending upon the discretion of the Secretary. At the current prices of silver the act provided for an increase in the amount of the government's silver purchases.

Silver-purchasing clause of the Sherman Act repealed by Cleveland's urgence

Under the terms of this act, more than $155,000,000 in notes were put into circulation. To this extent they increased the strain on the gold reserve, and made more difficult the task of maintaining the gold parity of our currency. The gold reserve had sunk very low, and efforts to restore it proved for a time unavailing.

To maintain the government credit in a period when the public treasury, like business in general, was hard pressed, President Cleveland insisted that the notes presented for redemption should be paid in gold, when, as was always the case, the noteholder preferred that form of payment. To have exercised the government's power of paying them in silver might have discredited our currency and have thrown it over to a silver basis. As the Sherman Act operated the government was expending gold, which it could ill spare, for enormous stores of silver which it could not force the community to use as money. Finally, in 1893, at the urgent insistence of President Cleveland, whose attitude during the whole episode was marked by a fine sort of stubborn courage, the purchasing clause of the Sherman Act was repealed.

Practically none of the notes now remain in circulation. By the Gold Standard Act of 1900 provision was made for their gradual retirement. From the bullion purchased with these notes standard silver dollars have been coined. Upon the basis of these dollars, certificates were issued, and as rapidly as treasury notes were turned in for redemption silver certificates were substituted for them. By this process treasury notes have virtually disappeared from circulation.

Our bank-note circulation, its advantages and its disadvantages

It remains to consider our bank-note circulation. In a preceding chapter the bank-note was described as merely one form of bank credit, one means by which banks may issue their promises to pay. So far as the liability of the bank is concerned there is no essential difference between the note and the deposit. In the one case the obligation of the bank is evidenced by a bookkeeping entry, in the other by a promise to pay written on a piece of paper which may pass from hand to hand and become a part of our general media of exchange. Whatever difference exists between the deposit and the note results from the greater "currency" function of the note. That is, the note tends to remain longer in circulation, and the bank's ability to redeem is not so continuously tested. A check drawn against a deposit, however, depends not merely upon the solvency of the bank but also on that of the one who tenders it. The check is speedily presented for redemption. The note, however, depends only upon the solvency of the bank and may remain outstanding for a considerable period of time.

It is because of its superior currency function that both the advantages and the disadvantages of the note proceed. The note may be tendered to persons unacquainted with the bearer's financial standing, and is, moreover, acceptable to those who have no easy access to banks. Farm laborers, in particular, demand notes or some form of currency to a larger extent than employees in a city factory, who are more likely to be paid in checks. But, inasmuch as the note remains longer outstanding, inflation of the nation's currency is more likely to result from an excessive issue of notes than by an excessive issue of deposit credit. We have already remarked that the ultimate result of any issue of paper is to drive out gold. For the issue of paper increases the ability of the holders to purchase foreign goods, and foreign payments must in the end always be liquidated in gold. An excessive issue of paper, be it the promises to pay either of the government or of the banks, may render extremely difficult the task of maintaining the gold standard.

Because of its greater inflationary possibilities, governments have been much more prone to restrict the right of banks to extend credit in the form of notes than in the form of deposit credits. In our country public recognition of the dangers of excess issues of notes is clearly evidenced. Our early experience with the loosely regulated issues of state banks had shown only too clearly their inherent dangers.

The dangers of loosely regulated issues of notes by state banks

The period before the establishment of the national banking system was in reality the dark age of American banking. The country was then flooded with a great mass of notes issued by state banks, some of them easily redeemable in "hard cash," some redeemable only with difficulty, others redeemable not at all. Many states placed virtually no legal restriction upon such issues, and banks came to consider as one of their inherent rights the privilege of putting out such currency without making ample provisions for redemption. He who attempted to force the banks to specie payments was often adjudged as virtually a public enemy. For was he not making it difficult for the banks to supply the public with the needed amount of currency?

In one case on record, a Boston broker was indicted by a grand jury in Vermont for demanding that a bank of that state cash its notes. Students of early American history will recall the unpopularity of both the first and the second United States banks because of their policy of sorting out the notes of the state banks which reached their counters and sending them home for payment in cash. The more difficult the access to a bank, the greater was the possibility of large profits. For the more likely were they to escape these demands for specie payments.

Only state bank-notes not readily redeemable left in circulation

In this period some of the states recognized clearly the nature of the bank-note and sought by law to regulate such issues. But this merely enlarged the field within which Gresham's law might operate. Notes of the strictly regulated banks were speedily presented for redemption. Notes of banks which did not recognize their specie obligations remained in circulation. The channels of trade were filled to overflowing with these depreciated issues. Under such conditions trade was severely handicapped. Notes received by merchants possessed different values, according to the bank of issue. Books were furnished merchants to apprise them of the values of the various issues, but no such book could be kept up to date.

The National Bank Act reforms due to fiscal difficulties of government

In 1863 the situation was changed abruptly, and curiously enough the cause of the reform was the fiscal difficulties of the government. The enormous war expenditures increased the necessity of large borrowings, and the banking system was revised in order to render such borrowing easier. In the National Bank Act provision was made for the incorporation of banks under the federal law. The new banks could only obtain the issue privilege by purchasing government bonds and depositing them as security with the Treasurer of the United States. In this manner a market was created for the government's securities. To drive out of circulation the notes of state banks a tax was imposed in 1865 of ten per cent. This tax virtually compelled banks to take out federal charters or give up the note issue privilege. Trade was no longer to be handicapped by the existence of a disorganized mass of partly irredeemable bank-note issues.

Under the national banking system the safety of the note issues has not often been questioned. They are secured by government bonds, and in the case of failure the noteholders have a prior lien on the assets of the bank. Criticisms of the national banking system have not stressed any possible lack of safety. Rather have they dwelt on the inelasticity of the note issues, on their inability to expand and contract sufficiently in volume to meet the needs of trade's seasonal demands. For regularly during the fall and spring planting seasons interest rates rose, security values fell, and banks in the interior withdrew their deposits from the money centers.

Our various forms of currency and how their gold parity is maintained

It has not been difficult to attribute the inelasticity of the notes to the bond requirement. The amount of notes which could be issued depended upon the total volume of bonds in existence. As the note circulation had increased in amount practically all of the available bonds had been absorbed. The note circulation represented a more or less definitely fixed volume of currency and was incapable of being adjusted to the varying demands of trade.

By the passage of the Federal Reserve Act in 1912, attempt was made to remedy this situation. Machinery was established for the eventual retirement of a large part of the old bond-secured notes. In a later chapter we shall see how this reform led to the creation of two new species of notes, Federal Reserve notes and Federal Reserve *Bank* notes.

We are now in a position to state in summary fashion our various forms of currency and to explain how the gold parity of each is maintained. Table 34.2 shows the circulation of each in July, 1924.

In one way or another all other forms of currency are interchangeable with gold. Coins smaller than a dollar are exchangeable at the Treasury for "lawful money," which includes government notes, silver dollars and gold coins. Government notes are redeemable in gold at the government treasury. There is no definite legal requirement that silver dollars be redeemed in gold, but the Currency Act of 1900 makes it the duty of the Secretary of the Treasury to maintain other forms of money at a parity with gold. This means in practice that he must exchange gold coins for silver dollars even if he should have to borrow funds with which to secure the necessary gold. The Act of 1900 gave definite and formal recognition to the single gold standard which, as we have seen, was implied by the Act of 1871 and which, in fact though not in law, had been in force ever since the Act of 1834 made it unprofitable to have silver coined at the mint.

Incorrect use of term "standard dollar"; what standard money really is

The silver dollars coined under the laws of 1878 and 1879, like those subsequently coined by the silver accumulated by the government, are sometimes incorrectly

Table 34.2 Stock of money in the United States, July, 1924

Gold Coin and Bullion	$4,490,807,000
Silver Dollars	503,755,000
Subsidiary Silver	277,614,000
United States Notes	346,681,000
Federal Reserve Notes	2,339,048,000
Federal Reserve Bank Notes	10,596,000
National Bank Notes	778,012,000
Total	$8,746,513,000
Percentage of Gold to Total Money	51.34
Money in Circulation	4,754,773,000
Circulation Per Capita	42.19

spoken of as "standard dollars." But silver is not freely coined on private account, and the silver dollar does not vary in its purchasing power according to changes in the value of silver. It is, therefore, a mistake to speak of a "standard" silver dollar. Standard money is the money in which all other parts of the circulating medium are ultimately redeemable. It may thus be defined as the money of ultimate redemption. It may also be said to be the one commodity whose price in terms of lawful money is fixed. Gold may be sold to the mint for dollars at a fixed price. Gold dollars may, in turn, be converted into gold bullion without loss in value. Such are the arrangements which make it proper for us to say that gold is the monetary standard.

So long as our present coinage laws remain in force, gold coins must always contain the same amount of gold per dollar. The dollar is defined as a coin containing 25.8 grains of standard gold. Since standard gold $\%0$ gold and $\frac{1}{10}$ alloy, there are 23.22 grains of pure gold in a dollar. At one time gold dollars were coined, but the coin was so small, so inconvenient, and so easily lost that its coinage was later abandoned. However, the present gold coins of the United States, which include the eagle, or ten-dollar gold piece, the double eagle, the half eagle, and the quarter eagle, contain precisely the stated amount of gold per dollar. The eagle, for example, contains 232.2 grains of fine gold. An ounce of gold, therefore, is worth $20.67 at the mint.

The currency system of the United States, it thus appears, is definitely based upon gold as the monetary standard. In fact, it should be a matter of pride that the United States, alone of all the world powers which participated in the Great War, maintained the gold standard throughout that period of financial storm and stress, even though it would not be wholly accurate to say that an absolutely free gold market existed in the United States during all of the war period. But the gold standard was not definitely accepted by the country until after a bitter controversy which followed shortly upon the repeal of the purchasing clause of the Sherman Act in 1893. Although forced upon Congress by the immediate necessities of the federal treasury, this action was regarded by the advocates of bimetallism as the successful culmination of the efforts of those mythical conspirators who were supposed to have dethroned silver and set up gold – a scarcer metal – as the world's monetary standard.

If the reader will turn to the table[1] on a previous page showing the course of the depreciation of silver between 1871 and 1900, he will note that just as, by an extraordinary coincidence, within three years after the act of 1871, silver, for the first time in the history of the world, became worth less than one-sixteenth as much as gold, so, immediately after the repeal of the purchasing clause of the Sherman Act in 1893, the value of silver became less than one-thirtieth that of an equal amount of gold. Undoubtedly the closing of the artificial market that the United States government had created for silver had something to do with the matter. But a continuing decline in the annual production of gold and other important factors, including the closing of the mints of India to the unlimited coinage of silver, must also be taken into account.

Money continued to appreciate, that is, prices continued to decline; business had not yet recovered from the slump following the great crisis of 1893; crops were poor; the farmers and the townspeople of the west had suffered heavily through precipitate declines in land values. The cheap money movement, which had been gathering strength ever since 1873, now reached its culmination. In the bitterly contested presidential election of 1896, William Jennings Bryan, the Democratic candidate, was supported by the advocates of bimetallism, whatever their previous party affiliations. His defeat by the Republican candidate, William McKinley, who had been supported by the advocates of the gold standard, marked the end of the last phase of the bimetallic movement. This was not, however, because the bimetallists were convinced that they were wrong or that their cause was hopeless. Bimetallism ceased to be a problem of political importance just so soon as the enormous output of the new gold mines of South Africa, by making gold cheaper, that is, by making prices in terms of the gold standard higher, ended the period of falling prices which lasted from the years 1873 to 1896.

From 1897 down to the eve of the Great War, the general trend of prices in all gold-using countries was upward. Cheap money movements are always children of periods of falling prices. Rising prices, by stimulating business activities, by favoring the borrower – the active user of capital – as against the creditor, do not breed general political and social disaffection, even though they may occasion as much economic injustice and in the long run may do as much harm as occurs in periods of falling prices. An ideal monetary system would be that which would give stability in prices. The gold standard, by this test, is far from ideal. Its strongest claim is not that it gives stability in prices, but that it is, one might say, automatic in its operations. If we must have general fluctuations in prices, alternating movements up and down, it is better that these should be governed by the changes in the output of a relatively stable commodity, like gold, than that they should be the outcome of political manipulation or of arbitrary adjustment of any sort whatever. It may be said for the gold standard, not that it is perfect, but that it is measurably "fool-proof."

Note

1 Table 34.1.

35 Mobilizing banking credits

The drastic reform of the banking system of the United States

Possibilities of the federal reserve

The Book of Popular Science (1924; revised 1929) New York: The Grolier Society. Group IX Ch. 33: 4437–46

In considering the factors responsible for the creation of the national wealth, statesmen and the public have often been far too prone to overlook the indispensable services of those institutions which assemble and distribute the credit resources of the country. Too often has the nation been depicted as merely a vast workshop in which the technique of physical production alone demands the thoughtful and continuous attention of the country's best brains. But without an adequate mechanism of exchange, production cannot function to its fullest capacity. General Francis A. Walker wrote indeed without exaggeration that it was much more important to the people of London to possess stable exchange relations with other countries than to keep in repair its largest bridge across the Thames; and a contemporary American economist has remarked that if the world were stripped of its telegraph wires it would not suffer more than if business should be obliged to conduct its operations without the use of credit.

In a previous chapter[a] we have noted the condition of credit in the days of "wild cat" state banks, days in which the country was flooded with currency in the form of the promises-to-pay of banks, promises too often disregarded. When the national banking system was established, a remedy was found in the impositions of so heavy a federal tax on the issues of state banks that they rapidly disappeared from circulation. But despite the admitted service of the national banking system, one cannot but wonder at the calm subordination of banking requirements to temporary political considerations at the time of its establishment.

Except for the financial difficulties of the government in consequence of the Civil War, the national banking system would probably not have been born. In its extremity, the nation was prepared to accept a banking system organized primarily to strengthen the market for government securities. A bill fathered by Salmon P. Chase, Secretary of the Treasury, provided for the creation of a set of banks chartered under federal law; and, as security for their note issues, required to purchase bonds of the United States and deposit them with the Treasury at

Washington. The successful banking system of the State of New York was taken, in a number of important respects, as a model. In this manner the government hoped to increase the market for its bonds.

But many of our institutions, illogically established, have in practice worked admirably. How was it with the national banking system? Before passing final judgment, it will be helpful to review the most prominent features of the act. In what respects did it build upon, and in what respects depart from the experience of earlier systems?

First, and of foremost importance, the act accepted the "currency" rather than the "banking" principle. These opposing viewpoints took root in earlier English banking experience. The currency principle stresses the analogy of bank-notes to government paper money, while the banking principle emphasizes the similarity of the bank-note and the deposit. From the standpoint of the banks' liability the banking principle secures its justification, for the note and the deposit are but different forms in which the banks extend their promises to pay.

But, on the other hand, advocates of "currency" principle argue that notes are apt to remain longer in circulation, and that harmful inflation of the currency was more likely to result from excessive issues of notes than from an expansion of deposits. In other words, the note possesses a greater currency function than the deposit, and its issue, it is accordingly argued, is attended with greater danger. The world had suffered in recent memory greatly from the irredeemability of government paper money. If, then, bank currency possessed the same inflationary possibilities, should it not be as strongly regulated by law? Should not the note issues of banks be more stringently restricted and guarded than their deposits?

This question was answered affirmatively in the National Bank Act. The amount of a bank's note issue was made to depend upon the amount of government bonds deposited with the Treasury. Furthermore, note issues were limited to the amount of the bank's capital stock. Finally, in case of insolvency, the government would assume responsibility for the redemption of the notes, but to safeguard itself, was given a prior lien on the assets of the failed bank. That is, in case of liquidation, the bank's resources would first be made available for the protection of the noteholders.

A second significant feature of the new system lay in the fact that nowhere was there to exist a central board of directors able to exercise a control over credit conditions throughout the country. In this respect, the United States departed from the experience of European countries where cash reserves were centralized in great central institutions. When further funds were required, a local bank would secure them by turning over some of its holdings of debtors' paper – their bills and notes – to the central institution. By raising or lowering its interest or discount rate, the directorate of the central bank can render it difficult or easy for the smaller banks to extend credit to their clientele. General credit conditions may thus to a large extent be determined by the single central institution. In the First (1791–1811) and the Second (1816–1836) United States Banks our country was fairly on the road to develop such dominating institutions, but these banks so aroused the fears and the hostility of the state banks and of the general public, that they were shipwrecked in the sea of politics. Public opinion in 1863 was not yet ready to sanction the reestablishment of any such all-powerful institution; nor was it willing to accept the dictation of any single central directorate. A federal officer, the Comptroller of the Currency, was at the head of the national banking system, but his duties were primarily administrative.

But even though it was not felt that the expansion of deposit credits should be restricted so rigidly as note issues, the national government was unwilling to leave the control of deposits entirely to the judgment and the discretion of the various individual directorates. Accordingly reliance was placed upon the unwieldy device of establishing by law certain minimum reserve requirements. That is, the upper limit of deposit credits was made to depend upon the amount of each bank's reserve of cash.

But ought not some banks to hold larger proportionate reserves than others? Country banks customarily kept funds on deposit in near-by city banks; these in turn made deposits in the larger financial centers. Should not the banks which held in greatest measure the deposits of other banks be obliged to hold the largest reserves? Clearly such institutions would be subjected to the greatest strain in any period of credit collapse.

Accordingly by law the national banks were divided into three general classes. Banks in New York, Chicago and Saint Louis, the central reserve cities, were required to hold a 25 per cent cash reserve. That is, they had to have on hand an amount of legal tender money equal to one-fourth of their liabilities to their own depositors. Banks in other large cities of the country, designated as reserve cities, were also required to hold a 25 per cent reserve, but half of this might be in the form of deposits with banks in central reserve cities. All other banks, the "country banks," were required to keep only a 15 per cent reserve, and deposits in banks in reserve cities or central reserve cities might count for three-fifths of this amount.

How our national banking system worked

With these few general provisions in mind, we are now in a position to examine the operation of the system and attempt to find explanation of those evils to which the credit mechanism of the country has clearly been subjected. The services of the national banking system in driving out the disorganized note issues of state banks, and in furnishing to state governments a model for regulating institutions of their own creation could not be gainsaid. But in no field of human activity had greater changes taken place than in that of commerce and business, and it could not but be felt that the development of credit and banking had lagged behind. Particularly inadequate did our banking system appear when attention was called to the frequency and severity of industrial crises in the United States. Such credit collapses did not occur with equal frequency or severity in European countries with great central banks.

The panic of 1907 leads to banking revision

Of all the crises of recent years, none called forth more popular discussion than that of 1907. To a greater degree than in previous periods of depression did it appear that the central difficulty was a faulty banking system, particularly as there had been no general crop failure, as in 1893, and since to all outward appearances the industries of the country had been sound and flourishing. To restore the tottering foundations of credit, gold was imported in enormous quantities from Europe, from countries where the per capita stock was less than in the United States. More strikingly than ever did it appear that our banking system was inadequately devised to utilize efficiently our vast quantities of gold in the support of the nation's credit. Never was there a crisis which was rooted more indisputably in monetary disorders, rather than in fundamental industrial weaknesses.

But save for one spectacular feature it may be doubted whether even this collapse would have been sufficient to overcome the inertia of the people and lead to a general demand for banking revision. In 1907, bankers in the interior found themselves unable to withdraw their deposits from New York City, and as a consequence, there was a country-wide tie-up. In August of that year, more than a third of the cash reserves of 6544 national banks were held in the vaults of the New York banks. If any such concentration of credit must exist, bankers and the public asked, would it not be preferable that it be controlled by banking institutions devised for the especial purpose of meeting the variable needs of business? Was not a publicly controlled centralization preferable to the irresponsible private concentration of the past?

The Aldrich–Vreeland Act of 1908

The panic had one immediate legislative result: the Aldrich–Vreeland Act of 1908. This act provided for an emergency bank note currency which might be called into being by the deposit of other collateral than government bonds. Since this provision was avowedly intended as a purely make-shift arrangement we need not consider its details here. In two ways, however, it gained historical importance. In the first place, although it was at first provided that the act should expire in 1914, it was later extended so as to cover the period until the Federal Reserve Act went into effect in 1915. The outbreak of the Great War in August, 1914, led to large shipments of gold to Europe and to a small-sized panic in the money market. To relieve the situation emergency notes to the amount of $386,000,000 were issued by 1363 different banks. It is very likely that the fact that the Aldrich–Vreeland Act was in effect prevented a serious panic like that of 1907. All of the notes issued under the act were retired before the act expired. They were subjected to heavy taxes which were increased as the notes remained in circulation, so that it was to the banks' interests to retire them as soon as feasible.

In the second place, the Aldrich–Vreeland Act is important because it utilized a machinery which, in earlier panics, the banks of large cities, organized in clearing-house associations, had improvised for themselves. In times of stress banks had sometimes been permitted to pay adverse clearing balances in instruments called clearing-house loan certificates, representing the joint credit of the banks associated in the clearing house, and advanced or loaned to the individual banks whose reserves were deficient. The borrowing banks gave security to the other clearing-house banks by depositing approved collateral. In the shortage of cash in the panic of 1907 these clearing-house loan certificates in many cities were issued in small denominations and were paid out by the banks and put into general hand-to-hand circulation. The Aldrich-Vreeland Act utilized clearing-house associations where these existed, and provided for corresponding organizations of banks in country districts. There is much in the present federal reserve system which, in a general way, is similar to these Aldrich–Vreeland provisions. In fact, although in the reform of the American banking system much was learned from other countries, notably from the central-bank systems of Europe and the elastic note issue of the Canadian banks, it nevertheless remains true that this great reform is based fundamentally upon the monetary experience of the United States, and that it utilized machinery which in one way or another has been shown to be particularly suited to the conditions that exist in the United States.

The Aldrich Bill fails to pass

A special section of the Aldrich–Vreeland Act provided for the appointment of the National Monetary Commission, – a body equipped with sufficient funds to undertake a thorough-going study of banking reform. Under the chairmanship of Senator Aldrich of Rhode Island, this commission heard the testimony of numerous banking and financial experts, and arranged for the publication of a number of works on important aspects of the money problem. At length it reported to Congress a bill for banking reform, a bill which became popularly known as the "Aldrich Bill."

The details of this bill need not detain us here, as it was not destined to secure the assent of Congress. To analyze the cause of its failure would also be unprofitable, save perhaps to mention that it ignored popular objections to a central banking institution in the election of whose directorate bankers' votes would be supreme. That it provided not for centralization but for banking cooperation was not sufficient to lull the general disapproval.

Defects of the old national banking system

After the failure of the Aldrich Bill, it appeared for a time as if banking revision would become a football of politics, particularly as in the political campaign of 1912 all three of the leading parties advocated banking reform in terms not ultra-precise and definite. But soon after the election of President Wilson, the study of banking reform was, at his initiative, begun anew. In 1913 the Federal Reserve Act passed Congress. To appreciate its real significance we must first understand the evils it was designed to cure. Of the defects of the old national banking system, those most emphasized in popular as well as in purely banking circles were the following:

1 Decentralized reserves. Cash reserves were parceled out among the vaults of 7500 individual banks.
2 Rigid reserve requirements, under which banks were compelled to refuse new loans when their cash reserves had fallen below the minimum set by law.
3 The inelasticity of the note issues, or the inability of our currency to adjust its volume to the varying needs of trade.

To many Americans unacquainted with centralized banking institutions, it was exceedingly difficult to apprehend clearly the operation of a system in which each individual bank was not the holder of a large part of its own cash reserve. But to the European, it would have been equally difficult to visualize the working of the American system. For the European has been accustomed to the great central banking institutions in whose vaults are held in large measure the nation's ultimate cash reserve.

It is not difficult to perceive the advantage of the centralized European systems in times of credit crises. If business can be carried over a threatened period of adversity, lack of business confidence may not become general and the soundness of credit may remain unimpaired. Through long experience, the leading bankers have learned that the only safe policy in such times is to lend freely, to convince the business public that the banks are prepared to throw their resources generously at the disposal of trade. Discount and interest rates will undoubtedly be raised in order to cut off the less urgent demands for loan accommodation; but the legitimate demands for credit must be met. Any other policy can only mean an accentuation of the public's fears. But such a policy requires courage. It is useless to ask each individual banker to go ahead blindly, in time of financial stress, risking the solvency of his own bank, perhaps. Somewhere in the banking system there must be some responsible, central authority to which the banks of the country as a whole may look for initiative and guidance in general banking policies and which, most of all, shall be in a position to assure individual banks that they are not incurring undue risks in holding to the right rather than the wrong financial policy. Thus the Bank of England, in announcing its official discount rate, virtually guarantees the other banks of that country that they can, at the stated rate, secure funds to maintain or to replenish their own reserves. But where under the old system were banks to obtain the funds for such an expansion of loans? Nowhere was there a central banking institution with funds husbanded for just such occasions. Least of all could one bank turn to another for aid. In time of threatened danger each institution set to work to put its own house in order, to diminish its loans so that the claims on its cash might be lessened. With each bank thus impelled to look first to its own interests, and with no means of effective cooperation among the banks, a general credit stringency might arise, which in its beginnings could easily have been handled had some means existed for placing the aggregate banking resources at the disposal of the threatened community.

How well the old system deserved the reproach, "Breeder of Panics," is indicated by the following remarks of Paul Warburg, a distinguished banker, for some time a member of the Federal Reserve Board:

> If after a prolonged drought a thunderstorm threatens, what would be the consequence if the wise mayor of a town should attempt to meet the danger of fire by distributing the available water, giving each house-owner one pailful? When the lightning strikes, the unfortunate householder will in vain fight the fire with his one pailful of water, while the other citizens will all frantically hold on to their own little supply, their only defense in the face of danger. The fire will spread and resistance will be impossible. If, however, instead of uselessly dividing the water, it had remained concentrated in one reservoir with an effective system of pipes to direct it where it was wanted for short, energetic and efficient use, the town would have been safe.
>
> We have paralleled conditions in our currency system, but, ridiculous as these may appear, our true condition is even more preposterous. For not only is the water uselessly distributed into 21,000 pails, but we are permitted to use the water only in small portions at a time, in proportion as the house burns down. If the structure consists of four floors, we must keep one-fourth of the contents of our pail for each floor. We must not try to extinguish the fire by freely using the water in the beginning. That would not be fair to the other floors. Let the fire spread and give each part of the house, as it burns, its equal and inefficient proportion of water. *Pereat mundus, fiat justitia!*

When we consider likewise the rigidity of our legal reserve requirements, many similar analogies might be made, all to the detriment of the old system. What would we think of a government which, having in time of peace established naval and military reserves, should insist that they should not be used in time of war, in order that the reserve forces should not be diminished? Would we regard a waterworks system as efficient, if, during a general conflagration, water could not be used when the supply in the reservoirs had fallen below what was normally regarded as the proper reserve for safety? Yet by our reserve law, banks were unable to utilize their funds to their maximum capacity at the very time when business stood in most urgent need for credit! Indeed, the United States was one of the few countries in the world which, by law, required a cash reserve to be held against deposits.

It was obvious also that the currency system of the United States was decidedly *inelastic*. Its volume could not vary according to the varying needs of trade. Particularly evident was this weakness in the period of greatest stress, the fall crop-moving season. In the late winter, banks in the agricultural districts found themselves with more money on hand than they needed. So large sums were shipped east, largely to New York, where a small rate of interest was paid on bankers' deposits. Along came the harvest season, and the need for cash in the interior annually caused a wholesale withdrawal of these funds. Each fall the principal banks of New York had been obliged to surrender about fifty millions of dollars to satisfy such demands. In addition, gold was often imported from Europe in large quantities. The high rates of interest on these foreign loans added to the real costs of moving the crops. Europe was exacting a toll for furnishing the funds which should have been forthcoming here.

The inelasticity of bank reserves the real crux

All of these defects of the old system – decentralized reserves, rigid reserve requirements and inelastic note issues – were merely different aspects of the single defect which we have placed second in the foregoing list, namely, the inelasticity of bank reserves. It is worth while, therefore, to further emphasize this particular point and to try and see its relation to the other defects of our old banking system.

The only reason for requiring that a bank shall maintain reserves equal to a certain specified per cent of its deposits or its note issue is to insure that the bank will be able to meet sudden demands for cash from its depositors and on the part of other banks. The rigid reserve requirements that we have already discussed provided that when reserves fell below 15 or 25 per cent, as the case might be, the bank should immediately cease lending until its reserves had been restored. This adequately served the purpose of protecting depositors. But so far as the extending of credit was concerned such a reserve was not a true reserve at all: it was a dead line beyond which the bank could not go. It might have to stop lending at the very time when courageous lending, even if at higher discount rates, was the only thing that would forestall a general crisis. In the practice of most other countries bank reserves are allowed to vary, the variation in the reserve ratio being accompanied by a sliding scale of discount rates fixed not by law but by the experience of the bank.

It is easy to see how this fundamental defect was linked up with others. If reserves were truly elastic it would not make much difference whether they were centralized or parceled out among individual banks. The real difficulty is that it is impossible that bank reserves should be elastic unless they are centralized. Again, if bank reserves had been elastic, the absence of elasticity in bank-note issues would not in itself have done any harm. The New York banks, for example, could have taken money from their vaults every autumn and shipped it to the West, knowing that in the course of the normal cycle of trade it would return in a relatively few months. For the time being, during the crop-moving season in the West, reserves might be low. But what of it? It would have been understood by everyone to have been a normal situation for that particular time of year, and one which would in a short time remedy itself.

But why, the reader may ask, did not the New York banks and the other large banks which held the major portion of the reserves of the country normally hold *more* reserves than were required by law? If the New York banks had normally held 40 or 50 per cent reserves, they could have absorbed the ordinary strains resulting from the movement of gold into the West, into the government treasury, or even to Europe, while retaining the ability to meet the real needs of the business community for loans. For such reserves would never, except in years when gold exports were large, have fallen to the legal minimum of 25 per cent.

The defect of decentralization

This question brings us back to the first of the three defects we have discussed, namely, decentralization. For even in New York City bank reserves were decentralized, that is, they were scattered among a number of different competing banks. In the nature of the case each bank was interested in doing the largest possible volume of business and in making maximum profits for its shareholders.

No one bank was responsible for the maintenance of the *surplus reserves* which would have given real elasticity to the American banking system. Just because no one bank was responsible, no one bank, as a matter of fact, ever attempted to maintain such reserves. When the return of money from the West, or imports of gold from Europe, or payments by the federal treasury, brought New York bank reserves above the 25 per cent line, this surplus lending power was at once utilized. There was always a sure market for call loans made at low rates to finance stock exchange speculations.

Call loans and speculation

Call loans are loans payable on demand. From the point of view of any one bank, a call loan seems to be a desirable form of credit, for when the bank reserves are threatened, or there is a demand for money for other purposes, repayment may be asked. But when some banks call loans, the borrowers put additional strain on other banks. Moreover, the general calling of such loans often forces speculators to sell their holdings to secure funds with which to repay their loans, just as the making of call loans at low rates generally stimulates *buying* of speculative securities on a large scale. In this way, such surplus reserves as appeared in the New York money market were absorbed in call loans, which led, in turn, to strong bull movements, that is, to rising prices on the stock exchange. When the reserves were brought down to the legal minimum, or in practice a little below, the tightening of the call-loan market often led to the precipitate selling of shares and a drop in stock market values. Altogether it will be seen that our inelastic reserve system worked in such a way as to bring about an unholy alliance between lending and speculation. The effect of fluctuations in the money market was felt in magnified form in the speculative market, while in turn, the ups and downs of speculation reacted upon the state of the money market.

The dominance of the New York money market is shown, even though not fully, in the accompanying table, which, speaking for a period several years earlier than the introduction of the federal reserve system, shows the disposition of the cash deposits and the reserves of the national banks of the country. New York, it will be noted, held more than one-third of the reserves of the country, and in

Table 35.1 Deposits and reserves of national banks (sums in millions of dollars)

Location	Number of banks	Deposits	Reserve Amount	ratios	Classification of reserve Lawful money in bank	Due from reserve agents	Redemption fund
New York	38	825.7	221.3	26.8	218.8		2.6
Chicago	14	262.9	66.6	25.3	66.1		0.5
St. Louis	8	116.8	27.6	23.6	26.8		0.7
Other reserve cities	306	1423.4	362.3	25.5	190.3	165.7	6.3
Country banks	6178	2627.2	443.5	16.9	199.6	226.7	17.2
Total	6544	5256.1	1121.4	21.3	701.6	392.4	27.3

addition, it should be remembered that many state banks, private banks and trust companies had deposits in New York which they treated as their own reserves. The deposits of other banks generally constituted more than one-half of the deposits of New York banks. Like an inverted pyramid upon its apex, the whole structure of bank credit in the United States rested upon the cash reserves of the New York national banks.

The importance of speculation in its relation to the money market is indicated in the accompanying table, which shows the character of the loans and discounts of New York national banks in 1890 and 1912. In interpreting the table, it should be noted that not only most of the loans made on call, but also some of the time loans made on collateral security, were for the purpose of financing speculative transactions.

The fundamental difficulty may be put in this way: *there was nowhere any slack or "give" in our banking system.* The whole system tended always to be in a condition of strain. Whatever slack might appear was at once taken up or absorbed in the speculative market. There was no possible remedy save in a more elastic relation between loans and reserves, and that was impossible without centralized control and centralized responsibility. Sometimes the best interests of the country demanded a banking policy which ran counter to the interests of individual banks. Such a policy in the nature of the case could not be the outcome of the operations of competitive banks, however public spirited.

Table 35.2 Loans and discounts of New York national banks: 1890 and 1924 (in millions of dollars)

Character of loan	1890	1924
On call	102	623
On time, with collateral security	43	475
On time, without collateral security	152	873

The federal reserve system

We are now prepared to examine the organization and the operations of the federal reserve system and to see how it has corrected the major defects of the old national banking system.

The system utilizes not one but twelve central banks. This avoids the traditional American objection to the financial and possibly the political power of a single central bank, and in view of the vast territorial extent of the United States as contrasted with most European countries, the system of regional central banks does not seem unreasonable.

These twelve great regional banks are owned and in part controlled by their member banks, which comprise all national banks within the respective federal reserve districts together with such state banks and trust companies as desire to join the system and which comply with certain required standards.

Coordination of the policies of all of the banks and a certain amount of control over each bank is in the hands of the Federal Reserve Board at Washington, made up of five members appointed by the President in addition to the Secretary of the Treasury and the Comptroller of the Currency. The boundaries of the different federal reserve districts together with the location of the different federal reserve banks and agencies are shown in the accompanying map [*Eds: not reprinted here*].

Functions of the federal reserve banks

The most important functions of the federal reserve banks are those of holding the reserves of the member banks and of rediscounting commercial paper for them. Under the old system, it will be remembered, a bank's legal reserve consisted partly of cash in its own vaults and partly of deposit credits on the books of banks in large cities, especially New York. To meet a drain of cash a bank had to take money from its own vaults or it had to draw upon its New York accounts. With inelastic reserves, a drain of cash into general circulation or large exports of gold necessitated drastic reduction in credit, frequently with disastrous results.

Now, however, when a member bank's deposits are as large as under the law its reserves permit, it may replenish its reserves by taking some of the commercial paper (loans and discounts) it holds and rediscounting or selling it to the federal reserve bank, which is always ready to assist in such operations, provided the paper is of approved quality. The result, of course, is a change in the form of the member bank's assets. Its loans and discounts are reduced, but its deposit credits with the federal reserve bank, constituting its legal reserve, are correspondingly increased. It is now in a position to go ahead and give its customers the further accommodation they need.

Or take the case where the member bank needs something that will serve as actual money. Local causes or the recurrence of the harvest season have led to large withdrawals of cash from the bank. In such circumstances the member bank again sells some of its loans and discounts to the federal reserve bank, but it takes the proceeds not in the form of deposit credit but in the form of *federal reserve notes* which will serve its customers as well as any other form of money would.

The federal reserve banks, in turn, may go ahead and increase their own deposit liabilities and note issues without any arbitrary restrictions. Of course the bills of exchange and notes which they take over from member banks must be of high quality and must be composed of relatively short maturities, that is, the credits they extend run for only a short time. At maturity, in case further accommodations are needed by the member banks, the paper which has been paid off may be replaced by new. The federal reserve banks are compelled to keep gold reserves equal to 35 per cent of their deposit liabilities plus 40 per cent of their note issues.

These provisions may seem at first thought to indicate that the United States has held to the old discredited policy of fixed and rigid reserves. Closer scrutiny reveals the fact that the present requirements in their actual wording are not at all like the old. In the first place, the centralized responsibility of the federal reserve banks makes it certain that in normal times they will secure elasticity in the credit situation by holding large surplus reserves – reserves of much more than 35 or 40 per cent of their liabilities. In the second place, the 35 or 40 per cent limits are not absolute dead lines, for by permission of the Federal Reserve Board the actual reserve may be permitted to fall below these points. A tax is imposed upon the amount of the deficiency to insure that the reserves will be restored as soon as possible to a normal level.

Taking the system as a whole, it will be seen that it gives a thoroughly elastic supply of credit. It has all of the necessary elements: elastic note issue, elastic deposits and elastic reserves. The assets back of the note issues of the federal reserve banks are in general like those back of their deposits; namely, commercial paper which has been rediscounted for or bought from member banks. Notes may also be issued upon commercial paper bought in the open market, that is, from banks outside the system, from note brokers and others. Federal reserve *bank* notes are to be distinguished from federal reserve notes. They are issued upon the security of federal government bonds which the reserve banks are required to purchase from such national banks as desire to give up their note issue privilege. Most of the government bonds held by national banks as security for note issue pay only 2 per cent interest a year, and, without the note issue privilege, they would be worth much less than par in the market.

Reference has been made above to the open market operations of the federal reserve banks. These are likely to prove of increasing importance in the future. It is urgently hoped that the federal reserve system may be able not only to lessen the acuteness of periods of financial crisis by insuring that in times of financial drought the springs of credit shall not be dried up, but also that it will be able to correct some of the defects in our economic system that are primarily responsible for our recurrent panics. If a man is to fall over a precipice, he is fortunate if his fall can be broken or cushioned in some way. But he would have been yet more fortunate if someone had held him back before he came to the edge of the precipice. A wisely ordered banking system would tend to check and dampen the periods of overoptimism and of too rapid business expansion, as well as to relieve the severity of the ensuing periods of depression. Just as it is a sound national banking policy to lend freely to necessitous borrowers in times of depression, so it is an equally sound policy to retard the flow of credit in periods when rapidly advancing prices are tending to overstimulate business.

Member banks *must* follow federal leads

If federal reserve banks are to be able to secure a larger measure of stability in American business, they must, like the Bank of England, be able to induce the banks of the country to follow their leadership. This is simple enough in periods of tight money when the other banks are dependent upon the federal reserve banks for funds. It is more difficult in periods of prosperity when each individual bank will feel itself competent to go ahead, extending its credits as rapidly as it pleases, without regard to the ultimate effect of a general credit expansion upon the welfare of the country as a whole. The open market operations of the federal reserve banks, if they can be developed on a sufficient scale, will put them in a position where they can say to the thousands of other banks in the country: "We come to your relief in time of stress by taking off your hands commercial paper which you are no longer able to hold, and by supplying you with funds so that you may continue the operations so necessary to the economic life of your own community. Now, when everything seems prosperous, we must ask you to take off our hands commercial paper which we think had better be held by you than by us. It is better that your surplus lending power be absorbed for the while in the holding of this paper than that you should be free just now to expand your credits further at low interest rates."

Putting on the brakes in time of danger

The open market, in other words, would enable the federal reserve banks to put increased burdens upon the other banks of the country, just as the mechanism provided by the federal reserve act makes it possible for them to relieve those burdens at other times. Increasing the burdens of the other banks would thus be the federal reserve way of "putting on the brakes" in a period in which credit was being extended at a dangerous rate.

Effect of new system during war

It was exceedingly fortunate for the United States that the federal reserve system was in operation during the Great War. The concentration of the reserves of the country in the federal reserve banks, together with the reduction of the reserve requirements in member banks, led to a tremendous expansion – a multiplication in fact – of the aggregate lending capacity of the banks of the country. The prodigious growth of governmental and private industries during the war, the enormous expenditure and borrowing operations of the government, the advances of billions of dollars to the other governments, would have created a strain that the old national banking system could not have borne. The monetary system of the United States, under the old conditions, would undoubtedly have gone the way of that of most of the countries of Europe. The gold standard would have disappeared, the currency would have been paper money and banknotes, both alike irredeemable in gold. The advance in prices would have gone much further and have been much more disastrous to economic welfare than was actually the case. In short, the federal reserve system, with its enlarged and more elastic supply of credit, saved the country from a great catastrophe.

Editors' note

a Chapter 32 of the Grolier *Book of Popular Science* entitled "Monetary System of the United States" (included in this selection as Chapter 34).

36 Dear and cheap money

The Bank of England and the mechanism of the London Money Market

How the foreign exchanges operate

The Book of Popular Science (1924; revised 1929) New York: The Grolier Society. Group IX Ch. 34: 4705–15

The Bank of England, today the most famous financial institution in the world, had a curious origin. At the end of the seventeenth century, when, as had often been the case before, England was engaged in a war with France, and when James II had but recently fled across the seas, the throne of William and Mary rested upon the support of the Whigs. The prosecution of war with France, the backer of the Stuart pretenders to the throne, called for money, and where was money to be had? It was in these circumstances that a company of Whig merchants of the City of London conceived the idea of forming a limited liability company to lend money to the government. At that time, of course, trading with limited liability was a rare thing, and the royal charter of 1694, which was issued by William III, establishing the "Governor and Company of the Bank of England," conferred an exceedingly valuable privilege.

The company or society thus named raised the sum of £1,200,000 (equivalent to about $6,000,000) by tempting the public with interest at 8 per cent, and so it came about that William III got his money for the war with France, the English National Debt began, and the "Old Lady of Threadneedle Street" was born. The whole of the money raised went to the government, and the company was given power to issue bank-notes for an equal amount, government security being thus behind the notes.

Not very long after its incorporation the bank was given a monopoly of joint-stock banking by a law which forbade other banking firms to have more than six partners. This monopoly was not canceled until more than a century later, and during the long interval banking was necessarily confined to the operations of private firms. In 1826 this law was repealed, but even then the Bank of England was given the exclusive privilege of issuing bank-notes within a radius of sixty-five miles of London.

The original loan of £1,200,000 was soon increased, as we may easily imagine. The Bank of England lent £11,015,100 to the State, and up to this sum it possessed the right to issue bank-notes upon government security. Beyond this it could issue notes upon its own private security. The original government debt of £11,015,000 remains to this day, and still figures in the weekly banking return of the Bank of England.

In 1844 the Bank Charter Act was passed to revise the conditions of note issue, to substitute Bank of England notes for the note issues of other banks, as far as possible, and at the same time to make the Bank of England note absolutely safe by insuring that it should be backed either by government security or actual gold.

The Bank Charter Act of 1844, commonly referred to as "Peel's Act," was the final outcome of a long controversy between the advocates of the so-called "currency" and "banking" schools, which had begun in the period of the Napoleonic wars, when the Bank of England had suspended specie payments, and when its notes, issued in large quantities, were at a discount as compared with gold. The act of 1844 embodies the "currency" principle, which is to the effect that a country needs a certain amount of money and no more and that, since bank-notes serve as money, their quantity should be definitely fixed by law. The gist of the "banking" principle is that the amount of money a country needs depends upon the volume of trade and that there can be no overissue or inflation of bank-notes so long as they are put into circulation to finance actual commercial transactions. The federal reserve system of the United States, like the banking systems of France and of Canada, embodies the banking principle.

The bank, in accordance with the act of 1844, has two distinct departments: the issue department, solely concerned with the issue of notes, and the banking department, which handles the ordinary business of banking. The workings of

Table 36.1 Bank return: January 9, 1924

Issue Department			
Resources		Liabilities	
Government Debt	£11,015,100	Notes Issued	£145,984,595
Other Securities	8,734,900		
Gold Coin and Bullion	126,234,595		
	£145,984,595		£145,984,595

Banking Department			
Resources		Liabilities	
Government Securities	£47,312,032	Proprietors' Capital	£14,553,000
Other Securities	77,040,564	Rest	3,338,068
Notes	19,708,380	Public Deposits	11,772,876
Gold and Silver Coin	1,823,449	Other Deposits	116,161,716
		Seven Day and Other Bills	8,765
	£145,884,425		£145,884,425

this system at the present time are clearly shown in the accompanying bank statement or "return" for January, 1924. The original government debt of £11,015,100 is held as an asset by the issue department to secure an equal amount of notes. "Other securities" are held to cover notes issued by the bank as heir to part of the privileges of note issue formerly enjoyed by certain other banks. But the bulk of the notes issued are covered pound for pound by deposits of gold coin and bullion with the issue department. The so-called "uncovered issue" is thus absolutely fixed in amount. Aside from this fixed amount, Bank of England notes are precisely like the gold certificates issued by the government of the United States. The amount in circulation will depend merely upon the extent to which paper money, rather than gold, meets the convenience and preferences of the community. When gold is needed for export, or for other purposes, notes will be presented at the bank and the gold withdrawn.

Before the war any person could go to the Bank of England and demand Bank of England notes in exchange for gold at the rate of £3 17s. 9d. per ounce. An ounce of gold, as we have already seen, really makes £3 17s. 10½d. in English money, but the Bank of England is compelled to pay gold for its notes on demand while it, in turn, has to wait for its coins when it takes gold to the mint. The margin of 1½d. per ounce is therefore partly interest and partly a commission paid to the bank as official agent for English gold money. When urgently in need of gold, however, the bank often raises its buying price somewhat above the legal minimum. The reader who has followed our account of the defects of the national banking system of the United States and of the improvements embodied in the federal reserve system will wonder just how under the handicap of an absolutely inelastic system of note issue the London money market has been able to achieve and retain its position of predominance.

For the explanation of the apparent paradox, we must look to three different sets of circumstances:

1 There are seasonal variations in the demand for money in England, but these variations are not comparable in magnitude to those occasioned by the crop-moving period in the United States and Canada. An elastic hand-to-hand circulating medium is therefore not so necessary in England.
2 A very large proportion of the business of England is transacted by means of bank checks. English bank deposits, as contrasted with bank-notes, are highly elastic. They are able to fluctuate freely with the needs of trade. During the fifty years preceding the Great War the supply of bank credit in the form of deposits subject to check was more perfectly elastic in England than in any other country in the world.
3 In emergency, the operations of the bank act may be suspended, so as to permit of an increase in the uncovered note issue of the Bank of England. This occurred in several earlier financial crises as well as during the Great War. Because of the possibility of suspension, the bank, by issuing most of its notes virtually in gold certificates, accumulates in normal times a store of gold in its issue department which can be utilized as a reserve for yet further

note issues in time of emergency. This explains the comment of Sir Robert Peel that the real merit of the act was to be found in the accumulation and preservation of a large stock of gold which could be made available by its suspension.

4 Now let us pass to the part of the bank return which is headed "banking department." That department, we repeat, is quite separate and distinct from the issue department. The strength of the bank is not determined by the size of its capital so much as by its peculiar position in the world's money market. The "rest" is a reserve fund corresponding to surplus and undivided profit in the statements of banks in the United States. "Public" deposits are those of the government, and "other" deposits comprise not only the accounts of private customers but also the accounts of other banks, for the Bank of England is a bankers' bank. Its cash reserves contain the greater part of the gold of England. Other banks keep a small supply of sovereigns and other coins on hand as till money, but most of their money is kept with the Bank of England and appears in the return under the term "other deposits." We should understand, therefore, that the really small amount of gold coin and bullion held in the banking and issue departments of the Bank of England is the foundation of the whole structure of English credit. More than that, this small store of treasure was before the Great War, and probably will be again, the world's central gold reserve. We may find it amazing that not only the hundreds of thousands of current domestic debts in England payable on demand in gold are backed up by such a tiny amount of actual cash, but that these same small hoards also constitute the means by which the balances arising out of international trade are in large measure paid.

The reader will now realize how great are the responsibilities of the Bank of England. The English economist Bagehot said: "On the wisdom of the directors of that one joint-stock company, it depends whether England shall be solvent or insolvent." We may go further and say that the smooth functioning of the great machinery of international commerce depends in no small measure upon the wisdom with which the Bank of England is managed.

The Bank of England is a private institution with public duties. It fulfills the most important functions, but it remains today as it always has been an institution fulfilling its responsibilities without acknowledging any formal duties or legal obligations in the matter. Its reserve, it is interesting to note, has increased, but not in proportion to the growth of the trade of England or of the world. In the 'seventies and 'eighties of the nineteenth century, it ranged from £12,000,000 to £15,000,000; in the 'nineties, it rose to over £20,000,000 and in 1912 it was £26,000,000. The real reserve of the Bank of England, the reader will observe, is equal to the amount of gold and Bank of England notes held in the *banking* department. Gold coins and bullion held in the issue department over and above the amount of notes in the hands of the banking department are offset, of course, by notes outstanding in the hands of the public. In the case of a sudden demand for gold, all the notes outstanding, except those already in the hands of the bank, might be presented for payment. But just in the measure that the bank holds its own notes, its gold reserve, thus free from prior claims upon it, is the basis upon which the enormous structure of deposit credit in England is based.

As to the Bank of England's view of its responsibilities, Bagehot, writing in 1873 in his famous "Lombard Street," remarked:

> All banks depend on the Bank of England, and all merchants depend on some banker. If a merchant have £10,000 at his banker's, and wants to pay it to someone in Germany, he will not be able to pay it unless his banker can pay him, and the banker will not be able to pay him if the Bank of England should be in difficulties and cannot produce his reserve. The directors of the Bank are therefore, in fact, if not in name, trustees for the public, to keep a banking reserve on their behalf; and it would naturally be expected either that they distinctly recognized this duty and engaged to perform it, or that their own self-interest was so strong in the matter that no engagement was needed. But, so far from there being a distinct undertaking on the part of the Bank directors to perform this duty, many of them would scarcely acknowledge it, and some altogether denied it.

These words are as true today as when they were written. The Bank of England does not admit responsibility, and yet it is responsible. Successive governments acknowledge that the subject is important, and pass on to less important matters.

How the Bank of England's reserve is affected, and how it matters to all

In view of the great importance of the subject, we must now see what it is that chiefly affects the bank's reserve of gold, and what the reserve matters to the ordinary man. Unfortunately, these things matter very much in the daily affairs of life; and while there are few newspaper readers who understand the money column there may be large groups of unemployed and business men bitterly suffering, because of things happening which are recorded in it – plainly for those who understand, obscurely for those who do not.

It is necessary first to show the part which gold plays in international trade and the foreign exchanges. Foreign transactions have much to do with the price of money. What do we mean by the "price" of money? How can money have a price? The answer to these questions is that the word here means something quite different from "price" as applied to goods. The price of a commodity means the amount of money for which it will exchange. The price of money means the rate of interest asked for the loan of it.

The way in which ordinary business is affected by the bank rate

When we speak of the "money market" we mean the places in which money may be borrowed. Very clearly, when money – i.e., loan money – is in plentiful supply, the rate of interest is low, and money is said to be "cheap." When money is scarce, and loans are difficult to negotiate, the rate of interest advances, and money is said to be "dear."

Of course, it matters a great deal to the business man what the price of money is. If a builder, for example, has to pay 7 per cent for money instead of 5 per cent, it makes a very great difference indeed to his chance of a successful venture. If the price of money rises, we have an immediate check to business; and, conversely, when money is plentiful, business is stimulated. Good business, by creating a demand for loans, tends to raise the price of money, and *vice versa*.

When gold becomes necessary to balance international payments

We showed in a preceding chapter[a] how goods are exchanged for goods in the same country by means of promises to pay gold, which we call "checks" – promises which are offset one against another by banks. This offsetting renders the passing of gold in business almost entirely unnecessary.

When we come to external commerce, the promises to pay gold take the form of bills of exchange, which are actually promises (or "accepted" *orders*) to pay gold at some future date. We do not pause here to explain the machinery of the bill of exchange in detail, for the reader will not be misled if he imagines the process to result in the same way as the exchange of checks, described in a preceding chapter.[a] It will be apparent, however, that if two countries, say the United States and England, trade with each other, it is highly improbable that at any given time the goods sold by Americans to Englishmen will be exactly equal in value to those sold by Englishmen to Americans. Therefore, it may not be at any given moment possible to set off paper promises to pay in such manner as entirely to resolve the transactions between the two nations. Of course, in practice the offsetting takes place between more than two nations, but it simplifies what we have to explain to fix our minds upon two nations only.

Imagine, then, that at a given time the goods sold by the United States to England, and due to be paid for, are worth \$25,000,000, while the goods sold by England to the United States, and due to be paid for, are worth \$24,500,000. It will be seen that, so far as \$24,500,000 is concerned, all that need be done is to offset promises to pay gold against each other, leaving a balance of \$500,000. Under these circumstances, the \$500,000 must be paid in actual gold shipped from England to the United States. It would thus become necessary to obtain gold from the Bank of England and to export it to New York. As a consequence, the reserve of gold at the Bank of England falls, and the English money market is affected.

Why the price of money is raised in London from time to time

How, then, does the Bank of England protect its gold reserve from such depletion? It has both to supply gold on demand and yet to prevent its reserve from falling to a dangerously low point. To give the answer in the simplest form, what the

Bank of England does is to *raise the price of money in London*. The means by which it effects this is by raising what is called the bank rate, i.e., the rate at which the Bank of England will discount first-class bills of exchange or lend money on good security for short periods. The official bank rate, because of the peculiar importance and power of the Bank of England which prescribes it, determines the market rate, or practical rate of discount, which runs a shade below it. Experience has shown again and again that the raising of the bank rate is effective in retaining gold in London or even in attracting additional supplies from other countries. The Bank of England has not infrequently thus to protect its gold reserve.

Thus, when in 1907 there was a financial panic in the United States, when business men were rushing to their banks for gold, and the banks in turn began to call on London for gold, the Bank of England raised its rate, and prevented too great a drain upon its resources.

So far we have avoided the difficulty that different countries have different coinage, but we must now consider this in detail, and see how foreign exchanges are in practice regulated.

It will be readily understood that as between the gold coins of two gold-standard countries the question is not what the coins are called, but what is the amount of pure gold in the coins. Considering this, what is called the "mint par of exchange" is arrived at. For example, what is the relation of the pure gold in the French pre-war coinage (napoleons) to the pure gold of the coins of the United States? This is easily calculated, and we find that a dollar has as much pure gold in it as rather more than five gold francs – the precise amount is 5.18 francs.

The causes of the rise and fall of the rates of exchange

Again, the mint par between the United States and England is 486.7 cents to the pound sterling. We hope we have made it clear that the mint par of exchange has sole relation to the amount of pure gold contained in the various coins. Obviously, as between a gold-standard country and a silver country, like China, there cannot be a mint par of exchange. Now let us suppose that as between two countries the claims for payment at a certain time are equal. That being so, exchange is at the theoretic par of exchange – i.e., if the two countries were the United States and England the claims would be settled at the exchange rate of approximately the English sovereign, $4.87. But, of course, it rarely happens that there is such an equivalence of indebtedness between any two countries; and it will be seen that if on a certain date there is more to remit from the United States to England than from England to the United States, there will be a considerable demand in the United States for bills of exchange as a means of remittance to London. Consequently, the price of a bill of exchange would rise in New York, or, in other words, the rate of exchange would rise.

To express it in another way, a bill on London would be at a premium; an American importer desiring to remit would be willing to pay more than the mint par of exchange – *i.e., more than 486.7 cents per sovereign* for it. There is, however, a practical limit to the premium he would be willing to pay. That limit is fixed by the cost of buying, shipping and insuring gold, and that limit is known as "the gold point." A moment's thought will show that this gold point strictly limits the premium of exchange, and is the point at which gold is paid instead of a bill of exchange, or promise to pay gold.

The insignificance of the commerce in gold compared with the bulk of trade

Now we see how it is that gold comes to be shipped in settlement of debts between one country and another. In relation to the enormous bulk of international transactions which take place, the shipments of gold are trifling. In point of actual size, however, the shipments of gold are great. For example, in the year 1924 the commerce in goods and gold of the United States was as shown in Table 36.2.

It will be seen that while in a single year our imports and exports of merchandise amounted in value to the enormous sum of $8,201,000,000, our inward and outward shipments of bullion and specie amounted to less than $400,000,000. It is plain, therefore, that the great bulk of the necessary payments were made by the transmission of bills of exchange, and that the shipment of gold played only a comparatively small part. Nevertheless, when transactions in gold are compared with the gold reserve at the Bank of England and other central banks we get a very different effect of proportion. In relation to the total volume of trade the commerce in gold is insignificant; *in relation to the bank reserves the commerce in gold is considerable and significant*. We see that it is large enough and frequent enough to have a very appreciable effect on the money market.

The daily table of foreign exchanges a thermometer of trade balances

We can understand, then, how important are the tables of foreign exchanges which appear in the money columns of the daily newspapers, and how closely they are watched. The movement upward or downward of rates of exchange with any particular country shows in which direction the balance of indebtedness is

Table 36.2 Shipment of goods and gold: 1924

	$
Imports of Goods	3,609,963,000
Exports of Goods	4,497,649,000
Exports of Imported Goods	93,335,000
Total Trade in Goods	8,200,947,000
Gold Imported	319,721,000
Gold Exported	61,648,000

Table 36.3 Foreign exchange

Sterling – Par $4.86 ⅝	Demand	4.26 ⅝
	Cables	4.26 ⅞
	Sixty-day bills	4.24 ⅝
Francs – Par 19.3 cents	Demand	4.64 ½
	Cables	4.65
Guilders – Par 40.2 cents	Demand	37.22
	Cables	37.27
Lire – Par 19.3 cents	Demand	4.34 ½
	Cables	4.35
Marks – Par 23.8 cents	Demand	.0000000000002
	Cable	.0000000000002
Norwegian Kronen – Par 26.8 cents	Demand	13.63
	Cable	13.65
Argentine Pesos – Par 42.45 cents	Demand	32.71
	Cables	32.76

tending. For example, Table 36.3 shows the rates of exchange as they were given in the daily newspapers of January 31, 1924.

Expressing the meaning of the table broadly, it is as follows: it shows the price which had to be paid at the time in New York for a demand bill payable at sight upon the leading money market in each of the different countries. The "cables" which are quoted in the table, are virtually demand drafts sent by cable instead of by mail. The price of cables, it will be noted, is generally a little higher than the price of ordinary demand drafts. This is not so much because of the expense of cabling – a relatively small matter in a large transaction – as because it takes some time for the ordinary draft sent by mail to reach a foreign country, and therefore a slight allowance for interest is made in the price. The price of 60-day bills on London, it will be further observed, is always lower than the price for ordinary demand bills. This difference also is to be attributed to discount or interest, the controlling interest rate in this case being the rate prevailing in the London money market. In general, a 60-day bill on London is worth in New York approximately as much as a demand bill on London with deduction for interest or discount for two months at the prevailing London rate.

The reader will note that the rates of foreign exchange quoted in the table are in every instance not merely below par but even far below what would ordinarily be the gold import point. The explanation is, of course, that in 1924 most of the countries of the world, not including the United States, were utilizing irredeemable paper currency as money. To pay the extraordinary expenses created by the Great War and of the period of reconstruction which followed, the governments of these countries induced their banks to issue notes in quantities so large that their redemption in gold was for the time being – and in some countries permanently – impossible. Before the war the franc was an actually enforcible right to demand a certain amount of specie in Paris, just as the mark was a real title to gold in Berlin. But with the changes brought about by the war, the franc and mark and other continental European currencies became simply promises to pay gold at some indefinite time in the future, – promises which it is wholly unlikely will ever be completely fulfilled.

Foreign exchange rates determined by supply and demand

Foreign exchange rates, like other prices, are determined by supply and demand. Exports create a supply of foreign exchange. Imports in a similar way create a demand for it. The American cotton exporter collects from his English customer by means of a bill of exchange drawn upon London. When such a bill is collected or sold in England and the proceeds put in a bank there, it becomes a credit upon which the United States can draw in payment for imports.

It must be remembered, however, that in exports and imports we include many other things than the commodities which figure in the ordinary statistics of international trade. *All things for which we have to pay other countries are imports. All things for which they have to pay us are exports.* Thus among the more important exports of the United States are commodities, American securities (bonds, stocks, etc.) and claims for the payment of interest and dividends on foreign securities owned in the United States. By such means, the United States builds up bankers' credits in foreign countries. Imports in turn include commodities, foreign securities, claims on the part of foreign investors to interest and dividends payable by American governments and by business corporations, expenses incurred by American tourists abroad, etc. Ocean steamship freights, payments for marine insurance and the earnings of the banks engaged in the foreign exchange business also enter into the true balance of trade on the one side or the other.

The significance of the larger meaning of exports and imports should now be clear. Whether or not a transaction involves the physical removal of a commodity from one country to another is immaterial. The wealthy American who pays a high price for an old Italian painting is of course an importer. But so are the other Americans who visit the picture galleries of Italy to see the works of the old masters. So far as the effect on foreign exchange is concerned, Italy may be said to export her climate and her art galleries quite as truly as she exports her olive oil and her silk. Some of the manifold and complex factors that enter into the true balance of trade are revealed by the accompanying estimate of the international balance of the United States for the year 1924. This estimate was made by Mr. Herbert Hoover, Secretary of Commerce, and it was published in a Department Bulletin in April, 1925. Speaking as it does for a year of financial confusion and turmoil, the statement includes a number of unusual items, but it is all the more instructive on that account.

Table 36.4 Balance of international payments of the United States: 1924 (in millions of dollars) (estimate made by Herbert Hoover, Secretary of Commerce)

Items	Credit	Debit	Balance
Merchandise	4,621	3,651	+ 970
Interest and dividends	614	150	+ 464
Ocean freights	76	68	+ 8
Government payments		5	– 5
Services to tourists	100	600	– 500
Charitable and missionary expenditures		55	– 55
Immigrants' remittances		300	– 300
Foreign loans, exclusive of refunding		795	– 795
Sale and purchase of outstanding securities	319	114	+ 205
Foreign bonds paid off	45		+ 45
Principle of interallied debt	23		+ 23
United States paper currency		50	– 50
Gold and silver	172	394	– 222
Total	5,970	6,182	– 212
Add increase in foreigners' bank deposits			+ 216
			+ 4

Gold shipments figure in this statement as exports and imports. In normal times when the currencies of the great nations of the world are based on a gold standard, it is better to take separate account of gold shipments, for they are really *the means by which the international balances are paid.* This will be clear if we reflect for a moment upon the operations of the gold points, as described above. If exports largely exceed imports, the supply of foreign exchange will be relatively large as compared with the demand for it. As soon as the price of exchange falls to the gold import point, however, gold will begin to flow in from other countries. The banks whose balances abroad have been increased by exports find it more profitable to exchange some of those balances for gold and to pay the expense of importing the gold rather than to sell their drafts or bills of exchange drawn against those balances at the low price prevailing in the market. This is the simple but extremely effective mechanism by which an excess of exports or imports, that is, a favorable balance of trade, necessarily leads to gold movements. Conversely, of course, if any country has for some time been importing more than it has been exporting, the demand in its markets for foreign exchange will be relatively large as compared with the supply. Under such conditions, the rate is sure to rise to the gold export point and gold will flow out in settlement of the country's adverse balance of trade.

To what conclusion the Ricardian principle of gold movements leads

This brings us to the consideration of one of the most important doctrines of economic science: the so-called "Ricardian principle" of gold movements. As a matter of fact the doctrine was well known before the days of the distinguished English economist, David Ricardo, but it was expounded by him in masterly fashion. We shall state first the conclusion to which the doctrine leads and then explain the reasoning upon which it is based. The conclusion is that no country can long maintain a favorable balance of trade. It is equally true of course that no country can for many successive years have an unfavorable trade balance. It will be understood that we are speaking of the *true trade balance* and not merely of the visible balance of commodity exports and imports.

And the reasoning upon which the conclusion is based

The reasoning upon which this conclusion is based is simple: A country whose exports exceed its imports drains gold from other countries. Its monetary circulation and its bank reserves increase. Money and bank-credit become relatively plentiful as compared with other things. Because they are more plentiful, their value decreases; that is, the general level of prices increases. The new and higher price level attracts imports from other countries and at the same time makes it more difficult to export successfully in competition with the cheaper goods of other countries. Through the operation of the increased supplies of gold, therefore, *the current of trade is reversed.* Imports come to exceed exports; gold is drained away by other countries who claim it in the payment of trade balances, now favorable to them; the price level moves downward again, and the cycle repeats itself. This doctrine, it should be understood, does not rest merely upon the basis of logic, of "pure reasoning." Like every other established scientific principle, it is accepted by competent experts because it successfully and satisfactorily explains the observed facts. Statistics of foreign trade and of gold movements square with the Ricardian doctrine. In fact, it is one of the most firmly established as well as one of the most important of economic doctrines.

We are now in a position to return to the Bank of England and to look into the mechanism by which the raising of its official discount rate safeguards its gold reserves. There is no magic in the official discount rate. In fact, it is hardly more than an official statement, a guarantee, that the bank stands ready to advance funds on high grade bills of exchange at the stated rate. As a matter of fact, most of the business of the London money market will be done at a distinctly lower rate. But the Bank of England expects that when it raises its rate, the rates prevailing in the general market will follow suit.

If they do not do so, it resorts to means of putting pressure on the market. For example, it may sell large blocks of its holdings of securities, thus absorbing the market's surplus funds and securing – through the collection of the checks paid for the securities thus sold – a transfer of funds from other banks in London to itself. Induced or forced to replenish their reserves – that is, their own credits at the Bank of England – the other banks turn to it for help. Then the Bank of England is in a position to name its conditions and to enforce what it holds to be the proper market rate of discount.

Effects of advance of discount rates by the Bank of England

When discount rates in the London money market have advanced as the result of the bank's initiative, what effects do they have? It is not true, as some have supposed, that high discount rates in themselves attract gold to the centers where they prevail. That is in truth their ultimate effect, but the mechanism by which they operate is roundabout and indirect. They attract gold because they *diminish and repel borrowing.* Some money, of course, will be borrowed at the higher rates. But other borrowers will prefer to wait and yet others will find that the high rates preclude profits from the enterprises they had in mind. The reduction of domestic borrowings in the London money market will in itself lessen the load upon the banks' reserves but the effect of the high discount rates is much more far-reaching than that. London discount rates, although extremely variable, are in general the lowest that obtain in any of the great money markets of the world. For this reason, London banks and money lenders normally hold large quantities of bills drawn to finance the trade of other countries in all parts of the world. Bills of exchange, like other commodities flow to the markets where they command the highest prices. To say that the discount rate is low is merely another way of saying that the price of bills of exchange is high. Thus, if the prevailing discount rate is 6 per cent per annum, the price of a 90-day bill of exchange for $10,000 is $9,850, while, if the prevailing discount rate is only 4 per cent, the price of the same bill is $9,900. Money lenders and dealers in bills of exchange sell them in the best markets. London, as we have said, normally holds many of them. But an increase in the London discount rate is equivalent to a decrease in the price paid for such bills in London. The flow of bills from other countries will be reduced or stopped, some foreign bills held in London may be resold to their home markets, and under extraordinary conditions, English bills may even be exported.

Important secondary reserve of London market in its holdings of foreign bills

The fact is that in its holdings of foreign bills, the London market has a secondary reserve of very great significance. The commercial paper which constitutes this reserve is a commodity the price of which varies exactly but inversely with the rate of discount. Slight changes suffice to turn it from an import to an export. It is thus an automatic mechanism by which England's trade balance is in normal times kept in a state of delicate equilibrium. When an adverse movement of the foreign exchanges threatens a drain of gold, the Bank of England, by raising its discount rate, avoids losses of gold by substituting for it a retarded inflow and an accelerated outflow of commercial paper and, on occasion, of investment securities. If, for example, the New York money market is demanding gold from London, London is normally able to transfer or pass on the demand to other countries by virtually saying to them: "We have changed our prices so that it will not be profitable for you to continue sending us bills of exchange and securities. In fact, you may find it profitable to take some of these things off our hands. Pay us, if you will, by sending New York the gold it is demanding." Thus the London money market in normal times should not be thought of as a gigantic financial center in which gold and investments are concentrated in enormous quantities, but rather as a sensitive intermediary or buffer through which the strains and stresses created by changes in the world's currents of international trade are transmitted and, in part, softened and absorbed.

London's international money market position cause and effect of low rates

It is a curious paradox that the London money market has been able to gain and hold this unique position largely because its discount rates are normally exceedingly low. For its discount rates are low partly because the banking business can be conducted in London economically. An enormous edifice of credit can be safely erected there on a relatively small gold foundation. London's low discount rate is thus seen to be at once the cause and effect of London's position in the international money market, and London's position in the international money market in a similar way is the cause and effect of her low discount rates.

Changes in relative importance of New York and London due to war

Notable among the many financial changes resulting from the Great War were New York's relative gain and London's relative decline as an international financial center. The positions of England and the United States were for the time being, at least, completely reversed. The United States suddenly became the world's greatest creditor nation, while England found itself, strangely enough, in the position of a debtor. The United States, thanks to the elasticity of the federal reserve system, was able to maintain the gold standard unimpaired throughout the war and the years of financial turmoil which followed. Moreover, during the early years of the war before the United States was a participant, American trade grew at the expense of the trade of the belligerent nations. Bills drawn upon New York rather than upon London came to be used in many parts of the world – in Latin America, for example – in financing a considerable portion of international trade. The demand for bills on New York as a means of paying European indebtedness also increased the prestige of the dollar at the expense of the pound sterling. With the general collapse of European currencies the stability of the dollar gave a further advantage to bills on New York.

Why London will probably never cease to be the world's clearing-house

Some of these changes are likely to be permanent. The New York money market, with the vast wealth of the United States and the largest gold reserves in the world behind it, was certain, some even thought, permanently to displace the

London market as the world's central foreign exchange clearing-house. Now there is no question but that in the future the international importance of the New York money market will be greater than it has been in the past, and that many international purchases which were formerly paid for in sterling will in the future be paid for in dollars, but these facts do not imply that London will cease to be the world's clearing-house. London's position is founded not so much upon the magnitude of English capital, of English trade, or of English gold reserves, as upon the highly organized and perfected machinery of the London money market, upon the elasticity rather than the sheer bulk of English banking reserves, upon the varied character and world-wide distribution of English trade, and upon England's geographical position, bringing London close to the other financial centers of Europe.

Editors' note

a Chapter 31 of the Grolier *Book of Popular Science* entitled "The Mystery of Money" (included in this selection as Chapter 33).

37 Insurance and speculation

How economic risks are diminished by combination and organization

The good and evil speculation does

The Book of Popular Science (1924; revised 1929) New York: The Grolier Society. Group IX Ch. 35: 4861–71

In popular discussion insurance and speculation are often confused with gambling. As a matter of fact, as we shall see, the individual differences and peculiarities of these three forms of activity are much more striking than are their similarities and likenesses.

Insurance is really the direct opposite of gambling. The peculiar characteristic of gambling is that it always involves the *creation* or *unnecessary assumption of risk*. If I gamble by tossing a coin or by throwing dice, I assume a risk and incur a chance of loss as well as a chance of gain in a manner that is wholly arbitrary and unnecessary. The coin need not have been tossed had I not so willed, and even if it had been tossed, I need not have entangled my personal fortunes with the outcome of the throw. In a horse race it normally happens that one horse wins and that the others are defeated. But this need not affect my personal fortunes. There is absolutely no risk to me in the outcome of any horse race unless I create the risk by betting on it.

It is not our purpose here to discuss the morality of gambling. We are merely concerned with its economic characteristics. We have seen that it is unnecessary, that it involves the creation of risk. And gambling has a further economic disadvantage. In the long run and on the average it necessarily involves *a net social loss*. The utility of gambling gains cannot offset the real disutility of gambling losses. To make the point clear, imagine that A and B both have incomes of $1000 per year. They wager one against the other $500 on the outcome of a certain event. A wins; B loses. A's income for the year is now $1500, while B's is only $500. For reasons which we have already discussed and which are so obvious as scarcely to need explanation, there is more difference between incomes of $1000 and $500 than between incomes of $1000 and $1500. Measured in terms of utility, A's gain does not offset B's loss. Unless successful gamblers are in general poorer men than unsuccessful ones, unless, in other words, gambling involves on the whole a transfer of wealth from the rich to the poor – an absurdly impossible assumption – it follows that gambling is responsible for a net social loss of utility.

Gambling is not merely nonproductive; it *destroys* rather than creates utility. This conclusion gains increased significance when we take account of the further fact that gambling gains are very commonly spent in a wasteful and extravagant fashion. The real costs, the hazards undergone, are forgotten. The winnings of gambling, easily got, are easily spent.

In economic analysis we thus find a strong case against gambling. And we have purposely taken no account of the fact that gambling very often weakens the moral fiber of the individual, although that fact has economic importance. Gambling makes men less inclined to the sustained and systematic effort which the work of economic production requires.

How, then, does insurance differ from gambling? Is not a fire insurance contract a wager between the insurance company and the insured? Does not the one virtually wager that the insured property will not be damaged by fire within the year, while the other wagers that it will? The analogy implied in such questions is wholly superficial. The man who does *not* insure his building against destruction by fire is the real gambler. He is virtually making a wager that the property will not be damaged by fire. Now when a man makes a bet, and later covers or cancels it by betting on the other side, he is, in his first transaction, a gambler, but in his second transaction he is destroying or annihilating the gambling transaction. The second transaction is technically termed a "hedge." Insurance, it will be clear, is really hedging. Subjected to actual and unavoidable risks of property losses from conflagration, from hail or drought, or from theft, the man who does not seek to remove the risk by hedging, that is, by insuring, is the true gambler. In a similar way, the man who buys a life insurance policy should not be deemed a gambler. He should not be thought of as wagering that he will die within a relatively short term of years while the insurance company wagers on his longevity! In truth of course, the actual unavoidable chance of his death subjects those dependent upon him for support to a real economic risk. Life insurance in some measure cancels or offsets that risk. It is a hedge.

The insurer not a gambler any more than is the insured

But, it may be argued, admitting that in both life insurance and property insurance, the insured should not be regarded as a gambler, is not the insurance contract always a wager so far as the *insurer*, usually an insurance company, is concerned? For the insured the risks in the case are unavoidable and necessary. Unlike the gambler's risks, they are not created nor are they arbitrarily assumed. They exist in the nature of the case. One has a choice between one of two alternatives: one may either carry the risk for one's self or one may shift the risk to an insurer. But to the insurer, we must admit, the assumption of risk is hardly necessary. Is not the insurer, therefore, a gambler? No, by reason of the curious paradox that as insurance is organized today the insurer, or the one who assumes risk, incurs little or no risk himself. Organized insurance really involves two principal elements, first, the insurance contract, by which risk is transferred from the insured to the insurer in return for a definite determined premium or price; second, the annihilation of the risks thus transferred from the insured to the insurer by their combination in large groups where scientifically predictable law, rather than chance, reigns. The blotting out of risk through the combination of risks is thus an essential function of insurance.

The law of large numbers the foundation of modern insurance

Whether a given individual will die today, a year from today or in twenty years, is a wholly indeterminate matter even though there may be certain probabilities in favor of one outcome or another. But in a large population the number who will die in a given year is, putting aside the effects of epidemics of unusual severity, predictable with a high degree of accuracy. This will be true even of the number of deaths among men of any given age, or in given occupations. It will be true in some measure of deaths from different causes. The death rate, in a progressive community, tends to decrease slowly through the years. But from year to year it is constant enough to make it suitable for use by insurance companies. The *law of large numbers* is the foundation of insurance. In some cases the law of large numbers seems to extend down into groups that are represented by very small numbers indeed. Comparatively rare events seem sometimes to come with remarkable regularity. One example quoted in books on the theory of probability is the number of Prussian cavalrymen killed each year by the kick of a horse. For the years from 1875 to 1894 the number of casualties per year varied only between three and eighteen, and their distribution among the different army corps was astonishingly regular. So the number of suicides or the number of murders among persons, say, of a given race, in a large city, will, year after year, bear an astonishingly constant proportion to the total numbers of the population affected.

Insurance is built upon the scientific principle that the combination of disconnected, individual, chance events gives an aggregate result that is so dependable that it can be used as a practical basis of calculation. Accident insurance, fire insurance, in fact, property insurance of all kinds, have a less adequate basis than life insurance, but as experience is increased and is more scientifically recorded and analyzed, the basis of rate-making in those fields is becoming more and more definite and satisfactory.

Insurance deals with necessary risks, gambling with unnecessary

We have said above that, in order that the result should be dependable and predictable, the events with which insurance concerns itself must be separate or disconnected. This condition is highly important. A great conflagration, such as that in San Francisco, will sometimes upset the calculations of fire insurance companies. In the case of such a conflagration the losses are not disconnected; the burning of one building follows from the burning of another. In their rates, fire insurance companies take account of this "conflagration hazard," as it is called, but its amount is necessarily conjectural. So in life insurance: it may sometimes happen that a great epidemic or a great war may introduce real variations – real risk, that is – but even under these exceptional conditions, the insuring of lives remains on the whole a business attended with as little risk as almost any other under the sun. From every point of view, we may conclude, insurance, as organized today, is not gambling. It deals with necessary risks, gambling with unnecessary risks. It creates utilities by distributing and thus softening losses that would otherwise cut deeply into the incomes of millions of individuals exposed to the manifold risks of life. It destroys risks; gambling creates them.

In law, insurance always means an insurance *contract*, an agreement by means of which risk is transferred from one person to another. In economic analysis, the *transfer* of risk is not so important as the reduction of risk to certainty by means of organization and combination. It is the economist rather than the lawyer who speaks when the phrase "self-insurance" is used. This refers to the practice of eliminating risk, or rather of reducing the range of uncertainty, by a wide distribution of investments or of other property holdings. Thus a large corporation with many plants located in different parts of the country may find it more economical to "carry its own insurance." That is, it does not enter into an insurance contract by which the risk is transferred to an insurer, nor is it even necessary that part of its annual earnings should be put aside into an "insurance fund" so that there will be something in reserve to cover large unexpected losses. The establishment of an insurance fund may be in a particular case a matter of ordinary business prudence; it is not on that account necessarily a part of self-insurance. The essential things in self-insurance are the number and the distribution of the company's plants or other holdings. Serious losses from fire are not likely to occur in any one week or in any one year to many of a company's plants, if they are located in different towns.

In the experience of American railroads, losses from fire and flood or from railway accidents have been found to be distributed evenly enough so that few companies have thought it worth while to establish special insurance funds. Such losses are commonly charged to operating expense and they are rarely large enough to lead to important fluctuations in earnings.

Self-insurance is not "putting too many eggs in the same basket"

In a similar way, the moneyed man who distributes his investments among many different types of securities is protecting himself by using the principle of self-insurance. Self-insurance in this case is simply obedience to the old injunction not to put all one's eggs into one basket. The use of this principle makes it possible for investors or endowed institutions, like universities and colleges, to secure a larger income than would be possible if they had to limit themselves to one or two classes of investments or securities. By holding a good many different types and classes of securities the private investor and the institution can afford to put a certain amount of money into securities which are not of the very safest order, and which for that very reason yield a higher annual rate of return. The large investor, it is clear, will do better to put his money into securities which yield a 6 per cent return, even if he occasionally meets with small losses, rather than to restrict himself to gilt-edged securities of almost absolute soundness which yield only 4 or 5 per cent return. The principle of self-insurance finds many other illustrations in the ordinary conduct of life. A housewife, closing her home for the summer, hid her silver in different parts of the house in the hope that if housebreakers entered they would not be likely to find all of it. In so doing, the housewife was applying the principle of self-insurance.

The important difference between destroying risk and eliminating loss

These examples make it clear that when we say that insurance destroys risk, we mean not that insurance prevents loss but that it *decreases the margin of uncertainty* with respect to the magnitude of unavoidable losses. Life insurance does not prolong a man's life. It does not eliminate the economic loss which families and the community suffer when men are cut off in the prime of their productive powers. It is certain that a fairly definite number of such men will die in each successive year. Insurance does not diminish the real loss; it distributes it in such a way that what would have been the uncertainty of the individual case is merged in the certainty of the common lot. The absolute unknown chance of death of a particular bread-winner is merged in the certainty that a certain number of bread-winners will die in a given year. There is an important difference, therefore, between destroying *risk* and eliminating *loss*.

It should be remembered, however, that by eliminating risk by cushioning and distributing the effect of the blows of adverse fate, insurance really lessens the net effects of loss. In fact, any institution or any system which leads to the more equal distribution of either gains or losses increases utility, just as gambling or any other activity that tends toward a more unequal distribution of wealth diminishes the sum total of utility. While insurance, therefore, does not prevent loss, it lessens the destruction of utility which accompanies economic loss.

Speculation gets a much worse reputation than it always deserves

We now pass from the subject of insurance to that of speculation. Is speculation merely a species of gambling? Is it, like insurance, gambling's opposite? Or is it neither one thing nor the other? Popular hostility and distrust of speculation are undoubtedly widespread. In the minds of many people the speculator is a gambler. The worth and value of insurance – the joint product of science and of business enterprise – has come to be accepted by the community: not so with speculation. Not only is it commonly classed with gambling, but it is charged with responsibility for all sorts of economic losses. The consumer holds that speculation is responsible for the fact that prices are high; at the same time the farmer is likely to be blaming it because prices are low. The businessman and the banker are likely to shift to the speculator blame for the crises which recurrently work havoc in modern industry and finance.

Now it must be admitted at the outset that there may be some truth in such charges. But on the whole, they are more nearly false than true. The individual professional speculator is often a gambler in the sense that he conducts his transactions in the gambling spirit. This adverse characterization is by no means true of all speculators, some of whom are scientific students of economic and financial conditions. But even if all speculators were as individuals no better than gamblers, it would hardly be fair on that account to bring a wholesale indictment against the institution of speculation itself. We are not concerned here so much with the morals of the individual as with the general and economic aspect of an institution.

The two essential differences between speculation and gambling

From this point of view, what are the essential differences between speculation and gambling? They are two. In the first place, as we have seen, gambling involves the creation of unnecessary risks. Speculation, like insurance, has to do with risks that exist in the nature of the case. The second difference is that gambling does not alter or affect the outcome of the event which is the subject of the wager. In an honestly conducted horse race the best horse will win whether or not he happens to be a favorite in the betting. The fact that a coin is to pass into the possession of a person who correctly guesses how it will fall after being tossed in no way affects the outcome of the toss. Speculation, on the other hand, actually affects prices. That is, it affects and in part determines the outcome of the particular event with which speculation is concerned. This will be made clear if we pause to consider the distinction between speculation and bucket-shop operations.

The distinction between speculation and bucket-shop operations

The operator of a bucket-shop usually maintains, to outward appearances, a broker's shop in which actual speculation involving actual buying and selling is conducted. The difference is that the operator of a bucket-shop does not execute the orders given him to buy and sell certain securities. He merely records these orders and pays his customers the gains and collects from them the losses which would have been theirs if the orders had been actually executed. In other words, the bucket-shop proprietor merely bets against his customers. He conducts a gambling establishment in which the gamblers are betting on the prices of commodities or securities instead of on the outcome of horse races or on the turn of a roulette wheel. The bucket-shop operator has a margin or advantage as against his customers in that he charges them a commission such as a reputable broker would charge on actual transactions. In addition, the bucket-shop operator knows that on the average his customers are more likely to be wrong than right and, moreover, he is sometimes able shrewdly to guide their operations so that they will be to his own ultimate advantage. It is unsafe to do business with a man whose profits come from your mistakes.

Turning to actual speculation, we find an entirely different state of affairs. Legitimate speculative transactions are actual and legally enforcible purchases and sales. As such, their influence on prices is precisely like that of any other purchases and sales. Speculative purchases and sales enter into and constitute part of the actual supply and demand of the market. It is on this very account, however, that speculation is sometimes condemned! Its influence on price is said to be unwholesome, arbitrary and in general disturbing. Let us examine some of these allegations and try to see what truth there is in them.

Some of the allegations against speculation in influencing prices

Take, for example, the common charge that speculative supplies of commodities – supplies which are added to the actual physical products available for the market – force prices down to an unduly low level. This kind of complaint is likely to come, in all honesty, from farmers and cotton growers who sometimes feel that the profits of their own toil go in large measure not to themselves but to speculators, whom they consider, therefore, to be merely economic parasites. Such critics are prone to point to the fact that the volume of wheat or of cotton sold by speculators is generally very much greater than the number of bushels of actual wheat or pounds of actual cotton available. It is this surplus or speculative supply which pushes the price of such products down to an unprofitable point, they say.

The error in this criticism is that it fails to take account of the fact that each speculative sale is accompanied by a purchase. Just in the measure that speculation increases supply, so also, in the same measure, it inevitably increases demand. We do not refer to the fact that all of the cotton or wheat that speculators sell on any given day must in some way find buyers, for it is easily possible that in order to induce persons to buy the quantities offered, if these happen to be very large, prices must be forced down for the time being to a low point. The important fact is that every speculator who sells wheat today must either have previously purchased it or he must purchase it later to cover his sale. Take, for example, a speculator who sells wheat today because he believes that the price is going to be lower later on. In such circumstances, the speculator might enter into a contract to deliver wheat two months from today. By his very selling operation, therefore, he has virtually committed himself to buy an equivalent amount of wheat within the next two months. His selling operations today may somewhat depress the price of wheat; his buying operations later on will in all probability have a corresponding tendency to raise the price.

In the long run speculation cannot affect general trend of average prices

There is no necessity for pushing this analysis much further. The fundamental point is simple and obvious. In the long run, through a period of successive years, speculation cannot possibly affect the general trend of the average price of wheat or of cotton or of any other commodity. So far as speculation affects prices at all, its force is spent in determining the *variations* or movements of prices in shorter periods of time, that is, in successive weeks or months, or of successive days. Whether the average price of cotton at the end of the third decade of the twentieth century is higher or lower than was the price of cotton at the beginning of that century is a fact wholly outside of the range of influence of speculation. The sole determinants are the actual supply and demand of the ultimate producers and ultimate consumers of cotton. But if we were to trace a diagram of the fluctuations of the price of cotton from 1901 to 1930, we should undoubtedly find it necessary to attribute many of the particular fluctuations or undulations of the line of prices to the effects of speculation. The further question at once suggests itself: Is the general effect of speculation upon the variations of prices wholesome or harmful? Does speculation tend to make prices more stable or more variable?

Tendency of prudent speculation to diminish variations in price

We are not yet ready to attempt a full or definitive answer to these questions. But of one thing we may be fairly sure: if speculators were, in general, well-informed and prudent in their operations, the net effect of speculation would diminish the variations of prices. This follows from the simple fact that so far as the speculator can foresee probable changes in prices, and just so far as he acts accordingly, just so far will his operations tend to eliminate those very changes. Suppose, for example, that the present price of wheat is $2 a bushel, and suppose that the general conditions of supply and demand are such that, in the absence of speculation, the price would inevitably drop to $1.50 per bushel at the end of three months. Imagine, now, that speculators, by careful market observation and analysis, have determined the facts and that they act accordingly. Using the mechanism afforded by contracts for future delivery, they will sell wheat today with the expectation of buying wheat later, say, three months from today, at a lower price. Now it is clear that this speculative supply, as it is called, coming into the market today, will lower the price considerably below $2 per bushel, while the purchase the speculators make later will increase the price of wheat three months from now to considerably more than $1.50 per bushel. In general, it is fair to say, these speculative operations will virtually move wheat from a time at which the demand for it as indicated by its price is relatively low, to a time at which the demand measured in terms of price is relatively greater. In so doing, of course the speculators will have performed a public service not only to agriculturists but to the consumer as well. When the price of wheat is low, some part of the supply may be devoted to relatively unimportant uses; when the price of wheat is unduly high, inconvenient and irksome economies may be necessary. By smoothing out the differences in prices of wheat at different periods, speculation tends to distribute its consumption in such a way that the best use is made of the aggregate supply. Speculation cannot alter the number of bushels of wheat in the market. But by operation upon the price of wheat, it may distribute the consumption of wheat in such a way that the utility of the total supply is increased. This is one of the ways, but only one of the ways, in which the speculator, so far as he operates wisely and shrewdly, is in reality a producer of wealth.

How every business man is a risk taker and therefore a speculator

Another of the beneficent results of organized speculation is that it makes it possible for those members of the community who are unwilling or unable to bear the burden of economic risk to shift such burdens to the shoulders of men whose business it is to assume them. *The speculator is a specialist in risk taking.* Risk in some form or another is found in all modern industries. In fact, from one point of view, it is wholly proper to say that every business man, every profit seeker, is a risk taker and therefore a speculator. He speculates, we may say, with respect to the kind of goods that the market will demand and the prices which the market will pay. He speculates with respect to the operations of his competitors and their effects upon his own business. In a host of other ways, too, he takes unavoidable risks. Some of these risks are inseparable from the business man's operations. Some of them he may get rid of by transferring them as we have said, to professional speculators.

How the manufacturer transfers some of his risks to professional speculators

Take, for example, the cotton manufacturer. The price of cotton fabrics, especially of the cheaper grades, necessarily fluctuates as the price of raw cotton fluctuates. In securing his annual supply of material the cotton manufacturer incurs the risk that, after he has bought, the price of raw cotton will drop to a lower point, that the price of his own product – cotton fabrics – will therefore fall and that he will incur large losses. If, on the other hand, it should happen that the price of raw cotton should rise, the manufacturer would gain by reason of the fact that he could sell his manufactured fabrics at a correspondingly higher price. But ordinarily the cotton manufacturer does not wish to subject himself to these particular risks of loss or gain. He is a manufacturer, not a professional speculator. He desires to devote his time and attention to the manufacturing and selling of cotton fabrics and, of course, he wants to secure such profits as he can get from those operations. He is not in a position to incur the chance of large losses from an adverse turn of the cotton market, even if there is an equal chance of correspondingly large gains. He prefers to pass these particular risks over to the speculator. He accomplishes this by the device known as "hedging." When he purchases raw cotton for his mills, he *sells* in the speculative market through a cotton broker an equal amount of cotton or of contracts to deliver cotton. Then as rapidly as the raw cotton in his warehouses is made up into finished cotton goods and sold at prices which are in large part determined by the then prevailing price of raw cotton, he *buys* an equivalent amount of cotton in the speculative market. When his stock of raw material is finally disposed of, he will have bought sufficient cotton through his broker to cover or offset all of the engagements to deliver cotton that he entered into in the speculative market at the beginning of his speculations. Any profits that he might otherwise have made from a possible rise in the price of raw material are offset by corresponding losses on his speculative transactions. On the other hand, the losses which he would have suffered if the price of raw cotton had dropped have been offset by the profits on his speculative transactions. He has freed himself from the purely speculative risks attending the buying and selling of cotton at the relatively small expense of the commissions he has had to pay his broker. Dealers in grain and other produce, millers and men in other industries are able, by hedging, to restrict their own chances of profit and loss to those necessarily connected with their business operations. The chances of loss or gain resulting from *price changes* are shifted to other shoulders.

There is no doubt that by the facilities it offers for hedging speculation performs a real service to many producers and dealers. This service, however, would not suffice to justify speculation if it were true, as some claim, that speculation itself is primarily responsible for those ups and downs in prices which are primarily responsible for business losses and for general business disturbances. One could hardly justify speculation on the ground that it affords facilities for hedging if it were true that the necessity for hedging or protecting one's self from the effects of unforeseeable price fluctuations were itself something for which speculation is responsible. We must return, therefore, to the problem of the effects of speculation upon the stability of prices.

Actual short-time fluctuations of markets originate in speculation

We have seen that in the nature of the case it can have no possible influence upon what we call the long-time trends of prices. For example, the general level of prices in the United States in 1913 was about 30 per cent higher than the average level in the decade from 1890 to 1900. Speculation did not and could not have had anything to do with this general change. At the other extreme, we find fluctuations in price which are of extremely short duration. Thus the price of wheat or of cotton or of the shares in a large corporation changes not only from week to week but from day to day and from hour to hour. These short-time fluctuations are in many cases the effect of speculative buying and selling. It is very likely that without organized speculation, that is, without stock exchanges and produce exchanges, short-time variations in price would remain, and, judging by past experience, it is likely that they would be more erratic and violent even than under speculation. But the fact remains that the actual short-time fluctuations of present-day markets originate in speculation. They are the results of the uneven operation of the forces of supply and demand, and in the modern market those forces very largely take the form of speculative buying and selling.

Tendency of organized speculation to correct seasonal price variations

But there is yet a third type of price variation and, from some points of view, the most important of all. There are variations not only from hour to hour, and from decade to decade, but from month to month and season to season. There is no doubt in the minds of competent and careful students of the problem that organized speculation in staple commodities reduces the range and the severity of these intermediate or seasonal variations in price. If it were not for speculation the price of wheat and cotton would be exceedingly low just after the harvest season, for demand would be small and supply would be large. Higher prices a few months later would be a comparative certainty. Some persons, it might be thought, would take advantage of the low prices of the harvest period and would buy commodities then and hold them for higher prices later on. This is true. But such operations *are* speculation. There is little doubt that farmers are able to get vastly more for their crops immediately after the harvest than would be the case if it were not for the great open markets where organized speculation is conducted. There market specialists buy and sell wheat and cotton and other commodities always with the constant purpose and effect of securing profits by taking advantage of any foreseeable variations in prices. Just so far as the variations they expect are real, just so far will such speculative buying and selling have the effect of reducing or eliminating them.

As a matter of fact, it is probably a sounder criticism of speculation to say that it too frequently *over-discounts* changes in price. Not only does it eliminate them, but it even in many instances reverses them! The competition of speculators may go so far that what would have been a period of falling prices may be turned into one of rising prices. It is likely, however, that this does not happen so frequently or on such a scale that it gives the basis for a really serious indictment of speculation.

More speculation than is necessary to accomplish best results

A more serious criticism is implied in the fact that there is vastly *more* speculation than is necessary to accomplish all the good that speculation can possibly do. In particular, there is too much uninformed, inexpert speculation; there are too many transactions which are conducted merely in the gambling spirit, or by men who are induced by "tips" and rumors to venture their money in losing operations. The speculation which accomplishes good is based upon expert and scientific analysis of economic tendencies. The speculation which does harm is that which is conducted by the ignorant and the ill-informed and, we must add, by the wealthy man who plays the game with loaded dice. When the large speculator plays with loaded dice, it is usually in one of two wholly different ways. He may be making use of inside information which is his as a director or officer of a corporation, – virtually, that is, as trustee for the stockholders. In such cases, he should be held accountable to them for his profits. Or he may make use of the sheer power of operations conducted on a large scale to crush the small fry who are in the market, and to manipulate prices for the time being to fit his own ends. No man is so wealthy that he can permanently depress or inflate the market for a particular commodity or security by buying or selling on a large scale. But financial power does make it possible to manipulate artificially the prices of commodities or of securities for the time being. In this evil, as yet unremedied, there inheres one of the principal defects of speculation as conducted today.

Foolish condemnation of dealing in futures, a necessity of modern business

Speculation is sometimes condemned on absurdly foolish grounds. Thus we sometimes hear it said that "dealing in futures" is something especially to be condemned. Future wheat and future cotton seem to be non-existing myths; trading in them has an appearance of unreality. Yet a moment's thought will show that modern industry is impossible without dealing in futures, and that the system of dealing in them permeates almost every nook and corner of modern business. The contractor who agrees to build a house for you at a stated price is dealing in futures. The steel mill which takes an order for rails or for structural steel is dealing in futures. Banking transactions almost without exception involve dealing in futures. The workman who accepts employment is dealing in futures; he is making a contract for the future delivery of his services. Some state legislatures have made fruitless attempts to prohibit dealing in futures. Any systematic and logical attempt to put such a prohibition into force would absolutely stop the wheels of industry.

Criticism of speculative buying and selling as not real, delivery being seldom made

Again, it is sometimes urged that speculative buying and selling are not real buying and selling because it rarely happens that actual delivery is made in fulfilment of speculative contracts. Now it is perfectly true that the amount of speculative purchases and sales is enormous as compared with the amount of commodities actually delivered, but the explanation is, of course, that through a *clearing* system speculative purchases and sales are canceled one against another – just as credits and debits are canceled on the books of a bank or in a bank clearing-house. Suppose a man buys a hundred thousand bushels of wheat for delivery two months later and then, within the intervening period, agrees to deliver a hundred thousand bushels at the same date. Let us suppose that *A* has bought from *B* and has sold an identical amount to *C*. Is the transaction less real, is it in any way tainted with immorality, merely because *A*, instead of taking delivery from *B* and turning the goods over to *C*, instructs *B* to make delivery directly to *C*, *A* merely paying his losses or receiving his profits on the transaction as the case may be? The clearing methods used in actual speculation are merely an enlarged application of this principle. In a group of twenty-six men whom we may represent by all the letters of the alphabet, it may happen that A is the only ultimate buyer and that Z is the only ultimate seller. Is there any reason why the commodities should change hands twenty-five times instead of being transferred directly from Z to A?

"Short-selling," the only effective bear move to influence market prices

Again, there are some critics of organized speculation who would prohibit "short-selling." On the produce exchanges, and in general on all of the exchanges of Europe, short-selling takes the form of contracts for future delivery entered into before the seller has bought the commodity or security which he has agreed to deliver. On the stock exchanges of the United States, a short sale is not a contract for future delivery, for actual delivery is made of securities borrowed for the purpose. To prohibit short-selling would be to weaken greatly the supply of "bear" side of the speculative market as compared with the demand or "bull" side. Thus the bears in the market who honestly believe that present prices are too high and that decline is imminent would have no effective way of utilizing their judgment in the market in such a way as to influence prices. The general aspects of short-selling are already covered by what we have said about dealing in futures. It is found not only in speculation but in business transactions of every imaginable type.

Exaggeration in fluctuation due to highly inflated bull market

We return to the fundamental fact that the peculiar difficulty with speculation is over-speculation. Too many men speculate on too slender a fund of information. One of the bad results of over-speculation is that the necessary ups and downs of prices are sometimes exaggerated. In the stock market, for example, when prices begin to move upward and especially when some speculators have made spectacular profits, outsiders are attracted to the market and buy, usually with no better basis for their buying than their belief that since prices have gone up, they must continue to go up! The increased buying of outsiders who are always attracted into a rising or bull market further stimulates the rise of prices. The apparent profits made from the continuing rise are reinvested in yet further purchases which put prices higher and higher. The net result is a highly inflated bull account or, in less technical language, a tremendous volume of over-purchasing.

Of course, just as soon as, for one reason, or another, prices begin to decline, some men sell in order to realize their profits before it is too late, while others are forced to sell because the decline in values makes it necessary for them either to sell or to deposit more money as security for the broker who is acting as agent for them or the banker who has advanced funds. As a result of such selling the decline of prices is likely to be even more spectacular and precipitate than was their rise. Thousands of men lose money and many industries are likely to be severely shaken.

The few who profit are wise professional speculators who have seen the same thing happen again and again and who have learned to profit by discounting the mistakes of the majority.

Speculation in stocks more dependent on money market than that in produce

These speculative swings are more common and more violent on the stock exchange than on the produce exchange. This is partly because speculation in stocks is much more closely dependent upon the condition of the money market than is speculation in commodities. This, in turn, is due to the American system of forbidding contracts for future delivery on the stock exchanges. When, as on the produce exchanges of the United States and on the stock exchanges of Europe, contracts for future delivery are permitted, a much larger volume of transactions are canceled or offset one against another. When immediate deliveries have to be made, as in the case of sales on the New York stock exchange, and when the speculative purchaser has to receive and pay for his security at once, there is certain to be an enormous demand for bank loans with which to finance these purely speculative transactions. In the United States, speculation, and especially stock speculation, is carried on with borrowed money to a larger degree than it is in any other country. This is one of the factors which undoubtedly is responsible for the speculative excesses we have already mentioned. Speculation is too closely allied to the money market; it is too sensitive and responsive to interest changes and discount rates. In turn, purely speculative changes react on general conditions in the money market and thence necessarily upon the general condition of industry. It is only fair to say, however, that since the inauguration of the federal reserve system many of the worst evils arising from the connection between the money market and speculation have been removed. But the fact remains that call or demand loans on speculative securities occupy a relatively larger place in New York than anywhere else in the world, and that the influence of this type of loan, subject as it is to a highly variable interest rate, upon speculation and the banking situation, is not wholesome.

Produce exchanges about only example today of perfect competition

Thus, we see that, despite the good that speculation really accomplishes, there remain real evils attached to it. Some of these, perhaps, are part of the price we have to pay for its benefits. Others can and should be remedied. We should not allow the presence of these admitted evils to obscure the fact that speculation performs a number of important economic functions. On the whole it exerts a stabilizing influence upon price, and in particular it reduces what we have called the seasonal variations of price. It makes it possible for the risks arising from price fluctuations to be shifted to a class of professional risk takers. It provides open markets in which, despite the occasional presence of short-lived attempts at manipulation, prices are determined in the long run by the powerful play of competitive forces. There are no more perfectly competitive markets, no markets in which the forces of supply and demand fix prices more definitely and accurately, than are furnished by the great organized produce exchanges. In fact, they afford about the only actual illustration of that "perfect competition" which is otherwise met with only in economic theory.

How great an advantage it is to have open and uniform prices, we are all in these days too likely to forget. Consider the position of an investor desiring to purchase shares in a certain corporation. Without the open speculative market there could be no insurance that the price he is asked to pay for a particular share is a fair price. There would be no single market prices. Men would have no real standard by which to measure the value of their holdings. They would be operating in the dark while now they operate in the light that open markets afford. Sometimes the light is a little dim, sometimes it does not shine as steadily as it might. But there is scarcely any other area in the whole wide field of economic life that is so well illuminated, as are the great organized speculative markets.

38 Money and prices

*How unstable prices work havoc to
industry and injustice to individuals*

The business cycle an economic
disease

The Book of Popular Science (1924; revised 1929) New York: The Grolier Society.
Group IX Ch. 36: 5109–20

The problems of economic science, unlike those of the natural sciences, have the
bad habit of getting into politics. Scientific questions cannot be settled by popular
vote. The ballot box is a useful instrument for its purpose, but it is not a piece of
scientific apparatus.

The fundamental difficulty with political solutions of the problems of economic
science is that they are likely to be arrived at not by scientific analysis but as a
result of a test of the strength of different opposed economic interests. It is one
thing to discuss the really scientific arguments for protection or for free trade; it
is quite another thing to decide to increase or reduce protective tariff duties
because stronger interests – those which for the time being control the most
votes – gain by the change.

In the same way it is one thing to try to reach scientific conclusions respecting
the defects in our present monetary system, while it is quite another thing to
introduce innovations in monetary policy born of nothing better than the
temporary political strength of certain economic interests.

It is unfortunate that the particular monetary problem which has most
often been the football of politics is perhaps the most difficult and elusive of
all economic problems, namely, the problem of the value or general purchasing
power of money. The conception of the value or general purchasing power of
money is nothing but a useful and convenient abstraction, – a tool of thought.
In actual fact, of course, money has not one value, one general purchasing
power, but many different specific purchasing powers. Thus, we may properly
speak, having in mind the prices of food, shelter and entertainment, of such
different things as the wheat-value of money, the beefsteak-value of money,
the grand-opera-value of money, the housing-value of money, etc. Probably
we should never have developed the conception of the general value or
purchasing power of money if it had not been for the fact that it often happens
that the different specific values of money vary together or in the same general
direction. The phrase "the value of money" is merely a useful tool in dealing

with problems that are created by these general or common trends in the different values or purchasing powers of money.

As a matter of fact, however, more serious problems are created by the fact that these different values or purchasing powers of money do *not* vary absolutely together. In a period of advancing prices some prices rise faster and farther than others. In a period of falling prices some prices lag behind, or even increase, while other prices are dropping rapidly. Students of the problem are coming to see more and more clearly that the major ills for which our monetary system is responsible are the maladjustments and dislocations of industry brought about by the fact that the army of prices, we might say, does not advance in even file; there is always a vanguard just as there are always stragglers and laggards.

Suppose that all of the different values of money change together and in the same degree. What harm would be done? The manufacturer's expenses of production would increase, but so would the selling price of his products. Consumers would find themselves confronted by higher costs of living, but in the same measure their incomes would also have increased. *Relatively* they would find themselves neither worse nor better off. We may set it down as a truism that just so far as business transactions are conducted on a cash basis the general rise or fall in prices could do no harm whatever, for it would effect no change in the relative positions of the different members of the community.

Debt-paying value of money falls with falling and rises with rising prices

The difficulty is, of course, that many transactions involve the creation of debts. Long-time debts make a particularly difficult problem. Debts are expressed for the most part in terms of monetary units, – dollars, in the United States and Canada. Even if all the other values of money moved up or down together, one particular value, which we may call its *debt-paying* value, would stand out as an exception. In fact, just so long as debts and credits are expressed in money, there can be no escaping the fact that debtors must lose and creditors gain in periods of falling prices, that is, in periods of increasing money values, just as debtors must gain and creditors lose in periods of rising prices. These circumstances give rise to the problem of the standard of deferred payments discussed in Chapter [33]. Debtors, it is fair to say, are usually more vocal, more insistent upon their rights, than are creditors. Prolonged periods of falling prices usually give birth to political movements for cheaper money, that is, for higher prices. But thus far, it has never been recorded that a period of rising prices has been accompanied by a political movement for dearer money. Either debtors are more conscious of their common interest than are creditors or rising prices bring certain advantages to the business community in which creditors, or a large part of them, share.

Before probing any deeper into the problems born of the fact that the different values of money lag, one after another, in periods both of advancing and falling prices, we must turn aside and inquire why prices in general should rise at certain periods and fall at others. Why is there not stability, if not in particular prices, at any rate in the general level of prices?

Variations in the value of money associated with changes in its quantity

From the beginnings of civilization almost down to the present day, wise men have never doubted but that the variations in the values of money were directly associated with changes in the quantity of money. Of course, there have been heretics and scoffers who have claimed that the number of monetary units in circulation has had nothing whatever to do with their value, but among thoughtful men the truth of the "quantity theory" has been generally accepted, and in recent years its truth has been verified by searching statistical investigations. A loose and easy way of explaining the relation between the quantity of money and its value is to say that the laws of supply and demand must apply to money as well as to other commodities, and that just as a large wheat crop has a lower value per bushel than a small crop, so a large supply of money must have a lower purchasing power per dollar than a smaller supply must have. There is nothing really inaccurate in this way of putting the matter, but it is not wholly satisfactory. There are substantial differences between money and ordinary economic commodities. Other commodities are valued because they satisfy human wants. Money directly satisfies no human want, except the morbid desires of the miser. The value of money is to us the *reflected* value of what money will buy for us. We sometimes say that we value things in terms of money. It is truer that we value money in terms of other things.

Increase in volume of money means increase in purchasing power of some persons

It is easy to see, however, just how an increase in the volume of money in a country must lead to an increase in prices. The simplest way of looking at the problem is to realize in the first place that every bit of money is someone's property. The particular bit of money may be the property of the government, of the bank, of the business corporation or of the individual.

Instead of thinking of a country's stock of money as an abstract sum, or as wealth belonging to no one in particular, like the climate or the landscape, picture that stock as divided among millions of individual holders. To its possessor money is purchasing power. One can not possibly increase the stock of money within a country without increasing the purchasing power of certain individuals.

Unless the annual production of wealth is increased, the use of a larger volume of purchasing power will inevitably send prices upward. The new dollars come into the market as competitors of the old. Dollars are the instruments by which their possessors compete for the nation's industrial product and divide it among themselves. If an increased purchasing power is offered for an unchanged volume of goods a rise in prices is an absolutely certain result. An increase in the quantity of money, therefore, leads to a decrease in the different values of money, not merely because there is a greater number of dollars but because a greater number of dollars *will be expended* for goods.

Average price per unit paid for goods depends on amount of money in country

There is another way of looking at the matter which some readers may find helpful. Let us put the reasoning in the form of a series of necessarily connected propositions: (1) the quantity of money and bank checks paid for goods in any year must be equal to the total number of units (pounds, yards, bushels, etc.) of goods sold during a year multiplied by their average prices per unit. (2) The amount of money and of bank checks paid for goods during a year equals the amount of money in the country multiplied by its average velocity of circulation or rate of turn-over plus the quantity of bank deposits subject to check multiplied by their average velocity of circulation or rate of turn-over. (3) Money will tend to be distributed between its two most important uses, hand-to-hand circulation and bank reserves, in fairly constant proportions.

These proportions will depend upon the convenience and the habits of the people with respect to the use of pocket money and bank checks, respectively, in making their purchases. (4) The volume of bank deposits is, by law and by banking practice, limited to a multiple of the amount of money in bank reserves. (5) Having seen that there tends to be a fairly definite relation or connection between the quantity of money in circulation and the amount of bank deposits subject to check, there remain only two other factors to be considered, namely, the rate of turn-over of money and the rate of turn-over of bank deposits. These factors undoubtedly will vary with the habits and customs of the community. But the reader who has followed the analysis thus far will have no difficulty in concluding for himself that *there must be some sort of connection between the amount of money in a country and the average price per unit paid for the goods bought and sold in the markets of that country.*

For ourselves, we feel that the foregoing method of analysis is on the whole less satisfactory than the simpler and more direct method of attack upon the problem which is based upon the fundamental observation that an increase in a country's supply of money is an actual increase in the purchasing power of buyers in that country. We do not mean that a doubling of the supply of money would necessarily cut prices in half, or that reducing the supply of money by 50 per cent would double prices. These results might follow if the economists' favorite phrase, "other things being equal," really described actual facts instead of being merely a convenient way of dividing a complex problem into its separate parts.

General tendency of the value of money in history always downward

It is important to observe that there are three different types of price movements. These may be distinguished from each other by the lengths of the periods of time

Table 38.1 Production of gold in the world from the discovery of America to 1924. Figures for the years 1493–1885 are based on the estimates of Dr. Adolf Soetbeer; for subsequent years, the figures are those of the U.S. Bureau of the Mint

Period	Annual Average for Period		Period	Annual Average for Period	
	Fine Ounces	Value $		Fine Ounces	Value $
1493–1520	186,470	3,855,000	1876–1880	5,543,110	114,586,000
1521–1544	230,194	4,759,000	1881–1885	4,794,755	99,116,000
1545–1560	273,596	5,656,000	1886–1890	5,461,282	112,895,000
1561–1580	219,906	4,546,000	1891–1895	7,882,565	162,947,000
1581–1600	237,267	4,905,000	1896–1900	12,446,939	257,301,000
1601–1620	273,918	5,662,000	1901–1907	18,441,690	382,696,466
1621–1640	266,845	5,516,000	1908	21,422,244	442,837,000
1641–1660	281,955	5,828,000	1909	21,965,111	454,059,100
1661–1680	297,709	6,154,000	1910	22,022,180	455,239,100
1681–1700	346,095	7,154,000	1911	22,348,313	461,980,500
1701–1720	412,163	8,520,000	1912	22,549,335	466,136,100
1721–1740	613,422	12,681,000	1913	22,249,596	459,939,900
1741–1760	791,211	16,356,000	1914	21,240,416	439,078,260
1761–1780	665,666	13,761,000	1915	22,674,568	468,724,918
1781–1800	571,948	11,823,000	1916	21,970,788	454,176,500
1801–1810	571,563	11,815,000	1917	20,289,546	419,422,100
1811–1820	367,957	7,606,000	1918	18,556,920	383,605,552
1821–1830	457,044	9,448,000	1919	17,695,037	365,788,796
1831–1840	652,291	13,484,000	1920	16,303,306	337,019,300
1841–1850	1,760,502	36,393,000	1921	15,959,643	329,874,000
1851–1855	6,410,324	132,513,000	1922	15,440,243	319,178,164
1856–1860	6,486,262	134,083,000	1923	17,790,597	367,764,279
1861–1865	5,949,582	122,989,000	1924	18,826,086	389,169,727
1866–1870	6,270,086	129,614,000			
1871–1875	5,591,014	115,577,000	Total	943,744,568	19,508,892,396

they occupy. In the first place, if we trace the history of money back through the centuries, we shall find that the general tendency of its value has always been downward. Prices in ancient times and in the Middle Ages seem to us ridiculously low.

Now these low prices reflect in part the relatively high value of the precious metals, and in part the relatively larger size of standard money units before the coinage had been subjected to successive adjustments. Thus, in the thirteenth or fourteenth century, sheep could have been purchased in England at about a shilling apiece. A sheepskin was worth about threepence in the money of the time, and the meat was probably worth not more than a farthing a pound. But even at such a price meat was a dearer diet for the people of the time than bread. The discovery of America and the exploitation of the treasures of the New World by the Spanish and the Portuguese, led to a general rise of prices throughout Europe. A veritable economic revolution ensued. Under the stimulus of the new and higher prices, industry and commerce advanced more rapidly than ever before in the world's history.

But even in the subsequent centuries the general curve of prices has continued steadily upward, interrupted only by occasional reverse movements.

But it is not the general upward trend of the price level through the centuries which is responsible for the problems that vex us today. Those problems are associated with two other types of price movements. In the first place, there are movements which continue for several decades or more and which generally reflect changes in the production of the precious metals, improvements in the organization of banking, or the increasing demand for money arising from the growth of industry and trade. These price changes are intermediate in length or duration between the long trends we have discussed above and the shorter cyclical changes which we shall discuss presently.

Thus in most of the western world, the general trend of prices (in terms of either the gold or silver standard) during the first half of the nineteenth century was downward. In the middle of the century came the great gold discoveries in California and Australia, leading to a world-wide rise of prices which reached its culmination in about 1873. Then, partly because the gold output did not keep pace with the increase of industry and trade and partly because, with the general abandonment of bimetallism in this period, there was a larger demand for gold as a monetary metal (for gold had to do a larger part of the monetary work of the world), prices declined, reaching a minimum – the lowest point in the century in fact – about 1896. Next came a period of rising prices, the enormous output of the gold mines of South Africa being the principal cause.

This period of rising prices extended from about 1897 to 1914. Then the Great War brought about a tremendous increase in the public expenditures of the nations of the world. The funds for these vast expenditures were secured in large part by monetary inflation. In most countries, inflation took the form of enormous issues of bank-notes. This period of sharply rising prices, which should be distinguished from the period immediately preceding, in which prices rose much more slowly, came to an end in about 1920.

It is true that in some countries still using irredeemable paper currency – Germany, Austria, Poland and Russia, for example – the price level continued to rise under the influence of further inflation. But, taking the world as a whole, gold prices began to drop or, in other words, the purchasing power of gold began to increase in about 1920.

Table 38.2 Prices and bank-note inflation: 1913–1919.

The general level of prices in 1919 as well as the bank-notes outstanding in that year are expressed as per cents of the corresponding figures for 1913; that is, prices and bank-note issues in 1913 are taken as 100.

Country	Bank-notes	Prices
France	652	429
Italy	667	457
Sweden	329	330
United States	172	214
Canada	251	236
Japan	289	365

So long as the gold standard or any other metallic standard prevails, price movements, such as characterized the periods from 1850 to 1873, from 1874 to 1896, and from 1897 to 1914, are self-corrective. They cannot continue indefinitely: they must be brought to an end by forces which they themselves bring into being. In a period of rising prices, for example, the costs of gold mining, like other costs of production, increase. If prices continue to rise, a point will be reached at which some mines – the poorer ones – will be forced to suspend operations. Few people realize how large a proportion of the world's supply of gold comes from low-grade ores. Securing profits from the mining of such ores is possible only by utilizing all possible operating economies. Relatively slight increases in productive costs are sufficient to reduce the gold output of the world very considerably. For this reason a period of rising prices must come to an end. The output of gold will be reduced and the trend of price changes will be reversed.

In a similar way, prices cannot continue always to move in a downward direction. The lower mining costs that accompany lower prices will make it profitable to mine low-grade ores and even, as in California, to dredge the sandy beds of rivers that drain gold-yielding lands. The gold standard, with all of its imperfections, thus has an automatic, pendulum-like action which helps to prevent extreme variations of the general price level.

We now come to the third, and by all odds the most important, type of general changes in prices. Examining the statistics of prices during the nineteenth and twentieth centuries with any care, we find that the longer movements of prices, up and down, are themselves made up of shorter wavelike movements succeeding one another in a curiously even fashion. Thus in England during the nineteenth century, the crests of the successive waves, though irregularly spaced, seem on the average to be between eight and nine years apart. In the United States the period has been more variable, so that no average could be named which would not be misleading. It is significant that the crests of these wave-like movements of prices coincide with the culminating points of periods of rapid and prosperous business expansion. The intervening valleys mark periods of business depression, often preceded by economic crises.

The observation of these facts has given a new scientific importance to the study of a very old problem: the explanation of economic crises. Everyone is familiar with these business convulsions. They seem to occur at fairly even intervals, apparently without warning. They are characterized by a cessation of buying and selling, by business failures, and by a tight money market. They are followed by long periods of depression, accompanied by all the evils of industrial unemployment. A hundred years ago, men commonly thought of a crisis as a collapse following a speculative "mania." They had in mind the results of such orgies of speculation and of such absolutely high prices as, in 1720, marked the South Sea Bubble in England and John Law's Mississippi Bubble in France. Crises, that is, were thought to be psychological in origin. Enthusiasm and over-optimism were contagious; expansion was carried too far; and the crisis itself might in turn be intensified by the similarly contagious qualities of pessimism. There are men even today who believe that psychology is the root of the matter, that business would be good if business men and buyers could only hypnotize themselves into believing it to be good, that the only thing responsible for a crisis is a general "loss of confidence."

Psychological factors not the fundamental cause of crises

Now, as everyone knows, the human animal is highly imitative, susceptible to suggestion and inclined to follow the lead of his fellows. It is very likely that if it were not for these psychological characteristics business expansion would not so often be overdone and business depression would not be so prolonged as, in

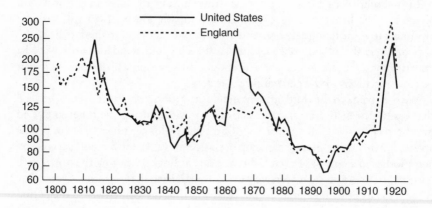

Figure 38.1 Commodity prices in the United States, 1810–1921, and England, 1800–1921
Prices in 1914 = 100

NOTE: This chart is reproduced by the courtesy of the Harvard Committee on Economic Research. The general movement of prices is pictured by stating prices in the different successive years as per cents of prices of 1914. This chart shows several different things very clearly: (1) International trade connects the different countries of the world in such a way that that their price levels must in general move together. (2) The general trend of prices was upward during the period of the Napoleonic wars, ending in 1815. Then prices moved downward until the discoveries of gold in California and Australia turned them upward in the middle of the century. (3) Prices reached the lowest point in the century in 1896. Then they increased under the stimulation of, first, the increasing production of gold, and, second, the monetary inflation of the period of the Great War. (4) The agreement on the movement of prices in England and the United States is especially notable in the case of the changes referred to above, each occupying a considerable number of years. The rise and fall of prices in the greeback period following the American Civil War had, naturally, no counterpart in England. The shorter swings or oscillations of prices, corresponding generally to the ups and downs of business cycles, often occur together in the two countries, but in some cases these shorter cyclical movements are peculiar to the one country or the other.

Table 38.3 Changes in the cost of living in the United States, 1913 to 1924

Item of expenditure	Per cent of increase from 1913 (average) to December of year stated								
	1915	1917	1918	1919	1920	1921	1922	1923	1924
Food	5.0	57.0	87.0	97.0	78.0	49.9	46.6	50.3	51.5
Clothing	4.7	49.1	105.3	168.7	158.5	84.4	71.5	76.3	71.3
Housing	1.5	.1	9.2	25.3	51.1	61.4	61.9	66.5	68.2
Fuel and light	1.0	24.1	47.9	56.8	94.9	81.1	86.4	84.0	80.5
Furniture and Furnishings	10.6	50.6	113.6	163.5	185.4	118.0	108.2	122.4	116.0
Miscellaneous	7.4	40.5	65.8	90.2	108.2	106.8	100.5	101.7	101.7
Total	5.1	42.4	74.4	99.3	100.4	74.3	69.5	73.2	72.5

actual experience, they generally have been. Psychological factors may increase the distance between the crest of the wave of prosperity and the trough of the valley of depression, but they cannot be fundamentally responsible for the *origin* of crises.

Economic crises follow each other with such apparent regularity that many men have thought that there must be in the external world some underlying physical cause. Neither human psychology nor human institutions, it seemed, could explain the regular recurrence of alternating periods of prosperity and depression. The most rhythmical, the most regular of recurrences in the physical world are those associated with the heavenly bodies. The problem might be solved, it was thought, by utilizing the facts of astronomy in combination with those of economics.

Jevons' sun-spot theory of crises

The most famous suggestion of this kind was made by W. S. Jevons, the brilliant English economist, in his "sun-spot theory" of crises. Jevons thought that the severe economic crises in England during two centuries had been about eleven years apart. He believed that this period agreed closely with the average length of the so-called "sun-spot cycle," during which the proportion of the sun's surface covered by spots increases and then decreases in a fairly regular way. The idea is by no means so absurd as it may at first appear. Many scientists have suspected the existence of some relation between the sun-spot cycle and climatic variations, although this connection has never definitely been proved. Variations in the annual rainfall would not have so large a *direct* effect upon the economic life of England as on that of other countries, notably the tropical countries with which England trades. Rainfall would affect English industry by affecting English trade. From sun-spots through rainfall, crops, English imports and English exports, was the route Jevons's speculations followed. Jevons's hypothesis has not been generally accepted, largely because it has been found that the average interval between

English crises has, in fact, been distinctly less than eleven years, while crises in other countries have occurred at quite different dates, and do not in general exhibit an eleven-year interval. But later research has shown that Jevons was right with respect to the length of the sun-spot period in the nineteenth century, although in earlier centuries, it seems to have been considerably less than eleven years.

Professor Moore's theory of association between rainfall and business cycles

Other writers have endeavored to find definite proof of a causal relation between climatic variations and the recurrence of economic crises. Thus, Professor H.L. Moore of Columbia University suspects that there is a recurrent cycle of about eight years in which the annual rainfall passes from a maximum to a minimum and back again. This, he thinks, corresponds with the length of the average business cycle. Although Professor Moore's work is marked by the careful use of scientific methods, his results cannot yet be accepted. The difficulty is that other competent students of rainfall statistics have thought that they have found quite different cycles, five years and fifteen years, for example. The truth is that the investigator intent upon finding a clue to these economic mysteries is likely to find cycles in almost any irregular series of figures! The series are really not long enough, and the cycles not pronounced enough to justify definite conclusions. But with respect to the *existence* of business cycles there can be no doubt, although we need not conclude that they tend to be of any particular length or that they are definitely related to any outward physical phenomenon. In fact, it seems highly probable that economic factors themselves are sufficient to explain the recurrence of crises and that we need not invoke sun-spots, rainfall or any other outside agent.

The economic factors which seem to be responsible are found in the operations of credit and banking. There could be no business cycle if there were no business contracts or no debts. A crisis occurs when men are unable to fulfill their contracts or to pay their debts. A primitive tribe using money or credit might pass through alternating periods of famine and plenty, but it could hardly pass through periods of business prosperity and depression. Just as the collapse of contracts and of credit characterizes crises, so the expansion of business undertakings, and in particular of business debts, characterizes the period of prosperity which precedes a crisis. With this important clue, we may proceed to look a little further into the problem. Let us begin by placing ourselves in imagination at the end of a long period of business following a crisis, just at the point where business recovery is beginning to make itself felt.

During the period of depression, the position of the banks of the country will gradually have been strengthened. The amount of their loans will have decreased and their cash reserves will have increased. The volume of business debts will have been decreased by bankruptcies or by settlements with creditors. The capitalization of many business undertakings will have been reduced. The drop in prices which followed the crisis will have led many men to "write down their inventories," that is, to put a smaller valuation upon their stocks on hand. In fact, during the period of depression, the position of industries and the banks will have become sounder.

When this stage in the cycle is reached, the banks will begin to feel justified in seeking more business. Like other business institutions, they will do this by lowering their prices. A bank's prices are its discount and interest rates. So soon as these are lowered notably there will be increased borrowing. Some foresighted business men will have been waiting for just such a turn in the money market before going ahead with their plans. Other business men will borrow money to use in operations which perhaps would not have been profitable if they had had to pay more for the credit they needed.

The result of increased borrowing will show itself in an increased volume of bank deposits, for bank advances are made largely in the form of deposit credit given to the borrower. But men do not borrow funds to let them remain idle in the bank. They expend them in productive undertakings. The expenditure of these funds constitutes a demand for steel, for lumber, for cement, for machinery, for raw materials and for labor. Influenced by this new volume of buying, prices begin gradually to rise. Wages generally do not begin to increase until later, for in a period of depression many men are out of work and most of these must be given employment before any considerable advance in wages will be possible. The new funds created by the lending operations of the bank are paid out in the various expenses of operating and extending the reviving industries of the country. These new funds pass finally into the hands of consumers in the form of wages, salaries, interest, dividends and rents. With their incomes thus increased, consumers enlarge their purchases. A new demand appears in the market, thus justifying those foresighted business men who had already begun to expand their operations.

What happens when period of recovery passes through expansion to inflation

The part of the economic cycle we have been describing may be termed the "period of recovery." Thus far all is wholesome. Industry is merely returning to normal conditions. If it could stop there or if it could be content with the natural progress which inevitably accompanies the growth of population and the march of invention and improvement, all would be well. But in actual fact it is just at this critical point that business seems inevitably to choose the wrong path. Recovery passes into expansion and expansion into inflation. It may be that this is inevitable under the operations of modern banking. The higher prices which have accompanied the recovery of business mean that business men will need *more dollars* with which to finance a given volume of trade. And the higher prices will make it possible for the bank to grant larger loans, for the business man's sales will, in terms of dollars, be bigger and his capacity to pay back whatever he borrows correspondingly larger.

Thus funds are made available for new and larger advances of credit. These, in turn, paid out in the form of the expenses of trade and production, pass into the hands of consumers. With incomes thus increased consumers' purchases are again larger, and so prices, bank loans, business operations, consumers' incomes and consumers' purchases all increase together. Bound together like causes and effects, the increase of any one of these factors leads inevitably to the increase of the others. And so business continues to expand and increase far beyond the point of safety.

Another factor, not yet mentioned, cooperates in the work of expansion. In a period of rising prices *business profits increase*. This is because many of the costs of production increase, if they increase at all, more slowly than do selling prices. Wages lag behind; rents, interest on bonds, taxes and other fixed charges may for the time being increase but little. Increasing profits lead in two different ways to the over-expansion of business activities. In the first place, a considerable part of these increasing profits will be *re-invested* in the extension of business operations where it is hoped they may form the basis of yet larger earnings. In the second place, for the time being, the interest rate lags behind the rate of profits. Money can be made by borrowing funds from the banks or by issuing bonds and selling them in the market and investing the proceeds in the extension of business operations.

These different factors working together make it practically certain that the process of business expansion will be overdone. Business recovery will become expansion and then inflation. But why, the reader may ask, should such a period of expansion come to an end? Why must it end in crisis and collapse? There seem to be two fundamental reasons.

New distribution of wealth tends to end a period of expansion

In the first place, the economic changes of the period of expansion are qualitative as well as quantitative. It is not merely the sum total of wealth produced which changes. It comes to be distributed in a new way. Consider for a moment the classes in the community that *benefit* from a rise in prices. They are the farmers, the mine-owners and the other producers of raw materials. They are the manufacturers, whose outlays for rent, interest and wages have not increased as rapidly as their gross incomes. They are the investors who hold stock in such industries. But other classes are adversely affected by rising prices. They are the owners of mortgages and bonds: the men who "live on their incomes." They are the salaried classes, the teachers and the government employees. They are the great body of wage-earners. Now, of course, such swift and dramatic changes in the distribution of wealth as accompany a period of sharply rising prices are in themselves unwholesome. And furthermore, these changes tend to undermine the solidity of the whole business structure. For the industries of a country are highly specialized. Rapid changes in the distribution of wealth result in unforeseen changes in the demand for the products of industry. With the relative growth of profits, for example, the demand for two classes of goods increases. These two classes are, first, capital goods – factory buildings, machines and the like – and second, the luxuries upon which the newly rich are prone to spend too much of their incomes. But because wages do not keep pace with the advancing price level, there is certain to be a *relative decline in the demand* for the fundamental necessaries of life. The analysis could be pushed much further, but these examples will serve. Rising prices lead to a new distribution of incomes, and these, in turn, to a new distribution of demand, which places uneven stresses and strains upon the industrial system.

Curtailment of banks' advances principal reason of collapse

The second reason why periods of rapid business expansion end in collapse is undoubtedly the more important of the two. It is that the banks of the country are brought to the end of their resources and have to curtail drastically their advances to business. The difficulty the banks encounter is not that the quality of the loans they are asked to make is perceptibly poorer. They are brought to a halt because their *reserve ratio* falls to the minimum which law or ordinary banking prudence prescribes. The reserve ratio in the case of a central bank, it will be remembered, is the proportion of its cash on hand to its cash liabilities in the form of notes and deposits. In the case of a local bank the reserve ratio is the proportion of the bank's own deposits in a central bank to the volume of its own deposit liabilities. Now it should be clear that rapid business expansion must decrease reserve ratios in two different ways. First, business expansion is accompanied by an increase in the volume of bank loans and this, in turn, by an increase in the volume of bank deposits. Second, the increase in consumers' incomes draws more money into hand-to-hand circulation. Saturday pay envelopes grow in number and in size. The receipts of retail shops increase. The average merchant keeps a little more money in the till just as the average buyer keeps a little more money in his pocket. This means that, with a given volume of money in the country, there will be less in bank reserves and more in hand-to-hand circulation. But this is not the only drain upon bank reserves. Rising prices invite imports and make it more difficult to export. Gold has to be sent to foreign countries to offset an adverse balance of trade. The gold comes from bank reserves and further reduces the lending power of the banks. It frequently happens that an adverse turn of the foreign exchanges is the first definite signal that the period of prosperity is approaching its end.

With their reserve ratios down to the minimum, and faced by continuing drains of cash for export as well as for hand-to-hand circulation, the banks have no alternative but to diminish very drastically the amount of their outstanding loans. The best way to accomplish this without unfair discrimination among different borrowers is to increase interest and discount rates so that all but the most necessary borrowings will be stopped. This increase of discount rates, often coupled in practice, it must be confessed, by flat refusals to lend, brings business to a sudden and demoralizing halt. The banks are not to blame. If they had not begun to contract their loans, the last penny of their reserves would have been drawn out and, although the final catastrophe might have been delayed, it would have been all the more devastating.

Crop failures in agricultural countries often precipitate crises

Very often a crop failure or some other unforeseen event may hasten or precipitate the crisis. Crop failure early in the business cycle is likely to do little harm beyond slowing up the period of recovery. But when business expansion has already proceeded well toward its possible maximum, a crop failure may bring it to a sudden end. A crop failure in agricultural countries like the United States and Canada may, by reducing exports, make the trade balance unfavorable and lead to a drain of gold from the banks. Again by reducing the purchasing power of the farmers, it will lessen the demand for the output of many industries. Finally, a crop failure in an agricultural country will greatly diminish the earnings of its railways. Thus there is undoubtedly more than mere accident that many great panics have followed upon crop failures, but we should not necessarily conclude that the crop failure is the real cause of the crisis. Coming at a time when the structure of business and credit is already over-expanded a crop failure may precipitate a crisis. But there have been important crises, like that of 1907 in the United States, with which crop failures apparently had nothing to do. The fundamental causes of crises, we repeat, are to be found in our credit system and not in agriculture.

Why economic crises were more common in the United States than elsewhere

The old national banking system of the United States, with its inelastic and rigid reserves, and with its lack of centralized responsible control, was especially bad in these respects. This, undoubtedly, explains why economic crises were both more frequent and more severe in the United States than in most other countries. One advantage, possibly the greatest advantage, of centralized banking systems such as European countries have long enjoyed, and such as the United States now has in its federal reserve banks, is that they make it possible for bank credit to be used in such a way as to lessen and even to counteract the oscillations which constitute a business cycle. A central bank, interested in the welfare of the country as a whole rather than in its own profits, will not ordinarily let its reserve ratio diminish down to that minimum point. It is not always necessary for such a bank to diminish its lending suddenly and drastically. After the end of the period of business recovery, when business expansion has proceeded some distance along its normal course, the bank may take measures *looking toward the future*. Slight and gradual advances in its interest and discount rates made long before its reserve is threatened will often serve the purpose. It will *put on the brakes* when it is seen that business expansion is beginning to proceed too rapidly. Then, if, despite the bank's efforts, a crisis comes, it will be less violent, partly because the volume of business commitments, and especially of bad debts, will be less, and partly because the central bank will not have to increase its discount rates so drastically as to give a sudden shock to business. Moreover, the ensuing period of depression will be shortened; recovery will be hastened because the central bank, with the adequate reserves it has been safeguarding for just such a purpose, will be able to give all of the help that is needed by legitimate and promising business operations. It may be too much to hope that the business cycle can be wholly eliminated by the efforts of the federal reserve system or in any other way. But there is no doubt that inflation may be held down somewhat and the ultimate collapse cushioned. The extent of the oscillations of prosperity and depression will be less.

With the advance of scientific study of the phenomenon of the business cycle, business men as well as banks have come to be more familiar with its problems. The extension of popular knowledge respecting the facts and the course of the business cycle is the surest way in the world of finally eliminating this disease from our economic system. Just so far as the business men or consumers can see the future, just so far will they discount it. And just so far as they discount it, they will change the future. The speculator who sees that the price of wheat is likely to go higher will operate in such a way as to make profits for himself. But his operations will have the effect of somewhat increasing the present price of wheat and of somewhat lessening that rise in its price which he foresaw. In the same way, just so far as the collapse which inevitably follows the periods of recovery and of expansion is foreseen, just so far will business operations be conducted in such a way as to minimize or perhaps to eliminate it. If this disease now inherent in our economic system is finally conquered, it should be considered as a signal victory for economic science.

39 An analysis of bank statistics for the United States

An Analysis of Bank Statistics for the United States (1928) Cambridge: Harvard University Press. Extracts from Chs I and II, pp. 1–32.

I: The national banks: 1867–1914[a]

The National Banking Act of February 25, 1863, required national banks to make quarterly reports to the Comptroller of the Currency, exhibiting their resources and liabilities "in detail and under appropriate heads." The Comptroller, in turn, was required to make annual reports to Congress, summarizing the reports made to him by the banks. The dates of the quarterly reports were fixed by law, so that there was opportunity for window dressing. But a statute of March 3, 1869, required the banks to make five instead of four reports a year, and the date of each report was to be set by the Comptroller.

In the annual Reports of the Comptroller of the Currency the United States has a unique record of banking operations. No other country has so complete a record covering a comparable period. Various investigators have dug into this rich lode of statistical material at one point or another, but as a whole it remains largely unexploited.

The present study has no claims to completeness. Its purpose is merely to put some of the more important figures in the Comptroller's Reports into such shape as to make them useful to students of present-day banking problems and in particular to students of the interrelations of the fluctuations of credit and of business activities. Except at points where there are obscurities or apparent anomalies to be cleared away, there is little or none of the interpretative analysis which the figures obviously invite. And although the fluctuations of various banking series are compared one with another, no comparisons are made of these fluctuations and the attendant movements of other economic phenomena. All of the series examined save one, the amount of money in circulation, have been drawn from the Comptroller's Reports. They are as follows:

1 *Capital and surplus: 1867–1914.* Sum of "capital stock paid in" and "surplus fund."

2 *Investments: 1867–1914.* "United States bonds on hand and other stocks, bonds, and securities, etc." Exclusive of United States bonds held to cover circulation and United States and other bonds held to cover government deposits.

3 *Loans and discounts: 1867–1914.* Overdrafts are included in loans and discounts reported at calls prior to December 1, 1898.

4 *Individual deposits less clearing-house exchanges: 1870–1914.* Obtained by subtracting "clearing-house exchanges" from "individual deposits" as reported by the Comptroller. "Individual deposits" do not include government or interbank deposits. Prior to April 26, 1900, however, some banks counted deposits made by savings banks as individual deposits.

5 *Net deposits: 1870–1914.* ("Individual deposits" less "clearing-house exchanges") plus (amounts "due to other banks" minus amounts "due from other banks"). The "due to" category includes amounts due to reserve agents, to other national banks, to state banks and bankers, trust companies, and savings banks. Under "due from" are included amounts due from reserve agents, from other national banks, from state banks and bankers, and from trust companies.[1]

6 *Circulation: 1867–1914.* "National bank notes outstanding," not "national bank notes in circulation."

7 *Lawful money in banks: 1875–1914.* "Specie" plus "legal-tender notes." Includes "United States certificates of deposit for legal-tender notes," prior to 1901; United States certificates for gold deposited, beginning April 24, 1901; "clearing-house certificates," beginning December 12, 1879. Figures for years before 1875 are not used because prior to June 20, 1874, when the five-per-cent redemption fund was instituted, national banks were required to hold reserves of lawful money on account of circulation as well as on account of deposits.

8 *Money in national banks: 1901–14.* "Total lawful money," plus "notes of other national banks," plus "national bank notes on hand."

9 *Estimated money in circulation, not in banks: 1901–14.* "Money in circulation" (as reported by U.S. Treasurer), adjusted to dates of call, with corrections for the period ending May 20, 1907, as indicated by the subsequent official revision of the annual statements of gold coin in circulation, less the amount of money in national banks increased by 50 per cent to allow for money in other banks.

All of these series except the last two (money in banks and in circulation) are given separately for New York City banks and banks outside New York City. This systematic separation is perhaps the most distinctive characteristic of the present study. Series for all national banks, in New York and elsewhere, are not given, because, first, by blending disparate movements these combined series cover up more facts than they reveal, and second, such series are easily available to the student. It is true, of course, that the fluctuations of the series for banks outside New York City are themselves blends of different regional movements. Figures for some of these regional variations will be brought together in a subsequent paper [(1925f)]. But even without further differentiation the distinction between banking operations in New York City and in the rest of the country has fundamental importance.

The different series are assembled for dates of call in Tables 1 and 2 [not reprinted], and the general movements of some of them are shown in the charts, which, however, represent annual figures. The characteristic fluctuations of the different series have been analyzed in much greater detail for the period from 1901 to 1914, inclusive, and the results of that analysis will be presented in a subsequent paper [(1925c), updated to cover 1915–26 in (1927e)].

Surveying the longer period as a whole, however, it is clear that the fluctuations of the series are of several different types. Seasonal movements have their effect on the magnitude of the items at different dates of call within a single year. Longer variations, of the type now commonly called cyclical, are also present. These seasonal and cyclical fluctuations are reserved for subsequent analysis. But in addition to them, and apart from the general upward trend of the different series, are other significant movements – variations of rates of growth, or breaks of trend. It is with these that the present discussion is largely concerned.

The significance of the changes in the general direction of the movements of the different series across successive decades is affected by the fact that they reflect the operations of national banks only. The picture they give of the progress of banking in the United States is distorted by the effect of the changing competitive fortunes of the national banking system....

II: Seasonal and cyclical fluctuations: 1901–14[b]

....

I pass to the discussion of the fluctuations of the different series which remain after their general trend and their normal or typical seasonal fluctuations have been eliminated. For convenience, I shall refer to these residual fluctuations as "cyclical." This should not be taken as implying that they are periodic, or that they are of one type, or that all of them are brought about in the same way.

....

In drawing inferences from Chart 10 respecting the cyclical fluctuations of the amount of money in national banks and of the amount of money in circulation, not in banks, certain cautions should be observed. The two curves, taken together, do not give an accurate picture of the cyclical movement of money out of circulation into the banks and back again, for they do not have a common trend. Between 1901 and 1913 the amount of money in circulation increased by 56 per cent, while the amount of money in the banks increased by 69 per cent.[2] The

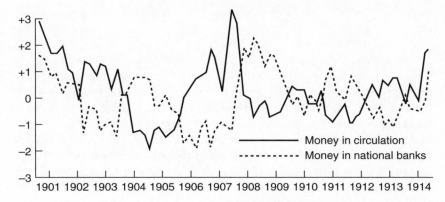

Figure 39.1 Cycles of money in national banks and of money in circulation, not in banks: dates of call, 1901–14 (Chart 10)

increase of money in circulation was more rapid in the earlier than in the later part of the period, so that the trend took the form of a parabola. In the case of the money held in national banks, a linear trend sufficed.

Furthermore, no larger significance should be attached to the position which these curves and those which follow them have with respect to the axis in the one or two years at the beginning and end of the period. The prolongation of a series in either direction might easily change the position of its trend sufficiently to alter substantially the relation of the figures to the trend in the terminal years.

Nevertheless, over the greater part of their course, the curves are dependable and instructive, if they be taken for what they are, namely, representations of the cyclical fluctuations of two complementary series, each shown in relation to its own trend. The general inverse correlation of the fluctuations of the two curves is, of course, inevitable. Equally to be expected, but nevertheless highly significant, is the continuous or even restless character of these inverse movements. Even allowing for the presence of the remnants of abnormal or subnormal seasonal variations, it is apparent that at substantially all times there was an unmistakable net movement of money either into or out of the banks. These movements, furthermore, have a cyclical character, which means merely that they reverse and then repeat themselves. The resulting cycles, however, vary to such a degree in respect of phase and amplitude that it is clear that the conjuncture of attendant circumstances is not always the same, or, in other words, that these cycles are not all of a kind. In particular the larger swings from 1905 into 1908, through the crisis year of 1907, are sharply contrasted with the smaller oscillations which follow. The disturbances of 1903 and 1913, moreover, appear to be on a larger scale than that of 1910.

The fluctuations of the amount of money in circulation show a remarkably close resemblance to the cyclical fluctuations of wholesale prices during this period.[3] They generally lag behind the price fluctuations, by an interval that is often as much as half a year. The fluctuations of the amount of money in the banks have, as one might expect, a fairly close inverse correlation with money rates.

....

The cyclical fluctuations of individual deposits and of net deposits may be considered together, for it is obvious at a glance that they are much alike. Their general similarity appears strikingly in the small diagrams – A and B – in Chart 15. Their seasonal variations, it will be remembered, differed considerably. It appears, however, that during the period we are surveying, there were no significant changes in the relation of inter-bank deposits to individual deposits, aside from rhythmical seasonal oscillations. Even across the years there was very little net change, as the equations of trend for individual deposits and net deposits (in Table 3 [not reprinted]) show.

When it is remembered that banks not in the national system were large depositors in national banks, both in and outside of New York City, the stability of the relationship between individual and net deposits appears especially significant. The agreement of the cyclical fluctuations is somewhat closer for outside banks than for banks in New York City. But even for the New York banks the general form and magnitude of the cycles of individual and of net deposits are alike. The differences are such as would be brought about by transient causes, like seasonal variations of more or less than ordinary magnitude.

The outstanding feature of the cyclical fluctuations of deposits is the predominantly inverse character of the movements in and outside of New York City. In the outside banks, however, deposits generally rose slowly and then fell rapidly. In the New York banks, they rose rapidly and then fell slowly.

The nature of the forces at work in these alternating movements is suggested by comparing them with the cyclical flow of money into and out of the banks (see Chart 15, C and D). The correlation of the cyclical fluctuations of the amount of money in all banks and of the net deposits of national banks in New York City is remarkably close. The movements of the net deposits of outside banks are somewhat like the fluctuations of the amount of money in circulation.

I have little doubt but that relations such as we are now considering lie at the very heart of the problem of the instability of the modern mechanism of bank credit and of those business activities which depend upon credit. The discussion of that problem falls outside the limits set for the present study.[4] Certain things, however, are obvious. Under the national banking system, the money forced out of circulation, in periods of low prices and stagnant trade, flowed to New York. There it generally served as the foundation of a rapid expansion of loans and discounts and investments on the one hand and of deposit credit on the other. The New York banks made advances to investors and to speculative buyers of bonds, and, usually a little later, to buyers of stocks. Large advances were commonly required to finance new issues of bonds. Low interest rates made such periods advantageous for refunding operations, for funding floating debts, and for issuing new securities to finance undertakings requiring large investments of capital in fixed and durable form.[5]

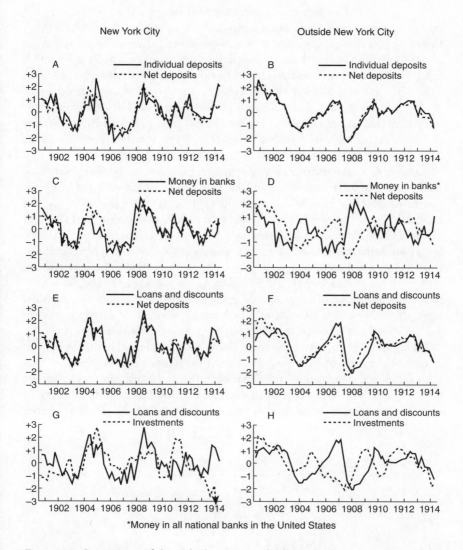

Figure 39.2 Comparisons of the cyclical variations of different banking series: dates of call, 1901–14 (Chart 15)

But a considerable part of the funds thus secured in New York could not be held there long. Payments had to be made to the *ultimate* borrowers in other parts of the country. Deposits were transferred to outside banks. The revival of industrial activity, with which these outside payments probably had something to do, led to increased lending by outside banks. An increase of prices and of the volume of retail trade draws money from New York, through the outside banks, into circulation. Just how far these different movements could go before reversing themselves appears to have depended upon a general conjuncture of circumstances. I see no basis for the belief that these cyclical swings, once under way, were never halted until the resources of the banks had been exhausted. Monetary factors undoubtedly have much to do with the cyclical fluctuations of business activities. Moreover, they set limits beyond which such fluctuations cannot go. But only in cycles of exceptional magnitude do such limits become effective. The greater number of cyclical fluctuations keep well within these limits. Crises are incidents, not of all cycles, but only of those which reach or approach their possible limits.

....

Another aspect of the process of alternating give and take between New York banks and outside banks is shown in Chart 16. While the expansion of loans and discounts in New York was, in considerable part, brought about by the accumulation of money in New York banks, the expansion of the loans and discounts of the outside banks reflects the growth of business activity. Money flows back to the interior, we might say, because loans and discounts have expanded there. Loans and discounts expand in New York because money has flowed there.

A reference to Chart 15 (E and F) will show how extraordinarily close was the relation of the cyclical fluctuations of loans and discounts and of net deposits, especially in New York. Outside of New York, loans and discounts appear to lag a little behind net deposits, although very little and not consistently.

One important phenomenon these charts do not reflect. That is the cyclical change of the ratio of loans and discounts to deposits.[6] The variations of that ratio follow the same general path that both loans and discounts and deposits take. Outside New York the ratio lags behind the fluctuations of its constituent series by an interval that is sometimes as much as a year. For New York banks the

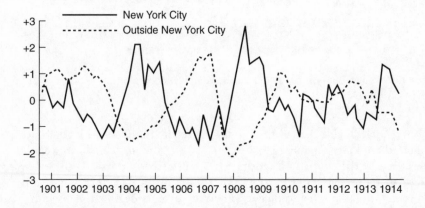

Figure 39.3 Cycles of loans and discounts of national banks in New York City and outside New York City: dates of call, 1901–14 (Chart 16)

fluctuations of the ratio appear to be inversely related to the fluctuations of the constituent series.[7]

Fluctuations of deposits have more effect upon the ratios than fluctuations of loans and discounts do, for the fluctuations of deposits are larger. For New York City banks, the standard percentage deviation of net deposits (corrected for seasonal variation) from the line of trend was 9.64; of loans and discounts, 6.80. For outside banks, the standard percentage deviation of net deposits was 3.41; of loans and discounts, 2.96. Furthermore, the volume of the net deposits of New York City banks is always notably larger than that of their loans and discounts, so that the difference between the absolute magnitude of the fluctuations of the two series is even greater than their standard percentage deviations suggest. It follows, therefore, that barring extremely large fluctuations of other variables, such as investments and money in the banks, which help to determine the volume of net deposits, the ratio of the loans and discounts of New York banks to their net deposits must be at a maximum when deposits (and, as it happens, loans and discounts also) are smallest, and at a minimum where deposits (and loans and discounts) are largest.

In outside banks, there is no large difference between the volume of loans and discounts and of net deposits. Before 1909 the former were generally a little larger,[8] subsequently they were generally a little smaller. The behavior of the ratio appears to have been governed very largely by (1) the selling of investments and the flow of money out of the banks while loans and discounts were increasing, and (2) the concurrent acceleration of the increase of other variable liabilities, such as undivided profits and surplus, – and in turn, of course, by the inverse movements which accompanied the falling off of loans and discounts.

The cyclical fluctuations of the investments of national banks in and outside of New York are compared in Chart 17. Leaving out of account the two first years, where the fit of the lines of trend is uncertain, it is obvious that there is less difference between New York banks and outside banks in respect of the timing of their investment operations than there is in respect of the timing of such other activities of theirs as we have surveyed. In only a very slight degree did purchases of investment securities by one group of banks have the effect of relieving the market at times when the other group of banks was selling.

In general both types of banks increased their investments most rapidly when their surplus funds were largest, that is, in periods when money had accumulated in their vaults. In such periods, of course, interest rates are relatively low and bond prices are high. The banks generally disposed of some of their investments, or, in any event, increased their holdings more slowly, after the prices of bonds had fallen. It does not follow, however, that these operations were disadvantageous to the banks. Investments were generally bought with funds which otherwise would not have found employment, and were disposed of as the demand for loans and discounts increased. Nevertheless, at the end of one of these investment cycles, as they might be called, the aggregate investment holding of the banks were usually larger than at the beginning. Probably a considerable proportion of the bonds owned by

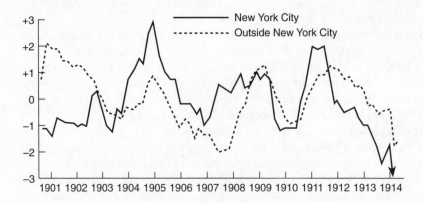

Figure 39.4 Cycles of investment of national banks in New York City and outside New York City: dates of call, 1904–14 (Chart 17)

the banks in 1914 had been bought at fairly high prices. It is to be observed, further, that purchases and sales by the banks were so timed as to increase somewhat the cyclical fluctuations of bond prices.

In Chart 15 (G and H) I have compared the cyclical fluctuations of investments with those of loans and discounts. There is a striking difference between the relation of investment operations to loans and discounts in New York City and outside of it. In New York the same conditions that led to an increase of investments led also to an increase of loans and discounts, no small part of which were advances to the security market. Outside of New York, however, investments were increased while loans and discounts remained low, and fell off as loans and discounts increased. The investment operations of the outside banks were, therefore, a factor making for the stability of their deposits and their earnings. But in this, as in other respects, the comparative stability of the operations of the outside banks was purchased by throwing upon the New York banks most of the stresses created by the cyclical flow of money into and out of the banks.

Notes

1 Net deposits thus computed do not agree with the "net deposits" reported by the Comptroller of the Currency, which are computed in order to ascertain reserve ratios. For that purpose, the amounts due from other banks and from the U.S. Treasurer, together with exchanges for the clearing house, checks on other banks in the same place, and notes of other national banks, were deducted from gross deposits, made up of individual and U.S. deposits, unpaid dividends, and amounts due to other banks. But the amounts due to and due from other banks were disregarded if, for a particular bank, the latter were the larger. According to a ruling announced by the Secretary of the Treasury on September 29, 1902, reinforced by status on May 30, 1908, U.S. government deposits were excluded from the "net deposits" against which the banks had to hold reserves. Further changes were made by the Federal Reserve Act, but these changes did not take effect during the period under examination.

2 Using averages of the amounts at the five dates of call in each year. The effects upon the proportionate distribution of the country's money was less than might be supposed. Assuming that in both years other banks held about half as much money as national banks did, the distribution was as follows: In 1901 national banks held 28.7 per cent, other banks held 14.3 per cent, and 57 per cent was in circulation; in 1913 national banks held 27.4 per cent, other banks held 13.7 per cent, and 59 per cent was in circulation.

3 See, for example, Professor Persons' chart in Persons, Warren M., (1923) "Review of the Second Quarter of the Year", *Review of Economic Statistics* 5, No 3 (July), 179–86.

4 I know of no better analysis of the essential instability of the volume of bank credit than is to be found in Hawtrey, R. G., (1923) *Currency and Credit* (2nd Edn.), London and New York: Longmans, Green and Co.

5 Low interest rates, furthermore, led to important shifts in the balance of international indebtedness. In general, New York became more of a creditor and less a debtor in the international money market. I have not, in this study, taken account of the important relations of external gold movements to domestic movements of money and credit. As a rule, New York was exporting gold while it was receiving money from the interior, and New York's gold imports generally coincided with the flow of money from New York to outside banks and into circulation. New York, one might say, had the position of an intermediary, transmitting variations in the country's demand for money to the international market. Cf. Andrew, Piatt, compiler (1910) *Financial Diagrams*. United States National Monetary Commission, 61st Congress, 2nd Session, Document No. 509, Plate 18: "Movements of Money To and From New York City – Weekly – 1899–1909".

6 Cf. Especially, Persons, Warren M., (1924) "Cyclical Fluctuations of the Ratio of Bank Loans to Deposits, 1867–1924," *Review of Economic Statistics*, vol. 6, No. 4 (October) pp. 260–83.

7 See Professor Persons' article cited above, especially his Charts 4 and 8. For New York, Professor Persons used the loans and investments and the net deposits of the clearing house banks. In respect of timing, even if not in respect of general shape and magnitude, the fluctuations of those series are much like those of the loans and discounts and net deposits of New York national banks. For outside banks, Professor Persons draws on the same sources that I have employed. He uses individual deposits, however, instead of net deposits. But, as we have seen, the cyclical fluctuations of individual and net deposits are much alike.

8 Before 1899 the difference was considerable.

Editors' notes

a This extract is from chapter I of Young's 1928 book on bank statistics. It was the first of a series of four articles that were originally published in the *Review of Economics and Statistics* (Young 1924f, 1925c, 1925f, and 1927e).

b Chapter II originally appeared as Young (1925c).

40 Branch banking in the United States

"Introduction" to Jean Steels, *La Banque à Succursales dans le Système Bancaire des États-Unis* (1926) Ghent: A. Buyens, vii–xx

Dr. Steels' monograph, I am very sure, will commend itself to students of the structure and operation of financial institutions. It has to do with an important and interesting subject, and it deals with that subject competently and illuminatingly.

Since 1913, as the world knows, the banking system of the United States has been drastically reorganized. In the same short period of years revolutionary economic changes – most of all the metamorphosis of the United States from a debtor to a creditor in the world's money market – have given a new international importance to that banking system. Fate has made the banks of the United States custodians of a disproportionate share of the world's reserves and dispensers of a correspondingly large portion of the funds which are available in the international capital market. Much depends, therefore, not only upon the wisdom with which the operations of the system are directed, but upon the structural soundness of the system itself and of its constituent parts.

Before the war the United States had what was undoubtedly the crudest and most defective banking system that could be found in any country that had achieved an advanced stage of economic culture. The causes responsible for that situation, as Dr. Steels observes, were undoubtedly of a political rather than of an economic order. But some of the most potent of these political causes had their roots in the conflicts of economic interests. The study of "sectionalism," of regional antagonisms, affords the most illuminating approach to an understanding of the political history of the United States. In the long struggle to determine the respective limits of the powers of the federal government and of the separate states, the interests of certain sections have made them favorable to greater centralization, while the interests of other sections have expressed themselves in the zealous defence of local autonomy.

So far as finance is concerned the most important cleavage has been the one between "creditor regions," supporters of "sound money" and of an effective centralized control of banking operations, and "debtor regions," partisans of "cheap money" and advocates of the largest practicable degree of freedom in the establishing and operating of banks. The recurrent "cheap money" movements that have characterized the political history of the United States have sprung from the fact that the opening up and developing of new lands have called for expenditures of capital in amounts far beyond the resources of the actual settlers. New regions have generally been debtor regions, and there is more than mere coincidence in the fact that demands for cheap money have always been voiced most loudly on the frontier.

In the field of banking the most important problems, from a political point of view, throughout most of the nineteenth century, had to do with issuing bank notes. Before the civil war there were, except in a few states, no adequate restraints upon the overissue of notes by particular banks, and no restraints at all upon the aggregate circulation of bank notes in the country as a whole. The wide expanse of territory, imperfect communications, and most of all the lack of any system for the prompt clearing and collection of the notes of local banks, contributed to make a situation in which the notes of local banks, once put into circulation, generally remained in circulation a long time. This situation gave an opportunity to unsound banks, for they could often get profits by creating liabilities, without being under any effective compulsion to make provision for the liquidation of such liabilities. Bank notes too often were merely the uncovered personal obligations of the issuing bankers. Both the First and Second Banks of the United States tried to return the notes of local banks promptly for payment, but these efforts were among the factors which led to the unpopularity of those institutions and to the consequent refusal of Congress to prolong their lives.

The establishment of the national banking system and the accompanying suppression of the note issues of state banks accomplished two things. In the first place, national bank notes were unquestionably "sound." They were always exchangeable at will for legal-tender money. In the second place, because no bank's circulation was permitted to exceed its capital, the aggregate circulation of the country could expand in any considerable degree only as the number and size of national banks increased. This closed the doors effectively to the possibility of any inflation of the currency on the part of the banks. National bank notes, whatever faults they might have, could not be issued in dangerous excess.

The fault most commonly imputed to them, in fact, was that at any one time their amount was too rigidly fixed, that it could not expand or contract with variations (especially seasonal variations) in the needs of trade; in short that the notes did not constitute a sufficiently "elastic" currency. In the discussions over banking reform, which began after the bimetallic movement of the last century had come to an end, the necessity of providing a more elastic currency was what was most commonly stressed. Not only minor seasonal perturbations of the money market, but even great crises, such as shake industry and trade to their very foundations, were attributed to the inelasticity of the currency. This was the fault which the Fowler plan was designed to cure, for which the Aldrich–Vreeland Act of 1908 afforded a temporary remedy, and which the more ambitious Aldrich plan, as its sponsors hoped, would eliminate permanently. All of these projects were profoundly influenced by the example afforded by Canada, – for the note issue of the Canadian banks showed a marked capacity to expand and contract in accordance with the notable seasonal variations of Canada's needs for currency. European experience, too, was drawn upon, particularly in the formulating of the Aldrich plan. But Dr. Steels is wholly right in emphasizing the importance as precedents of the methods of centralizing reserves and of providing emergency currency which had been improvised, as we might say, by the clearing houses of the United States at times of crises, and notably in the crisis of 1907. "Clearing-house loan certificates," quite as much as the notes of the Bank of France or of the Reichsbank, supplied the model upon which the federal reserve note was patterned.

Despite the historical importance of the problem of elastic currency, however, the inelasticity of the currency was not, in fact, the most serious defect of the pre-war banking system of the United States. It was, at most, a minor aspect of a larger problem, or one of the symptoms of a more deeply seated disease. This larger problem – or this deeply seated disease – was a consequence of the fact that nowhere in the banking system was there any definite allocation of responsibility for the maintenance of sound financial conditions or even for the maintenance of the solvency of the system as a whole. The system was atomistic and competitive. And the world's experience has been that banking is one field of enterprise in which unrestrained competition fails completely.

The atomistic nature of the system manifested itself at its worst in the operation of the legal requirements for the maintenance of stipulated "reserves" of "lawful money." Country banks found it unprofitable to hold larger stores of money than the law required. When trade was relatively inactive the money not needed for hand-to-hand circulation promptly flowed to the larger cities, and thence to New York. The "surplus reserves" (i.e., holdings of money in excess of the legal reserve requirements) were normally concentrated in New York. But – and this is the important point – the reserves of the New York banks were generally very close to the minimum specified by the law. "Surplus reserves," in fact, were commonly either exceedingly small or non-existent.

Prevented by the law from letting their reserves fall *below* a certain line, the New York banks found it individually profitable to permit any increase of reserves *above* that line to be absorbed by an extension of their liabilities – thus preserving the legal ratio of reserves to liabilities. There were times – as in the three years of depression following the great crisis of 1893 – when no lowering of discount rates would induce the market to avail itself of the surplus lending capacity of the banks. But such periods were exceptional. As Dr. Steels observes, the market for stock exchange loans in New York is large, elastic, and quickly responsive to the stimulus of lower interest rates. An expansion of such loans was often the first step in a process by which any surplus reserves which had appeared in the country's banking system were quickly absorbed.

With reserves normally fairly near the legal minimum, the money market was normally perilously close to a condition of strain. Always kept taut, it lacked resiliency, and was ill equipped to meet the additional strains put upon it from time to time by a demand for gold for export, by a movement of money into government treasury, or even by the annual seasonal flows of money into hand-to-hand circulation. In times of crises, the banks were often forced to make conditions worse by drastically contracting their advances, although it is a well tested rule of sound banking policy that at such times advances must continue to be available to solvent borrowers.

The pressing need, therefore, was not so much for a more elastic system of note issue as it was for a more elastic policy and practice in respect of reserves. A situation which permitted no increase of reserves except at the price of an immediate expansion of bank loans and often of stock exchange speculation, and which permitted no decrease of reserves except at the price of a drastic tightening of the money market, called imperatively for a remedy. The remedy of course, was the creation of an institution or group of institutions devoted to the public welfare rather than to competitive profit-seeking, to which the custody of the country's ultimate banking reserves should be committed, and upon which should be placed the responsibility of maintaining the solvency of the country's banking system as a whole. Such institutions, of course, would normally maintain, not "minimum reserves," but "surplus reserves," which would permit of reasonable variations without necessitating in the one case inflation or in the other a drastic contraction of credit.

Such a remedy was devised and applied in the creation of the federal reserve system. In the United States there is as yet no adequate recognition of the magnitude of this practical and economic achievement. It is a lasting testimonial to the dominance which, in 1913, Woodrow Wilson exercised over Congress and over his own political party, all the more notable because that party, throughout the course of American history, had been the traditional enemy of the centralization of political and financial power.

The expansion of credit during and after the war together with the subsequent enormous influx of gold have given the federal reserve system a severer test than its framers had contemplated. It has satisfactorily withstood that test. There can be no doubt that if it had not been for the federal reserve system gold payments would necessarily have been discontinued in the United States in 1917, or possibly even earlier. It is probable, furthermore, that without the federal reserve system, such enormous gold imports as came to the United States between 1922 and 1925 would have been attended by an excessive expansion of credit and an inordinate rise of prices, culminating, very likely, in a crisis of the first magnitude.

These larger aspects of the history of the federal reserve system are pretty well understood. Dr. Steels has wisely taken as a special subject of inquiry a less spectacular phase of the development of the system. The establishment and growth of the branches of the federal reserve banks have gone on so unobtrusively that they have well nigh escaped attention, even among American students. In fact,

Dr. Steels has given the first comprehensive and competent account of this important movement. He has accurately appraised its significance as a part of the process of fitting the somewhat artificial and cumbersome structure of the federal reserve system into the natural matrix supplied by the economic and financial geography of the country.

Dr. Steels acquits himself equally well in his account of the problems of "branch banking," that is to say the problems of the legal status and the comparative merits of a system of relatively small independent local banks and a system of large banks with numerous branches. In American banking history the question of "branch banking" has played a rôle only less important than the questions of the control of bank note issues and of the establishment of central banks. But the question has generally been discussed less on its merits than in terms of sectional antagonisms, of the danger to be apprehended from a mysterious monster called the "money power," and of "states' rights" versus centralization.

Dr. Steels' account of the present status of the matter is so adequate that I shall limit myself to some comments upon one aspect of the question which appears to me to have peculiar importance. The most significant difference between the administration of a local branch of a large bank and the administration of a small "unit" bank is the difference between a largely impersonal and highly personal administration of credit. In the United States the officers of a typical "unit" bank in a small city or town are commonly life-long residents of the place; the bank's "board of directors" is composed of prominent local merchants, manufacturers, and capitalists; the officers, directors, and other townsmen hold most of the bank's shares, and are accordingly the "proprietors" of the bank. Such a situation has possibilities both for good and for evil.

At its best the local bank identifies itself in various ways with the economic interests of the community. The intimate knowledge of local conditions which its officers and directors possess enables them to plan their loans safely and productively. Loans which the manager of a branch bank might have to refuse to grant, may sometimes be made – and wisely made – upon the basis of the confidence the officers of the bank have in the personal qualities – the honesty and ability – of the applicant. At its worst, however, the local unit bank may identify itself with one group of local financial interests. Borrowers outside of the favored circle may find it difficult to secure advances except on very unfavorable terms. If the bank has a local monopoly it may be able to exact unduly high rates of interest and discount. For the worst cases of extortion and discrimination in American banking practice, one must look, not to the large banks of the great cities, but to these small local institutions.

Moreover, just because most of its investments and loans are localized, the solvency of the small unit bank is dependent upon the continued prosperity of the community or the district within which it is situated. Speculation in land has always been an important factor in the economic life of the United States. In the face sometimes of legal restrictions, which often can be easily circumvented, many small commercial banks in the United States have put too large a proportion of their resources into loans made for the purchase of land, both agricultural and urban. In practice the evil of this practice has been found to reside not so much in the fact that land is not a liquid form of investment, that it cannot be disposed of quickly in time of need, as in the uncertainty which, under American conditions, attaches to the value of land. Fluctuations in land values, more than anything else, were responsible for the numerous bank failures which occurred a few years ago in some of the states of the Northwest, as well as for more recent failures in the State of Florida.

The dependence of a bank upon the prosperity of its own immediate district or region is particularly dangerous in a country where geographical economic speculation has gone as far as it has in the United States. In addition to this element of weakness, the small unit bank is constantly subject to a temptation to entrust an undue proportion of its resources to a particular industry or to a particular group of individuals. The laws have succeeded in restricting this practice, but they have not been able to exterminate it.

But even if, on the whole, the balance of advantage may be on the side of the large bank with branches, more impersonal in its administration of credit, the whole question, for the present at least, is largely academic. Branch banking on any large scale – more particularly on a national scale – is and promises to remain for some time a political impossibility in the United States. The immediate problems of branch banking with which Dr. Steels concerns himself have grown out of differences in the banking laws of the different states and of the federal government, coupled with the peculiar constitution of the federal reserve system with its unique device of "member banks." The ostensible purpose of the changes now under discussion is to establish an equality of competitive conditions as between national banks and state banks, and the federal government's power to determine the conditions of membership in the federal reserve system is being used as a lever to secure the desired result. A general undercurrent of opinion hostile to the growth of branch banking, however, undoubtedly has to be counted an important factor in the situation.

The unique constitution of the federal reserve system, with its "member banks," reflects the influence of the earlier associated activities of the member banks of the clearing-house organizations, of which Dr. Steels gives an account. In some respects this peculiar constitution is unfortunate, – although it has the great advantage that it has helped to make the general attitude of the local banks of the country less hostile to the central banks than otherwise it probably would have been. If the capital of the federal reserve banks had been supplied by individual investors, the political safety of the system would be far less secure than it actually is. If the capital has been supplied by the federal government, the danger would have been that attempts would have been made to dictate the policies of the system for political ends. But even though there may be no satisfactory alternative to the bank-membership device, it should be observed that it is by no means necessary for the continued success of the federal reserve system that the number of members should be large. It is necessary only that a reasonable number of important banks, especially in the large cities, should continue to be members and to have the privilege of borrowing or of rediscounting at the federal reserve banks. Funds supplied by the reserve banks flow promptly through various channels to the points at which the effective demand for such funds is most imperative. Nor is the privilege of membership in the federal reserve system worth so much to any one bank as to enable the federal government to forge its power to define the conditions of such membership into a weapon with which to put an end to the old conflict between its own jurisdiction in respect of banking matters and that of the governments of the different states.

I said in the beginning that Dr. Steels' monograph should attract the interest of students of banking institutions. But it will now be apparent, I trust, that the themes with which Dr. Steels deals belong to the fields of politics and government quite as much as to economics. The anomalous structure of the banking institutions of the United States reflects the peculiar political constitution of the country. The problems of banking organization which Dr. Steels discusses are modern instances of general types of problems that are as old as the country's history. I suspect, therefore, that I should have named students of law and of government along with students of economics in the list of those to whom Dr. Steels' monograph will have a special interest.

41 Downward price trend probable, due to hoarding of gold by central banks

The Annalist (1929) New York. Vol. 33: 96–7. January 18

What was true yesterday may be true today, but the truth which was significant yesterday may not be the truth which is significant today. When prices were slipping rapidly downhill in the deflation of 1920 and 1921, there were many who, sensing the fact that an artificial situation created by the war was disintegrating, leaped to the conclusion that there would be no stability until the pre-war price level was restored. As against an inference so little warranted, either by the history of earlier periods of deflation or by the character of the visible factors which might be expected to have a controlling influence upon the immediate situation, economists were altogether right in insisting that the rapid downward movement of prices could, and undoubtedly would be, stopped long before a level as low as that of 1913 was reached. Although confirmed by the subsequent course of events, that prophesy has now lost most of its significance for us.

Gradual downward trend of prices is probable

Fairly well assured that from month to month and from year to year the value of money will be comparatively stable, men are now looking further afield, and are asking what the value of money will be in 1940 or 1950. The answer is a matter of probability, not of certainty. Long-continued stability is improbable. A gradual downward trend of prices is probable.

Stability is a relative term. In the midst of the post-war convulsions of prices pre-war prices seemed to be almost unbelievably stable. But to any one who believes that "control of the general price level" is both practicable and desirable, and who therefore uses an unchanging average as a standard of reference, *instability* seems to have been a dominant characteristic of prices before the war. Stability, furthermore, may imply primarily the elimination or the lessening of those wave-like general oscillations of prices which economists have come to call "cyclical." Or it may imply the absence of those long, slow movements upward or downward which economists have come to call "trends." The distinction between these two meanings of stability is not merely academic. It is not made merely to serve the convenience of statisticians and other analysts. It rests upon real differences in the nature of the various forces which make for instability, and upon corresponding difference in the character of the measures which have to be taken if a larger degree of stability is to be secured.

It is generally agreed that under favorable conditions a central bank can operate upon the supply of credit and currency in such a way as to diminish the amplitude of a short-lived or "cyclical" general movement of prices. When gold is the general monetary standard, however, the central bank or banks of any one country, acting independently, cannot for more than a little while serve as a buffer against the slow pressure which a changing relation between the available supply of gold and the annual production of exchangeable wealth puts upon the general level of prices. On the one hand, how far a central bank can go in absorbing and impounding an excessive supply of gold depends primarily upon the extent of the marketable resources which it is in a position to exchange for gold. On the other hand, the efficacy of any attempts on its part to economize in the use of gold by keeping its own holdings down to a minimum will depend very largely upon whether the reserve ratios of other central banks are on that account maintained at a higher level than would otherwise have been feasible. Not much is accomplished by merely driving gold from one country to another.

There are only two ways in which, so long as the gold standard is retained, the natural effects of a changing relation between the supply of gold and the volume of other goods produced annually can be overcome.

Cooperation among central banks necessary

One way is to alter the size of the monetary unit from time to time by changing the mint price of gold in some such manner as Professor Irving Fisher has proposed. But this device, if it is to be practicable, requires that there should be an international agreement providing for concurrent action on the part of all the more important countries. The other method also calls for international agreements, but on the part of central banks rather than of governments. On the basis of such agreements, the central banks of the world could, if occasion required, go some distance in absorbing and sterilizing an excessive supply of gold, although there are obvious limits to what they could do. Similarly, on the basis of agreement, they might, if occasion required, reduce the downward pressure which a falling supply of gold exerts upon prices by effecting substantial economies in its use.

One naturally thinks of increased reliance upon the gold-exchange standard as the obvious means to that end, although, in fact, nothing so formal and rigid as the gold-exchange standard is really required. I mean that it is not necessary that a central bank which wants to exceed what would otherwise be a safe maximum ratio of liabilities to gold held should always eke out its gold holdings by acquiring foreign balances. It is necessary only that the central bank or (under some circumstances) the market in which it operates should be in possession of an adequate amount of assets quickly marketable in other countries, or of rapidly maturing claims against borrowers in other countries. Under exceptional conditions, an assurance that emergency loans can be obtained in some other country or countries without difficulty may be an important supplementary resource.

The vital purchasing power–wealth production relation

It will be observed that I put special stress upon the importance of maintaining – if anything like stability of the value of money over a long period of years is to be secured – a fairly stable relation between the rate of increase of the total volume of currency and credit, and the rate of increase of the annual production of wealth. There are some who hold that the thing with which the total supply of purchasing power should be compared is not the amount of wealth produced annually, but the aggregate volume of exchanges or transfers which call for money payments.

I believe that adherence to this latter view has put monetary theorist upon a false scent. It leads on the one hand to sterile truisms, such as that the aggregate amount paid for goods in the course of a year is equal to the number of units of goods sold multiplied by their average price per unit. It leads on the other hand – if one attempts to proceed beyond these sterile truisms – to confusion in respect of the meaning and effects of changes of the "velocity of circulation" or rate of turnover of money and credit.

The point at issue really calls for fuller explanation than can be attempted here. I shall merely ask the reader to observe, first, that the net money incomes of any group of people are a measure of the value of the amount of wealth which they produce; and second, that the amount of money (including bank deposits) which, on the average, they will find it convenient to hold at any given time will vary with the amount of their net money incomes. The first of these two points is familiar. The second many not be altogether clear at first, but I think that upon reflection its truth will become apparent.

Money–wealth relation not right

The relation between the amount of wealth produced annually and the amount of purchasing power needed if prices are to be kept at a stable level, is not fixed and rigid. It changes as business methods change, and as the general character of production and consumption changes, but generally it changes slowly. Nor, of course, is the relation of the total volume of the means of payment (currency and credit) to the amount of gold available for bank reserves or for other monetary uses wholly inelastic. It fluctuates within limits, as every one knows, with variations in the volume of production and the level of prices. Moreover, the upper limit of such fluctuations depends upon how banking is organized and upon the policies of central banks. Apart from possible changes in banking policies, however, we are justified in saying that the most important determinant of the future course of commodity prices is the relation between the annual production of wealth and the increase of the gold supply.

Now the average annual production of gold in the last few years has been distinctly less than the annual average (about $450,000,000) for the years immediately preceding the war. Even at that time there were indications that the upward pressure which the enormous output of the South African mines had exerted upon prices had pretty well spent itself, and that unless gold production could be increased or substantial economies could be effected in the use of gold, the price level would again begin to sag, as it had after 1873. Inflation, of a magnitude made possible only by departures from the gold standard, turned prices in another direction.

Gold reserves as adequate as in 1913

Now, with the gold standard generally re-established, the question of the adequacy of the gold supply has again become important. Central banks and governments hold about twice as much gold as was similarly held in 1913. The increase is large enough to account for almost all of the gold that was produced in the intervening period. If new production had been the only source of the additions made to these visible reserves, there would have been very little left to go into non-monetary uses. In fact, of course, the visible reserves have been augmented by the concentration of gold which was formerly in the possession of commercial banks or in hand-to-hand circulation, eked out at one time by some recovery of gold from other than monetary uses.

It is quite impossible to estimate such things at all closely, but I think that any one who looks at the available figures will agree that if banking economies (particularly the development of the Federal Reserve System) are taken into account, the gold reserves of the world are quite as adequate in relation to the present general levels of prices and production as the gold reserves of 1913 were in relation to the levels which prevailed in that year. Indeed, it is probable that there is more elasticity, more room for the growth of production without an accompanying fall of prices, than there was in 1913. The annual accretions from new production must also be taken into account. After allowing for the ordinary flow of gold into non-monetary uses, we cannot put the probable net annual additions to the world's gold reserves at more than from 2½ to 3 per cent of their present amount. Experts appear to be agreed that under present conditions the annual yield of the known gold mines of the world cannot be much increased without incurring sharply rising costs.

Dwindling gold supply less important than central bank policy

The rate at which gold reserves are growing is distinctly less than the rate at which the production of wealth is increasing in the United States, and is probably no larger than, and possibly not quite so large as, the rate at which production is growing in the commercially important parts of the world, taken as a whole. It should be remembered, furthermore, that a constant annual increment to the world's gold supply means a slowly diminishing percentage increase. In the long run it is the percentage increase that is important. Unless new factors such as cannot now be foreseen appear in the situation the increase of the world's gold supply will soon fail to keep pace with the growth of production. Indeed, it may already be lagging behind.

So far as the next few decades are concerned, however, the growth of the supply of gold is very much less important than the policies of central banks.

Sufficient gold, if wisely utilized

There is plenty of gold. Production and trade can grow without there being a general fall of prices, if only the central banks of the world will permit it. Just now, however, they appear to be afraid of prosperity. So long as they are, they will exert a retarding influence upon the growth of production. A few years ago, the Federal Reserve banks were accused of sterilizing gold, to the alleged detriment of the economic interests of Europe. From the subsequent course of events one might infer that the European banks merely preferred to do the sterilizing themselves.

The present situation is inexplicable on any rational grounds. If the fear of another war is any degree responsible, what the experience of the late war taught about the futility of accumulating large hoards of idle gold has been forgotten. If the European banks are merely trying to make their own solvency secure, they forget that gold is not the only liquid asset for which there is an elastic international market. If they are purchasing confidence and prestige, they are paying a high price. If the Bank of England is attempting to regain a larger portion of its pre-war "supremacy," those directing its policies have forgotten how before the war the gold reserves of London were smaller than those of any other large central money market. To attempt, under present conditions, to build up a large idle hoard of gold, whether in London or elsewhere, is generally only an expression of financial nationalism, and financial nationalism is an expensive luxury. It should really make very little difference to any country just where the bulk of the world's gold reserves are kept, provided that there can be complete assurance that claims upon those reserves will be honored without difficulty.

No thinking person wants another period of inflation. But the high-gold-reserve-ratio fetish ought not to have the influence which it now has upon banking policies. A gradual downward trend of prices is probable, not because the supply of gold is or will soon become inadequate, but merely because the central banks of different countries will probably try to maintain their separate hoards of gold.

42 The French franc

"Introduction" to Eleanor Lansing Dulles, *The French Franc, 1914–1928* (1929) New York: Macmillan. Pp. xi–xvi

Miss Dulles's book has a twofold significance. In the first place it is a history. It gives an account of an important episode – or series of episodes – in the recent history of France. In the second place, it is an essay in monetary theory. It presents the results of an inquiry into the behavior of prices, exchanges, production, and trade under a régime of inconvertible paper money. But the reader will find that Miss Dulles draws no sharp line between her account of the various specific factors which shaped the fortunes of the franc and her analysis of the quantitative relations between the variations of the currency and the fluctuations of other economic phenomena. This, I think, is one of the principal merits of her book.

It is no longer profitable to inquire into the working of a depreciated currency with no other end in view than that of finding a fresh confirmation of established monetary principles. No intelligent person who has given any attention to the matter any longer doubts that there is a fairly dependable relation between the amount of a country's currency and the purchasing power of a currency unit. An inquirer's time and energy can be given more profitably to problems which as yet have not been so fully disposed of. Among these problems are such matters as the degree of rigidity or elasticity which may appear under particular conditions in the relation between the quantity of money and prices, the nature of the mechanism by means of which – again under particular conditions – that relationship is maintained or changed, the direction in which the controlling forces run and the way in which they get their initial impulse, the manner in which the whole interrelated system of prices is affected, and the resulting effects upon different forms of economic activity. It is to difficult questions such as these that Miss Dulles, so far as she deals with monetary theory, has addressed herself. When one pursues questions of this order at all closely one inevitably passes from the field in which general theorems, of the nature of economic "laws," are applicable to a field in which the search must be for the particular explanations of particular happenings.

Moreover, when a country's money is depreciated and is fluctuating in value, and most of all when its future depends upon the needs of the government and the nature of the financial expedients to which the government resorts, the behavior of producers and consumers, traders and bankers, lenders and borrowers, in transactions which involve transfers of money, is affected. The ordinary practices which lie back of and which, in a sense, give meaning to theorems which express the necessary mathematical relations between the quantity of money and the level of prices are not wholly to be relied upon. The theorems remain true, but when severed from their factual background they become mere truisms. There is the danger that if they are pressed into service in the study of the phenomena of depreciated currencies they will carry their old associations with them and will suggest wrong inferences with respect to the nature of the forces at work and the order of causal sequences. The task which confronts the investigator, therefore, is not that of putting the new body of experience into the old formulas, but involves a mixture of historical appraisal and economic analysis. There must be an account of what was done and, so far as possible, of why it was done, and there must also be an examination of the interrelations of the different things which were done and of their visible consequences. Such considerations both explain and justify the methods which Miss Dulles has used and the general course which her inquiries have taken.

The stress which Miss Dulles puts upon psychological attitudes, particularly as they manifest themselves in speculative operations, is, I believe, not disproportionate to their real importance. It will be understood, of course, that Miss Dulles has in mind something much more far-reaching than the technical processes of organized speculation or the transactions of professional speculators. Just as the housewife who buys sugar in advance of her needs because she thinks that if she waits she will have to pay a higher price is a speculator in sugar, so every person who spends or accumulates money or who borrows or lends with a view to securing gains or avoiding losses attaching to changes in its purchasing power is a speculator in money. The most striking instances of speculation in money occur when a sudden loss of confidence in the stability of its value, arising from the disclosure of a disappointing budgetary situation or from other developments which are likely to affect the national finances adversely leads to a "flight" from a country's money in the form of the precipitate buying of foreign exchange. The return movement which sets in when stability appears to be in a fair way to be achieved or even when the financial prospect is in any considerable degree altered for the better is of course also speculative in character. In the early stages of currency depreciation, when hope of a fairly early return to the former gold parity has not yet been abandoned, forces which again are properly to be called speculative, showing themselves in an increased demand for money for holding rather than for spending, sometimes help to bolster up its value. Monetary speculation appears in domestic markets – in the markets for commodities, for land, and for equities in industrial undertakings – as well as in the markets for funds payable in the moneys of other countries. For various reasons, however, these last markets are more quickly sensitive to shifts of speculative opinion. It is possible, of course, to put all of these phenomena into the conventional formulas, and to dispose of them as changes in the demand for money or in the velocity of its circulation. But we get closer to the roots of the matter if we put our emphasis in the first place upon changes in the hopes and fears and in the calculations of those who use money rather than upon the formal consequences of such changes.

One should beware of thinking that speculation in a depreciated money and speculation in a commodity must operate in much the same way and have much the same sorts of effects. It is not true, for example, that the effects of speculation in money are necessarily short-lived and that the ultimate determinants of its value remain unaffected. Under the conditions which usually attend the use of inconvertible paper money there are no fixed limits to the amount which can be supplied. A fall in its value, whether attributable to speculative operations or to any other cause, leads to a larger volume of expenditures and hence to a demand, on the part of the government as well as on the part of industrialists and traders, for larger supplies of money. Larger advances by the banks to industry and trade will be justified by the increase (in terms of money units) of their assets, of the volume of their transactions, and of their prospective profits. The amount of advances which will be made to the government will depend upon its needs, and what its needs are will depend in considerable part upon what its fiscal policy is. But they will always be increased by a fall in the value of the currency unit. There is no "limiting" or "ultimate" supply of inconvertible money apart from such restrictions as the government may choose to impose upon itself or upon the banks. Speculation in an inconvertible currency, therefore, by helping to bring about the result which it anticipates, may sometimes operate cumulatively in one direction, in a way for which speculation in wheat or cotton affords no parallel.

The results of two years of residence and study in France show themselves not only in Miss Dulles's knowledge of details and in her command of sources of information but also in her interpretation of the character of the problem with which she deals. That problem, as she sees it, is not merely a matter of the changing quantitative relations of certain economic variables. It is first of all a problem of public policy, and it is a problem which is related to the interests of the country and of its people in many different ways. Impressions and appraisals, as well as economic inferences, have their place – and a proper place – in her book. It adds to the value of her work that she writes as a friendly and sympathetic historian. I wonder, however, whether she does not at some points go rather too far in her defense of the fiscal policies of the French government. The economist, if he is to fulfil his own proper function, cannot deliver himself over completely to historical determinism. It is not for him to say that conditions being what they were all doors were closed to any better solutions than were reached. I have no patience, I confess, with those who say that during the war and the years immediately following it France, or any other country similarly circumstanced might have got along without inflation. Such a statement either is a pointless platitude or is nonsense. But there were times, I think, when French fiscal policy was not shaped entirely by the compulsion of circumstances, but was built partly upon illusions – as, for example, in respect of recoverable reparations or the possible return of the franc to the prewar gold parity – which were clung to even after they were known to be illusions.

The stabilization of the franc might not have had to wait until 1928 if the problem had been attacked in the same way and with the same determination six years earlier. But these are matters of conjecture. What is certain is that the monetary experience of France since 1914 affords a particularly inviting opportunity for the study of the behavior of an instrument which men have created for their own purposes, but which they have not yet fully learned how to control and to use. Miss Dulles has made good use of that opportunity.

Part V
Growth and fluctuations

43 Industrial fluctuations

"Nicholas Kaldor's Notes on Allyn Young's LSE Lectures, 1927–29," *Journal of Economic Studies* (1990) 17, 3/4: 76–85

Under this heading we may group analysis of the fluctuations of prices; the value of money; the mechanism of wage-fixing; and unemployment. The study is therefore important in itself. Further this study has given rise to a new approach to economics. Hitherto, economists have been chiefly interested in adjustments towards equilibrium, but this problem is one of pathological economics yet supplementing, and in no way displacing, the classical studies of economic harmony. The classical social standpoint, strengthened by the reaction from mercantilism, led to excessive sophistication of the facts in so far as it viewed money prices as merely superficial, as in truth [*they are?*] manifestations of the fundamental social mechanisms of communal co-operation in the production of wealth. Heterodox views soon appeared, accusing the orthodox of confusing acquisitive with productive actions, of stressing the harmony of interests at the expense of explaining their opposition. Sismondi was one of the first to interest himself in this "disharmony" (also Lauderdale, Malthus, Daniel Raymond). At the present time take Effertz, "Arbeit und Boden," Landry in his *Manuel d'Économie Politique*, and Davenport.

Earlier investigations regarded trade cycles merely as manias, forming the basis for the later "psychological theory" of waves and optimas and pessimas. Some sort of rhythm is assumed in human temperament. Pareto could see no other explanation than this, and Pigou now gives great weight to it. (Compare the crude seven-year "turnover" theory in biology.) But why should these waves coincide, as between different individuals? This periodic movement is explicable only as the result of contagion due to some external cause and then, admittedly, mental states may accentuate "real" fluctuations. Amongst suggestions for these external causes note that of "vital fluctuations," – infra-red wave fluctuations (v. [W.B.] Hexter, *Social Consequences of Business Cycles*, preface by Young, 1925. Also, [D.S.] Thomas, *Social Aspects of the Business Cycle*.) The evidence relies chiefly on doubtful correlation of time-series, i.e. vital series and economic series. Question: to which economic wave, the preceding or the succeeding, should any one vital wave be attached?

Then come the overproduction theorists. J. B. Say pointed out that absolute overproduction was impossible; supply and demand are the same thing viewed from different angles. What is commonly called overproduction is merely ill-balanced production. But this involves (i) that the supply of money increases correspondingly with production for, otherwise, prices may fall, leading to decreased profits for producers. (Objection raised by J.S. Mill.) (ii) A view of the world as a whole. Taking each country by itself it may overproduce relative to the world demand for its products. cff. Chile, post-war. Ricardo and Senior also employed the "Say" approach.

Then come the socialist overproduction theories; Owen, Rodbertus, Marx, Proudhon. These, based on the Marxian value theory, saw that since labour was paid less than the full value of its product, it could not buy its full product. The surplus product of labour accumulates, only slightly relieved by the production of luxury goods, until the glut of goods in the market produces a crisis, and international rivalries. This curiously lives on in some modern theories not based on Marxian doctrine, but which emphasise that purchasing power does not keep pace with the output of goods at rising prices, i.e. Hobson's "over-saving" or overproduction of capital. But men do not "overproduce" because of power to do so, but because of mistaken estimates of investors. Different forms of income do not vary at the same rate, and doubtless it is true that changes in production are not elastic enough to coincide with changes in consumers' demands.

Those that seek extraneous causes turn first to agriculture. Now it is true that crises in countries largely agricultural have been attended with crop failures. Yet the inelastic demand for agricultural products leaves a larger surplus for exports in the good years. Further, certain kinds of activities vary directly with the volume, and not the value of the crop – e.g. milling, transport. Explanation of periodicity is usually sought outside human institutions, e.g. Jevons' sun-spot theory, a courageous attempt to give a scientific explanation of industrial fluctuations. He thought that the sun-spot cycle corresponded with the average interval between crises; he also studied weather cycles in India. The period for the study of crises is something less than a hundred years, and some of the material for the early part is very inadequate. Jevons' mistake was, when he found that he had to fit in ten crises to satisfy an eleven-year period of sun-spots, he found crises which anyone considering a shorter period than 99 years, or with different hypotheses, would not have counted as crises. Also, he paid no attention to the actual interval between crises, but merely took average interval, which may be purely arbitrary, and no indication of the central tendency. Finally, periodicity in agricultural production has not been successfully located. Moore finds an eight-year period. So far as periods can be found from studies of price changes, "the" period seems to be nine years.

"Variations of profits" were emphasised by Mitchell, and early Pigou. Given industrial fluctuations, this explains why they continue. When prices rise, profits increase more than wages, interest, etc.; but, after a point, when surplus stocks and contracts are exhausted, costs of production rapidly rise, overtake prices, and lead to a crisis. But consumers' incomes must increase as producers' costs of production, so that one would expect a concomitant increase of prices. To explain the difference between prices and costs, we have to look at monetary theory, and credit: there is further disequilibrium between articles produced and those demanded.

April 24, 1928 'Over-investment, over-saving' theory:

It has two general forms.

(a) The standpoint that the production of wealth is such, and that savings of persons is such, that it is disproportionate – in excess – to the community's need for capital, and so saving has to be pulled up short once in a while. But could there be so large an accumulation of wealth that capital equipment would be so increased that its product could not be sold profitably? The problem revolves round the question whether the product of capital can always be sold profitably, and how to define "profitably"? Now notice that we would here expect the rate of interest to be low, which should re-act upon people's desire to save. When we say people save willingly, we must bear the rate of interest in mind. So large saving need not mean over-saving, it is not in itself fatal. It is not because the expected rewards are low, but because actual rewards are low, expectations are not realised, we have a crisis. People do not over-save, they miscalculate.

(b) There is something in the mechanism of modern industry which leads men to miscalculate.

Here there are sub-variant theories.

(i) In a period of prosperity – large profits, – however induced, men's judgement deserts them; i.e., there is psychological optimism in a general endeavour to get their shares in the increasing level of profits. So a disproportionate amount of saving is tempted and drawn out. That is [in figure 43.1], an increase in profits, δP, calls forth an increase in savings, δS; so that δS is not proportionate to δP:

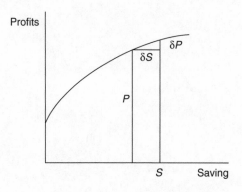

Figure 43.1

(ii) This rests upon the fact that profits are the largest single source of saving. So that with the redistribution of the communal income during times of change, (a) more goes to those who habitually save, and (b) the change in itself offers increased temptation to saving by this group. The shortage of demand in consumers' markets makes it impossible to sell the increased output. (a) Consumers' demands decrease relatively to renewing demands. (b) The increased supply of capital increases the supply of consumers' goods. But all this assumes the trade-cycle. What starts the movement? The explanation of the trade cycle must start outside the trade cycle.

(iii) This is a development from various heterodox monetary theorists. (cff. Douglas Martin[a].) The money-income of consumers is created largely by the outlays which producers make in the expenses of production. ("Producers" – a wide term. "Expenses" – wages, rent, interest, profit.) These consumers' incomes are augmented by borrowing by producers via the banking process. Then lately there has been a great increase in the expansion of credit to consumers. So far as purchasers allow their consumption to go beyond their money-incomes (via banks indirectly) the money income of the community is increased. The amount of money in circulation depends on the extent to which new money incomes are created by bank borrowing.

(1) The money put into circulation by the producer will not suffice to pay for the goods which are being produced at prices profitable to the producer. (Expenses are but expenses, so that if consumers only pay back the producers' expenses paid to them, then producers *as a whole* can never make profits; i.e. expenses = incomes. Hence one producer profits at the expense of another; each producer is a parasite on other producers.)

(2) The expansion of industry increases consumers' income for a time faster than it increases the product of industry. Supply is not increased relative to demand. An increase in investments, anyhow, causes this. It gives a cumulative effect, which, so long as it continues, leaves industry in a prosperous state. Then, when a shortage of bank credit, or sudden increase in goods, appears, goods equal purchasing power, and a crisis follows (Figure 43.2).

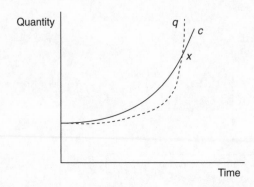

Figure 43.2

But (i) this is an incident of the process not a fundamental cause. (ii) In a stationary state there would be no pure profits, and business profits would remain constant. Now make the state "static." Then the increased consumers' income is quite safe so long as the proportion of saving remains constant. We can conceive of a state of steady progress where consumers' income, investment, and the production of goods all increase at the same rate. So that if there is no trade-cycle to begin with, sub-variant (iii) does not exist in fact.

April 26, 1928

(v. Warren Persons, *Quarterly Journal of Economics*, 1927, "Classification of Theories of Industrial Fluctuations." Mitchell's book repeats theories which have no virtue but that of being vaguely connected with industrial fluctuations.)

Unadjusted statistics definitely suggest irregular and diverse types of industrial fluctuations. We can imagine fluctuations as a result of some regularly recurring phenomena like tides or wave motion of light, and the study of wholesale price fluctuations in England since 1850 show fairly marked group periodicity, but this is not true of the first half of the century, nor of prices in France and Germany, nor is it true of statistics of foreign trade, and bank-clearings. In fact those period movements which can be detected do not seem to be general, or other than fortuituous. Now this statistical investigation shows that perfectly level progression in industry is rare. There are series of more or less regular variations, small, then suddenly a vastly larger fluctuation, – the crisis, trade cycle, *et. al. nom.* This gives rise to the regular fashionable classification of "trade cycles," – depression, recovery, prosperity, reaching a climax, crisis, depression etc. But owing to the difficulty of locating a crisis in every case it has now been abandoned in favour of "regressions" some of which are so severe as to be called a crisis. When we take studies in different countries we find that no two lists agree as to the crisis years. There is now reason to go back to the older view that crises do occur from time to time, without any attempt to fix them to any cyclical movement. We should consider crises as something different from these "regressions."

Crises: Sudden collapse of industry; unemployment; shortage of bank-credits; breaking down of contracts; bankruptcies and failures on a large scale; and generally falling prices and accumulations of goods.

As a result of this definition, a crisis could not exist in an agricultural economy. In the Middle Ages, for example, it could only have occurred in a big money market. Notice that recent excavations re Sumerian civilization show highly complex monetary organisation, and records give an account of an unmistakable crisis. The essential feature of the crisis is that the people are unable to fulfil their contracts. – Possibly as a result of inability to sell goods, maladjustment, but that is not an essential feature. – There are many possible causes.

(i) Extraneous circumstances: cff. war, or, in a country depending largely on agricultural produce, serious crop failures. Perhaps the crisis may begin from quite a trivial cause. e.g. USA 1907 panic. Industry was inflated – prosperous –

and it was assumed it would become more prosperous, then one bank failed, there being a prejudice against the management of this bank, other banks would not help; a general lack of confidence in the banking system was precipitated, heavy drawings on the banks. Loans called in, crisis.

A man's ability to meet his creditors obviously depends on the ability of his debtors to meet theirs, so that a crisis may occur on account of the credit network breaking down anywhere. But still, unless the condition of industry is somewhat strained, or especially, inflated, there is no crisis. It seems possible that the contract system may break down merely on account of excessive complications, inherent, and without any extraneous causes. That is, the supply of many raw materials, and of labour and bank-credits are inelastic, and, in the short run, not expansible beyond a certain point. One of these shortages applying may be sufficient. – This is not certain. – But above all, to repeat, notice that the extraneous circumstances are not sufficient without strain in the industrial position. "Strain": (a) various maladjustments, (b) various short-run inelasticities and shortages. Commitments may have been undertaken on the expectation that profits will continue, or even increase, but profits may be squeezed out through increased cost of labour, raw materials or bank-credit. These are not, that is, in themselves a large element of strain, unless they run counter to general expectations. (c) In conditions of rising prices various redistributions of purchasing power take place. Berridge's work in U.S.A. found that the number employed times average wage fitted in fairly well with the price curve. That is, that the total purchasing power in the hands of labour increases at about the same rate as the production of industry. The redistribution that is important is from those who receive fixed incomes. That is, there are changes in consumer's demand, and changes in the relative proportions of consumer's spending and spending for production. This is particularly important because thirdly, the greater part of the profits of business supplies the fund for further expansion, and the greater part of saving out of profits is not necessarily well spent. It does not seek the investment market, but is put back into the so-far prosperous industry which has produced it. In other words, there is a tendency for prosperous industries to trade too far upon their prosperity.

May 1, 1928

Strain in industry is always necessary, possibly a sufficient condition. The petering-out of bank-credits is probably not sufficient to precipitate a crisis unless industry is operating upon the assumption that prices and profits are going to continue to increase.

The most important factor of "High Conjuncture" is the "competitive illusion". (cff. Bull movements on the stock exchange. The ordinary demand curve must be inverted for speculation: the higher the price the greater the demand.) The business of production is undertaken by entrepreneurs not one of whom has a complete view of the situation. Buying, the giving of order, rises cumulatively, and justifies itself for a time, – providing no one industry is expanding out of all proportion to the others. As a result, over-production of equipment goods, (sometimes) over-accumulation of stock, either in the market for means of production, or in the consumers' market. Those operations which are prompted by expectations that prices will change, as opposed to those prompted by an apparent opportunity not due to price changes, seem to be the principle factor. They cause just the effects which one finds in the trade-cycle.

Thus, an industrial fluctuation = something starting a belief in price changes, then "bull" commences; then either (i) inherent strain (ii) external factor, brings about the collapse. This question of the cause starting the belief in price-changes demands the closest analysis. Now genuine leadership in industry is rare; there is a flock behind any successful leader, and the thing is overdone. But does not Schumpeter overemphasize "originality"? It is not so important that someone should go ahead. This suggests that the natural state of industry is depression. (cff. Veblen.) He insists upon something "adventitious" as starting industry out of depression; further, his "normal" is the lowest extreme. Surely it should be more near to the statistical average? Then, are purely adventitious circumstances sufficient?

How about the monetary situation? During the depression reserves accumulate in the banks, so that interest rates fall. Now do not these falls in interest rates attract industrial enterprise until industry expands again? (cff. Keynes, Cassel, Hawtrey.) But actual industrialists (and bankers) deny that variations in the rate of interest influence the extent of their operations, providing their competitors pay the same. It is the "market" on which they count. Hawtrey emphasizes the middleman, wholesaler, – a small difference in interest rates should greatly influence him. Does not seem to be carried out in fact. Yet all this is part of the explanation. A continued low interest and discount rate does have one effect: long-time borrowing by companies looking ten or twenty years ahead is more feasible. – Their debentures can be sold at a higher price when rates are low: small variations in the rate greatly affect the total cost of raising capital. So perhaps the British depression continues as high, rather than low rates are going on? Now when an expansion of borrowing takes place, [it is?] larger than it would have been otherwise: "actual" amount depends on contemporary amount of real saving; – and under present conditions, that leads to an expanded demand for the products of industry, and so improves its position; i.e., so long as there are reserves of credit and labour. The small regular movement has merely not gone far enough to be "bulled."

May 4, 1928 Remedies for industrial fluctuations

On the one hand are those who seek palliatives and preventatives; on the other, those who hold industrial fluctuations are inherent in the existing system, and hence advocate complete replanning.

(i) Thoroughgoing industrial combination

The individual producer has a very limited view of existing conditions and is so much swayed by existing economic activity that he cannot sway the channel of events himself. Both these evils industrial combination would tend to reduce, especially if carried to a monopoly extent, i.e. competition qua competition is abolished. However, an historical survey shows that big combinations are no better able to foresee events than are an agglomeration of small traders. (cff. Germany pre-war.) Then it is argued that big combinations can stabilize prices. This is true as regards such things as steel, – where the combination (i) controls the supply of iron ore; (ii) the price of the raw material is not a very large element in the final price, – but not in oil, etc. where the price of the raw material immensely affects the final price (e.g. contrast stability of railway rates, with variations in shipping). The argument is altogether unsound. If price stability is due to preventable causes then obviously prevent instability. But if price instability is due to inherent qualities of the economic system, then the best that can be done is to make the economic system elastic. cff. agricultural products. It is impossible to stabilize prices "economically." In the world market, the general market expenses, transport etc., are fairly well fixed. So the variable element in world agricultural prices is the element due to the farmer, so that, in general, x percent variation in market price has meant $x + dx$ percent in farmers' prices. One may conclude that so far as the price system is inherently unstable, an artificial stabilization of a section of it leads to greater instability elsewhere. Where one commodity competes with another, if the price of one is fixed fluctuation will be thrown on to the other.

(ii) Timing of governmental expenditure so as to go contrary to general movement

But in a period of depression Government expenditure, and hence taxation, increase would only lower the purchasing power in the hands of consumers in general. Unless savings are accumulated, and taxes tap these. – So one must assume the government finances (i) by borrowing directly from the banks, (ii) by issuing stocks to be taken up by the public or banks. – Involving slight extension of bank-credit. In other words, what is needed is a little inflation. On economic grounds there is no objection except that in itself, after a crisis it would not be sufficient without an "inconceivable" amount of government expenditure. – Thus it is a palliative. – But there are political difficulties. Instructions to the government to spend heavily, and then to throw cold water during the boom, would lead to great difficulties eg. in deciding what industries are in a boom.

(iii) Industrial fluctuations controllable by controlling the supply of bank credit

Note: It is not necessary to assume that industrial fluctuations are a function of variation of bank-credit. cff. pre 1844 act. The banking school demand elastic currency, otherwise curtailment of bank credits [would be] necessary, hence crisis. Then currency school: you can never have that degree of industrial expansion to bring about a crisis if you have an inelastic currency. Note Bagehot's advice, but only a palliative.[b] The modern idea is that if the supply of credit is properly regulated there need be no expansion to a crisis extent. It has various forms. For example, central bank regulates credit so as to keep some index number of prices constant. (Fisher; Keynes' *Tract on Monetary Reform*.)

Now it is impossible for banks in one country alone – apart from foreign aid – to regulate prices. Besides, a "fictitious" average maintained steady is nothing worth bothering about. In any case a certain elasticity is necessary, otherwise apart from the statistical average immense variations may take place elsewhere. Stability means something far more than the stability of an index-number.

Then what is the real power of the banks? The banks of the western world taken together would have an immense power over prices, but not those of any one country. Some say the Federal Reserve System was the chief controlling influence of prices in U.S.A. but Burgess (Federal Reserve Banks) contends that the policy of Europe has been more important.[c] There are differences too in the way in which the reduction of discount rates causes business expansion; it is assumed that there is always a negatively inclined curve for loans. Now variations in a discount rate in one market will increase borrowings in that market, – shifted from elsewhere, – but otherwise we are uncertain of the general increase.

May 8, 1928 Business forecasting

To a certain extent, forecasts of industrial fluctuations would, apart from positive factors of change, level out the foreseen fluctuations. Juglar has suggested an economic meteorological office. One Babson has made a good thing out of selling forecasts based on a line of normal growth. But it is obviously *a posteriori*. The conception is an empirical one based on a study of past movements and cannot be projected into the future. Babson assumed that fluctuations will be equally dispersed about the line of normal growth. Developing from Babson we get Persons' system, Harvard Economic Research.[d] (Note book written by Young in collaboration with Persons, mathematical statistics, recently unauthorised translation into Russian.[e] Preface warns Russian readers to interpret "profits," "capital," etc. in a "symbolic sense.") This method seeks for correlations between different series. They found three general classes out of some fifty types. They had to do with

(i) The condition of trade and industry, – "volume of business activity." For this, bank-clearings after eliminating those that represent speculative rather than industrial operations (note new banking statistics U.S.A.) give the best single index. In addition Persons relied mainly on wholesale prices.

(ii) Fluctuations of the money market. Ultimately decided on interest rates.

(iii) Speculations on the stock exchange. The number of shares sold, and the condition of prices on the exchange.

When investigations for time-lag were made the banking series went pretty closely, and so did the volume of trade and speculation. But each group of series had its peculiar movement. Generally [stock] exchange preceded business activity, then came the money market. (Or start where you will.) The time correlations were stable pre-war, then spoilt by the war, and now have reasserted themselves in the last seven years. But it is a method of forecasting obviously most uncertain and quite illogical if resting purely on past statistics. Yet Persons had a "law" or relation. If there were a two points rise in loans over last loan price (this) showed stock exchange prices at peak [sic]. But the experience of last year discounts this. Yet certain Americans continue to seek the "philosophers' stone." (cff. Karsten re application of the method of quadrature.)

That "industry requires secrecy" is a ridiculous maxim. If further information were compelled from industry, as regards stocks, prices etc. there is no doubt that further "wholesome" competition would be fostered which would make better use of the country's resources, and stand in the way of destructive competition. Thus (a) more economic theory, (b) more information regarding the state of industry is needed.

Editors' notes

a Sic. Perhaps Major Douglas

b See Bagehot, Walter (1915) *Lombard Street* (14th edn.), London: Henry S. King & Co., especially Ch XII, "Principles Regulating Bank Reserves," and Ch XIII, "Conclusions," where he refers to his proposals on bank reserve requirements as "humble palliatives" (p. 315).

c Burgess, W. R. (1927) *The Reserve Banks and the Money Market*, New York and London: Harper & Brothers. Reviewed by Young in *Economica*, vol. 8, June 1928, pp. 229–31.

d Persons, M. *Indices of General Business Conditions*, Cambridge, Harvard University Committee on Economic Research, 1919.

e This probably refers to Henry Lewis Reitz (ed.) *Handbook of Mathematical Statistics* (1924) Boston: Houghton Mifflin, to which both Young and Persons contributed (separate) chapters.

44 Particular expenses and supply curves

"Nicholas Kaldor's Notes on Allyn Young's LSE Lectures, 1927–29" *Journal of Economic Studies* (1990) 17, 3/4: 41–8

Particular expenses and supply curves

The interpretation of the ordinary supply curve (as shown in Figures 44.1, from Cournot, and 44.2 from Marshall) depends on the period of time taken into account. If one takes a limiting curve, one corresponding to the short-period demand curve, it shows an instant of time. It will be like the hypothetical demand curve as it will show the prices at which different quanta of goods would be supplied. However,

(1) If we abstract the actual social-economic mechanism, i.e. the distinction between producers and consumers, and have mere members dealing with one another, then this supply curve may be considered as a demand curve. Suppliers are people who want other commodities. Each supply curve is the reciprocal of a demand curve, so it could be represented by an ordinary demand curve for money. There is no difference in principle between short-period demand and short-period supply curves.

(2) If we look at it from the social-economic standpoint there are people who sell not because they want other commodities for themselves. Then the supply

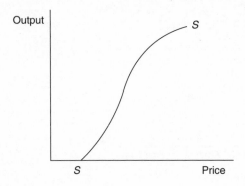

Figure 44.1

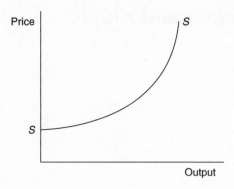

Figure 44.2

curve is not quite like a demand curve. The important thing in shaping this curve is not the diminishing utility of money to suppliers; yet the curve would rise, not because of ultimate costs of production, but because of (i) a physical shortage of supply so that, in a short period, to bring further goods into the market is expensive; and (ii) dealers have the distribution of demand through time in mind. Take the agricultural products speculative market; the circumstances which determine whether the dealer will sell now depend on his estimate of what he would get by waiting. This supply curve is related to a normal distribution of demand in time curve. In other words, it does not bear much relation to any long-period supply curve (i.e. the stock and produce exchanged in day-to-day transactions for a short period are not much help in finding what determines long-period prices). It is most important not to confuse this supply curve with a particular expenses curve of Marshall (Figure 44.3).[1][a]

OH is the amount produced annually; *AH* is the equilibrium price. The producer of the *OH*[th] unit has no differential advantage, but the producer of

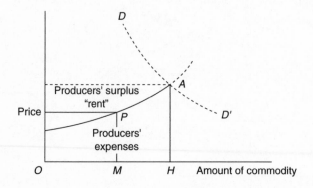

Figure 44.3

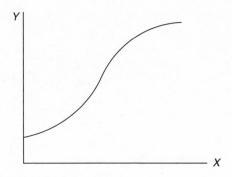

Figure 44.4

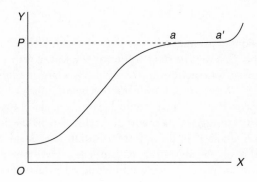

Figure 44.5

the OM^{th} unit has such advantages which permit him to produce at a cost of MP. The particular expenses curve is the locus of M, the greatest advantages being at the right (left?)[b]. The curve rises from the fact that not all producers have the same costs. If there were a random distribution of costs, average costs would be distributed normally and the curve would appear as in Figure 44.4.

Empirical evidence – government figures – has shown that the actual curve is frequently as in Figure 44.5. It gives concrete significance to the concept of marginal firms, from which the considerable bulk of the product comes. (Marshall has no such figures.) But it cannot be interpreted as a supply curve. It does not follow that those producing at the lowest expense will sell at the lowest price. On the contrary, they may sell at the highest price and it is the maximum-cost people who would be willing to sell low. The lowest cost producers are in a position to hold out. If there is any correlation between this and a supply curve, it is probably an inverse correlation[c].

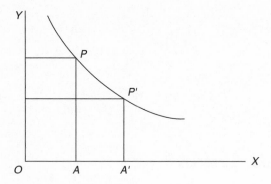

Figure 44.6

Lecture XV

Curve of supply of an industry under given conditions (Figure 44.6). If the price *AP* is sufficient to evoke a supply *OA*, then, given a sufficient amount of time for the necessary enlargements and reconstructions of the industry, a larger supply can be produced at the price *A'P'*. We abstract outside improvements, unexpected developments, etc., those improvements which would have taken place apart from the growth of the industry – though it is a moot[d] point how far these exist. Take the so-called "revolutionary changes" of the industrial "revolution". Modern economic history emphasises the way the increasing markets led to development. It is an interesting question how far pure science is a function of industry, and how far it goes under its own momentum. (Note thesis, "Connections between the Growth of Pure Science, Applied Science, and Increasing Returns"). It might be a good thing to drop the word "invention" from our vocabulary; the adapting engineer is the important man. But this must not be understood as preaching a deterministic theory of inventions.

Yet this curve gives rise to many difficulties:

(1) It relates not to a particular establishment, but to a particular industry. If it is applied to firms, monopoly would be the outcome.
(2) Sometimes it cannot even be related to an industry, but to a particular product. For sometimes the splitting up of an industry is the only way increasing returns can be obtained (e.g. printing trades, as described in Young's Presidential Address[1928]). Differentiation is more characteristic of modern industry than integration. Integration is only characteristic of certain special industries[e]. (Thesis, "Study in Economic History on the Basis of Successive Censuses of Occupations"[f].)
(3) But sometimes even the product will not do. Products change, and new products appear. Social change takes place partly by the substitution of new products which achieve the same end (e.g. the carriage, automobile;

manuscript, printed book). There then follows the question as to how far we can relate the changing product to something more fundamental than the external object – e.g. utility, psychic income. This is a fundamental problem when measuring different welfares in different periods. But where possible it is better to keep to the product.

Then there is the question of what is the relation of this curve to short-time curves. How can this be shown graphically? And would you take this curve to mean average costs or marginal costs of production? (Marginal costs here meaning the costs of production which, at any given time and price, it is just worth bearing.) Marshall took, in effect, average costs by using the "representative firm". He distinguished between its average and marginal costs but apparently held that the distinction became blurred in the long run. The Representative Firm is merely an expository device to aid in understanding this curve; it is the vehicle through which external economies – those outside a particular industry but to which the representative firm has access – affect supply. (Robbins'[g] article is "overcritical"; he does not appreciate it as an expository device; the question is perhaps one "hardly worth wasting an article on in the *Economic Journal*".)

Seeking for equilibrium conditions under increasing returns is as good as looking for a mare's nest. Certainly the matter cannot be explained by this curve apparatus, which does not see things "in their togetherness". For example, how variations of the cost of *M* (the good considered in the curve) affect other goods and their prices.

If, in Figure 44.7, the demand curve *DD′* cuts *SS′* as given, and does not change, there is no particular difficulty. Equilibrium is at *X*. That is, this construction is all right so far as the forces taken into account go. But it is a highly abstract situation, for *DD′* is closely connected with the supply curves of other industries, and if the demand for these other supplies is elastic, then increasing production of *M* is likely to alter the supply of other goods, and so *DD′* tends to shift (indefinitely) to the right, (v. Glasgow [British Association]

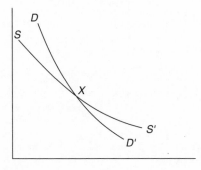

Figure 44.7

Address). But there may be equilibrium at any given time, dependent not only on the production of *M* but of other goods. The main point is that *DD'* is the reciprocal of supply curves in other industries, showing alternative uses of productive resources.

Where the situation is as in Figure 44.8, slowly increasing output causes increasing difference between supply price and demand price. So is the price set between the limits of the two prices? It is a very important problem in the sense that many times in the history of modern industry, especially in times of rapid expansion, a situation arises where the cost curve moves away from the demand curve, giving chance for profits. Now,

(1) This "sellers market" invites middlemen to insert themselves into the situation. This should be contrasted with the optimistic view held by some writers of the distribution of resources by competition. Under dynamic conditions there are always, at any given time, large elements of maladjustment from an equilibrium situation. The extent of the departure is disguised by the creation of new and socially unnecessary costs. The usual theory of profits overemphasises that taking of risks; some profits, such as those, represent merely picking plums. The middlemen create costs, and look as if they were earning their living, which of course they are from an individual but not social standpoint. The position gives rise to a false appearance of prices equalling costs where, rather, costs tend to equal prices (e.g. goods with special characteristics, branded goods sold at a high price; cff. also banking theory). "In times of industrial prosperity the world is full of such people." (Compare the number of middlemen during the currency troubles in Hungary.)

(2) The second effect is that producers themselves try to take advantage and increase production. If they follow the *SS'* line (shown in Figure 44.8 or 44.9) the maladjustment will merely increase. But in fact they use plants to a maximum, etc., taking short cuts to increased production. The curve *SS'* assumes warehousing, labour supply, etc., increase at the same rate as the industry, and that the industry is adapting itself as regards management, etc. So that in fact the cost curve actually turns up (see Figure 44.9)

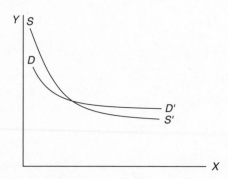

Figure 44.8

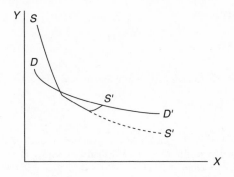

Figure 44.9

Marshall says the original (Figure 44.8) *SS'* curve represents the fact that cost per unit of output may be reduced as output grows, given time for the organisation of industry. But that is exactly the problem: how much time? The Marshallian statement is really meaningless. The "period of time" is relative to costs, and the costs are relative to the period of time. Otherwise it is clear that if *OA* can be produced at price *OP* and price *OA'* at price *OP'* (see Figure 44.6) what is there to prevent it from being done? In other words, why not follow the counsel of some rationalisers and "put British industry in shape"? But, even if one could see ahead, and plan and co-ordinate industry – each growing industry supplying a market for the other's goods – it would not be done. For the changes made are costly, and how costly depends on how long a time is taken. Say it is carried out in ten years, it would disrupt the social life of the country. Some industries would be abandoned, unemployment would occur, the population would need to be shifted from one place to another. And there would be enormous capital costs. The amount of capital required would be immense; for a time the country would need to live on next to nothing. You would cut far too deeply into the supply of present goods.

On the other hand if it was undertaken over a long period, by the time *OA'* was arrived at, changes in demand and invention would make it, perhaps, all worth nothing. If the period is too short, costs are too high; if the period is too long, advantages are lost. What is the right time? In fact it is determined by what industrialists can see looking ahead, versus costs as appearing in the form of the rate of interest. The market balances displacement costs against the increased product visible just ahead in the future.

Given any point on the graph there are a myriad of (future) supply curves according to the period selected. A long-period supply curve is meaningless apart from the particular length of time considered: the curve is relative to the rate at which increasing returns exist. On the other side you cannot postulate a constant demand curve for a good over a long period. It would shift as a result of the very forces which are shifting the supply curve. We need a theory of an equilibrium rate of progress. Probably the optimum rate of progress which will keep the supply curve close up to the demand curve.

Note

1 Marshall (1920) *Principles*, Appendix H (8th edn.), London: Macmillan.

Editors' notes

a The appendix is entitled "Limitations of the Use of Statistical Assumptions in Regard to Increasing Returns". Figure 44.3 is drawn directly from Marshall's Appendix H where there is extensive discussion of the "representative firm", internal and external economies, and increasing returns, to which Young is alluding in these lectures.

b *Sic*. Kaldor's marginal handwritten note. The puzzle is resolved by reference to Marshall's own discussion of this diagram, in which he states: "For convenience the owners of differential advantages may be arranged in descending order from left to right; and thus *SS'* becomes a curve sloping upwards to the right." This must mean that the greatest advantages are at the left, as Kaldor has suggested here.

c This cryptic paragraph perhaps warrants a clarificatory note. Young appears to be saying that when price is high it is because costs (of the marginal producers) are high, so supply (and demand) is low. When price is low it is because costs are low, so supply (and demand) is high. Thus the supply curve (along with the demand curve) is downward sloping. (Later Young explains that supply is greater when demand is greater because of the "increasing returns" that are associated with a larger market size, which affords greater scope for internal and external economies, and for specialisation in all its manifestations. Microeconomic analysis then merges with macroeconomics and the theory of economic progress.) Marshall himself (Appendix H) says of the upward sloping curve in Figure 44.3 that it is not a true supply curve; but modern textbooks usually conceive it thus, and ignore Marshall's many reservations.

d The word "moot" has been changed to "most important" in a hand-written amendment to Kaldor's manuscript.

e These ideas were examined in greater detail in Young, A. (1929) "Big Business: How the Economic System Grows and Evolves Like a Living Organism". (Reprinted as Chapter 46 in this selection.)

f The reference is obscure, but see Young's article, based on such an approach, "Economic Changes since the War: Their Meaning and their Lessons". (Reprinted as Chapter 45 in this selection.)

g See Robbins, L. (1928) "The Representative Firm", *Economic Journal*, 38, September.

45 Economic changes since the war

Their meaning and their lessons

The Book of Popular Science (1929) New York: The Grolier Society. Group IX Ch. 37: 5239–48

Men learn from experience, but, in the field of economic science, the experience which forces itself upon their attention and which calls insistently for explanation, is not the routine experience of uneventful years. It is that which takes us unawares or that of momentous changes into which we probe in order that we may learn from it. The economic changes which followed upon the World War were both sudden and momentous, and upon economic science there devolves the task of inquiring into them so as to explain them, to discover their meaning, and to extract from them the lessons which they hold for the future. First in importance among these new developments is the shifting of what might be called the center of gravity of the world's economic life from Europe towards America, – a shifting which manifests itself in industry, commerce and finance. The war, it is sometimes said, ushered in the era of America's industrial supremacy. The word "supremacy," however, is badly chosen. Despite the attempts which nations make to gain economic advantage at the expense of other nations, and despite the hold which the notion of "international economic rivalry" has upon the imaginations of men, it is truer to say that the modern world is a world of international economic coöperation than to picture it as one in which some nations have industrial "supremacy," others are economically subservient. "Primacy," or "leadership," is a better word.

The following table is taken from a document prepared for the International Economic Conference (the first of its kind in the world's history) which met at Geneva in April, 1927. Some of the figures are only approximations, but nevertheless they give a reliable picture of certain aspects of the changes to which we have referred. The figures, it will be observed, are in *relative* form; that is, population, production and foreign trade in 1925 are expressed as *percentages* of the magnitude of population, production and trade in 1913. The changes shown in production and trade are real changes. That is, they are changes in the physical volume of production and trade, not changes in their money value, which, of course, was much larger in 1925 than in 1913, because prices were much higher:

Table 45.1 Population, production and foreign trade of different regions in 1925 as compared with 1913 (Magnitude in 1913 = 100)

Region	Population	Production[1]	Foreign Trade
Europe, including Russia[2]	101	105	89
Europe, excluding Russia	104	105	94
Northern North America	119	126	137
Southern North America[3]	107	170	128
South America	122	135	97
Africa	107	139	99
Asia[4]	105	120	136
Oceania	116	123	132
The world	105	117	105

Notes

[1] Foodstuffs and raw materials only.
[2] Union of Socialist Soviet Republics, including Asiatic Russia.
[3] Mexico, Central America, and West Indies.
[4] Excluding Asiatic Russia.

Consider some of the facts which stand out most impressively. (1) In the face of pessimistic forecasts to the contrary, the world's production of foodstuffs and raw materials increased more rapidly than population. This remains true even after allowing for the fact that 1925 was a year of exceptionally good harvests. (2) International trade recovered from the effects of the war more slowly than production did, whereas before the war international trade was growing *more* rapidly than production. Currency disorders were partly responsible for this reversal. When a country's currency is falling rapidly in value, and especially when the movements of its relative value, compared with the values of the currencies of other countries, as reflected in the foreign exchanges, are uncertain and unpredictable, a hazardous element of speculation is introduced into international trading, and the flow of goods from one country to another becomes irregular and intermittent. Moreover, the purchasing power of some countries had become so far reduced that they offered very poor markets for foreign goods (Russia is an outstanding example). Such things have cumulative effects. Every country which found the outlet for its own exports diminished became a poorer market for the exports of other countries, for it had been accustomed to pay for its imports largely with its exports. Such countries, therefore, produced fewer goods for export and began to produce at home some of the things which they had been accustomed to import from abroad.

The new industries which began to grow up in this way, as well, too, as the new industries which had been brought into existence either by reason of the special demands of the war or as a result of the war's interference with international trade, clamored for a sheltered position under the protection of high tariff barriers. The new spirit of self-assertive nationalism and of international distrust which the war had aroused was another factor making for high protective tariffs and for misguided strivings for national economic self-sufficiency and isolation. The world, as though in a fit of childish petulance, was deliberately throwing away some of the advantages of international economic cooperation. It was because some far-seeing men – including in their number industrial as well as political leaders – were alive to the follies and dangers of such a course, that the International Economic Conference was convened at Geneva in 1927. (3) The backwardness of trade as compared with production was localized and confined for the most part to those regions which had been most directly and seriously affected by the war. The trade of North America, Asia and Oceania (including Australia and New Zealand) showed large gains. The changes in the relative shares of different regions in the world's trade are given in Table 45.2.

Put in the form of modest percentages these figures are likely to fail to impress the reader with the magnitude and importance of the changes which they reflect, changes which amount in some instances to thousands of millions of dollars. In another way, too, these figures may be misleading. Although arranged by regions, the figures are for *international*, not for inter-regional trade. Europe's preponderating share, which, even after her losses, amounted in 1925 to about half of the world total, is partly explained by the circumstance that it includes intra-European trade, such as that between England and Germany or between Austria and Hungary. If the figures for Northern North America had included (as they do not include) the trade among different American states or different Canadian provinces, the share of that region would have been made to appear very much larger. Or if the figures for Europe had included only the trade between the continent of Europe and the British Isles on the one side, and the rest of the world on the other side, those figures would have been very much smaller.

What is the relation between these changes in relative positions and the changes which might normally have been expected if the war had not intervened? How far is the new position of America in the production and trade of the world an unearned position? How far is it a real net gain? How far does it merely reflect the misfortunes of other regions, the enforced retarding of their economic growth? One cannot say with certainty. Certain probable inferences can be made, however, upon the basis of what we know about the general direction of the changes in production and trade which were taking place before the war. (1) The increase of production in the United States and Canada, even if manufacturing industries are taken into account, has probably been less and almost certainly no greater

Table 45.2 Relative shares of different regions in the world's trade in 1925 as compared with 1913 (percentages)

Region	Imports		Exports		Total	
	1913	*1925*	*1913*	*1925*	*1913*	*1925*
Europe, including Russia	61.6	55.1	55.2	44.7	58.5	50.0
Europe, excluding Russia	58.0	53.9	51.0	43.7	54.6	48.9
Northern North America	12.4	16.2	15.8	20.6	14.0	18.3
Southern North America	1.9	2.3	2.4	3.0	2.1	2.6
South America	5.7	5.2	6.7	6.2	6.2	5.7
Africa	4.0	3.9	4.5	4.2	4.3	4.1
Asia	11.9	14.1	12.7	17.9	12.3	16.0
Oceania	2.5	3.2	2.7	3.4	2.6	3.3

than it would have been if there had been no war. America has gained in wealth, not because of it, but in spite of it. (2) Even without the war, America's *relative* share in the world's production of wealth would have been larger than it was in 1913, for production in America was growing faster than in Europe. The war, of course, by impeding Europe's progress, increased America's relative gain. (3) America's proportion of the foreign trade of the world is much greater than it would have been if the war had not destroyed a large part of Europe's commerce and if its after effects had not made the re-establishing of that commerce slow and difficult. (4) The absolute or actual amount of America's foreign trade is probably no greater because of the war. About as large a proportion of the wealth annually produced in the United States is exported to other countries as would have been if there had been no sudden change of the trends or tendencies which appeared to be discernible before the war. Even this much would have been impossible, in view of the comparative poverty of some of the countries which were large buyers of these exports, if the United States had not been able not merely to increase its annual output of goods but also to finance its own export trade and to advance large sums of money to other countries; thus, in effect, selling a considerable part of its goods on credit.

We shall now look a little more closely at these related subjects, the production, trade, and financial position of the United States.

The figure already given for the increase of production in Northern North America (the United States, Canada, Newfoundland, etc.) between 1913 and 1925 (26 percent) referred to foodstuffs and raw materials only. For the advance in manufacturing production in both the United States and Canada was much more notable, – so much so indeed in the United States as almost to deserve the name of a veritable economic revolution. We say "almost" because, after all, the advance of manufacturing industry in the United States was a continuation of a long period of steady growth. As a result of that growth the United States now has the highest average per capita production of wealth which the world has ever known, and consequently the highest general level of welfare. What have been the causes? Not the country's endowment of natural resources, rich as that endowment is, for Europe, taking the continent as a whole, is quite as well supplied. Not any special or distinguishing quality in its people, for they are of European stock. Not any superiority in scientific achievement, for save in a few special fields, scientific leadership still remains with Europe. What then is the explanation of America's swift rise to industrial primacy?

Something may he conceded to the general diffusion of education in America. Some weight must also be given to the democratic organization of society, to the absence of rigid barriers between different classes, to the relatively better chance which a man of real ability has to rise from a place in the ranks to a position of responsibility and leadership in industry. Account must be taken, too, of the practically complete absence in the United States of those remnants of old feudal prejudices which, in Europe, often prevent men of high capacity from looking at industry and trade as offering opportunities for a useful and honorable career. But these things, taken in the aggregate, are very much less important in explaining the phenomenal advance of American industry than is a simple economic principle. Adam Smith, writing in 1776, reached the heart of the matter when he said: "The division of labor depends upon the extent of the market."

The division of labor, however, has come to be something very much more far-reaching than that specialization of tasks among different skilled crafts which Adam Smith had particularly in mind. It manifests itself in our intricate system of industrial organization, with specialized plants located at favorable points, with the making of complicated products broken up into a large number of separate *processes* (thus facilitating the use of machinery), and with an increasing use of roundabout and indirect methods, such as call for large preliminary outlays for highly specialized equipment. In their modern forms the economies of the division of labor are largely identical with the economies of "capitalistic" methods of production.

Now a little reflection will serve to convince anyone that the extent to which it is economical to use roundabout, or capitalistic, methods depends upon the amount to he produced. It would be wasteful to make a hammer to drive a single nail; it would be better to use whatever awkward implement lies conveniently at hand. It would be wasteful to furnish a plant with an elaborate equipment of specially devised jigs, presses, lathes, drills and conveyors to build a hundred automobiles. The methods appropriate to large-scale production are the most economical methods, but the same methods would he absurdly uneconomical if used in producing goods on a small scale. "Mass-production," with its attendant economies, has been carried further in the United States than in other countries largely for the reason that producers here have access to the largest domestic market in the world, a market in which the movement of goods from producer to consumer is unimpeded by tariff barriers. Automobiles, for example, are built at a smaller cost in the United States than in any other country. The costs are low because the output is large.

The most important aspect of these economies is that they operate cumulatively; that is, the increased productivity of any one industry means an increased demand for the products of other industries. Every step forward in the specialization of industrial pursuits opens the way for increased specialization in other parts of the industrial structure. The division of labor increases the size of the market just as (and because) it increases the average per capita product of labor. A people producing more is a people demanding more. Increased demand thus leads to increased industrial efficiency, and increased industrial efficiency leads to a further increase of demand. With a given population and with a given state of technical knowledge there are, of course, limits to this process, but there is no reason to suppose that in a country such as the United States these limits have been reached or even approached. The largest hope for the future, however, is that the progress of science and of technical knowledge will continue always to keep the improvements which are possible a little ahead of the improvements which have been achieved.

In its biennial census of manufactures the United States has a more nearly continuous record of its industrial progress than has any other country. We shall

Table 45.3 Growth of manufacturing industries in the United States: 1914–25

	1914	1925	Percentage increase
Wage earners (thousands)	6,896	8,384	21.6
Wages (millions of dollars)	4,068	10,729	163.7
Primary horsepower (thousands)	22,291	35,735	60.3
Value of products (millions of dollars)	23,988	62,706	161.4
Value added by manufacture (millions of dollars)	9,710	26,775	175.7

content ourselves, however, with some figures showing the net progress achieved between 1914 and 1925 (the year to which the figures for the production of foodstuffs and raw materials, already given, refer).

The figures for 1925 and some of the figures for 1914 do not include establishments whose annual products had a value of less than $5,000, but this does not really affect the significance of the comparisons.

The most important item is "value added by manufacture" (i.e., the total value of the product less the value of the materials used). Part of the extraordinary increase of 175.7 percent is attributable to the higher level of prices which prevailed in 1925. If prices had remained as low as they were in 1914, the value added in manufacture would have been about 70 percent greater in 1925 than in 1914. While this enormous expansion was being accomplished the number of wage earners increased by only 21.6 percent, and at the same time there was a substantial reduction in the average length of the working day. The average product per wage earner increased by about 40 percent, while the average product per working hour increased by 50 percent or more. Part of the explanation is that the average factory worker was better equipped with power-driven machinery in 1925 than in 1914, – the increase of the supply of prime movers was enough to give just about one horsepower more per worker. An extraordinarily large proportion of the value of the increased product went to labor in the form of wages. The average factory worker was paid more than twice as many dollars in 1925 as in 1914. Allowing for the increase in the cost of living, it is safe to say that his real wage (the purchasing power of his money wage) was at least a third more. In addition, he had more leisure. In the years immediately following 1925 the industrial worker made yet further gains, for the cost of living fell off somewhat, while there was a further increase in the general level of money wages. In the first years of the second quarter of the twentieth century the average American workman had attained a higher position than workmen ever had before, at any time in the world's history. He was able to maintain a higher standard of living, to command more of the comforts and minor luxuries of life, and in many occupations he had an opportunity, through his savings, of becoming a capitalist in a small way on his own account. In particular industries and in certain localities, however, the general brightness of the picture was dimmed, as in earlier years, by intermittent or semi-chronic depression, attended necessarily by a lack of opportunity for the full employment of the available supply of workers. The solving of the problem of industrial maladjustments – themselves in part the fruits of industrial change and progress – remains one of the major tasks of economic science.

Reference has been made to that important factor in the economic progress of the United States – the increased use of sources of mechanical energy. In 1927 the total capacity of the prime movers in the factories, mines and electric plants of the country was not less than 80,000,000 horsepower, and electric plants accounted for about as large a part of this total as factories did. Even more striking is the fact that the United States now supplies about a third of the world's annual production of coal, seven-tenths of its production of petroleum, and has a third of its developed water-power. Moreover, the amount of those sources of heat and power consumed in the United States is approximately equal to the amount produced, the whole being equal (measuring petroleum and water-power in terms of their coal equivalents) to not much less than 1,000,000,000 tons a year. Domestic uses and the consumption of gasoline in the operation of automobiles account for only a minor part of this enormous total. The greater part goes to supply the industries, the railways and the local lighting and power plants of the country. Without this abundance of sources of power the present amazing productivity of American industry could not have been attained.

In respect of its foreign trade the present position of the United States is somewhat paradoxical. The annual value of its trade is now considerably more than twice what it was before the war. Part of the increase is accounted for by the general advance of prices, but there has been a gain of about 50 percent in the *quantity* of goods exported and imported. The United States now has a larger foreign trade than any other country in the world, while before the war it was a rather poor third, being surpassed by both Great Britain and Germany. But in no other of the great countries of the world is foreign trade of smaller relative importance as compared with the sum total of the country's economic activities. Not over five or six percent of the total amount of wealth produced annually in the United States is exported, and not over 10 percent of the annual production of the kinds of goods which conceivably might be exported (including the products of industry, agriculture and mining) reaches foreign markets. As compared with the figures for the ratio of the foreign trade of other highly industrialized countries to their aggregate production of wealth these are small proportions. They mark the degree in which the United States, with its vast area – and its varied resources, is economically self-sufficient and self-contained. What may be more surprising, possibly, is that these proportions have changed very little over a long series of years, and are no larger now than they were before the war. From one point of view, therefore, the notable increase of the foreign trade of the United States merely reflects an equally notable increase in in the general scale of its economic activities.

The proportion of the total output which is exported varies, of course, for different commodities. Among the important products for which the export market absorbs a fairly large percentage of the total output are: lard (30 to 40 percent), wheat (15 to 30 percent), leaf tobacco (35 to 50 percent), cotton (40 to 50 percent), rosin and turpentine (40 to 70 percent), kerosene (30 to 40 percent), lubricating oil (about 30 percent), copper (about 40 percent), cigarettes (15 to 20 percent), agricultural machinery (15 to 20 percent), sewing-machines (20 to 30 percent), motor-cycles (40 to 60 percent), cash registers (10 to 20 percent), typewriters (30 to 40 percent), locomotives (10 to 30 percent). On the other hand export markets take less than 10 percent of the total annual production of such important commodities as oats, corn, lumber, coal, boots and shoes, automobiles, tires, rails, structural steel, cotton goods and pianos.

Although the magnitude of the foreign trade of the United States has thus maintained an extraordinarily stable relation to the annual volume of the country's production of wealth, its character or composition has changed materially. The degree of change, however, has not been so great as people who do not take the trouble to look at the figures sometimes appear to think. For a long period of years before the war, crude raw materials generally constituted between a fourth and a third of the country's exports, and were more often over than under 30 percent, raw cotton being the most important variable item. The proportion now is a little, but only a little, smaller, ranging from 25 to 30 percent. The relative importance of exports of unmanufactured foodstuffs fell off rapidly in the last quarter of the nineteenth century, increased rapidly during the war and the years immediately following, and has now dropped to its pre-war level of between six and nine percent. Exports of manufactured foodstuffs, however, which were relatively much smaller just before the war than they had been before 1900, have declined still further in relative importance – from about 14 percent, the pre-war proportion, to about 11 percent. Partly manufactured or semi-finished goods, other than foodstuffs, had been gaining rapidly in relative importance for half a century or more – and just before the war made about 16 percent of all exports, as compared with about 14 percent in recent years. The proportion that finished manufactures make of aggregate exports, however, has continued to grow, having passed the 30 percent point before the war, and standing now at about 40 percent. These *relative* changes should not be permitted to obscure the fact that since the years just before the war there has been an *absolute* increase not only in the monetary value but also in the actual amount of each of these great general classes of exports. In becoming a great industrial nation the United States has not ceased to be a great agricultural nation. The new forms of economic activity have not displaced the old; they have merely been added to them.

The most important of the commodities which have gained a relatively larger place among the country's exports are petroleum products, machinery, automobiles, rubber manufactures, cotton manufactures, coal, wheat and fruits. Exports of lard, copper and tobacco are also larger than they were, though they have not quite kept pace with the general growth of the country's trade.

Imports, viewed generally, have grown quite as rapidly as exports, – which is, of course, a perfectly normal and wholesome situation. In fact, during the last few years, imports have gained notably upon exports. This is a natural reaction from the abnormal conditions which prevailed from 1915 to 1921, when imports, measured in money value, were little more than half as large as exports. For a period of twenty years before the war their value was generally between two-thirds and three-fourths of the value of exports. Since 1921 the corresponding proportions have had an ordinary range of between 80 and 90 percent. Although with the growth of the domestic market the value of every class of imports has grown, the most notable increase has been the imports of raw materials for American industry. Imports of manufactured goods, although they increased in value, have fallen off somewhat in quantity. The imports which have increased most rapidly are crude rubber (for which the United States now pays something like $500,000,000 a year), raw silk, coffee, sugar, paper and wood pulp, crude petroleum, wool, tin, copper, vegetable oils, oilseeds, fertilizers and lumber. Other important imports are furs, hides, burlaps, cotton and woolen manufactures and diamonds. But rubber, raw silk, coffee and sugar, taken together, account for nearly a third of the country's total imports.

There have been some striking developments in the geographical distribution of both the export and the import trade. Two factors are largely responsible for these changes: first, the growth of the relative importance of industry as compared with agriculture in the United States; second, the slow recovery after the war of the productive capacity and purchasing power of Europe. Formerly over three-fifths of the country's exports went to Europe, but now Europe takes only about half of the total. She formerly supplied half the country's imports, but now she furnishes only 30 percent. The amount of the trade with Europe is little if any smaller than it was (its monetary value has increased substantially). The diminished importance of trade with Europe merely means that that trade, important as it is, has not grown as has trade with Canada, Latin America, and Asia. Trade with Canada (measured in dollars) has multiplied about two and a half times since 1914, trade with Southern North America has multiplied two and a third times, with South America it has nearly trebled, with Asia it has had a five-fold increase, with Oceania and Africa (though still relatively small) it has quadrupled. The most striking change has been the increase of imports from Asia, which are now greater than from any other continent. Rubber from the British and Dutch East Indies and raw silk from Japan and China are the principal items in this enormous inflow of goods from the Far East, the annual value of which is well over $51,000,000,000. Coffee comes from Brazil, Colombia and Central America (to name only the principal sources of supply); tea from the British East Indies, Japan and China; cocoa beans from British West Africa, the West Indies and South America; sugar from Cuba and the Philippines; hides from Argentina and Canada; goat and sheep skins from India and New Zealand; furs from England, China, Canada and Australia; cheese from Italy and Switzerland; flax seed from Argentina; cotton from Egypt; cotton cloth from England; wool from England, Australia, Argentina and Uruguay; pulp wood and wood pulp from Canada and Sweden; paper from Canada; tobacco from Cuba, Holland and Greece; petroleum from Mexico; burlaps from India; copper from Canada, Mexico, Peru and Portuguese Africa; tin from the Straits Settlements; sodium nitrate from Chile; diamonds from Holland and Belgium.

Among the larger items in the outgoing stream of exports are cotton to England, Germany, Japan and France (naming again only the most important markets); wheat to England, Japan and many countries of Western Europe; flax to England, Holland, Cuba and Brazil; tobacco to England and China; cigarettes to China; hams, bacon and lard to England, Germany, and Cuba; cotton cloth to the Philippines, Canada and South and Central America; gasoline to England, France, Australia and Canada; illuminating oil to China, Japan, Australia, Brazil and Western Europe; fuel oil and lubricating oil to England, France, Italy, Germany, Panama and Canada; refined copper to England, Germany, France, Belgium and Italy; automobiles to Argentina, Brazil, Mexico, England and all of the British Dominions.

Despite the changes in the geographical distribution of the country's foreign trade, the general situation with respect to the balance of trade with different regions remains very much what it has been for many years. There is a very large "favorable" balance (excess of exports over imports) in the trade with Europe, and smaller ones in the trade with Canada and Australasia. These "favorable" balances are partly offset by "unfavorable" balances in the trade with Latin America and by a very much larger one in the trade with the Far East, whence the enormous imports of rubber, raw silk. tin and burlaps come. Through the mechanism of the foreign exchanges the credit balances which accrue to banks of the United States by reason of the excess of exports over imports in the trade with Europe are available to importers for meeting that part of the expense of bringing goods in from Latin America and Asia which is not covered by the funds created by exports to those regions. We look at precisely the same facts from another angle when we say that Europe meets part of the deficit which arises out of her trade with the United States by drawing upon the proceeds of an export surplus in her trade with Asia and Latin America. But this is not all there is to the matter, however, for after all of its imports are offset against its exports, the United States still has a large annual uncovered credit balance against the rest of the world. How is this balance paid? This question leads us to an examination of the new position which the United States has attained in the world of international finance.

During most of its history the United States has been a debtor country. That does not mean that its people have been improvident, but merely that the productive possibilities of the country were so great that capital was attracted from overseas. Much foreign capital, for example, went into the building of American railways. After 1895, the United States gradually reduced the amount of its indebtedness to other countries, but just before the war the net amount was probably as much as $5,000,000,000. Then there came a financial revolution. Confronted by enormous public expenditures and in urgent need of supplies, the people of Great Britain and of other European countries asked the people of the United States to take off their hands a considerable part of their American investments. Soon the governments and then the industries of European countries turned to the United States for loans. A large amount of borrowing on the part of other countries which had ordinarily been done in Europe was deflected to American money markets, especially in New York. Visible evidence of these revolutionary developments appeared in the form of the largest "favorable" trade balance which any country had ever had, amounting in the seven years ending with 1921 to well over eleven and a half billions of dollars. Even after allowing for the inflated prices of that period this is an amazing figure.

So great an expansion would have been impossible without the elastic supply of credit and currency which the newly established Federal Reserve System was able to provide. It would have been impossible too, if the margin between the amount of wealth annually produced in the country and the amount consumed there or retained within its borders had not been increased in unprecedented degree. This was accomplished partly by speeding up production and partly by consuming a smaller proportion of the total amount produced. Some of the increased saving which helped towards this result was involuntary; that is, it was imposed upon people whose incomes did not increase as prices rose.

Retarded for a while by the world-wide depression of industry in 1921, the outward flow of American capital again quickly grew to large proportions, although not attaining the extraordinarily high levels of the period of war and post-war monetary inflation. During the last few years, it is important to note, the movement has been normal, in the sense that the annual national saving which it represents has not had the artificial stimuli of rising prices and an abnormally high level of business profits. Several years ago the United States had not merely ceased to be a debtor in the international capital market; it had become a creditor in an amount equal to or larger than the amount of its pre-war net indebtedness to other countries. Since that time its foreign holdings have been still further increased.

So new is this position that some Americans have been made uneasy, and have begun to wonder whether these debts will ever be paid. They are concerning themselves with an unreal and, in a sense, a meaningless problem. It is in no way necessary that debtors in other countries, taken as a whole, should be able to repay all of their American creditors within any specific period of time. It is only necessary that each individual American creditor could be able at any time to sell all or part of his holdings of foreign securities at a fair price whether in the American market or abroad. To this end it is necessary, as a general rule, that each foreign debtor should be able to pay what he owes, even if he has to "refund" his debt by borrowing again, whether in America, or in his own country, or in some other market. If he borrows again, but does not borrow in America, he may perchance displace some other borrower, and the latter may then turn to the American market for a loan, in which event the net amount of the foreign investments of the United States would not be reduced. In view of the cumulative nature of the forces which are responsible for the growth of wealth production and capital accumulation in the United States, it is much more probable that for an indefinite period in the future those foreign investments will increase than that the rest of the world, taken as a whole, will find it expedient to pay its debts.

There will, however, be changes in the character and the geographical distribution of the debt. The inter-governmental debts which now figure so largely in public discussion arose out of the exigencies of war. They may be paid or they may be canceled, but they will not be renewed. Again, the loans which have been made to the industries and the cities of Germany and of other European countries were sought for because of a temporary shortage of capital in those countries – a shortage attributable in part to the wastes of war, in part to needs incurred in connection with the restoration of stable currencies, and in part to a demand for funds to be used in paying reparations or other abnormal debts. This situation is artificial, in the sense that it has not grown out of the normal processes of production and trade. Capital generally flows to countries where natural resources are plentiful or where labor is especially cheap, and where opportunities for the profitable use of capital are therefore particularly inviting. In the future a larger proportion of the exports of capital from the United States will go to other parts of the American continents, to Asia, and even to Africa.

Not by borrowing only, however, has the rest of the world been able to buy more goods from the United States than the United States has bought in return. Enormous payments – payments so large as to be altogether unprecedented – have been made in gold. Two circumstances, first, Europe's urgent need for goods, and second, her enforced abandoning of the gold standard, combined to make gold of relatively less value to her than goods. During the twelve years beginning in 1915 over two billion dollars in gold poured into the United States, while outgoing shipments of gold were barely a fifth of that amount. The gold stock of the United States recently stood at about four and a half billions of dollars, and constituted more than half of the world's aggregate monetary stock of gold. With the stabilizing of European currencies and the restoration of gold monetary standards the situation has changed. The central banks of European countries are husbanding their stocks of gold, and their present policies are calculated to prevent such an expansion of credit (that is, such a multiplication of rights, in the form of bank notes and deposits, to demand gold from them) as might lead to renewed gold exports. In fact, many of them are trying to increase their stores of gold. In the meanwhile some of them eke out their supply by holding stocks of "gold exchange" in the form, for example, of deposits in New York banks, or bills of exchange payable in New York.

Under the old American banking system, an inflow of gold as large as that of recent years would almost certainly have led to an enormous expansion of credit, accompanied by a spectacular rise of prices and a feverishly speculative "boom" of business activities, followed by collapse and depression. In fact the inflow of gold could not have gone so far as in fact it did, for the expansion of credit and the rise of prices and of interest rates would have attracted imports of commodities and impeded exports.

It would, of course, be going too far to attribute all of the wholesome stability of prices and of industry in recent years to the wisdom with which the Federal Reserve Banks have used their power of controlling the supply of credit. But that without the Federal Reserve System the present economic situation of the United States and of the world in general would be more troubled and less promising than in fact it is can hardly be a matter of doubt to any thinking man.

46 Big business: how the economic system grows and evolves like a living organism

What will become of the small retailer?

The Book of Popular Science (1929) New York: The Grolier Society. Group IX Ch. 38: 5387–94

The vast and intricate system of economic organization, by means of which the varied needs of modern life are met, is mostly a product of a continuous process of evolution. In only very small part is it a result of conscious collective planning or devising. It grows and changes unceasingly as men, in their work as producers and money-makers, try to find new and more economical ways of providing consumers with goods which they are willing to buy. Every innovation, whether in the technique of production or in the organization of business, affects in some degree the conditions which govern the activities of other producers. The economic system grows and evolves, like a living organism, by means of successive adjustments and adaptations. But change breeds change, and every new adjustment paves the way for another.

So complex is the world's economic organization and so inconspicuous, at first, are some of the changes which finally lead to veritable economic revolutions, that it is dangerous to generalise about the nature and probable outcome of the economic tendencies which are at work in the contemporary world. One tendency, in particular, has again and again been made the basis of generalizations which thus far have proved to be unsound. That is the observable tendency towards an increase of the size of the average business undertaking. Because of that tendency many men have been led to prophesy the final doom of the competitive system and the complete extinction of the small business undertaking.

Thus Karl Marx, who formulated the creed of modern revolutionary socialism, held that the small property owner was fated to disappear, and that wealth and the control of industry would become concentrated in the hands of a relatively small number of people. But during the last 50 years the general course of events has been so far out of line with Marx's forecast that, among the socialists, only his most loyal disciples now insist upon its truth. There have been a host of minor prophets, too, ready when any new industrial amalgamation is announced, or when any large industrial undertaking achieves a striking success and grows rapidly larger, to proclaim the approaching end of competition as a factor in trade and industry, and the coming dominance of monopoly. The railway, such prophets once held, was to supplant all other agencies of transport. Yet the railway itself now has to face the powerful competition of motor transport. Immediately before and after the beginning of the present century, a very large number of industrial combinations or "trusts" were formed (a recent writer lists 90 combinations, large and small, which were formed in the United States between 1898 and 1904). There was no lack of prophesying that a new industrial order was being ushered in. Only a relatively small number of these combinations, however, proved to be successful. Some of them, in fact, were formed merely in order that their securities might be sold at inflated prices to investors who overestimated the profits that would result from combination.

Does the new order hurt the old?

When department stores were new there were many who foretold the ruin of the small shopkeeper and his disappearance from the field of retail trades. In recent years the growing activities of mail-order houses and of systems of chain stores have given rise to similar forebodings. Are the new prophets of economic revolution any more likely to be right than the old?

No one dominating principle shapes the course of economic evolution. It is, as we have seen, always a matter of successive adjustments to a situation which is forever new because it is forever changing. The advantages of unified or large-scale industrial management are not absolute. There are disadvantages as well as advantages. Which are preponderant in a particular industry cannot be determined upon the basis of abstract considerations alone. Everything depends upon the characteristics of the particular industry, upon the nature of its products, and the size of its markets. Let the reader ponder the reasons which account for the circumstance that agriculture, the world over, remains a small-scale industry together with the reasons which explain why the manufacture of steel, the world over, is mostly in the hands of gigantic corporations. It will not do to evade the issue by holding that agriculture, as contrasted with steel-making, is inefficiently organized. In the first place, there is no real evidence to that effect. In the second place, no farmer, not even the most efficient farmer, could continue very long to enlarge the scope of his operations, by acquiring and operating one adjoining farm after another, without losing money. After all, the real test of efficiency as a producer is the capacity to bid enough for land, labor and other productive agents to keep them out of other employments and then to use them profitably. This is an unfair test only when a particular producer enjoys special privileges, not available to his would-be competitors, or when he is strong enough to be able to afford to suppress competition, whenever it begins to show itself, by attacking it ruthlessly and at whatever cost.

Enlarging the market

There is one elementary distinction which ought never to be neglected, for its neglect always leads to confusion. That is the distinction between the economies which may be gained when the market for a particular product is enlarged, so that it can be produced in larger quantities, and the economies which a particular firm secures when it increases the scale of its operations.

The history of the securing of the first of these two kinds of economies makes a very important part of the history of modern industry. To appreciate the nature and significance of these economies, one must fix one's eyes, not upon the activities of a particular firm, but upon the operations of an entire industry, or, better yet, upon the operations of the whole group of related industries which contribute to the making of a single product. Producers of raw materials, of fuel, of auxiliary supplies, of machines, together with railways and other transport agencies are all in the picture. Consider, for example, the printing industry. The average printing establishment is not, even today, a very large affair. Back of it, however, and, as one might say, reaching the final consumer only through and by means of it, are the type-founders, the makers of linotypes and monotypes, of printing presses and of other specialized machines, of inks, of wood pulp, and of paper, together with the industries which, in turn, supply equipment and materials to those which are immediately auxiliary to that of printing.

Thus the books, the magazines, the newspapers, and the multitude of printed forms which appear to be so important a part of the paraphernalia of modern life are seen to be the products, not necessarily of large printing establishments, but of an intricately organized system of industries, operating, as an aggregate, on an exceedingly large scale. Sometimes the various stages of a series of industrial operations are brought together into what is called an "integrated" industry. The United States Steel Corporation and the Ford Motor Works, are as good examples as can be found anywhere of integrated undertakings. In no case, however, can the integration of successive industrial processes be altogether complete. Nor are the conditions common which make any large degree of integration economical or feasible.

Economies of the big plant

Turning now to the large undertaking or large establishment (as distinguished from the large industry or large group of related industries) let us try to discover whether any general explanations can tell us why, in some fields of industry and trade, the average successful undertaking is very large, while in other fields the small enterprise continues to hold its own. We shall arbitrarily exclude from consideration such undertakings as railways and local "public utilities" (water, gas, and electric light plants, street railways, telephone service, etc.). In this particular field of enterprise, almost any undertaking requires a considerable initial investment of capital, and, furthermore, the special conditions under which such undertakings operate make monopoly (either controlled or owned by the public) more economical than competition. Outside of this special field, then, what industrial and trading activities lend themselves best to large-scale and what to small-scale management? As we have already seen, the general conditions which business enterprise has to meet change so continuously and so rapidly that any single generalization, and especially any definite forecast, is likely to be wrong. There is one observation, however, which appears to be supported by all of the experience which we have had up till now with such matters. Unified management and large-scale undertakings succeed best when the product itself can be standardized (so that one unit is like any other unit) and when the processes of production, however complex, can be reduced to an ordered succession of routine operation.

Industries of a different class

Some of the products of agriculture are fairly well standardized – so well so, indeed, that they are commonly sold by weight or measure. But the conditions under which farms have to be managed do not lend themselves to routine, in the sense in which routine pervades the operations of many manufacturing industries. The farmer has to know the qualities of his land and the various peculiarities of his different fields. He has to contend with the vicissitudes of the weather. He has to meet one small emergency after another, and, so far as may be, he has to keep his plans flexible and adaptable. In farming, *management* (responsible directing and deciding) has to concern itself with a multitude of small details. It cannot successfully spread itself over a very large field. This is one reason (the circumstance that agriculture still remains in some degree a *family* industry may be another) why the average farm is not a very large undertaking. How different the controlling conditions are in the manufacture of steel billets and beams and rails will be obvious to anyone. Look again at the printing industry. Its products are almost infinitely various. That is one of the reasons why the industry of printing is not in the hands of a relatively small number of establishments of great size. Book printing, newspaper printing, and commercial printing are different trades, requiring (in part) different sorts of equipment, and each calling for a considerable amount of managerial supervision of details. The markets for many kinds of printing, furthermore, are local. It might be quite as uneconomical for a resident of a small town to have all of his printing done in a great manufacturing centre as to send there for all of his small purchases or for his plumber or his barber. But even the "one-man" shop of the small printer who combines the functions of craftsman and retail dealer is one of the channels through which the operations of the great industries which are auxiliary to the printing trade serve to meet the wants of the buyers of printing.

An industry may approach the status of a "handicraft," as we have seen, either because of the insistent demand of buyers for special and particular characteristics in the things which they purchase or because of the variability and instability of the conditions with which producers have to contend. At one end of the scale is art in all of its varied forms. The artist has to manipulate stubborn and refractory materials into new forms, which will convey meaning and a sense of beauty to the observer. He has to acquire a "technique," which means that he has to achieve a difficult mastery over his own faculties. His task is as far removed as one can imagine from the processes which are utilised most economically in "mass-production," and which therefore lend themselves best to large-scale organization and management. The artist is first of all a craftsman. And the farmer, it may be observed, is, and has to be, rather more like a craftsman than like a manager of a "standardized" industry. Modern large-scale industry – where it can – tends to eliminate the craftsman, and to substitute the engineer, the machine, and the machine operator. A penetrating observation by Werner Sombart, a great German economist, has been summarised by Professor Wesley Mitchell in the following words:

> Modern technique seeks emancipation from the hobbles of living nature. So far as possible, it chooses inorganic materials in place of organic – metals replace wood, coal-tar dyes replace vegetable dyes, mineral lubricants replace animal oils, and so on. Similarly with prime movers: man power and animal power are replaced by steam, electricity and the internal combustion engine. Working processes undergo a like transformation. For the ordinary processes of nature, modern technique substitutes artfully arranged chemical or mechanical processes, designed to convert standardized materials into standardized products through a continuous series of operations on a quantity basis.

The field of standardization

Standardization has to contend, however, with the infinite variety of human needs and with the human passion for novelty and for change. Its largest field is found somewhere *between* the variety and instability of the natural environment, on the one hand, and the varied requirements and caprices of human nature itself, on the other hand. It is no accident, therefore, that with certain notable exceptions its greatest triumphs have been in the "heavy" industries, which supply "semi-finished" products. Out of these products a multitude of specialized industries fashion the bewildering varieties of goods, which are sold in the world's markets. There is an appearance of paradox in the circumstance that never before in the world's history has so large and varied an assortment of goods been within reach of the average man as in these days of "standardization!" Some of the industries which take over the standardized semi-finished products and convert them into a diversity of finished products are themselves very large industries, composed of large establishments, while others are small. As a general rule, however, and as we should expect, the typical establishment which has a specialized product (i.e. a product fitted or adjusted to the particular needs of a particular body of consumers) is not as large as the typical establishment producing semi-finished or "inter-mediate" goods.

Determining factors of size

Distance, and the modern methods of transport and communication by means of which distance is overcome, are among the most potent of the circumstances which determine the optimum size of an individual undertaking within a given industry. If raw materials are both widely dispersed and bulky, so that transport costs are large, a number of small plants, distributed so as to draw upon different local sources of supply, may be more economical than a few large plants. If the *finished* product is bulky, perishable, or for some other reason difficult to transport, the advantages of small plants, near to different markets, may be great enough to offset whatever technical economies might be secured by the concentration of manufacturing operations in a very few large plants, necessarily remote from some, at least, of the principal markets. The cheapening and improving of transport and communication during the last hundred years has had the effect, in many industries, of enlarging the area from which raw materials can be obtained economically; as well as the area within which the products of a particular establishment can be sold profitably. These changes have operated to make the average establishment, in such industries, larger than otherwise it would have been.

Shifting retail trade centres

The organization of retail trade, also, is influenced by distance and by improvements in transport and communications, for retail trade has to adapt itself to "market areas," and these, in turn, are larger or smaller according as distance is a smaller or larger obstacle. Almost every retail establishment occupies a site which gives it some sort of advantage, however small that advantage may be. Just what particular sort of site gives the maximum advantage depends upon the character of the goods which are offered for sale and the nature of the market which is sought for them. A shopkeeper may be satisfied, according to his capital and his ambitions, with the casual patronage of passers-by, or with some part of the patronage of a neighborhood. He may try to secure for himself a share of the trade of an established "shopping district," and he may even hope to attract "pilgrims from afar." In rapidly growing communities, however, and especially in American communities, retail markets are never stable for very long. A shopping district becomes congested, so that some enterprizing firm decides that it can do better by establishing itself elsewhere. Other firms may follow its example, and a new shopping district may soon be created. The old district may survive, or it may be given over to a wholly different class or group of business activities. Much economic waste, it may be observed, often accompanies this process of restless change. American cities have only recently come to realize, what most European cities learned long ago, that a city's growth must be planned, that it must not be left to the haphazard forces of shopkeepers' competition and real estate speculation. A city is like a living organism, but unlike a healthy unitary organism, it does not have within itself those magical properties which preserve a due balance of the parts and organs and which prevent the development of abnormalities and excrescences.

　　Let us return, however, to our own proper problems. The fears, once prevalent, that great department stores would secure a monopoly of all retail trade have pretty completely disappeared. In the first place, anything like an effective monopoly of retail trade is impossible for there is no way in which competition in that field can be effectively suppressed. Even though certain great department stores have been amalgamated, so that they are units or links in "chains" of stores, competition on the part of department stores themselves remains keen and effective. In the second place, the department store has not displaced the smaller establishment. Not merely do these survive, but with the growth of our towns and cities, their numbers continue to increase. Most of them are comprised in one or the other of two distinct classes: first, the specialized shop, offering a limited and distinctive type of goods; second, the neighborhood store (observe that the "neighborhood" may be either a business or a residential district), conveniently accessible to a fair number of possible customers.

The department store

Some of the advantages of the department store are obvious. Shopping under one roof is convenient. A single credit account will cover a considerable part of a buyer's needs. The department store can be and usually is arranged like a great bazaar, with a visible display of very large samples of the goods offered for sale, so that the buyer who enters the store for a particular purpose may find his interest attracted to other goods. From time to time certain "lines" may be offered at bargain prices, so as to achieve the purpose of attracting customers into the store. These advantages suffice, up to a certain point, but beyond that point they fail so that room is left for that persistent competition of which we have already spoken. The "overhead" expenses (rent, light, heat, etc.) of a department store are likely to be quite as large, in relation to the gross volume of sales, as those of a smaller establishment. Every effort has to be made to keep the "rate of turnover" (i.e. the ratio of sales to the average amount of goods held in stock) as high as possible. One great and profitable American department store, in accordance with a definite policy, accepts a net loss (which, of course, it tries to minimize) on that part of its business which is housed, in its imposing building, on and above the street level, getting its profits out of enormous sales of cheaper goods in its "bargain basement." The losses of its other departments thus constitute, in a curiously literal sense, part of the "overhead" expenses of its profitable activities. The mere size of a department store does not always enable it to buy its goods more cheaply than similar goods can be bought by an alert manager of a smaller and more highly specialized establishment, for the latter's annual sales of a particular class of goods may be quite as large as those of the department store. In short, the department store has advantages, but it also has its limitations. It has an important, useful, and often profitable place in the general field of retail merchandising, but it can occupy only a certain special part of that broad field.

The chain store development

Chain stores, which have had a spectacular development in recent years, present some striking contrasts with department stores. In respect of the sheer magnitude of their operations some of the great systems of chain stores equal and even surpass the largest department stores. But whereas the department store brings together different activities and an amazing range of commodities under one roof, the chain of stores is often content to handle only one particular class of goods, and in place of one great central bazaar to which all customers must come, it maintains a large number of relatively small outlets, located in each instance in accordance with a careful calculation of advantages. A recent federal census of Distribution, revealed the surprising fact that 28.7 per cent of the total volume of sales in the eleven cities covered by the census had fallen into the hands of the chain stores. Their sales for a year, in those eleven cities, amounted in the aggregate to more than $1,200,000,000. For the United States as a whole, according to figures gathered by the Chain Store Research Bureau, the value of the goods sold by chain stores in a recent year was over $5,000,000,000. In 1928 nearly 4,000 "chains," large and small, were operating, there being as many as 860, some local and some operating on a nationwide scale, in the grocery trade alone. Among the other enterprises which are being operated successfully as "chains" are boot and shoe stores, clothing stores, restaurants, bakeries, drug stores, and those extraordinarily interesting and successful establishments which resemble miniature department stores, but where nothing can be bought except at small fixed prices, such as 5 or 10 cents, or 10 or 25 cents, or within a somewhat larger range, but not exceeding a dollar.

Any large economic development of this kind has back of it, of course, the vision and initiative of individual men. But it should not be forgotten that changing conditions create the opportunities of which enterprising men take advantage. The chain store system is no "belated" discovery. It is not as though men had suddenly devised a way of securing economies which before had always eluded them, so that an economic waste of long standing could finally be eliminated. No, the chain store is merely another example of adaptation and adjustment to a new situation. Fifty years ago chain store systems would probably have been unprofitable, except in a few narrowly circumscribed fields.

The telephone in retail shopping

Barely a generation ago the general introduction of the telephone brought with it a notable change in the conditions to which retail trade had to adapt itself. *Some* of the advantages of location which small retailers possessed were lost, for the telephone helped to overcome some of the disadvantages of distance. Particularly was this true of what is sometimes called the "better-class trade" in staple kinds of groceries and provisions. An established reputation for reliable goods and for prompt service came to count far more, with certain classes of consumers, than a certainty that the prices asked were as low as the market afforded. The consumer in fact was willing to pay a certain price for relief from the inconvenience of personal shopping. Many grocery stores, although affording facilities for the personal inspection of goods, came to be largely warehouses from which goods were delivered, upon order, to the customer's home. The system of making sales upon credit, already well established, extended still further as a result of the introduction of the telephone. These changes did not and could not greatly affect the buying habits of the poorer classes in the community, and as time went on some of the advantages which people with moderate incomes had secured from them began to be whittled away.

Increase in selling costs

Modern capital-using methods of manufacturing goods greatly increase the productivity of the labor employed in industry. For that very reason they are responsible for a corresponding increase of the *cost* of employing labor in other pursuits. With the steady increase of the productivity of labor in industry the cost of personal services has increased, and will continue to increase. An increasing pressure, therefore, is put upon retailers, as upon those engaged in other fields of enterprise, to economize, so far as they can, in their use of labor, particularly when the labor is not directly aided by "labor-saving" machinery. As compared with the costs of manufacturing goods, the costs of handling, displaying, selling and delivering have become *relatively* greater.

Influence of the automobile

These costs fall upon the consumer, and the consumer of moderate means has reached a point where he is willing to adjust himself to a system by means of which these costs are reduced, even at the expense of some personal inconvenience to himself. The well-nigh universal use of the automobile, affording a quick and flexible means of transport, has been another very important element in the new situation to which both dealers and consumers have had to adjust themselves.

The problems which the different retail trades have to meet are not, however, all alike. One of the earliest of the great chains was established to sell cigars and tobacco. Taking account of the circumstance that many men buy their cigars or cigarettes in small quantities, and at whatever place is most convenient, careful studies were made of the average number of people passing certain possible sites for retail stores (certain corners, for example) per hour or day. Other considerations were, of course, taken into account, but when once the managers of the chain were convinced that a particular location was the right one, hardly any rent, no matter how high, was regarded as too much to pay. The location of those vendors of curiously assorted goods, the chain drug stores, are determined on much the same bases. Different considerations, however, often govern the choosing of locations for chain grocery stores. The margin of "a profit on the turnover" is generally fairly low, and, to make a profit, overhead costs have to be kept low, too.

Choice of location

Nearness to the homes of possible customers counts far more than proximity to important business districts or a large number of passers-by. Nowhere, however, does the influence of the new situation created by the general use of the automobile (which has enormously increased the possible range of "cash and carry" trade) show itself more plainly than in the selection of the locations of the great new retail stores which have been opened in a number of American cities by firms which formerly confined their activities to the mail-order trade. The locations selected have generally been away from the crowded business and shopping districts, where access by automobile is difficult and where parking space is not to be had. This new development is a particularly interesting example of adaptation to new conditions. It may be the beginning of a considerable overturning of the principles which have hitherto shaped the growth of American cities and the organization of American retail markets.

The economies achieved by the chain stores do not stop with their elimination (generally, though not universally) of the expense of delivering goods and of losses from bad debts. The accounts of chain grocery stores have been compared by the Harvard Bureau of Business Research with the accounts of ordinary retail grocers. The chain stores, it was found, were able to buy more cheaply. On much of their trade the wholesaler is virtually eliminated. They have their own brands, and some of them manufacture or prepare a considerable part of the products which they sell. Their operating costs, also, are kept at a relatively low figure. By keeping reserve supplies in central warehouses, and by confining themselves mostly to trade in a selected but limited line of staples, their different outlets are able to get along with relatively small stocks, so the "rate of turnover" (a fundamental factor in the economy of retail trading) is relatively high.

It must not be supposed, however, that there is any magic formula for business success, whether in large industries or small, in chain stores or in the ordinary single-unit establishment. Some large industries have faded and not all systems of chain stores have succeeded financially. Intelligence, imagination, persistence and courage are needed in these fields, as elsewhere. One of the real advantages of large-scale units in industry and commerce, is that they make it possible for intelligence and managerial ability of an exceptional order to be spread, as we might say, over a larger field of activities. But how far it is economical to go on enlarging the scale of the business unit, even when the best of brains are behind it, depends, as we have tried to show, upon, first, the characteristics of the particular industry or field of enterprise, and, second, the character of the general economic situation into which every business undertaking must somehow be made to fit.

47 Bibliography of Allyn Young's writings

Ely, Richard T., Adams, Thomas A., Lorenz, Max O. and Young, Allyn A. 1908. *Outlines of Economics*. Revised edn. New York: Macmillan.

—— 1916. *Outlines of Economics*. 3rd edn. New York: Macmillan.

—— 1923. *Outlines of Economics*. 4th edn. New York: Macmillan.

—— 1930. *Outlines of Economics*. 5th edn. New York: Macmillan.

Reed, Harold Lyle (with Allyn A. Young). 1925. *Principles of Corporation Finance*. Boston: Houghton Mifflin.

Riley, Eugene B. (with Allyn A. Young). 1925. *Economics for Secondary Schools*. Boston: Houghton Mifflin.

Watkins, Myron W. (with Allyn A. Young). 1927. *Industrial Combinations and Public Policy: A Study of Combination, Competition, and the Common Welfare*. Boston: Houghton Mifflin.

Young, Allyn Abbott. 1900. "The comparative accuracy of different forms of quinquennial age groups." *Quarterly Publications of the American Statistical Association* 7 No. 49/50 (March/June): 27–39.

—— 1901. "The enumeration of children." *Quarterly Publications of the American Statistical Association* 7 No. 53 (March): 227–54.

—— 1902a. Review of *L'Utilité Sociale de la Propriété Individuelle*, by Adolphe Landry. *Journal of Political Economy* 10 No. 4 (September): 631–3.

—— 1902b. Review of *The Theory of Prosperity*, by Simon N. Patten. *Journal of Political Economy* 11 No. 1 (December): 137–41.

—— 1904. *A Discussion of Age Statistics*. U.S. Bureau of the Census. Washington, DC: Government Printing Office.

—— 1905. "The Birth-Rate in New Hampshire." *Publications of the American Statistical Association* 9 No. 71 (September): 263–91.

—— 1906. "Age." Pages 130-174 in *Supplementary Analysis and Derivative Tables. Twelfth Census*. Washington, DC: Bureau of the Census.

—— 1909. "California Vital Statistics." *Publications of the American Statistical Association* 11 No. 87 (September): 543–50.

—— 1910a. "The Census Age Question." *Publications of the American Statistical Association* 12 No. 92 (December): 360–70.

—— 1910b. Review of *Report on National Vitality, Its Wastes and Conservation*, by Irving Fisher. *Economic Bulletin* (American Economic Association) 3 No. 1 (March): 51–3.

—— 1911a. "Mr. Mallock as Statistician and British Income Statistics." *Quarterly Journal of Economics* 25 No. 2 (February): 376–86.

—— 1911b. "Some Limitations of the Value Concept." *Quarterly Journal of Economics* 25 No. 3 (May): 409–28. Reprinted as Ch. 10 in Young (1927b).

—— 1911c. Review of *The Common Sense of Political Economy*, by Philip H. Wicksteed. *American Economic Review* 1 No. 1 (March): 78–80.

—— 1911d. Review of *The Meaning of Social Science*, by Albion W. Small. *American Economic Review* 1 No. 2 (June): 311–2.

—— 1911e. Review of *La Théorie des Marchés Économiques*, by Bernard Lavergne. *American Economic Review* 1 No. 3 (September): 549–50.

—— 1911f. Review of *Die monographische Darstellung der Aktiengesellschaften*, by Otto Warschauer, and *Syndicats Financiers d'Émission: Organisation, Responsabilité*, by M.E. Thaller. *American Economic Review* 1 No. 3 (September): 583–7.

—— 1911g. Review of *The New Dictionary of Statistics*, by Augustus D. Webb. *American Economic Review* 1 No. 4 (December): 890–1.

—— 1912a. Review of *An Introduction to the Theory of Statistics*, by G. Udny Yule. *American Economic Review* 2 No. 1 (March): 174–6.

—— 1912b. "Jevons's *Theory of Political Economy*." *American Economic Review* 2 No. 3 (September): 576–89. Reprinted as Ch. 11 in Young (1927b).

—— 1912c. Review of *Control of the Market*, by Bruce Wyman, and *Corporations and the State*, by Theodore E. Burton. *American Economic Review* 2 No. 3 (September): 643–5.

—— 1913a. "The Vote on the Single Tax in Missouri." *American Economic Review* 3 No. 1 (March): 203–6.

—— 1913b. "Pigou's Wealth and Welfare." *Quarterly Journal of Economics* 27 No. 4 (August): 672–86.

—— 1913c. Review of *La Distribuzione dei Redditi nelle Provincie e nelle Grandi Citta dell'Austria*, by Franco Savorgnan. *American Economic Review* 3 No. 1 (March): 182–4.

—— 1913d. "Street Car Transportation in St. Louis." *American Economic Review* 3 No. 3 (September): 712–4.

—— 1914a. Review of *Laws of Wages*, by Henry Moore. *Annals of the American Academy of Political and Social Science* 51 (January): 282–4.

—— 1914b. "Railway Rate Making: Discussion." *American Economic Review* 4 No. 1 Supplement (March): 82–6.

—— 1914c. "Depreciation and Rate Control." *Quarterly Journal of Economics* 28 No. 3 (May): 630–63. Reprinted as Ch. 8 in Young (1927b).

—— 1914d. Review of *Foreign Companies and other Corporations*, by E. Hilton Young. *American Economic Review* 4 No. 2 (June): 391–3.

—— 1914e. Review of *Intorno al Concetto di Reddito Imponibile e di un Sistema d'Imposte sul Reddito Consumato*, by Luigi Einaudi. *American Economic Review* 4 No. 3 (September): 679–80.

—— 1915a. "Personal or Impersonal Taxation." Pages 336-345 in *Proceedings of the Ninth Annual Conference of the National Tax Association*. Ithaca, NY: National Tax Association. Reprinted as Ch. 7 in Young (1927b).

—— 1915b. "The Sherman Act and the New Anti-trust Legislation." *Journal of Political Economy* 23 No. 3–5 (March, April, May): 201–20, 305–26, 417–36. Reprinted as Ch. 9 in Young (1927b).

—— 1915c. "Public Borrowing for Road Building." *Cornell Civil Engineer* 23 No. 6–7 (March/April): 301–15.

—— 1915d. "Concluding Comments [on Depreciation and Rate Control]." *Quarterly Journal of Economics* 29 No. 2 (February): 395–400.

—— 1916a. "Nearing's Income; King's Wealth and Income." *Quarterly Journal of Economics* 30 No. 3 (May): 575–87.

—— 1916b. Review of *Graphic Methods for Presenting Facts*, by Willard C. Brinton. *American Economic Review* 6 No. 1 (March): 181–2.

—— 1917a. "Do the Statistics of the Concentration of Wealth in the United States Mean what they are Commonly Assumed to Mean." *American Statistical Association* 15 No. 117 (March): 471–84. Also in *American Economic Review* 7 No. 1 Supp. (March 1917): 144–56. Reprinted as Ch. 6 in Young (1927b).

—— 1917b. "Discussion [of Two Dimensions of Productivity]." *American Economic Review* 7 No. 1 Supp. (March): 58–9.

—— 1918. "National Statistics in War and Peace." *American Statistical Association* 16 No. 121 (March): 873–85.

—— 1919. "Practical Basis of Germany's Bill." *New York Times* (August 10).

—— 1920a. "The Economics of the Treaty." *New Republic* (February 25): 388–9.

—— 1920b. Review of *Currency and Credit*, by Ralph Hawtrey, and *Stabilizing the Dollar*, by Irving Fisher. *Quarterly Journal of Economics* 34 No. 2 (April): 520–32.

—— 1921a. "Commercial Policy in German, Austrian, Hungarian, and Bulgarian Treaties." Vol. V Ch. 1 pt. 3 in *A History of the Peace Conference*, edited by H. W. V. Temperley. London: Institute of International Affairs.

—— 1921b. "The Economic Settlement." Pages 291–318 in *What Really Happened at Paris*, edited by Edward M. House and Charles Seymour. New York: Scribner's.

—— 1921c. "The Measurement of Changes of the General Price Level." *Quarterly Journal of Economics* 35 No. 4 (August): 557–73. Reprinted as Ch. 13 in Young (1927b).

—— 1922a. "Introduction." In *Foreign Exchange, The Financing Mechanism of International Commerce*, by Edgar S. Furniss. Boston: Houghton Mifflin.

—— 1922b. Review of *What Next in Europe?*, by Frank A. Vanderlip. *Atlantic Monthly* 129 No. 4 (April).

—— 1923a. "Fisher's 'The Making of Index Numbers'." *Quarterly Journal of Economics* 37 No. 2 (February): 342-64. Reprinted as Ch. 14 in Young (1927b).

—— 1923b. "The United States and Reparations." *Foreign Affairs* 1 (March 15): 35–47.

—— 1923c. "The Trend of Prices." *American Economic Review* 13 No. 1 (March): 5–14. Reprinted as Ch. 4 in Young (1927b).

—— 1923d. *George Henry Colton*. Hiram, Ohio: Hiram College.

—— 1924a. "Commerce: The Market-place of the World". 36 chapters in *The Book of Popular Science*, edited by Dexter S. Kimball. New York: The Grolier Society, 1924.

—— 1924b. "Index Numbers." Ch. 12 in *Handbook of Mathematical Statistics*, edited by Henry Lewis Reitz. Boston: Houghton Mifflin.

—— 1924c. "War Debts, External and Internal." *Foreign Affairs* 2 No. 3 (March 15): 397–409. Reprinted as Ch. 2 in Young (1927b).

—— 1924d. "Germany's Capacity to Pay." *American Statistical Association* 19 No. 146 (June): 242–6. "A Rejoinder." *American Statistical Association* 20 No. 150 (June 1925): 260–1.

—— 1924e. Review of *Currency and Credit* and *Monetary Reconstruction*, by Ralph Hawtrey. *American Economic Review* 14 No. 2 (June): 349–52.

—— 1924f. "An Analysis of Bank Statistics for the United States: I. The National Banks, 1867–1914." *Review of Economics and Statistics* 6 No. 4 (October): 284–96.

—— 1924g. "Marshall on Consumers' Surplus in International Trade." *Quarterly Journal of Economics* 39 No. 1 (November): 144–50. "Consumers' Surplus in International Trade: A Supplementary Note." *Quarterly Journal of Economics* 39 No. 3 (May 1925): 498–9.

—— 1924h. "Economics Defeats Politics in Europe." *New York Times* (August 24), Section 8.

—— 1925a. "Hungary in 1925." Unpublished mimeo. Reprinted as Ch. 3 in Young (1927b).

—— 1925b. "Introduction." Pages vii–xii in *Social Consequences of Business Cycles*, by Maurice Beck Hexter. Boston: Houghton Mifflin.

—— 1925c. "An Analysis of Bank Statistics for the United States: II. Seasonal and Cyclical Fluctuations, 1901–1914." *Review of Economics and Statistics* 7 No. 1 (January): 19–37.

—— 1925d. "The Trend of Economics." *Quarterly Journal of Economics* 39 No. 2 (February): 155–183. Reprinted as Ch. 12 in Young (1927b).

—— 1925e. Review of *The Mathematical Groundwork of Economics*, by A. L. Bowley. *American Statistical Association* 20 No. 149 (March): 133–5.

—— 1925f. "An Analysis of Bank Statistics for the United States: III. Regional Differences, 1901–1914." *Review of Economics and Statistics* 7 No. 2 (April): 86–104.

—— 1925g. Review of *Papers Relating to Political Economy*, by F. Y. Edgeworth. *American Economic Review* 15 No. 4 (December): 721–4.

—— 1925h. "Introduction." Pages ix–x in *Labor Problems*, by E. S. Furniss. Cambridge: Riverside Press.

—— 1926a. "Introduction." Pages iii–v in *Economic History of Europe, to the End of the Middle Ages*, by Melvin M. Knight. Boston: Houghton Mifflin.

—— 1926b. "Economics and War." *American Economic Review* 16 No. 1 (March): 1–13. Reprinted as Ch. 1 in Young (1927d).

—— 1926c. "The Aged Poor of Massachusetts." *Quarterly Journal of Economics* 40 No. 3 (May): 549–54.

—— 1926d. "Introduction." Pages vii–xx in *La Banque à Succursales dans le Système Bancaire des États-Unis*, by Jean Steels. Ghent: A. Buyens.

—— 1926e. "The Economics of Farm Relief." *The Independent* [New York] 117 No. 3972 (July 17): 64–6.

—— (with H. Van V. Fay). 1927a. *The International Economic Conference*. Boston: World Peace Foundation Pamphlets, Vol. 10, No. 4.

—— 1927b. *Economic Problems New and Old*. Boston: Houghton Mifflin.

—— 1927c. "Depreciation and Reproduction Cost." *Quarterly Journal of Economics* 41 No. 2 (February): 345–9.

—— 1927d. "The Structure and Policies of the Federal Reserve System." *The New York Times Annalist* (May 6 and May 13). Reprinted as Ch. 5 in Young (1927b).

—— 1927e. "An Analysis of Bank Statistics for the United States: IV. The National Banks: 1915–26." *Review of Economics and Statistics* 9 No. 3 (July): 121–41.

—— 1927f. "Economics as a Field of Research." *Quarterly Journal of Economics* 42 No. 1 (November): 1–25. Reprinted as "Economics" in *Research in the Social Sciences*, edited by Wilson Gee. New York: Macmillan, 1929.

—— 1928a. "Introduction." In *Economic History of Europe, in Modern Times*, by Melvin M. Knight et al. Boston: Houghton Mifflin.

—— 1928b. *An Analysis of Bank Statistics for the United States*. Cambridge: Harvard University Press. Reprint of articles in *Review of Economics and Statistics* (October 1924, January 1925, April 1925, July 1927).

—— 1928c. "English Political Economy." *Economica* 8 No. 22 (March): 1–15.

—— 1928d. Review of *London Essays in Economics: in Honour of Edwin Cannan*. *Economica* 8 No. 22 (March): 113–7.

—— 1928e. Review of *The Reserve Banks and the Money Market*, by W. R. Burgess. *Economica* 8 No. 23 (June): 229–31.

—— 1928f. Review of *On Stimulus in the Economic Life*, by Josiah Stamp. *Economic Journal* 38 No. 150 (June): 286–8.

—— 1928g. Review of *An Economist's Protest*, by Edwin Canaan. *Economica* 8 No. 24 (December): 370–2.

—— 1928h. "Increasing Returns and Economic Progress." *Economic Journal* 38 No. 152 (December): 527–42.

—— 1929a. "Downward Price Trend Probable, Due to Hoarding of Gold by Central Banks." *The New York Times Annalist* (January 18).

—— 1929b. "Capital", "Economics", "Labour", "Land", "Price", "Rent", "Supply and Demand", "Utility", "Wages", "Wealth", "Value." *Encyclopaedia Britannica* 14th edn. Reprinted in *Journal of Economic Studies* 17 No. 3/4 (1990): 115–60.

—— 1929c. "LSE Lectures 1927–29." Published in *Journal of Economic Studies* 17 No. 3/4 (1990): 18–114.

—— 1929d. "Economic Changes since the War: Their Meaning and their Lessons." Ch. 37 in *Book of Popular Science*, Vol. 15, edited by Dexter S. Kimball. New York: Grolier Society.

—— 1929e. "Big Business: How the Economic System Grows and Evolves Like a Living Organism." Ch. 38 in *Book of Popular Science*, Vol. 15, edited by Dexter S. Kimball. New York: Grolier Society. Reprinted in *Journal of Economic Studies* 17 No. 3–4 (1990): 161–70.

—— 1929f. Review of *A Study in Public Finance*, by Arthur C. Pigou. *Economic Journal* 39 No. 153 (March 1929): 78–83.

—— 1929g. "Introduction." Pages xi–xvi in *The French Franc, 1914–1928*, by Eleanor Lansing Dulles. New York: Macmillan.

Index